PHILOSOPHY AND FREEDOM

Edited by
DAVID G. PEDDLE AND NEIL G. ROBERTSON

James Doull's remarkable legacy as a teacher, scholar, and thinker has left behind a profound and challenging examination of the philosophical and historical roots of contemporary thought and politics. His life's work was devoted to reflecting on freedom in its philosophical and historical context and, more specifically, to looking beneath the commonly accepted forms of North American and Continental thought and discovering a deeper theoretical and practical development. David Peddle and Neil Robertson have collected Doull's essays on the history of western thought and freedom, from the ancient period to the post-modern era, and have provided an introduction that places them in the context of Doull's overall project.

Commentaries on his intricate works by twelve former colleagues and students explore various aspects of Doull's history and place it within the context of contemporary scholarship, allowing the reader to judge the depth and rigour of Doull's writing. Together, the texts and commentaries provide a long-overdue introduction to and analysis of Doull's thought, offering further insight into a longstanding and significant dialogue in Canadian philosophy and classical studies, and bringing out a penetrating analysis of the philosophical underpinnings of the contemporary world.

(Toronto Studies in Philosophy)

DAVID G. PEDDLE is Assistant Professor in the Department of Philosophy at Sir Wilfred Grenfell College at the Memorial University of Newfoundland.

NEIL G. ROBERTSON is Associate Professor in the Foundation Year, Contemporary Studies, and Early Modern Studies Programmes at the University of King's College.

James Doull

Philosophy and Freedom

The Legacy of James Doull

Edited with an Introduction by
David G. Peddle and Neil G. Robertson

UNIVERSITY OF TORONTO PRESS
Toronto Buffalo London

Toronto Buffalo London
Reprinted in paperback 2016

ISBN 978-0-8020-3698-8 (cloth)
ISBN 978-1-4875-9277-6 (paper)

Printed on acid-free paper

National Library of Canada Cataloguing in Publication

Philosophy and freedom : the legacy of James Doull / edited with an introduction by David G. Peddle and Neil G. Robertson.

Includes bibliographical references and index.
ISBN 978-0-8020-3698-8 (bound) ISBN 978-1-4875-9277-6 (pbk.)

1. Liberty – Philosophy. 2. Liberty. 3. Doull, James – Contributions in the philosophy of liberty. I. Peddle, David, 1965– II. Robertson, Neil G.

B824.4.P54 2003 123′.5 C2002-905798-1

University of Toronto Press acknowledges the financial assistance to its publishing program of the Canada Council for the Arts and the Ontario Arts Council.

University of Toronto Press acknowledges the financial support for its publishing activities of the Government of Canada through the Book Publishing Industry Development Program (BPIDP).

Cover photograph: Philip Coblentz/Brand X Pictures/PictureQuest

To
JAMES ALEXANDER DOULL
In Memoriam

... namque omnem, quae nunc obducta tuenti
mortalis hebetat visus tibi et umida circum
caligat, nubem eripiam

Aeneid 2, 604–6

I'll tear away the cloud that curtains you,
and films your mortal sight, the fog
around you. (trans. Fitzgerald, 1990)

Contents

Part Four: The Post-modern State

Acknowledgments

In the course of putting this book together we relied on a number of people and institutions for one form of support or another. Most prominent among these were the following, to whom we are extremely grateful. For financial support: Department of Classics of Dalhousie University, Memorial University of Newfoundland, Sir Wilfred Grenfell College, University of King's College. For advice throughout the course of this project: Floy Doull, F.L. Jackson, Graeme Nicholson, Henry Roper. For technical support: Sharon Brown, Pat Dixon, Pam Parsons, Calle Stewart, Nick Thorne. Finally, we must thank Floy Doull and the journals *Animus*, *Dionysius*, and *Dialogue* for permission to publish articles. It has been a genuine pleasure also to work with Suzanne Rancourt, Editor, Humanities Division, University of Toronto Press, as well as Barbara Porter and John St James, who have been extremely supportive throughout. We owe a debt of gratitude as well to two unknown reviewers who offered many constructive suggestions which much improved this volume. As always our deepest debts are to our respective wives, Louise McGillis and Patricia Robertson, and to the substance they provide in our lives. Errors are solely the fault of the editors.

Preface

The setting that is most appropriate for philosophy in modern times is the seminar. The philosopher who is conducting a seminar presents a paper, and the seminar participants, having absorbed the argument, discuss it and question it, both with the speaker and with each other. In the ideal setting, one of the participants will then offer a second paper that can respond to the first one, extending it or replying to it, initiating a further discussion. It was in this setting that James Doull philosophized over a period of more than forty years. The editors of the present book, former participants in seminars conducted by Doull, have succeeded in creating here a replica of that experience of philosophy, recognizable to anyone who participated in the seminars in years past: nine 'papers' and eleven 'commentaries,' with an 'essay' offered as introduction. One of the conditions for a philosophical seminar is that the participants share with the philosopher some common understanding of what philosophy itself aims to be and to do, a commonality of mind that is abundantly in evidence throughout this book.

In all his doings, it was Doull's aim to bring before his contemporaries the highest idea of philosophy itself, a thing so rarely pursued nowadays that in his presence one was constantly made to think, not of contemporaries, but of Parmenides and Socrates, Aristotle and Hegel. For Doull, philosophy was not some sort of meta-discourse that would assemble the results of other discourses and then add on its own reflections as a supplement – as if there were, first, an empirical encounter with the real for which thought then furnished logical forms and categories; or as if we acquired actual knowledge from the sciences, whose results philosophy would then analyse. On the contrary: for Doull, philosophy itself accomplishes the direct knowledge of being and of that which is. There is no screen or barrier that closes off the real from the gaze of philosophy. Doull saw philosophy incorporating *within* itself all the science that is alive in a given age, and likewise, whatever art and religion are alive in a given age. Not a discussion *about* science, law, art, and religion, but rather, recognizing them all as ways of knowing, philosophy absorbs their knowledge into itself.

Another thing you did not find with Doull was that path, so often taken nowadays, that confines philosophy to a merely practical or directive role, operating in morality and law, but concedes to the special sciences everything that is cognitive.

For Doull, philosophy is the direct and comprehensive knowledge of reality. That reality is freedom. Here is the ground for the thoroughgoing modernism of Doull's thought. But this freedom, when it is known philosophically in its reality and truth, is not merely an attribute of the singular subject. It is that of course, but the idea of freedom incorporates as well all the conditions whereby such a free individual can exist in the first place, all the history, law, art, religion, thought, and science that have constituted the modern subject and the forms of freedom that are now possible. Philosophy does not discover reality and truth by some sort of sudden ambush, but always along with all these mediating data.

Doull's own specialty was the history of philosophy. For it is clear that the reality of freedom was *always* known, in different and particular ways, wherever there was philosophy. Doull's amazing attention to the details of ancient, medieval, and modern philosophical thought leads us to apprehend not only the forms and categories of bygone systems but also the reality and the truth that the philosophy of those times had disclosed: the visage of freedom itself in the infinite variety of ways in which it became evident to thought. And so the first chapter here discusses the God of ancient Israel, moving on from that topic to open up the gods of Greek epic, tragedy, and comedy, the beginnings of a story which, running through a vast labyrinth, comes to its end in the final chapters with our contemporary civilization, law, and politics. Some of the most astonishing parts of this odyssey appear in chapters 2 to 5, where Doull exposes his most specialized research on Plato and Neoplatonism. The commentators throughout this book have, it seems to me, risen to the occasion, and incidentally, at certain points, have rendered Doull's own argument easier to follow than in the original.

A true philosopher cannot suppose that reality is completely unknown and unrecognized outside his seminar. Students who attended Doull's seminars could always sense that in their own unshaped and inarticulate views of reality there was something that he was addressing, some pre-philosophical intuition that was in accord with his philosophy. I remember one evening in 1954 when he gave a paper on Plato's *Phaedo*, on the way in which Socrates' argumentation came to grips with, and surpassed, the intuitions of the Orphics and the Pythagoreans. For me, this was like a visitation from the *logos* itself. That there was a type of thinking that was fit to operate in the domain usually claimed by religion and belief, that a form of thinking almost mathematical in character might yet reveal harmonies of the universe and of the soul, that some such power of soaring might even be slumbering within myself! All this I surmised that evening, although I could not possibly have expressed it. It turned me around. Doull was able to gain the trust and the love of his students because he knew and understood that which was their own ground and their own being. Philosophy is the cognition of that which is – for instance, ourselves – by way of a concept and an idea. But the ground for that cognition is that which has already been informed by a concept and an idea from the start.

Graeme Nicholson
Trinity College, University of Toronto

Editors' Introduction

1. Situating James Doull

James Doull died on 16 March 2001, leaving behind a remarkable legacy as a teacher, scholar, and thinker of astonishing breadth and remarkable depth. Doull's life work was devoted to a reflection on freedom in its philosophical and historical context – to uncovering beneath the commonly accepted forms of North American and European thought a deeper theoretical and practical development.

Doull's legacy is marked by what might be called an 'untimely timeliness.' In an age which thinks itself beyond the necessity of philosophical thought Doull has sought to recover the speculative ground of contemporary freedom. In this pursuit he brings to light a paradox that characterizes the contemporary world: on the one hand, the contemporary sees itself to be revolutionary in its puruit of an immediate freedom, seeking to escape what it perceives as the fixed and oppressive character of metaphysical categories; on the other, the contemporary is unable to recognize the fullness of its own freedom. A result of this paradox is that twentieth-century freedom appears in opposed, antagonistic forms such as Marxism and National Socialism, or, more recently, liberalism and communitarianism. In Doull's view, contemporaneity finds itself torn between an assumed confidence in its own infinite liberating power and a growing inability to establish this freedom in the world in stable and effective forms. For Doull, then, the nature of contemporary freedom is not adequately expressed in and by contemporary self-understanding, and particularly not in contemporary philosophy.

Doull's work is thus timely in that it calls us to reflect more deeply upon the assumptions present in contemporary freedom. His work is untimely in its unapologetically philosophical and speculative approach which questions these assumptions at a fundamental level. It is only such an approach, Doull argues, that can bring to light the ambivalent character of contemporary freedom: that it is both the fulfilment of the whole development of Western culture and also a corruption in which the fullness of that tradition has fallen into one-sided abstractions. So far as the contemporary takes itself to be immediate – by defining its freedom in opposition to philosophy and its tradition – Doull argues we must reach behind this self-understanding to uncover the deeper mediations – historic, institutional, and speculative – that ground and sustain contemporary freedom. His central thesis is that the contemporary world has an underlying philosophical basis and that the divisions in 'revolutionary' thought (first made explicit in the opposition between Marx and Nietzsche) are but moments of a concrete thinking in whose unity the truth of both resides. Though inaccessible on contemporary assumptions, in Doull's view, this unity is implicit in Western social institutions and their relation to human subjectivity.

Doull's untimely timeliness is perhaps most succinctly expressed in his claim, made in an exchange with Emil Fackenheim, that 'Hegel now alive would be a Hegelian still.'[1] The peculiar difficulty and intellectual power of Doull's writing resides in the singular challenge of expounding such a Hegelian standpoint. Doull's account of the contemporary rests on his claim that the post-Hegelian developments of the last 150 years, far from undermining the Hegelian standpoint, rather fulfil it more completely. Doull claims that only from a Hegelian standpoint can we gain both an objective account of our own age and a philosophical recovery of the historical mediation that made possible our age and is sustained in it. The difficulty of Doull's texts is that we as readers are asked not only to free ourselves of the common paradigms of contemporary thought, but also to think the contemporary and its history from the standpoint of the speculative logic of the Hegelian philosophy. For anyone reading Doull's writings for the first time, they can thus appear foreign and surpassingly complex.

These strange contours of the Doullian position in large measure account for the peculiar fact that while the importance of his thought has been recognized by thinkers such as Hans-Georg Gadamer, John Findlay, Emil Fackenheim, and George Grant, Doull nevertheless remains a somewhat obscure figure, a maverick in academic circles – never publishing a book for example – and yet having a sustained influence on three generations of scholars. As Wayne J. Hankey notes in his contribution to this volume: 'Not many in Canada can be compared to James Doull as the creator of a philosophical school based in an interpretation of the whole history of Western philosophy. When one adds that his school has continued to reproduce itself for a half a century through several generations of students, that it remains central to the life of vibrant institutions, and that this power of regeneration stems from its union of a linguistically and philologically disciplined reading of texts with a total system of philosophy, Professor Doull's accomplishment is virtually incomparable in our country.'[2]

James Doull established his 'school' through his long tenure as a professor in the Classics Department at Dalhousie University. After graduating from Dalhousie himself in 1939 with a degree in Classics, Doull spent several years both before and after the Second World War in various graduate schools – at the University of Toronto, Harvard, Oxford – educating himself in the tradition of Western philosophy and theology, influenced in particular by his studies under the supervision of Charles Cochrane, the great classicist at the University of Toronto. In 1947, Doull, along with George Grant, took up an appointment at Dalhousie University. The two – Doull in Classics and Grant in Philosophy – established an astonishingly vibrant intellectual context for philosophic education. Grant would later say of Doull: 'Of all the Canadians of my generation, he certainly has the clearest intellect of any I have known. Nothing I would ever have to say about philosophy will compare to his knowledge of it.'[3] While Grant moved to McMaster University in 1960, Doull stayed on at Dalhousie, and played a central role not only by establishing his distinctive approach in the Dalhousie Classics department and its academic journal, *Dionysius*, but also, through his many students, in giving shape to the Foundation Year Programme at the University of King's College.[4] Likewise, Doull's influence has been formative in the Philosophy Department of Memorial University and its Sir Wilfred Grenfell College Campus, and in Canada's first Internet journal of Philosophy, *Animus*. His recent death is a great loss to the Canadian academy, but his influence and significance are substantial.

2. The Question Concerning the Contemporary

Doull saw his own project, though thoroughly immersed in the long history of Western thought and freedom, as fundamentally contemporary. According to him, the need to question the one-sided and immediate forms of contemporary freedom arises as a demand from within the contemporary itself. In a 1984 article about the origins of contemporary institutions, Doull describes the problematic character of contemporary understandings of freedom that motivates his philosophical project:

> The common assumption of recent times has been that institutions exist to protect and to promote the rights of their individual members. There is assumed to exist a free individual who can expect as of right from the state, from the economy, from the family, the satisfaction of his needs and desires in increasing measure, approximating his full satisfaction. These and other institutions are thought to derive all their authority from individuals so defined. Because the measure of justice lies in the particular will and opinion of individuals, not in the objectivity of institutions, in universal ends, the distinction of state from economic society, of family life from participation in the work of society, is in great part obliterated. Marxist and liberal are in perfect agreement that a former elevation of the state above society – the realm of particular interests – has been superseded, as also the family which was once thought the principal interest of women, who were therefore excluded from the productive and progressive work of society. The questions are asked in this inquiry, what is the origin of this assumption? Is it well founded? What are its limits? To ask about the origin and foundation of what has been, one may say, for a century and a half an ever more fixed and settled dogma is not without difficulty. It may appear to be only an antiquarian inquiry, curious but without practical interest, or else what is thought intolerable, to recommend a return to the institutions and beliefs of an unliberated age. But the necessity of the inquiry can no longer be disregarded: it becomes always more deeply felt and recognized that this contemporary society can give no account of its principal assumption, of the confidence that once animated the democratic and socialist revolutions.[5]

Doull's writings provide a careful, philosophically precise examination of how contemporary freedom is related to and situated in the context of the larger development of the West. Doull's interest is not to bring against our time the freedom or virtue of an earlier age, but neither is it simply that we be reconciled to contemporary self-understandings. Rather, he would have us recover by a careful study the stages of freedom that belong to the Western tradition so as to grasp more fully the character of freedom that belongs to the contemporary. Doull's attempt to recover the history implicit in contemporary freedom is, however, marked by an extreme difficulty. On the one side, unless we know their place in the

Western tradition we will be victims of the divided and abstract forms in which contemporary freedom articulates itself; on the other hand, these very forms, because they have emerged in explicit rejection of the tradition, inhibit its objective appreciation. Thus, Doull calls for a two-sided movement of thought: contemporary self-understanding needs to be corrected through a relation to the tradition, and, simultaneously, our relation to the tradition must be freed of contemporary presuppositions. For Doull, the possibility of a recovery of the Western tradition lies in our capacity to discover in ourselves the elements not only of contemporary presuppositions, but also of the history that underlies and informs these assumptions. This requires a viewing forward and backward that will constitute at once our recovery of the past and our engagement with the present. This view is similar to Gadamer's 'fusing of horizons.' Like Gadamer, Doull sees the need to break down the assumed disjunction between past and present. However, by contrast with the Gadamerian view, for Doull the speculative power of philosophy provides access to a completed circle beyond the endless character of hermeneutical self-understanding.

Doull's standpoint, then, is specifically Hegelian. On his view, Hegel's philosophy is the most complete working out of philosophy per se, and it is only from this standpoint, of speculative reconstruction, that both the Western tradition and its post-Hegelian reaction can be understood objectively. As Doull puts it, 'Philosophy is the "lingua franca" in which we can dispute with Plato and Aristotle and the wise of the times without need of an interpreter.'[6] The papers by Doull collected in this volume can be read in their interconnection as just such a speculative reconstruction of the Western tradition. Equally, they provide a speculative recovery of the totality of contemporary freedom through the recognition of the continuing presence of the tradition even in the contemporary reaction against it.

According to Doull, this speculative recovery is thoroughly concrete, grasping not only past thought but equally the logic that animates art, religion, political institutions, and historical life generally. Following Hegel, Doull argues that philosophy gives access not only to an ideal realm, but to the very reality of historical life and institutions. To engage in a philosophical study of this history is to study the history of the truth itself in its creative, theoretical, and practical expression. From this standpoint, Doull's approach to current assumptions is three-pronged: first, he argues that contemporary forms, both intellectual and practical, cannot find stability in their own terms. Second, he painstakingly articulates the logic of contemporary intellectual and cultural forms and shows them as derived from and animated by the larger logic at work in the Western tradition as a whole. Third, he provides careful philosophic readings of texts from the history of philosophy as both an act of resistance to the contemporary claim that philosophy is impossible and also a necessary corrective to those readings which distort the tradition in the mirror of contemporary dogmatisms. All three of these themes can be seen singly and in concert in the pieces gathered in this volume and in the commentaries which accompany Doull's writings.

In all of this Doull is certainly a student of Hegel; yet Doull's recovery of Hegel in a post-Hegelian age cannot simply reproduce the position of the master. The recovery of a Hegel not adjusted to and distorted by contemporary assumptions is itself a demanding task. But Doull's concern is not with a merely scholarly retrieval of a past position. Rather, his claim is that Hegelian thought expresses the deep and living roots of the history in which the contemporary world has its place. In this task Doull has moved beyond recovery to the active development of Hegel's position. He has had both to explicate the development of post-Hegelian philosophy from Hegel's standpoint and to respond to the critiques of Hegel introduced by post-Hegelian developments, such as those of the young Hegelians, and of Marx, Nietzsche, and Heidegger. This recovery and defence of Hegel has in its turn required of Doull that he articulate aspects of the pre-Hegelian development not exhaustively considered in Hegel's own writings. In particular, he has articulated more fully than Hegel the philosophical character of medieval thought, especially in relation to the logic implicit in the writings of Augustine. Finally, and perhaps of most direct interest to many, Doull has before him historical developments which Hegel did not. For example, for Hegel, North America could only be 'the land of the future.'[7] Over a long career, Doull has thought deeply about the character of both Canadian and American political forms and freedom, and as well about the significance of the demise of the nineteenth-century European nation-state. Thus, we find in Doull a reflection on the post-national states of North America and the argument that they are capable of realizing human freedom more adequately than the nation-states of Hegel's world.

Doull's position then is not a mere repetition of Hegel, but a contemporary rethinking which is beyond historical limitations that circumscribed Hegel's own system. Again, the whole thrust of Doull's view is to shed light on contemporary thought and institutions. He insists on showing how a fuller appreciation of the spirit of contemporary institutions and their history would clarify certain contradictions of the contemporary world and make possible a more developed philosophical spirit.

3. Philosophy and Freedom: Text and Commentaries

Since 1967, Doull has published a series of significant studies ranging over the whole of the Western tradition. His retirement from Dalhousie in 1982 only increased this output of publication and reflection. Indeed, several pieces in this collection are appearing in print for the first time.[8] Doull's essays were written over the course of a long career, but while these articles took form on different occasions and for differing purposes, they nevertheless display such consistency of argument that a careful selection produces a philosophical history of Western thought and freedom, from its sources in antiquity through its present developments.

Philosophy and Freedom presents Doull's history of Western thought and freedom with illuminating commentaries on his often difficult but always rewarding texts. These commentaries are written by twelve colleagues and former students of Doull, from the disciplines of history, theology, classics, and philosophy, who are intimately acquainted with his work and who continue his legacy in universities across Canada and the United States. These commentaries are invaluable to the reader's exploration of Doull's thought, which is rendered difficult by its logical depth, historical reference, and terse style. Collectively, they help to illuminate and enrich Doull's consideration of that tradition as a whole. But in their own right they also serve as explorations of the different aspects of Doull's history of the Western tradition. Further, several of these commentaries place Doull's interpretations within the context of contemporary scholarship, allowing one to judge the relative depth and rigour of Doull's own accounts. Together, the texts and commentaries which this volume comprises provide an introduction to Doull's thought, to a longstanding and significant dialogue in Canadian philosophy and classical studies, to the school which Doull founded, and to the differences which animate its heritage.

The first text in this volume, a lecture given to the Foundation Year Programme at the University of King's College, Halifax, in 1999, provides in direct and popular form an overview of the argument that develops in the rest of the work. This volume is then divided into four sections: 'The Ancient World' (chapters 1–3); 'Medieval to Renaissance' (chapters 4–5); 'Hegel, Modernity, and Post-modernity' (chapters 6–7); and 'The Post-modern State' (chapters 8–9).

Doull argues in chapter 1 that Judaism developed an extremely articulate vision of divine creative freedom and, over the course of a long history, gave voice to a profound conception of the relation of human freedom to its divine source. Nonetheless, it was in Hellenic Greece that such a relation became the basis for a political life which in its institutions, art, and religion made manifest the union of God and humanity as conceived by its citizens. In the context of the Hellenic culture of Homer and the great dramatists, Doull finds the thought of Plato of peculiar interest: it is at once fully a part of this culture, but at the same time in tension with it so far as it emphasizes the division between the divine and the human. In this first chapter, Doull focuses on this tension and its kinship to the divisions of the Jewish standpoint – divisions which, Doull suggests, it is the work of Aristotle's thought to overcome.

In the first commentary on this chapter, Paul Epstein argues that Doull's account of the logic at work in Hellenic culture provides, over and against certain contemporary perspectives, a comprehensive account of the development of ancient tragedy and comedy. Epstein provides an analysis of the tragedies of Aeschylus, Sophocles, and Euripides and of the comedies of Aristophanes, in a way which demonstrates that the historical course of Greek drama can be understood as a two-sided articulation of the relation of divine to human freedom.

Angus Johnston, in the second commentary on chapter 1, interprets the argument of Plato's *Republic* as a philosophical image of Hellenic freedom. Johnston argues that this is the specific import of books 8 and 9 of the *Republic*, and sees his reading of Plato as complementary to Doull's sense of the inadequacy of Plato's account to Hellenic culture. For both Johnston and Doull, Plato's logic is unequal to the content he seeks to express, but while Plato provides only an image of dialectic, he is also aware of the limits of image.

Doull, in a dense and difficult reading of Plato's *Parmenides* in chapter 2, brings out the development in Plato's thought which, distinct from that of ancient Judaism, moves towards the Aristotelean conception of the relation of the many and the One, of the human and the Divine. Doull finds in Aristotle's philosophy the fullest expression of this logic, a logic comprehensive of the freedom manifest in Greek culture and institutional life. According to Doull, however, the ironic result was that having achieved philosophical expression of this freedom, the Greeks fell into a Hellenistic subjectivity (scepticism, stoicism, and epicureanism) which was unable to comprehend the mediations present in Hellenic institutions.

Dennis House, in his commentary on Doull's analysis of Plato's *Parmenides*, makes the remarkable claim that even Plato would find in Doull's analysis a superior understanding of the integrity and logic of the *Parmenides*. In a detailed reading of Doull's interpretation, House articulates the logic of the *aporiae* which begin *Parmenides*. House argues that, having given poetic expression to the relation of the One and the many in such dialogues as *Republic* and *Symposium*, in *Parmenides* Plato seeks to give this relation logical form.

In chapter 3, Doull concludes his presentation of ancient freedom by considering the logic of ancient Rome. Here the subjectivity discovered in Hellenistic culture can be related to and grounded in an actual *imperium*. In Rome the depth of ancient freedom is made manifest in a developed universality, but together with this manifestation comes an experience of the limits of ancient freedom: its incapacity to hold together human subjectivity and political institutions.

For Colin Starnes, the Roman world gives practical realization to the theoretical unity of thinking and being accomplished among the Greeks. Starnes, following Doull, finds in Virgil's *Aeneid* the most developed expression of the principles which ground the unique stability of the Roman regime. Starnes's commentary points to the relentlessly practical character of Rome's 'eternity,' which, betraying the limits of the ancient world, points toward the deeper spirituality of Christianity, particularly as expressed in the thought of Augustine.

Chapter 4 indicates how, according to Doull, Augustine discovers a human subjectivity, deeper than that found in Hellenistic culture. In relating this subjectivity to a Trinitarian God, Augustine develops a conception of human freedom beyond that available to the ancient world. For Doull, Augustinian subjectivity was to have a complex history: in part it will ground the new spiritual freedom of the Middle Ages and be the basis of medieval institutions; but more fundamentally, a renewed Augustinianism will be the basis of the modern critique of medieval spirituality. From this latter perspective, Doull finds in Augustine a logic that exceeds the Neoplatonism of both antiquity and the Christian Middle Ages.

The commentary by Robert Crouse provides a subtle examination of Doull's account of Augustine. Crouse is simultaneously extremely appreciative and highly critical of Doull's consideration. While Crouse and Doull may provide differing accounts of Augustine which have, in turn, important implications for their consequent interpretations of the medieval and modern worlds, there is a shared perception that Augustine's spirituality must be distinguished from the pagan forms, in particular from those found in pagan Neoplatonism.

In chapter 5, Doull provides a history of the development of Neoplatonism, from its first formulation in late antiquity through to its various reformulations in medieval and Renaissance Christianity. Doull's argument is that this history moves toward a relation of the One to what is other than it such that it is comprehensive of this otherness. At this point, the long development of Neoplatonism is completed and there occurs the transition to modernity in the emergence of a 'cartesian subjectivity.'

Wayne Hankey's commentary on Doull's account of the history of Neoplatonism succinctly situates Doull's argument in terms of contemporary scholarship. Hankey suggests that Doull's position is one-sided, and that this one-sidedness rests in his claim that, in modernity, Augustine triumphs over Dionysian Neoplatonism. For Hankey, what is problematic is the central Hegelian claim that Augustinian subjectivity is comprehensive. Hankey suggests that post-modernity brings to light the suppressed Dionysian aspect. On his view, the recent interest in Dionysian Neoplatonism and the reappraisal of Augustine in post-modern philosophy and theology stem from important philosophical movements beyond Hegel.

In chapters 6 and 7, Doull presents Hegel's philosophy as both the culmination of modern thought and the origin of post-modernity. For Doull, Cartesian subjectivity is beyond Neoplatonism and is also comprehensive of Reformation religion. In modernity the completed spirituality of the Middle Ages, through a renewed Augustinianism, is reconciled to the world and is able to construct institutional forms whose legitimacy consists in their deepened expression and comprehension of the inward freedom of the individual. 'Enlightened' civil society is the practical fulfilment of the subjectivity in which Descartes grounds science and philosophy. Doull considers Hegelian thought as in principle comprehensive of the modern divisions of citizen and institution, subject and object. In both 'Hegel's *Phenomenology* and Post-modern Thought' (chapter 6) and his debate with Fackenheim (chapter 7), Doull responds to the contemporary rejection of modernity and its Hegelian fulfilment. He provides here a reading of Hegel's philosophy, both as comprehensive of the history of Western freedom since antiquity and as capable of reconciling post-Hegelian developments which are themselves seen as falling within the logic of Hegel's system.

Lin Jackson's 'The Hegelian Idea,' commenting on Doull's treatment of the *Phenomenology* in chapter 6, brings to the forefront the Hegelian logic which underlies Doull's approach. Jackson's vigorous account indicates how for Hegel and for Doull 'freedom is not only the principle of spirit, of human psychological and ethical life. It is also, in another form, the principle of nature, and beyond that again it is the idea that forms the inspiration and object of all artistic, religious, and philosophical expression.'

In his commentary on chapter 7, Ken Kierans investigates the 1970 debate between Doull and Emil Fackenheim, 'Would Hegel Today Be a Hegelian,' which centres on the status of Hegel's philosophy in the contemporary world. Kierans focuses on the accounts of evil which Doull and Fackenheim formulate. For Fackenheim, Hegel's account of evil falls short of the realities of post-Hegelian history, especially the Holocaust. Kierans suggests that Fackenheim's understanding of evil and his reading of Hegel is akin to that of Schelling. Through a sensitive reading of both sides of the argument, Kierans indicates that Hegel and Doull both speak from a standpoint that can give philosophical expression to the horrors and despair of post-Hegelian history.

In the concluding chapters of this volume, Doull brings to light the limitations and ambivalence of recent articulations of Western freedom, showing the relevance of his philosophical history to the pressing concerns of contemporary political discourse, especially in the context of the Canadian constitution. In chapter 8 Doull examines difficulties in the concept of freedom inherent in Heidegger's *Being and Time* and finds Heidegger's thought an inadequate guide to the complexities of North American freedom.

Graeme Nicholson's commentary, however, argues that while Doull has rightly characterized the contemporary as a unity fallen into divisions of the natural and ideal, he has mistaken the character of Heidegger's philosophy relative to this. Nicholson suggests that rather than occupying one side of this division, Heidegger partakes of both. Thus, for Nicholson, Heideggerian thought, without claiming a standpoint comprehensive of contemporary divisions, is nevertheless beyond them and, therefore, beyond Doull's account of post-Hegelian philosophy.

Chapter 9 is a fitting conclusion to this volume. Together with the history of Western philosophy and freedom from its antique origin to its expression in the Hegelian system, Doull's primary concern throughout his scholarly life was with the foundations of Canadian sovereignty. Here

Doull's philosophical history illuminates the basis of the Canadian constitution. Canada is artfully drawn into this history, and shown to be held by self-understandings inadequate to its own political life. For Doull, the recovery of a logic that is comprehensive of contemporary forms of thought is more than an intellectual exercise; rather, it is part of a deeper appropriation of the freedom that is properly our own and crucial to our constitutional reconciliation.

The development and character of Doull's political thought is the subject matter of the last two commentaries. Henry Roper considers Doull's political writings up to 1983, and suggests that, in spite of a deepening pessimism about practical remedies, especially in Canada, Doull's position through to 1983 was remarkably consistent: rational freedom was attainable only by institutional forms capable of resisting and ordering the naturalisitic individualism of the consumerist economy of the United States.

David Peddle and Neil Robertson reflect on Doull's political thought from the mid-1980s to the present. They suggest that there is a crucial development in Doull's later political thought. Doull came to a deeper sense that a rational freedom was actual in North American political institutions. Crucial to this new stance was a re-evaluation of the United States, where he perceived a constitutional order capable of relating and ordering the divided nature of contemporary life. Nevertheless, he still makes fundamental distinctions between those forms of North American institutional life appropriate to the United States and those appropriate to Canada. What is required, to resolve Canada's constitutional uncertainty, on Doull's view, is a more comprehensive understanding of Canadian freedom and an institutional life more adequate to its expression.

Through its exploration of the thought of James Doull, it is hoped that this volume contributes to a deepened sense of the history of the contemporary world, its thought, and its institutions – to a better sense of the requirements and possibilities of our own age and country.

Notes

1 Chapter 7.
2 Chapter 5, Commentary.
3 William Christian, *George Grant: A Biography* (Toronto: University of Toronto Press, 1993), 139.

4 See M. Heller, 'The Foundation Year Programme at King's College,' in M. Nelson and Associates, eds, *Alive at the Core* (San Francisco: Jossey-Bass, 2000), 234.
5 Doull, 'The Christian Origin of Contemporary Institutions Part Two: The History of Christian Institutions,' *Dionysius* (Dec. 1984), 53.
6 See 'Freedom and History,' p. 5 below.
7 Hegel, *Introduction to The Philosophy of History*, trans. Leo Rauch (Indianapolis: Hackett, 1988), 90.
8 This book was begun before Doull's death. Appearing here for the first time are the introduction 'Freedom and History: From Antiquity to Post-Modernity'; section 2 of 'Plato's *Parmenides*' – 'The Hypotheses of Plato's *Parmenides*,' which was written especially for this volume; and 'Heidegger and the State.'
9 *Philosophy and Freedom* thus completes in a certain way Doull's project in his 'Christian Origin of Contemporary Institutions' articles.

PHILOSOPHY AND FREEDOM

The Legacy of James Doull

An Introduction by James Doull – Freedom and History: From Antiquity to Post-modernity*

What, if anything, can be learned in our present age from a comprehensive study of former ages and of itself? By 'learned' I do not mean what store of curious information you have acquired and can talk and argue about subtly and entertainingly, but whether you have in some measure been educated to a better understanding of the present time in which you live and make your way – a better understanding, that is, than is contained in the current dogmas you brought with you and everyone repeats. It seems at first sight that you can have learned nothing from the Foundation Year Programme, and that for two reasons. The first is that former times are commonly thought to be knowable not as they were, but only through the medium of current language or at the extreme as they are for each of you uniquely. The second is that the present age has found that it cannot know itself. Philosophy is supposed to be the self-understanding of an age, and we have discovered that for us there is no philosophy.

As in the course you moved from one age to another, the beauty and clarity of some former time may have invited you, as the Sirens invited Odysseus and his crew, to live there in your own time: ancient Greece perhaps, or Dante's ascent to Paradise, or the aesthetic freedom of the Renaissance. But then are you not like some Don Quixote, giving to the things around you, even to the point of folly, another sense than they generally have for those of your own time. Regarded in this way, the Programme would not have educated but rather unfitted or deranged you for the world in which you inevitably have to make your way.

*Originally presented as the final lecture, Foundation Year Programme, University of King's College, April 1999.

Or stay with the present age, and what by its own account you learn from it in the end is a kind of sophistic resembling that of Gorgias, who declared that there was nothing; that, if there were, it could not be known; that, if known, it could not be spoken. Regarded in this way, the Programme, it seems, can teach you nothing about this or former times. You have apparently either a quixotic learning or none at all.

This paradoxical result appears inevitable if we consider for a moment the general constitution of those former ages, in which you might be tempted to live quixotically, and that of the present age. At least for peoples who had come to a sense of their rational freedom there was God or gods, nature as in some manner dependent, man as in and dependent on nature, but also in relation to an eternal order, both his end and the origin of his ordered temporal freedom. In your study of the ancients you saw the several forms of this constitution pass into and find stability in the Christian world, to which you had an introduction through Augustine. That structure with important variations, in the course of its history, continued through the Middle and Modern age. Then you found that God-centred world humanized or historicized, as though we had come to be confined in a sort of Platonic cave, from which we could make conjectures but had no knowledge of what might be beyond it. The former unification of man as both a natural and a universal or thinking being which we had through that older constitution and its history we took ourselves to have immediately and to be empowered to realize it temporally outside that larger context. But then we found this humanized world to be divided and ourselves in it: either we had an existential freedom in some natural particularity or in an indifferent equality we would know and control all the conditions of life, and thus provide for every need and desire. Then we discovered an incorrigible conflict between these constituents which were assumed to make up one world. And both these abstractions, each in itself and in their relation, showed themselves endlessly divided and incapable of the unity they were assumed to have. From that experience we have the current sophistic and end of philosophy.

This conclusion likely does not agree with your experience of the Programme. Have you not learned much about other times? And have not current dogmas lost something of their hold on you? But if that experience be not illusory, there must be some medium of exchange between this and former ages. Some have thought to find in language a hermeneutic which could interpret the new and the old to each other. But we have begun to know again what was already known to the

Ancients, that language is not the house of being but needs its own interpreter.

Let us consider what it means when we say there is no philosophy. We are not to take it generally but in a particular context. So limited, the statement is true: philosophy as pursued within the bounds of our post-metaphysical culture has been defeated by the endless negativity or difference of things. Analysts, Phenomenologists, Existentialists, and whatever other sects have held the stage in this century have failed in their promise at last to provide a scientific philosophy. There is not such a philosophy as was intended. As to whether generally there is and has been philosophy the statement says nothing. The conclusion from this impasse is not that of Richard Rorty, that, though philosophers know nothing, they deserve honour and reward all the same as good talkers. Sophistic has a far greater importance, and for this Rorty and others who have reduced seeming philosophy to sophistic indeed deserve honour and a living. As has been said, if there had been no Phrynis, there would have been no Timotheus: that is, if there had not been such a sophistic, there would not again be philosophy.

Put to Parmenides the conclusion that there is no philosophy. He could just as well reply that not philosophy but the endless finitude that stands in its way is illusory. The Platonic Socrates went beyond this abstract response and proved to a reluctant Protagoras that they were engaged in the same work. Protagoras not only played games with being and not-being but undeniably knew their objective conjunction in the pleasure he had in his art. For pleasure has implicit in it its negation, which is pain. This immediate conjunction of contraries, giving way to more stable conjunctions, is the thread which could free the prisoners from the dogmas of the Cave.

Philosophy is the 'lingua franca' in which we can dispute with Plato and Aristotle and the wise of the times without need of an interpreter. In the reading of poetical and other texts and in the general understanding of another age, it is the surest corrective of anachronisms. We can learn to distinguish what of our own time fell within the interest of another time and what did not, and to see past ages as not only past but also present and partially coincident with our own, It thus appears possible that you have learned something of the past from the Programme, and something pertinent to an understanding of the present age.

In your studies you have observed that the desire to be liberated from the burden of authority, tradition, institutions is not uniquely of our time but occurred also in other ages. That from which one would be liberated is not the same in one age and another, nor is the liberated state. But these differences fall within a common structure: there is a negative movement, then in the completion of that movement an interest is awakened to know that from which one has been liberated.

Let us take as perhaps the simplest illustration the Greek world. In Homer you saw its elements as present but still loosely related to one another. One epic is about the family, the other about the political order. The two are not drawn into one action as later in the dramatic poets. The political order as it appears in the *Iliad* is inchoate: monarchic, aristocratic, even democratic polities are there in a rudimentary way. There is an underlying tension between the mortality of the living individual and the desire through heroic virtue to find relation to the immortal life of the gods. The living individual and his desired universality are brought nearer together in the 'polis' as political power tends to pass from aristocracy to the wealthy and to the many. In the Athenian democracy all these elements are present and have reached a certain balance, which you may read in *Eumenides* and other plays. Then in the great war of the Athenians and the Spartans this customary order breaks down as democratic individuals find themselves the support of the state and in this relation take the objective order to be their possession.

The individual in the immediacy of that relation takes himself to be the measure of all that before was measured by the balanced order. The sophist was liberated from the human and the divine order, which had for him only such being as he might choose not to deny. He was in the contradiction of being, at the same time, beyond the former order – liberated from it – and incapable of knowing it. Philosophy, as Diotima explained to Socrates, begins in poverty, need, and thus in the desire to satisfy itself in a freedom which knows as its own what one had been liberated from.

Let us suppose that our liberated, post-modern world is in this negative or sophistic phase, from which it has not come to an understanding of itself and that from which it has been liberated. With us this sophistic phase is far more comprehensive than in ancient Greece. The individual who is free from a former divine order and its imprint on human institutions is a member of two societies – of a linguistic and cultural community, and of a 'global society.' His rights are assumed to be primary in relation to both societies, but are divided as are those societies. In the one he has a right to life and to a natural particularity of language and culture; in the other these differences are subject to an equality which tends to obliterate them. In an older nation state, which was under a divine order, opposed national and economic societies were in one way or another united.

For a time each of these societies sought to subject the other to it, the national as what one calls 'fascistic,' the economic as Marxist. These have given way to a democratic nationalism and a pluralistic, corporate economy. In this change, and necessary to it, has appeared the beginning of a common state – in Europe at least, where this whole revolution began and has gone through its logical development. In this turning to a state which is eventually to unite these divided components one may discern the approaching end of this negative phase.

The revolutionaries of this and the last century never believed that the Owl of Minerva takes flight only as the evening darkens. They took the negative phase they were in positively, and saw it as a realization of former ages which knew itself and could control its course, as many today, extrapolating from unstable assumptions, imagine they know the shape of the approaching century and millennium. Philosophy, as has been said, knows only the actual, but that as rational. Past ages for the philosopher belong neither to museums only nor, as we reach out to them in nostalgic desire, do they like Creusa's ghost ever recede and elude our grasp. They belong to our actuality, as that through which what we are directly liberated from took shape. Our bat-like vision can only approach that actuality by degrees. The way then by which you can learn something about the present age is to look forward and backwards at the same time – to learn both what some earlier time has given us, and in what it is insufficient to where we are.

Let us then consider briefly a little of what you may have learned from the ages your reading and the clarity of your teachers have brought before you. On the ancient peoples who did not know the self-conscious freedom you first encountered in Jews and Greeks only one element. You should have learned from them to question the prevalent dogma of the present time that primitive peoples with only the rudiments of a rational culture enjoy a natural freedom, are guardians of nature, not destroyers of it, are peace loving and not, like those of a European culture, brutally dominant; etc. I assume that you have learned how by a harder work than to found the Roman race some came, as with Gilgamesh, to know and lament their unfreedom. The Mexicans at least of our American aborigines know better their relation to the European conquerors. They set forth even pictorially for everyone to see how the Europeans brought them both the benevolent Utopia of Thomas More and the avaricious cruelty of the 'conquistadors.' From the one they derive, at whatever cost, an inner rationality and a capacity for self-government.

Ancient Judaism

In reading something of the Old Testament you may have learned the first conclusion of this struggle to be freed from the domination of natural powers. The self-conscious freedom we both assume and flee from in our contemporary culture began in the knowledge of nature as created in the divine freedom and that freedom imaged in man before he fell into evil ways. It was likely also brought to your attention that there was here only the beginning of a rational freedom – a submission to the primacy of the universal, not a freedom which pervaded the finite and united it concretely with the universal.

You perhaps observed the folly of those who would leap from Heideggerian 'being' to the God of Exodus, from an existential freedom which finds the source of evil in the universal to the pure universality of divine thought; a folly in which one fails to see in Heidegger's 'being' the existentialist nationalism which came near to destroying the Jewish people and which thus passes over a long historical mediation.

Hellas

In your study of the Greek world I hope you have learned to respond to the misconstructions of Nietzsche, Heidegger, and other existentialist writers who treat philosophy, especially since Socrates, not as an understanding but as a desertion of an earlier poetical vision. That is to construe that world in post-modern terms, and so to derive from it nothing you do not already know. It being hard to know when and how far your poetical imagination differs from that of Greek poets, the surest guide to an objective reading of their works is the philosophical understanding of the same world by Plato and Aristotle.

Let us not be drawn into that world for fear we would not in the time we have get beyond it. It must suffice to comment briefly on its limits. In the poets from Homer on you found a company of gods at once free immortal beings and in the bodily form of mortal humans. These elements were joined for an aesthetic vision. Humans aspired to a like aesthetic embodiment of self-conscious freedom. Nature for this aesthetic vision was neither divinely created, nor was it on its own. It was matter for an imagination which would make it the home of free self-conscious beings, so far as that was possible.

As the looser Homeric world developed into ordered self-governing 'polis' and a unity of ends constrained the multiple relations of humans to themselves and the plurality of free divine beings, this aesthetic view reached its limit. In the dramatic poets interest passes from this plurality to the whole relation of rational freedom to individuals in their natural particularity, who had their substantial basis in the family and the eternity of the underworld. The result in the end was to bring into one these relations, in an individual holding in his self-relation the particularity of the aesthetic presentation. On the divine side, the gods, who for the artist had a natural particularity grounded in themselves, had this concreteness for themselves. In this the divine plurality passes into one God. In the God of Aristotle the abstract unity of the Jewish religion and the particularity of the Greek coalesce. But this result is not for the free individual or person who can only approach the divine unity by the negation of all particularity.

We find an affinity with the Greeks as the first people to have known democratic self-government. Democracy is not government by consensus merely but by a consensus of rational individuals. It was for the Greeks the natural result of their historical development – of a religion and culture which knew natural differences as grounded in self-conscious freedom. But Greek democracy is not democracy as we know it. There is nothing of individual rights in it, nor is there anything of a civil society, of a private freedom having also common ends. Again, when democracy came fully into its own among the Greeks it degenerated into 'ochlarchy' or mob rule, where individuals lost their sense of the common good. Why this was so and how we could avoid the same result you may have learned from the Programme.

You find in Plato and Aristotle a logical division of polities or constitutions which has remained in political philosophy: monarchic, aristocratic, oligarchic, democratic. In the Modern Age these are rather distinctions within the unity of the state than existing independently. With the Greeks these polities tended to follow one another in succession: political power passed from a patriarchal monarchy to an aristocracy, to the wealthy, finally in democracy to the many. In this succession previous forms, and the virtue which could maintain them, remained in the later and gave them stability. But, as there was no unity comprehending them, this ordered relation was precarious. Private interests broke away from the political good and corrupted the several polities. With the corruption of democracy the cohesion of the state was lost.

You find in Plato and Aristotle the clearest understanding of these relations in their first principles and as related to the primary distinctions in the human soul. The limits of Hellenic freedom are evident in the ways in which they would stay, if only for a time, this process of corruption. In Plato's *Laws* one finds an ordered relation of polities, but set over it the 'deus ex machina' of a 'nocturnal council' which, like an inquisition, would prevent the emergence of an immediate individual freedom, in this forgetting the initial relation of his philosophy to sophistic. With Aristotle the best polity would have stability through the dependence of a highest practical freedom, where one was an end to oneself in the contingent, on the contemplative knowledge of an absolute divine freedom which knew all division and finitude as its own – the heroic virtue of the poets which reached beyond itself to the gods. The government of a 'polis' which could remain in this relation would be an aristocracy, and those who were occupied with particular ends, where private interest draws one from the political good, would best have the status of slaves. What are the conditions of a modern democracy? And do we retain them in our post-modern culture which cannot so much as understand the ancient?

Rome

You have read in the *Aeneid* where Jupiter confers on the Romans 'imperium sine fine.' The Roman state would not be subject to the successive movement and corruption of polities, nor would individual freedom be destructive of the political community. What causes then belied Jupiter's promise and led to the decline and fall of the 'imperium Romanum'? Great books, one knows, have been written on this subject. But let us consider for a moment what gave to it this incomparable stability.

The poet tells that Rome was founded by Trojan exiles who, after many wanderings and mistakes as to who they were, became one people with the Latins, an uncorrupted rustic people. The Trojans to find unity with the Latins had first through their leader to descend into Hell, know the hold of evils on the soul and a purgation underlying them. Then this potential good had to be forgotten as Aeneas reentered the world of the living by the ivory gate, by which 'falsa ad caelum mittunt insomnia manes.' Then this inner good had to be made actual as in a difficult war with part of the Latins and their allies evil passions on both sides were at length subdued. Finally in the rage of avenging his friend a political will is restored in Aeneas, and in Turnus the evil will which opposed the union of the Trojans and Latins retreats reluctantly to the realm of the dead: 'vitaque cum gemitu fugit indignata sub umbras.'

The poet rightly defined the immovable attachment of the Romans to the 'res publica,' by which they could subdue the known world. The several polities which the Greek state could not unite were contained in that relation. The political good was the prime motive for individuals, who would not be corrupted by their particular interests. This strong unity was expressed in the Roman religion: the gods were not the free concrete spirits of the Olympian religion, but particular ends deified. Or if they borrowed from the Greeks the many gods had only a superficial independence from the imperial will of Jupiter.

This structure was imperfectly realized in the mature Republic, where an aristocratic Senate of former magistrates controlled a legislative democracy through the regal power conferred on annually elected magistrates. This arrangement assumed that the aristocratic element would not be seduced by private interests and its authority over the people weakened – as happened when once the most dangerous external enemies of the state had been destroyed. A long civil war eventually made evident the true logic of the constitution, that the magisterial 'imperium' had to be conferred on one man. Virgil saw the positive side of this revolution – the absolute unified will of the preeminent magistrate as imposing peace and habitual obedience to the law on all peoples.

This restoration exposed however the original defect of the Roman state. Its coherence was through an abstract will which subdued nature and the passions. The emergence of these forces had been the corruption of the Republic, and they remained in the Principate and Empire. The free individual or person had this division in his self-relation. The many individuals within their relation to the sovereign individual were a society whose members, being excluded from an active part in government, gave themselves over to their particular interests. But in this they discovered an incorrigible division between an abstract Stoic will and an ever elusive otherness, and dissolved into sceptical boredom and vanity. The same division appeared in the state: an abstract oppressive bureaucracy and an imperial will which might be benevolent and might be an arbitrary tyranny.

The unified end which the divided individual could not find temporally in the state became the interest of a contemplation which sought a point in which thinking and its object passed into undivided unity. In that light temporal images of that unity might appear in an aesthetic vision. The state and political virtues were but an imperfect image of that eternal world. The 'res publica Romana' was no longer one's 'patria.'

Some see in this flight to an intelligible unity from Roman scepticism a cure to the scepticism of our post-modern world. In this they treat modernity as though it had never been, though from it we derive democracy, individual rights, the sciences in which we probe the secrets of nature, the application of their discoveries to human needs, etc. Their negative theology has this various content of which they can give no account. Negative theology has however another importance in that, retracting the assumption that there is a world independent of thought, it renders one receptive of a logic through which this content can be known as no longer an impediment to self-conscious freedom, the logic, that is, of modernity.

The Middle Age

In Eriugena one reads that between true religion and the Neoplatonic philosophy that he accepted from the Greeks there is no difference. Augustine in his *City of God* disposes of Neoplatonism halfway through that work as a reflection on the Roman world, and for the rest subsumes that contemplation, which does not cure the division in his soul, under a 'sapientia' he draws from Scripture of creation, fall, the conflict of the two cities and their final separation. A philosophical grasp of the Trinitarian principle moving in this history can only be remotely approached through the Trinitarian relation of the rational powers of the soul. On the human side the limit to a Platonic theology appears most strongly in the doctrine of grace and predestination he opposes to the Pelagians. Aspects of Augustinian thought which cannot be taken into a Platonic framework only come fully into their own in the Reformation of the sixteenth century which was no longer confined by that philosophy.

What is true in Eriugena's statement is that an incomplete Augustinian philosophy can be given systematic form through late Neoplatonism, further that this form contained what of Augustine was useful to a somewhat Pelagian church in its work of forming barbarous peoples to a rational relation to the religion they accepted and presupposed. The means to this formation was the philosophical culture of late antiquity, and the agent a sacred clergy, bearer in virtue of its office of the religious truth which it conveyed to the laity through sacraments externally given and received.

You have entered into this formation at certain points of its history. The *Divine Comedy* has always, I think, had a central place in the Medieval section of the Programme. There you followed the ascent of the poet from the collapse of a knightly virtue he celebrates in the *Convivio*, which could not stand on its own, to what absolutely sustains it – the Aristotelian principle which, self-moving, moves all else, and to his unified spirit reveals faintly the triune God of his belief. Guided by Virgil through Hell he learns the negativity concealed in the virtues, and then in a Stoic structure the purgation and original unity underlying this division of virtue and vice. Then Beatrice, the departed object of his ideal human love, takes him through a contemplation of the virtues thus unified in which by degrees nature and reason are drawn together. There remains still a multiplicity and division, subjectively unified through the theological virtues, and objectively disclosed through Bernard's contemplation, perfected in his devotion to the virgin mother of Christ, of nature and thought absolutely unified in a vision of the Aristotelian God no longer detached from humanity. On the historical side this unification is reflected in the emergence of an emperor who will subdue the evil passions and ambitions which set Church and Empire against each other and brought discord into all political relations.

Thomists who find in Aquinas and Dante a model even for our time appear to forget this passing historical situation. One has in these writers a wondrous work, but should not, as Dante himself in his denunciation of Philippe Le Bel, turn away from the reality of Dante's emerging emperor: emperors and kings, while they can unify, are strengthened also by this unity to pursue their ambitions for power and conquest. The human comedies of Boccaccio, Chaucer, and others have place in your initiation to the Middle Age as complementary to the *Divine Comedy*.

In philosophy as in the world there was need to hold thought and existence more strongly together and not simply assume with Aquinas that there were sensible substances from which our intellect could abstract the form. You could not have had time to look at the difficult arguments of Scotists and Nominalists on form and individuality, which intellectually prepare for that Renaissance in which ideal and sensible image concretely combine as not since antiquity. To the aesthetic vision it is as though the otherness of things did not impede the expression of their ideality. The content expressed was drawn alike from the realm of belief and from ancient myth and history. The unifying form was the

Neoplatonism which let the finite or divided stand only to pass to its truth in the mystical unity where thinking and thought were no longer distinguished. Historically in that Renaissance world the kingship which barely came into view for Dante brought under its power noble and commoner alike as their unifying end.

We can find respite from our turbulent, irrational culture in the tranquil clarity of Renaissance art. At the same time we know it is not the art of our time, in which this inner unity appears impressionistically, fragmentarily, or in mad Dionysian ecstasy. At such times as also intellectually differences recede for us into that primal unity, we can find in the Neoplatonic philosophy of the Renaissance the true theology of the Christian religion, there more fully than in Aquinas and Dante. But to live really in that age would demand a frivolous disdain of the devoted benevolence which, along with titanic arrogance and lust for wealth and power, moves in the arts, sciences, trades of this present age for the ease and improvement of human life. Beauty and negative theology can give rest from contemporary freedom and add elegance to life, but are not comprehensive of it.

Modernity

This Renaissance culture also in its own time was found insufficient to itself. The ancient thought by which Virgil and then Beatrice could guide Dante to the earthly paradise and through the heavenly spheres where he could receive the Christian truth, as it developed farther the relation of its ideal and sensible poles had its own completeness – and in it Eriugena's assimilation of Augustine to late Neoplatonism failed. The Vicar of Christ became a secular prince, competing with others for earthly goods, maintaining his power by the maxims of Machiavelli, selling spiritual goods to feed his love of beauty. The greatest need was felt to find a relation of this world to Christian truth without a Platonic mediation. You have no doubt read something of the two-fold reform of the Church: the one which, remaining within the structure of clerical government, drew on Aquinas, Scotus, and other medieval doctors; the other which retracted the equation of Augustine with Neoplatonism and replaced clerical mediation with 'justification by faith alone.'

In this latter Reformation was the beginning of a new age. The primary structure is not, as with Eriugena, of an ideal and sensible finitude receding as to its absolute truth into an infinite unity, but of a division comprehended within the infinite. Human self-consciousness, responding to this divine movement, was no longer content with an abstract mystical union but, as inwardly reconciled to the world, can enter into its institutions and works, not as descending to an inferior life, but as to that through which it can make actual its inner freedom.

How Augustinianism as thus informing a positive relation to the world is itself altered and how it came to be situated in a new philosophy independent of Scripture and authority are questions too difficult for a first initiation into these matters. Let us attend only to a few points which can clarify the relation of this modern world to post-modernity. For about this relation extremely divergent opinions are current. Some look to the Modern Age from the Medieval and through its assumptions. When did it begin? In the secular interests that take shape after Aquinas and Dante? In the Renaissance of the fifteenth century? Its philosophy is then a continuation and confusion of the older period. Or read Heidegger from among the post-moderns: it is the last, self-destroying inanity of a thought which has forgotten 'being' – an epilogue to Scholastic philosophy. These are external views which speak about the beginning and nature of they know not what. Considered from within, the beginning of a new philosophy is with Descartes, and the place of its gestation is the restored Augustinianism, which was a trouble to the old Church until in Jansenius it was expelled, while it was creative of the new.

For an existing world formed in the light of the new philosophy one can best look to the United States. There remains there a continuing relation to the first phase of this philosophy where a subjectivity certain of itself had true knowledge of the world in the light of a divine substance and one remained within the Christian religion. There is also a negative phase, which one calls Enlightenment, where the free subject and a community of such subjects are an end to themselves and realize in finite ends their divinely given rights to 'life, liberty and the pursuit of happiness.' And, connecting the two, is a moral will which can exceed private and communal interests.

The relation of these aspects is however not fully worked through in the Republic – not to speak of the presence in it of a post-modern culture forgetful of its history. The division and return is more deeply illustrated in Goethe's elaboration of the Faust story. The negative phase goes there into the extreme opposition of good and evil and the overcoming of it both in the free individual and objectively. The argument is nearer the Augustinian form but as responding to Enlightenment brings into one the contingent Humean subject and the rational subject. With that, as already earlier in Leibniz, disappears a final division of elect and damned.

The movement of this philosophy in its historical embodiment is of the formation of a society of free individuals [civil society] who regard the state as founded by a contract among them, who recognize free universal relations or rights in relation to one another and to the state, and in the end bring society under the state.

Post-modernity

We post-moderns do not live in an enlightened age, but without it the tensions and divisions in our age are incomprehensible – existential individuals and linguistic-cultural communities which assume themselves to be comprehensive of division or otherness and experience that they are not; the universal economic community which would be and is not effective of the whole good of the living individual; individual rights which as unified are assumed to underlie the state and other communities and are not united but in a primary division of life and equalized freedom.

Our post-modern world is called also post-Christian. Neither the Middle nor the Modern age could think itself post-Christian. The negative phase of the former was opposed not to the religious attachment as such but to a certain extraneous mediation of it. Enlightenment was opposed not to faith but to a subjective unfreedom in relation to it. Feuerbach, Marx, and other precursors of the post-modern age saw the content of religion as having become the possession of the existential individual or of humanity.

Post-modernity derives from Modernity, the division of state and economic society from an antecedent unity of them. Here as in other cases this result is only binding for a certain point of view – for one within this negative phase from which is concealed the mediation which made it what it is.

Again, when we say that individual rights are antecedent to government and the state, we forget that they derive from oppositions in civil society itself and its relation to the state. When rights are presupposed, society and state appear as subservient to particular interests, which they regulate bureaucratically, that is, abstractly, while individuals as bearers of rights are an anarchic force.

After Post-modernism

There is much to be learned from the past. In question is whether we in our present culture can be receptive of it. Let us look again for a moment at that culture in its most developed form. A half century and more ago the existential and universal aspects of it inspired a most destructive war between them. Following that war they lost in western Europe their apparent independence of each other. In what has become the European Union both nation states and a common economy have become subordinate to a common state. However incomplete that subordination is, it has tamed nationalism and modified somewhat the global economy in the interest of the Community. The divided national and economic aspects as related to that unity expose the relativity and otherness or difference which could be concealed in their supposed independence. It is of great importance that a recognition of this relativity appears to have undermined the attempt of Heidegger and others to maintain the integrity of one aspect or the other.

Europeans these last years have been disturbed to see that the national passions which overpowered them three-score years ago are alive in all their savage ferocity among their Balkan neighbours. Moved by the moral will of Americans they are attempting these last days to break this evil spirit in the Serbian people.

With the Europeans this subordination of national communities to a common state is very difficult. National independence is given up and not given up. Government is ambiguously centred in the Union and the national states.

We in Canada are not in that ambiguity. Particular sovereignties and a common sovereignty have long coexisted in our Constitution and the history of our federation. We are all Canadians but with differences having political form as provinces. What does it mean when Lucien Bouchard (Premier of Quebec) the other day said that, walking along a street, he saw many 'ethnics' but no Canadians? Prime Minister Jean Chrétien, if he walked the same street, might say he saw many politically correct equals but no Canadians. Both eliminate our history and our political constitution. This post-modern culture, though largely borrowed, is of great importance to us, as the negative phase without which we cannot grasp what we are. Multiculturalism and the global economy are either the end of us or that through which we come to an understanding of the federal union we already are through our history. It should be easier for us than for Europeans to resolve the contradictions of post-modern society – that is, if there is anything of an independent intellectual spirit in Canadians. So far as there is, there is not only much to be learned from the past, but we are capable of learning it.

PART ONE

The Ancient World

chapter one

Tragedy, Comedy, and Philosophy in Antiquity[1]

Ancient Judaism

In ancient Judaism the beginning of a liberation from nature which is found in the great Indic religions may be said to be completed. There is no longer the endless process towards liberation from natural necessity, no longer the bondage of immutable natural and inherited differences in the ordering of human life. The individual has assumed instead the attitude of one freed from a Platonic cave to knowledge of the universal, knows the world as created and sustained by a free, self-conscious principle according to ideas. The end to which human life should be directed is a knowledge of this creative principle, of the universal good through which created beings exist and find their appointed goods. The Jewish law in its elementary provisions aims at maintaining a community unified, drawn out of subjection to the passions, to natural powers, through relation to the one God.

The standpoint of this religion is not easily intelligible. It is not to be approached by a pragmatic logic adapted to everyday uses and to the discovery and control of contingent relations in nature.[2] Nor is it enough to have reverted from these interests to knowledge of an Eleatic being. The absolute of Judaism is not simply being or unity. If the world is a nullity in relation to the creative God, it is also thought to manifest his power and goodness through finite goods and principally through the dependence of these on the primary good. There is present in this position a dualism of good and evil, intelligible and sensible, but also the negation of it in the principle. Ideal and sensible being are, as Plato says, only hypotheses, have not their ground in themselves but in the good itself, which 'exceeds in dignity and power both being and truth.'[3] The good is the universal ground and origin to which thought has referred all being and itself as the knowledge of being. In this Platonism, which was perceived in antiquity to be the philosophical theology of Judaism,[4] the concept of the one creative God is made intelligible.

The negation of all externality and natural necessity in the service of the one God is the source of the wondrous trust and inner freedom of the Jewish and then of Islamic peoples.[5] It is not the subjective freedom of the Stoic, not the consciousness imperturbable in itself against the fatal course of the world. Human freedom here lies instead in the knowledge of the divine creative freedom, in the primacy of this knowledge over finite cognitive and voluntary relations. It is the freedom represented constantly in the Platonic myth of the soul aspiring to knowledge of the ideas, capable of this knowledge and held from it by its involvement in the sensible world, where the resolution of this division is not in the soul itself but objectively in the good.

The unification attained in relation to the good is the beginning and condition of a free subjectivity. But how this unity is the nature and possession of the human individual also in finite relations is not available to this standpoint. In another language it does not belong to this religion that God has a Son. Of first importance in relation to the origin of Christianity is how this limit, that there is not present an actual human freedom, could come to be known as a deficiency, how the desire to overcome it could be formed. To answer this question it is necessary to attend to the historical existence of this religion, how it is constituted in relation to the service of the one God.

Of this consideration there are two parts: first, the form of the older or original Judaism; secondly, how this form was affected by an awakening subjective reflection. It is this later form of which it is to be said that Plato provides the philosophical theology. The philosophical interest found in the Judaism of the last centuries before Christ should be thought an intrinsic growth, a receptivity of Hellenic influences which had its origin and need in that religion itself. The religion whose object is the God who can freely give existence to the world, in which the knowledge of this principle, the subjection of human finitude to it, is the highest concern, because it has in it the beginning of human freedom, provides a development of this freedom, even if this be as a subjectivity which does not maintain itself in the end in the face of the divine subjectivity. This religion tends, one may say, to a spiritual form, which is, however, impossible of realization without development of its unitarian principle.[6]

Judaism, though in its idea related to man as thinking, as inwardly free, thus to all men, is the religion of a particular people. Since this people has its freedom not in its natural existence but through its religion, it is said to be 'chosen.' This relation is not immediate: there was an original natural unity with God, then a fall and expulsion from the earthly paradise, the assertion of a particular human will against the divine creative will, then the reception of the people into its peculiar relation to this will and a human service to it through the revealed law. In return for a faithful obedience to the law the Jewish people is promised prosperity and continued possession of a land to dwell in.[7] Primarily natural human interests are given up in devotion to the one true good.[8] Then these interests are restored conditionally. The condition which stabilizes the relation of the two, of the absolute good to the desires of the soul and their objects, is the law.

The tension between the external life and prosperity of the chosen people and their inner freedom and relation to the good is easily known from the historical books of the Old Testament. The recurrent lapses of the people to cults more congenial to a sensuous will, then chastisement and return to obedience the prophets collect into a more stable relation: the sufferings of the Jews in their outward life has for its purpose to show to the gentiles the true and universal divine government. In these prophetic visions there is the beginning of an independent subjectivity, able to refer to itself the fall and return, the good and evil, of the chosen people. Separated from the absolute content of prophesy, this becomes the questioning subjectivity of the author of *Job*: is there indeed for the just the reward of a prosperous life? If the question is in the end answered affirmatively it is only after a sceptical dialectic forces the argument back to the absolute good which is beyond the opposed positions. To be consistent with the argument the conclusion would be that the correlation of justice and earthly rewards had to be abandoned. Instead, having discovered the ground of this conviction in the primary adherence to the one God, the author allows to stand the external correlation which his argument has undermined.

A like reasoning appears still more explicitly in *Ecclesiastes*, where out of the sophistic or sceptical experience that just and unjust, wise and foolish fare alike in the world the lesson is drawn that one must hold to the observance of the divine law. The argument has the same defect as in *Job*, that the negative aspect of it is rather lost than accounted for in the conclusion.[9] Since the resolution of the problem is only in the relation of the opposition to God as before their division, the coherent conclusion would be what is found in Philo, that the true Judaism is not to be found in the external life of the people or in Scripture literally taken but in the contemplative knowledge of the One who cannot be revealed truly in what is other than himself.[10]

The philosophy to which Judaism tends when once a free individuality begins to emerge from the common life of the people has its adequate exposition in Plato. In *Republic* the question of Job and the preacher made current among the Greeks by the Sophists, whether justice is more than a name destabilized by whoever cares to show the deceptiveness of language, is answered by taking the argument back to the good itself. It is necessary to show that those who assume that there exists on its own an economic community supplying useful goods and desired luxuries are mistaken. If animal communities can exercize their instinctive arts of building, hunting, gathering, and storing their food to the limit of their natural need, human desire has an endlessness which must receive its limit from the rational soul. This same endlessness is found in the active aggressive temper of a ruling class, in the ambiguous mixture of ambition and service to the common good, which not even so extreme a measure as the abolition of private households is sufficient to eradicate. To discover an end in which private and public goods are undivided it is necessary to turn to the universal, to the ideas and finally to an object – the good itself – on which hangs all division of the ideas and their difference from the thinking soul.

The question whether there is a true justice which is the good alike of the individual and of a community living according to a rational law has its answer thus in a principle beyond both. The question accordingly takes the form how this principle can be realized, how it can impart limit to the multiple, divided, endless, which, in the soul or in a human community, has otherwise only an illusory stability and peace properly considered. The polities usually recognized and the virtues which order the soul to them are only a decay and falling away from the good polity in which law and virtue are ordered to the undivided good.[11] But of the reality of justice and the true polity *Republic* treats only generally and obliquely: a people must be elevated beyond private interests to a pure devotion to the law, and the laws themselves must have in them an inner identity and unity of purpose, whose absence in ordinary communities exposes them to sophistic criticism and destruction.

The question how the good polity can exist is treated further in *Politicus* or *Statesman*. In that dialogue, as in others nearly related to it, Plato has before him the Eleatic conclusion that there is no true finitude but only the One itself.[12] In *Sophist* he has shown how there can be a definite otherness or finitude for a theoretic thought, namely by a limitation of indeterminate difference in relation to an absolute identity. In this way is constituted both an unchanging ideal world of genera, and their species, and a changing sensible participation in this order.[13] In *Politicus* the same question is asked about a political community: how can its ideal ordering to the good – its constitution – exist in a sensuous will moved by needs and struggling to find a self-relation against them? The answer given is that it can exist in two ways: either good government is a theocracy where there is an immediate submission of the passions to the good and the law and constitution defining the relation of human animals to it, *or* on the human side there develops out of the arts or particular applications of a teleological reason a universal political reason, which takes on itself to order the passions to the good.[14] The theocratic ideal has the defect that it has no room for human freedom, for a human participation in the divine freedom which is its principle. To realize the ideal humanly there is need not only of a legislator to disclose the true constitution to a people, but also that the legislator rule, that in him be present the activity of applying the law to the unpredictable variety of particular cases. The ideal human ruler thus does consciously with knowledge what the divine ruler accomplished immediately.

But how does this orientation to the good exist in human passions? Plato answers that in the passions there is a principal division between the passive and the active.[15] Not that the passive is without an active, the active without a passive aspect. But a disunity and imbalance of these aspects is the source of indeterminateness and evil in the soul and in the state. The principal work of the ideal ruler is to find a synthesis and limit of active and passive powers in the irrational soul. In this way the soul is rendered receptive of the mutual limitation of affirmative and negative which is the logical basis of law as of ideal finitude generally.

This profound consideration of the nature of government, whether and in what ways freedom can be present in the direction of human affairs, has in it the inconsequence pointed to above in relation to Judaism. In the theocratic form there is lacking a consciousness of the discrepancy between the absolute divine good and the desire and search for a natural well being. Where a knowledge of this difference is awakened and the desire to bring the two together into one relation, this unification is only found possible by suppressing the desire at its source, namely in the tendency to a free subjectivity. In looking for a natural balance of active and passive powers, the legislator-ruler of *Politicus* intends to prevent the emergence of a self-consciousness which, as with the Sophists, should take itself to be their absolute unification.[16] From this subjectivity and an attendent scepticism the escape and remedy is in effect a return to the theocratic relation, but now with the knowledge that an ordered human life can only be sustained in unfreedom. The Platonic state in which are worked out the implication of this conclusion is found in *Laws*. In the state there designed legislator and ruler are no longer one. But only by an imposed orthodoxy can the citizens be saved from lapsing into false opinions about the world, from giving priority to the contingent over the necessary in nature, which can lead to a knowledge of soul and the divine.[17]

The restored theocracy of *Laws* has the same instability as the Judaism of the Preacher. It depends on an awakened self-consciousness which is required to negate itself. Give place to this self-consciousness and it will dissolve the finite into its abstract elements, into affirmative and negative moments whose unity can be found only in the good itself. Deny it place and human life is separated in its particularity and natural existence from its absolute end. Plato has the fullest lucidity about the problem: he has asked how there can truly be anything but the One or the good; but to this question he finds no sufficient answer, only that the contrariety which is the nature of the divided, is suppressed in the positivity of the finite, its negativity being present as otherness. But the otherness is implicitly contrariety, and shows itself as such at the point where the relation of the finite to the One or the Good comes to light. There is not on the side of the finite a unity of contraries, save as a synthesis or mixture, but only in principle.[18]

The same matter can be spoken of in the concreter context of law. It was known to Plato since his early Socratic dialogues that the legalistic adherence to a particular positive injunction rests on a blindness to the negativity and, at the extreme, contradiction which is also present. The great sophists were perfectly aware that this was so, and made an art of sorts out of this knowledge. Socrates and Plato find refuge from this art by transferring the problem to the absolute. The Platonic dialectic is a kind of sophistic in the service not of a liberated individual but of the good itself.[19] The interpretation of the law in this view cannot be left to the judgment of the virtuous citizen, but must be done for him by one versed in the good, not the sophistic, dialectic. In this manner of thinking the casuistry of Rabbinic and Islamic lawyers has its origin, where law cannot be separated from its religious ground and must remain the possession of a sacred order. The same is found in Plato's *Laws*, where underlying the ordinary application of the laws is partly the authority of the original legislator, partly a nocturnal council, watchful against the appearance of a radical human freedom, doubtfully corrigible once it knows too much.[20]

This argument is of the highest importance in relation to the origins of Christianity, in that it exposes fully the limits of a Judaic monotheism. The naturalism of a divinely sanctioned attachment to land and a prosperous life in it passes into an abstract legalism. These moments are unified in God, but this unity is not revealed in the creature. What is unspiritual in this religion is negated. There is the principle of a spiritual religion, but of this there can be no development without first a deeper knowledge of human freedom, a knowledge that division, contrariety, necessity are negated not only in the divine principle but also in human thought, in a free subjectivity which is not critical or sceptical merely, as in sophistic, but knows the concretion of opposites, the unity of form and matter, as constituting natural substances and subjectivity as the highest substance. But this knowledge has its origin elsewhere, in a religion where this human freedom is presupposed, develops into free political institutions, is brought to light in aesthetic experience and finally in philosophy.

Hellenism

The ancient Greek religion is as difficult of access to the contemporary student as the Judaic. It is not only that in Hellenistic times this religion had lost its older sense and had become a matter of culture. The long alliance of this Hellenistic-Roman culture with Christianity appears in turn to be dissolved in recent times.

About the relation of Hellenism to Christian theology there have been many opinions. It can appear that through Hellenic philosophy an original, more existential Christianity was transformed into an intellectual system remote from the experience of the Christian community.[21] It is forgotten in such accounts that the idea of an incarnate *logos*, alien to Judaism, has already from the first all the philosophical difficulties of the later theology.[22] If in Christianity this idea could be grasped as completing the Judaic monotheism, as bringing division and concreteness into the concept of the one absolute God, whereby an adequate revelation of the divine nature was possible, it is inconceivable that this development could occur directly out of Judaism. That God was revealable and revealed was rather known first to the Greeks. In the Hellenistic world this knowledge took the form of a radical human freedom severed from its divine origin. There was, however, a point in the discovery of this freedom where it could as well be said that everything was Zeus – that the human went over to the divine – as that the sovereignty of the gods had passed to man. In the older Hellenism, and there only, is it possible to follow the formation of the second element of Christianity, namely of a concrete and adequate *logos*, or determination of the one God.

It can be useful to consider first the end of this Hellenic development, where it was given a precise conceptual formulation by Aristotle. One can bring thence to Hellenic religion and art, where the same idea of a free humanity first appears, an objective measure, evading thus the assumptions of a contemporary aesthetic and science of religion. As against the Platonic good, in which thinking goes beyond itself to an inner freedom before division and difference, the *prakitos nous* intellect is for Aristotle an end in itself.[23] Its finitude is that it operates in that which can be other than it is, in the contingent. The modes of its operation, the ethical virtues, are limitations of contrary affections of the soul, of contrary possibilities of its action. The ends of the practical intellect as thus defined may be realized or may be frustrated; the virtues have in them partially the conditions of their realization, partially their realization depends on contingencies beyond their scope and on the necessary course of nature. To *eudaemonia* belongs both the ordered satisfaction of human desires in actions according to the ethical virtues and the actuality of the practical intellect itself, which is exempt from the contingencies of the particular virtuous ends. But to the latter it belongs principally, and this thinking activity which is for itself is what it is to be human.[24]

This human freedom is to be distinguished from that of the sophist, who if indifferent to contrary possibilities, is all the same subject to them, in that he thinks nothing, which is beyond their division, is the subject of contraries. The Aristotelian practical freedom is a mode of operation of the theoretic nous which knows that, in thinking beings in the many ways in which they are for it, it thinks primarily itself.[25] Thinking in this account is neither wearied by an empirical endlessness nor does it find its limit in contraries as the end of analysis, but sets before it the unity of contraries as substance and perceives a dependence of substantial necessity on the unmoved self-relation of thinking.[26]

Aristotle's ethical treatises and the *Politics* can only be ambiguous, perplexing, and in the end unintelligible if they are abstracted from a theoretical interest. Before there were philosophers the Greeks were accustomed to place their practical life, this as constituted by the relation of free individuals to the substantial institutions of family and political community, in the universal context of religion, of the relation of men to gods and of both to an invincible fate or necessity. The poets taught at once the ruinous consequences of a human hybris that would overreach the due limits of human life and a knowledge of fate which raised heroic individuals to the level of the gods. Ethical and political questions for Aristotle as for Plato are about the form of that limited human good which stays short of the deepest conflict of good and evil. Plato, as shown above, had not discovered how this finite human realm could have a certain separation and independence from its absolute foundation, how there could be present in it an actual human freedom which was all the same limited. Nor again had he discovered, what is constantly assumed in the poets and was historically the case, how the family could be thought to have its own end, state and family being neither confused nor the one subordinated to the other. Aristotle is true to the Hellenic tradition in dividing family from state, in finding in both a human freedom stabilized against immediate reduction to an absolute theoretic freedom.[27]

Plato had perceived rightly that the Hellenic family, which had its independent relation to the gods and could expect an unqualified attachment from its members, was the final impediment and threat to the formation of a political community which should know and be obedient to the good and a just ordering of human interests to it. The difficulty he observed is analogous to that experienced generally at the present time between an absolute right of individuals to the satisfaction of their particular interests and the possibility of government not paralyzed by competing and contradictory pressures from the governed. Were there what is called a pluralistic society, it might be thought the problem of a unification of interests need hardly arise. But what is so designated is in truth a society where only a formal unity is sought, such as is amenable to computation, to a logic which only superficially integrates concept and reality. There is then, however, no true community, no consciousness of common and private interest reconciled, but rather of division endlessly extended or a Hinduistic flight from uncomprehended particularity. Plato has before him instead, as observed already, an ordering of particular goods to one supreme good, the formation of a community where particular interests will not settle into independence but be held dependent on the one true good. The abolition of the family for the ruling class he so far modifies in the *Laws* as only to forbid private cults. What is intended by these provisions is illustrated best by Judaic institutions, where a patriarchal unity of family and state can contain and bring back to itself the hardening and isolation of particular interests.

What Plato would evade as destructive of any stable peace in human affairs, namely that there should be two equal and opposed relations to the highest good, occurred in fact among the Greeks, being indeed the essential structure of Hellenic institutions. Homer had presented in the *Iliad* a conflict of individuality and heroic virtue which could not be resolved until there was awakened in the principal hero a knowledge of the nullity of both, that love and friendship and the pursuit of honour, these and the gods themselves, who sustained these goods and conferred them on mortals, were comprised in an underlying fate or necessity. The finitude of human desires and goods being thus revealed, it was possible for the hero to return to them, to live within an ordered finitude. In this relation human goods were known to the hero as a mixture of good and evil. He who sought them inordinately brought to light the contrariety in them, experienced their contradiction as the extreme of human evil, and knew its resolution only as implacable necessity.[28]

This is another knowledge of necessity than is found in Plato and in Judaism. There it appears as a recognition of human impotence, of the division of human from divine, then as an elevation of thought to the knowledge of a creative divine self-consciousness beyond the opposition of being and truth. Necessity is not in this view the end of the argument, where nothing remains but to acquiesce in what cannot be otherwise, but is transitional to an inner freedom in the knowledge of the one God. In Greek religion, necessity appears as beyond the definite intentions of the gods, as destroying the relation of human and divine subjects. But there is also present here implicitly a more developed relation of human and divine than in Judaism. Achilles is not, as with Job, simply restored in the end to his former happiness, but in returning to his virtue is also freed from its finitude. It remains that he should know the division of universal and particular in human interests not simply as negated in fate or necessity but as contained in a purified relation of human and divine subjects.

Plato brought against Homer and the other poets that they showed the gods as the cause as well of evil as of good, also as taking on themselves an immediate and deceptive human form.[29] These are true objections by a Judaic measure but mistake the nature of the Hellenic religion. To know with Job the one God, the absolute good, is no doubt a higher knowledge than Achilles attains, but is at the same time less developed on the human side. The Olympian gods are themselves so far more Christian than the one Judaic God in that there is in them an actual unification of divine and human, not the principle only of a unification. The goods which the gods bring about in human life are mixed with evil; virtue is bought at the price of life, the political good with the ruin of family. But the gods stand back from human strife and the failure of their own purposes, know the fatal connection of good and evil as beyond their definite purposes but not beyond themselves. For the Hellenic gods, no less than the one God of Israel, are known as free subjects. They are not natural forces invested with a superficial subjectivity. Subjectivity is their nature, and the moving spirit in this religion is to discover a relation of humans as free individuals to this divine subjectivity. With this discovery vanishes the sensible individuality of the gods, the love and seduction of mortals and other such offensive manifestations.[30]

If the *Iliad* brings to light out of the struggle of war the conflict of virtue and life, fate or necessity as the true and primary object, the *Odyssey* shows the truth of the family to lie in the same object. It is necessary to the enlightenment of Achilles at the end of the *Iliad* that his seeming freedom to choose between winning glory at Troy and returning to a happy life in his family be removed, as is done through the death of Patroclus. Between him and Achilles was a friendship having like obligations to those among members of a family. To Patroclus dead and departed to the potentality of Hades Achilles has the inescapable obligation of revenge. He returns to his political obligations to the Greeks first as to the only means of revenge. His return restores to the Greeks the unity and undivided favour of the gods they had sought for vainly since the beginning of his quarrel with Agamemnon. His savage mutilation of Hector's body and the sacrifice of Trojan prisoners provoke the resentment of the Olympians. Achilles' choice has now the objective form of a conflict between the Erinys of Patroclus and the Olympian gods. The resolution is not that of the *Oresteia*, where Athena and the Areopagite court determine the honour due to both. Here Achilles and Priam are raised momentarily above the division of family and state, but not so that this inner unity is known as a subjectivity which can order the relation of individual to state.

That inner principle underlying the division of individual life from the common political good, as this division is presented in the objective form of a difference of divine powers, is what the poet means by fate or necessity. That this is implicitly subjectivity or free individuality is more easily discerned in the argument of the *Odyssey*, which is directly about the individuality the *Iliad* treats of not for itself but in relation to strife and division in the Greek army, to the sources of unity and order of a political community. Odysseus in a way knows well the end which moves him to return home against every obstacle. Penelope likewise knows in a way why she continues to resist a misalliance with one of the suitors in the face of their depredations and the practical certainty of Odysseus' death. In another way the end is unknown and has to be defined by the course of the argument. The domestic good is assumed to be different from that sought in the common enterprise against Troy. But if it lie in the satisfaction of the living individual as against the universality of honour, may the hero not be spared the labours of many years and the unfailing hostility of Poseidon? With Calypso he can enjoy a natural immortality, the good of the Biblical paradise. Among the Phaeecians he is offered the enjoyments of civilized life. With such goods the wise hero cannot be contented, but is guided homewards by Athena herself. The Hellenic family has its ground not in nature but in thought. The final evil with which the restored family has to contend is the Erinyes of the slain suitors. But Zeus and Athena cause an oblivion of the lust for revenge among their relatives, whereby peace is restored between them and Odysseus.

The conclusion of both the great Homeric poems is in general the same: between the desire of honour, the universality of fame, and the saving of one's individuality there is at the extreme a destructive conflict, of which there is no actual resolution in human life. There is liberation from it only by participation in the inspired knowledge of the poet who can bring forth from himself the fatality of human life, in this freeing himself from it. This knowledge Achilles can enter into, but only then to return to the pursuit of honour, whose nullity he has already experienced. In the *Odyssey* there is, however, the difference that this inner liberation is shown to be the nature of the family, is so far actual and enters into human life. It can appear curious that in that poem Odysseus should be led by Athena, not to the various exercise of his resourceful spirit, but to an inactive domestic tranquillity. But then, as the poet knows, the ground of intelligence is in the inwardness and potentiality of memory, before the dividedness of Odysseus' clever sophistic wit.[31] The correction of this division he finds in Penelope, and to that Athena directs him in his return. This good Odysseus can only enjoy by the intervention of Zeus, who restores a political order between him and the relatives of the suitors. To this end he does not appease the Erinyes but causes them to be forgotten. In the argument of the work the political order remains, as said, in the background, is presupposed; the particularity which asserts itself against it is negated at the point of extreme opposition – in the Erinyes of the suitors or with Odysseus in relation to the virtue of Penelope.

The Homeric muse thus presents an actuality of divine ends in human life and also a knowledge of the limits of those ends. Before this imagined world and its principal division into Olympus, the realm of the gods, earth, the field of contingent human purposes, and Hades, the resting place of the dead, is the muse which brings it forth from the depths of memory. This moving spirit of the whole does not itself appear, while those who hear the poems are referred beyond the action of men and gods to fate as the truly actual, and to a potentiality before division as the substance of the family. The poet has articulated and given a total context to a human desire to come to oneself, out of change and mutability, not only to a formal law, but to an *ethos*, to law which is not abstract, but the end and moving principle in the passions. But he has directed this desire for an actual freedom also beyond it to a self-relation which is inward and potential only. Out of this contradiction and the desire to dissolve it in an actuality adequate to the potentiality can be understood the further course of Hellenic poetry. It suffices for the present purpose to attend to tragic and comic poetry, peculiarly the creation of the Athenians. This is the poetry of an ordered community where family and state are assumed to constitute one whole, where a *theoria* of their division is possible, a subsumption of it under their unity and a knowledge of this as the one true actuality into which pass the multiple divine and human purposes and fate or necessity itself. Of this actuality one poet will say 'And in all this action there is nothing that is not Zeus' (Sophocles, *Trachiniae*, 1278); another, what seems altogether opposed, 'All that was Zeus's of old now is our hero's alone; Sovereignty, partner of Zeus on his throne, now is forever his own' (Aristophanes, *Birds*, 1752–3).

In these opposed ways, which Plato saw to complete each other,[32] tragic and comic poets overcame the distance between myth and self-conscious reason, between fate and freedom, human and divine, discovering thus the ground of a spiritual religion. The tragic poet presents an action in which the spectator, experiencing both sympathy with heroic agents and fear before the fatal course which leads them to destruction, is purged generally of passions responding to the division between the purposes and suffering of the heroes and remorseless fate, is awakened to a knowledge of his freedom. In tragedy the agents at most come to the point where they know their fate as themselves, where their suffering is converted into a movement from themselves in which they are no longer deceived by a hidden negativity or error implicit in their virtue, their character. The comic action begins instead with a vulgar subjectivity which has fallen away from virtue and the fatal consequences to which it is liable. As Aristophanes tells in *Symposium*, the comic agent is the result of division from a unity to which he would return.[33] This return is a purgation of his immediate individuality, of his vulgarity, to an individuality which is the subject of the original division. Tragedy shows thus an assimilation of human to a universal, divine self-consciousness, comedy rather the human pole of the same relation.

Aeschylean tragedy, if one take the *Oresteia* to realize best its full intention, is content to resolve the extreme division of state and the Erinys of the individual, which has its existence in the family, in a subjectivity present in the state, in an Areopagite court inspired by the wisdom of Athena. The Athenians, contemplating the fate of Agamemnon and its consequences, might learn what was in the blind passion for conquest and military glory, the violation of family which lies in it,[34] of the madness which pursues political action unpurged of the lust of private vengeance,[35] how there is political reason which transcends and can order the division between abstract law and the profoundest offense to the heart, to the sacred right of the Erinyes.[36] Out of that reason can come a reconciliation of thought and feeling, of political man with nature, not an immediate unity with nature but a concretion which has come out of the deepest division. This reason which can arrest the fatal necessity in which unthinking human action finds itself caught they learn from Aeschylus' presentation, how they might participate in it through reverence for the Areopagite court, the guardians of established law, the remnant of an aristocratic constitution giving way to democratic equality.[37] There is room for tragic poetry which can discover also to the many who are prone to put their judgment before traditional authority that their nature is this concrete self-conscious reason.

The Orestes of Sophocles has no need to be acquitted by a court or to be exiled, to be excommunicated for a time from the political community. His matricide is not only authorized by the Delphic god, is not only in principle pure as the due exercise of his kingly office, but is also through the perfect collaboration of Electra at the same time the work of the family spirit, of an undefiled, undivided Erinys.[38] In an action which thus unites the sacred right of the individual, the right of the dead in the potential existence of Hades, with the active reason of the political community, the Athenian spectator could find no guilt. Where Euripides supposes instead a debased Electra, sunk into selfish interest and forgetful of a simple obligation to the spirit of her murdered father, so direct a liberation of Orestes is not possible.[39] Even when the Areopagite court has acquitted him, he is presented in another Euripidean play as only abstractly free, as subject to possession by a wild animality, which has still to be united with his rational soul.[40] Of this unity he becomes capable through his sister Iphigenia, she perforce the priestess of a barbarous cult in which the lives of captured strangers are sacrificed by her hand to Artemis. From this involuntary savagery she is inwardly free, purged in it from resentment against her own sacrifice to the same goddess, intended by her father but frustrated by divine intervention. Thus reconciled she desires to return home, which she accomplishes with her brother, who has been freed not only from the external negation of his animality by sacrifice to the goddess, but inwardly also through the humanity of his sister.

The logic of this tragic purgation appears nowhere more completely than in *Oedipus Coloneus*. Presupposed in its argument is the ruinous fatality which drove the wise king in the earlier play to discover his birth and inexpiable offenses against his parents, to blind himself, cutting off the sources of a knowledge found useless to him, and to impose on himself permanent exile from Thebes.[41] The spectator of that play had contemplated not only in the one man the simultaneous ruin of kingly power and of family but also his active inquiring intelligence coalescing with the prophetic vision of the blind Teiresias. There is the beginning of a self-consciousness which knows fate or necessity as not alien to itself,[42] and there *Coloneus* begins. The wanderings of the blind Oedipus have led him to the sacred grove of the Eumenides at Colonus, where he senses he is called by the gods to end his life. His daughters have served as guides to him, his relation to the visible world. Through the argument of the play there is formed in him a self-direction; a passive, inspired knowledge of his end is converted into an active movement to it, a voluntary passing to the gods. To this movement the impediments are his pollution, his sin against the Eumenides, and the collapse of his once confident political intelligence, the elements of the fate which destroyed him. What is known incipiently from the other play must here become explicit to him, that this fatality does not fall outside his self-consciousness.

That Oedipus is already reconciled with the Eumenides is beyond the piety of the Attic elders who make up the chorus of the play to understand. Time and exile are not enough to obliterate the memory of his offenses, but only the oblivion of Hades, to which he is turned. In that relation, in the pure inwardness and potentiality of his soul, he is free from the fate that has driven him restless in his exile. He is able to subordinate fate and necessity to a consciousness of his freedom and regard his sins as suffered rather than done.[43] That this is so Theseus can accept from him, who has himself descended to Hades and, returned, knows the relation of the living individual to the potentiality of death. If one compares this play with *Antigone*, Oedipus has here such a knowledge as Creon in that play might have attained, if upon his ruin he had discerned the principle of the family piety maintained against him by Antigone. He would then have corrected the abstractness of his active political reason and come to know its origin in an immediate relation to the oblivion of Hades.

It remains that Oedipus should be seen as freed also from the division of reason from nature and individuality in the political community, from that division which had been his own ruin. His sons contest the kingship of Thebes, the one on the natural principle of his prior birth, the other on the rational principle of general approbation by the people. The impossible device of an annual alternation of the two in power having failed, Polyneices raises an army against his country and his reigning brother. The resolution of the conflict, the ground on which the opposed principles might be reconciled is to be found in Oedipus. The brothers compete for his favour, for possession of his person, though neither had thought to put a term to his exile and restore him to a place in his political community. The brothers in this show themselves ignorant of the condition of peace between them, namely an absolute respect for the undivided unity present in the family. It is not so, as Plato would reason, that the family is the origin of faction and disunity in the state. Nor is it true that the best state is the most unified where division has been suppressed in the highest degree.[44] The poet shows instead through his Oedipus how the state can sustain a difference of general and particular interests, if this difference be known as derivative, as from a prior unity in the family, as able therefore to be given up in the state and not maintained unconditionally. Oedipus invokes destruction on his sons who are incapable of this wisdom and have in themselves no basis of reconciliation. To Theseus who has known why to respect him, has given him citizenship and place of burial in Athens, he can impart the highest political wisdom, the secret of true kingship, which can tolerate and encourage diversity without losing itself in faction and an ungovernable plurality.[45]

This enlightenment Theseus can only fully receive at the moment of Oedipus' death, which he alone witnesses. Though between Oedipus and his daughters there is a perfection of family virtue, perfect devotion requited by a love equal to it, they cannot accompany him all the way to the place of his death. The nature of his death is not to be known in that immediacy of family love. For in it Hades and Olympus are as one, oblivion and the intelligence which knows fate and itself as prior to it. To speak of Oedipus' departure as death Theseus knows to be inappropriate.[46] It is rather death and resurrection undistinguished. To Theseus is given an intuition of the unmoving principle which moves in the extreme division of human life, to which humans are related through their fundamental institutions, the end into whose self-relation is dissolved even fate or necessity. This knowledge it would be impossible for Theseus to communicate to the citizens of his state. The ordered life of political and domestic communities rests on the difference of family and state, of Eumenides and Olympian gods, of finite ends and overpowering fate. These differences at the same time vanish into a unity of human and divine. The spectator is led thus to a freedom beyond the limits of his religion and institutions, in which he can no longer find full satisfaction, but has need to discover an order in which there will be place for this free human subjectivity.

In Sophoclean tragedy there thus appears a resolution of the problem and fundamental interest of the ancient Hellenic religion: the division between a concrete unity of human and divine ends or, its historical equivalent, of institutions and individual freedom, – this and the loss of these goods in a fatality stronger than divine and human purposes. Here fate or necessity is shown as only the appearance of an infinite divine freedom. This argument returns to the one God of the Hebraic religion, to whom the true human relation is now no longer immediate but mediated by the difference of human and divine. This difference is lost, however, in the result, which, with Aristotle, one may express thus, that God's knowledge is not of what is other than himself, since then it would be of the divided, of the base as well as the good, but a higher knowledge in which the divided and other has become self-knowledge.[47] This result is only so far distinguished from the Christian concept of God that there the other and finite has not only receded into the divine self-knowledge but develops out of it, having through this reversion become adequate to it. For this development to become revealable it is also necessary that on the human side the disparity between a self-knowledge originating in this older Hellenism and a content inadequate to it should be experienced as a scepticism and loss of nature.[48]

What in the tragic presentation appears as a negation of the difference between human and divine is in the comic rather the formation of a rational human individuality or personality, the humanity of the Hellenistic-Roman world where will be felt in due course a need of the Christian religion and a dissatisfaction with its seemingly more plausible and natural rivals. The comic poet, as said already, assumes a vulgar individuality which seeks its private good, is in conflict with the ethical order, is, as the poet openly declares in the 'parabasis,' no other than the ordinary spectator himself.[49] The purgation effected by this poetry is not through the relation of the 'demos' to heroic characters of greater than ordinary virtue but directly of itself. The same content as in the tragic purgation is here referred to this ordinary individual as its subject. One who brings to Aristophanes' comedies the characteristic assumptions of contemporary culture will find there some mixture of censorious conservatism and pornographic indulgence. It is thus forgotten that there was not at that time a subjectivity so assured of itself that it could live thus in an opaque plurality of interests. There was no principle present which could sustain a radical opposition of virtue, of adherence to the ethical order of family and state, and the instincts of a mob democracy. The incomparable interest and importance of this comedy is that, complementing tragedy, it could reveal this principle of free subjectivity or personality.

The dividedness and the desire to reconstitute a former unity which Aristophanes in *Symposium* declares to be the nature of *eros* – to be human nature – appear as a breaking away of particular interests from the common end to which the citizens were formed by the old virtues, as this division and a movement in the individual to return to the former unity. Plato describes a like movement in *Republic*, the inevitable course of corruption of the good state to the extreme point of a tyrannic individuality, in which the primary desire of the good in the soul is obscured by illusions but remains. This division of the soul from its true end one can regard as a corruption, but also as the formation of individual freedom. For the free individual or person is he who has in himself his relation to the good and his finitude and difference from it. Plato knew this individuality in the superficial form of sophistry, as a relation of the division in its pure abstraction to the individual, a knowledge of himself as measure of the being and negativity of all things. Whether as an assertion of sensuous immediacy or as a universal rhetorical art, sophistry did not know the Socratic desire of the good, of the return to unbroken unity. To Plato it was as though division and otherness should not have been, but only the good. If in image and language and not conceptually, the comic muse shows better than either the relation of individual to the good or undivided.

The comic purgation begins with the lapse from virtue, with trivial and divided characters, then awakens in the spectator the knowledge this dividedness is absurd, that is, contradictory and a nullity. The poet may bring about this purgation through a content itself close to his own purpose, as when he sets against each other the Socratic analysis and search for the universal and the tendency of this criticism to dissolve ordinary virtue. The spectator of the *Clouds* assuredly misjudged Socrates, but through him might be purged for the moment of his own self-serving abuse of reason. A better subject of the comic art is the demagogue who promotes an aggressive public policy to make a career for himself, the confusion of justice and private motives in Athenian judges, of the love of peace with the self-interest which generates war and faction. For in these characters are combined the terms of the division which in *Clouds* are distributed between Socrates and those who would abuse the lessons of his 'phrontisterion.'

Of all the surviving comedies *Birds* exhibits most fully the nature of this purgation, the disclosure of an individuality freed from the division between an abstract good and its more confined interests. When the Athenians first contemplated the action of this play they were engaged in the greatest and most ruinous of their follies, the conquest of Sicily. To adhere to the advice of Pericles and fight a limited war with the Lacedaemonians, which they could prudently expect to win, supposed a virtue in their rulers which knew its limits, which respected the ethical order of family and state. In this enterprise the 'demos' showed itself to be wholly possessed by the divided spirit which would get beyond its division by indefinite aggression and expansion. In these circumstances the poet makes the people in the whole scope of their political life the subject of his comedy. The chief characters of the piece, a plausible talker and his gullible companion, themselves thus fully in the spirit of this society, cannot bear its oppressive business. They would find for themselves instead an animal life where desires could be satisfied without the complications of human society. In this they revert to the primitive presupposition of Hellenic religion and its ethical order to a veneration of natural powers, irrational vitality, which one learned from Hesiod and other poets had been succeeded by other gods, and last by the Olympians. In comic form this beginning of the action is equivalent to the pseudo-aristocratic Nietzschean reaction of a Critias or a Callicles to Athenian democracy. In *Birds* it appears as an inarticulate, immediate individuality, in flight from the dividedness – the 'nihilism' – of society but able when developed to comprehend it, to be free of its endless otherness.[50]

The fanciful bird-city which those unlikely heroes found has need of arts they left behind, but has in it, what Athens lacked, the power to correct the ensuing corruption, to expel or discipline immigrants come for the same reasons as themselves. Having separated themselves from the divided life of Athens, they are capable of a knowledge of the division, are no longer merely in it. When war breaks out between the new city and its nature gods and the Olympians, the first defector to them is Prometheus. How is it to be taken that Prometheus, who had gone over from the Titans to the Olympians, from irrational brutality to divine reason, should now defect to the nature-city and its gods? Not assuredly to bring blessings to mankind through the arts, for what Aristotle will say of *techne*, that its end is in the product and not the maker, who therefore is unfree, had long before been expressed in the Prometheus myth: the divine liberator of the human race from immediate dependence on nature was himself bound in the chains of necessity from which he was only freed by submission to Zeus, to the *praxis*, which is its own end.[51] A merely technical society divides men from nature and cannot restore the unity it has broken; there is not a common end of reason and desire present but an endless expansive striving towards it. From an Athens which had fallen from political virtue into just this division the founders of the bird city had fled. If Prometheus will join them it is not to be bound again, but because he will find the arts there and the desires they stimulate and serve, immediate individuality and reason united.

In the bird city there is not only a liberation from Promethean necessity, from the contradiction of freedom and servitude in the arts, but also from the necessity stronger than the purposes of the Olympians. For what is it that a war between men and the gods ends with the transfer of sovereignty to Peisthetarios, to the ordinary Athenian? It is not a victory of nature over reason, of nature gods over the Olympians. The war is with all the gods; the ambassadors who come to treat for peace with men represent both the barbarous nature gods and the Olympians, and with them is Heracles in whom human and divine are united. It was an old story that Zeus would be cast from his throne by a son stronger than himself; that, warned by Prometheus, he avoided this overthrow by giving up a design of marrying Thetis. In the offspring of this marriage nature and self-conscious intelligence would be more adequately united than in the Olympians or in the sons and daughters of their casual alliances with mortals. Sophocles can present the human and mortal in Heracles as transfigured into the divine.[52] But for the comic poet he is then only a bastard son and not true heir to Zeus: he is not as individual divinized. In this comic war the implicit unity of nature gods and Olympians in Heracles is explicated, and for the spectator in Peisthetairos, and so in himself.

The nature of the old comedy is perhaps still more evident in the last surviving plays of Aristophanes. It may be said that the revolutions which, following the Sicilian expedition, destroyed beyond repair the balance of traditional virtue and democratic freedom which Athens had enjoyed for a time, left a public no longer tolerant of a criticism sparing no folly. That the comic muse is thus responsive to social opinion and not rather formative of it has in it sociological assumptions of later time. After *Birds* had shown the Athenians a free subjectivity underlying all the content and primary distinctions of their religion and public life, what remained for this comedy to do that would be more than repetitious of the same? The genius of Aristophanes found material still, but of another kind. Tragedy, the other form of the Dionysiac theatre, could itself be treated comically. Both dramatic forms bring to light a relation of human individuality to the divine subjectivity of the Olympians, prior to necessity and the finitude of their purposes. But this is an inspired knowledge which neither poet nor those enlightened by him can take with them from the theatre to ordinary life. This same knowledge as separated from an aesthetic embodiment and become the possession of pure thought is what the Greeks called philosophy. To make the tragic movement from man to god subject of the art which knows how to relate the divine to man is to go some way towards this philosophical separation. In *Frogs* Aristophanes weighs against each other and submits to the judgment of Dionysus (the subjectivity the Attic poets knew how to clarify from a Nietzschean immediacy to its true nature) the objective direction of Aeschylus' tragedy and the Euripidean tragedy which can approach nearly the subjectivity of comedy.

In *Ecclesiazusae* and *Plutus* the separation is completed. The one, as in Plato's *Republic*, equalizes the division of male and female, bringing to light a common rational subjectivity. The other discloses a rational freedom through the contingency and necessity of economic life. Of the latter a commentator observes, 'The stately Parabasis is gone; the beautiful lyrics which elevated the whole performance into a higher and purer atmosphere have altogether disappeared; the great historical personages, literary and political, the poets, the philosophers, the demagogues, the generals ... have faded not only from his own satire, but almost from the very recollection of his audience: ... the performers might almost be treading, so to say, the boards of some provincial theatre.'[53] Truly said, save the last point: *Plutus* belongs still to the Old Comedy in that it does not yet find matter for comedy in the complications of private life. The interest of the piece is how nearly explicit is the subjectivity which, once established and presupposed, will invite the comedy of Menander and his successors.

Towards a knowledge of Christianity it is of the highest importance to distinguish this older Hellenism from the subsequent Hellenistic-Roman culture. In the former, there is discovered a relation of man to God which is not mediated, as in Judaism, by a simple negation of the finite but by taking the finite into an infinite spiritual relation. In the universal Hellenism of the Roman Empire one has the result of this discovery but no longer the way to it. A spirituality is attained with the loss of an older content, the need of a content adequate to the new principle. The older Greek religion, the imagery of the arts, institutions which required but could not contain free personality, all this passed into an immediate spiritual unity of human and divine. The transition became, however, the object of a philosophical thought which freed it from the instability of language and imagination, which knew nature and human finitude, their difference from and relation to God, through categories or pure distinctions of thought.

From the above argument easily emerges the standpoint of the Aristotelean philosophy, as also its relation to the Christian religion. The original Aristotelianism is neither, as is congenial to contemporary criticism, an empiricism contaminated still with a mythological remnant, especially in its theology and psychology, nor is it the Neoplatonic Aristotelianism which in its various forms was an invaluable servant to Christian theology for many centuries. It could not be the former, since there was not then a reason so well settled into finite interests as to see the principal questions of an older philosophy as mythical, linguistic, speculative in a bad sense; to take as standard a mathematicized logic which had lost the power to discriminate categories; to look for a knowledge of the soul through its powers fragmented and frozen into various empirical attitudes. The interest of that time was to discover a humanity which could stand in relation to God, which did not show itself a nullity in religious and practical experience. In what is called philosophy in recent times this independent humanity, though always assumed, remains mostly unknown. To Neoplatonism Aristotle provided a finite or discursive moment which receded into an intuitive unity, itself categorially indeterminate, not as originally determined to be self-knowing as against knowledge through other categories, spoken of therefore by preference in the abstract categories of being and unity. Here again the spirituality in which the Aristotelean philosophy ends is assumed, but abstractly and not as in the Christian religion.

Plato, asking what it was for sensibles to participate in the ideas, was led to the conclusion that the two worlds were related in the good itself, prior to their distinction. The difference of ideas and sensibles being once assumed, what appeared to be a relation of the two dialectic could always show to be illusory, to be rather an endless otherness.[54] Himself unsatisfied with that result, Plato supposes as well a divine thinking whose activity combines the undivided and divided principles, produces an ideal world and a sensible image of it.[55] If in this way he would show the good to be actual, the actuality is not by this account its nature but posterior to its undivided unity.[56] Aristotle was not alone among the first Platonists in seeing that a revision of principles was necessary.[57] Some might think to find an actuality of the undivided principle in ideal or qualitative number. Here, however, the dyadic principle was presupposed: in these numbers its endless divisibility should be arrested, not shown as derived from the undivided. Others instead therefore abandoned the ideas and would treat all that was posterior to the good as in truth quantitative, as number. Here there was indeed continuity or self-identity and endless divisibility, not the two as activity. The thinking which regarded the continuity and discretion of quantity was only more obviously external to its objects than Plato's divine intelligence.[58]

The impediment which divided the good from creative divine activity Aristotle saw to be the common assumption that everything finite was composed of contraries.[59] No further advance was possible unless what thinking knew as other than itself was comprehensive of contraries. The *nous* knows first the categories. The accidental categories it knows as related to substance, which, while remaining itself, is capable of contraries. The categories are for *nous* a being in thinking which it thinks itself.[60] Its self-knowledge is not immediate only and before division, but also a mediated knowledge. The categories are genera, prior to, but susceptible of, division and contrariety. In the categories thinking knows itself, knows its self-relation and division as making one whole. The accidental categories integrate these distinctions imperfectly as successive or as abstractly related. In substance thinking all but has possession of itself: form and matter are nothing but potencies to their relation; the difference of individual and universal falls within their relation. To this category the others tend, on it they depend, since only with substance do division and connection of the divided appear as moments of an intrinsic activity.[61] Asking therefore whether there can be a science of all the causes – such a science as that of Plato's creative divine intelligence – Aristotle answers there can be such a science, if substance is the first genus of being to which the other genera are related. Only in substance does it become thinkable how the creative activity can unite the formal and material conditions of a teleological production, and not rather be dissipated in the endless divisibility of matter.[62]

But the doctrine of categories is only the beginning of Aristotle's universal science. The categories are prior to division, to the distinction of true and false. But is this distinction to be thought a determination of the categories, of this first realization of the good, or does it fall to a finite knowing subject? Plato's demiurgic intelligence is said to create the visible world looking to the *cosmos noetos.* But what is this intelligence? Not the *nous* which turns from its relation to the ideas to the good which is prior to that relation. It is rather the thinking of a world composite of the good and divided principle. If it is shown in the *Sophist* that negation or otherness belongs as well as being to this world, this is in the end only the negativity of a dialectical reflection, an untruth which dialectic disengages from truth in its analysis of the composite.[63]

Aristotle asks whether the primary science is of the principles of demonstration as well as of the categories, whether logic comes under its consideration or is only the abstracted general form of the methods of the several special sciences. Is there only the attitude of an empirical understanding which Aristotle recognizes to be appropriate to *phusike,* in its several parts, or is this a secondary and derivative attitude? The question is of the highest importance if one would know how Aristotle came to think there was a *phusis* or intrinsic moving principle in all things, whose operation was analogous to the productive arts. For this is a knowledge which appeared also in later times to exceed the limits of scientific inquiry. If Aristotle can discover the presence of an unmoved mover in all the genera of nature, that is because division and syllogism, as well as the categories, are for him the form of what is other than the divine self-thinking. Through this logical form the demiurgic intelligence remains one with itself in the specification of natural genera and their actualization in individuals.[64]

Through the logical form the theoretical understanding knows itself one with its objects. But the creative divine intelligence is not theoretic only. Nor again, is it productive in the manner of the human arts, which suppose an appropriate matter and where product is separated from producer. Nor is the divine freedom that of the practical understanding, which through its own end has for its content contingent purposes which can as well be realized as frustrated. As the poets already taught, God knows the necessary as himself. Aristotle asks how it is possible there should be a universal science of all natural genera. His answer is that all genera are related to the prime entelechy through the same principles – form and matter or form and privation – that the variety of species in a genus, the manifold differences of individuals are all comprehended in the same relation to the unmoved mover or divine self-consciousness. This relation is manifested in the total activity of the genus; e.g. in the rest and movement of the four elemental bodies, the continuity of the genus in their unfailing generation out of one another.[65]

The *phusis* or moving principle, through which, for example, the corruptible elements seek their place, is part of this total activity. As with the arts this *phusis* moves on condition a body is in a certain state. Its spontaneity is conditional; having come to rest, it receives from another its power to move again. If one asks how God renews the finite powers operative in a genus, sustains its actuality, the answer is that he moves as desired, as end. The sense of this answer is that the difference of nature from God, the separation and need which is the origin of this movement, is divinely caused: the desire animating nature is the end from which it has fallen. The recurrent movement in all genera is through stages, by which the division of rest from movement is converted into the divine actuality where rest and movement are one.[66]

The inner unity which is before division in the category of substance is imparted to individuals by the divine causality. The demiurge of *Timaeus* in giving actuality to the ideas is impeded by an external necessity; the products of his work are a mixture of reason and necessity. The Aristotelean teleology realizes its end without hindrance, combining absolutely the determinate genus with all the material conditions of its realization. In its product the divine intelligence is reflected into itself, the contrariety of the genus which appears in the difference of form and matter being negated in the individual. In this result division and mediation have passed into the self-identity of the individual substance. In this self-identity Aristotle finds at the same time a realization of the Platonic good and the surest principle of finite knowledge.[67]

If nature is thus one with the divine causality in its first production, it is also divided from it. If one ask the reason of this division of the product from its causes, the answer is that one has here only the first entelechy, immediate unity of cause and caused. Their difference appears as a separation of the effect from its causes; the answer is that one has here only the first entelechy, immediate unity of cause and caused. Their difference appears as a separation of the effect from its causes. The early Greek philosophers had not distinguished nature from God. With Plato began a separation of nature, but as falling away from the undivided principle. Aristotle's nature, as comprehensive of division, has present in it the absolute actuality. The relation of the finite substance to the divine thinking is, however, at first abstract or immediate: the negativity which belongs also to the relation is concealed as the *steresis* or privation which is an element with form in its composition. This negativity then appears as the external involvement of the substance, a dividedness and otherness distinguished from its self-relation. The *phusis* or inner moving power of the substance is its effort to overcome this division and regain its simple self-identity.[68]

But in this natural movement the impulse or desire of the substance is only partially appeased. Its full relation to the unmoved mover is not disclosed therein. Most revelatory of this relation is the movement of the heavenly bodies; this relation is not obscured by a manifold externality and contingency. These bodies remain ever self-related, difference only occurring in their circular movement to be immediately negated in the uniform relation of centre to circumference. If these bodies thus reveal an unmoved mover as their principle, they also fail to show its nature fully. They are many and externally related to one another, moving and moved. Only the cyclic movement of the heavens shows this negativity as reciprocal, as the division and necessary connection of one movement. So regarded the substantiality of the heavenly spheres is nothing but a self-identity which is just as well a privation explicitly present and actual as well. In this contradiction the unmoved principle is known as comprehending in its self-consciousness all the difference of the first heaven from itself.[69]

All the genera of nature have this same structure. The argument shows them in the end to be a nullity, to pass into the divine self-consciousness. God is spoken of as the highest substance, besides whom there are the many natural genera. God and nature are different, but then the independence of nature is found to be in truth, as in the Hellenic religion, the fate or necessity which is the form of its relation to God as free self-consciousness.

To this reduction of nature to God in the full disclosure of its negativity there is found one exception.[70] The true division of God from himself which can stand in free relation to him is the rational soul. Aristotle's science of the soul begins, as do his other natural sciences, as a search to define the genus in its first or immediate form. The soul which lives merely, without sensation or thought, is distinguished from other natural forms as the active principle of an organized body. A plant in this view has already a certain freedom from natural necessity: there is in it not the abstract self-relation merely of the simple body, nor is it a mixture and harmony of simple bodies, but the differentiation of its parts and functions is resolved into one end. The plant is an end to itself at the same time as it is bound to its vegetative processes without such separation as would permit a sense of itself, of its self-relation, and of something other than itself.[71]

The development of this principle is very different from that of other natural genera. There the self-identity which the substance at first sought to maintain passed to a discovery of necessity. Here the development is of a concrete teleology, unconscious of itself and having its activity immediately in the maintenance and growth of its body, to a self-conscious activity knowing its external relations and embodiment as itself. The powers of the soul which appear in this development are not faculties of a substance but the unfolding of the substance itself.[72] Each of the principal distinctions is the whole substance, less and more explicit to itself. These distinctions reduce to two, which contain the rest: the soul seeks to know, to find itself in what is presented to itself as other; and to move, to initiate from itself its relations to another. The end sought in the whole development is to overcome the contrariety of these desires. While these cognitive and appetitive powers are divided, the soul, though betraying even as vegetative an incipient freedom, is subject to necessity. The resolution of its contradiction is not in God only, as with other substances, but also in itself.[73]

It is enough for the present purpose to indicate the course of this resolution as it occurs in the rational soul, in the soul which has attained to spontaneous activity, as knowing and as practical, and does not react only to changes in its sense organs and its body generally. In its 'epistemic' or scientific thinking the soul knows the content of sense and imagination as comprised in its concepts, its division, and reasonings. This content it has received into itself as potential. Its thinking is then the explication of this potentiality, so that in the end even the individual thing is known primarily as the subject of logical contraries, as that about which demonstrations are made. The active *nous* which has thus related all its content to its self-consciousness as principle may be spoken of as breaking in upon the soul from without.[74] It is the manner of Aristotle's science to regard the higher thus from the side of the lower, which the argument shows as passing into it. It is only necessary to attend to the structure and movement of the whole argument to know that Aristotle only provisionally measures the higher thus by the lower.

Of the practical *nous* Aristotle is able to say that it is its own end, is free in its labour to conform the world of its particular interests to its freedom, especially through the common work of domestic and political institutions. Of the evils attendant on this laborious freedom there is nothing to be added from this Hellenic standpoint to what the poets have taught. Practical freedom has for its definite content contingent purposes, which may or may not be fulfilled. The virtues which relate these ends as stable attitudes to the practical *nous*, mediate between extreme possibilities. There is a negativity latent in virtuous actions, which the poets have shown comes to light fatally in heroic characters. The logic of this fatality is given in Aristotle's treatment of practical understanding.

The *nous* as practical is free, is for itself, does not, as technical reason, lose its activity in an alien product. This freedom is natural in Aristotle's sense: that to which the soul tends, which it acquires actually by the ethical virtues and the prudence which can resolve conflicts among them in the light of the *prakton agathon* as such. This common human good has its reality in the political community. There is a common rational work; each is an end at once to himself and to others, is purged in a true *paideia* of the deceptions of the passions and of partial virtues. But this virtue in a Creon or an Oedipus betrays its finitude in an opposition to the family. Considered in relation to the soul, this is first the opposition of *phronesis* to what one may call natural feelings, the unformed feelings of the individual, presupposed in his education to virtue. When virtue attains its completion in practical thought, this immediate presupposition stands out against the universality of that attitude. This natural individuality has its rational good in the family, which if it be called the natural community as against the state is among Greeks a free community.[75] The individual belongs to both communities, but in relation to them is exposed to a profound division in himself. In this division appears the limit of practical freedom, where it confronts a necessity in which the individual can only find himself free by returning to a theoretical attitude.[76]

How do natural feelings, the natural individual, and practical wisdom belong to the one soul? Taken simply as other than practical wisdom, the affronted feelings of Antigone or Haemon appear as unformed youthful passions, not yet subject to rational control. But the soul, if it is not to succumb to the experience that its practical freedom is abstract and illusory, has need to bring before its view both attitudes, to know them as in one relation belonging to itself. As theoretical, it knows itself through the division of thought and sensibility. It can likewise find itself in the division of the practical soul, in the knowledge that sensuous and rational desires are one power. Practical thought, in that it can order and chose among ends, knows this unity, but abstractly: this unity is realized in a plurality of ends. But these many ends, as realized, may be compared in their logical form with the celestial spheres: there is in them a negativity which corrects the appearance that they are self-identical and freely executed; they are found in their consequences to limit and impinge on one another.[77] The soul is constrained to discover how they are compatible, not destructive of one another. How, as Plato asked, can the soul find peace in itself? In Aristotle's formulation, how is the unmoved mover, *to prakton agathon*, related to the moved mover, that is, to *orexis* or desire?[78] The answer to this question can be seen in an immediate form if one ask how the soul, human or animal, moves its body. It is insufficient to answer with Plato that soul can move bodies because it is self-moving. In the movement of animals there is an alternation of rest and motion in the limbs, a reciprocity in which appears an unmoved self-relation of the animal.[79] The thinking soul is similarly unmoved in the movement of desire, when this is freed from every particular content and known as bringing forth from itself an alternation of positive and negative moments. The practical soul, like the theoretical, comes thus to the knowledge that its particular interests, the world of its desires and realized ends, is the possession of its thinking self-consciousness. Unmoved mover and desire are one actuality in this relation.

Aristotle's science of the soul reverts at this point to its beginning. In the course of the argument the unconscious organic life of the vegetative soul was shown to pass into a division of the soul from its body and natural environment. Then this division in the sensitive and imaginative soul was found to be comprehended in the theoretical self-consciousness. The practical soul finally could sink into the immediacy of animal desire and unite that immediacy with its rational freedom. Through these stages the soul has not separated itself only from its embodiment, as was sought in the Platonic philosophy, but has found in its universality and the immediacy of its embodiment and externality one actuality.[80]

In the conclusion to which the Aristotelian philosophy comes the standpoint of the old Hellenic religion no longer remains, but has passed into the relation of human individuals, freed from division and necessity, to a God who knows himself in natural necessity. The divine thinking which comes thus to itself out of nature is then intelligible to itself, is its own object, in a thinking which in division and difference is not subjected again to necessity, but goes over to an otherness adequate to itself.[81] So likewise human life in the result, being unified out of the extreme division of universality and natural immediacy, does not revert to this division. In going over to life and nature it has an otherness and finitude which in its development is found to be a form of its original self-identify and not an alien necessity or fatality.

The concept of God to which Aristotle comes is an incipient knowledge of what will afterwards be called the Trinity in Christian theology. Nature and humanity are comprehended in this concept. Plato in *Timaeus* had sought to explain the creation of nature as primarily the construction of soul by divine intelligence looking to an ideal model. Nature is thought to be the intelligible world, not as for thought, but as universal life. Aristotle has come to this same concept of nature and its origin. He has made it intelligible – what the demiurgic intelligence is which, regarding the total idea, creates soul and all nature as its image; what again the image is, namely, the otherness or difference of the divine thinking as divided from it; how man in turning from nature out of desire to know the divine idea does not therein fall into division between his universality and particularity, but rather finds these moments unified in his individuality.

But this knowledge was mediated by the Hellenic religion and the dividedness of human life in the Hellenic family and state. Without this mediation the conclusion, as formulated by Aristotle, was no sooner attained than it became unintelligible. Already to Aristotle's first successors his philosophy had become problematical. Between the standpoint of the conclusion and the way to it Theophrastus finds a gulf he does not know how to bridge.[82] To Strato nature appears a mechanism severed from the divine mover.[83] The need is felt by these Peripatetics of new development from the concrete spiritual standpoint which came into sight in Aristotle's conclusion. The beginning of this development is not, however, with them, but is made by the Stoics and the other Hellenistic schools. In Stoicism the unification of divine and human, the reduction of a dispersed plurality of genera to one living nature, which Aristotle had come to, appears in the immediate form of a pantheism. In this collapse human freedom is no longer a speculative knowledge of life and thought as concretely united, but abstract personality, the self-identity of the individual maintained against passion and particular interests.

In Stoicism and the other schools there is such a collapse and incapacity for philosophy as occurred again in the nineteenth century and is still the form of contemporary culture. Then, as afterwards, there was the illusion that a rational freedom undivided from nature was attained, or else might be attained by the domination of an abstract thought. Plato and Aristotle became as unintelligible to this standpoint in its several forms as are the philosophies of the older modern period to contemporary schools. But in antiquity this natural concreteness was felt in due course to be rather division and loss of nature. There emerged out of it the need to know what it thought to have possession of more directly, as in more recent times thought was to be superseded by 'praxis,' which in turn is experienced as a need of thought. So regarded, the Hellenistic philosophies can be thought the beginning of an intrinsic development of the new standpoint in which Aristotle ends his inquiry. The first Peripatetics, one may say, are paralysed and cannot move because they do not know their principle in an external and sensuous form, out of which they might come to a mediated knowledge of it.

But this development is not to be looked for so long as the subjective freedom of Hellenistic culture remains nostalgically attached to older forms even when it has freed itself from them. Alexander indeed and his successors establish empires to which Greeks and Hellenized barbarians belong rather as individuals and as cosmopolitan than as Athenian or of some other 'polis.' It is the Roman people who make a new beginning with this abstract freedom, for whom it is the principle of their religion and of their domestic and political institutions. The Roman conquest and domination of the other Meditaerranean peoples has the immense importance of giving reality to the abstract practical spirit already present in Hellenistic culture. In this way the implications of this standpoint are made known and felt, not in language and education merely, in what we call 'culture,' but as historical reality. Somewhat similarly it may be said that the implications of the contemporary technological society are only truly known in its Marxist form. The adequate mediation of the concrete spiritual principle, of which there was a first and passing vision in the Aristotelian philosophy, the argument will show to occur in Christianity. A consideration of Roman religion and institutions can reveal how a desire of the Christian revelation and a capacity for it came into being.[84]

Notes

1 Extracted from 'The Christian Origin of Contemporary Institutions Part One,' *Dionysius* 6 (1982), 131–41.
2 Feuerbach, *Wesen des Christentums,* chap. XI.
3 *Republic,* 509b.
4 Philo on Moses and Plato, see references in Zeller, *Philosophie der Griechen,* III, II, 393f.
5 Hegel, *Phil. der Religion,* II, 98.
6 Ibid., 62, 66.
7 Genesis 16.
8 Abraham's willingness to sacrifice Isaac; see Genesis 22.
9 Ecclesiastes 12: 13–14.
10 On Philo's allegorization of the Jewish law, see see Bréhier, *Philon d'Alexandrie,* 35–61; Judaism as contemplation of the One, in which all predicates are negated, ibid., 69–83.
11 Politicus, 300dff.
12 *Parmenides, Sophist,* and *Politicus* all have in common that they are about the Platonic 'stoicheia' or elements: Findlay, *Plato,* 210ff.
13 *Sophist,* 266aff.
14 *Politicus,* 271c–275a.
15 Ibid., 305e–311c.
16 Ibid., 310dff.
17 Legal orthodoxy, *Laws* 10.
18 Aristotle, *Metaphysics,* 1071b.
19 Ibid., 1004b 25.
20 *Laws,* 961aff.
21 Cf. David Strauss, *Leben Jesu,* esp. section 144.
22 John 1: 1.
23 Aristotle, *Eth. Nich.*, VII, 4 and 5.
24 Ibid., 112b 31.
25 Aristotle, *De Anima,* III, 5.
26 Aristotle, *Physics,* VII, 9–10.
27 Aristotle's concept of the family, *Politics,* I, 3–13.

28 *Iliad* 24, 525–33.
29 *Republic*, II, 378e–383c.
30 As shown, for example, in the relation of Creousa to Apollo as treated in Euripides' *Ion*.
31 On the whole relation of Athena to Odysseus, Sophocles' treatment in *Ajax* is most instructive.
32 Socrates and Aristophanes on comedy and tragedy at the end of *Symposium*. The proof that the two forms have a common principle was given in the dialogue in the twofold relation of Socrates to Diotima and to Alcibiades.
33 *Symposium*, 189dff.
34 *Agamemnon*.
35 *Choephoroi*.
36 *Eumenides*.
37 Aristotle, *Ath. Resp.*, 25.
38 Sophocles has no need of a following play to complete the argument: Orestes in exacting vengeance is in the very act freed of guilt. Cf. the final comment of chorus.
39 Orestes at the end of Euripides' *Electra* must suffer exile and purification.
40 *Iphigenia in Tauris*.
41 *Oedipus Tyrannus*.
42 Ibid., 1455–8.
43 *Oedipus Coloneus*, 266–7.
44 Aristotle, *Politics*, II, 2.
45 *Oed. Col.*, 1643–4.
46 Ibid., 1647–55.
47 Aristotle, *Met.*, XII, 9.
48 Treated further in relation to Roman-Hellenistic culture.
49 In the comic parabasis the action of the play passes into direct relation of poet to spectator.
50 For an exact and detailed exposition of *Birds*, see an unpublished Dalhousie thesis by P.D. Epstein.
51 So in Aeschylus' Prometheus trilogy.
52 Sophocles, *Trachiniae*, at the end.
53 B.B. Rogers, introd. to *Plutus*, Loeb, vol. 3, 361–2.
54 So the hypotheses of the *Parmenides* are to be understood.
55 Criticism of Parmenides in *Sophist*.
56 Aristotle, *Met.*, XII, 6.
57 Speusippus and Xenocrates contributed to the Aristotelean criticism, the one by reducing the ideas to a quantity, the other by attempting to express them through the category of quality.

58 Aristotle on mathematical number, *Met.*, XIII, 2–3.
59 *Physics*, I, 5.
60 *Met.*, IV, 2.
61 *Met.*, VIII, 6.
62 *Met.*, IV, 3.
63 *Met.*, 1089a 15–32.
64 Aristotle, *Physics* II, where the argument has passed from the discussion of substance as unitize of contraries in the previous book to the determination of *phusis* and causality.
65 *Met.*, IX, 6–8.
66 *Met.*, XII, 7.
67 *Met.*, IV, 3.
68 *Physics*, III, 1.
69 *Met.*, XII, 8–10: reduction of the independent celestial movers to one primary mover.
70 When the whole argument of *De Anima* is gathered together to the conclusion implicit from the first, this is evident.
71 Vegetative soul, *De An.*, II, 4.
72 *De An.*, II, 3.
73 *De An.*, III, 9.
74 *De Generatione Animalium*, 736a 28.
75 *Politics*, I, 13.
76 *Eth. Nich.*, X, 8.
77 *De An.*, III, 11.
78 *De An.*, III, 10.
79 *De An.*, III, 10; *De Motu Animalium.*
80 *De An.*, III, 12–13.
81 *Met.*, XII, 7–9.
82 The urgent problem of Theophrastus' *Metaphysics.*
83 Strato accepts a separation of nature from God (see Zeller, II, II, 904 for surviving evidence as to his doctrine).
84 *Editors' note*: See chapter 3 of this volume, in which such a consideration is provided.

COMMENTARY ONE
The Unification of Gods and Men in Greek Tragedy and Comedy

PAUL EPSTEIN

About twenty years ago I was discussing the difficult last scenes of *Birds* with Professor James Doull. The main character had staged a successful war against the Olympian gods, and Zeus was about to lose his cosmic kingship. I was excitedly repeating two salient moments of the action: the god-man Heracles could not be the true heir of Zeus, and an actual man instead would inherit his rule. As Mr Doull listened quietly, I announced that the question of the proper mediation between the highest god and man in *Birds* very much resembled the same question in the Christian religion. A brief pause followed. He then replied, 'You might say, Mr Epstein, that Comedy is the religion of God the Son, just as Tragedy is the religion of God the Father.'

Several years after this exchange, in his article 'The Christian Origin of Contemporary Institutions,'[1] James Doull gave precise and extended meaning to what he had earlier so briefly said. In that article he argues that 'in the older Hellenism, and there only, is it possible to follow the formation of the second element of Christianity, namely of a concrete and adequate *logos* or determination of the one God.'[2] In the world following upon the decline of the strictly Hellenic world, the knowledge of this 'took the form of a radical human freedom severed from its divine origin.'[3] Nevertheless during the last years of Athenian flourishing, 'There was ... a point in the discovery of this freedom where it could as well be said that everything was Zeus – that the human went over to the divine – as that the sovereignty of the gods had passed to man.'[4]

The first of these poles, the receding of all things into Zeus, Doull understands as best realized in the tragedies of Sophocles, while in the comedies of Aristophanes he sees the fulfilment of the second, the passing of sovereignty to man.[5] This article will seek to illustrate this view by tracing the history of the dramatic poets, both tragic and comic, that causes this result. The article will fall into four main divisions. First, it will indicate the limits of contemporary views compared to that of Doull. Second, it will locate the possibility and occasion for a history of the dramatic poets in the Hellenic account of the gods' origins, on the one hand, and the relation of the drama to the Athenian polis that both presents and watches the drama, on the other. Third, it will examine this history among the tragedians: a movement toward the tragic pole of divine-human unification in Aeschylus, its attainment in Sophocles, and a certain loss of this unification in Euripides through the arising of a more comprehensive human subjectivity. Fourth, it will argue that three analogous stages within the plays of Aristophanes define the attainment of the comic pole of human-divine unification.

As briefly indicated above, James Doull's interpretation of Greek drama, both tragic and comic, is based on two fundamental insights. He has seen, first, that the two forms of drama present complementary, contradictory, and necessary forms of the movement toward, and achievement of, a divine–human relationship, and, second, that this relationship arises through the dramatic antagonist's experience of the institutions of the polis. Contemporary critics, following Nietzsche, being incapable of this comprehensiveness of view, tend to make one aspect of this spiritual universe the centre of their interpretations. Some examples of this, drawn from both comedy and tragedy, are instructive. In both, the best that contemporary criticism can discover is a kind of free, self-subsistent individuality, widely believed in contemporary culture to be the true ground of all things.

Here Nietzsche's *Birth of Tragedy*[6] has a special importance. His first book not only offered an interpretation of Greek drama but also declared his own view of the true nature of human individuality. For him tragedy is the discovery by the human individual that his true existence is inseparable from that of ultimate being, which is perhaps more accurately called becoming. The real interest of Nietzsche's view lies in its idea of human individuality, since as a description of Greek tragedy it is thoroughly ahistorical. It is grounded in a distinction between the Apollonian and the Dionysian,[7] which, having no reality in ancient mythology or poetry, is entirely of Nietzsche's own imagining. The former is the *principium individuationis,* the latter is the ground of the individual's sense of a direct connection to being. On Nietzsche's account, while these two principles usually operate separately, in tragedy they are drawn together. There, he argues, the veil is removed from the eyes of the human being in his assumed individuality and he discovers that his true existence is nothing less than being itself.

'The excellence of Nietzsche's view lies in his knowledge that Tragedy reveals a truth not previously known about human nature, and that this truth is the relation of humanity to ultimate reality.'[8] The analysis by which Nietzsche has arrived at this view, however, is not true to the actual existence of Greek tragedy; his Apollo and his Dionysus are very one-sided portraits of these gods. Apollo does not simply represent a *principium individuationis,* nor Dionysus simply the union with Being. In *Oedipus the King,* Apollo illumines not only the man who solves riddles by human reason, but also the seer who has an unmediated knowledge as a servant of the god. Apollo is the god both of the individual par excellence and of him who proves to be his nemesis. Nor is Dionysus alone the god who leads men to find their individuality in a mystic union with nature. As the patron of both tragedy and comedy, he leads men to a deeper sense of that individuality, in tragedy to know their dependence on the Olympian gods whom they imitate, and in comedy to know themselves as the true actuality of these same gods.

Nietzsche represents nevertheless in some ways the high-water mark of contemporary critics. The others have in general even more partial views. Denys Page can set his own sense of what is suitable against the poetical theology of Aeschylus as developed in the *Oresteia* and pronounce the reconciliation of Athens and the Furies in it 'an artificial contrivance.'[9] From what intelligible standpoint this decree has been issued would be hard to say.

Sir Richard Jebb in a different way cannot understand Sophocles' presentation of the gods in *Antigone.* He calls it a conflict between the law of the state and the law of conscience.[10] This might be a fine description of a collision in a nineteenth-century novel, but it completely overlooks the fact that both Creon and Antigone are constant in their appeals to the gods, whether of the upper world or the lower. In still another form of overlooking the gods, E.R. Dodds says that the play *Bacchae* shows the human need for Dionysian experience.[11] In the play the god Dionysus so inspires a woman with his ecstasy that she kills her own son unawares. The play ends with the conundrum that neither civilization nor a rejection of it for a mystical union with nature is satisfactory for human life. This is something more awful than a need for Dionysian experience.

The criticism of comedy has suffered from the same inability of the critics to understand a divine–human relationship mediated by the comic hero's experience of life in the city. There has persisted the feeling in many quarters that comedy is a poor cousin of tragedy, and therefore does not deal with higher matters. As a result, no general exposition of comedy that serves at the same time as an existentialist manifesto has in modern times captured the general imagination as *Birth of Tragedy* has.

Nevertheless, there has arisen a view of comedy that sees it as presenting the triumph of a particular individual who bends the institutions of the city and even the will of the gods to his own private ends. Cedric Whitman has propounded this view in his book *Aristophanes and the Comic Hero.*[12] Whitman accurately describes, one might say, the first half of an Aristophanic drama, in which the hero pursues, and succeeds in, his attempt to make all things subject to his sensual desires. Whitman does not seem capable of seeing that in the second half of the drama, the comic hero must gradually surrender his purely private interests and become a rational individual.

The view of Leo Strauss[13] is one-sided in a manner complementary to that of Whitman. He finds in the plays of Aristophanes a presentation of what belongs to the objective requirements of the polis as the limit to human subjectivity. It is true that the foundations of the city are discovered by the comic hero in the course of his career. Yet these transcend the city itself. In *Birds*, for example, the hero discovers them only in marrying Basileia, the principle of Zeus's rule over both nature and the human city. In marrying her, the hero displaces Zeus and is declared the highest of gods. Thus, the city itself is not sufficient to answer the hero's subjectivity; only a divine subjectivity can do this.

Even more partial in their views are those who find in the comedies a topical interest or fantasy. These views take their departure from the undoubted fact that each comedy does have its beginning in some contemporary reality or event. Gilbert Murray regards this topical element as the centre, and he especially interested himself with those plays that touch on the question of the Peloponnesian War. Murray regards these plays as a direct appeal to the audience, and the comic element as something designed for Athenian groundlings.[14]

The limit of the topical view lies in the fact that while all the plays of Aristophanes begin with something topical, they certainly do not end with the topical. For example, *Frogs* begins with the fact of Euripides' death. It ends, however, with the return of Dionysus from Hades with Aeschylus, who will presumably revivify the city with his poetical teaching. This difficulty of the topical school has caused some to speak of the element of fantasy in Aristophanes. For example, J. Henderson speaks of the re-establishment of peace between Sparta and Athens at the end of *Lysistrata* as an element of fantasy.[15] Certainly this event is not historical, but that does not make it fantasy. The argument of the drama indicates that the title character is a kind of human Athena, and through her all the citizens of the two city-states come to possess the attributes of the goddess. The action of the drama, then, is a possibility within Greek religion, if its ideas be developed in a certain direction.

The above exposition of the limits of contemporary criticism can illustrate Doull's view only in a very preliminary and external way. Only the fuller exposition indicated above can attempt to bring out its salient point, that a divine–human relation arising from the main character's experience of objective institutions animates both comedy and tragedy. Now, all Athenian drama assumes both the cosmology of the Hellenic religion and the ordered life of the fifth-century polis. First, the Hellenic account of the gods' origin is found in the *Theogony* of Hesiod and begins not with God himself, as does the Jewish account of the beginning, but with the various nature powers, and other archaic forces within the human world; out of these are born the Olympian gods, with Zeus at their head, who preside over the world of nature and of spirit. Man in the Hesiodic account is not depicted as being made by the highest gods, although every important aspect of his life as a familial, political, or intellectual being has a god who presides over it. These Olympian deities are said to have triumphed over the earlier powers in a war; this war has shown that those later in time have nevertheless a deeper rational quality.[16] Further illustrating this movement toward a deeper spiritual reality are those beings born of Zeus, both divine and human, who surpass him, even though he is the chief of the gods, by being free of a natural beginning. Athena, born from Zeus's head, represents a wisdom complete in itself. Heracles is the son of Zeus and a mortal woman; as the saviour of man from various monsters, he has a more active virtue than his father. Dionysus, also the son of Zeus and a mortal, can communicate the life of the gods to men more completely than any of the purely divine beings; in comedy and tragedy, both presented under his auspices, a total view of the divine relation to men is presented for the latter's contemplation.

This history of the gods provides a certain limit to the sovereignty of the gods, since all things can recede into the divine but cannot be presented as having originally proceeded out of the gods. This has of course opposite consequences for tragedy and comedy; a tragedy is complete to the extent that it depicts all things as dependent on the gods, while the excellence of a comedy depends on its capacity to show humanity as the true heir of an ultimately limited divinity. In tragedy, there are three possibilities. First is the kind of drama that reveals a movement toward the spiritual presidency of Zeus in affairs both human and divine, and this defines the plays of Aeschylus. Second is the equalization of human life to Zeus conceived as the reality of all gods; this defines the plays of Sophocles. Finally, the natural beginning point of the gods allows the possibility of the nature powers' again appearing in a certain independence of the Olympians, and this animates the plays of Euripides. An analogous history for comedy falls entirely within the plays of Aristophanes. The first plays all show the career of the comic hero as falling within the governance of the Olympian gods. *Birds* then is the turning point; the hero's reversion first to a nature religion, and then his emergence from it allows him to attain a subjectivity deeper than that of Zeus. The remaining plays, assuming this discovery, then show it in relation to the institutions of the city.

The other occasion for there being a development within drama lies in the fact that all Athenian drama is in one sense a mirror of the fifth-century polis. That is, the action assumes an ordered city-state in which the family and state are the essential institutions, and the hero, whether heroic or vulgar, defines his being in relation to these institutions, and the gods whom these institutions instantiate. In tragedy, the setting is the mythological past, in which the main characters experience the consequences of their heroic virtue. In comedy, the vulgar main character shows the consequences of a contemporary collapse of the institutions that animate the polis. It does not, however, belong to the tragic action itself to declare that it is a mirror of contemporary life. As much as the spectator sees the elements of his own world playing before him, it belongs to his consciousness that what he sees is also the work of a poet. This does not mean for the ancient Athenian that the play is a fiction, wholly invented by the imagination of the poet. In this religion, however, the poet does have a part in giving form even to the gods themselves, who exist in a religion of beauty. Therefore, even if in the action the whole life of the hero is brought under the government of Zeus, there is an unresolved duality between the god's self-consciousness and that of the poet.

In comedy the work of the poet has been equalized with contemporary life. The main character explicitly represents a tendency in the life of Athens, and the audience sees itself playing on the stage. Nevertheless, this view appears only on the comic stage, at the festival of Dionysus. Since tragedy and comedy were presented at the same festival, the comic vision would never be the sole poetical vision presented.

Aeschylus begins the tragic side of this dramatic history, which ends with a certain divine priority in the human–divine relation. He fulfilled the requirement that each tragedian write three plays for the tragic festival by making each one an act in a more comprehensive trilogy. The

Oresteia is the only full trilogy that we have remaining to us, although we have other single plays. Beginning with a tremendous collision between kingly authority and maternal and wifely right at Argos, the trilogy ends with the unification of the familial and political under the presidency of Athena, at her city of Athens. It represents at once the overcoming of human and divine collisions. A conflict between Agamemnon and his wife Clytaemnestra is clarified by being seen also as a conflict between the Furies and Apollo. The trilogy begins with the hybris of Clytaemnestra, since she imagines that she is doing justice by avenging herself on Agamemnon both for having left her, in order to lead the Greek forces at Troy, and for having sacrificed their daughter to the same end.[17] His arrogance, which culminates in attempting to introduce his mistress Cassandra into his household, certainly merits punishment, but his wife is hardly guiltless. Although without doubt she is the instrument of divine justice against her husband, she has committed regicide in so being. This allows the cosmic element to appear, as Orestes is commanded by the Delphic oracle to kill his mother.[18] The circumstances of his doing so make him subject to his mother's Furies, and the great divide between the orders of Greek gods becomes a part of the action. Apollo is an Olympian god; the Furies belong to the pre-Olympian order and regard the killing of Clytaemnestra as a violation of their rights. Thus, the collision between Titans and Olympians is recapitulated in human life. Neither order is capable at this level of composing their dispute, and so when Orestes flees to Athens, Athena establishes a court of homicide to hear his case.[19] The jury is divided, showing that the city recognizes both orders of deities; Athena breaks the tie on behalf of Orestes, thus freeing him. She then threatens and persuades the Furies, henceforward the Eumenides, to be the guardian spirits of the city. The Chorus then sing of the reconciliation as one effected by a concord of Zeus and Moira.[20]

One can say of the trilogy equally that it is a human collision solved by the gods or a divine collision solvable only through human institutions. That is, the original conflict between Agamemnon and Clytaemnestra can be resolved only by the divine founding of a court. Yet the true sovereignty of the Olympian gods cannot simply be the 'overthrow' of the old gods. Still, their integration into the Olympian order cannot happen only at the divine level, but must be complemented by humans who make real what these older gods preside over. Nevertheless, the final ordering of affairs both divine and human rests with Athena, the tutelary god of Athens.

Although only one play of the Prometheus trilogy is extant, a pattern similar to that of the *Oresteia* presents itself. The Olympians have only 'recently' overthrown the Titanic powers, and the Titan Prometheus is now being punished by Zeus for his gift of fire to men. One presumes that, in the missing plays, Prometheus is freed and through the city of Athens, he comes to have his place in the Olympian order. Through the polis the integration of the overthrown gods into the rule of Zeus is accomplished.

Sophocles does not concern himself with the 'consolidation' of the Olympian order, and his collisions are thus not between a divinity of the old order and one of the new, or between humans who incarnate these orders. Instead, the collisions occur between equal and competing claims within the Olympian order, generally those that belong to the oppositions of the family and state. Thus, whereas in *Libation Bearers* the Furies originally defend the blood right of the mother, in the plays of Sophocles the family appears from the beginning as a spiritual institution; in burying her brother, for example, Antigone defends an ethical bond.

Tragedy results from the collisions between the absolute claims of these realms, and the heroes who experience these collisions undergo a variety of fates. In *Electra*, Orestes is able to restore political order through killing his mother and without having to suffer the penalty of a matricide. Oedipus saves his country by discovering the ruinous truth about his relation to his mother in *Oedipus the King*. In *Antigone* both central characters think that they truly worship Zeus, although Antigone identifies him with the family and the underworld, and Creon thinks him uniquely devoted to the state and the world above. Their opposition leads them to destruction, and also to a certain insight into the unity of the two realms.

In general Sophocles presents a deeper integration of human life with the gods than does the *Oresteia*. The jury in dividing exactly over the guilt of Orestes give equal place to the Furies and to Apollo as moments of Athenian life; only Athena has in her the totality of the divine life at Athens. No god appears in manifest sensuous form to conclude the drama and declare the relation of men to the gods in either *Oedipus the King* or *Antigone*. Oedipus's whole experience shows at the same time both the totality of human possibility and its inseparability from the divine being and government. He has experience of kingship and family, human glory and misery, and at the end he knows that in all he has done, character and destiny are one.[21] *Antigone*, by showing the complementary experience of Creon and Antigone, reveals the whole range of human possibility and activity as made real in the family and state; their catastrophes show that they are not self-subsistent, but that both are dependent on the Zeus that they worship.

With Euripides, the Sophoclean collision between the family and state has vanished. Instead, the opposed elements tend to be an abstract reason within the realm of the state and a direct passion that tends to the destruction of ethical institutions. This latter is not as with Aeschylus a power that belongs to the Titanic realm, but one that falls within the Olympian gods. In *Hippolytus*, for example, the title character worships Artemis; he is devoted to the hunt and is indifferent to the love of women. Hippolytus's passions are thus ordered through inner suppression and external conquest. His stepmother is moved by Aphrodite in a fearful form; she desires her stepson. Passion appears in her as a perverse desire, which poisons the ethical order. Especially notable in this regard is *Bacchae.* The people of Thebes have not accepted the divinity of the god Dionysus, and he is resolved to show himself a god; he tells the audience of this resolve at the beginning of the play.[22] The drama shows the terrible ambiguity of this divinity. The god encourages and makes actual for his devotees a direct unity with the realm of nature. Agave, who had earlier rejected the god, leaves the city in order to worship him. Having then experienced a oneness with nature, she eventually kills her own son, Pentheus, confusing him with a wild beast.[23] While her initial flight from the city is seen as necessary, the catastrophic consequence shows the insufficiency of this flight to a fully human life. The god had initially addressed the audience, giving the action a certain immediacy for its members; presumably they leave the theatre with a deep sense of the unresolved tension between ethical institutions and Dionysiac experience.

Comedy takes up the poetical argument from Euripides and is capable of uniting man to both orders of gods and the spectator with the dramatic action in a different form. Aristophanes' dramas show the activity of a divinized humanity as comprehending both the Titans and Olympians while limning the essential forms of contemporary life. The reality of this radical comprehension also marks, in the development of Aristophanes' dramas, the self-dissolution of the religion within which comedy has arisen. Each comedy achieves this comprehension through the activity of a central character, who like many or all of his fellow Athenians, finds life in the contemporary polis oppressive.[24] He feels deprived of one or another natural good by the current arrangements within various institutions of his polis, and to overcome this division he seeks to make all that oppresses him serve his enjoyment of that natural good. Having overcome the division in this way, he then finds it incomplete. The remainder of the play shows the central character finding that he can enjoy his natural good only through a reason that moves in it, and he discovers this reason in the realms of *techne*, family, and state.[25]

Thus, every play unites common life with the inspired imagination of the poet, and so unifies nature and reason in one subject such that the Hesiodic division between nature powers and spiritual powers is overcome. First, the comic poet does not have to look to a mythic realm in order to describe the varied relations of a human subjectivity with the substantial powers; he has only to describe his own contemporary world. The spectator, as a result, sees no alien hero but his own self playing in the drama before him. Second, by his alienation from the elements of polis-life and his return from that, the central character has experienced in one action what the Titans and Olympians experienced dividedly.

Although every play thus tends, through the comprehension of these dualities, to the equalization of man with the gods, not every play can make this completely manifest. The difference lies in the particular form which the central character's alienation from the polis and his return to it take. This cycle can describe the relation of one individual or class of society to certain aspects of polis-life or the relation of individuality itself to the foundations of polis-life. Thus in *Wasps*, for example, a son wishes to save his father from jury duty and to encourage him in the enjoyment of private life;[26] eventually the son learns that he cannot govern his father or keep him away from the law courts, if only as a defendant.[27] The son, therefore, experiences his relation to the city through his peculiar relation to family and state. When Lysistrata and the women, however, find themselves deprived of the joys of Aphrodite, they revolt against the division of life into a male and female sphere and do not rest until they have secured the government of all Greece and the direction of both family and political life; the conclusion of the play indicates that their activity incarnates the life of Athena. Thus, the cycle of alienation and return here indicates the women's total appropriation of the foundations of life in the polis.

Where this equalization between the individual in his cycle of alienation and return and the foundations of polis-life has occurred, the dissolution of the Olympian religion becomes manifest. Here not only has the individual, through this cycle, a deeper subjectivity than the substantial powers, but a content equal to them. Thus, human subjectivity makes actual the being of the substantial powers. The history of the plays of Aristophanes is the progressive search for this equalization. The five plays before *Birds* show a form of revolt in which the content of the naturalistic revolt falls short of reproducing out of itself the full content of the objective institutions against which it has revolted.[28] *Birds* is the first of the eleven extant plays in which this equalization occurs. All the plays thereafter show a human subjectivity whose activity is the fullness of the life of the gods. *Birds* and four of the plays after it indicate the contrast, direct or implied, between purified human subjectivity and the being of the gods.[29] In *Ecclesiazusae*, the gods have vanished, and one sees the total human appropriation of those essential institutions, family and state, which earlier the gods had been depicted as animating.

A discussion of *Clouds*, *Birds*, *Frogs*, and *Plutus* will indicate the stages of this process. *Clouds* is typical of those plays that are moving toward but have not attained the equalization indicated above. Then *Birds*, *Frogs*, and *Plutus* mark the three stages of this equalization. In *Birds*, the central character unifies the moments of the divine life through a revolt against the political order. In *Frogs*, through Dionysus's wish to make his desires as a spectator govern that festival of tragedy over which he presides, it becomes clear that human activity makes possible human participation in the life of the gods. Finally, in *Plutus*, the well-being of man, those riches and that justice which define his total well-being, is seen as the entire interest of the gods, whose rule is secure only because of the activity of men.

In *Clouds*, a certain Strepsiades is at first willing, in order to repulse his creditors, to deny traditional religion and morality; he comes to be the strongest supporter of these after experiencing the consequences of his denial. The play begins with his contemplating the financial ruin which confronts him.[30] He has married a woman of aristocratic connection, and their son, having not the character but the external habits of an aristocrat, has run up large debts by an excessive devotion to horses. Strepsiades, having sent his son to learn the dialectic of the sophists, repulses his creditors with complete trust in his son's power to best them, if necessary, in a lawsuit.[31] The same thinking-shop, however, which had taught him dialectic has also instructed him in atheism, a belief in the primacy of nature, and contempt for the traditional family.[32] Strepsiades, therefore, experiences a short triumph, since his son proposes, on the basis of his new learning, to beat both his mother and father as part of their education. Strepsiades now repents of plotting to rob his creditors, and to extirpate the source of the evil, burns down the Thinking-shop itself, to punish, he says, many evils but especially blasphemy against the gods.[33]

Strepsiades has learned that the stability of his family life depends not on sophistical cleverness but rather on belief in the gods. He has experienced the consequences of denying them, and so his final adherence to them is mediated by that awareness. To the extent that Strepsiades has gone through this cycle of naive adherence to the Olympian gods, then a naturalistic rejection of them, and finally a return, he has experienced the life of the gods more deeply than they have themselves. These latter have overthrown the nature powers in order to be what they are. Strespaides has experienced their being overcome from the standpoint of one who has experienced these nature powers more directly. However, because he has made his financial needs the measure of his life in the polis, his naturalism has not sought to replicate the Olympian order. He has felt oppressed by the order of the polis not in its entirety but through his family and creditors. Thus both his alienation from, and his return to, the Olympian gods are mediated through these and have a partial character. He has exceeded them in the form of his experience but not in its content.

This partial character marks all the plays before *Birds*. Even in *Peace*, where the hero journeys to Olympus to compel the gods to make peace, he feels oppressed not by the gods themselves, but their failure to end the Peloponnesian War.[34] This partialness belongs to comedy in its first expression. In tragedy, the *pathe* of the central characters reflect the totality of the divine life. Since comedy looks for the substantial realm in the contemporary world, with the former as the measure, it inevitably follows that initially the contemporary world cannot replicate its model. *Birds* marks the first comedy in which the activity of a representative character is equalized with the whole realm of the polis and with the gods who govern it and the cosmos. Two Athenians, Peisthetairos and Euelpides, leave Athens, not because of this or that felt deprivation, but because they find the life of the city itself as depriving them of the free exercise of an untrammelled natural enjoyment. Under the leadership of Peisthetairos, they decide that only a city of the birds, that is, a city based on natural feeling, can satisfy them.[35] Birds are declared not only the basis of life in the polis but the original gods, who thus have dominion over all. All men, including the audience, are invited to join the bird-city by becoming birds themselves. Thus nature, divinity, polis-life, and human individuality are seen as united in the city of the birds.

Once this complete naturalism has been attained, Peisthetairos begins to feel its limits. The arrival of would-be birds from earth allows him to govern natural impulse through *techne*, and *techne* through the *nous* that belongs to political life, the exercise of which Peisthetairos now says is the true meaning of being a bird.[36] This achievement is capped by the arrival of Prometheus, who announces the end of Zeus's rule; bird-mania has meant the end of sacrifice to the gods, who, incapable of Peisthetairos's integration of natural impulse with reason, are now hungry and will soon send ambassadors to sue for peace with the bird-city, that they might eat again.[37]

Prometheus's going over to the bird-city shows that it has integrated the realm of *techne* into itself more deeply than have the Olympian gods. As one knows from Aeschylus, although Zeus has the sovereignty over *techne*, Prometheus has the direct experience of it, beginning as a Titan and advancing toward the Olympian realm. Here Peisthetairos has the experience of both Zeus and Prometheus; thus, at least *in potentia*, the rule of the Olympians has already been transferred to men.

The arrival of an embassy from Olympus confirms this transfer.[38] This embassy mirrors the divine order, consisting of Poseidon, a Titan-like god called a Triballian, and the god-man Heracles. Thus, the embassy includes a ruling Olympian, a nature deity overthrown by the Olympians, and a hero who has a deeper unity of reason and nature than either is capable of. The Triballian has no love for the Olympians, Poseidon no inclination to surrender the sovereignty of the Olympians, and initially Heracles has no desire to see their overthrow. When Peisthetairos indicates to him, however, that as one born of a human, he cannot be the true heir of Zeus, he defects to the human side, and by his vote the embassy gives Basileia to Peisthetairos.[39] She has in her that complete dominion over nature and life in the polis that has given Zeus his authority; when she is given to Peisthetairos to marry, the transfer of authority is complete. It belongs to humankind to enjoy the unified dominion which she represents, and the coming of the three ambassadors shows that this dominion exists dividedly for the Olympian order and is united in Peisthetairos.

Peisthetairos is married to Basileia because he and no god has united all that belongs to her in his activity; since the gods have no real subjectivity, and their nature is fixed, neither Zeus nor any of the ambassadors can directly experience that unity of reason and nature that belongs to her rule. Peisthetairos, however, as a man, can and does experience them all. His subjectivity, and through him that of all humankind, is thus seen as the actuality of the divine life.

Once the activity of the individual who revolts against those institutions based on the Olympian gods is equalized with those institutions, then he has in effect overthrown the gods. Until that equalization has occurred, the activity of men is balanced by the superior substantial existence of the Olympians. Through this equalization, however, the whole substantial reality of the gods is comprehended by human activity. This relation between the human individual and the substantial realm marks all the plays after *Birds*. In *Lysistrata*, human activity arising from the Peloponnesian War and its settlement is seen as the actuality of the chief deities. In *Thesmophoriazusae* and *Frogs*, the relation of humankind to the self-communication of the gods in religious festivals is explored. In both these plays, it is indicated that human activity makes actual this self-communication.

Frogs makes this point even more deeply because its hero, Dionysus, a god-man, makes actual the self-communication of the gods through his humanity. As the play begins, Dionysus, who presides over tragedy, is distraught at the recent death of Euripides and prepares to bring him back from Hades.[40] He thus makes his desire as a spectator of tragedy the measure of his activity. Dionysus is dressed as Heracles, seeking to imitate him in his trip to Hades.[41] He thereby unites in his own person the elements of tragedy. In imitating Heracles, he takes on the role of a tragic hero while the end to which he undertakes this is the fulfilment of his desire as a spectator. Thus, he wishes to have both the potentiality of the spectator and the activity of a tragic actor.

As Dionysus and his slave, Xanthias, journey to Hades, it becomes increasingly evident that while both of them have the potential to imitate the whole range of spiritual reality from slave to god, neither has the actual virtue of these forms.[42] The first part of the play thus has an unexpected conclusion. Not in his imitation of Heracles but from the side of potentiality Dionysus unifies the two original sides of his enterprise. He is capable of imitating all human and divine beings, as does drama itself.

The remainder of the play shows Dionysus learning how to clarify this mimetic capacity for the benefit not only of himself, but of all who go to the theatre. This involves his surrendering his idea that he can choose a poet to suit his own private whims as a spectator. Rather he must choose a poet whose plays will enable the spectators to achieve their true end. A contest between Euripides and Aeschylus for the title of best poet indicates that the true end of spectators of a tragedy lies in their attaining a heroic and thus complete devotion to the life of the city. A spectator who sees plays that depict a heroism of that kind will be moved to imitate it. Thus, Dionysus chooses Aeschylus and not Euripides, that poet less thoroughly devoted to the imitation of the heroic, as the one to bring home with him to Athens as the saviour of the city.[43]

Thus Dionysus has achieved the true presidency of the theatre. He has united in himself and will cause the spectators to unite for themselves, the life of the gods of the Underworld and that of the gods of the Upperworld. The god and the spectators will have experienced the pure potentiality of which Hades is the locus, and the realization of that, which is Olympian heroism. Dionysus has attained this unification through his human nature, through the purification of his desire as a spectator. Moreover, it will be other humans who will enjoy this unification, while the realms of gods remain separate. The true enjoyment of the unification of the gods belongs to men.

In *Plutus*, the last extant play of Aristophanes, the comic argument reaches its limit. Previous plays had shown the relation of a representative Athenian to the Olympian religion as it historically existed. *Birds* had represented the overthrow of Zeus; *Lysistrata* had seen human action as making real what the goddess Athena stood for. *Frogs* had shown the relation of the god Dionysus to the theatre he presided over. *Plutus* presents the relation of men to a poet-devised god whom the play shows to be the one true god of Athens, and who has as his end nothing other than the communication of wealth and virtue to men and women. Even the Hesiodic division of gods into Titans and Olympians is in a way rewritten, since Plutus is posited as having a unity of rational and natural ends in himself, prior to the reign of Zeus.

The play falls into two essential divisions. An Athenian is worried about his son and how he will make his way in the world. The virtuous are all poor, and the rich, villainous. Perhaps he should encourage his son in a career of villainy, so that he too can enjoy the benefits of wealth. He asks the oracle at Delphi what he should do, and he is told to follow the first man that he meets.[44] He follows a man who proves to be the blinded god of wealth. It seems that Plutus had planned to enrich only the virtuous, and that Zeus had blinded him for his intent. Thus, there exists potentially a god who has in him the communication to men of both natural and rational goods. The Athenian decides to restore Plutus to sight, who out of fear of Zeus has to be persuaded.[45] Thus, the Athenian is willing to defy Zeus and Plutus in order to restore Plutus to his sight.

Many are drawn to this scheme, from love not of virtue but of wealth. 'Poverty' objects to the scheme, on the ground that she alone compels men to the efforts necessary to the securing of wealth.[46] Her pleas are rejected, because what is desired is wealth without any of the mediation necessary to attain it.[47] Wealth is restored to his sight at a shrine of the healing god, and this restoration marks the turning point of the play.[48]

Now, to enjoy the benefits of wealth, one must first share in virtue. All Athenians flock to Plutus, and as a result the cult of Zeus is neglected. Finally, not only the priest of Zeus but also Zeus himself join Plutus; the statue of Plutus is erected as the true god of Athens. Only a god who can afford them the benefits of virtue and wealth united can reign at Athens, and only a god whose reign is mediated by a human life that overthrows the rule of Zeus, who will not allow such a unification.

Thus, the last extant play of Aristophanes has taken the comic argument to its extreme point. It describes a human individual who has made himself the measure of a divine world whose very being is the definition of that individuality. That is, the concrete individual enjoys both virtue and wealth. In order to present a divine guarantor of that individuality, the poet has substantially rewritten the existing poetical history of the gods by positing a pre-Olympian concretion of rational and sensual goods in the being of the god Plutus.

Thus comedy and tragedy, taken together, conclude the Greek religion. The religion does not begin with a unified spiritual god as the cause of all else. Instead, it posits various nature powers out of which develop the ruling Olympians. This finitude or process in the arising of the Olympian gods makes it necessary that the two forms of the dramatic art reach contradictory conclusions. The one teaches the receding of all things into Zeus, and the other shows the actual individual to be master of all things, even the gods. While comedy could examine tragedy and even show it as included within itself, the city did not therefore end the presentation of tragedy nor imagine that it could live without its teaching. The contradiction could not be fully resolved, either in Greek religion or even within the Hellenic world.

Notes

1 J.A. Doull, 'The Christian Origin of Contemporary Institutions Part One,' *Dionysius* 6 (1982); reprinted here in chapter 1.

2 See above, 28.

3 Ibid., 28.

4 Ibid., 28.

5 Ibid., 33.

6 F. Nietzsche, *The Birth of Tragedy & The Genealogy of Morals*, trans. F. Golffing (New York: Doubleday, 1956).

7 Nietzsche, *The Birth of Tragedy*, 19–24.

8 Cf. my 'The Recovery of a Comprehensive View of Greek Tragedy,' *Animus* 1 (1996).
9 *Agamemnon*, ed. Denys Page and J. Denniston (Oxford: Clarendon Press, 1957), xxii.
10 Sir Richard Jebb, ed., *Sophocles*, Part III (Amsterdam: A.M. Hakker, 1971), xx.
11 E.R. Dodds, ed., *Bacchae* (Oxford: Clarendon Press, 1960), xiv.
12 Cedric Whitman, *Aristophanes and the Comic Hero* (Cambridge, Mass.: Harvard University Press, 1964).
13 Leo Strauss, *Socrates and Aristophanes* (New York: Basic Books, 1966).
14 See Murray's *Aristophanes: A study* (New York: Oxford University Press, 1933).
15 J. Henderson, ed., *Lysistrata* (Oxford: Clarendon Press, 1990), xxxiv–xxxv.
16 Hesiod, *Theogony*.
17 Aeschylus, *Agamemnon*.
18 Aeschylus, *Libation Bearers*.
19 Aeschylus, *Eumenides*, in *Aeschylus*, ed. H.W. Smyth, 2 vols. (Cambridge, Mass.: Harvard University Press, 1926).
20 Aeschylus, *Eumenides*, 1046.
21 Sophocles, *Oedipus the King*, ed. Sir Richard Jebb (Cambridge: Cambridge University Press, 1887), 1329–31.
22 Euripides, *Bacchae, Euripidis Fabulae*, ed. Gilbert Murrary (Oxford: Clarendon Press, 1913), 3: 1–62.
23 Agave discovers what she has done at ll.1284–9.
24 Peisthetairos in *Birds* and Lysistrata in the eponymous play are cases in point.
25 Peisthetairos rediscovers the city by re-experiencing these realms in *Birds*; in *Frogs* Dionysus discovers the nature of tragedy both as a craft and as educating the citizens.
26 *Wasps*, 54–135. All line references to the plays of Aristophanes are taken from *Aristophanis Comoediae*, ed. Hall and Geldart, 2 vols. (Oxford: Clarendon Press, 1907).
27 *Wasps*, 1444–5.
28 *Acharnians, Knights, Clouds, Wasps, Peace.*
29 *Lysistrata, Thesmophorizusae, Frogs, Plutus.*
30 *Clouds*, 11–13.
31 *Clouds*, 1131–1302.
32 *Clouds*, 1321–1475.
33 *Clouds*, 1509.
34 *Peace*, 50–62.
35 *Birds*, 1–554.

36 *Birds*, 1325–1470.
37 *Birds*, 1513–33.
38 *Birds*, 1565.
39 *Birds*, 1646–87.
40 *Frogs*, 66–70.
41 *Frogs*, 45–6.
42 *Frogs*, 460–673.
43 *Frogs*, 1500–27.
44 *Plutus*, 750–6.
45 *Plutus*, 120–253.
46 *Plutus*, 507–16.
47 *Plutus*, 609–12.
48 *Plutus*, 750–56.

COMMENTARY TWO
The Origin of Constitutions in the *Republic*

ANGUS JOHNSTON

In his 'The Christian Origin of Contemporary Institutions' James Doull brings out two central aspects of Platonic thought. The first is the difficult position which he finds to be at the heart of Greek theology more generally, that in fate and necessity there is the otherness which provides the divine with a completed self-consciousness and which allows the human to partake in that very self-conscious freedom. The second is, in contrast to the first, that Plato recognized the necessity for such finite freedom yet did not see how it could be thought to be one with the divine. Another way of putting this is that he saw that there must be free individuals to form a true state, but could not find a unity of the individual with the state except in an internal and ideal unity, in philosophical wisdom. This wisdom Professor Doull relates to the wisdom of Judaism, for only in the Good is the contradiction between finite and infinite overcome and yet the Good is known as the creator of that very finitude. In this light Doull contrasts the Greek view of necessity with the Platonic view.[1]

This paper will treat of Plato's effort to think the connection between the individual and the state, and thus to think the connection between finite necessity and its principle. Thus, the emphasis here will be on that side of Plato which in Doull's treatment leads to Aristotle. The decline of the states in the later part of Plato's *Republic* is an attempt to think external necessity as one with self-conscious freedom and to bring out ways in which human practice can itself overcome the contradictions between the finite and the infinite. Plato argues that it is only after one has seen these ways that one can answer the sophistic question: Which is better, the just or the unjust life?[2]

In the paper I consider books 8 and 9 of the *Republic*, the decline from Plato's just state through the constitutions which are less and less just. I treat these books in relation to the problems of the dialogue as a whole and especially in relation to Plato's intention for this part of the work. In order to do this, I find treatment of the central metaphysical images in books 5, 6, and 7 inevitable and I find the distinction between 'degrees of reality' and 'kinds of reality' – adapted from deVogel and Vlastos[3] – useful.

In *Politics* V, 12 Aristotle discusses Plato's treatment of the change of states. There is no cause which particularly explains the first transition from the rule of philosophers to timocracy. Plato argues that nothing is abiding and Aristotle finds this inadequate. Further, Aristotle questions the adequacy of the other changes in Plato's account and the order of those changes; in fact, he argues, change is usually to the opposite state rather than to one which closely resembles what has been.

These criticisms are in keeping with Aristotle's general point against Plato that he does not explain why things participate in the form. If the *Republic* has disclosed the form of justice and its relation to a first principle, then Aristotle's demand is that the various states that are, their kinds and their changes, should be understood through and by that form. Why are there many rather than one?

Aristotle is only the first to question the 'realism' of the Platonic account. The question hangs upon the relation of the principle – in this case the form of justice – to that of which it is a principle – the various forms of injustice which are evident in the sensible world. This is also bound up with the realism of the ideal state – to what extent one can see the form itself in the sensible world. There are three positions which interpret this 'participation' of actual states in the form. First there are those, like Aristotle, who judge that Plato intended the forms of injustice to be known through justice but also judge that he failed to show how this was so. Vlastos's argument that Plato got surprising results from a 'degrees-of-reality' theory 'while all he needed was a kinds-of-reality theory' is the more general expression of this criticism, for the degrees imply a causal connection, which is exactly the question at hand.[4] Second are those who acknowledge that the form and the formed are not united, but who argue that that is as it should be. Allan Bloom argues that Plato outlines an impossible city 'to show its impossibility.' This, for Bloom, moderates moral indignation – makes impossible communism and Fascism – and thus America is born like Athena from the head of the philosopher king. 'Socrates' political science paradoxically is meant to show the superiority of the private life' – the best city is only a myth but the best man 'exists actually.'[5] So the connection between the ideal and the other degenerate forms can never be complete and the degeneration is the display of the impossibility of the ideal in anything but the soul. In a more developed way Martha Nussbaum also argues that the reality of the Platonic state and its degenerate forms must remain problematic. The display of states makes clear the criteria by which Plato is judging virtue and the whole affirms the completeness of the philosophic life as against other forms. She argues in a more self-conscious way than Bloom the relation of Plato's thought to Nietzsche. Put in Nietzschean terms our question becomes: Is there an irreconcilable conflict between the ascetic ideal and the life of passion and poetry – that is, between the just state and the others – which leaves the two opposed? Plato does and does not overcome this conflict in Nussbaum's view – he does intend to take up what is opposed to the principle, but nevertheless a serious contingent value conflict is left unresolved, at least in the *Republic* between the vision of the form and the formed.[6] Ernest Barker comments on Nettleship's contention that these books constitute the first attempt at a philosophy of history: if they are not history they explain history, and show why history is a record not of the perfect 'idea of the State, but of its various and successive perversions. They show, that is to say, that history has not been made by the full mind of man, acting in the proper hierarchy of its parts, but created as it were by fragments of mind.'[7]

The third possible argument is that with all the difficulties involved, the degeneracy of the just state is meant by Plato to be a real display of participation and that, properly understood, he brings it off. Guthrie admires the realism of the Platonic account on empirical grounds, DeVogel on dialectical grounds – that is, she argues that the account has a completeness about it which leaves particular states necessarily connected to and grasped through a unity.[8]

I will argue that in relation to Plato's intention the place of these books in the dialogue as a whole supports the first and third positions – that is, the intention is not the exaltation of philosophical ideals above all but the display of the form in all states. And I will argue that if the books are understood as a poetic expression of dialectic in the Platonic sense, the unjust states are best understood as degrees of reality – and thus a connection of the so-called real and ideal. At the heart of the argument here, as I see it, are the two points cited above from the Doull article. If one understands Plato to be uniting the sides of fated necessity and free self-consciousness, one can agree with Aristotle that Plato seeks a unity of the finite forms in the form of justice and yet understand that in seeking that unity through external change, an accidental necessity, and an assumption of that externality, Plato is dealing with the problem of self-conscious freedom in a way which is fundamental to Greek theology.[9]

In order to consider the place of books 8 and 9, we must consider the work as a whole, but especially books 5, 6, and 7. Why Plato treats of their content in the middle of the *Republic* is of course one of the fundamental questions concerning the work. By book 5 we have a definition of justice – we have then what in some sense was sought from the beginning of the work. And that definition does not change despite all that goes on in the rest of the work. Plato suggests (505a) that without the knowledge of the Good any other knowledge – even the knowledge of justice – will not profit us, for we will not know what justice is for. If this is so and the dialogue is about justice the central metaphysical images of the *Republic* should give us some sense of the dialogue as a whole.

The image of the sun and the wonderful treatment of light as thought in book 6 bring the whole earlier discussion of knowledge and ignorance to the conclusion that knowing and being are one in the Good – and this principle is more than being and being known. The line analogy begins from this unity of thought with its object and delineates the four levels at which this unity occurs. The image of the cave unites the two images in that it is an image of motion from one level to another through the desire for the single unity beyond them all – that is, the sun again. But for my purposes here, the divisions of the line will serve best, and I will accept that the cave and its stages (treated in book 7), correspond to the line.

Plato asks us to take a line and divide it unequally, then divide it unequally above and below the first division in the same proportion. Let the first division be that between the sensible and the noetic or intelligible realms. Let the division of the sensible realm have for its smaller part *eikasia* – a realm of likenesses, of images, of guesses. Let the next part represent *pistis* – belief, trust, confidence, persuasion – the completion of *doxa* or opinion. The object of the first is the shadows and likenesses of sensible things, of the second the actual things in the sensible world. Let the intelligible be divided similarly first into the mathematical – strictly, that thinking which uses the imitated in the sensible world, the real things, as images now, arguing from hypotheses to conclusions. Plato says that this is the nature of the mathematical sciences and it is the pursuit of *dianoia.* The object of this form of thought, then, is the hypothetical or mathematical reality. Finally, the highest stage of the line is the dialectical, moving from hypotheses not to a conclusion simply but to a first principle, and that without the use of those other realities as images. Unhypothetical principles are the result, and a mark of this dialectic is that it will draw out what follows from the principle again and in order: by forms through forms to forms and finally concluding with forms.

There, then, is the part of the dialogue which perhaps reflects the whole. Is this order at all applicable to the dialogue itself? Related is the question of the dialogue form and its relation to philosophical argument. This is a monstrous question. Dialogues are reasonable images – they are poetic and philosophical at the same time. There are characters and their interplay, there is argument, there are show and rhythm and diction, and in a sense plot – all of the aspects of drama according to Aristotle's *Poetics.* But Aristotle argues strongly that all other aspects serve plot, the drama, the action, what is done. Here all serves thought. But in this poetic form there is this difficulty: the order of thought is not necessarily the order of the poetry. When Plato introduces a character to argue, say as Thrasymachus does in book 1, his argument occurs in the right place in relation to other arguments if the work is well done. But the character is introduced in relation to the whole work and its requirements. That is to say, poetically the whole dialogue is already a poetic dialectic with the whole vision which that would imply. The poetic images and developments of the dialogue are participating, if you will, from the beginning to the end in a movement of forms. If, then, one is to relate the parts of the dialogue to an order of thought such as that presented through the line, it will be necessary to see that order in its poetic form – as imagination portraying stages in the unity of thought with its object: as eidetic poetry.[10]

I find four major divisions in the *Republic.* The image of the line lies in the third. It is the hypothesis here that the divisions of the line correspond to the divisions of the dialogue. This hypothesis becomes intelligible when one conceives the *Republic* as a work of poetry and considers the dialectic in this light. Then the intention of books 8 and 9 becomes clear. The parts of the dialogue themselves suggest to me at least that this hypothesis is more than a rude abstraction.

The first book presents likenesses of or guesses at justice. One would never argue that the whole content of the book is simply such likenesses or shadows. For as I have argued above, there is a sense in which the whole dialogue is wholly present in the imagery of its parts. The arguments of justice among thieves, justice as the virtue of the soul as vision is of the eye, and the objective character of techne – these are in one sense more than shadows, as for Plato they are steps towards something more complete. But within the first book these arguments are left as fleeting glimpses, as presumptuous analogies and ultimately as a confusion between the ideal and the real; what justice is and what it is for are not clear – that justice is real seems only clear for Thrasymachus.

In the image of the cave Plato suggests how painful it will be for us to look away from the shadows to the reality of this visible world. Socratic argument has brought us, at the end of book 1, to the point where confusion has led to ignorance, self-conscious ignorance. The myth of Gyges completes the blindness – one is forced to look to the reality of the soul itself. But one can do it at this point only through the assumed reality of this visible realm – we will seek the just in the necessary growth of a state. In doing so we are approaching the highest form of *doxa* and the most trusted. From an assumed beginning point in needs and abilities among humans we move in books 2 and 4 to a developed notion of the state and the soul. The city that seemed only to serve natural needs becomes, through the limitless character of these needs, something unnatural and reasoned – the appetites themselves make necessary the guardians, and thus the rulers, and through their education the appetites are brought to a limit and order. So, says Plato, the city will grow in a kind of circle, bettering its citizens and being bettered by them.

In this state and, through it, in the soul we find definitions of the virtues, thoughtful in character and subtle in application. Has the dialogue not then attained the forms of these virtues – in terms of the line have we not begun dialectic? Again I would suggest that in relation to the dialogue as a work of art, dialectical or complete reason is present in the art – in the presentation of this self-circling state. Because this is so, the definitions are true. But they are not known to be true at this point in the work. They are known through *pistis* and belong, in my view, to that stage of the line. Again, the transition point is noteworthy. Why the three waves? Justice is that each do the work suited to each. But there seems to be no more radical distinction among humans than the sexual distinction. But no, this distinction Socrates likens to baldness – it is accidental, shadowy. The first wave – that men and women perform the same tasks – reveals that the source of the state we have generated is still only given, natural in some sense and assumed. The wave is so serious because this fundamental assumption is brought to light and makes explicit that we have at this stage only developed opinion. This whole relation of the state to that which is given, to that which comes to be and dies is put in question through the second wave, where the institutional foundation of the state in the family, in the Furies of Hades, in Antigone, in Penelope is broken down, leading us beyond natural birth and even death (hence the discussion of war). The universal implied in the state we have outlined is not adequately represented in the assumed realities of the visible world. We must see it in a different light – perhaps from a different sun.[11] It is at this point that the big wave strikes: Is justice actual? Can the just be at all?

Out of the waves and the transition they represent comes the images sun, line, and cave. And a great deal else too. If the hypothetical argument has made any sense, one should expect, at this point in the dialogue, the mathematical. But again it is not mathematics itself but the poetic presentation of the movement between opinion and knowledge. The sun, the line, and the cave are mathematical images – that is, they are using the real objects of the visible world as images of dialectical thought. They present hypotheses which Plato acknowledges must remain here hypothetical. The glory and the frustration of the images becomes clear if they are seen in this light. As images they present us with dialectic, but as images they remain as imitations of that only. As mathematical images, then, what do they accomplish in relation to the dialogue? Three points are clear: First, they call the mind to a form of reason which grasps first principles in a way which explains what is other than the principle. This is the sun and its relation to the being and knowing of things. Second, they call the mind to determine this relation in an ordered reasoned account – one looks to the line and its ratios and distinctions. And third, the relation of the good to what is other than it is found in the soul and the state. This is at the heart of the image of the cave and of the treatment of education (mathematical, practical, and dialectical) which forms so much of book 7.

The images have raised the thought of the dialogue up to the invisible realm. If there is to be a knowledge of justice, there is now the demand that the form (1) must ground what is other than it; (2) must do so in a reasoned, articulated way; and (3) must be seen to ground the life in the soul and the state, which up until this point was assumed. This is exactly the character of the arguments in books 8 to 10. Watching the decline of the constitutions in book 8 is like watching the light of the sun fading in the distance, until the just state has become its opposite, complete injustice. In the decline, this opposition remains external, as do its stages. Yet the stages are articulated and ordered; they come out of one another by a reasoned necessity wholly in keeping with the stages of the line, and are more and more external views of the principle – that is, of justice. Still, the grounding of injustice in justice is not complete until the just and the unjust lives are compared, the explicit demand of book 2. The comparisons are in relation to happiness, to knowledge, and finally to true pleasure. All are forms of overcoming opposition in increasingly developed ways, and all in relation to an end. In relation to happiness, and to the being of the soul and the state, what is, is one in justice – its very nature is that all parts must be each in its own way. Injustice must assume this being, but in division – a household of slaves is Plato's image. The second argument is that only the just soul will know the pleasures of the whole soul, so that only he can judge, an argument which appears in the same logical form in the *Philebus*. Finally, just pleasures are those which involve no opposite. They are ends themselves, and thus what justice is for becomes a limited question. This is a hint of independence from the Good which is also the relation of justice to it.

The decline of the states is put in ironic parentheses in Plato's text: ironic because it seems to me that Plato is thinking in two directions at once. Consider the obscure mathematics which outline the miscalculation of the positions of the stars which lead to the decline, and the obscure mathematics by which the ratio of advantage of the just over the unjust life is calculated at the completion of the decline. These are mathematical frenzies marking the decline to the visible and changeable perhaps, but at the same moment, in my view, they are images of the transition to dialectic, mathematical quotations as the mediation setting off something higher. Here I find Plato on the way up and the way down all at once: a remembering in forgetting.

In Parmenides, dialectical method is described as laying down first that something is and then that it is not. The move in the *Republic* to the mathematical realm came out of the question of the being or not-being of justice. It is a mark of the power of the dialectic in books 8 and 9 that the question simply does not make sense anymore. Justice is known and affirmed each time a contrary form is proposed. For what Plato has shown is that in being and in being known and in goodness as an end, all other constitutions are, are known, and are good or profitable in so far as they are just.

I am suggesting that albeit in this poetic way of a dialogue, the form of justice has begun to appear, that the various states will be an endless show of its possibilities. And the soul will be immortal through this, its virtue – because of the power of justice to ground injustice, the soul can never be destroyed by its vice. The suggestion by Socrates that the soul and justice may be simple and not complex at all is an indication not that our argument has been opinion only, but that a more fundamental unity underlies the eidetic images of a dialogue. Through poetry we are approaching the source of the poetic. And poetry will be reborn from this true source – again, this means that the form will have a power over what is other than it, the very images themselves. The myth of Er is this poetry. Heavenly spindles present nothing but the possibilities within justice. In this vision all of reality is shown, as in the line and the cave. But now reality has become a judgment: for the soul will suffer reality or enjoy it. By striving to express the whole we must chose the part, and it is by that whole, the form of justice, that the part will be judged. This is to present the true as a choice and this reality of practical choice is justice, as against what is, in a way, beyond choice: the Good or the One. There is present here a grasp of the unity of opposites in finite praxis, as Doull puts it.

The *Republic* is about the relation of one individual Form to the many – to the dyad. As such it only requires an image of the relation of the forms to the One or Good. This relation of Justice to the good is left as it should be left in the *Republic* as hypothetical, as mathematical. But Justice, through the dialogue, through the decline of the states, becomes unhypothetical and real in all that seems opposed to it. In relation to Plato's intention, I am with deVogel – he intends to ground the possibilities of all states and he does this by the relation of degrees of realities which precede our notions of 'kinds' of realities, and our empirical experience of states in the world; they are seen through the form. And instead of the war of the philosophical with the practical, as in Bloom's account, philosophy and practice can be seen as mutually affirmative. And the contingent which seems to cause the first decline, the contingent so rightly stressed by Professor Nussbaum, is taken up by the decline into an ordered whole related to the judgment that justice always grounds injustice. Aristotle's objections do not affect the truth of the dialectical decline of these states, but rather suggest that this temporal decline is a faulty image of justice – in the end Aristotle will argue that all the states are present in every state. Decline and fall is an image of 'participation' and is unclear because its unity is outside of it.

Finally, in relation to James Doull's treatment of Plato, the arguments which end the decline of the states, the comparison of the just and the unjust life, bring out ways in which finite practical human life can overcome the oppositions present to us; states and individuals are returning to justice or moving from it, but in doing so there are the unities of happiness, of knowledge, and also of pleasure which are actually good, which are what the other degrees are for, and more, what they are.[12] As Plato puts it, we are only caught up in contradictions because we look at the middle of justice and mistake it for the heights. Doull emphasizes the way in which, for Plato, our vision is raised to the true heights by the law, by tablets on mountains. This is reminiscence by faith. But for Plato, as Doull shows in his treatment of the transition to Aristotle, there is also the unity with the principle which is the decline and cycle of states and the soul: reminiscence by forgetting.

Notes

1 James Doull, 'The Christian Origin of Contemporary Institutions Part One,' *Dionysius* 6 (1982), especially p. 128 (p. 30 above).
2 See Doull's treatment of sophistry in the same article, 137 (pp. 38–9 above).
3 Gregory Vlastos, *Platonic Studies* (Princeton: Princeton University Press, 1973), 58–75, and C.J. deVogel, *Rethinking Plato and Platonism* (New York: E.J. Brill, 1988), especially her discussions of dualism and also on John Findlay's view, 68–9.
4 *Platonic Studies*, 75.
5 Allan Bloom, *The Republic of Plato* (New York: Basic Books, 1968), 415.
6 Martha Nussbaum, *The Fragility of Goodness* (Cambridge University Press, 1986), 158.
7 Ernest Barker, *Greek Political Theory* (London: Methuen, 1947), 177.
8 W.K.C. Guthrie, *A History of Greek Philosophy* (Cambridge: Cambridge University Press, 1975), 4: 543–4; deVogel, *Rethinking Plato and Platonism*, 98–9.
9 For a position diametrically opposed to Professor Doull see Michael Despland's treatment of Lev Sestov in *The Education of Desire: Plato and the Philosophy of Religion* (Toronto: University of Toronto Press, 1985), 262ff.
10 In 'Findlay and Plato'(1985), James Doull praises the work for its division of the major dialogues, especially in relation to the division between the middle dialogues, which concern the forms, and the later dialogues, which consider the *stoicheia* which lie behind the forms and give them a scientific ground: 'they do not give a science of the state or the soul or whatever but rather an eidetic reflection on these matters in the light of unifying principles which remain themselves in the background' (256). I am interpreting the *Republic* in this light as a middle dialogue, and thus primarily eidetic, concerning forms.
11 The question here is also in Euripides' *Bacchae* and its two suns: can one face the extreme of human evil, as Doull puts it (p. 30 above), and know its resolution in more than 'implacable necessity'?
12 This is the Platonic beginning from which comes the Aristotelian notion that pleasure is beyond time.

chapter two

Plato's *Parmenides*

Section One: The Argument to the Hypotheses in Plato's *Parmenides*[1]

The reader of *Parmenides* should put himself in the place of the Clazomenian philosophers who have come to Athens to hear the great argument of Socrates with Zeno and Parmenides as recorded in the memory of Antiphon. From it they would learn what Anaxagoras had not made clear, how the *nous*, alone unmixed, could relate to the atoms in each of which were all difference, the endless process of separating their differences from the original mixture. Of the atoms in this endless process nothing could be said distinctly that would not show itself as other in further division.

Zeno gave general form to this recurrent same and different: the contraries themselves would have both to be united in the individual, and in that contradiction must be annulled. Parmenides would thus be shown to have said rightly that thinking and being were immediately one and that negativity or not-being was unthinkable.

Socrates had however given up the separation he found in Anaxagoras of the pure, unmixed *nous* from its work of distinguishing and ordering the atomic individuals. As the good, the *nous* was determination of itself and ordered its determinations to itself. This unity of the divided and the undivided Socrates could not think directly but had discovered a method by which a true finitude could be known. The confusions of sense perception and opinion or ordinary language, where the being of things has ever a negativity lurking in it, he thinks to be eliminated in 'separate' ideas – 'separate' in that, like the *nous* of Anaxagoras, they are 'pure' and 'unmixed,' self-identical. In these objects Socrates had perhaps discovered the true finitude which Zeno thought to be impossible.

What the Clazomenians will hear reported to them by Antiphon is an examination of this 'true being' by Parmenides, whether and in what way it can sustain the argument of Zeno that all division and finitude ends in contradiction and nullity.

127a–130a: Introduction

What the dialogue is about is indicated more distinctly by the place and occasion of the meeting of Socrates with the Eleatic philosophers. Parmenides and Zeno have come to Athens to celebrate the Great Panathenaea. In Athena poets and other artists embody aesthetically the self-conscious reason which knows opposed positions, can stay and reconcile thus what would be mutually destructive conflicts – the circumspect reason which exists humanly in Odysseus, her favoured hero; which gives Achilles pause when in just anger he would kill Agamemnon, first among the Greek commanders; can order the conflicting demands of Apollo and the Eumenides; which drives to madness and suicide in the soul of Ajax conflicting heroism and slighted dignity, where time and the reflection of an Odysseus would have saved him. In the last example, or in the mad Heracles, Zeno's contradiction as the truth and nullity of extreme division occurs, as also a possibility of surviving the contradiction. Athena one should suppose to preside over the division between Zeno and Socrates and to know a resolution adequate to both.

A brief exchange between Socrates and Zeno states the opposed positions whose relations, and in the end their unification, will occupy the remainder of the dialogue. Zeno has read his book, which then for the first time became known in Athens, to an interested audience, among whom was Socrates. The reading finished, Socrates, to be sure he has grasped rightly the logic of Zeno's proofs that there cannot be a plurality of beings, asks him to read again the first hypothesis of the first argument, and, that being read, states what he takes to be its meaning: 'if beings are many, they must be both alike and unlike, which is impossible; for neither can unlikes be like nor likes unlike.' Zeno confirming, he goes on: 'that being so, it is impossible that there be many; for if there were, they would suffer impossibilities.' Is it the common intention of all your arguments to contend against all the ways one speaks of a plurality that there are not many? Zeno confirms that Socrates has understood well the meaning of his whole book.

Thus all the forty 'paradoxes' of Zeno's book *On Nature* are comprised in one formula and taken into the discussion. Omitted in Socrates' statement of Zeno's logic is the counter hypothesis that there can be nothing that is neither like nor unlike. That one must attend also to negative hypotheses enters the argument of the dialogue when Socrates' response to Zeno has been stated, its meaning drawn out, and the problems of participation gone through. They will be shown by Parmenides to be no less necessary than the affirmative hypotheses about unity and being to a knowledge of the relation of a 'separate' intelligible world to a sensible world.

Zeno, so understood, appears to Socrates only to repeat in other words what Parmenides has already said, that a multiple world was an unthinkable, that is, contradictory, not-being. His many arguments were in effect a deception, by which, saying the same as Parmenides, he seemed to be saying something different. Zeno disallowed this reading of his intention: his purpose was neither to deceive nor to propose another than Parmenides' philosophy, but polemical only. He would show to those who thought it absurd that there was only being that, supposing a plurality, they were involved in equal and greater absurdities. Socrates, one might say, saw Zeno as a Sophist, as one who could at his will obliterate the difference of contraries. Zeno's clarification allows Socrates to state his position not against 'sophistic' but in relation to the being of Parmenides.

Socrates takes it to follow from Zeno's adherence to the undivided being of Parmenides that they have common ground: 'Tell me this, do you not think there is an *eidos* by itself of likeness and another, its contrary, which is unlike; and that in these, which are two, you and I and the rest which we call many participate? Neither Zeno nor Parmenides has conceived such an ideal plurality. It occurs to Socrates to expect that Zeno has made this assumption because he for his part has another concept of being than the Eleatic. Being for Socrates is another name for the good, and the *eidh* are determinations of the good. Individuals, it seems clear to him, can have part in contrary *eidh* without contradiction. When Sophists say of something that it is 'like and unlike,' 'one and many,' they fail to distinguish in what comparison or in what respect the two belong.

The true difficulty for Socrates lies in the implications of a unified relation of the 'separate' *eide* to individuals, which will not fall in the shifting comparisons of an extraneous subject or be in one respect and not another. In *Phaedo* where he tells how he came to the hypothesis of separate universals he speaks of them as substantial causes, e.g., of the union of soul and body which constitutes the human individual. But as not only separate and in themselves but present in individuals, universals are also mixed with one another. Nature is the process of mixing and separation. And this negativity and circulation of contraries is not only in changing and corruptible individuals but in their unchanging ideal basis, and through this individuals have a mediated relation to the good.

Socrates would marvel greatly if someone began by distinguishing and setting apart such universals as 'likeness' and 'unlikeness,' plurality and unity, rest and motion, and then showed them able among themselves to mix and be separated – if someone could show the same *aporia* among objects attainable by reasoning as Zeno showed among sensibles, contraries mutually entwined in every sort of way. As Zeno's arguments proved the being of Parmenides to be the only truth of the sensible world, so would the concurrence and mutual exclusion of contrary universals prove the primacy of the good. So one might take the analogy. But for Socrates, as said, being has become the self-identity of the good. The good is not only in itself but divided and different from itself and relating its determinations to itself as to their end. And so he reads Zeno as showing among sensibles the multiple relations everyone assumes them to have, not their nullity.

It makes a difficulty in reading *Parmenides* that in speaking of the good, Plato uses abstract Eleatic concepts – unity and being. What these concepts signify for him is plain from the context, whether one think of the transition in *Phaedo* from the intelligence of Anaxagoras which separates extraneously the mixed individuals of a material world to an intelligence which moves 'for the best,' or of the good of *Republic* toward which are ordered alike the divisions of the state and the soul. Zeno's arguments had for their purpose to show that nature or the material world which humans commonly suppose to be there, and themselves to be in it, is, for a thinking which has just begun to know itself, a nullity. How from this abstract beginning 'the one' came to be 'the good' in which is centred in the sensible and ideal totalities Plato treats only elusively. From his standpoint it is not possible to write such a history of Presocratic philosophy as one has in Aristotle, which supposes that the substantial unity of the ideal and sensible world, toward which Plato's thought tends, has been discovered, and with it the division of being into primary genera or categories. The history of philosophy can then be regarded as a history of the discovery of the elements of substance.

This Aristotelian view of the movement of philosophical thought from Parmenides and Zeno to Plato is itself too narrow. The opponents of Parmenides appear in it as accomplishing something, if obscurely and without direction. The source of the instability of the several positions and the recurrent need to begin anew is seen to lie in a groping after the stability of substance as the category which alone remaining itself is receptive of contraries. Implicit in the history is therefore a relation to Zeno's common criticism, as one has it in *Parmenides*, of all who supposed they could think a multiple and finite being. But to bring out this relation clearly one would have to say of the successive attempts to think the finite that there was in them not one or more of the causes but them all and an incapacity of the category constitutive of a particular position to contain them. In all the positions until Anaxagoras, unless transiently in Heraclitus, thinking either with Parmenides and Zeno cannot find itself in the world that is there for it, or entering into it finds the logical forms in which it would think it inadequate to itself. Anaxagoras first brings the two sides in their strong separation together and would know them as one totality. But thought stands in an extraneous relation to the supposedly true entities of Anaxagoras' world. The endlessly recurrent relation of their togetherness and their separation, as for the unity of the thinking which divides and orders them, is subject to Zeno's criticism and, as 'ex hypothesi' independent of thought, first shows itself a contradiction and nullity.

Between Zeno and Parmenides in their own historical situation at the beginning of Presocratic philosophy and the application of their principle to Anaxagoras at the end, there is this difference, that then the nullity for thought of nature as simply there is immediately asserted without proof; now after successive attempts to think the finite were made and given up, the whole relation of thinking to its assumed world became explicit. Or, one might say, the Eleatic principle had its complete proof. On this understanding, Plato's use of Parmenides and Zeno in the dialogue as that against which Socrates presents his discovery of a true finitude can be taken as an abbreviation of Presocratic philosophy generally.

The result of Presocratic philosophy was not what Zeno would require, were his principle to be applied to its several forms and especially to Anaxagoras. Instead the thinking which knew itself one with being, with Socrates and the Sophists passed into the form of self-consciousness – a thinking which knew the positive and negative moments of what was other than itself as related to each other and to the thinking subject. There was no longer the thinking which knew being but not its division and multiplicity. One had in its place first the self-conscious subject which knew itself as 'measure of the being of beings and of the not-being of not-beings.' Or with Socrates the new principle took the form of a universal being to which belonged all negativity and difference. This principle Plato called 'the good.' Regarded in its simple unity, apart from its division and multiplicity, it might be called 'one' or 'being.' And the reasoning which considered the relation of this unity to its determinations might be extraneous and not expressive of a teleological relation.

To use the Eleatic forms, abstract and inadequate to what one would think by them was indeed inevitable for Plato so long as he took for principles the 'one' and the 'indeterminate dyad' and on the assumption of their difference sought their unity through an external reflection and did not know their relation as the intrinsic self-determination of an original unity or as actuality. In *Parmenides* one sees the genesis of that concept, which begins to appear in the criticism of Eleaticism in *Sophist*.

130a–e: Of what are there ideas?

The argument then passes to the Platonic Parmenides for whom 'the one' is 'the good' and is assumed capable of showing the relation of all things to that principle. Ascertaining first from Socrates that the explanation he has given of a sensible plurality as 'participating' 'separate' ideas was not a thesis merely but for him the ideas are separate and self-identical, Parmenides would first learn whether it is intended universally or to apply only in some cases. By Aristotle's account it was held in the Academy that there were not separate *eide* of negations, privations, relations, or where there was a prior and posterior.[2] That is, the ideas were properly essences or substantial natures, 'by themselves' or self-identical, without the types of negativity and otherness mentioned. Always included as well were unity, being, like, unlike, and such pure universals. The Socrates of the dialogue had not fully clarified the position, but was beyond the historical Socrates who was occupied with definition and with virtues and the good or beautiful as the end sought by them. He was beyond that Socrates who had not 'separated' these or any universals from language and 'opinion,' whose ambiguities he disclosed. Here he had 'separated' and knew these forms as self-related objects of a universal thinking.

The Socrates of *Phaedo*, to discover what that unmoving independence of the soul was from all its mutable relations to the world, 'separated' universals from their unstable presence in the objects of sense and imagination. He came to this knowledge by correcting a view of the soul as simply in the natural cycle of birth and death, coming to be and perishing, or as having the continuity of a harmony of the changing elements of the cycle. In this reflection he comes to a knowledge of the ideas through mutable nature and has not, or has only begun, to relate the 'separate' ideas to that way through which thought came to them. Asked by Parmenides at that point whether there were ideas of 'man' as embodied soul or of the elemental natural bodies he would no doubt be perplexed. And it would appear absurd that there be ideas of 'hair,' which protects animal bodies from externals, or of 'mud,' 'dirt' and such unordered mixtures of the elements. The thought came to Socrates sometimes that there must be one account in all cases, but from it he falls back for fear he be destroyed in an 'abyss of absurdity.'

The 'abyss of absurdity' from which Socrates recoils is a loss of that stability his thought has found in a knowledge of the ideas. That certainty and himself as a thinking self-conscious being appear to be lost in that comprehensive idea to which Parmenides' questions have led him. The true being he had in the ideas will rest on a common idea inclusive also of that of which thought has not a certain knowledge. That which is self-identical and as such true for thought will also be not itself and untrue. This consequence is for Socrates absurd, that is, contradictory.

But Socrates, Parmenides observes, is still a young man and as such respects overly the opinions of men. He is not yet capable of what is not a human but rather a divine knowledge. The discovery of the ideas is the beginning of a science, of a knowledge of what the scientific understanding is. But there is also a dogmatism of the understanding, a common sense not easily moved from its certainty. But in Socrates, Parmenides discerns a philosophical enthusiasm which in his greater maturity will break through that barrier.

131a–e: The first **aporia** *of 'participation'*

After intimating to Socrates that, having separated the ideas, he cannot stop short of a total idea reflecting all externality, Parmenides questions him on how one is to understand 'participation' or the relation to ideas of the individuals of the sensible world. This inquiry develops further Socrates' problem how self-identical ideas can be interconnected. For now not only has all the diversity of the sensible world been brought under one identity, but one asks how that identity can be individualized. In this and the previous line of questioning there is taking shape the structure of the ideal world, as this will be treated in the hypotheses about the relations of an absolute unity to a divided totality.

Parmenides begins by asking whether individuals participate a whole idea or a part of it or in some other manner, that is, can 'participation' be understood through the relation of parts to whole, or if not, through some other relation of the many to the unity of the idea. One will observe that the question, so formulated, takes up from where the questions on the content of the ideal world ended: how is that comprehensive idea related to the individuals of the sensible world.

Socrates in his answer shows that he knows well the sense of the question. 'Participation' is like the diffusion of light, which while remaining undividedly itself is spatially extended even to individuals. Elsewhere Plato compares the diffusion of the good to that of the light from the sun in the sensible world. But is not that identity, considered in its relation to individuals, rather like a sail spread over many individuals, touching each with some part of itself? 'Participation' would then not be of the whole, as Socrates' image intimates, but of the part.

The relation thus described one should compare with that of a unified thought to extension in the philosophies of Descartes and Spinoza. The difference lies in this, that the light in the image is thought to have division and difference in its identity, as on the other side the sail is not simply the continuity of extension but as partitioned among a multitude of individuals. Here a like relation to that of the moderns emerges as one seeks the truth of a presupposed world. The particularity of the many has not given way to the abstract form, as later it will (as already in a manner in the matter of the Stoics) but is to be united with it. The argument then passes from the relation of parts to whole to the 'some other way' mentioned.

Parmenides begins the exposition of this more developed relation with the question whether an idea can truly be partitioned and remain one. Socrates accepting that to be impossible, Parmenides presents to him a way in which it can be thought possible. Consider the contrariety of 'great' and 'small' and an 'equality' which neutralizes their difference. In this relation one has the conditions of a unified process. The reflection of the self-diffusing unity and that process into each brings the process or becoming to a momentary halt and permits that first apprehension of being which is called aisthesis.[3] The conditions of this relation are here simply set before Socrates, who apprehends both an immediately stabilized unity of the divided and the undivided and the need to go beyond it to a more than evanescent truth, and thus to a second account of 'participation.'

But before passing to the second and subsequent explanations of 'participation' a general observation on their common structure. In every case 'participation' is through a certain relation of the Platonic 'principles' – undivided unity and the indeterminate dyad. From one to another there is a strict logical development towards an adequate relation of the principles – a relation in which both have explicitly the same total content. In *Republic* one has the image of a divided line, whose divisions represent relations of thought to being, at each division more adequate than the last, 'hypotheses' by which one ascends to the good – the 'unhypothetical' principle in which being and thought are no longer divided. Neither the logic of that ascent is there given nor how a 'dialectical' or 'hypothetical' thinking can exceed itself in an 'unhypothetical' principle. *Parmenides* will supply both. In the several *aporia* of 'participation' it will attend not only to a positive relation of thought and being at each grade but also to a negativity in which they are divided. The negativity present at one grade is at the next taken into the positive relation, only to recur in another form. The series is not endless but in four stages reaches a point where the object of thought is seen to be the principles themselves. Hence there are four *aporia*, the last leading to the 'hypotheses' about unity and being or the relations of an ideal and a sensible totality.

The endlessness which for Zeno nullified immediately a plurality of beings is here limited, allowing at each level an apprehension of finite being, a truth more stable as one ascends, until with the 'separate' ideas the relation appears to be absolutely stabilized.

The insufficiency of this first account of participation, which appears when its logical constituents have been brought out, is not further examined here. It is enough to have given the basis of the criticism of sense perception as knowledge which is amply set forth in *Theaetetus*.[4]

131e–132c: Second aporia

Socrates avowed that to define 'participation' was more difficult than he had supposed. The first attempt, that is, resulted for him in a renewed separation of individual and universal and the forming in his mind of a new relation. The object of his thought is not one individual but a multitude, and when he regarded them all there appeared to him one idea over them all. The multitude, that is, was not for him an indefinite plurality but implicitly under a universal. The many he regarded from the side of the universal into which the unstable content of *aisthesis* returned as to a stable and true being, as in that relation he could regard all the individuals of a kind, e.g., great things. And when he so regarded them there came into view for him one idea over all. In that way was formed for him the attitude of thought to being which in *Theaetetus* is called 'true opinion.'

Socrates accepts from Parmenides as true this account of how he discovered separate ideas. But the multitude being thus unified, what is the relation of the idea or universal to the many 'participants'? Parmenides sets before Socrates the difficulty of that relation. In coming to this position one has circumvented the indefinite plurality of things which makes true universals appear the unattainable end of an endless process. In this unification the idea has been separated from all the individuals, and it appears evident that there can be no 'participations.'

Socrates counters this difficulty with the proposal that the ideas be regarded as objects of thought which occur nowhere but in souls. In *Theaetetus* the attempt to find in the soul a bridge between universals and individuals is examined at length. The constituents of the sought mediation are memory, recollection, and imagination – a mediation attempted not for the last time in the history of philosophy, though decisively defeated in *Theaetetus*, where it is shown that a determinate relation of individual and universal is not to be found in the collaboration of these psychic powers.

Here Parmenides simply points to the consequence of Socrates' interpretation of the position – that the ideas as in the soul would save their universality, while through the soul related to endless division. To which Parmenides objects that each of these thoughts taken in itself would be a thought of nothing. Socrates concedes that a thought must be of something that is. Of some one object which that thought, being present to all the individuals, thinks, namely the one idea as being. The true being and the relation to it of all the individuals, with which the formulation of this position began, appear to be restored. But in a peculiar and impossible sense: the same necessity as thus conjoins the idea and all its participants also divides them and imposes a choice between an absorption of all the many into the thinking of them – where one will say that all things think – or a separation of thoughts from thinking – where one will say that all things are unthought thoughts.

The same division is treated in *Theaetetus* under the proposed definition of knowledge as true opinion with a *logos*. The *logos* both inwardly unites all plurality with the universal and is externalized into a dispersed multitude of parts, an externalized universal and a relation of individual to that universal. The elements of thought are thus materialized and as such unthought. So ends in that dialogue the attempt to equate knowledge with true opinion, by itself or with a *logos*. The whole argument in its barest essentials is given here in a few sentences. Its result is that an adequate account of 'participation' has not been found. For if the alternatives one is left to choose between are combined, the multiplicity and difference which *ex hypothesi* have their stability and truth in the ideas are rather obliterated in the *logos* so taken. There is demanded a *logos* which inwardly and in its explication contains all differences within a unity of form.

132c–133a: Third **aporia**

This reasoning awakens in Socrates what in consequence of it appears the best explanation of participation: there are unmoving 'paradigms' in nature, 'the others,' i.e., all the many individuals, resemble these and are likenesses of them; their participation in the ideas is nothing else than imaging them. In this he adopts the standpoint of a 'dianoetic' or reasoning thought which in treating of universal objects refers its proofs to sensible individuals in which are imaged the intelligible objects of which alone they are true.

Socrates takes 'participation' to be a positive relation, a likeness, of these individuals to the true objects of thought from which unlikeness has been excluded. He assents to Parmenides' statement that the relation must be reciprocal. But with that a negativity appears in the relation which demands a new idea to assimilate the two sides, a demand which repeats itself indefinitely, so long as all the variety of the many instances are not seen to have their truth in the one idea. Socrates sees the conclusion that 'participation' cannot be by 'likeness.' You see, observes Parmenides, how great is the *aporia* if one posit self-subsistent ideas. The transition from the scientific understanding of which for Plato the only model was geometry to a philosophical science was the most difficult. But only in that science could the relation of individual to universal be made clear and not subject to endless division.[5]

133a–135c: The fourth **aporia**

Socrates is at the edge of the greatest and most difficult *aporia* for one who has separated ideas from the sensible world. The preceding problem demands for its solution that the division in 'dianoetic' thought between the true objects of its necessary reasoning and the many sensibles it uses to represent them and this multitude be replaced by one idea. Thought will then have for its primary object the identity and division of the idea itself, in which will be contained the sensible multiplicity.[6]

The *aporia* which occurs here is that if one take this new relation of thinking to being as an identity of the two sides, there appears against it their division – an unbridgeable gulf between thinking and its objects. The equivalent in the older modern philosophy is the division of the rationalist and the empiricist. For Plato it is the division between the philosopher and the sophist. Protagoras speaks like many since when he says that the shortness of life prevents one from knowing whether there are gods, that is, an endless division and otherness makes inaccessible such knowledge. But the later rationalism and empiricism have a common root and, as Plato will show in *Sophist*, so have philosophy and sophistic.

In *Parmenides* the *aporia* is given the form that the sensible and intelligible worlds are incorrigibly separated and also are not separated, in that each side has the other in it. Humans are cut off from the ideal or divine world and can know nothing of it. The gods, likewise, as Epicurus will teach, are in their realm and can know nothing of human affairs.

But if humans have no knowledge of ideas or universals there can be no unified direction in their lives. As Plato elsewhere elaborates, the state would disintegrate, justice would be the will of the stronger. Or rather there would not be justice or a political community at all. Even in the arbitrary will of the tyrant there is a residual reason. And Protagoras for whom truth is the immediacy of feeling Socrates proves to be a calculating utilitarian. The sophist who is the measure of being and not-being has reason in him. In a later age Hume for whom 'impressions' were the primary truth had in him a reason which knew the universal and divine, and that his empirical self could not attain to what he knew. The division between empirical and rational, as between sophist and philosopher, is a subordinate distinction.

As to the ignorance of the gods, it is in the transition from the 'dianoetic' to the unified knowledge of ideas that this has in it, and in truer form, a knowledge of the sensible world. In all the forms of knowledge criticized there in the previous *aporiai* there has been a conjunction of ideal and sensible worlds. In this last form, fully explicated as it will be in the 'hypotheses,' the ideal and sensible worlds are known as complementary totalities. The *aporia* lies in the contradiction between the omniscience of the gods and their ignorance, which follows from the separation of a human or empirical world from a world true for thought. The resolution is in a recognition that the separation of the two is impossible.

How Plato saw the relation of human and divine he tells elsewhere in mythical language, especially in the great myth of *Phaedrus*. The life of the gods is a contemplation of all nature, within which is the human world. This contemplation is not of something alien, but of that through which the knowledge of their world is actual, is separated, and the separation negated. Humans from their being in the world strive to participate in the divine contemplation of the unity of the two worlds, but even if they attain something of it, are drawn back from it to their world and the assumption that on its own is the prime reality. In *Parmenides* and other late dialogues the mythical vanishes and the interest is to give this content the form of thought.

135c–136c: Revised Zenonian dialectic

The conditions on which such a philosophical thought is humanly possible were spoken of at length in *Republic*. From the standpoint the 'aporetic' argument has here reached, it is only necessary for *Parmenides* to impress on Socrates the necessity of being thoroughly practised in dialectic. One has to be freed from a sophistic use of dialectic in the service of ambitions and particular ends or as the strongest defence against philosophy. For philosophical thought to be possible dialectic must have become a purely objective contemplation of ideas, of divisions and interconnections not imported but found in them. That dialectic Socrates had in the wonder which is the beginning of philosophy. But despite the strong philosophical spirit moving in him he will never discover the truth unless he has made his own that dialectic which is the method of its discovery.

On that method, before he consents to apply it to unity and being, the primary Eleatic concepts, Parmenides makes several comments, important if one would follow him. The dialectic is that of Zeno, his own principle with the negative moment by which one does not immediately declare the many nothing but shows their intrinsic contradiction and nullity. It is Zeno's dialectic applied, in response to Socrates' 'separation' of ideas and his difficulty concerning them, to the self-identical ideas. Through the *aporiai* which applied this method to particular relations of being and knowledge, the method has become known in its universality. Applied in this form to the relations of ideal and sensible totalities the method itself undergoes a certain change. In the earlier *aporiai* the method drew out the affirmative and negative moments of the forms of being, reflected on them, and separated ideal and sensible components. There were not affirmative and negative 'hypotheses' separated and about the same totalities. Here where there is, to use analogically the *Phaedrus* myth, a going over of divine knowledge to its reflection in a sensible world and then a retraction and return to itself, the one movement can be followed through affirmative, the other through negative hypotheses. And on the human side there is a like alternation between an affirmative relation of rational and sensible moments, and one in which the difference of the moments is negated. The negative hypotheses have thus in the original a definite meaning which Neoplatonic commentators laboured vainly to discover from their standpoint, which had nothing in it of Plato's dialectical method.

Section Two: The Hypotheses of Plato's *Parmenides*

Introduction

The reader of *Parmenides* has been prepared to embark on 'the grand sea of discourse,' which the hypotheses are, by the earlier part of the dialogue. It may be useful to summarize that preparation:

(1) The argument began with the dialectic of Zeno which showed that what appeared other than the being of Parmenides – the immediate unity of being and thinking – was a co-presence of contraries, a contradiction and nullity.

(2) Against this position Socrates proposed that a sensible plurality and its various determinations could be saved from that consequence if there were 'separate' ideas or universals which they participate, for in that relation the transition of contrary into contrary was halted. The ideas were immovably self-related, their being exclusive of negativity, and the many 'had part in' this separate being. Zeno seemed thus to be answered.

But about this explanation Socrates had misgivings: the ideas, to be participated, it occurs to him, must stabilize the movement of the many and thus be themselves not only self-identical but different, a relation and circulation of contrary movements. But how can the immutable being-in-themselves of the ideas be also different from itself.

(3) The beginning of an answer to Socrates' problem is to know that the ideas are not of some sensibles and not others, but everything in the sensible world is reflected into the ideal. Even the most trivial and

contingent entities are not just themselves but in a certain relation of the sensible to the ideal world.

(4) On this understanding it is possible to ask what participation is – a far more difficult matter than the Socrates of the dialogue supposed. The question must first be asked 'aporematically' – by opposing to each other affirmative and negative positions as to the relation of individuals to the ideas. No resolution is given to the opposition, but it is taken from it that a new explanation is required. The *aporiai* continue to the point where there is a complete separation between an ideal world and a 'divine' knowledge of it, and a 'human' knowledge of an apparent world.

(5) Parmenides then proposes a method by which the *aporiai* as thus developed can be resolved. It is plainly insufficient, as in the *aporiai*, to carry to the extreme an analysis of the identity and negativity of things – to pure identity and pure division and difference. For how does that result apply to the world in which the two aspects are mixed? And even if there is a conjunction of the two in the ideal world, will this, as the last *aporia* intimated, be beyond our world? Parmenides' method is not purely analytic, but will consider also the consequences of supposing that the ideal unity 'is not' – that the division and difference have not only an underlying identity but are themselves a contrariety of positive and negative moments, unified in the absolute negativity of that identity. This negative reflection he would show has the consequence for the entities of our world that their apparent otherness than the ideal world is altogether dissolved.

The method he describes as that of Zeno, for Zeno did not adhere to an immediate unity of 'being' and 'thinking' simply, but attended also to the nullity of a supposed sensible plurality. The method as applied to Platonic ideas and supposedly 'participating' individuals has another meaning than for Zeno. The intention is not to defend the simple being of Parmenides against his pluralizing opponents, but to discover a unity of ideal and sensible worlds as prior to their apparent difference.

Both the problem to be solved in *Parmenides* and the method of its solution are thus clearly given. The long succession of Neoplatonic commentators on the dialogue had another problem, and the method appropriate to its solution was different. For them the problem was the relation of the free individual or person to an adequate end, and the method to resolve the finitude of that end and the knowledge of it so far as the two were divided from each other – to discover as primary a 'one' before the division of thought and thinking. For Plato there was not yet such a free individuality, unless as the sophistic subjectivity destructive of the ordered life of the political community. Plato's interest as against the sophists was to discover a true objectivity.

Parmenides responds to difficulties in the relation to individuals of the 'true being' of the ideas, which the image of 'participation' rather concealed than clarified logically. If by 'ideas' were intended the substantial natures of things, and 'participation' meant the relation of these natures or essences to individuals, both the structure of the 'ideas' and their individuation were at first indeterminate. Neither as Socrates sought to give definite form to the ambiguities of opinion or language in regard especially to virtues nor when in *Republic* and other 'eidetic' dialogues the ideas serve to order to one end by degrees the boundless content of soul, state, love, language, do questions about their relation to individuals impose themselves directly.

In these inquiries one looked for true knowledge of assumed entities. *Parmenides* begins with the Eleaticism for which there is no world or finite totality. It asks whether the ideas as earlier formulated provide an adequate response to that Eleatic doctrine. From a 'separation' of the ideas the argument of *Parmenides* looks to their relation to that from which they were supposedly separated. 'The others,' as the sensible plurality is called in the dialogue, are shown by the affirmative and negative 'hypotheses' to be only apparently, not in truth, 'other' than the ideas. That conclusion is the basis of the inquiry in *Sophist* whether there is a true 'otherness' and an undeceiving knowledge of it, such as one thought to have in the 'separate' ideas.

One has thus in *Parmenides* the beginning of an argument, among the most difficult and the most important in the history of philosophy, which reaches its conclusion in the Aristotelian philosophy – the true meaning of 'participation' is found to be substantial unity. And the conflation of thinking and thought in a higher unity, as spoken of in *Republic* and remaining in *Parmenides* and subsequent dialogues, passes into a separation of the thinking which is its own object from finite actualities and their relation to that infinite thought as mover.

The argument as it here unfolds is after Aristotle long concealed. The categories and the logic generally which were discovered in the development from *Parmenides* to Aristotle remained as known and assumed in Stoicism. In Neoplatonism this logic of the finite was subsumed under the relation of undivided unity to the divided and different. Aristotelian logic might be given more or less weight within this 'Platonic' context but the meaning of its distinctions – their relation to the unity of thought – could not be an object of inquiry so long as these Eleatic abstractions stood as primary. Only when it became the interest of a new philosophy to find place for a logic of the finite within the unity of thought, while at the same time remaining free of it, could this ancient argument again come into view for another standpoint.

For other reasons *Parmenides* and the continuation of its argument in other dialogues can hardly be other than opaque from within our contemporary world, where one assumes an existent individual freedom, and for the use of such free individuals collects and sorts out contingent relations through a mathematized logic. The unity of thinking and being with which Parmenides initiated an older philosophy does not find place in this culture, though it may be sought in the pre-philosophical medium of language. Thus the necessity Plato met with to separate universals and the consequent problems of 'participation' do not occur, unless the need arises to know what our freedom is, and first how its beginning in self-consciousness can contain an endless otherness. Being beyond philosophy we are also before it and have to make a new beginning in which the problems of Platonism are bound to recur.

A concreteness in the medium of language is exposed to an endless otherness, from which it takes flight. A self-reference of that endlessness falls into Zeno's 'paradoxes,' which, if one take not as an affront to common sense but allow to occur, constitute the beginning or background of *Parmenides*. As against that Eleaticism the argument of the dialogue would discover a thought which in its self-relation was comprehensive of division and difference. Such a thought is present in the *aporiai*, where one would find the identity of a plurality of various individuals and then attends to their difference from this abstraction. The movement of thought in the successive attempts to define the participation of 'the many' in the self-identity of the ideas is to correct the initial abstractness of the idea, until all the negativity of the many is seen as belonging to it. The reflection on the difference of 'the many' from the ideas takes correspondingly the form, not of an identity within which falls all difference, but of a unified relation of the two aspects of the divided – of a negative unity.

The argument of the hypotheses brings into one reflection the affirmative and the negative unity. The division and difference contained in this comprehensive relation is not, as the last of the *aporiai* demanded, only the difference of a divine or ideal thinking from its identical object and the negation of this difference in its self-relation. The apparent being of a sensible world as other than this intelligible world and the knowledge of it the argument shows to be the appearance of the ideal.

This appearance is found first to rest on the positive unity of the reflection and then to pass into the negative unity and self-relation of the positive and negative aspects of the difference as opposed and exclusive.

The first and second hypotheses taken together constitute the positive unity of undivided identity and division and difference. This positive unity as immediate is a temporal appearance and only comes to what it properly is as the inner reflection of this temporal and spatial externality. The negative hypotheses taken together show the unity of the temporal appearance as not only inner but as the negation of its own contrariety.

Through the affirmative and negative hypotheses the presupposed 'others' whose 'true being' was the separate ideas are found to be indeterminate division externalized, this as positively self-relation and as self-relation through the negation of the indeterminate division or form.

First hypothesis (137c–142a)

In the *aporiai* there was need to move from one to the next because against each proposed identical relation of individuals to ideas a negativity or non-identity occurred. Neither in the object considered nor in the thinking of them did a unity of the identity and the recurrent difference come to light. The 'logos' in this aporematic inquiry was divided between Socrates and Parmenides. In the 'hypotheses' the movement is unified both on the side of the object and in the thinking of it, where the argument is borne by Parmenides and a passive respondent only receives and assents to it.

The affirmative and negative moments in the *aporiai* connected for thought a multiple content. From one such relation to the next the content was more strongly unified with the form, until in noetic thought the many were drawn from their dispersion into one idea. But against paradigmatic ideas was still a negativity and appearance. The final *aporia* demanded that this last difference of the many and the ideas be seen as reflected into identity. Such is the standpoint of the first hypothesis: a unity in which rests everything of the sensible world. The object is no longer a plurality of 'paradigmata' but the common identity of all the ideas and their participants, and thus an ideal world altogether separate from the sensible or 'human' world.

The argument has passed from the ideas and their participants to the 'principles' or 'elements' of the ideas, and first to an undivided principle absolutely identical with itself. That there is also a 'dyadic' principle will come to be known when the consequences of the first hypothesis have been fully drawn out. Knowledge of the first 'principle' and then of the second is hypothetical. The object, that is, does not stand on its own but is laid down or supposed by a thinking which, when it has attended to the consequences of its supposition, will complement it by another until it comes to an 'anhypothetos archē,' in which the several hypotheses and the partial thought which supposes them are united. Such a principle, beyond the division of thinking and its object, one knows is called in *Republic* 'the good.' The 'one' of the first hypothesis is not that principle, but the supposition that it is pure self-identity only and a supposition which will be found not to exhaust the nature of the hypothesis is not the Eleatic principle. It is not an immediate identity of thinking and being, as against which all finitude is illusory opinion and in truth nothing. The principle assumed in this hypothesis has resulted from the examination of Socrates' response to Eleaticism – from the more complex relation of thought to the 'true being' of the ideas. It is a partial apprehension of that on which the self-identity of the ideas rests. After the development of the successive and complementary hypotheses of *Parmenides*, Plato on that basis will undertake to show in *Sophist* that there is such a true finitude.

Against the principle of the first hypothesis is not 'the one' of Neoplatonists. That 'one' is not hypothetical but rather the unhypothetical beginning on which all else depends. That not indivision but a dialectical unity of indivision and division or finitude is the true account of the principle is not what they read in the Platonic texts. *Parmenides* serves another than its original interest in their numerous commentaries, which however interesting they may be philosophically in another context, are an unreliable guide to the structure and meaning of the dialogue in its own right.

The first hypothesis begins by supposing the 'archē' to be 'one' or undivided and asks what follows from that assumption. The meaning of the assumption one knows from the conclusion of the *aporiai*: the principle is pure self-identity – the positive aspect in the *aporiai* into which has finally passed all division and negativity. It is the self-identity of the ideal world, an incomplete concept of it as accounting neither for its own diversity and fullness nor for its relation to a temporal and changing world. But these further relations will only be truly known if they are found to be consequent on this beginning – on the 'true being' of the ideas taken in its universality.

But how are these consequences from a beginning which seems from the first to eliminate all plurality and difference? In its first enunciation the principle can be taken to be the Eleatic. To Neoplatonists 'if the principle is one, then it is not many' stated the transcendence of the infinite divine unity over all division and finitude.[7] But this beginning states the meaning of the hypothesis only immediately: it does not make known that the unity of the principle is not immediate but mediated by the negation of all forms of division and difference, so that its self-relation is in truth a pure negativity and capacity for division and difference. The hypothesis only comes to be known as what it properly is by the successive negation of those forms of being in which self-relation and difference are opposed and finally of division itself and plurality. What the *aporiai* demanded to be recognized if there was to be a 'true being' not as well untrue – a self-relation in which was division and difference, this has to be known from the relation of these 'elements' themselves to each other. The consequences of the hypothesis that the principle is self-identical in their full development are that the principle is also divided. The counter assumption of the second hypothesis, that the principle is a duality, will in turn through the argument of that hypothesis be found to have the consequence that it is undivided.

The proof of the reciprocal relation and unity of these two hypotheses is not without difficulties. Each hypothesis from the first immediate statement of it develops at the same time itself and its relation to the other through a series of contrary relation. The series is not indefinite but completed in three stages. Each of these is a unity of contraries, but not the unity of the 'principle.' The logic here is not that of Zeno in which the unity of contraries is their contradiction and nullity. Nor is there an open otherness or difference which does not reach complete division or contrariety.

It is the logic of which one form is the 'sophistic' which relates to the knowing subject a primary contrariety of its objects – the subject which 'measures' the being of the things that are and the not-being of things that are not, or concludes from this relativity that nothing is or can be known or expressed. In the other or Socratic form the division is stabilized on the affirmative side in the 'true being' of the ideas, in which relation occur the difficulties exposed by the 'aporia,' namely of the unity of individuals and the ideas. The first hypothesis supposes this division radically resolved in a one-sided way in a primary identity into which has passed entirely the division of individual and universal or idea. In this is only the beginning of a resolution of the problems of 'participation,' where one supposes a difference of the two sides which is somehow to be bridged. In place of 'participation' the question is now of the relation of the identical principle to all that is unified in it. The question is asked from the side of the ideal world in relation to which 'the many' of the sensible world are radically unified how this unity is constituted. In the ideal world which has emerged in the *aporiai* as the totality of itself and the sensible what are the many individuals and the contrariety of their self-relation and otherness or negativity? Not a sensible world but a certain unity of this and the ideal in which their difference and relativity has not been taken fully into their self-relation.

In the development of the hypothesis its consequences are the stages in which a first abstract unity of the two worlds which does not contain their difference is converted into an inner unity capable of individuation and relativity of the many. What is negated of the hypothesis thus assumes by degrees the identity of the undivided principle and the difference of 'the many' the form of a division and difference of the principle.

Thus the 'one' of the hypothesis is first declared not to be 'many.' Then not the 'sameness' and 'difference,' the 'likeness' and 'unlikeness' of this plurality, since in these relations, against the hypothesis, the 'one' would be divided. Nor is an equality in which these oppositions are negated adequate to the unity of the principle, since in this relation is also division and inequality.

In time there is a unity of divided moments, and in the reflection of time into itself the transition of its moments is brought to rest. But the relation of time or of becoming to being has also division and difference in it and is not the identity of the hypothesis.

The division in this relation is unified in the being which is for a subject in the several forms of knowledge. The division is in an identical relation, which prevails in the knowledge of the ideas. But of the hypothesis the difference in knowledge of self-relation and difference, the elements of reasoning or the 'logos' have also to be negated. There is thus only the hypothesis itself, a conclusion unacceptable to the thought which has developed its consequences and knows it as the result of the three reflections which successively developed into one identity and division.

The logic by which the consequences of the hypothesis are drawn out is more explicit in the second hypothesis, which begins with the division of the undivided principle. For then there is present in the argument both the undivided and the divided. The unities which mediate the hypothesis with itself in which self-relation and division are brought into one are not extraneous to the hypothesis as in the first, where they are rather assumed and one attends not to their whole structure but to the division in them – to that in which they are not one. For this reason a closer treatment of them is best deferred to the second hypothesis, where their logic is more fully explicated.

Second hypothesis (142b–155e)

'Would you like us to go back to the beginning of the hypothesis to see whether to us on going back it will appear different?' With this question Parmenides points to a transition in the argument to a new beginning. The argument in negating all division of the hypothesis has returned to the beginning.[8] But through the consequences of the hypothesis this unity is known as not immediate but through division and negation of the division. Division and difference are not only for a thinking which negates of the undivided principle a presupposed finitude but the principle itself is the result of this negation.

All division has passed into the self-relation of 'the one.' 'The one' in the immediacy of this result is other than the way to it. This transition is the beginning of a new hypothesis, that 'the one is.' The relation of 'is' to 'one' has behind it all the divisions of the first hypothesis through the negation of which one came to know the full meaning of that hypothesis. The meaning of this hypothesis, as the full development of its consequences will make clear, is that the division of 'is' and 'one' rests on their unity. The true account will then be the unity of the two – the 'logos' which goes into division and in its division remains itself.

The division of 'is' and 'one' is a new hypothesis, related to the first but not as a consequence of it. It originates in the first but that original unity falls at once into a division other than the unity. The relation of the division to the unity is at first indeterminate: between 'being' or self-relation and that in which all negativity is united falls an ever-recurrent difference of positive and negative. Such is the second Platonic principle, the 'aoristos dyas.'

That which is other than the identical principle was taken as dyadic – as an indeterminate relation of contraries – and not rather as itself primarily unified Aristotle found to be fatal to the Platonic philosophy, as having for its consequence that the ideas dissolved into a Pythagorean relativity and this into an Eleaticism in which there was strictly nothing other than 'the one.' This result is, however, logically a long way off. The second hypothesis will develop the relation of the undivided and the dyadic principle from their initial separation to where within it is contained everything of the ideal and sensible worlds. All that the first hypothesis was not is here that through which it comes to itself, as the undivided unity of all that is divided. The argument thus moves through unities of the undivided and the divided, at first incomplete, to a unity in which is contained all their difference.

The first consequence of the hypothesis is an endless fragmentation of the being which is not one. In the *aporiai* participation first appeared to Socrates as like the diffusion of light, everywhere present while remaining identical with itself. Parmenides sets against this image another which expressed the relation of an abstract being to a plurality having an indefinitely small part of it. So here the being which is not the one with all plurality and difference but abstract self-relation is indefinitely diminished and mixed with otherness or negativity as present to individuals. This fragmented being of individuals is also undivided and, as the first hypothesis assumed, the many units are nullified in the undivided principle.

The identity which the first hypothesis assumed is here to be shown as from the unified relation of the dyadic principle to it. This first integration of the undivided and the dyadic principle is by three stages. The first, as indicated, is the indefinite division of being. The second is through the relation of continuity and discontinuity in numbers, the relativity and primary unity of these moments. The third stage is the unity of the first two: the qualitative fragmentation and that of numbers, which by the second stage rests in the unity of self-relation and division, are one and the same movement of division and recapitulation of the divided.

The exposition suffers from categorial confusion and unclarity. So it must, since a separation of categories was only possible through a reformulation of principles in which undivided and divided were known as abstract moments of a comprehensive unity. That the principle in which ideas and participants are united is not the quantitative unity of the Pythagoreans Plato knew well. But taking as dyadic the principle of difference and then attempting to express conceptually the relation of the dyad to the undivided he availed himself of concepts inadequate to his meaning, but sufficient for a reader to follow the course of his thought. For the result of the threefold argument which discovers a determinate relation of the dyad and the undivided is that the relation of the sensible world to the ideal is that of parts to whole. The quantitative unity was understood to have drawn all being into a comprehensive unity – by intention the unity of the undivided principle. The partitioning of this unity is into parts which in their division and relativity express their inner identity now known as the whole.

Part–whole, 142e

The relation of parts to whole [142e–], as it has come out of the previous argument, does not at first have in it the stages of that argument. Taken immediately, all the parts are found to be comprehended in the whole and the endless divisibility of 'being' limited. But when one considers how the whole is in the parts, these as limited are incapable of receiving its unity. The whole is present in the units but not in any, some, or all of the parts of the endlessly divisible being. The whole ever overreaches the parts, so taken. By Zeno's argument being in the units is to be in 'nothings.' The 'one' is in another, not in 'nothings' but in a unity and first determinateness of indeterminate being.

Movement and immobility, 145e–146a

That first determinateness is through the relation of pure mobility to the immutable unity of the divided in the 'one': the eternal rest of what is ever in another. The division of being and unity is thus a division in the undivided. Endless division reaches its term in a contrariety of 'same' and 'different' as their immediate division in the 'one' comes to rest in different and opposed relations to it. The argument passes to a reflection on this relation.

The result of the reflection on the relation of parts to whole is expressed in the question whether, if such is the nature of the 'one,' it is not necessary that it both be at rest and move. Not, as in the sensible world, an alternation of rest and motion, but an eternal rest and opposed to it an eternal division and mobility.

'Same' and 'different,' 146b–147b

The relation of the ideal and sensible worlds to each other is next considered as constituted by the contrariety of 'same' and 'different.' First this relation is distinguished from that of parts and whole – not simply as another opposition but as that which must succeed the other if it is insufficient. The 'one' is to itself not in the relation of part to whole, nor is it different from itself. Therefore it is the same as itself. But the previous argument showed the 'one' as thus in itself to be in another – elsewhere than it is, the present argument expresses it – and this 'in another' as the condition of it being 'in itself.' But this otherness of the 'one' which is the same as itself, when it is not the spatial otherness of the sensible world but the otherness of the 'one' itself, makes with it a contrariety whose terms are repugnant to each other. Not even momentarily can the different be in the same. 'Same' and 'different' are thus essentially divided – separated from each other in one relation.

In consequence of this radical separation of 'same' and 'different' their seeming concurrence in the entities of the sensible world must be thought illusory: neither from themselves can entities not radically one derive this association nor from the different. But in this radical separation of 'same' and 'different' neither can the things that are not one have part in unity. As already known they cannot be related to the 'one' as parts to the whole, nor the 'one' to them as wholes. It remains that the 'one' which was found different from itself and the 'others' be the same as itself and the 'others.'

With this argument begins the retraction of the initial assumption that there are sensible and ideal worlds each independent of the other: the sensible 'many' resolve into the mutual exclusion of 'same' and 'different.'

'Like' and 'unlike,' 147c–148d

But within the unity of these contraries, the 'one' appears like and unlike itself and the 'others.' In this opposition the terms do not take flight from each other but are divided within a common unity. The question is how this unity affects the relation of the ideal and sensible worlds. The 'one' is neither more nor less different from the 'others' than are they from the 'one.' The two sides are thus similarly different. The difference which the one and the 'others' have similarly is not temporal and changing but has ever the same meaning and applies to all things. 'In what way the "one" has been rendered different from the "others" in this way everything would be like everything, for everything is different from all things.'

But the one was before found the same as the 'others.' If different made the 'others' like, the same should have the contrary effect of making them unlike. But the effect of the 'same' should rather be to make its recipients not unlike but like, and the different should correspondingly make unlike. The sum of the argument is that both as different and the same, the two relations taken together or separately, the 'one' is like and unlike itself and the 'others.'

The sense of this reasoning is that the relation of the ideal to the sensible world is not through the contrary moments of the 'divided one' but is a unified relation. The sensible plurality is not there on its own but is constituted by this unified relation.

'Contact' and 'non-contact,' 148d–149d

'Contact' and 'non-contact' in a mechanical account of nature might appear to pertain to the mutual relation of bodies and not to their relation to an ideal world – until one has begun to ask how they move and act on one another, in which question it emerges that they are not only separate or as parts of a whole but in their division together and not together. Underlying this relation, as the argument to this point has brought to light, is a unity of form or an indivision of the divided. The question the cumulative logic of the hypothesis poses now is how an implicit formal unity is related to a plurality as divided.

The argument discloses a negativity in the plurality in 'contact' with one another and with the 'one' – without which relation there would not be a mutual 'contact' but as the last 'logos' showed, the many would collapse into nothing. The negativity has the form of a 'contact' between many which ad infinitum exceed by one a connecting relation or 'contact' among them.

From this result emerges the conclusion that this relation also is insufficient to unify the sensible and intelligible. There is demanded a relation comprehensive of the recurrent negativity of 'contact' and 'non-contact' – a relation where so to speak the 'non-contact' falls within the 'contact.'

'Equality' and 'inequality,' 149d–151e

The question whether the 'one' is 'equal' or 'unequal' to itself and the 'others' is found to elucidate farther the relation of the two worlds. It brings into view on both sides a unity of the divided form and the undivided. If the 'one' is 'greater' or 'smaller' than the 'others,' or the 'others' 'greater' or 'smaller' than the 'one,' it cannot be from their own distinct natures but must be because they participate 'equality,' 'greatness,' or 'smallness.' But these forms independent as universals each of the 'others,' when they are considered in relation to the 'one' and the 'others,' disclose their true nature as complementary moments of quantity. Each appears to exercise in the participants not only its own power but that of the others.

This result being rejected as impossible, the three universals are taken to be separate and unparticipated. One has then only the 'one' and the 'others,' but such that nothing falls outside this relation. 'Great,' 'small,' and 'equal' are not separate universals only, but within the relation of the 'one' and the 'others' determinations of that relation. Numbers are ever equal and a given equality ever diminished and exceeded.

The conclusion is drawn that the 'one,' as it seems, will be equal and greater and smaller in number in relation to itself and the 'others.' This contradiction and the inner unity of the elements of a quantity, their unparticipated unity, have to be brought into a more comprehensive relation.

'Time,' 'being,' and 'becoming' of the 'one,' 151e–155c

The relation of the ideal to the sensible world is further clarified through the forms of 'time,' 'being,' and 'becoming.' In these forms, taken severally, there is a totality of form – division of an original unity and a negative return of the divided to its origin. And the temporalized and the reflected or ideal whole are related as one activity. The relation is not that of actuality, as Aristotle understands that concept. But, as becomes explicit fully in the third hypothesis, the undivided and divided principles as immediately unified are in Plato's thought the origin of time and the externalization of the ideal world. The argument is moving toward the standpoint of the third hypothesis, where all the content of the ideal and sensible worlds is contained in the relation of time to eternity. At this point in the argument the relation is only formal. The remaining arguments of this hypothesis will show by what stages the content is taken into this relation. The hypothesis concludes with an integration of the two worlds through the graded relations of 'being' and 'knowing.' For that reflection one has first to discover the unity of 'being' and 'becoming' – of self-relation and process towards it.

The argument begins by assuming that 'being' is in 'time.' A reflection on their unity in the 'now' of the divided moments of time converts the relation of 'being' and 'time' to an eternal presence. The next consideration is the relation of that eternity to natural development, in which the realized end is last to appear, the end of a process of 'becoming.' That result as well is incomplete, in that it neglects the negativity of 'being' which was there in its omnipresence.

In this reflection 'being' is itself absolutely unified. There is no 'before' and 'after' or, in Plato's more concrete language, 'older' and 'younger' in the relation of the 'one' to itself and to the 'others.' In the first reflection into itself of temporalized being there was an equalization of 'younger' and 'older,' so that the 'one' was neither 'older' nor 'younger' than itself and the 'others' but of equal age. While one stayed with the original assumption that 'being' was 'time' or 'time' was 'being,' the 'one' was found 'older' and 'younger' than itself and the 'others.'

The argument to this point corrects the first assumption and by the two stages mentioned puts in its place as first the presence and thus absolute dividedness of the undivided. This contradictory result is the beginning of the final question of this section, what of 'becoming'? One can no longer assume a confluence of 'being' and 'time' but must ask how 'becoming' has its origin in the 'one' – in the relation of its indivision and division. The question has thus two parts, according as the 'one' imprints on all else its being or the unity in which the division of being and negativity is negated. In the one view the initial difference of 'time' between the earlier born or 'older' and the later born or 'younger' must ever remain the same. But if 'becoming' is considered as reflecting the negative unity of the 'one,' the initial difference of 'older' and 'younger' is rather a relativity of the terms and an endless approximation to their unified relation to the 'one,' which has its division in its self-relation.

The sense of the whole argument of this section is that through it both the assumption that 'being' is 'time' and that of an inner unity without relation to time and becoming are abstractions which demand that that which contains them be discovered. The brief final section of the second hypothesis responds to that demand.

The 'one' as determinate and for knowledge, 155c–d

The 'one' as it emerged from the relation just considered is reflected in the pure form of time and its division into 'is,' 'was,' and 'will be.' On both sides is the unity of division and indivision. Within their relation fall the finite determinations which in several gradation of clarity and distinctness are for a self-conscious knower – a knower having division and difference within its self-knowledge. 'There would be understanding of the "one" and opinion and sense perception, all which forms we are exercising in our present discourse.' To the 'one' pertain 'name,' 'logos,' and all such cognitive relations as we apply to the 'others.'

The context of these remarks is the ideal world within itself in the relation of the two hypotheses generative of the idea of the sensible world. Through these relations there is the unification of the undivided and divided hypotheses. The *aporiai*, one should recall, were constituted by a contrariety of 'being' and 'negativity' which recurred in all forms of knowledge. To discover a unity comprehensive of this division, which made all knowledge ambiguous and uncertain, Parmenides had to carry the argument to the ideal world and consider these relations in their pure universality. The undivided and the divided are the foundation on which the *aporiai* will be seen as resolved not only in the ideal world but in the relation to it of an existent sensible world.

The forms of finite knowledge as they occur at the end of this hypothesis bring into the relation of the inner unity of the divided and the undivided, and time as the immediate unity of the same moments, all the sensible and ideal content. What was divided in the *aporiai* is in this reflection within the undivided, from one to another of the graded relations of being and knowing, more fully subsumed under that unity.

Third hypothesis (155e–157b)

On the assumption that the principle of all things was an undivided 'one' identical with itself, that principle was not 'many' nor any relation of an ideal and a sensible totality underlying which was division and multiplicity. If one supposed instead an original division of unity and being, there followed from that supposition an endless difference and a succession of limitations of this difference and ordered relations to the undivided principle. The last of these relations was that of the forms of knowledge in which being and negativity are both exclusive and in undivided unity. The two hypotheses at that point all but coalesce: all that the undivided 'one' was not it now is if divided. For the two hypotheses to be one it remains only that the original division itself be known as resting in the unity at first assumed to be simply undivided.

This unity of the first and second hypotheses is not a consequence of either, but a new beginning – a third hypothesis. Hypotheses are laid down or supposed by a thinking subject. The hypotheses which give direction to an empirical inquiry may succeed one another indefinitely. Here the hypotheses are about the principles at once of what is known and the knowledge of it. The series has its completion in an *anhypotheloi arche* where there is no longer a division of the known and the knowledge of it. With the third hypothesis which now ensues on the first and second, thinking and its object are fully unified – but that at first immediately and on the side of the universal.

In the first hypothesis thinking is an external reflection on the relations of the principle assumed to be simply identical with itself to an ordered plurality, which Socrates had taken to lead to it, but was defeated by the recurrent negativity of the *aporiai.* The hypothesis was completed in a first unification of the extraneous reflection and the identical principle. In this unification the division for which the successive predicates were negated of the principle is ascribed to it: the identical 'one' is for thought divided. With the 'one – is' begins a new hypothesis, that is, a new relation of thinking to thought.

In the second hypothesis the same ordered finitude as was negated in the first principle as pure identity becomes a succession of determinate relations of the undivided and the 'dyadic' principles. The reflection here is again external in that the unities discovered of the two principles are for the thinking subject: the unity of the divided and the undivided is not known as a unity of the principle itself. In the full development of the consequences of the hypothesis that the principle is divided as well as identical the division is known as negated also on the side of the known. In the several relations of thinking and being, being is truly known so far as the division latent in it, to which the *aporiai* pointed, is division in an identical relation and thus a radical separation of being and negativity. The stabilized positivity of the 'noetic' knowledge has been given its foundation through the developed implications of this hypothesis. With this result a new hypothesis is demanded – a return to the identity of the first, not as other than all the divided but as underlying division, the source of endless difference and the limitation of it.

The *logos* passes to a third hypothesis, is no longer an examination of the second but a new beginning. The principle in this third hypothesis is both one and many and neither one nor many. Taken immediately, the relation of these contradictory moments is temporal: in that the 'one' is at one time, it partakes of being; at another time again, in that it is not, it does not partake of being. It cannot at the same time partake and not partake of being. Only as partaking at one time and not at another does it escape the contradiction.

But different from either state is the time of transition from not-being to being or from being to not-being. The times of participating and not participating are not only different but also one as the continuity of the process in which participants come to be and perish, coming to be is a unification of their multiplicity, perishing a passing into multiplicity. The contraries predicated in the second hypothesis of the 'one being' are here as in that present unity a becoming like and unlike, of growth, corruption, and equalization. There is the same succession of predicates as in that hypothesis but also the presence of a unity which belongs not only to a subjective reflection but to its object as well.

After 'great,' 'small,' 'equal' the argument of the second hypothesis passed to 'time,' 'being,' 'becoming.' There is here the same transition, but with a different and extended interest. Through the relation of time to eternity, and within it of being to time and becoming, the limitation of endless 'dyadic' division was brought into a comprehensive form capable of containing the division, as were not the whole of parts and the other relations earlier considered. As within the division of this comprehensive form, the ordered finitude was the relation of a sensible and an ideal world. Through the relations of thinking to being this division of the two worlds was known by degrees as that of the ideal world and its appearance – in truth one world. The interest of the third hypothesis is to give primacy to that unity, allowing place within it for the difference of the two totalities of the finite.

The coming into being and perishing of a multitude, which have only 'in another time' the identity and difference of opposed predicates, at the point of transition from the one to the other relation are 'in no time.' The hypothesis whose implications the present argument follows is that the 'one' is neither and both of contrary predicates. The two sides of the hypothesis meet at the instant of transition from the positive to the negative aspect of becoming or of the negative to the positive. At that instant there is neither the before nor the after of time and thus no time at all. The identity of the 'one,' in which according to the first hypothesis it is neither of contraries, is present in the contraries which the second hypothesis in the full development of its consequences referred completely to the 'one.' 'The strange nature of the instant is situated between motion and rest, being in no time, and into this and from this the moving changes to rest and the resting to movement' (156d–e). The nature of the instant is strange as annulling the certainty before expressed that the contrary states of becoming and perishing can only be present 'in another time.' The contradiction there evaded as impossible is now found present in all forms of change. The ideal world is the inner reflection of this unified world of becoming.

The argument of this hypothesis reaches beyond the duality of principles as this occurred in the second hypothesis to an inner identity externalized as an extended identity and related to the inner identity in the moment of time. One will recall the expression of this relation in opposed images as the first of the *aporiai*. In *Sophist* this enveloping relation is spoken of as 'one idea everyway extended and a plurality comprehended from without.' Within this idea fall the total reflection of becoming into the being of the ideas. This finite totality *Sophist* describes as 'one idea through many wholes held together in one.' The 'wholes' are the several relations of the sensible and ideal worlds whose course the second hypothesis followed through and are now known in this hypothesis as in an identical relation.

How the hypotheses affect the 'others' (157b–160b)

The difference of these two comprehensive ideas of *Sophist* appears more explicitly when one asks how this third hypothesis – and with it the first and second as unified in it – affects the 'others.' As already indicated, the two reflections on the relation of the 'others' to the ideal and sensible worlds thus unified are not hypotheses.

The hypotheses have for their end to resolve the *aporiai* of participation. The meaning of the question how as so far developed they affect the 'others' is, in what way have they resolved the *aporiai*? The first hypothesis as altogether separating the 'one' and the 'many' might appear to give no solution. But the argument of the hypothesis showed this separation to be of all finitude from undivided unity, and the true object of thought to be not one side and the other but a relation of the two. There is thus already in this hypothesis the beginning of a solution. The second hypothesis shows all ideal and sensible finitude to be constituted by relations of the undivided and the divided principle. The separate ideas and the negativity neglected in this separation are contained in this relation. The separation of positive and negative moments in the relations of sensibles and ideas belonged to an abstract thought which did not know what division was and that both its moments enter into the constitution of all the finite. In the 'wholes' considered in cumulative succession in that hypothesis sensible and ideal, as constituted of the same elements, are ever more fully integrated.

It remained that in the third hypothesis the reflection on the relation of the two principles and the drawing of all ideal and sensible finitude into that relation should be regarded as not only for the thinking subject but in the objects considered. The 'one' is neither and both of contrary predicates: Not abstract Eleatic being, with which it might be confused at the beginning of the first hypothesis, but an identity of indeterminate division of the second hypothesis. Zeno's argument, that if there were 'many,' 'the many' must be both of contraries which was impossible, applies here in another way than originally intended. Here to be neither of contraries is rather to be both. So for 'the one' itself and for 'the others,' which to participate must first be other, and as absolutely other have to be before division and thus relation to 'the one.' Their multiplicity, which they have from the dyadic principle, is annulled in this separation, and they are identity externalized or pure extension. All that falls between these extremes – the ordered relations of the sensible and ideal worlds – is not here taken to be nothing. But the affirmative hypotheses and the relation to them of 'the others' at this point in the whole argument of the dialogue leave unresolved the divided relation of 'the one' and 'the others' to themselves and to each other.

The relation of 'the others' to 'the one' falls into two parts just as did the third hypothesis itself. 'The others' are related to the ordered finitude in which endlessness is their own nature as wholly deprived of unity. They are also related to the instant of becoming, which is neither of the contraries by which they were limited in the first relation, and to the being or reflection into itself of the instant.

The argument of the first relation may be stated succinctly as follows:

(a) That 'the others' are not wholly deprived of 'the one' is a consequence of the third hypothesis in that the endlessness of the dyadic principle does not escape the radical separation of its moments therein. This presence of contraries or complete division in the dyad is considered first in the relation of parts to whole. The terms of this division have no meaning except as relative. If in imagination one considers the dyad divided beyond every limit, the terms of the division are ever parts of a whole.

(b) This relation of parts and whole to the dyad is not only in a subjective reflection or comparison of the two but applies universally to what is compared: the two sides are like or positively related in their unlikeness.

(c) The self-relation or positivity of the relation limit each other. This mutual limitation applies by the same argument to rest and motion and all the contrarieties elaborated in the second hypothesis.

From the hypotheses follow also other consequences if the participants before they participate are wholly other than 'the one.' The 'indeterminate dyad' is related not only to its terms as separate and mutually limiting but to the pure identity of 'the one' which is neither of contraries.

(a) 'The one' and 'the others' are wholly separate. They being all that is, there can be no third relating them.

(b) 'The one,' having neither parts nor whole, cannot be in 'the others' through this relation. Nor can they participate as parts or having any plurality, being altogether deprived of unity.

(c) Nor can 'the others' participate as like and unlike or through any other contraries: participating not even one they can participate no form of duality.

(d) 'The others' are thus neither identical nor different, mobile or immobile or any of the contraries which they participated according to the other reflection.

Both results following of necessity from the hypothesis and the two being incompatible, how are they to be combined in the further course of the argument?

First negative hypothesis (160b–163b)

The affirmative hypotheses and 'the others' in relation to them so far resolve the *aporiai* that the recurrent division of being and negativity which gave rise to them was found to revert to a primary identity. That is a one-sided resolution in which the division is only implicit, not a resolution which has place for and contains the division. The negative hypotheses and 'the others' as formed by them will provide that resolution. But there 'the others' are lost finally in an absolute negative unity, and the question remains for subsequent dialogues how, that resolution being assumed, there is also otherness or finitude.

The affirmative hypotheses, taken in their developed relation to the others, are found to be incomplete and to demand a further hypothesis – an hypothesis which will have room for division and difference, of itself and in relation to 'the others.' The new hypothesis arises immediately from where the reflection on the affirmative hypotheses ended. "Is the not-being of "the one" the same as the not-being of the "not-one"?'

The 'not-one' with whose not-being the affirmative hypotheses ended is the divided or dyadic: 'the others,' it was finally discovered, could not participate 'the one' unless they were first radically separated from it, not only partially deprived of unity. As related to 'the one' in 'the instant' they were only partially deprived. In relation to the inner reflection of 'the instant' they were excluded by their contrariety from it. The not-being of 'the one,' it is answered, is altogether contrary to that of the not-one.

Before laying down formally the new hypothesis and examining its consequences the dialogue treats briefly of its meaning. The argument has reached the point where 'the one' is unknowable, not as at the conclusion of the first hypothesis, because abstractly one, it is nothing at all that has division and plurality, but because the plurality taken into the argument in the second and third hypotheses can on its own account only have relation to it as not not-one–not divided. The not-being of 'the one,' as against this result, has otherness and is knowable. The two predicates are inseparable: the one is knowable as not simply being or not being but as also neither of the two. So with greatness, smallness, and other such contraries: as well as through each other they are each something and known as such. The negated one has meaning not as name merely or connection of names, not for an immediate or intuitive knowledge, but as unity of contraries. But, as will appear in the second negative hypothesis, this unity, which the argument here requires, recedes in the full explication of the first into an absolute negativity without relation to being. There remains, that is, an externality in the relation here of the negative one to contraries, at the same time as the *logos* demands recognition that to this one belongs otherness as well as knowledge.

The movement of Plato's thought is to a concretion of the undivided and the dyadic principle – an end which continued to elude him, for which a reformulation of principles was necessary. One should not fail to observe that for him this 'one' which is articulately knowable is not inferior to a 'one' which is simply beyond division. For Neoplatonists coming to *Parmenides* with that assumption, the negative hypotheses defy clear interpretation and are redundant: from the affirmative hypotheses and their consequences can be taken already that 'the one' is before division and all things a descent from it and without it nothing.

The new beginning being thus given meaning, Plato asks what follows from it. First, 'knowability' and 'otherness' by which the new hypothesis 'if the one is not' was separated from the affirmative hypotheses, from being in a subjective relation, are now given objective form and treated as consequences of the hypothesis. On these first and the other consequences of the hypothesis some general observations can perhaps make it easier for a reader to follow their course. The order and succession of predicates of the negative one are that of the second hypothesis but from another standpoint. There the argument moved through relations of the dyadic to the undivided principle from the more abstract to where the difference of the sensible from the ideal world has been taken into their unity, and the argument passes to the third hypothesis which supposes this unity. In the affirmative hypotheses this subsumption of all the divided under the unity is for an extraneous reflection, which having discovered through the first hypothesis the transcendence of the undivided principle cannot in the second rest short of a comprehensive unity of the divided with it. In the negative hypothesis the division of the ideal and sensible worlds is regarded as rooted in the comprehensive unity to which the affirmative hypotheses led – as a division of that unity, an otherness negated in it. The negation of this otherness is at first abstract, then by degrees collects into it everything of the ideal-sensible division. There thus occur in the negative comprehension the equivalent of the part–whole, equal–unequal, being–becoming relations of the second hypothesis.

The first consequences of the hypothesis are thus its 'knowability' and its 'otherness' in general or its relation to a plurality separate from but belonging to it. This otherness is that of the part–whole relation treated in the second hypothesis. But here there is present also the unity in which the division is negated – the unity which before fell to a thinking for which was the division. The negative unity is 'knowable,' as not only beyond but mediated by the division – as 'greatness,' 'smallness,' and the terms of other such contraries are known not only in their relativity but each in itself. The knowledge of this 'one' as self-related against all otherness is of the highest or 'epistemic' form.

The 'otherness' related to this 'one' is not that of 'the others' only but its own 'otherness': 'the others' are not other than its unity, but of it as divided. There is a contrariety of the two sides by which they are other, and the 'otherness' is at the same time 'to' and 'of' the related terms, which are thus particularized.

So considered, the difference or otherness of the universal and sensible sides of the division belongs to both sides, as in the relation of parts to whole as treated in the second hypothesis, but the relativity of the two sides as such has not come into view. That supposed independence is undermined in the next reflection, in which they are treated as like and unlike. For in this relation is not only, as thus treated, a reflective sameness and difference of whole and parts, of each to itself and mutually, but the terms of that relation as fallen together, united but only partially so.

Where in the second hypothesis the movement of the argument was to exhibit the relativity of 'parts' and 'whole' and the following contraries and thus bring into view an underlying identity, in which finally in the third hypothesis all the many were nullified, here the division at each stage, while different from the negative unity, appears as contained in it. Using the images of the initial *aporia,* one will say that in the second hypothesis the light which remains itself in its diffusion prevails, while here in this negative hypothesis also the sail and the difference of 'the many' from it has place in relation to the negative one. It is thus here, as Parmenides indicated, that one has the full resolution of the *aporiai.*

The negative one has in it being or self-relation, the difference from it of a plurality and the negation of this difference. The development of the hypothesis at the same time stabilizes 'the many' – imparts to them a being having in it their difference – and negates this relation. The term of this development is at the transition to the second negative hypothesis, where the being of the negative one and the relations of 'the many' to it are taken wholly into the negative moments. The stages of it are the formation of the several grades of being and a negativity in which falls also the otherness or difference of these forms of being. 'Participation' or the relation of sensibles to universals is thus clarified through the relation to each other of the undivided and divided principle, the undivided having the twofold form of indivision before division and as negation of it.

The negative 'one,' as thus constituted, was at first an immediate relation to its elements. It was self-related, and thus known, and also different, and between 'the many' and these aspects were various 'participations' or relations. The second consideration, of 'likeness' and 'unlikeness,' enlightens the second *aporia,* where 'the many' had at the same time a common universality and were also different from that identity and from one another. The difficulties of that relation were examined at length in *Theaetetus* under the question whether 'true opinion' was knowledge. How were the relations of 'the many' in which they were like and unlike also unified? The 'opinion' of 'the many' true and not deceptive? In *Theaetetus* an answer was sought and not found in memory and recollection – a difficulty expressed succinctly in the third *aporia.* From the first negative hypothesis follows a unity of the two *aporiai*: the positive identity of like and unlike and the negative unity of thinking, in which, in the words of the third *aporia,* all things became thinking or else, though objects of thought, remain unthought. In consequence of the hypothesis, the divided positive and negative moments, which in *Theaetetus* appear to be incorrigibly divided, are seen as together constitutive of the object. In this unified view of the *aporiai* the way to a solution becomes more evident: the abstract identity of like and unlike and their negative unity have to be more deeply integrated, so that the one has division implicit in it and the other negates the division in relation to that identity. The result of that transition underlies the next *aporia,* which is of the ideas as *paradigmata.* But the transition has in it a great difficulty, which in *Theaetetus* has the form of asking whether 'true opinion' with a *logos* rightly defines knowledge and examines that proposal without discovering a clear solution. The solution lies in knowing the attitude of 'true opinion' to be contained in the *logos*, this as not accompanying 'true opinion' merely. As treated under this negative hypothesis the logic of this transition becomes clearer.[9] The formation of a *logos*, of a unity, that is, comprehensive of division, takes place here in a reflection on the greatness, smallness, and equality of the negative one. For the likeness and unlikeness of 'the one' and 'the others' to come into the form of a *logos*, the positive and negative aspects of this relation have to expose their underlying contrariety or complete division. The argument has then to bring to light not only the identity in which the contraries are divided, but in relation to the negative one their relativity and dependence on the deeper relation of being and negativity which follows next in the development of the hypothesis.

On the side of 'the others' the *logos* has first the form of an external unity, in relation to which the particularity is dissolved and 'the others' are reflected immediately into an inner unity and the origin of their division known to lie in the difference of affirmative and negative unity. In *Parmenides* this argument has the form of a comprehension of the endless divisibility of great and small within an equality of the two. The examination in *Theaetetus* or the assumption that knowledge is 'true opinion' with a *logos* moves to the same result through what is essentially the same reflection.

Next and last among the consequences of this first negative hypothesis is that the 'negative one' is, and that in this immobile self-relation it also moves and changes. The reflection on 'equal,' 'great,' and 'small,' as that elsewhere on the relation of 'true opinion' to a *logos*, drew separate positive and negative moments into a pure contrariety of being and negation, in which division is stabilized and as division and difference also negated – that is, into a *logos*. Such is the logic of the transition from 'opinion' to 'true being' or the separate ideas. This relation taken simply in its aspect of identity gave rise to the fourth of the *aporiai*, the negativity and difference which separated individuals from the ideas. The affirmative hypotheses brought to light the unity of idea and participant on the side of identity. The interest in the negative hypotheses is to discover a unity from the side of division and difference – a negative unity. In this unity taken with that which the affirmative hypotheses disclosed would be a complete solution of the *aporiai*.

The argument here demands first that one know the being and the negativity following from this hypothesis as each what it is through not being the other. The *aporiai* belong to an analytic thinking which does not know what it abstracts from as belonging to it, that is, that the truth is the *logos* comprising both. That knowledge in all its forms is a concrete grasp of its object it is the whole interest of *Parmenides* to show. The *aporiai* are logical obstacles to this insight very difficult to break through. Plato to do so has to revert from the ideas to their principles or elements and to find that an affirmative unity of all things – of an ideal and a sensible totality – and a negative unity are complementary and only together the full account.

As completing the affirmative hypotheses, the negative hypotheses show how the *aporiai* are solved. So Parmenides indicated at the beginning of his exposition. Here, in treating the being of the 'negative one,' the argument has reached a point of the greatest interest where the separate being of the ideas and the negation of that identical being come together in relation to the 'negative one.' The ideas in their plurality do not enter the argument directly, but the affirmative and negative aspects of the principles approach a concretion. The being of the 'negative one' can only be completely what it is – identical and itself unchanging, for knowledge undeceiving – through the negativity excluded from it, as this can only be completely what it is as not identical. This relation in which the difference of contraries all but vanishes and dissolves into pure contradiction is for the 'negative one.' This one is not the negative unity of the *nous*, of thought itself. *Nous* does not as such enter the Platonic argument until *Sophist*, where it has behind it the whole result of *Parmenides*. Here one follows the genesis from the principles of that noetic relation of thought to being.

The next question as following from the hypothesis is about movement and change as pertaining to the mutually sustaining relation of being and negativity just considered. That relation taken immediately has in it a difference of the terms and thus movement and change which, even if it has the temporal identity of circular motion and change, is other than the ideal immutable identity.

The course of the argument, which will recall the treatment of being, time, and becoming in the second hypothesis, is to regard the being and negativity of the 'negative one' temporally united in change and motion as disclosing an immutable identity. Then motion and change are regarded as different from that foundation, and finally these moments as in a negative unity comprising their difference. There is taking shape here that relation which after a further logical development *Timaeus* can describe as an ideal world for a universal intelligence and the sensible world as a moving image of that idea. Here however the consequences of the first negative hypothesis – that the 'one which is not' is and is different from the others – are at this point completely drawn out, and this passes into a second negative hypothesis.

The second negative hypothesis (163b–164b)

The first negative hypothesis, beginning with the difference of the being and otherness of that hypothesis from its unity, finally in the succession of its consequences reached a point where this difference, having then within it the contrariety of separate ideas to their sensible appearance, disclosed a unity underlying that division. Into that unity was absorbed this last and all the previous consequences of the first negative hypothesis. The argument returned to a new beginning – a negative unity in which there was altogether nothing of being. Nothing of being and the otherness attending it in the previous hypothesis.

The meaning of this hypothesis, generally stated, is that there is a unity in which all differences of the ideal and sensible worlds has been negated. The result of the affirmative hypotheses was that all ideal and sensible finitude was in an underlying unity. According to the second negative hypothesis all finitude as other than that affirmative unity is negated in relation to it. The argument is moving to, but has not reached, the Aristotelian standpoint of actuality, where the separation of ideal and sensible is known as within their unity, the sensible known as realizing the potentiality of the universal and returned to it in its difference. Here the affirmative and negative unities are primarily unitive of the undivided and indeterminate division – of the principles – of finitude constituted of their relative secondarity. The relation of the affirmative and the negative hypotheses to 'the others' is therefore twofold: the 'others' both participate the ideal finitude and have relation to absolute unity. Only when these divided relations are unified or, what is the same, the principles so received that the 'dyad' is known, not as a principle, but as a moment in the relation of the positive to the negative unity does one have the Aristotelian relation of potency to act.

When the explanation of 'participation' given in the third of the affirmative hypotheses is taken with the being of the 'negative one' in its first form, one has a resolution of the *aporiai* so far as that is possible within the Platonic principles. Or the latter alone, as following on the third hypothesis and having on its own the opposition of positive and negative moments and thus their unity, is sufficient to their resolution. For the *aporiai* were formed by a reflection which opposed to the positive accounts of 'participation' a neglected negativity. For a solution the separate positive and negative aspects of the relation have to be unified, and the unity itself must be not only positive but inclusive of the opposition of the two.

There remains however the question how this unity in relation to the 'negative one' belongs to individuals. The word 'participation' supposes subjects wholly separate which then acquire relations to what is not thus separate or individualized. The others than the affirmative unity, when so considered, were found a nullity. This nullity is the point of connection of the 'others' with the 'negative one' – its externalization and that as absolutely divided or as units. In that relation the two apparently exclusive images of the first *aporiai* meet.

The second negative hypothesis is in its consequences the development of this relation. The previous hypothesis was of a 'negative one' to which belonged being and otherness. The content of that relation was finally the 'true being' of the ideas in relation to their negativity. At that point for the unity of the 'negative one' with being and otherness to be completed this content breaks down into the formal opposition of being and negativity – this in relation to a unity in which even this division is negated. The third of the affirmative hypotheses supposed similarly a unity beyond the ordered and knowable content of the second and all division. To that affirmative unity this second of the negative hypotheses joins an absolute negative unity.

This development of the argument will remind the reader of the final *aporia*, which is no longer about the relation of ideas to their participants, but about the total separation of a divine world and the knowledge of it from our human knowledge of a sensible world. Neither can the gods know anything of our world nor we of theirs. The resolution of this *aporia* is through the principles.

The course of the whole argument might be briefly summarized as follows. (1) In the third of the affirmative hypotheses the ordered relations of the undivided and the dyadic principles as developed in the second are known as in a momentary and a reflected unity. In this relation the endlessly divided moments of the 'dyad' – the nature, it is said, of the 'others' as such – are radically separated. The 'others' thus enter into relation to the ideas or participate, from which the negativity which obstructed their participation is excluded. (2) But to enter this relation the 'others' must be wholly deprived of unity, not as in their dyadic nature having something of it. In the final consideration there is no participation but complete separation of the 'others' and the ideas.

(3) In the first of the negative hypotheses, the 'nothings,' that is, pure unrelated individuals, are related to the 'negative one' by contraries not only exclusive, but so connected that each is fully itself as not the other – in the relation expressed by the law of excluded middle. The others and the ideas seem strongly bound to each other in this relation.

But the secure knowledge of the divine ideas which seems to have been gained in this relation this second negative hypothesis dissolves step by step in reverse order to that in which it was formed in the first. The hypothesis supposes a negative unity in which nothing of being or positivity remains. In the relation of immobile being to motion and change, with which the first negative hypothesis ended, being and negativity are not only bound together but the two appear as at once together or contradictory. The ordered content of the relation dissolves into an immediate relation of the 'one' and the 'others' as nothings or pure individuals.

Where the previous argument had moved through the grades of being from the least stable to the ideas, here the argument would separate the formal relations of being and otherness with which that hypothesis began from their successive and strengthening integrations.

First consequences for 'the others' of the negative hypotheses (164b–165e)

As with the affirmative hypotheses, what is meant by the consequences of the negative hypotheses for 'the others' is the relation to individuals of the ideal world as itself comprehensive of division and difference – the ideal world thus concrete, as temporal and externalized, immediately present to individuals. Individuals are 'the others' to the ideal world in that the argument has not come to an Aristotelian unity of form and matter, where the two as separate are known as abstractions. 'Participation' is the word used to express the relation of individuals to ideas where a supposed otherness of the two sides has not dissolved into their primary unity.

In the consequences for 'the others' one has thus a resolution of the *aporiai* so far as the hypotheses can provide it. The resolution which followed from the affirmative hypotheses was defective in that the individuals to participate had not only to be related to an inner identity of their dyadic nature but to be wholly separate from that identity, not partially separate only, as in the first consideration of their relation to the ideas. But as wholly separate the individuals were 'nothings.' In the consequences of the negative hypotheses they will again be found to be 'nothings,' but 'nothing' in another relation to indeterminate division and in their radical separation related to the negative one.

The first reflection on the relation of 'the others' to the negative one attends to the altered status of their dyadic nature. Where before this was found through one aspect of the dyad to give to 'the others' a being and through it a participation of the ideas, now the divided terms of the dyad in relation to the negative one give only an illusion of being which as images in a dream endlessly recede if one would stay them in conscious knowledge. In this 'the others' reflect the mutual exclusion of contraries which followed from the first negative hypothesis, this as in the absolute negativity of the second. A seeming unity of the exclusive contraries is rather an endlessly recurrent cancelling of each by the others. From this process as an endless repetition of the same terms, the true result is the negation of them as different. So the first negative hypothesis passed into the second, where the exclusive contraries were nullified. The endless difference of opposed moments of 'the others' likewise gives way to their pure negativity or nullity.

Such is the general form and result of this illusory participation. Within this relation fall those successive totalities through which the first negative hypothesis came to its full development in the relation of contraries sustained by their mutual exclusion – that and the reduction of the same totalities to their simple logical form in the second negative hypothesis. In relation to 'the others' both movements occur, as they appear both to participate and not participate these several unifications of indeterminate division.

Second consequences for 'the others' of the negative hypotheses (165e–166c)

The negative hypotheses supposed first a negative opposed to the not-being of the not-one, to which belonged being and otherness, then secondly a negative one in which this finitude was altogether negated. There remained to be considered how this comprehensive unity was related to the plurality of individuals which to participate the affirmative hypotheses have first to be wholly separate from them, were thus deprived of all being, and were nothing. To the negative one they were opposed as that in which vanished all the indeterminate and determinate division and difference of 'the others,' that is, the not-one, an external to an inner ideal nullity. The movement of the argument is to a unity of these extremes, where the being and otherness which was drawn into the negative one is negated also of 'the others.'

The first reflection on the relation of 'the others' to the negative one was then as endlessly determinate and indeterminate, as was the second negative one, in which was undone even the seemingly unbreakable bond maintaining the difference of exclusive contraries. All the difference of 'the others' from one another and their relations to universals are destabilized. 'The others' are an unresolved contradiction, in which is exhibited in them the absolute negativity of 'the one.' That inner unity is not itself present to 'the others' and the contradiction resolved also on their side.

'The others' than the negative one, in which has been negated all their finitude, are simply its relation to empty unity from which it is immediately reflected into itself. One assumed hitherto in the argument that there were in some way others, and asked how they could be thought to participate the ideas. At this point 'the others' are simply for the negative one its negativity externalized, an externality in which it is immediately returned to itself. Taken together with the first reflection on 'the others,' this reflection does away altogether with a supposed *chorismos* or separation of the two worlds.

The way to this conclusion is first to regard 'the others' as though without the presence of 'the one' they had something of being on their own. But 'the others' so regarded, being without the one, are not so much as ones, and so neither can they be many. They are neither of these, and, one might add, of any other contraries. Thus they are nothing.

But, secondly, in this reduction is disclosed what 'the others' are. They are nothings as self-related units which have no communion with the 'not-beings' which, as first considered, they were taken to be. None of the 'not-beings' in any of 'the others.' 'Nor is there an opinion (*doxa*) or image (*phantasma*) of "the not-being" with the others, nor can "the not-being" be in any way the object of "opinion" for "the others."' On the side of 'the others' than the negative one fall also their relation to a would-be finite knowledge. 'If "the one" is not, "the others" neither are nor are "opined" to be either one or many.' Not to them belong any of the contraries which in the first reflection on the relation of the negative one seemed to, but in truth did not, fall within the relation. There remains only the negative one returned instantly to itself from its dispersion. The two images with which the *aporiai* began pass into each other.

'Then in sum if we were to say that, if "the one" is not, nothing is, would we be speaking rightly?' The respondent concurring, Parmenides both accepts this conclusion and qualifies it. 'Let this be said, and also that, as it seems, whether "the one" is or is not, itself and "the others," in relation to themselves and in their mutual relations, all altogether both are and are not and appear and do not appear.' To the conclusion belongs also the whole course of the argument which led to it. The affirmative hypotheses, after finding 'the one' separate from all finitude even being, then founded the being and ordered finitude of 'the one' and, these two relations of 'the one' to division and finitude being found complementary, it followed that 'the others' both participated the ideal world and, as wholly separate, appeared and did not appear to participate. The negative hypotheses then founded a being of the negative one and of a plurality related to it. Then 'the others,' after the appearance of a relation to the negative one, receded from that appearance into pure negativity.

The simple conclusion that nothing is has to be taken with the being of an ideal world and a sensible world related to it, and with what the argument brought out with equal force, that this relation of the two worlds is an appearance and the vanishing of that appearance. The Aristotelian problem that, if unity and being are taken to be the principles of all things, it is difficult to show how there can be anything other than the principles themselves, applies precisely to this whole result of *Parmenides*. And this difficulty Plato addresses directly in *Sophist* in the question how there can be a true otherness. It is also evident from the conclusion of *Parmenides* how close Plato is to the Pythagorean position in which Aristotle takes his philosophy to end, namely that the ideas are numbers. For numbers and in general quantity, having contraries, are also beyond them. But Plato in dialogues after *Parmenides* first examines other ways in which within infinite unity there is place for ideal and sensible finitude.

After Parmenides

An outline of what Plato would think philosophically is given in the myths which supplement the argument of many dialogues. The more his thought can draw into it of the content of the myths, the nearer it approaches what he principally desires to think. In *Parmenides* there is nothing of the mythical unless in the occasion of the dialogue, that it was coincidental with the great festival of Athena. Likewise, the dialogues which take their point of departure from it – *Sophist, Philebus, Statesman* – do not disclose a mythical background, which however reappears in a manner in *Timaeus*, which treats altogether concretely the relation of universal thought to soul and nature.

The myths are about this concrete content – noetic thought and its existence as soul, the human individual as uniting life and thought, the gods as for an aesthetic vision being this unity eternally. This unity and the necessity which obstructs it even for the gods one knows has been the dominant and continuing theme of the poetic and other arts among the Greeks. Their domestic and political institutions, in their general structure and historical development, express likewise the division of life and thought and a striving to discover a unity underlying their division.

In Platonic dialogues the *nous* or intelligence of Anaxagoras did not remain separate merely from the 'mixed,' which as endlessly divisible it would and cannot order. The 'divided' and 'mixed' is known as related to thought and their difference stabilized – not, as for 'sophistic,' collapsing into an immediate unity of thinking with itself. As observed in *Phaedo,* this stable being, which the Socrates of the dialogue separates from changing sensible participants, as against the blinding light of an immediate knowledge of *nous,* understood as 'the good,' permits an indirect access to it. The form of an ordered ascent from the sensible world to 'the good' or 'the beautiful' is given in *Republic* and *Symposium.* These dialogues each in its way show this ascent to be imperilled by a negativity which in its most developed form is the tyrannic subject centred on itself against the universal good. In *Republic* the just life may be shown preferable to the unjust, but a unity of the positive and negative movements is in the end only expressed mythically. *Symposium,* though with the aid of Diotima, who as a *deus ex machina* instructs Socrates in 'mysteries' beyond the positivity of his philosophy, brings the objective good and the independent subject into a closer relation. A unified relation of the two is pointed to in the question whether the same poet is capable of the tragic and the comic inspiration – of bringing to light an objective resolution of the primary division humans are subject to and as well showing the division as closed in a unified self-consciousness.

In these 'eidetic' dialogues the whole relation – the affirmative and negative aspects of it – of this second best way to 'the good,' to that end to which it leads, is not given philosophically. Nor can it be given so long as one remains with the word 'participation' to cover the relation of sensible individuals to the separate ideas. How positive and negative moments are opposed and united in that method is not explicated, how it thus leads to a self-knowledge of *nous* and to the existence of *nous* as life and soul. One learns from *Republic* that 'the good' exceeds in 'dignity and power' the divided relations of thinking to true being and the grades of being less clear. How thought passes from this divided relation to the purity of the intelligible light, and how to this belongs the mediation which led to its disclosure does not enter the argument. A simple transcendence of 'the one' or 'the good' over the finite or divided, as in a Neoplatonic reading, does not belong to Plato's thought: the thinking which can rest in that unity is that of the person or rational individual who would find the stable ground of his freedom. The Platonic *logos* does not know but would discover that freedom.

Through the succession of affirmative and negative hypotheses and their relations to participants, the argument of *Parmenides* has explicated the object in which thinking thought the several grades of 'the line' could find identity with being. Those relations occur in the development of the second hypothesis, encompassed in the relation of that to the first hypothesis. These hypotheses as united in the third situate in the one object all that was contained in those relations of thinking and being. The affirmative hypotheses show the division of the undivided and divided principle, an ordered finitude through their relation, and how 'the others' out of their endlessness are drawn into that order or 'participate.' In this the 'principles' are united on the side of being or identity, not in the negative unity which in the finite relations of the 'line' fell on the side of thinking. This negative unity of division and contrariety is exhibited by the course of the negative hypotheses and their relations to 'the others.'

The successive hypotheses are laid down by a thinking which responds to a recognized incompleteness in the implications of the previous hypotheses. All the hypotheses belong to one reflection which in them is dispersed and lost, it seems, in its object. The conclusion of the dialogue awakens a dissatisfaction with the conclusion that 'nothing is' or that there is no otherness than 'the one.' This is a far different dissatisfaction than that with the conclusion of the first hypothesis, which gave no place to division and difference. There the dissatisfaction is that all the forms of being, appearance, not-being that have unfolded in the course of the argument are not for the subject which attended it but only the negation of it. In *Sophist* begins a criticism of the Eleaticism of *Parmenides* for which all things in truth ever rest in one identity or are ever the negativity of a self-related motion. There is knowledge for the hypothesizing subject that the ideal and the sensible world are one but not that to this world belong as having the same complete reality thought, life, and soul.

The argument demands these concepts if there is to be a true knowledge of the finitude constituted by the relations of the two principles for a subject itself related to the unified result of the hypotheses it has posited. The transition from the argument which has treated unity and being not as predicates of existent beings but as themselves substantial and all else as comprehended in their relations to a true knowledge of the finite, or in *Philebus* to true determinations of 'the good,' or as in *Timaeus* to a total knowledge of nature as a moving image of a divine idea, is among the most difficult. Of all the *aporiai* which block the way to one who would enter his philosophy, Aristotle takes this transition to be the most difficult to resolve and the most necessary for a knowledge of the truth. If unity and being are the substance on which all things rest, it is hard to show how there is knowledge of anything but the substance. But suppose as first an existent world. It results from the history of philosophy that there is no true knowledge of it unless through unity and being as substance.[10]

For Aristotle a resolution of this *aporia* is only possible through the concept of actuality – a unity of the ideal and sensible worlds which is not only, as in *Parmenides*, for a thinking which comes to self-knowledge by negating through the hypotheses the duality of principles and a finitude constituted by their relations, but can discover in its object this active unity and know division as a moment in its realization and return to itself. He sets in the way of one who would grasp this unity of the Platonic principles and the priority of the actual to the potential a further *aporia*, that of numbers, as what in the end must be thought the substantiality of ideas and sensibles. This Pythagorean Platonism, which in *Met.* A, 6 Aristotle takes to define Plato's contribution to the discovery of the 'causes' and returns to in M and N after the exposition of his own philosophy, has for him a crucial importance not easily grasped.

In the criticism of Eleaticism, that is, of *Parmenides*, in *Sophist* this doctrine does not appear; nor in *Philebus* is the unification of the principles in the constitution of the good and its determinations subjected to this Pythagorean doctrine. The reduction of all things to number and quantity is nearer the surface in *Timaeus*, though the soul is more than a 'self-moving number,' and the physical elements and their mixtures, if constituted of triangles, are not analysed further into numbers, points, and lines. To bring thought, life, and causal relations, finite truth and finite goods into the Eleatic unity of ideal and sensible of *Parmenides* evidently seemed at first more easily done than a more accurate reflection permitted.

In the argument of the three dialogues mentioned there is a common difficulty which becomes more evident from one to the next. The difficulty is that the division of the identical and divided principles, which the hypothetical reflection of *Parmenides* negated, here recurs. In advancing beyond that dialogue there is also a certain retreat from its conclusion. The active principles which extend the argument appear as a third principle after absolute unity and the ordered relation of the dyadic principle to it. Their activity is in relation to the affirmative hypotheses, their consequences, and effects for the others and not to the whole argument and conclusion of *Parmenides*, that there is nothing.

Difficulties occur in the relation of *nous* and *psychē* to what is prior to them, how the finitude resting on the positive relation of the principles belongs to their activity. It is useful, if one would enter into the difficulties, to regard them from the point of their solution. Aristotle in the aporematic introduction to his philosophy in *Metaphysica* B asks, first, whether there can be one science of all the causes – of the essential structure and activity of its objects – and, secondly, whether the same science can treat of the relation of knowledge to those objects – the logical principles.

There is a beginning of these questions in *Sophist*. As against 'sophistic' which, in the extreme form Gorgias gave it, agreed with the negative conclusion of *Parmenides*. Plato there discovers an 'otherness' of true and false for the knowing subject. This 'otherness' is founded on the relation of the two comprehensive ideas as developed in the affirmative hypotheses of *Parmenides*. Contraries there are wholly separated from each other in relation to the undivided principle – not exclusively opposed in relation to the negative one, as in the first of the negative hypotheses. Contraries which do not combine – rest and motion, same and different, being and not-being – are found in the argument of that dialogue to provide the basis of true and distinct knowledge of more ambiguous linguistic statements, and even of images – which, against the Sophists, have something of objective determinateness.

The argument moves to this result from the initial question, what is the 'sophist'? After several attempts to define 'sophistic' as an exclusive species of several genera of *technai*, none of which can contain the mixture of particular objective and a subjectivity which is for itself, the inquiry is forced back to the elements of definition – generic identity and complete division of species. There is a point in this purgation of 'sophistic' from its particular content where the philosophical reflection which would define and what it would define have a common structure, and the question occurs whether 'sophistic' and 'philosophy' are the same. Plato has known well the kinship between the two and that where the education of the young has moved from poetry as its medium to abstract thought only a strong habitual orientation towards the objective good can save the most from the deceptive liberation of the easier choice. In the argument of *Sophist* the two separate at once into an immediate subjective knowledge for which there is no truth but its own self-relation and knowledge of a true objective finitude.

The true otherness thus discovered in opposition to 'sophistic' has in this exclusion its own limit, and that in two ways. The definition attained of 'sophistic' as 'maker of images' neglects the negative unity of the sophistic scepticism which makes itself 'measure of all things' – a unity which in universal form the negative hypotheses of *Parmenides* had discovered. Definition, secondly, as itself defined in this argument is not through division of a genus which has that division implicit in it as already negated in the analysis which discovered the genus. It is definition by limiting dyadic division and bringing it under contraries which do not combine. The consequences of this method are set forth problematically at *Met.* B, 998a20–999b23. The relation of individuals to the definition is indeterminate, from which occurs an uncertainty which has priority, the genera immediately predicated of them or the most remote and universal genera. The 'otherness' by which as against 'sophistic' the subject can discriminate true and false does not suffice for a determinate knowledge of the object. The impediment is an acceptance of the relation of principles found in the affirmative hypotheses of *Parmenides* and a retreat from the negation of that relation through the negative hypotheses.

The deepest interest philosophically of *Sophist, Philebus,* and the attempted philosophy of nature in *Timaeus* is how from one dialogue to the next the argument approaches and makes more evident the revision of principles *Parmenides* required. *Philebus* treats of the good in a manner analogous to the treatment of the true and false in *Sophist.* From when the Cyrenaics and the Cynics first gave to the Socratic good the opposed content of pleasure and abstract virtue, the relation of the two had been examined in various Platonic dialogues, but not so that they were known as gradations of the one good. In *Republic,* where one has the most ample treatment, it is shown how the soul in its three 'parts' can be directed to the good as its primary end through the virtues. But lurking in this *paideia,* and emerging most strongly at the point of its completion, was a subjectivity which by degrees eroded the objective order of the *polis* and made its immediate satisfaction or pleasure its primary good. The 'good life' might in its total satisfaction far outweigh the bad life. How the bad life in its immediacy could be thought a mode of the good life required another examination, for which again the affirmative hypotheses of *Parmenides* provided the method.

The elements of the argument by which the good will be thus ordered are 'limit,' 'the unlimited,' 'the mixed' or the two as related to the individual, and *nous* as cause to the mixture. *Nous* has for its end not only the good as beyond all division but the ordered relation of the dyadic principle to this unity, as followed from the second hypothesis of *Parmenides*. The self-relation of *nous* is third to this twofold relation; only through this mediation is it an end to itself. *Nous* not only knows this composite end but as practical realizes it in the soul, this as will appear in *Timaeus*, the same self-related composite as *nous*, but as potential and having its realization in relation to an external world.[11]

The good as this composite object is not simply an abstract measure of finite goods but in a threefold relation: first as absolute unity and its instantaneous presence in the moment – the *kairos* or immediate determinateness of the end; secondly as symmetry, the harmonious or beautiful relation of the divided to the one end; thirdly as truth or what for *nous* is separate. This threefold good *nous* imports into soul, informing its immediate relation to the world as pleasure, its reflected or imaginative relation as pure pleasure, its collected and thinking relation as the active realization of particular ends.[12]

This ordered structure of composite goods and the relation of *nous* and *psychē* as subordinate to it is the basis of Plato's later political writings (*Statesman* and *Laws*). In these one does not remain, as in *Republic*, with a dependence of the polities animated by the lower parts of the soul on a government by philosopher kings, if such are to be found, and then the lapse of this order into the rule of tyrants – individuals immediately an end to themselves. It is a great advance in political philosophy to have discovered instead a synthesis of the polities which allows a participation in the government of the state to the several classes, in all of which there is an active relation to the good. This synthesis of polities has however an instability in it: the mutual limitation of the classes might break down into a direct relation of self-consciousness to the one good and this freedom fall into 'sophistic' and tyrannical self-will. On this account in Laws the ultimate secrets of power have to be concealed from the citizenry, who have to be protected from this fall and the atheistic materialism attending it by strong laws.[13]

So in *Philebus* the tripartite concept of the good, whereby the free self-consciousness, which is *nous*, is subordinated and not related directly to the undivided good, guards against the same ruinous freedom. But, as in

Sophist, the subjective freedom one would contain is still there and can break out. The inexorable movement of the Platonic *logos* is to break down that limit and to prepare the way for a thinking comprehensive of 'sophistic.'

Aristotle points to a difficulty in the treatment of the good in *Philebus* which emerges more distinctly in *Timaeus*, in the *aporia* whether the principles of the corruptible and the incorruptible are the same or different. Plato, bringing *nous* and *psychē* into the argument in *Sophist*, did not inquire whether the undivided and the dyadic principle were in their composition adequate to entities having apparently a spontaneous activity. What is *nous* in *Philebus* as posterior to an ordered finitude? Or what was soul in relation to the threefold good and to the three levels of psychic goods? *Timaeus* gives an answer to the latter question in the construction of soul by the demiurgic *nous*. Soul is composed of the same relations of the dyadic to the identical principle as inanimate beings – the sameness and difference and being of ideas and of sensibles. With that an unending power of self-movement has been imparted to it by the *demiurgos*.

The same difficulty in another form pervades the whole exposition of nature in Timaeus. The physical elements and composite bodies are constituted of triangles having contrariety in their shape, and the mobility of bodies themselves is from a like contrariety – a mobility in which an original indeterminate motion is limited. There is not in bodies an intrinsic *physis*, nor is soul itself unless in name. But with this construction of nature from the Platonic principles another tendency competes – to carry further the analysis of bodies into triangles to lines, points, and numbers, and thus a mathematization of nature.[14]

Already in the second hypothesis of *Parmenides* the ordered relation of ideas to individuals has underlying it an endless division of unity and being and its first product is an attempted generation of numbers. There is more in Platonism Pythagoreanized than a return simply to that standpoint. In *Sophist* the negative conclusion of *Parmenides* was avoided in that the negativity for which was a true finitude was that of a theoretical knowing. In *Philebus* the determinations of the good were for a practical subject. 'Soul' occurred in the reasoning of that dialogue but was not directly its interest. In *Timaeus* the object contemplated is the ideal world, therein a demiurgic *nous* for which is the ideal world as *paradeigma*, as externalized, or as nature. This standpoint is for Plato not wholly philosophical but reason enclosed in a myth. The recurrence of myth is necessary because the *nous* of *Sophist* and *Philebus* as subordinate to the principles and their ordered composition can enter into a theoretical and a practical relation to it but not a unified contemplation also of itself and its realization as soul. In this altogether objective contemplation the Platonic principles were strained beyond their capacity. Nature as constituted according to those principles was for a thinking which held division and difference within its unity. Between this thinking and the contrariety governing its objects was a tension and the need to overcome it.

Aristotle in the order of his introductory *aporiai* places directly after the question whether unity and being are the principles of all things – the standpoint of *Parmenides* – a question whether numbers should be accounted the principles. *Aporiai* arising from the standpoint of *Sophist*, *Philebus*, and *Timaeus* precede. In this Aristotle has the true insight that after *Parmenides* the problem to be resolved was how contraries in their negative relation did not dissolve into contradiction and nullity simply but were contained as moments within a concrete unity. Plato in taking the ideas to be numbers came as near as possible to this Aristotelian solution if he would save 'the one' and 'the dyad.' But also in that position it became evident that a new beginning was necessary. If the conclusion to which the dialectic of *Parmenides* led seemed unthinkable, the subsequent argument of *Sophist*, *Philebus*, and *Timaeus* led back to the same unthinkable conclusion, and that in a stronger form where no evasion was possible, unless with Speusippus and Xenocrates one were to revert to a Presocratic Pythagoreanism. If from the hypothetical reasoning of *Parmenides* one could turn in *Sophist* and the following dialogues to *nous* as its origin and centre, now for *nous* itself the same contradictory result of the Platonic principles emerged.

One has need to attend to the logic of this movement. In *Sophist* the principles are not only negated in that the contraries which do not combine, through which there is definition and true judgment, are for the negative unity of the *nous*. In *Philebus* the determinate forms of the good are within an encompassing relation of *nous* to its own existence as soul. This primary relation is concealed so far as *nous* is taken to be third after the undivided good and the good as *symmetron*, *teleion*, *hikanon* – as the total idea. But this subordination is broken through at the point where in the explication of the goods 'in the soul' *nous* is reflected into itself out of its finite teleology and knows as primary the relation of the unified end to soul.

In *Timaeus* the *nous* as demiurge is no longer third but has the composite good in its relation to the undivided good, and can thus be said to contemplate the comprehensive good as the *paradeigma* of soul and nature. As the practical *nous* of *Philebus* its causality was not in this way originative but to bring limit into the unlimited. *Timaeus*, as said, is partly mythical in that it cannot separate logically its primary standpoint and the construction of soul and nature through relations of the undivided and the divided principle. But the soul first in its intrinsic mobility and negative unity brings into the form of contradiction the contraries of which it is a harmony. And the elements and mixed bodies in their cyclic movement are a like contradiction, concealed only as their motion is seen as either derived from the spontaneous *movement* of soul or from an unordered movement of matter.

That the ideas are numbers is, one might say, a last defence of the principles against the contradiction to which the negative hypotheses led. Through them the *nous* is related to the good and to soul and nature through a unity of form in which determinate structure is reduced to its most abstract elements, before body is plane and linear geometrical form and before that number. Or the soul is a number and its structure and content are reduced to quantitative relations. But the reduction stops short of pure quantity and would have minimal quanta or a residual qualitative difference. Or the soul is one with itself beyond division and yet divided. A unity having difference within it is sought, but not that of numbers whose differences are extraneous to the pure relation of discrete to continuous, and not difference as grounded in substance or as in a teleological relation where differences are already potentially in the end to be realized.

Quantity in the present argument is the most abstract concept the *nous* finds to express a unity in which is division and difference and the negation of it – an image thus of the unity of thinking which has otherness within its self-relation. The object which was thought in the most external manner by this concept continued to be the good. But as so thought the good or the concrete unity of the ideal and sensible was first quantity which did not have the properties of that concept, then quantity proper or the object of mathematized thought.

The *nous* in this quantitative concept of soul and non-living nature and the relation of both to their ideal ground had overcome or all but overcome the assumption that all things were a composition of the principle. The argument had read into the composite a negativity in which division, difference, contrariety passed into contradiction, as in the negative hypotheses, but also into a resolution of it. What was primarily for thought was not the relation of the undivided and the divided but *genē tou ontos* or categories in which difference and contrariety were variously within a generic unity. Quantity in which the Platonic argument began to grasp such concrete unities was not *genos* in which the ideas and their realization could be thought, but rather 'substance,' which while remaining itself was capable of contraries, and actuality.

At the same time as *nous* through this revolution had for it not ideas and participants but substances having in their negative unity the *physis* or principle of rest and motion – the impulse to pass into division and contrariety while remaining self-related – it also was freed from subordination to a composite good and life and soul as its actuality from confusion with relations of contraries and an extraneous causality.

In the dialectic of *Parmenides* and the reflection on it in the following dialogues and in the mathematicized Platonism reported by Aristotle is to be found the genesis of the Aristotelian philosophy. The argument which led to the discovery of the Aristotelian categories and the traditional logic generally, to the actuality of this logic in natural substances, to the infinite actuality of the divine substance and the relation to it of human life and thought – this argument is among the most difficult.

In its own time the Aristotelian philosophy responded fully to the primary interest of the older Greek culture – to discover a relation between the mortality of the living individual and his rational freedom. In that context the Platonic philosophy could be understood as leading to the clarification of that end for thought as above all in the tragedies of Sophocles it had been clarified in and for the poetic imagination.

When in later antiquity the Platonic and Aristotelian philosophies became the interest of free individuals who from the scepticism and despair of a subjective culture found in those philosophies an infinite end beyond division, neither the Platonic dialectic nor the relation to it of the Aristotelian philosophy had any meaning for them.

The Aristotelian logic detached from its origin became a tradition – the true method of reasoning, unless when it gave way at the highest level of speculation to a Platonic logic of unity and division. The Aristotelian metaphysics might serve, as in Thomism, to found a finite human order, from which might be inferred a Neoplatonic theology. Or the subjective freedom moving in that world might break through that limit to an abstract Scotist or Nominalist logic. And that in turn might prepare for a more direct access to the underlying Neoplatonic thought. And for this the original relation of Platonism to the Aristotelian philosophy was ever reversed.

Only in the modern age when a self-consciousness, certain of itself, discovered in the logic of the understanding a method for the investigation of nature, and experienced the contradiction between the necessity of nature and its own freedom did a dialectical thought recur and knowledge of the meaning and origin of traditional concepts lost in an inert tradition since Aristotle.

Notes

1 Section One of this essay originally published in *Animus* 4 (1999). Section Two was written by Doull, especially for this volume, in 2000.

2 *Met.*, 990a34 – 991a8 and elsewhere.

3 The argument here, dense from its brevity, will be explicated fully in the second hypothesis. For the general sense of it one may reflect on the difficulty in early modern philosophy of passing from the abstract relation of extension to thought to their relation in sense perception. Plato brings into one a rational and an empirical beginning of knowledge.

4 That criticism turns on the relation of the world as it is for the philosopher's contemplation to the world as measured by the clock.

5 Not that Plato has here fully in view the logic of geometry: his criticism is in relation to that middle position he assigns to mathematics in *Republic* and, as in the other cases, the method is a Zenonian dialectic.

6 *Republic*, 510b–511d.

7 As, e.g., in Proclus's commentary. Victor Cousin, *Procli Commentarius in Platonis Parmenidem*, 1064ff.

8 So regarded, the unity is not simply assumed but is known as that in which the last division of the separate ideas from their participants is unified. The hypothesis in this return appears to be not only its absolute indivision but this as mediated by the difference of being and unity.

9 The argument of that dialogue presupposes the unity of the sensible and the universal as this results from the reflections on the principles in *Parmenides*. In that light *aisthesis* and *doxa* are treated to appearance only problematically, but conclusively to one who knows *Parmenides*. The argument here is clearer in the sense that one follows the formation of the presuppositions.

10 *Metaphysics* B, 1001a4 – 1001b25.

11 *Philebus*, 23c–27c.

12 *Philebus*, 66a–67b.

13 *Statesman*, 305e–311e; *Laws* X, 891c–910d; XII, 951c–e, 961a–c.

14 *Timaeus*, 52a–c: initial relation of the ideal world to place; ideas, numbers, and geometrical form.

COMMENTARY

The Criticism of Plato's Doctrine of Participation in *Parmenides*: A Propaedeutic to the Platonic Dialectic

DENNIS HOUSE

I

The inquiry that is both the hardest of all and the most necessary for knowledge of the truth is whether being and unity are the substances of things, and whether each of them, without anything else, is being and unity respectively, *or* we must inquire what being and unity are, with the implication that they have some other underlying nature. For some people think they are of the former, others think they are of the latter character. Plato and the Pythagoreans thought being and unity were nothing else, but this was their nature, their essence being just unity and being ... If we do not suppose unity and being to be substances, it follows that none of the other universals is a substance; for these are most universal of all, and if there is no unity-itself or being-itself, there will scarcely be in any *other* case anything apart from what are called the individuals ... if there *is* to be a being-itself and a unity-itself, there is much difficulty in seeing how there will be anything else besides these – I mean, how things will be more than one in number. For what is different from being does not exist, so that it necessarily follows, according to the argument of Parmenides, that all things are one and this is being.

Aristotle, *Metaphysics*, 1001a2–1001a35

Just as we do not rule over the gods by virtue of rule as it exists in our world and we know nothing that is divine by our knowledge, so they, on the same principle, being gods, are not our masters nor do they know anything of human concerns. But surely, said Socrates, an argument which would deprive the gods of knowledge, would be too absurd.

Plato, *Parmenides*, 134d

To this let us add the conclusion: it seems that whether one is or is not, both it and the others, in relation to themselves and to each other, both are and are not and both appear and do not appear to be, all of these things in all of these ways.

Parmenides, 166c

The problem *Parmenides* presents to its interpreters is not simply consequent upon Plato's manner of articulating his standpoint, but is more significantly a reflection of the fact that he was on his way to a standpoint which he had yet to reach. Plato, in *Parmenides* 126a–137c3 (hereafter 126a–137c3 will be referred to as P1 and the remainder of the dialogue as P2), reaches the conclusion that his 'second best method,' which he followed in the *eidetic* dialogues, may not be a method of inquiry at all. As a result, Plato cannot begin from the assumption of the Ideas and a multiple world that participates in them. He, at this point, is without an object except in the sense that he has given definite form to the impasse that blocks his path. The only way forward is to lay down hypotheses, which, unlike the hypotheses of the middle dialogues, are properly hypothetical and not fixed stable points of departure, and then to determine what consequences follow from them. The Platonic Parmenides has a method to the extent he can exhaustively determine logically what the hypotheses are and what is consequent upon them. But the task of discerning the status and relation of the various hypotheses, if they are not to be taken simply as a discrete series, falls to the commentator to explicate. This is not to say that the grounds for discerning the connections both in the case of the *aporiai* and the hypotheses are not to be found in the text. Doull, in his commentary, articulates what Plato left unexpressed in the dialogue itself – how the series of *aporiai* and hypotheses are to be understood as integrated into a structured, ordered, and coherent argument.

'One source of perplexity,' Sayre writes, 'is that this latter portion [P2] fails to exhibit any obvious continuity of subject matter with the first part of the dialogue ("*Parmenides I*"), making it difficult to determine what the dialogue as a whole is about.'[1] Doull argues that P1 precisely sets forth the problem P2 addresses. The present paper is limited to considering P1 and its relation to P2 and Doull's treatment of the same. With the exceptions of Aristotle's comments on the Platonic philosophy and Hegel's treatment of the *Parmenides*, on almost every detail of interpretation Doull presents a reading of the dialogue which significantly differs from what is found in other commentaries. I will examine the following points of interpretation where Doull stands alone or with the very few in his reading of P1:

1 The problem *Parmenides* addresses is indicated by the audience to the dialogue – the Clazomenian philosophers who have come to Athens. How is Anaxagoras's *Nous* as pure and unmixed related to the finite as a mixture?

2 Zeno and Socrates are to be understood as holding opposed positions and the unification of this opposition occupies the remainder of the dialogue.
3 The order and structure of the *aporiai* follows the fourfold division of the line in *Republic.*
4 When Socrates introduces the 'day image,' the reader is to understand this as the 'light image' of the *Republic.*
5 131c–132b is not a separate *aporia* but is to be taken together with 132b–132c as forming one *aporia.*
6 Although Plato uses the abstract Eleatic concepts of Being and Unity, the reader is to understand by the terms the Good of *Phaedo* and *Republic.*
7 There is one point of difference between Doull and most other commentators concerning P2 which must come into view in considering P1: that 155e–156b, rather than being a corollary or appendix of H2 (hereafter the hypotheses will be referred to as H1, H2, H3, etc.), is the Third Hypothesis.

> The reader of *Parmenides* should put himself in the place of the Clazomenian philosophers who came to Athens to hear the great argument of Socrates with Zeno and Parmenides.[2]

Doull notes that Plato uses a device to indicate to the reader the perspective in which the dialogue is to be read. Doull comments that in the *Theaetetus,* for example, the argument is for Euclides and his friend Terpsion.[3] The reader is by this device invited to regard the dialogue from a Megaric standpoint and will not go astray in his interpretation if he follows this guide. Plato internalizes his audience in several other dialogues. In the case of the *Parmenides,* the audience are Clazomenian philosophers. Doull concludes from this, and finds it confirmed in the course the argument follows, that their interest in the argument of Socrates with Zeno and Parmenides is to solve a problem which Anaxagoras left unresolved.

Plato, in the *Sophist,* declared that it is necessary to question the pronouncement of the great Parmenides and argue that what is not is and what is is not.[4] Parmenides presented a problem which his Presocratic successors found it necessary to address but impenetrable: 'For never shall this be forcibly maintained, that things that are not are, but you must hold back your thought from this way of enquiry, nor let habit, born of much experience, force you down this way, by making you use an aimless eye or an ear and a tongue full of meaningless sound: judge by reason the strife-encompassed refutation by me.'[5]

If one asks of Parmenides' argument 'why Being Itself or Unity Itself?' the answer is that it is logically necessary that Being is and not-being is not. Here we have the law of non-contradiction or principle of identity as the controlling principle. Parmenides introduced for the first time a pure principle of thought. What is thinkable is, what is unthinkable is not. The problem which Parmenides' successors, Empedocles, the Atomists, and Anaxagoras, addressed arose as a consequence of Parmenides' principle. They were committed to the tenet that 'nothing comes from nothing.' Melissus had laid down the terms required by Parmenides' principle on which the existence of plurality, finitude, could be maintained: 'If there were a many, they would have to be such as the one is.'[6]

Consider Empedocles for a moment in respect to what Aristotle calls his 'lisping expression' rather than 'according to its meaning.' He avoids falling into the contradiction that contraries combine by maintaining that his four elements are eternal, unchangeable, autonomous building blocks and by limiting change to the aggregation and segregation caused by two opposed, equally balanced principles which take turns holding dominion in a cyclical succession. What Empedocles cannot show is how there can actually be a unity of the diverse elements as a result of their aggregating in which one has one thing that is which is more than the sum of its elements. An Empedoclean element does not have an inner relation to what is other than itself (the other elements), but immediately is itself. What is aggregated has not integrated the difference of elements from each other into a unity.

The Atomists proposed a pluralized Eleaticism, but with the flaw that neither do the atoms themselves have any nature which out of itself would connect them to each other nor does the void have any nature of its own which would out of itself contain the plurality of atoms within a unity. It falls outside of this account to answer the question 'why' things are the way they are, because it is denied as a beginning point that there is any inner connectedness in reality, any unifying principle, any purposeful ordering in nature. The Atomists explicitly affirm the nature of their principles to be mechanical principles. The difficulty these attempts confronted is that once they accepted Parmenides' principle of thought, they could only rescue the sensible world of identity and difference in terms that left it unthinkable. Doull writes, 'In all the positions until Anaxagoras, unless transiently in Heraclitus, thinking either with

Parmenides and Zeno cannot find itself in the world that is there for it, or entering into it finds the logical forms in which it would think it inadequate to itself.'[7]

With Anaxagoras a problem that before him had been hidden comes into full view. Again, the requirement is accepted that one must remain consistent with Parmenides' dictum that contraries do not combine and that nothing comes from nothing. *Nous* is pure, unmixed, has all knowledge about everything, and starts the creative eddy in motion which is responsible for what is and shall be. What is other than *Nous*, matter, is impure, ruled rather than self-ruling, 'all things together,' 'everything in everything,' such that what comes to be through the creative act of *Nous* comes from what is and not from not-being. Like comes from like and not unlike from like, and thus Anaxagoras seems to avoid offending Parmenides' principle.

Anaxagoras has taken a step Empedocles and the Atomists avoided: his 'everything in everything' at once affirms the total manifold of differences, the dividedness of being, and affirms that the divided and distinct mix together with the result that at every point there is one thing that is many things as intermediate between the manifold differences. Aristotle, in book IV of the *Metaphysics,* writes, 'While the doctrine of Heraclitus, that all things are and are not, seems to make everything true, that of Anaxagoras, that there is an intermediate between the terms of a contradiction, seems to make everything false; for when things are mixed, the mixture is neither good nor not-good, so that one cannot say anything that is true.'[8]

Anaxagoras has avoided joining with Heraclitus against Parmenides, but with a result which is equally perplexing. 'Everything in everything' is a mixture of what is one and self-identical with the endless dividedness and difference of 'the many,' and taken as a whole is neither one nor not-one and is both and neither. The act of Anaxagoras's *Nous* separating out from the original mixture is endless because what is separated is itself ever endlessly divisible. If one asks what is this 'everything in everything,' which Doull speaks of as 'Anaxagoras' atoms,' nothing fixed and distinct can be said. What is the same as itself as one thing is endlessly divided and different from itself as all things.

In the *aporiai* of P1, Socrates asserts the side of identity – 'the many' participate/share in their Idea and as such are one and identical. Against this, Parmenides shows that the many sensible individuals are divided and endlessly different from their Idea. In the final *aporia* sensible and ideal being fall apart into two isolated worlds. Like Anaxagoras's *Nous,* mind, thinking cannot find itself in the multiple world of sensible individuals. The Ideas, as conceived of in P1, are pure and unmixed, while the sensible individuals are mixtures in a comparable relation of Anaxagoras's *Nous* to all things mixed together, and the problem in both cases can only be solved if one can show how there can be a unity of the undivided and divided, of ideal and sensible being.

I would suggest here something which Doull does not say and might well disagree with for reasons which will be indicated later. The problem the Clazomenian philosophers have to work out is the relation of H1 and H2. Quite simply, the One of H1, to use Anaxagoras's language describing *Nous*, is alone by itself, pure unmixed, while the One-Being of H2 is one and many, same and different, like and unlike, etc., and the problem that presents itself is how to bring the two together, which is the problem the Clazomenians have before them. Doull is correct in finding that the audience to the dialogue comes to the discussion with the problem it addresses precisely formed both in respect to the *aporiai* and in respect to the question which is being addressed through the hypotheses – in P2 the problem of how there can be a concretion of a One and Dyadic principle.

I believe Anaxagoras thought he had conceived of the relation of *Nous* to what is other than *Nous* in a way that did not leave his account a victim to Zeno's dialectic. He avoided saying, as Heraclitus did, that all things are and are not, but said positively in anything is all difference. The problem, then, is whatever is is endlessly something else and never is just what it is. This has the consequence that Anaxagoras has fallen directly into Zeno's trap. The reason *Nous* can never get to what is and is one, save directly as what is immediately one, itself as unmixed, is because what is one is infinitely many, what is the same as itself is different from itself and for there to be any individual other than *Nous* itself, these contraries would have to be united in the individual, and as such contradictory, with the consequence that the individual is annulled.

Nous itself so understood is open to the consequence of losing itself in what is other than itself in a mobility that might be compared to the flux of Heraclitus. Anaxagoras recognized this problem and addressed it in a way that highlights the difficulty rather than solve it. He expressly said that *Nous* not only started the creative 'eddy,' but is responsible for what is and shall be. Once *Nous*, according to Anaxagoras, has set matter in motion, which forms the vortex according to an intelligent law, there is no need for *Nous* to interfere further. The 'intelligent law,' in fact, is mechanical and produces a world which mind, divine or human, cannot find itself in. In the *Phaedo*, Socrates rejects this separation of *Nous* as principle from the principled and identifies it with the Good as a teleology principle. Reason he sees as intrinsically ordered to an infinite end – the Good Itself. What is the reason things are the way they are? Because it is best that they be that way. In this relation of thinking or reason and being, Socrates finds cause to hope that he can find his way into the world he is in and that is there for him. The problem Anaxagoras left unclear is 'how the *Nous*, alone unmixed, could relate to the atoms in each of which were all difference, the endless process of separating their differences from the original mixture.'[9] It would seem reasonable to suppose that the Clazomenian philosophers are to be thought of as hoping to find in Socrates' response to the argument of Zeno and Parmenides a solution to the difficulty formed in Anaxagoras's position. Presocratic thought has reached it limit with Anaxagoras.

> Athena one should suppose to preside over the division between Zeno and Socrates and to know a resolution adequate to both. A brief exchange between Socrates and Zeno states the opposed positions whose relations, and in the end their unification, will occupy the remainder of the dialogue.[10]

Doull, in his commentary on the *Parmenides*, as also on the *Theaetetus*, attends to the importance of taking note of the place (Athens) and occasion (the Great Panathenaea) of Socrates' meeting with the Eleatic philosophers in order to discern what the dialogue is about. In this section of the *Parmenides* (127a–130a) Doull finds that the answer to the question of what the dialogue is about is distinctly stated. Namely, it sets forth the opposed positions of Zeno and Socrates and their relation and ultimately shows them to be unified. What this means is by no means immediately evident.

What is the opposition between Socrates and Zeno? It would seem that Socrates is not opposed to Zeno as Heraclitus would be. He would marvel greatly if likeness and unlikeness, plurality and unity, rest and motion could be shown to be able among themselves to mix and be separate. In fact, Socrates does not oppose Zeno directly, but holds to the position he expressed in the *Republic*: 'It is obvious that the same thing will never do or suffer opposites in the same respect in relation to the same thing and at the same time.'[11] Socrates' response to Zeno's argument is to propose a position which, as Doull notes, neither Parmenides nor Zeno had conceived of.[12] The identity of thinking and being which the latter found in Unity Itself or Being Itself, Socrates suggests is also present as a plurality of ideas which are each in turn self-identical, unchanging, simple, unmixed, directly known, and so on. Thus Socrates, so far as this goes, does not regard himself as holding an opposed position to that of Zeno's but as sharing a common ground with him. If granted the plurality of Ideas, Socrates believes it is possible to say that something is like and unlike so long as one distinguishes what that something is compared to or distinguishes the respect in which it is like and unlike, without offending the requirements of Zeno's argument.

Doull distinguishes two steps in the brief exchange between Socrates and Zeno.[13] At first, Socrates viewed Zeno as a sophist. The sophistic art deconstructs the belief in Ideas as stable and determinate essences or natures; what is taken to have a fixed nature by one person has the opposite meaning in the perception of another, or what has a certain nature in one relation has the opposite in another relation, and from this it is concluded that nothing is determinate in and through itself. Zeno could be mistaken for a sophist because in the sophistic view thinking collapses into an immediate unity with itself.[14] Socrates' response to Zeno regarded as a sophist would embark on the argument that establishes the doctrine of Ideas and distinguishes them from their manifold and contrary appearances.

What Socrates learns from Zeno's response is that Zeno's argument is to be taken as polemical, that is, he accepts the distinction of contraries such as 'like' and 'unlike' and on the basis of such a common understanding shows that what is constituted out of such contraries, namely a plurality of beings, is contradictory, unthinkable, and thus a nullity. His intention is not to argue that 'like' is 'unlike,' 'unlike' is 'like,' and to obliterate all distinction. Zeno, in other words, is saying something very definite about a 'multiple world': if the finite world is, it is sheer contradiction. Indeed, the possibility that there be contradiction requires that there be fixed and stable meanings and it is only on the assumption of such finite distinctions that there can be an argument for the Parmenidean One. Thus Zeno says his argument is polemical and not sophistic. Zeno is understood by Socrates as arguing that a multiple world is a nullity while accepting distinctions such as 'like' and 'unlike,' 'one' and 'many,' and so on. One might say that what Parmenides asserts positively, Zeno attempts to demonstrate through an objective dialectical reflection of the Idea of 'plurality' and historically also in terms of the Idea of 'motion' and 'becoming.' Unity Itself or Being Itself is known as precisely what is not the subject of contraries. In this way, Socrates is able to recognize that Zeno's dialectic is not sophistic. The question then becomes focused on the difference between the dialectic of the *eidetic* dialogues and Zeno's dialectic. Doull brings out accurately the common ground between Socrates and Zeno and the point of their opposition.

The second step in the discussion between Socrates and Zeno is that it occurs to Socrates that he has a different concept of being than the Eleatic. Doull argues that Socrates understands Being to be another name for the Good and the *eide* are the determinations of the Good.[15] Socrates believes he can save a sensible plurality against Zeno's argument by distinguishing from it an ideal plurality and understanding the former as participating in the latter. Contrary Ideas cannot combine, but a sensible individual can participate in contrary Ideas because the sensible individual stands in one relation to one contrary and in another relation to another contrary. Sensibles have multiple relations to the universal Ideas. The criticisms which follow in the next section of P1 partly bring out the problem that the relating of the universal Ideas and the sensible individual is abstract in the sense that it does not account for the difference of the two; their connection is made by an 'extraneous subject' who views them in one relation and not another.

Socrates' response is sufficient in order to allow the argument to proceed. However, what Zeno requires as a response to his argument is that it be shown how difference and identity can meet in one individual. Do Socrates' sensibles break down to a multiplicity of unrelated or extraneously related relations, and if that is the case, can the sensibles themselves be said to be in any sense at all? The problem also occurs for Socrates' ideal plurality. If the Ideas are to be thought of as the determinations of the Good Itself, how is their identity and their difference from the Good and from each other to be understood? No solution can be found by reverting back to an atomist position. 'The good,' Doull writes, 'is not only in itself but divided and different from itself and relating its determinations to itself as to their end.'[16] How this can be the case is precisely what must be shown in response to Zeno's argument, not only in the relation of the Good to the Ideas but also in the relation of the Ideas to their appearances or sensible individuals.

What does Doull mean by 'the opposed positions of Socrates and Zeno whose relations, and in the end their unification, will occupy the remainder of the dialogue'?[17] Do we have here opposed positions? Socrates' doctrine of 'participation' attends to the side of the being and identity of 'the many' through the affirmative relation to their Ideas, while Zeno focuses on the difference and negativity between an assumed 'many' and the Ideas Socrates posits. Zeno assumes that there are finite stable distinctions in order to annul them, while Socrates' assumes 'the many' in order to show that so far as they are they are one and identical. Doull's interpretation is confirmed by the course the movement through the *aporiai* follows in the last part of P1. Socrates asserts an identical relation of the many individuals to idea and against that Parmenides, taking up the argument from Zeno, brings into view their negativity or non-identity of 'the many' and their idea. Plato is equally with the Zeno and the Socrates of P1 and in that with neither the one nor the other.

'In the *aporiai*,' Doull writes, 'there was need to move from one to the next because against each proposed identical relation of individuals to ideas a negativity or non-identity occurred. Neither in the object considered nor in the thinking of them did a unity of the identity and the recurrent difference come to light.'[18] P2 begins with the result that so long as one stays with the simple opposition of pure identity and pure division or difference there can be no solution to how there can be either a sensible or ideal world. For there to be either world it must be shown how identity and difference combine. Plato rejects both Zeno's view that identity and difference are simply opposed and contradictory and Socrates' response that identity can be separated from difference and division because it leaves unexplained that from which the Ideas have been abstracted or separated.

In a sense, both sides of the problem are in Eleaticism, if Parmenides and Zeno are seen in their difference from each other. In Zeno's view, if the finite (ideal or sensible) is, all things mix including contraries. Parmenides' One can only be known as an abstraction from the divided and different and then he must deny that from which it came to be known ever was or was known. Parmenides' view concludes that nothing mixes. The result of either holding that everything mixes (Anaxagoras's 'atoms') or that nothing mixes (Anaxagoras's *Nous*) was expressed in Gorgias's famous argument that nothing is and if something is it cannot be known and if it could be known it could not be communicated. The alternative to accepting Gorgias's conclusion Aristotle found in the category of substance as the category which alone remains one with itself while being receptive of contraries. Plato, of course, does not have before him Aristotle's doctrine of substance, but he has reached the very definite point at the end of the *aporiai* in P1 that all difference must somehow be taken into identity and identity into difference. The abstractions of Eleaticism must somehow be broken through. The assumption from *Phaedo* that the Ideas are simple, incomposite, which Socrates hoped would provide a solution to Zeno's argument, is abandoned as a result of the *aporiai* and they are rather understood as constituted out of the primary elements or principles of the One and an indeterminate Dyad.

> It makes a difficulty in reading *Parmenides* that in speaking of the good, Plato uses abstract Eleatic concepts – unity and being ... How from this abstract beginning 'the one' came to be 'the good' in which is centred in the sensible and ideal totalities Plato treats elusively.[19]

> The argument then passes to the Platonic Parmenides for whom 'the one' is 'the good' and is assumed capable of showing the relation of all things to that principle.[20]

Here we meet with a pivotal point in Doull's interpretation of the *Parmenides.* He supports his view that when Plato uses the terms 'the One' or 'Unity Itself' or 'Being Itself' the reader is to understand 'the Good' by saying that the *Parmenides* must be read in the context of *Phaedo* and *Republic.* The reader knows from the middle dialogues that the Good 'is not only itself but divided and different from itself and relating its determinations [the *eide*] to itself as to their end.'[21] If the One of H1 is to be taken as a Parmenidean One, then it follows that the One of that hypothesis is other than the finite but not greater than it. In other words, the finite is assumed and then negated and the One is simply other than, not the finite. If, however, as Doull does, one takes the One as the Good Itself, not in the sense of being beyond the division of being and truth, but as what 'is not only itself but divided and different from itself,' then it is greater than and not simply other than all limited determinations. How one interprets H1, for example, will depend upon how one understands the negation of all finite forms in that hypothesis. Is the negativity of the One there to be understood as merely a way of asserting its immediate identity and transcendence or, alternatively, is it to be taken, as I believe Doull does, as a pure negativity in which through successively negating all division and difference it is known to be comprehensive of it. On H1 Doull writes, '[T]he unity of the principle is not immediate but mediated by the negation of forms of division and difference, so that its self-relation is in truth a pure negativity and capacity for division and difference.'[22]

And this leads to another more difficult question. Has the argument, as Doull contends, through the *aporiai* prepared the reader to view the hypotheses as each in turn 'laid down or supposed by a thinking which, when it has attended to the consequences of its supposition, will complement it by another until it comes to an "anhypothetos arche?"'[23] In this perspective the logic of *Parmenides* is dialectical. Or, should the dialogue be read analytically, in which case, for example, H1 would be seen as lacking self-consistency (lacking 'being' and thus the One is not). In this view, H1 is abandoned and one moves to H2 as addressing the problem brought out in H1, but in a way that does not require that the pure negativity of H1 be maintained as an essential moment in the development of the argument. In other words, is Parmenides only able to move to H2, on the basis of the insight from H1 that the One is only able to be all things (H2) because it is not anything (H1) like Anaxagoras's *Nous*, or is the argument of H1 simply directed against the One of the historic Parmenides? One is only able to make sense of Doull's interpretation of the *Parmenides* once one has accepted the identification for Socrates of the One with the Good and that as accepted by the Parmenides of P2. Plato, one might say, knows what he wants to articulate, but is perplexed when he attempts to find the logic by which it can be expressed. Hegel writes: '[T]his determination consists in the one being identical with itself in the other, in the many, in what is distinguished. This constitutes the only truth, and the only interest for knowledge in what is called Platonic philosophy, and if this is not known, the main point is not known.'[24] The argument for this does not depend upon referring the reader to the middle dialogues but is made quite explicit through the course of Parmenides' criticisms of Socrates' theory of Ideas.

II

The *aporiai* are to be read as presenting a step-by-step development in which the final *aporia* leads 'to the "hypotheses" about unity and being or the relations of an ideal and a sensible totality.'[25] There is a common structure which runs through what Doull takes to be the last three *aporiai*. Namely, Plato has before him the question of how there can be an adequate relation between his principles – undivided unity and the indeterminate dyad. One might comment that in this interpretation, Parmenides is able to consider the theory of Ideas critically because he regards the Ideas and their appearances as constituted out of more primary elements and can therefore set against each other their identity and difference or dividedness. This may appear to have the problem that his criticisms are from an external standpoint, since the Ideas are not taken as separate undivided primary beings but as derivative from more primary elements. But Plato, in the *Phaedo*, already was aware of the problem when he presented his 'second best method.' The logic by which the many Ideas in their separate identities and differences from each other were to be related to the undivided Good or the many sensible individuals to the Idea(s) they participate in involved regarding both the universal forms and sensible individuals from the perspective of an assumed external subject. The dialectician could view sensibles as sharing in and not sharing in their Ideas and view the Ideas as determinations of the Good Itself and as different from each other and the Good. One might say that the reason Socrates spoke of his method as a 'second best method' is because in the best or in a truly scientific knowing one would have to be able to show how these elements objectively belong to the Ideas themselves and to their appearances. What is present in the doctrine of participation, but hidden in it, is the problem of how one objectively brings together both in knowing and in the known the elements of identity and otherness or difference. The language of 'sharing and not sharing in' hides the fact that the connection of the positive and negative moments is not expressed. That these moments are only related by an external subject had the consequence that Plato had not completely advanced beyond a sophistic attitude.

Doull comments that the divisions of the line in the *Republic* mark relations of thought to being. At each higher level the externality of the two sides is more deeply reconciled until one reaches the 'unhypothetical principle' in which thought and being are no longer divided. The measure of adequacy or inadequacy, it might be added, both on the side of knowing and of being and of the two taken together is a measure of the degree of a concretion of the terms, unifying form and content or the undivided and divided. In *Republic*, Doull writes, '[n]either the logic of the ascent is there given nor how a "dialectical" or "hypothetical" thinking can exceed itself in an "unhypothetical" principle. *Parmenides* will supply both.'[26] The limitation of the account given in the *Republic* is that one has an image or picture. In *Parmenides* Plato does not reject what is given in the image but explains it. Indeed, Doull argues that the *aporiai* follow one after another as sense perception (*aporia* 1) is followed by true opinion (*aporia* 2), and it is in turn followed by 'dianoetic' or reasoning thought (*aporia* 3), and the development ends in the unified knowledge of the Ideas which has in it a knowledge of the sensible world or, at least, the recognition of the same negatively (*aporia* 4). The grades of the line of *Republic* provide the steps in the *aporiai*. The logic by which the steps are connected involves showing how the lower is taken up in the higher. 'The negativity present at one grade is at the next taken into the positive relation, only to recur in another form' until one reaches a final end, 'where the object of thought is seen to be the principles themselves.'[27] The 'negativity' is the not-being or difference of the universal form from the sensible individual(s) in the relation of participation. The separation or negativity that is brought out in the first *aporia* is overcome and the sides are positively united in the second *aporia* and then another 'negativity' appears which is resolved in the third *aporia*, until a final end is reached and the reader is prepared for the hypotheses concerned directly with unity and being.

The article which is most useful in assisting in the reading of Doull's commentary on the *aporiai* of P1 is his commentary in *Dionysius* on Plato's *Theaetetus*. I will limit my comments to certain critical points in following Doull's commentary on this section and points where a different line of interpretation might be thought possible. The essential standpoint of Doull's interpretation of the *aporiai* is stated from the beginning of his commentary: 'The argument then passes to the Platonic Parmenides for whom "the one" is the "the good itself" and is assumed capable of showing the relation of all things to that principle.'[28] The problem of the 'separation' or *chorimos* of the Ideas from what participates in them appears in two stages. First, there is the question of whether the Ideas are exhaustive and comprehensive of the manifold kinds of being or for some kinds there are not Ideas. Second, once they are taken to be comprehensive, the problem of their self-relation to what is other and different from them becomes the focus.

In the section 130a–e, where Parmenides asks Socrates to indicate of what there are Ideas, Doull refers the reader to *Phaedo* in order to show the meaning of Parmenides' question. The advance beyond dialogues which are intermediate between the Socratic and *eidetic* dialogues such as *Protagoras* and *Gorgias* involved as the first task separating Ideas as stable essences or natures from the shifting appearances which the Sophist could oppose to each other and conclude that there is only being-for-another and not being in and for itself apart from particular measuring subjects. In *Phaedo* the response to the neo-Pythagoreans, whom Socrates addresses, requires that he show that soul is not the subject for the succession from one contrary to another – from its being or life – to its not-being or death. Soul and the Ideas are taken as sharing in common that they do not admit of their opposites and are thus distinguished and separated as beings from the natural cycle of the particular objects of Becoming. The Ideas, as pure self-identical beings, are at once separated from the realm of object of becoming in which there is a mixture of being and not-being, and are taken to be causes of the same.

The difficulties of the doctrine of participation which Parmenides sets forth in the *aporiai* all have to do with the nature of the otherness of sensible individuals from the Ideas. Once one has separated the Ideas from the sensible multiplicity, how does one relate them back in their difference from it?

Socrates in *Parmenides* is certain that there are Ideas of logical contraries and also Ideas by which individuals and communities order themselves and their world in relation to universal ends such as Justice, the Good, and Beauty. But when asked whether there are Ideas of the natural elements (fire and water) and composite individuals such as man, he says that he is puzzled. He recoils from the possibility that there could be Ideas of hair, mud, and dirt. Socrates is perplexed and, at first, more ready to imagine that there are certain sensible objects which somehow are, without having an Idea to participate in, than to allow that the operation of the Ideas is comprehensive of what seems to fall away from the intelligible into what would belong to the natural in absolute difference from the intelligible. In this view, the Ideas would not only be separate and independent, but also at the extreme remove from the intelligible world would be a natural world separate and independent, a world in which mind finds itself at home and a world of the senses. Socrates' fear is that he will fall into an 'abyss of absurdity.' How, if the Ideas are comprehensive of all that belong to the sensible, do the Ideas themselves not lose their universality, which is necessary for there to be thought, and how do the Ideas not get caught in the mobility of becoming and lose their stability?

Parmenides comments that Socrates still 'has a regard for the opinions of men.'[29] The attitude of opinion assumes that there is the being of the many sensibles and a being of universals and the two are connected externally in the act of opining rather than united objectively. Doull comments: 'He is not capable of what is not a human but rather a divine knowledge. The discovery of the ideas is the beginning of a science, of a knowledge of what the scientific understanding is. But there is also a dogmatism of the understanding, a common sense not easily moved from its certainty.'[30] Indeed, this is not only true in respect to Socrates' resistance to the notion that there is an idea comprehensive of all externality, but is also brought out in how he is still confident that he can solve the problem of 'the one and many' by viewing the sensible individual in two relations. Parmenides' criticisms of the doctrine of participation have the precise form of leading Socrates to the recognition that 'human knowledge' (the 'second best method' of *Phaedo*), in other words, the mediation of the difference between unified Ideas and a sensible plurality by an external subject, leaves the division endlessly unresolved; the resolution of the *aporiai* is then known only to be possible if there is a dialectic that would show the Good as principle or 'divine knowledge.'

The discussion continues on the understanding that 'the many' are to be seen as totally dependent upon the Ideas as their comprehensive self-sustaining foundation; the Idea is not an abstraction from 'the many,' what can be separated out as their common identity, but is the cause of their being as becoming. An Idea is at once none of 'the many' that participate in it and all of them. The *aporiai* Parmenides brings against the doctrine of participation begin with the assumption of Socrates' acceptance that the Ideas are comprehensive of all multiplicity and difference. The separation is at once to be asserted and negated.

At the risk of over-interpreting Doull's account of this preliminary inquiry, I suggest the structure that will come out in the first three hypotheses of P2 has already been indicated in the discussion between Parmenides and Socrates. Socrates has separated the Idea from its participants. As such the Idea is radically other than 'the many' – being none of 'the many' as what is purely self-identical like Parmenides' One of H1. At the same time, the Idea is comprehensive of 'the many' – is all of them – as the being in becoming. The One-Being of H2 is a becoming as well as a being. The possibility that the Idea can be comprehensive of all difference (H2) depends upon its pure negativity – that it is not any one of 'the many' (H1) and one might reasonably anticipate that a third hypothesis would then be required to show that the Idea, or more properly 'the principle,' is 'both one and many and neither one nor many.' Doull quite correctly restricts himself to stating what comes out of the argument as it develops and avoids interpreting the discussion from a later vantage point. However, he does show that the structure of what follows in P2 is already laid down in P1.

131a–e: The first aporia *of 'participation'*

The difference lies in this, that the light in the image is thought to have division and difference in its identity, as on the other side the sail is not simply the continuity of extension but as partitioned among a multitude of individuals.[31]

To appreciate the direction of Doull's interpretation it is useful to contrast his account of the first *aporia* with one he would reject. The commentator who takes the One of H1 to be the One of Parmenides purified of all externality and accidents (other than but not greater than what is other than it) might reasonably see in the 'day image' a close connection with the One of H1. The image of 'the day,' in this view, indicates a common identity in which the difference and division of what it is the identity of is excluded from it – an identity in which all difference is lost. The One of H1, if one follows this interpretation, has the relation to all finite beings in their manifold determinations of simply not being any or all of them.

The 'sail image' would then be taken as prefiguring H2. In the 'sail image' what is at first taken to be continuous shows itself to be endlessly divided and different, with the result that the original identity or unity is lost. The commentator committed to this line of interpretation would find that once one starts with division – One-Being – what follows is itself divided and endlessly divided in a succession of forms including being 'in itself and in another.' In the sail image the participants are each 'in itself and in another.' In the first image one has the immediacy of a moment in time and in the latter, the externality of space. In the former thinking and discourse are impossible because nothing mixes; in the latter, because everything mixes with everything (the great is small and the small is great, etc.).

Now the advantage of the above interpretation is its simple reading of the text. The One is the One or Unity Itself and not spoken of directly as the Good Itself and the day image is simply that of '*one and the same day*, which is many places *at the same time*.'[32] Doull interprets the 'day image' as the *Republic* image of the light of the sun in sensible world which is there compared to the diffusion of the good. Light 'while remaining undividedly itself is spatially extended even to individuals.'[33] Doull goes on to say that 'the light in the image is thought to have division and difference in its identity.'[34] If the intention of Plato is to have Socrates respond by giving 'the light image,' why does he instead have him speak of 'one and the same day,' where a temporal moment or limited duration is related to a diversity of places? In the *Republic* light is understood to be the cause of the seeing and the appearing of sensible objects as the Good is to knowing and known. Light while remaining one with itself in its diffusion is the cause of the manifold differences of colours appearing and being seen. This is a very developed image. Socrates' intention in giving 'the day image' is to avoid the consequence that Idea or 'whole' would be separate from itself. One can think of the light image as having division and difference in its identity because its identity is the cause of such. But one can only think of 'the day image' as having division and difference in its identity in the purely external manner that an observer can note the co-presence of the same day and many places.

Thus if one presses the image harder, as Parmenides does in 'the sail image,' and asks how are the parts related to the whole *as parts*, the whole itself turns out to be not a whole at all but what is indeterminate. One has in 'the day image' a totally external and abstract notion of a continuity or commonality that runs through the many things and in 'the sail image' there is discontinuity or a partitioning of the one Idea in which the Idea dissolves into a multitude of contrary parts which can be connected neither with the original Idea nor with each other. Parmenides explains that if one divides Largeness Itself, the parts are to be large by a part of Largeness smaller than Largeness Itself, which would be *alogos*.

Socrates and Parmenides view the relation of the whole Idea and its relation to the many things that participate in it from opposed sides. Socrates' 'day image' takes account of the identity 'the many' participate, but cannot provide an account of what in the nature of the many distinguishes them from the Idea Itself. Parmenides' 'sail image' observes what is missing in the 'day image': he attends to the difference of the many from their Idea. If this is all that is to be said about their respective positions at this point in the argument, one could be satisfied with the account given above, which I believe Doull would reject.

The two images bring into view the opposed perspectives which are present in each of the *aporiai* that follow. It is not that Parmenides and Socrates simply ignore what is in the other's account. From Socrates' standpoint to imagine that 'the many' are separate is mistaken; the Ideas are separate but not 'the many.' It is only because 'the many' participate that they are. So Socrates immediately negates the difference of 'the many' from their Idea. The difference of 'the many' from their Idea, in this view, is the total dependence of 'the many' for their being and self-relation upon the independent, self-identical Idea. Apart from the participated the participants are not at all. Parmenides' beginning point is to view 'the many' in their difference from their Idea and bring into view the nature of their otherness or finitude. To participate partially in the Idea has the consequence that 'the many' are contradictory and unthinkable and as such cannot be.

Is Socrates image of 'one and the same day' to be taken as a temporal image or as implying the 'light' of day and that interpreted as it is in the *Republic*? What the image is intended to show, however you take it, is how the Idea is not separate from itself in its participants. The light image in the *Republic* served to show how the Good is not separate from itself as the effective cause of what is other than itself. The sense in which Socrates may be taken to understand the difference of 'the many,' as indicated above, fits with the light image. Without light, 'the many' are not and are unknowable, with light they are and are known, which for Socrates is understood as what participation effects. Taking the 'day image' as referring to the 'light' serves to bring out fully what Socrates intends.

The advantage of understanding the image as simply temporal is that one can more easily understand why Socrates, with some reluctance, would allow Parmenides' spatial image of the sail to be accepted as an interpretation of his 'day image' and consider, so to speak, the many places as at first separate. Perhaps what is indicated in the 'light image' of the *Republic* can only be achieved if one were to bring together into one view the continuity expressed in the 'day image' with the discontinuity expressed in the sail image.

Doull finds in this *aporia* the attitude of sense perception. He comments in a footnote that the argument is 'dense from its brevity.' I am only able to offer a few remarks which are at best suggestive of how Doull understands the matter. So far as Parmenides, in his reflection on the 'sail image,' might be imagined to allow that 'the many' are at all, 'the many' would be the Idea as divided and self-contradictory. It would be the unstable Heraclitean flux. Socrates' 'day image,' and here we must mean 'light image,' focuses on the unity of the Idea before it is divided and contradictory and would know the finite as nothing but the unified idea diffused. Doull writes, 'The reflection of the self-diffusing unity and that process into each brings the process or becoming to a momentary halt and permits that first apprehension of being which is called *aisthesis*.'[35] For the full development of this account he refers his readers to the *Theaetetus*, and one should add his commentary on that dialogue in *Dionysius*.

131e–132c: Second aporia

It was noted earlier that Doull understands the *aporiai* to follow the fourfold structure of the line in the *Republic*. The section from 131e to 132c might be interpreted as containing two distinct *aporiai* and not just one. By viewing this section as constituting a single *aporia*, Doull preserves its continuity with the account given in the *Republic*. Is there in 131e–132c one *aporia* or are there two? And if two, can they still be understood as corresponding with the second division in Plato's line?

131e begins with the abandonment of trying to understand participation in terms of a relation of parts to a whole. So understood the Ideas are not really separated from 'the many,' but there is rather a certain coalescence of the two which from either side results in the impossibilities indicated above. Parmenides proposes a way in which Socrates can address this problem by reflecting upon how the Ideas came to be known in the first place. From the observation that there are some number of things that seem to be large, one distinguishes out the common character – largeness – and takes it to be a single Idea. The difficulty which Parmenides then puts before Socrates is that the supposedly unitary Idea turns out to be indefinitely multifarious rather than one. The Idea of Large that covers the many large things in turn must cover both itself and the many large things and in turn must cover the original Large and the many large things and the large that covered the former two and so on. So the Idea so understood turns out to be indefinitely many or, in a word, not an Idea at all.

This criticism is itself open to criticism. Why is it necessary to proceed beyond the first idea of large to one that would take account of that idea and the many large things that share in the abstracted idea it denotes? Is the abstracted common quality 'largeness' different from the quality in the many large things? If not, the process is complete in the first instance. If so, the idea of largeness has never been separated, but is one more instance among the many different instances of the never to be reached idea of 'largeness itself.' The force of Parmenides' argument, strictly interpreted, is that abstraction of a common quality is impossible because a quality as it is present in the many things is endlessly different and cannot be resolved to a single identity. His criticism is that of the Sophists, who attack the abstract universals of opinion by opposing appearances to each other and showing their difference and thus destabilizing the universal as denoting a determinate nature or essence.

Doull's account of this section is very compressed: 'In coming to this position one has circumvented the indefinite plurality of things which makes true universals appear the unattainable end of an endless process. In this unification the idea has been separated from all the individuals, and it appears evident that there can be no "participations."'[36] I can only guess at what this means. The true universal is unattainable so long as one takes as the object of thought the endlessly different many things. Socrates gets around that problem by looking at all the many things at once and finds a common quality. 'Participation' would be impossible because the unified idea that has been separated from all individuals was found to belong to them in the first instance and not as an Idea that is other than 'the many,' such that there can be the relation of participated to participant. The problem is that there is no distance or otherness between 'the many' and their Idea(s). My account given above differs with what I am taking to be the meaning of Doull's interpretation in that it is there suggested that Parmenides' criticism requires that the abstracted quality be seen as at once identical with the many instantiations of that quality from which it is abstracted and as different from them, such that the one Idea becomes an indefinite multitude. In other words, Parmenides treats the position as both having 'circumvented the indefinite plurality of things' and precisely as not having 'circumvented the indefinite plurality of things,' In either account, there can be no 'participation.'

On a simple reading of the text it would seem that 131e–132b forms a separate and distinct *aporia* from what follows in 132b–132c. Doull treats 131e–132c as one criticism and, I believe, is alone among commentators in doing so. So far Parmenides, in the second *aporia*, has presented what he takes to be Socrates' position and received his approval, and then Parmenides goes on to interpret the position and show it to be problematic. It is at this point that Socrates jumps in to explain how the position may be interpreted otherwise. In other words, the original position under consideration remains the same. The difference lies in how it is understood. By Parmenides' account the idea or quality is regarded as an abstraction from the original, the many sensible individuals differing in quantity as more comprehensive than the many instances – as all of them together – but still on an ontological same plain. Socrates regards the abstracted quality as in the soul and thereby the difference between it and what belong to the sensible individuals is brought into view. It might be argued, as I believe Doull does, that the second *aporia* really begins at this point once the confusion of 131e–132b has been cleared up. Parmenides' criticism as expressed at the beginning, as noted above, was itself open to criticism. If one allows that we have here one *aporia* and not two, there are altogether four *aporiai* which, as Doull argues, correspond to the structure set out in the *Republic.* The strongest argument for treating what on the surface at least appears as two distinct *aporiai* as one is that the whole section is concerned with the attitude of true opinion.

The correction which is made from one *aporia* to the next involves Socrates redefinition of 'the many' and Parmenides' response, which turns on a new difficulty concerning the separation of 'the many' from their identity. Socrates' reply to Parmenides' criticism in the first part of the second *aporia* is intended to show how the Ideas do not themselves have the indeterminate character of 'the many' which they are to explain. In the first part of this *aporia* the abstractive process by which the universal Idea is to be discovered turned out to be endless, with the result that a single universal Idea is never reached. Socrates' response is to take a step in the direction of inverting this movement. In a sense, rather than viewing Idea as an abstraction from 'the many,' 'the many' are to be viewed as being what they are in their relativity to the Idea and nothing in themselves. By taking the Idea into the soul, Socrates is now able to start straightway with the immediate possession of the Idea. What then are 'the many' of which the Idea, as a thought, is their identity? 'The many' are not to be taken as the sensible individuals. Of what is the thought in the soul to be the unifying principle? Socrates accepts that it cannot be a thought of nothing but must be of something that is. The thought must be a thought or a thinking of thoughts or universals. Each thought or universal is and is unique. How then can there be an identity (one thought) of a plurality of thoughts or universals? The difficulty is that what unites (the one thought) is also what divides, since each thought is unique and determinate. This leaves the impossible choice. Each thought must be imagined to think all the other thoughts and the *logos* by which all the thoughts are thought by each will negate their determinate difference from each other or one will say that all things are unthought thoughts and as such without a *logos* connecting them.

Doull refers the reader to *Theaetetus*, which he does throughout his commentary, and here the reference could not be more helpful and necessary. Clearly, as he indicates, the attitude of true opinion is what is being consider here. 'The *logos* both inwardly unites all plurality with the universal and is externalized into a dispersed multitude of parts, an externalized universal and a relation of individual to that universal. The elements of thought are materialized and as such unthought.'[37] Doull concludes his consideration of this *aporia* with comment that '[t]here is demanded a *logos* which inwardly and in its explication contains all differences within a unity of form.'[38]

One might wonder whether the sense of this *aporia* can be properly understood as a problem already expressed in the Socratic dialogues. Consider 'virtue' as the idea of the particular virtues. The problem now is the relation of the idea of the whole, 'virtue,' and of the parts – the particular virtues. Are we to understand that the unity of the whole – 'virtue' – requires that each particular virtue think all of the other particular virtues. This, in a way, is Anaxagoras's 'everything in everything.' Or, are we to say that the parts of the Idea of 'virtue' are not integrated into the unity of a whole – are discrete and separate like Empedocles' elements or, more correctly, Plato's Ideas considered apart from their integration into the Good Itself. In this case, one would have unthought thoughts. One has the impossible choice between allowing that everything mixes (each thought thinks all other thoughts) or nothing mixes (unthought thoughts).

132c–133a: Third aporia

Doull's treatment of this *aporia* is very brief. I will present my own account of it, which so far as I am able to understand is not altogether incompatible with his view. He quite accurately shows that the step from the last *aporia*, which considers the structure of true opinion as understood in *Theaetetus*, is followed by 'dianoetic' or reasoning thought as in the ascent through the line of the *Republic*. In the arts the product made resembles the pattern. Perhaps more to the point here is how in geometry the drawn diagram is related to the concept it represents. Once Socrates allows that the relation of the fixed patterns in nature and their sensible likenesses involves a symmetrical or reciprocal relation, there is no escaping the problem of 'the third man argument.' If one is not following the argument accurately, one might say that the criticism is weak because it comes out of a concession which Socrates should not have allowed – that the relation of the two sides is symmetrical, when he should have maintained that it asymmetrical.

Plato has another interest in the argument which is closely connected with how the hypotheses in P2 are to be understood. The problem of circularity leads to 'the third man argument.' The *paradeigmata* are intended to explain their images but are themselves explained by their images. The difference between a *paradeigma* and its likenesses is that between the Idea and its appearances as the sensible individuals, between Being and Becoming. The defect of the logic of participation is that it holds two perspectives apart – the image is like its *paradeigma* and unlike it, the *paradeigma* is like its image and unlike it, the same as and different than. To stop this circulation of contraries, the requirement is that one come to the One or identical principle in a way that it contains the contraries of like and unlike, sameness and otherness, being and becoming. The reason the logic of participation is subject to 'the third man argument' is that each new 'third Idea,' which is to account for the difference or otherness of the terms of the prior division, in comprehending the identity of those terms does not negate or annul its own difference from them, and in not doing so fails to show itself to be One and comprehensive of both being and becoming, likeness, and unlikeness and so on.

133a–135c: The fourth aporia

In the introduction to the presentation of the *aporiai*, Parmenides commented that Socrates resists allowing that the Ideas are comprehensive of all multiplicity and difference because as a youth he is still held by the authority of opinion and philosophy has not taken hold of him as he was sure it would in the future. The third *aporia* began with the hope that in a *paradeigmatic* relation between the identical Idea and its images there might be a beginning to a human knowledge of the Ideas. That path was cut off because there appeared an endless reciprocal difference between the *paradeigmata* and the images. Any advance would require a new beginning in which the difference or division is contained within a prior unity. 'The *aporia*,' Doull writes, 'which occurs here is that if one take this new relation to being as an identity of the two sides, there appears against it their division – an unbridgeable gulf between thinking and its objects.'[39] The fact of their reciprocal difference from each other so understood has the consequence that not only are the Ideas themselves by themselves but so also the sensible individuals are themselves by themselves.

Unlike the earlier *aporiai*, the final *aporia*, the greatest and most difficult, does not begin with the proposal of a solution to the problem raised in the previous *aporiai*, but rather states fully the consequences of the difficulty brought out in the third *aporia*. Doull first observes that the division between what is spoken of in the *aporia* as between the human relation to its world and the divine relation to the absolute Ideas corresponds to the division in older modern philosophy of the division between the empiricists and the rationalists and within Plato's writing between the sophist and the philosopher. He then observes the consequences for the human world were this division to stand firm: '[T]here would not be justice or a political community at all.'[40] This is a problem

Plato was well aware of in the transitional dialogues like the *Protagoras, Gorgias,* and *Meno.* In *Symposium* Plato addressed the problem of the *chorimos* or gulf between the Ideas and the multiple world as it appeared in the *Phaedo.* The dialogue begins with Apollodorus, who is viewed by his companions as something of a tragic figure. He seeks the undivided good, but knows it only negatively as the nullity of all finite interests and involvements. Apollodorus, in turn, sees Glaucon and such individuals who are occupied endlessly with particular and finite pursuits as somewhat comic characters. They think they are doing something when they are really doing nothing. Doull next comments that '[t]he division between empirical and rational, as between sophist and philosopher, is a subordinate distinction.'[41] Even in the extreme remove of the arbitrary will of the tyrant 'there is a residual reason.'[42] Plato's refutation of a Callicles or Thrasymachus had the form of showing that human servitude and freedom is not of man to man but of man to the gods. The logic by which that is the case Plato begins to disclose as early as *Symposium.* The solution there took the form of showing how the finite realm of human activity and inquiry is related to the divine realm in which there is an actual possession of the absolute Good by the gods. The solution was found in the notion that in *Eros,* as intermediate between human and divine beings, and *eros* as the moving principle in the human soul, there is at once a poverty or negativity and a plenty or possession of the end. In this way, it was thought that one had found how the Good is in what is other than itself. The seeming contingent realm of finite being was to be understood as held in the sustaining ground of the Ideas, as the becoming of the Ideas, a becoming in absolute being. The limitation of that argument is that it still has the form of an image which permits one to imagine contraries coexisting without annulling each other and is expressed in *Symposium* as successive moments. Eros is at one time poor and destitute and at another time rises up and is resourceful and filled with plenty.

Doull concludes: 'The *aporia* lies in the contradiction between the omniscience of the gods and their ignorance, which follows from the separation of a human or empirical world from a world true for thought. The resolution is in a recognition that the separation of the two is impossible.'[43] Now once that point is reached the assumptions which lead to the separation will have to be given up. The reader and Socrates are now prepared to consider that if the Ideas and 'the many' are not separate and independent of each other, then the alternative path to follow would be to consider the hypothesis that they are relative to each other and sustained in their relativity by an identical principle.

The *aporiai* were introduced by Parmenides' observation that Socrates is still young, respects too much the opinions of men, and, as Doull comments, is still incapable of what is not a human but rather a divine knowledge. The *aporiai*, as Doull shows, follow the steps of the ascent in the line and Cave of human knowing from *aisthesis* to *doxa* to 'dianoetic' or reasoning thought. The necessary next step is to divine knowledge beginning from first principles and what is other than the principles known as belonging to them.

Plato, I suggest, would find in Doull's commentary on the *Parmenides* an account of his argument which understands its distinctions and integrity with greater precision than even he himself did. Plato showed little mercy on his readers when he wrote *Parmenides* and Doull has followed Plato's example in his commentary on the same. In both cases the reader is presented with the abundant issue of two long lives devoted to philosophical inquiry.

Notes

1 Kenneth M. Sayre, *Parmenides' Lesson: Translation and Explication of Plato's* Parmenides (Notre Dame: University of Notre Dame Press, 1996), xi.
2 Doull, chapter 2 above, 93.
3 Doull, 'A Commentary on Plato's *Theaetetus*,' *Dionysius* 1 (1977), 9.
4 *Sophist*, 241d.
5 G.S. Kirk, J.E. Raven, and M. Schofield, *The Presocratic Philosophers* (Cambridge: Cambridge University Press, 1957), 248; Plato, *Sophist*, 242a; Sextus, *Adv. math.* VII, 114.
6 *Presocratic Philosophers*, 400.
7 Doull, 87, above.
8 Aristotle, *Metaphysics*, 1012a 25–9.
9 Doull, 83.
10 Doull, 84.
11 *Republic*, 437b.
12 Doull, 85.
13 Ibid.
14 Ibid.

15 Ibid.
16 Doull, 86.
17 Doull, 84.
18 Doull, 100.
19 Doull, 86.
20 Doull, 88.
21 Doull, 86.
22 Doull, 102.
23 Doull, 101.
24 Hegel, *Hegel's Lectures on the History of Philosophy*, vol. 2, trans. E.S. Haldane and F.H. Simson (London: Routledge & Kegan Paul, 1974), 67.
25 Doull, 91.
26 Ibid.
27 Ibid.
28 Doull, 88.
29 *Parmenides*, 130e.
30 Doull, 89.
31 Doull, 90.
32 *Parmenides*, 131b; emphasis added.
33 Doull, 90.
34 Ibid.
35 Ibid.
36 Doull, 92.
37 Doull, 92–3.
38 Doull, 93.
39 Doull, 94.
40 Ibid.
41 Ibid.
42 Ibid.
43 Doull, 94–5.

chapter three

Virgil's Rome[1]

The Roman religion is in certain respects similar to Judaism. In both there is a preoccupation with external goods at the same time as absolute submission to the authority of abstract thought. The Jewish law as the command of the one God is of its nature universal, but the peculiar possession of the chosen people, who can expect by its careful observance to prosper in their external interests. The relation of the faithful obedience to the law to prosperity is to be sought in God. Humanly the two may be separated beyond comprehension, as with Job. In the Roman religion the relation of the two is made explicit. There the service of the supreme god is through devotion to a universal human end, the 'res publica,' to which all particular interests are to be sacrificed, not in inward piety only, but by obedience to a magisterial authority. This service of the state the Romans call piety; the hero of the Roman epics is the 'pious Aeneas.' In piety there is demanded of the individual an abstract unification of ends. Many and even trivial ends are also divinized, are seen to have in them a relation of man to God in which he knows himself as free self-consciousness. These many ends are not comprehended in the one political end, but rather subjected to it. The necessity which was above the Greek gods is here the externality and constraint experienced in this utilitarian relation. The limit of this religion and of the Roman state is that the individual should free himself of this necessity, should know himself as a free person possessed of rights.

In the Roman religion there is not that division of state and family, of political virtue and natural affection found in the Greek religion. Nor are Roman institutions patriarchal as with the Jewish people, where the state can be regarded as an extended family. The individuality capable of both the domestic and the political relation in the division and contrariety of the two, which in the end was discovered among the Greeks, is present in the Roman religion and institutions. Though with the Romans family and state are strongly separated, there does not occur between them the conflict of opposed religious principles of Eumenides and Olympians. There is one principle of both institutions, namely the subjectivity of magistrate and 'paterfamilias.' How state and family are related, the logic of essential collisions between them, cannot be presented within the limits of Greek tragedy.

The *Aeneid* is of all writings the most instructive on the nature of Roman religion and institutions. The poet knows perfectly that his subject, namely the fulfilment of Roman history in the Augustan empire, cannot be treated epically in the manner of Homer without altering profoundly the concept of the gods, of fate or necessity, of the relation of humans to the one and the other. His subject comprises the domestic as well as the state religion of the Romans. A divided epic treatment of private and public life, as in the Iliad and Odyssey, would not be possible where the common ground of the two has become explicitly known. There is not only the fatal connection of the two institutions which the Greek tragic poet knows how to reveal, but the root of this fatality in self-conscious freedom is already discovered, is the principle in Roman institutions. The Roman poet does not have to disclose a self-conscious principle, an unmoved mover, beyond all the finite, but can present a subjectivity for which fate and necessity are not beyond it but occur in the fulfilment of its purposes.

The Roman Jupiter is not Zeus, who is impotent to control the fatal course of human events but must sorrowfully give up cherished purposes. Fate is instead only the form and process of fulfilment of Jupiter's will. He is not to the other gods the first among equals but exercises over them an 'imperium' to which in the end they must bow, even if, as Juno in the poem, they invoke against it all passions, good and evil. The human embodiment of this absolute will is not an Achilles conscious of the conflict of virtue and morality, but the triumphant consul or, most completely, Augustus, in whom, after vanquishing his enemies and bringing to an end a century of civil discord, all military and civil power is effectively united. To a contemporary culture where the *logos* of Christianity is largely contracted either to 'praxis' or to intuitive immediacy, the preparation of it in Roman religion and institutions is not easily grasped. What is there the principle and moving interest is likely now to appear only abhorrent, unnatural, and beyond belief. But in Roman authors is expressed the desire to overcome nature and mortality, not abstractly as in Judaism, not theoretically as in Greek religion and philosophy, but in history and external reality.

The labours of Aeneas as those of Heracles are ascribed to the hostility of Juno or Hera. One might look for a similar conclusion to the argument of the *Aeneid* to that of Sophocles' *Trachiniae* or of Euripides' *Hercules Furens.* The differences are very instructive. The former of these Hellenistic works ends in the apotheosis of Heracles, his death and divinization being simultaneous.[2] The Heracles of Euripides survives the extreme labours of his descent to Hades, his madness and the murder of his children, to enter painfully at the end into a rational benevolence, where the destructive conflict of virtue and natural individuality is brought to rest.[3] Virgil's hero descends likewise into Hell, but is not on his reascent afflicted with madness. He is rather from that point in himself exempt from Juno's rage. Her continuing hatred works instead through the Latins and their allies. Through Allecto, the spirit of mad unreason, she inspires the Latins to refuse alliance with the Trojans contrary to repeated signs of the divine will.[4] The Latins in the poem live still in rustic simplicity. Their religion is of Saturn and other nature gods, not of the free, dominant will which is Jupiter. It is they, and not Aeneas, who are subject to a wild confusion of purpose, where they are unable to acquiesce in the divine right of Aeneas to rule, but must suffer a reduction of their natural will to the point where they know submission to be necessary and liberating.

Aeneas in his wanderings carries the Penates with him.[5] He is not an Odysseus returning home to Penelope, and then also to the ancient Laertes. His wife, by whom he would be attached to Troy, is lost there in the sack of the city. As founder of the Roman race, he is appropriately subject to the authority of his father Anchises, whom he carries from the burning city.[6] The family for him is centred in this paternal relation.

After the death of Anchises in Sicily, Aeneas is not at first capable of the paternal authority which falls to him. He is distracted at Carthage by an alliance with Dido, founded on nature and passion, which obstructs his pious obedience to the plan of Jupiter, that he should found a people able to rule themselves and others by reason and law.[7] Superficially considered, his separation from Dido is like that of Jason from Medea. But in the cold Stoical reason which dismisses Dido there is not calculating ambition, but pious acceptance of a still inarticulate movement to a principle of rational freedom.

In the following book he approaches some way to the knowledge of this principle.[8] In the funeral games on the anniversary of his father's death Aeneas and the Trojan men, honouring the dead hero, are turned to the sources of human authority in Hades. But they are powerless in this relation to restrain the rebellious desire of the Trojan women to end their wanderings, to settle in Sicily. For them, as for Antigone, family piety has its existence among the living in the natural love of women for those closest by blood, a pure devotion of the living to the implicit eternity of the dead. Roman domestic piety should exist rather in a living individuality itself freed from nature. The Trojan women would live in a Hellenic piety in Sicily. This being refused them, they can be instigated by Juno to burn the fleet. In this contest between family piety and political reason there is not mutual destruction but victory for the state.[9] But to consolidate that victory and to know the principle in which it is grounded, Aeneas must make his descent to Hades.

Aeneas learns from Anchises, not what was necessary merely to a homecoming, as did Odysseus from the ghost of Teiresias, nor what was needful towards finding a promised land in Latium, but the whole source of Roman history to Augustus.[10] His journey through the underworld to Anchises among the purged spirits in Elysium prepares him to receive that account. As in a Platonic myth all the corruptions imprinted on the soul by an irrational life are exposed to him, and the purgation of the passions by which some are made capable of a just and benevolent life. Aeneas comes to know the nature of the soul, the opposition of good and evil in it and the 'amor fati'[11] as its primary desire, which moves it to desire to cross over from the living to the kingdom of Dis, and thence, when all passions and beneficent interests have sunk into the pure potentiality of Lethe, to return again to the labours of mortal life. In this knowledge is seen the true sense of the Roman 'patria potestas,' the relation through it of the individual to the inner divine principle which sustains the division of reason and sensibility. In the language of the ancient Greek religion Anchises departed would be called a 'hero,' protective of the living as Theseus and Oedipus at Athens. But here the nature of the protection is more explicit: Aeneas, having learned fully what is in this piety to the Penates, is thereby made capable of founding the Roman state. For this work is nothing else than to make of Trojans and Latins one people in whom uncorrupted nature and political reason will be united. Family and state have the same end, namely the knowledge that fate, the necessity which, as well in the realm of Dis as in that of Jupiter, ever annuls the division of natural will from reason, – that fate is not alien to human freedom but the process in which it is realized.

The vision of Roman history Aeneas receives from his father is expressed in the language of Stoic pantheism. Returning from that dreamlike inspiration to his political task, he both carries with him and has forgotten that knowledge.[12] It is with him as the end to which in the contingencies of human life he must find his way with the ambiguous guidance of signs and oracles. The end of his labour is to establish a people who will in the fulfilment of their history realize a benevolent Stoic humanity. Aeneas as founder of the Roman race has to fuse together into one the elements of this people. These are first the passivity of an original garden, an idyllic state, of which the poet had written already in his *Eclogues*. The second element had been the subject of his *Georgics*, an austere life in the laborious agricultural arts, where luxury and an indefinite proliferation of desires were unknown. With these qualities of the Latins is to be combined the ruling will of the Trojans, itself purged from the passions by acceptance of family discipline and adherence to the primary political end. Against the formation of this people, who should not aspire only to a peace, such as the Judaic prophets announce, but should impose peace on the nations, Juno will incite, first, all the evil passions of the soul. The fallen or evil state is the individuality which, involved in its passions, would make itself its end as against this system of utility. As her final weapon will remain the reluctance of the Latins to submit their rustic independence, with its multiplicity of ends, to the political reason which knows one primary end, the resistance of Saturn to Jupiter Capitolinus.

By these forces Juno animates the Latins and their allies against the Trojans.[13] She incites first among them a wild bacchanalian folly, the beginning of subjective freedom, preventing thus the conclusion of an alliance of Latin and Trojan, which the wise Latinus knows by many a sign to be the inevitable will of the gods. This spirit had to be subdued in the Latins before they will be capable of a stable political will, such as they will receive when they are one people with the Trojans. The defeat of the Latins is at the same time their education, a purgation of the passions. After this spirit has been defeated, there remains the deeper and more settled opposition of Turnus, the revolt of nature against the authority of abstract reason.[14] Amata, wife of king Latinus, is unable to follow him to this extreme and kills herself. His ally at the end is his sister Juturna, a nature spirit, between whom there is the same immediate sympathy as Achilles received from Thetis, his divine mother. In the Hellenic religion the Olympian gods wrested sovereignty from the older nature gods, who, if banished to Tartarus, had still their relation to humans in the opposition of natural feeling to reason and political virtue. Saturn and the other primitive nature spirits of the Roman religion will be integrated differently with the higher gods. As in the family so in the state religion, nature is to be subjected rigorously to an abstract sovereign reason, to be preserved and given place on that basis.

Likewise the political education of Aeneas and the Trojans is incomplete until they have taken into themselves the powers which Juno directs against them. The Roman hero, returned from the underworld and forgetful of the knowledge there received, might be compared with the Oedipus who was destroyed by his disregard for the instinctive prophetic vision of Teiresias. In the Roman religion this moment of unformed intuitive feeling is present, but firmly under the authority of the magistrate, who can use it for the purposes of the state. The poet therefore has Aeneas initiated into this primitive wisdom by the Arcadian Evander settled on the site of the future Rome. Evander knows both this unformed religious sense and a freedom from it in the simplicity of rustic life, where particular human ends are realized and laboriously maintained against the opposing forces of the natural environment. In this life, which Virgil has celebrated in the *Georgics*, there has not emerged a subjectivity which has become its own end and set itself against these particular ends. It is the tendency to this subjectivity – to an individuality which can free itself from the dutiful life of the farmer and the citizen soldier and give itself without scruple to its immediate interests and desires – which Aeneas, like an old Roman aristocrat, must be able to recognize and suppress when it makes its appearance among the people. What Evander has shown him, Aeneas makes his own in the war with the Latins.[15]

In the first part of the war, where the Trojans are besieged in their camp, Aeneas, thus inwardly prepared by his visit to Evander and allied with him, confronts the blind strength of Dionysiac fury. This subjectivity has its complete embodiment in the sadistic tyrant Mezentius.[16] Aeneas is not, like the Pentheus of Eurpides, destroyed by a spirit more concrete than his own. Tyranny was for Plato the extreme point in the corruption of the good polity, where the destruction was complete and a new beginning necessary. At that point a negativity or otherness had appeared which the state could not contain. The Roman state has a greater stability. Against its ends, a plebeian individuality, concerned with its everyday interests, has the same impotence as is felt now by a like individuality against an uncontrollable 'technology.' The individual who knows himself more than finite ends is powerless against them, is made the servant of his own creatures. Why this is so becomes plain in a further consideration of the Roman state.

In the second part of the war,[17] where the Trojans advance in turn to besiege the Latin capital, Turnus is moved neither by his former Dionysiac unreason nor by any prudential reflections but out of despair. If the Jewish people were promised a land of their own in return for obedience to the one God, in Turnus is expressed the despair of the conquered peoples who had to surrender to the Romans the independent possession of their lands. Aeneas in the final battle is like Achilles who could not rest until he avenged the death of Patroclus on Hector. But Pallas is not to Aeneas the Patroclus whose friendship Achilles esteemed above duty to the Greeks. He is the son of Evander, the faithful Arcadian ally, who has wisely submitted to the Trojans. The Olympians found it necessary that Hector should die by the greater virtue of Achilles. The necessity to which Turnus succumbs is the implacable political will of the founder of the Roman race. In contemporary language there is here the relation of an existential subjectivity to the utilitarian objectivity of a Marxist society. The further development of the relation of individual to state among the Romans is therefore peculiarly instructive.

The Aeneid celebrates the Augustan principate as a renewal of the golden age. The sense in which this is true, and not rhetorical adulation of an imperial patron, has been indicated. To the Christian, Christ is the second Adam, in whom an original animal life in unbroken unity with nature and human reason in its whole capacity for good and evil are brought together. The Roman poet shows these elements to be more strongly combined in the Roman republic than among other nations: the subjectivity to which the Jew and Greek is awakened by the logic of their institutions, and leads beyond them to a higher contemplative life, appears to have a practical satisfaction in Roman institutions. There is here, one might say, a 'praxis' beyond theory. But the limits of the system are already conspicuous in Virgil's account. Aeneas, to be capable of his work, must attain to an independent subjectivity, and Turnus must either come to this same radical independence of all natural attachments or be destroyed. The argument of the *Aeneid* is that the Roman 'res publica' is for this subjectivity a sufficient end, that indeed there cannot be a higher end which might be preferred to it. But in this argument the negativity in this end is neglected, the evil which the individual also experiences in it. The principate itself, which appears to Virgil the perfection of the republic, imposes also a reflection on this negativity. The dominant class in the state are made to feel their impotence to know the universal practical end of advancing the power of the republic as also their dependence on the whim of an imperial master. In relation to the same end the highest freedom and the deepest debasement and servitude are experienced by the senatorial class in the first century of the principate. The logic of this experience is the same as that of a later time, when humanity and the revolution appeared a sufficient end and was ever found instead to be destructive of personal freedom. What comes to light in this is the inadequacy of external ends, even the most comprehensive, to subjective freedom.

Among the Roman multitude this inadequacy appeared as a disintegration of political and domestic institutions, as a loss of interest in the state and a preoccupation with immediate satisfaction. The nature which had been constrained and brought into the service of the political good was released. Political and domestic virtue appeared abstractions, though there was lacking then the psychology which could designate their rejection as 'liberation.'

This corruption of Roman institutions is to be seen as intrinsic to them. The Roman order appears in the Aeneid as resting on a concrete spiritual principle, which can be spoken of in the language of Stoic pantheism. Human freedom in this view is to have its end not in external goods only but in the universal creative *logos*. But there is here the same difficulty as in Marxism and other contemporary forms, that an underlying universal reason in which men would be delivered from alienation, at home in the world, has its realization in the external ends of a practical attitude, in which individuals can find either an abstract, repressed freedom or a limitless pursuit of contingent goods.

Out of this experience was formed in antiquity a criticism and rejection of the practical standpoint as primary. The individual might attempt to find his freedom in Stoicism itself, holding to the principle of the practical attitude and regarding the unreason he met with everywhere in the actual course of life as a foolishness which should not be. One would in this way maintain a positive relation to the practical world. This attitude informs what is best in Roman literature of the silver age. A deeper reflection is found in sceptical philosophy, which virtually knows the corruption as a dividedness in the soul itself, as an independence which is also, in all human arts or definite purposes, an incorrigible dependence and alienation.[18] The Sceptic still holds, like the Stoic, to his abstract freedom, but has in fact exposed this freedom as contradictory and unstable. The same result would be everywhere evident in contemporary 'praxis' but for the residual momentum of an empiricism which can regard its logic as arbitrary without knowing this to be scepticism.

The scepticism of the Roman Empire is to be distinguished from the sophistic which greatly occupied Plato's attention, against which he and more definitely Aristotle could show how knowledge of true being was possible. The principle remains the same: a subjectivity conscious of its own infinity, as knowing the distinction of being and not-being related to itself. The scepticism of Protagoras and Gorgias had for its object the language of persuasion, of the assembly and the courts, or else was merely formal and without a determinate object. To this scepticism, Plato could oppose a dialectic able to discover in the good an objective principle of the finite. Against Aristotle's science of the finite, which knew the extremes of finite division as united in substance, and therein stabilized, this formal scepticism was to no effect. The later scepticism has power over Aristotelian science for the reason that its principle is implicitly the concrete subjectivity which Aristotle had shown to be the highest genus of substance. The Stoic or Sceptic who places the good in *ataraxia* or tranquillity of mind has freed himself negatively from the alienation of involvement in external ends. He falls short still of what Aristotle knew, that there is an intelligence which is its own end as comprehending the being of its objects and its own division. But reflecting on its own dividedness and contradiction, and the contradiction of possessing its objects and being lost in their externality, this subjectivity discovers again an ideal world and knows the genera of that world as in its thinking self-consciousness. The nature of the practical Roman spirit only comes to light in the Neoplatonic idealism which can again regard the outer direction of intelligence to a presupposed sensible world as a subordinate attitude. In Judaism the interest of humans in worldly ends belonged to a fallen state, unless it were corrected by obedience to the law and knowledge of the one God beyond finitude and division. In this relation the opposition of good and evil, as of being and not-being, is not seen as intrinsic to human nature but rather as a separation from God, which ought not to have been. The restored relation of man to God, as already treated above, entails in this view a negation of difference: human finitude and individuality is without ground in the one God. From the Hellenic religion and the philosophical theology which developed out of it was derived a knowledge of God as comprehending division, and of man as related to God through the difference and unity of his sensuous and rational being. In this result, one might say, the restoration of the fall is not abstract but inclusive of human individuality. In Roman religion and institutions this concrete attitude, in which the older Hellenic religion and philosophy terminate, would be realized practically. But this practicality appears in the end as the way in which an implicitly concrete subjectivity comes to itself, overcoming both the negativity of external ends and its own dividedness. Fall and return, good and evil, appear thus as not external but rather as constitutive of a concrete nature. It can be said therefore that in the Roman religion the preparation for the Christian religion is complete.

The Kingdom of God

The scepticism in which the Roman religion ends, if negatively it is an alienation from the world of finite interests in which this religion has its reality, is also the possibility of a spiritual relation of man and God in which their difference will be contained. In the Judaic religion there was the knowledge that the true relation of man to God was beyond the finite, in the knowledge of the one transcendent God. The Hellenic religion sought a finite unity of human and divine and came at the end to a purified spirituality in which the natural and finite was comprehended. The Roman religion was a conflict of this infinite spirituality with a universal worldly end, where finally this end appeared as a pure negativity, as the separation of purposive activity, the relation of purpose, means, and realized end from all content. Out of this purgation appears then as the underlying truth of this religion the infinite spiritual relation which is its own end.

This result may be taken, as in Neoplatonism, as the immediate intuitive relation of self-consciousness which has freed itself from the finite distinctions to the One, this known negatively as beyond division and finitude. But in Judaism there was already present a knowledge of God as thus beyond all finitude, and of a separation of man from this transcendent One. In relation to the Judaic God, this self-consciousness has not to overcome its own dividedness but its separation from God. The negation of division has the objective form of a development of the one God to the concept of God as concrete subjectivity.

The creativity of this principle is not, as in stoicism, of a world whose finite content is ever lost in the process of its return to the creative principle. Nor again is God the initiator of a world where the creature dissolves in the face of its transcendent creator. The creature is instead the manifestation of the creator, in that division and finitude is a moment of its triune form. The creature is thus not exposed as a nullity only to a sceptical thought, but is the object of a thinking which knows it as true, as disclosing truly its idea or concept.

Man in relation to this principle is neither divided from what he knows as his true end nor does he seek it in the immanence of practical activity.

His finitude and need is rather a difference in which his infinite good appears, an otherness which is not for itself but manifests its origin without dissolution into it. The developed concept of God in this new religion is as the Trinity, as a thinking which knows the *logos* by which it creates as equal with itself in its absolute difference. The true relation of man to this principle is through a thinking which knows it as the origin and end in which human finitude subsists.

That God was revealed in Christ has no meaning within the original Judaism, since the one God is not such as to be revealed in any creature. In Neoplatonism knowledge of the One is mediated by the universal procession and return. There is a spiritual relation of human and divine, but at the point where division is transcended and passes into intuitive unity. In the Christian religion the mediation is not thus evanescent, but division and difference belong to the spiritual relation itself. This doctrine can be seen by Christians as the fulfilment of Judaism and found implicitly in the Old Testament. There the fall of man from an original animal perfection is related but, as also in the Roman religion, is thought to be corrected by submission to a law, by establishing the difference of a good and an evil will. As against this abstract correction Christ is for Christians the second Adam, in whom the division between the law and the natural will is comprehended. The law is to be fulfilled, and not replaced by the unreason of an immediate individuality. As in the Aristotelian psychology, man is at once an immediate sensuous individual and universal; these moments, taken separately, are abstractions. As one with himself in the radical division of nature and thought, Christ is the full and adequate revelation of the God who is neither simple unity only beyond division nor limited by any presupposed being, but knows all that is different from him as himself.

This religion is announced as the Kingdom of God. It does not exist humanly as the political reason of the Roman state, nor as a Jewish theocracy, as the authority of a law which should be antecedent to human reason. Nor again is the Kingdom of God thought to be revealed in an anarchic will, which holds to earth and nature against abstract thought. The ruler appropriate to that attitude is the 'Fuhrer' or 'charismatic' individual. The divine government spoken of in the Gospels is rather the relation of the individual collected out of division to concrete unity to the Trinitarian God known as the principle of this concrete individuality. In this relation all institutions and human authorities become a matter of indifference, since they pertain to those to whom power, wealth, and other external goods are a care, as having independent being.

The proof of this divine kingdom could not be in words only, or in the thought only of the philosopher who knew what was true in Hellenic polytheism, but in the life and death of Christ. For thus the negativity and evil of human life, at the extreme the separation of man from God, and the negation of this separation, the concept of the Kingdom of God, could have the form of fact, of immediate, empirical proof. The factual proof is proof only for those who knew its mediation in the teaching of Christ; it is for the Apostles proof of what they received in the universality of language. That word and fact together express the unity of the concept, the truth of the teaching, is the knowledge of Christ which had absolute authority for the Apostles and through them for the Church. The Church knows the life and death of Christ only by report and on the authority of the Apostles. The externality and incorrigible uncertainty of this knowledge of fact it completes by presenting to the community of believers the total doctrine of the God whose concept is to be revealable adequately in the man who is the universal *logos*, who dies and is risen, whose unity with the Father the Church participates as the Spirit which brings it to its true nature.

The ancient Church knew no institutions other than itself which could be called Christian in more than an ancillary sense. But this ancillary relation was not easily discovered with the institutions which most nearly occupied the same ground as itself, namely the universal empire, whose *logos* also was thought to exist in one man. The Church might be indifferent to political ends or might apologetically commend the virtue of its members to the state. The state might persecute or tolerate the Church. It was evident after some centuries that the practical and political virtue of the Roman state was not alien to the Church, but a human reason requiring to be completed by an ampler Christian reason. The state could in turn find support from the Church, such as neither the merely practical spirit of its official religion would afford nor the many religions of the nations, which were not capable of a secular political will. In this Augustinian solution, as it may be called, the illusion is dispelled that the Church can maintain another and purer virtue than the world. The 'civitas Dei' and the 'civitas terrena' are inextricably involved with each other. But it lies in the concept of Christianity that this separation of an ancillary human reason and work from the divine work could not persist. The 'civitas Dei' and the 'civitas terrena,' if they stand in this external relation, must the one draw to itself the primary interest of Christians, the other corrupt the Church and draw it again into the realm of finite ends against which it was originally constituted. Partly the desire to be free of this division had its satisfaction in a monastic life, where worldly interests could be renounced at their root by giving up family, the competitive work in useful pursuits, the illusions of personal freedom. But participation in the Christian good through this ideal life must be abstract. There was lacking to it what the Christian knew to have been realized in the life and death of Christ: external immediacy, need, the evils of the fall, were not there rejected but revealed as one substance with the universal.

To the Church the formation of a secular life which would be neither ancillary to it nor abstract has ever been difficult to understand and accept. But the moving cause of a Christian secularity is in the Christian belief itself, the desire of an 'intellectus fidei,' not theoretic only but also active. The root of this desire is in the difference between the revelation itself, the divine idea in its absolute concreteness, and the representation of it in language and image, in the participation in it sacramentally. The 'intellectus fidei' seeks an assurance which would not be historical only, not in sacramental reconciliation only, to which is opposed the experience of common life. Christianity was revealable originally in the completion of an historical mediation, where it could be known as actual, in the unity of thought and external reality, in 'the Word made flesh.' Word, image, and sacrament are the likeness of an original, which they may truly express, but not give certain knowledge of it.

What then are Christian institutions? It must remain for another occasion to give more than the general concept of them, as this emerges from the whole argument. Family, economic society, state can be thought Christian so far as they have a spiritual form, have their end not in external goods themselves, but in these as the appearance of an idea or concept. One will thus say that when the ideality of monastic life loses its abstractness and becomes the end and moving form in those goods which the monk renounces, then there is a beginning of Christian institutions. 'Civitas Dei' and 'civitas terrena' begin to have a common Christian end when an emperor directs all orders.

> Ut pax sit et concordia et unanimitas cum omni populo Christiano, inter episcopos, abbates, comites, iudices, et omnes ubique seu maiores, seu minores personas; quia nihil Deo sine pace placet, nec munus sanctae oblationis ad altare, sicut in evangelio ipso Domino praecipiente legimus ... Diliges proximum tuum sicut te ipsum ... In hoc enim praecepto discernuntur filii Dei et filii diaboli; quia filii diaboli semper dissensiones et discordias movere satagunt; filii autem Dei semper paci et dilectioni student.
>
> Caroli Magni Capitulare Ecclesiasticum, Anno 789 (*M.G.H. Leges*, I, p. 63)[19]

Notes

1 Extracted from 'The Christian Origin of Contemporary Institutions Part One,' *Dionysius* 6 (1982), 151–64.
2 Sophocles, *Trachiniae*, at the end.
3 Euripides, *Hercules Furens*, 1313–1429.
4 *Aeneid* 7.
5 *Aeneid* 2, 717 and elsewhere.
6 *Aeneid* 2, 767ff.
7 *Aeneid* 4.
8 *Aeneid* 5.
9 *Aeneid* 5, 654ff.
10 *Aeneid* 6.
11 *Aeneid* 6, 313–4; 745–51.
12 *Aeneid* 6, 894–900. Aeneas emerges from Hell by the ivory gate, by which pass false dreams. In this way the poet explains how the hero, instructed by his father, is all the same exposed to the uncertainties of empirical knowledge.
13 *Aeneid* 7.
14 *Aeneid* 11.
15 *Aeneid* 8.
16 *Aeneid* 7, 10.
17 *Aeneid* 11.
18 On the nature of ancient scepticism, see Hegel, *Gesch. Phil.*, I; II, D; for its difference from the more recent scepticism, see D.K. House, unpublished Liverpool thesis on Sextus Empiricus.
19 So this peace should be both concord and unanimity with all the Christian people, amongst bishops, abbots, electors/counts, judges, and all everywhere whether major or minor persons; because nothing to God is pleasing without peace, not even the office of holy oblastion at the altar, just as in the gospel we read of the Lord himself teaching ... Love your neighbour as yourself ... In this very precept are distinguished the sons of God and the sons of the devil; because the sons of the devil always have their hands full to move dissentions and discords; however the sons of God always are eager for peace and love.

COMMENTARY

The Eternity of Rome: Virgil's Doctrine and Its Relation to Plato

COLIN STARNES

> But in Roman authors is expressed the desire to overcome nature and mortality, ... not theoretically as in Greek religion and philosophy, but in history and external reality.
>
> J.A. Doull[1]

At the start of the *Aeneid* Jupiter explains to Venus his plan for the yet-unfounded city of Rome. Aeneas's descendants, he says, shall be called Romans, and '[f]or these I set no limits, world or time,/ But make the gift of empire without end' (I, 374–5).[2] In other words, Virgil is saying that Rome, once founded, will be eternal by the will of the supreme deity which nothing in the universe has the power to disturb. The thought of Rome as the 'eternal city' is of such long standing that the revolutionary aspect of Virgil's teaching can easily pass us by. At the same time, we are perhaps tempted to dismiss it as mere poetic or chauvinistic hyperbole since, as *we* know, Virgil was wrong. *His* Rome, the city of which he spoke, did not prove to be eternal, but instead eventually declined and fell to Christianity.

Plato had taught that no city could last forever but that, by an inexorable logic, even the ideal commonwealth was forced to decline through all the various possible forms of government to the lowest, tyranny, and from this to rise again, ascending eventually back to the true republic in a never-ending cycle.[3] It is against the background of this position that Virgil's doctrine is revolutionary. He perceived that Rome possessed a principle of stability that could both control, and was proof against, any unforseen circumstance. In terms of this power he saw Rome, alone of all cities, as exempt from the Platonic cycle. In this paper I will show why Plato maintained that no form of government could last forever, why Virgil thought Rome was eternal despite Plato's reasons, and, finally, why Virgil, though right in relation to Plato, proved wrong when his city came into conflict with Christianity. Unless we can do this it will not be possible to maintain the truth of all three positions.

1. The Cycle of Justice in Plato's *Republic*

At the start of Book II of the *Republic* Plato turns to a consideration of the state because he thinks that it may help in discovering the nature of justice. By the end of Book I difficulties have been found in all the main contemporary opinions about its nature as expressed by Cephalus, Polemarchus, and Thrasymachus. But even though, in questioning the others, Socrates seems to know what he is talking about, *he* concludes that, 'for me the present outcome of the discussion is that I know nothing' (354b). He has been able to bring certain seemingly valid objections against the prevailing views and yet, because the argument has not revealed the nature of justice in itself, he has no way of knowing whether his objections are informed by a true intuition or if they merely come from some ingrained prejudice that is as open to question as those of the other speakers. It is at this point that Socrates suggests they look for justice not in the individual but where, as everyone agrees, it is to be found on a larger scale and thus, presumably, will be easier to discern – that is, in a city or state (368d).

This extremely important transition determines the whole of the rest of the argument. At first blush it seems like a startling non sequitur. We can agree, like Adeimantus, that we *do* speak of justice in a man and in a city (368e), and we can also be prepared to follow Socrates' plan of looking for justice in a city and then turning to see if it is the same in an individual (368d), but in doing this it seems that Socrates's analogy becomes the real starting-point of the argument. He has this flash of insight that justice might be the same in both a city and in an individual and the argument proceeds from there – but in this case why did Plato start with the discussion of the first book?[4]

Through the first book Socrates has shown by his questions that the opinions about justice held by Cephalus, Polemarchus, and Thrasymachus are contradicted by other opinions which both he, and they too, in some sense hold. At this point the two sides are simply at loggerheads, for even though 'Thrasymachus blushed' (350d) at the answers Socrates has been able to elicit from him – because they are the clear contrary to what he began with – he complains that he has been forced to agree with Socrates. He does so reluctantly, without conviction, and merely because Socrates has, as it were, been able to fight with his own choice of weapons. Thrasymachus maintains that Socrates won't allow him to speak freely but merely poses his questions, and that all he, Thrasymachus, is permitted to do is to 'nod assent and dissent' (350e) – as if he had only to read the lines of a play scripted by Socrates.[5]

Socrates knows this and knows that if the situation were only a little different, so that Thrasymachus could pick his own methods – barely contained threat of force, anger, sarcasm, bald assertion, and bluster[6] – he too would find himself in an impotent position similar to the one in which he had managed to put Thrasymachus. In other words, Socrates has no more liking for Thrasymachus's methods than Thrasymachus does for his. For this reason the conclusion of the first book – that justice is virtue and wisdom (350c, d) and leads to a happy life (354a) – is fragile and unstable even though Thrasymachus has in some way agreed to it. This instability is why Socrates says he is unsatisfied with it.

Somehow, if the inquiry is to proceed, a way must be found to get beyond these conflicting opinions – which is to say that Socrates must find some method of inquiry that is acceptable to all. This is what his analogy with the state is intended to provide. He proposes a fresh start at a point before all the various prejudices and opinions which each of the speakers, himself included, possess – and one from which all can proceed by means of a thinking which is common to all. He does this by turning to a labour in which all can join, which is the construction – in thought – of a city. Socrates begins as it were from the ground up where nothing is established and where, at each stage, each of the building blocks and each of their relations can be examined in thought. Thus, when he suggests the analogy of the city, it is to move the discussion not towards concrete reality but in the opposite direction – away from that and towards the intelligible. In other words, the entire discussion of the city is purely theoretical. It would not serve his purpose if anything that followed was to be taken as referring to some particular city that either was, is, or will be – for in this case the whole realm of the particular would find its way back into the discussion and the conflict of unexamined and ungrounded opinions in the first book would simply repeat itself.

Now the great objection to this procedure is that while one might allow that a city so constructed in thought is indeed the best, it does not follow that 'what is proposed is possible' (450c). Socrates' answer comes down unflinchingly on the side of the theoretical (cf. 472d–473b). In short, he takes it for granted that, as actions 'partake of exact truth less than speech,' it is impossible for the ideal city to be embodied in action without some diminution of its intelligible nature – and here we must think chiefly of its eternal stability. What Socrates has in mind is that the essence of anything as recognized by thought – say, for example, of a circle – can only be embodied in a greater or lesser degree in earthly circles drawn in sand or turned on a lathe which are, on close enough inspection, only imperfect copies of the ideal and which, because of their natural matter, are liable to decay and corruption while the ideal circle is incorruptible and eternal.[7] For this reason he holds that even in the best of circumstances the ideal city of thought can only be approximately embodied on earth, and consequently, for his argument, it is enough if he can show that the ideal city could be approximated in the world and what it would look like.

Socrates is very clear about the standard against which the ideal city must be judged if it is to avoid the charge of being irrelevant to human affairs. He says:

> [N]either city nor polity nor man either will ever be perfected until some chance compels this uncorrupted remnant of philosophers, who now bear the stigma of uselessness, to take charge of the state whether they wish it or not, and constrains the citizens to obey them, or else until by some divine inspiration a genuine passion for true philosophy takes possession either of the sons of the men now in power and sovereignty or of themselves. To affirm that either or both of these things cannot possibly come to pass is, I say, quite unreasonable. Only in that case could we be justly ridiculed as uttering things as futile as daydreams are. (499b, c)

The rule of the philosopher/king, which the argument has shown to be the 'smallest change that would bring a state to this [true and just] manner of government' (473b), is safe from the charge of irrelevance if it is conceded that it could possibly come to pass in the world and among men. Socrates goes on to specify the exact sense in which he means his words to be interpreted:

> If, then, the best philosophical natures have ever been constrained to take charge in infinite time past, or now are in some barbaric region far beyond our ken, or shall hereafter be, we are prepared to maintain our contention that the constitution we have described has been, is, or will be realized when this philosophical Muse has taken control of the state. It is not a thing impossible to happen, nor are we speaking of impossibilities. That it is difficult we too admit. (499c, d)

In other words, the discussion of the ideal city in the *Republic* would be a 'futile daydream,' a mere 'wish-thought' (450d) or fantasy – which Socrates himself scorns – and impossible in Plato's sense, only if its realization depended on something that lay demonstrably beyond the capacities of human nature as defined; for in this case it would not be a community of humans, but of gods or of some other species. However, beyond guarding against logical errors of this sort, Plato is quite unconcerned to show how his state can be realized in the world. It is enough provided that his listeners agree that it could be, given *infinite time and place.* Circumstances, individuals, and in short the whole realm of particulars may not have been right at the time in Athens – or anywhere else in Greece – for a philosopher/king to come to power in a city 'adapted to his nature' (497a), but, as Socrates says, no one can reasonably say that it is utterly impossible and could not happen anywhere in the world given an infinity of time.

These changing and unforeseeable circumstances, which are the very things that make it possible to say that the ideal state might someday and somewhere be approximately realized, are also the things which Plato, with strict logic, recognizes as making it impossible for any embodiment of the ideal state to remain forever – granted that it has actually come into existence. A very unusual set of conditions is required for the true state to come into the world. Somehow the rarity of a genuine philosophical nature must have been properly nurtured yet have escaped the corruption to which it is prone (492–495) – perhaps through the accident of exile or illness (496b, c). And then, since that nature can do nothing unless there is 'an element [in the state] having the same conception of its constitution that [the philosopher has] in framing its laws' (497d), the citizens of an existing, corrupt, state would have somehow to be content to let the philosopher reorganize it in order to produce such an element – which Plato, with heavy irony, imagines as happening most speedily and easily if all its inhabitants over the age of ten agreed to be sent out into the fields (for manual work) while the philosopher was given a free hand to bring up *their* children in *his* way (541a). Plato recognized that such things were beyond any human power to engineer because, as particular and changeable, they could not be foreseen or controlled with infallible certainty, and for this reason he teaches that an approximate embodiment of the ideal state would necessarily depend on some happy fortune or else on the intervention of the gods. In either case, it depends on things that are beyond what is in our power to know and control.

It is this dependence on particular circumstances beyond our ken that will also lead inevitably to the degeneration of the true city once it has been established. Plato discusses this degeneration in relation to the one point where reason and nature must come together perfectly and without fail if the ideal city is to continue – that is, in the begetting of those with a philosophical nature to be its rulers. As Socrates says: '[T]he laws of prosperous birth or infertility for your race, the men you have bred to be your rulers will not for all their wisdom ascertain by reasoning combined with sensation, but they will escape them, and there will be a time when they will beget children out of season' (546b).

In modern terms, the problem is that while *in general* the rulers can do everything in human power to reproduce men of like nature to themselves, mating the best with the best, etc., *in particular* they cannot, as it were, know exactly *which* sperm should unite with *which* egg. Insofar as our knowledge does not extend this deeply into the hidden secrets of nature's particulars, we cannot say at what precise moment the union must be accomplished to achieve this end, and thus, sooner or later, Socrates says,

> guardians, missing this, [will] bring together brides and bridegrooms unseasonably, [and] the offspring will not be wellborn or fortunate. Of such offspring the previous generation will establish the best, to be sure, in office, but still these, being unworthy, and having entered into the powers of their fathers, will first as guardians begin to neglect us, paying too little heed to music and then to gymnastics, so that our young men will deteriorate in their culture, and the rulers selected from them will not approve themselves very efficient guardians for testing Hesiod's and our races of gold, silver, bronze and iron. And this intermixture of the iron with the silver and the bronze with the gold will engender unlikeness and an unharmonious unevenness, things which always beget war and enmity wherever they arise. 'Of this lineage, look you,' we must aver the dissension to be, wherever it occurs and always. (546d–547a)

Socrates goes on to describe the exact course of the degeneration of the embodied approximation of the ideal city through its main forms, which he distinguishes as timarchy, oligarchy, democracy, and, finally, tyranny. We have no need to follow Plato any further except to note that, as the realization of the true city lies beyond human power – being dependent on the particulars of nature which we cannot know and thus, as he puts it, on chance or the inspiration of the gods[8] – his real focus of interest is not in the institutional embodiment of the city as such, but in the *cultivation* of justice in the individual soul. Thus, in his famous simile, he speaks of the philosopher who discovers that there is nothing 'sound or right in any present politics' (496c) as one who has fallen among wild beasts and, though unwilling to share their misdeeds, is unable to hold out singly against the savagery of all. For these reasons, 'the philosopher remains quiet, minds his own affair, and, as it were, standing aside under the shelter of a wall in a storm and blast of dust and sleet and seeing others filled full of lawlessness, is content if in any way he may keep himself free from iniquity and unholy deeds through his life and take his departure with fair hope, serene and well content when the end comes' (496d, e).

Socrates is clear that this is no great thing in comparison to what a true philosopher could do both for himself and his city in 'ideal' conditions – but it is the best a philosopher can hope for if he does not have the good fortune to live in a state adapted to his nature (497a). Nevertheless, as he says later, it matters little whether the ideal city is found anywhere on earth, since there is 'a pattern of it laid up in heaven for him who wishes to contemplate it and so beholding to constitute himself its citizen. But it makes no difference whether it exists now *or ever will come into being*. The politics of this city only will be his and none other' (592b – emphasis mine).

Thus, in the end, the argument of the *Republic* returns from the consideration of the city back to the individual soul where, in the Myth of Er, through the right ordering of the soul's three parts, analogous to the right relation of the three elements of the ideal city, it is shown *to be possible* for each of us to pursue justice – regardless of the nature or condition of the particular city into which we have been born (614b ff.). This is what lies within our power and it was here and only here that Plato taught that justice could be realized by each of us. Thus, the turn to the discussion of justice in the city (from Book II onwards) does not so much supersede the quest for justice in the soul as it serves to prove that since it cannot find permanent embodiment in any human community it can only be held, reliably and abidingly, within the soul of the individual.

2. The Eternity of the Roman State

The Roman relation to this question is very different, as we see in Virgil's *Aeneid* – which, with Professor Doull, I take as the most explicit and developed statement of the Roman principle.[9] Virgil teaches that Rome is the true and just form of the human community valid for all peoples and for all time. This claim is extraordinary in both aspects – that is, that Rome is a universal city adequate to the needs of *all* peoples and that it will be so for *all* time. How could Virgil make such a statement? It appears to be so outrageous, so arrogant, that it seems we must either take it as poetic exaggeration or preposterous chauvinism. Nevertheless Virgil had good reason for making both claims.

The assertion of Rome's universality is not our primary interest but, since it is based on the same reason as the claim for its eternity, it will help us to appreciate the latter if we first understand the easier case of universality. Virgil shows the meaning of a universal city first in relation to Dido's Carthage. This is the chief (and only) characteristic Rome shares with her greatest enemy – and it is the reason why Carthage was her greatest enemy. Although the principle of universality was different in Rome and Carthage – the former being inspired by Jupiter and the latter by Juno[10]– they do share this much, in distinction from the exclusivity of all other forms of the ancient city where nation was irreconcilably opposed to nation, as the Greeks to the Trojans, the Persians to the Greeks, and the Hebrews to the Egyptians, and so on.[11] The signs of the universality of Carthage are everywhere present – from Juno's desire that her favourite city 'would be the ruler of the world' (1, 28) to the fact that the shipwrecked Trojans discover on the walls of its temple, still under construction, scenes, not from the history of the Phoenicians, but from the Trojan war, showing mutely, but unquestionably, that these people are not limited by any provincial outlook or narrow exclusivism but recognize all human fame and accomplishment as their own, whatever its origin (1, 605f.). Above all, there is Dido's generous and sincere invitation to the Trojans to join her city and people on absolutely equal terms: 'Or would you care [she asks Ilioneus, even before meeting Aeneas and thus before her romantic attachment to him]/ To join us in this realm on equal terms?/ The city I build is yours; haul up your ships;/ Trojan and Tyrian will be all one to me' (1, 776–9). In the tragedy that ensues Aeneas eventually rejects Dido's offer, and with it the Carthaginian version of universality.

As the traders of antiquity, at home everywhere and nowhere, the Phoenicians had a genuine indifference to matters of race, creed, colour, and other like particulars. They cared nothing for the quarrels of particular peoples – of Trojans and Greeks – and could as happily do business with each as they could recognize the greatness of both. In this there was the basis of a universal city, founded on the commonality of human appetites which they knew themselves to be capable of satisfying. This was the ground of Juno's hope. But what neither she, nor Dido, nor Carthage as a whole could understand or prevail against was the one other possible version of a universal city, with its basis in reason rather than the appetites. When these two came into conflict it became clear that Dido could not prevail against Aeneas nor Carthage against Rome, nor Juno against Jupiter, because among men and gods – that is, beings endowed with reason – reason rather than nature *is* the primary governing principle.

The Romans were able to impose their version of the universal city on virtually all of the known world, uniting in a single empire a vast diversity of peoples from India to Spain and from the North Sea to the Sahara. They did this by recognizing the common rationality of all mankind in virtue of which all could be brought under a single rational order (expressed in the Roman law), and of which Aeneas was the first servant in his unflinching obedience to the command of *fatum.*[12] This was *the* Roman virtue, as Anchises tells his son in the underworld: 'For your arts are to be these; to pacify, to impose the rule of law, to spare the conquered, battle down the proud' (6, 1152–4).[13]

The abstract unification of all the nations of the earth in a single community under the rule of one law was finally achieved in the extension of Roman citizenship, by the emperor Caracalla, to all freeborn males in the empire in AD 212. This was certainly an astonishing achievement, but we have less trouble in understanding it than the parallel claim that Rome would be eternal. In the first case there is the proof of the historical record, while in the second Rome was clearly replaced by another order at least from the time when, in AD 330, Constantine transferred the capital of the empire to Byzantium; by the middle of the sixth century ancient Rome was dead.

Nonetheless, Virgil was correct in predicting the eternity of Rome, as we can see if we understand the reasons for his judgment. He begins where Plato ends – with the recognition that there is a divine rational principle in the universe which ultimately governs the affairs of men. Plato calls this the 'Good,' and for him it was the highest object of philosophical knowledge: in Virgil it is *fatum,* or the absolute divine command issued to men and gods by Jupiter. There is no search for this principle in the *Aeneid* as there was in the *Republic.*[14] It is assumed from the first sentence where Aeneas is described as *fato profugus* (1, 2) – 'driven on by *fatum.*' That is, his task and calling are determined by the rational order of the universe. In principle the rest is simple. Aeneas has first to discover the nature of the just city which he has been ordered to establish. He comes to this in the course of his wanderings (books 1–6), where he experiences, in a practical sense, the limitations of every other possible form of the human community, both in this upper world and in the underworld. He arrives eventually at the place and the idea of Rome by a process of exclusion. Once this is known – that is, once he has discovered the form of the city which is in accord with the rational principle of the universe – it follows that, since this principle is stable and unchanging, the city that is in perfect accord with it must also be eternal.

Plato, who taught that there was an eternal 'pattern [of the true city] laid up in the heavens' (529b), would have had no quarrel with the first half of Virgil's teaching: what he denied was the claim that Rome, or any other city, could be such a perfect embodiment of that pattern that it was beyond every possibility of corruption. We have seen his reasons. They have to do with the random, irrational aspect of nature that is in principle impenetrable to human knowledge because we can only have a sure and certain knowledge of what is both fixed and universal – that is, the Forms or Ideas.

There can be no doubt that Virgil both understood and agreed with this in the most profound sense. And yet he held that Rome had so completely overcome this deficiency that it would be eternal. How is this so? For the answer we must turn to the second half of the *Aeneid.* In his treatment of Allecto in book 7, Virgil gives incomparable poetic expression to the problems which Plato recognized as leading to the inevitable downfall of the true republic, although here they are presented as the difficulties Aeneas must overcome on the way to establishing that city for the first time in the history of the world.

The seventh book is the start of a new topic in the argument of the *Aeneid.* Here Virgil makes a new invocation to the Muse,[15] saying that, in comparison to what has gone before, 'A greater history opens before my eyes,/ A greater task awaits me' (7, 58–9). This half of the poem is no longer concerned with the knowledge of the nature of the true city but with its practical realization in the world of concrete particulars. It is 'greater' because it is concerned with matters of life and death, with arms, and with the institutional embodiment of the divine truth rather than with the truth in abstraction from the particular exigencies of life and the sensible world.

In Dido's suicide, Juno recognized that her version of the universal city could not prevail against the one willed by *fatum.* It was not the case that someone other than Dido could have represented her cause any better. Dido had gone as far as anyone could go to win Aeneas to her side. She had used all the means at her disposal, all the attributes of Juno – her beauty, her intelligence, her generosity, her maternity, her pathos, and her ferocity – and yet she had come to this end. There was no ignoring this truth or fudging the issue: there simply was no other universal city Juno could prefer instead of Carthage – if not Rome – and she recognizes this from her first appearance in the seventh book.

> I am defeated [she says]
> And by Aeneas. Well, if my powers fall short,
> I need not falter over asking help
> Wherever help may lie. If I can sway
> No heavenly hearts I'll rouse the world below.
> It will not be permitted me – so be it –
> To keep the man from rule in Italy;
> By changeless fate (*fatum*) Lavinia waits, his bride.
> And yet to drag it out, to pile delay
> Upon delay in these great matters – that
> I can do: to destroy both countries' people,
> That I can do. (7, 422–38)

In calling the dread figure of Allecto from the underworld – hated even by her father, Pluto,[16] Juno unleashes all that the side of nature, the irrational, and the particular can do to prevent the realization of the ideal city – and Virgil presents this side with a power and clarity beyond anything in Plato, who did not postulate an active maliciousness from nature but only an *indifference* to rational ends and its impenetrability to human knowledge. Allecto is much more than this: hers is an evil will that positively *delights* in the irrational. She is moved by '*lust* for war,/ For angers, ambushes, and crippling crimes' (7, 445–6). This recognition of voluntary evil – which is not merely a matter of curable ignorance – is thoroughly Roman in its sober realism.[17] It means that Virgil understands, even more deeply than Plato, what there is in the universe that can work against the true city – and he places all of it in Aeneas's path.

Allecto, 'Daughter of Night' (7, 443), from the dark bowels of earth at the farthest possible remove from the realm of Olympic reason, does those three things which can most impede the realization of the true city. Using the infinite particulars at her command she picks just those which will stir up human irrationality in its three main forms – female (the passive), male (the active), and that of the mob (communal). She goes first to Amata and uses her 'womanly anxiety and anger' (7, 474–5) at what the Queen can only see as the loss of her daughter to the vagabond Aeneas, who, she fears, may take Lavinia away forever just as easily as he had come out of nowhere. Concerned only with the natural link between herself and Lavinia, a part of her own flesh and blood, Amata has a mother's anxiety to keep and protect what is hers and cares nothing for the divine command that her daughter must marry a foreigner. When her spurious arguments fail to move her husband, Latinus, she divides the city by hiding Lavinia and leading the women – that is, those, either potentially or actually, with maternal concerns similar to her own – into secession. She does this in the most effective way open to her by *feigning* Bacchic possession – that is, by a calculated appeal to the natural impulses of the women of the city insofar as they seek release from their subordination to the rational ordering of society. Without exception the Latin women respond to her call to protect the family from dissolution at the hands of Latinus and his god. They remove en masse, leaving the city divided along its most basic suture, which is the union of its men and women in a common enterprise.

Allecto goes then to Turnus and, in the disguise of an old crone who claims to be giving Juno's command to the hero, plays on his male pride at being thwarted in anything he has undertaken. At first Turnus makes light of her concern, scorning to be guided by a woman: 'Men will make war and peace, as men should do' (7, 613). In other words, he says she should mind her own business, reminding her that she has no cause for worry because the affairs of state are in his hands. But then, as the purport of her words sinks in, Allecto reveals herself in her true hideous form and Turnus is driven wild by the irrational thought, with no care for the right or wrong of the matter, that his honour is impugned by a woman and that he will be thought a coward. This is more than he can bear.

> Enormous terror woke him, a cold sweat
> Broke out all over him and soaked his body.
> Then driven wild, shouting for arms, for arms
> He ransacked house and chamber.
> Lust of steel raged in him, brute insanity of war,
> And wrath above all ... (7, 631–6)

An active and violent passion has been stirred that nothing can quell short of force itself.

Finally, and with the most damaging effect, Allecto causes Aeneas's son Iulus to have the misfortune of mortally wounding the pet stag of the Latins. Iulus and his party had been hunting for food when he startled a deer which had been 'floating down/ A river, keeping cool by the green bank' (7, 679–80). Iulus would not have shot if he had known the animal was a pet and, having shot, his arrow might have missed its mark but for Allecto who, like an invisible puff of wind, guided the arrow to its target, where again, and unfortunately, it did not kill the beast outright, in which case the conflict might have been avoided, but hit in such a way that, though wounding beyond cure, left the stag able to make for home. 'Groaning, he found his stall,/ And coated with dark blood he filled the house/ With piteous cries, as though imploring mercy' (7, 688–90). It was an innocent mistake but, in the sudden passions that were aroused on the Latin side – to kill the monsters who had done this – and on the Trojan side – to defend their lives – there was not the slightest chance for reason to prevail. In a flash, from this unlucky accident, the two sides were irrevocably at war.

No one can say that Virgil ignored or made light of those irrational particulars which Plato recognized as the humanly insuperable obstacles to establishing his ideal city – and as inevitably destroying it even if, by some lucky chance, it were ever founded. Raw passion ungoverned by reason, a passion which itself is often essential to survival (as when the Trojans had to defend their lives against the sudden attack of the Latin farmers), and such unfortunate and unforeseeable chance events are ineluctably part and parcel of this world, and they have the effects both Plato and Virgil describe. Yet Virgil teaches that the Roman empire will be eternal beyond anything that passion or chance can disturb. How can this be so?

Virgil's answer is found in the terms of the reconciliation between Jupiter and Juno in the twelfth book, where the Roman principle is finally made explicit. It consists in a separation of the two sides (the rational/universal and the sensible/particular) that, according to Plato, must be joined if the ideal city was to be embodied. Instead of abandoning the effort to give institutional form to this fragile and unstable union by concentrating on the cultivation of justice in the individual soul, Rome would embody the ideal city in all its essential characteristics – but would seek nothing further than this. The whole side of nature would be left free to pursue its own ends without hindrance so long as these did not conflict with the demands of reason. In this Jupiter (speaking for universal reason) does not crush Juno (speaking for the side of nature) but recognizes her legitimate place in the total scheme of things. Just as she (or nature generally) has not, in the end, the *power* to rule over Jupiter (or reason), so too it would be *wrong* for him to destroy her since they have a common parentage and share an identity in spite of their differences. The question is how their conflicting interests can be reconciled – and the Roman answer is that once the side of nature has been brought to see that it cannot govern, the side of reason can willingly allow nature to follow its own ends in everything except government.

Jupiter, in turning a blind eye to Juno's appeal to Allecto, has allowed her every particular she can muster against Aeneas and the Trojans. But the moment Juno's resistance goes beyond what particulars can do – as when Juturna actually rearms Turnus with the sword he had carelessly misplaced – Jupiter draws the line, as he must do if the whole cosmos is not to collapse into chaos. Juno accedes to his will when he finally says, 'I forbid your going further' (12, 1092–3). She does so because she recognizes that the whole side of nature, her interest, can only exist in an ordered cosmos. This is why she does not carry her opposition to Jupiter and the rational order any further – recognizing that she and nature are limited and that, if nothing prevents a sword moving from one place to another with no cause, then there is nothing to prevent the whole of nature falling into a chaos in which she would lose not merely her beloved Turnus, but everything else as well. Here she reveals her kinship with Jupiter, for she does not want nature – in the sense of an undifferentiated chaos – nor the return of Saturnian rule, any more than he.

But, within these essential limits, Juno begs Jupiter not to impose his will in matters that are not *necessarily* governed or dictated by the universal reason (*fatum*).

> But one thing not retained
> By fate I beg for Latium ...
> Never command the land's own Latin folk
> To change their old name, to become new Trojans,
> Known as Teucrians; never make them alter
> Dialect or dress. Let Latium be.
> Let there be Alban kings for generations,
> And let Italian valour be the strength
> Of Rome in after times. Once and for all
> Troy fell, and with her name let her lie fallen. (12, 1111–23)

In other words, while acknowledging that Jupiter (or reason) as the victorious ruler *could* impose on nature in every particular, Juno nevertheless, politely, beseeches him not to do so in those cases where it is unnecessary – as for instance in matters of name, dialect, and dress. Her point is that as long as he has the essence of what he wants – as long as it is his version of the universal city that will prevail – it is not a matter of essential importance to him if the people are known as Italians or Trojans, whether they speak Trojan or Latin, or if they wear the clothes of the East or West. But to her, to the side of nature, these particulars are of *essential* importance. Jupiter willingly accedes to this request, waiving his own preferences, because he knows that if she (or nature) is not satisfied in this way then there can be no lasting peace between them. Juno is after all his sister, a divine power co-equal with himself in all but his primacy, and an aspect of reality that must be given its due. Not to do so, where he has no reason to refuse except for his personal preference, amounts to using raw power to force her compliance. This is just the state of affairs in which, sooner or later, the side of nature, by a tiny deviation unnoticeable to men, will eventually destroy the city – just as a single unnoticed seed of grass lodged in a tiny crevice will lead to others that can eventually destroy a solid concrete wall. Jupiter is thus true to *reason* when he abjures the use of force and answers,

> Sister of Jupiter
> Indeed you are, and Saturn's other child,
> To feel such anger, storming in your breast.
> But come, no need; put down your fit of rage.
> I grant your wish. I yield, I am won over
> Willingly. Aussonian folk will keep
> Their father's language and their way of life,
> And that being so, their name. (12, 1126–33)

'To all this Juno nodded in assent/ And gladdened by his promise, changed her mind' (12, 1141–2). She has gotten the essence of what she wanted, though not what was unessential in it – that is, the desire that her city should rule the world. In just the same way, Jupiter has what is essential to him – the rule of reason – though not what is unessential, which would be the (Platonic) identity of reason and nature in every particular.

This separated relation of reason and nature was the basis of Roman rule. By recognizing the common rationality of all people the Romans brought the whole world together in a single order under their law. But, aside from this one point of contact in an abstract reason common to all mankind, the Roman system had absolutely no interest in the concrete content of the lives they governed. Indeed, the utter indifference of Rome to the natural interests of its subjects – as long as they obeyed the law – constituted the second 'principle' of their rule and was on the whole as scrupulously observed as was the law itself. It had to be – for both elements were necessary to Rome's stability, which was based, first, on an absolute, soulless, and heartless insistence on the law[18] and, secondly, on an equally strict indifference to everything else – to all that, in Juno's phrase, was 'not required by any law of destiny' (12, 819; translation mine).[19] The one side is enshrined in that long list of the heroes of the Republic from Junius Brutus and Lucretia to Marcus Regulus and Cato the Younger who, without the slightest thought for their natural interests, preferred the law above all other things. On the other side stands Rome's unrivalled ability to tolerate intact a countless host of outlandish deities, customs, and traditions which she welcomed into the city and adopted with enthusiasm – provided only that they did not conflict with her laws, which gave the widest possible scope to the free expression of every conceivable particularity. Both sides are present from the earliest days of the Republic in the standard formula which Rome imposed on her defeated enemies. They could continue to have their own municipal government, traditions, and deities, but must have the same friends and the same enemies as Rome.[20] The natural differences were thus preserved and protected within the empire: Greeks did not have to cease being Greek in order to be Romans – nor did Spaniards, Britons, Gauls, or Egyptians – and yet none could turn against any other in the ceaseless conflicts of nation against nation.

Based as it was on these two principles, Virgil was correct to speak of Rome as eternal. Instead of seeking, in Platonic terms, for the rare and fragile coincidence of reason and nature to embody the ideal state, Rome would be that, and would govern all mankind by reason, through the expedient of refusing to concern herself in any way with the side of nature except in the rare and extreme cases when nature sought to transgress her laws. At these points the whole weight of the state could be brought to crush those who threatened the state with irresistible and unrelenting force. Where Plato saw that the unknowable things of nature worked, in all but the rarest circumstances, to prevent the establishment of the true city, Rome was supremely indifferent to them because she did not attempt to govern and control them in every particular. And because she was satisfied with the rule of an abstract reason that did not reach too deeply into the natural lives of her subjects, she had nothing to fear from the side of nature – her rulers did not have to be philosophers, indeed they did not even have to be sane, and there was no passion and no unforeseen chance that could conceivably disturb her rule for the simple reason that she did not seek to rule what she could not control.

But what she did rule – the essential but abstracted reason of mankind – she could control absolutely and with the full force of the divine rational order that had given man this aspect of his being in the first place. Virgil had good and sufficient reason for claiming that Rome was the institutional form of the ideal city and that it was both universal and would be eternal. It was, as he says in the *Fourth Eclogue*, 'the pattern of the age to come' (4, 46–7).

3. Conclusion: The City of God and the Finitude of Virgil's Rome

We know, with the advantage of hindsight, that Rome did not last half a millennium beyond Virgil's day, and so it seems that he must have been wrong. In part this is correct – but he was not wrong in his own terms. Virgil recognized that the separation of reason and nature – while capable of providing to the Roman state a practical stability that other nations lacked – did not produce a humanly satisfying solution. This is shown in the *Aeneid* where, in the end, Aeneas is reluctantly unable to grant the *clementia* his father had recommended because of the demands of the divine law imposed on him by Evander – that he requite, in blood, the life of his son Pallas.[21] Aeneas's hesitation shows that he understands that it is a shame to have to sacrifice Turnus now that he was freely willing to become a citizen of Rome. But this *was* the price which Evander had earned by the unstinting and uncomplaining aid he had freely offered to the Trojans and which the divine law required.

Of the humanly unsatisfactory nature of the Roman solution Professor Doull writes:

> [T]he limits of the system are already conspicuous in Virgil's account. Aeneas, to be capable of his work, must attain to an independent subjectivity, and Turnus must either come to this same radical independence of all natural attachments or be destroyed. The argument of the *Aeneid* is that the Roman 'res publica' is for this subjectivity a sufficient end, that indeed there cannot be a higher end which might be preferred to it. But in this argument the negativity in this end is neglected, the evil which the individual also experiences in it ... What comes to light in this is the inadequacy of external ends, even the most comprehensive, to subjective freedom.[22]

In short, the stability of Rome, which was achieved only at the cost of the radical separation of reason and nature, brought to light a problem that

Virgil recognized, as had Plato before him, as one which was not able to be resolved by any created agency. In this sense then, as Doull points out, 'It can be said therefore that in the Roman religion the preparation of the Christian religion is complete.'[23] That is, the experienced inadequacy of ends that must forever remain external had prepared the Roman world to hear and appreciate the new possibilities which opened up with the Christian claim that Jesus is the Word of God incarnate – in whom nature and reason are absolutely united. In this teaching a new principle appeared that had its basis not in any human activity but in the divine self-revelation. In the course of a few centuries, as millions of men and women voted with their feet, it proved preferable not only to the separation of reason and nature on which Roman stability was based, but also to their actual but temporary union in Plato's embodied ideal city. It could do so because it combined both the coincidence of reason and nature which the Plato recognized as the theoretical goal *and* the practical stability which Rome had realized. This was to be the City of God – with its start in time and its end in eternity – whose fundamental structure Augustine was the first to discern and describe both in its distinction from Roman practice and Platonic theory and in its divinely granted union of their ends.[24]

Notes

1 'The Christian Origin of Contemporary Institutions Part One,' *Dionysius* 6 (1982), 153. This paper is concerned with matters considered in '[Part] C. The Roman res publica' (151–61), in the lengthy and remarkable two-part article by Professor Doull which has become for many a kind of manual on the origins of modernity. See 'Virgil's Rome,' above, 167–80.

2 Unless otherwise indicated, translations from the *Aeneid* are those of Robert Fitzgerald, *Virgil, The Aeneid* (New York: Random House, 1983).

3 See *Republic*, 544c ff. Quotations from Plato are from the translations in *The Collected Dialogues of Plato*, ed. Edith Hamilton and Huntingdon Cairns (Bollingen Series LXXI; Princeton: Princeton University Press, 1961).

4 Some recent interpreters, moved by this consideration, have dismissed Book I as irrelevant to the real argument. See, for example, N.P. White's widely used introduction *A Companion to Plato's Republic* (Indianapolis: Hackett, 1979).

5 Cf. 350d–354a.

6 Cf. 336a ff.

7 See, for example, the argument in Letter VII at 342b ff.

8 See the text (499b–c) quoted above (184), and also 497a.

9 'The *Aeneid* is of all writings the most instructive on the nature of Roman religion and institutions.' 'Christian Origin,' 152. See above, 168.

10 The opposition between Rome and Carthage is that between the two possible versions of a universal city – i.e., Rome, or Jupiter's city, in which reason is primary and the appetites secondary, and Carthage, or Juno's city, in which the opposite is the case.

11 The 'classic' exposition of this natural enmity of peoples is found in Aeschylus's *Oresteia*.

12 *Fatum*, which is usually translated as 'fate' or 'destiny' can easily be misunderstood since, for many today, these words convey the sense of an irresistible, unknowable, and therefore, from a human point of view, essentially arbitrary force that governs our affairs. Virgil agrees that it was irresistible, but for him it was in no sense arbitrary, being the very opposite of *fortuna* (see this opposition in the speech of Nautes at 5, 709–10). *Fatum* is the word for the divine rational principle that ultimately governs all things in the universe from the gods themselves to nature. Jupiter is its chief spokesman. The word is the past participle of the defective verb *for*: it means 'a thing having been spoken' and thus implies a rational principle of which it is the utterance. In the Christian idiom it corresponds to the Word, or *logos*, of God.

13 'As founder of the Roman race, [Aeneas] is appropriately subject to the authority of his father Anchises, whom he carries from the burning city. The family is for him centred in this paternal relation ... Aeneas learns from Anchises ... the whole fatal course of Roman history to Augustus ... Family and state have the same end, namely the knowledge that fate, the necessity which, as well in the realm of Dis as in that of Jupiter, ever annuls the division of natural will from reason, – that fate is not alien to human freedom but the process in which it is realized' ('Christian Origin,' 154–5; 169–70 above).

14 'The Roman poet does not have to disclose a self-conscious principle, an unmoved mover, beyond all the finite, but can present a subjectivity for which fate and necessity are not beyond it but occur in the fulfilment of its purposes.' 'Christian Origin,' 153; 168 above.

15 See 6, 37ff., where Virgil invokes the help of the muse of love or desire, Erato, because, presumably, she is the one who best knows about the natural particulars that move us to love and which are the concern of books 7–12.

16 See 7, 327: *odit et ipse pater Pluton.*

17 'The fallen or evil state is the individuality which, involved in its passions,

would make itself its end as against this system of utility.' 'Christian Origin,' 156; 171 above.

18 The adjectives come from Hegel's brief but incomparable exposition of Rome in his *Philosophy of History*.

19 *Nulla fati quod lege tenetur.*

20 The terms of this 'Cassian Treaty' (about 495 BC) may be found in Livy, *Ab Urbe Condita*, II, 33, 4.

21 11, 178.

22 'Christian Origin,' 158–9; 173 above.

23 Ibid., 161; 176 above.

24 Though written to demonstrate that the Christians were not to be blamed for the decline and fall of Rome – which it proves if one limits one's regard simply to the responsibility that can be attributed to human agency – the *City of God* nevertheless shows more clearly than anything else that it was in fact the appearance of Christianity that brought into the world a new understanding of the aim and end of the human community which was, over the centuries, to prove preferable, for millions of men and women, to that proposed by Rome. And it was one which Rome, for all her power, was unable to resist since it was based on the revelation of the concrete unity of God and world which the Roman principle denied and was consequently unable either to assimilate or extirpate. An account of Roman impotence in the face of this new religion may be found in J.J. O'Donnell, 'The Demise of Paganism,' *Traditio* 35 (1979): 45–88.

PART TWO

Medieval to Renaissance

chapter four

Augustine[1]

The congruence of theological thought with the faith of the church which began with Athanasius is completed in the work of Augustine. What stood in the way of this congruence was a thought which did not have the form of its object, which treated it according to abstract categories whose movement and mediation was not in themselves but in the subject. In the belief of the church the movement does not fall to a subjective reflection but is of the Trinity itself. That theological thought remains thus separate from its absolute object has its source in this, that the movement of return from the human side is abstract. Augustine in his *Confessions* describes a return or conversion of the individual to God through which, because it is concrete, this residual subjectivity is given up and the Trinitarian standpoint of the church established. This conversion is first of himself, but because the forms through which it moves are universal, he writes of it also for others.

The first nine books of the *Confessions* treat of his conversion. They remove the 'hypotheses,' to speak Platonically, which separate the individual from the objective or the divine standpoint. In the tenth book he brings the whole course of his conversion under the end to which it led. All the 'hypotheses' which impeded his relation to God thus removed, in the immediacy of this result the subjective movement passes into the objective or divine prior in itself. This transition is only distinguished from the like movement in Neoplatonism by the concrete subjective integration which prepared for it. Augustine has thus reached the standpoint where the scriptural revelation is open to him, where the creation and the spiritual return to the creative principle in Christ and the community of the faithful are for him in an objective systematic Trinitarian movement. Such is the content of the last three books of the *Confessions.*

The language of Scripture was opaque to Augustine so long as he took the linguistic and imaginative medium – the letter – to be primary and not the truth it conveyed, which was most clearly disclosed to a spirit which both believed and thought the content of its belief.[2] There is not here a philosophy which is distinguished from theology and gives to it its method. Theology is the work of a thinking which has the same structure as the faith. It is not separated from the scriptural revelation but is a thinking and not only a believing relation to it.

The moments or successive 'hypotheses' through which the conversion of Augustine took place can only be noticed very briefly here.[3] The argument begins with his infancy, where he is in the same relation to the end in which he will have rest as the infant Jesus in whom the church believed the divine *logos* to dwell. From this immediate relation in which there appears already the beginning of a subjectivity which can oppose itself to its universal good, the child begins to articulate its relation to the world. Of interest here to the argument is first the formation of a division between the order the child finds given and imposed, and an arbitrary freedom to reject it, a freedom which as set against the universal is simply evil.[4] The next stage in the development is that the opposition of good and evil should be not merely thus external but be a division of the free individual himself. Such is the form of Augustine's Manichaeism, where his relation to the world is divided between a sensuous immediacy forever overtaken by the otherness of the world to him and a universality in which his self-relation is freed from this otherness. This division is for him an external material embodiment, the opposition of light to darkness. His relation to the world is like that of a behaviouristic or Humean psychology, where the division of the will is without a unifying self-conscious centre, simply factual.[5] From this pseudo-scientific mentality Augustine finds next the beginning of a liberation in the Academic scepticism by which he can withhold assent to the deceptive alternation of an independence from nature and submission to it of the Manichees. In this sceptical freedom he both continues in his former interests and is indifferent to them. But the contradiction of this relation gradually makes itself felt: his particular interests both are and are not ends for him. Towards them he sinks into a languor and immobility, since they are not interests of the sceptical reason which withholds its assent to them.[6]

The next stage in his conversion is that he should be freed from the presupposition on which this division of rational freedom from natural interests rests. That is the materialism of Stoic and sceptical philosophy and generally of the Roman world. Not only finite ends but the externality and necessity to which they succumb come before him as resting on an endless self-identical matter. In that relation his inner indifference to the world is realized in the indifference and nullity of the world itself.[7] This completed scepticism is the point of his conversion to the Platonism which knows the sensible world and contingent human ends in relation to it to have their ground in a world of substantial ends containing all the conditions of their realization. This ideal realm discovered through the negation of the former division of thought from its world is no longer alien to the free rational subject.

But there occurs at this point a new difficulty for Augustine. His relation to this ideal world is mediated only by the former sceptical position. The new standpoint itself is unmediated, is an end immediately known without the way to it. Platonism does not move him because he does not know the *logos* as incarnate, as united with the natural individual.[8] What separates him from the end is the finitude of the rational powers of the soul, intellect and will. For these powers there recurs a separation of sensible and ideal. The unity of the worlds has been discovered to him, but is also beyond the scope of his rational powers. The course of the integration is again in this form, that the sensuous will, taken as different and in conflict with the rational will, should appear as a nullity, as a moment of one will comprehending their difference.[9] In the vanishing of this division there remained no further impediment for Augustine to the belief of the church. In Christ the beginning of his conversion and its end meet, the immediate unity of the human individual with the *logos* and that mediated by the whole course of their separation. The thought which through intellect and will would unite the ideal and the sensible, not immediately but through their difference, saw the end it sought realized in the revelation.[10]

The argument of *Confessions* is destroyed unless one sees the first nine books as introductory to the remaining four. Through these the subjective movement of the individual to God becomes the beginning of an objective contemplation of the creation, fall, and redemption – the whole content of the faith. The other forms in which the Christian religion was known, the original revelation and the apostolic faith, had the same structure: a subjective conversion to the infinite divine purpose, then to this standpoint the revelation of nature and human finitude as comprehended in this purpose. The difference of these forms lies not in the structure or content, but in the way it is known. The *Confessions* thus brings into view the whole Augustinian theology. Other works will begin from the objective standpoint to which the argument of the *Confessions* has led.

In the *Trinity* he treats of the divine principle in itself. As in the *Confessions* the revelation was grasped in its full concreteness, so the Trinitarian principle as there treated is the reflection of this concrete revelation. The method of the work is to study the Trinity first through Scripture, then through nature but especially in the movement of the rational creature to a unification of its powers, which was also its conversion to the Christian revelation. The Trinity as known through the agreement of these complementary methods is no longer as for the Greek Fathers, in a tension between the difference of the persons and their unity. The persons are the moments of an absolute creative thinking, where the unity of thinking with its object is not primarily before their division, but equally in the *logos* and the spiritual return.

When the human creature is considered not only in the process of his conversion and unification but also in relation to the completed process, where he is in principle conformed to the revelation in Christ, there is discovered the Augustinian doctrines of grace and predestination, which he elaborated in controversy with the Pelagians. The relation of human freedom to the divine will was not of equal concern to the Greek theologians, for the reason that the integration of the two was conceived by them rather hierarchically than as comprehension of the finite in the infinite divine freedom, towards which first the 'hypothesis' of a separate finite freedom had to be radically negated.

What pertains more directly to the present inquiry is the concept of a 'civitas dei,' the church considered in relation to grace and predestination, neither in the finite relations of authority and moral discipline nor, with Dionysius, as a hierarchic order of dependence on a primal unity. The 'civitas dei' is the community of Christians in whom the end sought in the conversion from the fall is operative. All other polities rest on a partial integration of human ends into the divine. For this reason the peace and justice which they seek is found in the course of time to be unstable and illusory. The 'civitas dei' however, being defined as the community in which the difference of the human will from the divine is overcome, is an idea without historical existence. For it belongs to an historical community not only that there be in it a moving end but also that there be a separation from the end, the need and the labour of attaining it. The evil of former communities, which is an idea overcome in the 'civitas dei,' is that this difference and separation does not have its origin wholly in the intended end, is not that end as immediate and undeveloped. The end rather was more or less abstract; the political good and the particular goods of individuals and classes were only superficially harmonized, so that civil wars could with difficulty be suppressed unless in the face of external enemies.

The 'civitas dei' is not the medieval church which will compete with the Empire for the government of humanity. It is the spiritual part of the church, through which the worldly part is sustained and the ministrations of its clergy have validity.[11] The relation of the two parts to the church itself has a like difficulty to that of other worldly communities to the 'civitas dei.' The Augustinian doctrines of grace and predestination, if not rejected by the church, must first be accommodated to a Pelagian doctrine of human freedom. The worldly aspect of the church is assumed to have an independence of the spiritual, though in relation to it.[12] The 'civitas dei' will only have historical existence when the difference of these parts is not seen thus externally but as within the one moving end.[13]

But the realization of the 'civitas dei' is a new beginning. The interests and passions of men, their natural life, are in the belief of the church and its theological thought integrated into the infinite divine purpose. Their difference from this end has now the status of an otherness in which the infinite divine purpose is implicit, of the means through which it will be disclosed. At first in this beginning the natural will is related immediately to its ideal end. That is the condition of barbarous peoples who succeed to the dying power of the western empire. Roman virtue, the product of another religion and culture, cannot enter into this immediate but concrete relation to the end.

The church also, while it remains Augustinian and not in an external Pelagian relation to the faith so defined, sinks into an immediate relation to it.[14] The mediation of the individual with his absolute end becomes external to him; the means of grace are seen as things; the clergy, the universal element in the church, are deeply separated from those who live in their unformed passions. The reason in the church, though occupied with the content of the Augustinian theology, is not Augustinian. The Augustinian content is approached through the abstract logic of the Dionysian system.[15] The interest of the thinking part of the church is no longer to find an 'intellectus fidei' which should have the structure of the faith, but to approach the faith through a philosophical reason separate from it. The object of philosophical interest is the content of the fate which is assumed, but the relation of reason to this content is indeterminate as is the form of this reason. The Dionysian

Platonism of Eriugena is not held to in its integrity but falls into opposed idealistic and nominalistic fragments.[16]

The 'civitas dei' in this first realized form is the paradigm of a new secular order.[17] The barbarous tribes, being converted to Christianity, and knowing there a substantial end to which they would conform the unstable passions of the natural will, establish also a secular end for themselves in a sacred kingship. In relation to this they both give up their natural freedom and would retain it.[18] As their particularity is believed to be contained in the absolute end of their faith, so the kingship would rather save their particular freedom than enslave it.

Notes

1 Extracted from 'The Christian Origin of Contemporary Institutions Part Two: The History of Christian Institutions,' *Dionysius* 8 (1984): 97–103.

2 *Conf.* V, xiv, 24.

3 The reader can fortunately be referred to Colin Starnes, *Augustine's Conversion: The Argument of the Confessions Books I–IX* (Waterloo: Wilfrid Laurier Press, 1986).

4 Cf. *Conf.* I, vii, 11 and *Conf.* I, x, 16.

5 Light and dark, good and evil, are thought in the Manichaean system to be objective distinctions. The world in which humans find themselves is a mixture of the two, of the affirmative and the negative. The difference of this position from a Humean or from a behaviouristic psychology is that in these the mixed unanalysed condition is taken as the real. Where one is thus more content with the immediate, a sceptical spirit is less easily awakened.

6 In Book VI; cf. especially xi, 18–20.

7 VII, i, 1–2; vii, 11.

8 VII, ix.

9 VIII, viii, 19–xii, 29.

10 VII, xii, 29.

11 The spiritual church and the general body of the Catholic church with its clerical government are held together in Augustine's thought: the second tends to the first as its end. Because the relation of the two is considered universally in the medium of thought, not empirically, he can avoid the sectarian separation of the Donatists. On this relation is founded his doctrine that the sacraments even if administered by unworthy priests are valid, so also the authority of the 'praepositi, per quos ecclesia nunc gubernatur' (*Civ. Dei.* XX, 9, 2).

12 'Et ita semper gratia dei nostro in partem bonam cooperatur arbitrio atque in omnibus illud adiuvat, protegit ac defendit' (Cassian, *Coll.* XIII, 13). The Augustinian doctrine prevailed against its opponents at the Synod of Orange, AD 529.

13 The church of Gregory the Great is distinguished from that of Augustine in that this unification has taken place: the government and sacramental life of the church rest on an Augustinian basis, but to this they are related in an external and immediate way: *Dial.* IV, 58; *Mor.* XI, 14, 22; XIII, 18, 21; XXXV, 8, 12; etc.

14 From this the realistic and symbolic interpretations of the Eucharist, which could continue together in the ancient church, tend to collapse into the doctrine of an immediate, objective transmutation of the elements, as in Robertus Paschasius, 'Liber de Corpore et Sanguine Domini' (Migne, *Patr. Lat.*, 120).

15 Eriugena, *De Divisione Naturae.* The Augustinian system will only assume an independent philosophical form in modern philosophy. Those aspects of Augustinian theology which have generally seemed most repugnant since Arminius and Enlightenment have their source in the immediate relation of thought there to the scriptural revelation.

16 Medieval philosophy begins in Eriugena with the Platonism of Dionysius and ends with it in Cusanus. In it lies the inner connection of the various opposed positions in early medieval philosophy.

17 The anarchic individual freedom of the northern peoples, Celtic and Germanic, through Christianity became capable of an ordered relation to an end comprehensive of it.

18 Kingship and popular freedom subsist together in an undeveloped form especially in the Anglo-Saxon kingdoms, which were less subject to the traditions of Roman government.

COMMENTARY
The Augustinian Philosophy and Christian Institutions

ROBERT CROUSE

'We study history ultimately in order to know institutions,' said Adolf von Harnack, great modern historian of ancient Christianity; 'nothing at all ... makes a lasting impression on the human community that has not taken form in institutions.'[1] And since 'all institutions originate in ideas ..., so also all of the history of institutions is unprobed as long as the motivating ideas are unknown.'[2] In that perspective, Harnack focused his attention upon the theology of St Augustine, and saw there both the fulfilment of the intellectual quest of the ancient world,[3] and the basis of all that has been distinctive in Western Christendom down to modern times: 'Along with the Church he served, he has moved through the centuries.'[4]

Similarly, James Doull, in his study 'Christian Origin of Contemporary Institutions,' looks to the Church Fathers, and especially to St Augustine, for an explication of the principles informing Western civilization. 'Patristic theology may appear to be remote from the history of human institutions in medieval and modern times,' he observes, 'but in truth only by this long argument did the Christian belief in the reconciliation of man with God receive the form in which it could be the presupposition and basis of finite institutions.'[5] As he makes the point in another essay:

> The contemporary question and that of the Fathers are also greatly different, as is our society from that of the Empire. The differences do not, however, touch the primary logical form of the problem, how an integrity of the elements is possible in human life. The contemporary theologian has, therefore, essentially the same question as when Augustine, beginning from a like diremption of the natural and the rational, reflected in his *Confessions* on the logic of his conversion – that is, of his knowledge that the concreteness of the elements is the true principle.[6]

It is from the standpoint of that contemporary question – 'the diremption of the natural and the rational,' 'the division of rational freedom from natural interests,'[7] the conflict between 'human freedom and servitude to nature,'[8] that Doull seeks in the Fathers, and especially in St Augustine, 'the Christian principle' in terms of which the contrary elements may be so combined that neither diminishes or absorbs the other.[9] In contemporary life the conflict of contrary elements may be seen in the opposition between the total claims of technological reason (as with Marx), on the one hand, and the total claims of the natural (Nietzsche, Heidegger), on the other.[10] But this, says Doull, is logically the same conflict as constitutes the story of St Augustine's *Confessions*, and the problem, now as then, is to grasp the principle in which the opposed elements are reconciled.

A principle of reconciliation belonged to the Christian religion, of course, from the beginning. But, according to Doull's argument, that 'inner, felt reconciliation in the apostolic faith' is extended to the world in the working out of 'the agreement of faith with the *intellectus fidei* ... virtually complete in the Augustinian theology.'[11] It is in a succinct and profound analysis of St Augustine's *Confessions* (here, and also in his essays on Augustinian *sapientia* and Augustinian Trinitarianism) that Doull endeavours to show how the young Augustine's experience of multiple forms of the conflict between reason and nature in his own life prepared him for a concrete grasp of a revealed principle of reconciliation, in which Word and flesh are united. In the final three books of the *Confessions* the point is reached where 'the creation and the spiritual return to the creative principle in Christ and the community of the faithful are for him in an objective, systematic Trinitarian movement.'[12] 'The *Confessions* thus brings into view the whole Augustinian theology. Other works will begin from the objective standpoint to which the argument of *Confessions* has led.'[13]

Doull speaks of an important difference in method between the *Confessions* and *De Trinitate.* Here the methods are spoken of simply as 'complementary'; elsewhere the difference is attributed to a difficulty, not fully appreciated by Augustine, 'that his experience terminated in a principle no longer philosophically accessible to him.'[14] Thus, that agreement of faith with the *intellectus fidei*, necessary if Christian belief is to become the basis of finite institutions, is only virtually complete in the Augustinian theology. The further requirement is that the intellectual or philosophical form should be separated from the religious, should stand on its own. 'An independent thought which takes itself to have the same content as the Christian religion appears at the end of the Patristic period.'[15]

From Doull's standpoint, 'Patristic theology is not philosophy, in that it presupposes a revealed truth. It is however the genesis of a philosophy, in that its movement is towards an intellectual relation to the content of that presupposition.'[16] That is to say, it is a matter of faith seeking understanding. Certainly, in terms of a much later definition of philosophy which would see it as independent of faith and divine revelation, there is no Patristic philosophy. But for St Augustine, true philosophy (*nostra philosophia*)[17] involves a continual interrelation of *fides* and *intellectus* in the 'hermeneutic circle': *credo ut intellegam, intellego ut credam.*[18] The understanding finds, that faith may yet continually seek: *et inveniendum quaeritur et quaerendum invenitur.*[19] For St Augustine, the religious form and the philosophical form are not alternative, but complementary and always interdependent.

The *Confessions* is, as Doull wonderfully demonstrates, a profoundly philosophical work. Yet, it is at the same time profoundly religious, and the resolution of its philosophical dilemmas depends entirely upon the revelation of the Word made flesh, accepted in the humility of faith. The *De Trinitate* undertakes to explicate – indeed, according to St Augustine, to demonstrate rationally – the first principle of the true philosophy.[20] But the only secure starting point for that demonstration is divine revelation, and the first four books are occupied with biblical exegesis. In books five to seven, the doctrine is given logical definition, and becomes the basis, in the remaining eight books, for an *itinerarium mentis in Deum*, as the soul ascends towards its principle, understood not as an absolute thinking, but as a relational unity of equal moments of being, knowing, and loving. While the Neoplatonic (especially Porphyrian) trinity of being, life, and thought may be seen as a certain explication of the Aristotelian doctrine of God as self-thinking thought as manifest in the hierarchy of finite reality, St Augustine's anti-subordinationist doctrine insists upon the perfect equality of the eternally distinct hypostases of being, knowing, and willing.

For all it may owe to the hypostatic doctrine of Plotinus or Porphyry, St Augustine's argument is essentially an exposition of the trinitarian doctrine of Nicaea, and constitutes a philosophy radically different *in principle*: in some sense Neoplatonic, but a post-Nicene, post-Porphyrian, distinctly Augustinian Christian Platonism.[21] The Augustinian philosophy is essentially a dialogue between the rational soul and the Word of God revealed: 'It is your Word, who is the Principle, who also speaks to us. Thus, he speaks in the gospel to bodily ears ... that we might believe and seek and find within, in the eternal truth, where the one good master teaches all his disciples.'[22] In that dialogue, faith and understanding are inextricably allied, and faith remains a necessary condition of understanding throughout man's wayfaring existence. There is here no independent philosophy.

Nor is there to be found any independent philosophy at the end of the Patristic period. One speaks of early medieval philosophers, such as Boethius, Pseudo-Dionysius, and Eriugena as 'Neoplatonic' or 'Procline,' but there is equivocation in such designations. Boethius knew something of the works of contemporary pagan Neoplatonists and their predecessors, and made limited use of them; Pseudo-Dionysius was influenced in some measure by Proclus; Eriugena knew none of the works of the major pagan Neoplatonists directly. Whatever their complex relations to such sources,[23] these are philosophers for whom the doctrines of the Christian religion have fundamental importance. Neither they nor, indeed, their pagan Neoplatonist contemporaries could think of a philosophy independent of divine revelation.

One may speak of early medieval thought, with Werner Beierwaltes, as 'an intensive symbiosis of philosophy with theology,'[24] although that is (as he recognizes) to introduce a distinction not yet present to the history. The possibility of an independent philosophy does not appear until the thirteenth century, with St Thomas's formal distinctions between faith and reason, theology and philosophy,[25] distinctions against which the most notable Augustinians of the day argued vehemently.[26] While St Thomas himself, in the *Summa theologiae*, in spite of his distinctions, made a thorough synthesis of philosophical and theological elements, others, in the aftermath of the 'Averroist' crisis, sought to establish the independence of theology. A theology *sola fide* (as with Occam) had as its inevitable corollary a philosophy *sola ratione.*

James Doull may be right in claiming that 'the Augustinian system will only assume an independent philosophical form in modern philosophy.'[27] Indeed, there is currently much interest in arguing for the 'Augustinianism' of Descartes.[28] But perhaps the very circumstance of independence means that the position can be only equivocally Augustinian.[29]

There is no direct translation of the Augustinian philosophy into the institutional life of medieval Christendom. Yet, as Christopher Dawson remarks, St Augustine's role was decisive in 'depriving the state of its aura of divinity and seeking the principle of social order in the human will. In this way the Augustinian theory, for all its otherworldliness, first made possible the ideal of a social order resting upon the free personality and a common effort towards moral ends.'[30] According to James Doull's Protestant view of medieval history, however, the influence of St Augustine is not so decisive: 'The reason in the Church, though occupied with the content of the Augustinian theology, is not Augustinian. The Augustinian content is approached through the abstract logic of the Dionysian system,' which, according to Doull, dominates medieval philosophy from Eriugena to Cusanus.[31]

That Pseudo-Dionysius was a very significant influence in medieval philosophy, especially after new twelfth- and thirteenth-century translations of the *corpus*, is beyond question; yet Dionysian Platonism was always one among several forms of Christian Platonism: Boethian, Calcidian, and, above all, Augustinian. In the early medieval centuries, the Dionysian influence was sometimes strong (as in Eriugena), and sometimes weak or non-existent (as in St Anselm); in the later Middle Ages, it was an important element in the speculative syntheses of such thinkers as Albertus and Thomas, and in the mystical theology of such as Bonaventure, Eckhart, and Cusanus. But ever-present (beginning with Eriugena) is the difficult question whether Augustine was being interpreted in Dionysian terms, or vice versa. For the high Middle Ages, the interpretation of both Augustine and Dionysius was further complicated by the Aristotelian revival, partly by way of Arabic texts and commentaries with an important admixture of Neoplatonic interpretations. Can all this complex history (and more) really be included under the rubric of 'Dionysian Platonism'?[32]

According to Doull's argument, the role of Dionysius in relation to Augustine's Trinitarian doctrine is clear: 'to know the abstract principle thus discovered as principle of all the finite, theology had to be given a Neoplatonic structure. That was provided by Dionysius latinized by Scotus Eriugena and by his own systematic works.'[33] The effect was that 'the division in St Augustine's *De Trinitate* between the objective treatment of the revealed doctrine and the subjective approach to it vanishes in one objective and systematic view,'[34] a 'direct concentration on the infinite principle' which is 'the opposite pole to the existential naturalism with which Augustine's conversion began.' But 'if in religion all particularity was absorbed into a relation to the absolute principle, a like inarticulate unity was the character of secular life,' and thus 'the Trinitarian principle had its existence in the intuitive freedom of barbarous peoples,' insofar as 'the barbarians themselves sought to combine in their political communities individual freedom with devotion to the universal.'[35]

In what sense, or to what extent, this represents a 'secular development' is a difficult question. There is always a temptation to presuppose modern distinctions between the religious and the secular. Are there really any secular institutions in the early Middle Ages? Is Charlemagne a secular monarch? A contemporary mosaic (surviving from Pope Leo III's triclinium) represents him receiving his commission, together with Leo, directly from St Peter. His shrine at Aachen (commissioned by Frederick Barbarossa) shows him (now canonized) as a hieratic golden figure, flanked by the smaller attendant figures of Pope Leo and Archbishop Turpin. Are the Norman kings, Roger II and William II, secular monarchs when they cause themselves to be represented in mosaics at Palermo and Monreale as being crowned directly by Christ? Is the Emperor, Frederick II, a secular monarch when he claims to be the new King David, the Messianic king, as well as the new Augustus, and hails the little town of his birth as the new Bethlehem?

The beginning of secular institutions, indeed the development of the very concept of the secular (along with the concept of an independent philosophy) would depend upon philosophical and theological developments far beyond both Augustine and Dionysius. Nevertheless, as Doull suggests, the Augustinian Trinitarian doctrine is concretely present in the combination of individual freedom with devotion to the universal manifest in those vows (monastic as well as feudal) in which the most fundamental of early medieval institutions were constituted. And it is the characteristically Augustinian formulation of the doctrine, with its emphasis upon the relative equality of intellect and will, which translates thus into social institutions. The wisdom of Oliver and the ardour of Roland are the coordinate principles upon which depends the integrity of both individual personality and communal institution.

'The realization of the *civitas Dei* is a new beginning,' says Doull,[36] and in the promised continuation of his study we may anticipate a fuller and more nuanced account of medieval institutions and the philosophy which informed them. In preparation, what we still chiefly need from St Augustine is a fuller explication of the conception of *civitas Dei*, particularly in terms of the philosophy of *amor*, which is its principle. 'Two loves have founded two cities.'[37] Indeed, the concept of *amor* is fundamental throughout the system of St Augustine, not least in the *Confessions*, which is all about the ordering of love: *pondus meum amor meus.*[38] The problem for institutions, as for the individual soul, is the problem of the ordering of loves, which is ultimately the trinitarian question of the interrelations of truth and love. That question is at the heart of the Augustinian philosophy.

Perhaps the most perfect medieval vision of the Augustinian *civitas Dei* is Dante's *Paradiso*, where all finite ends, temporal and spiritual, and all particular interests, however mundane or exalted, all earthly and heavenly loves, preserved in their distinctions, are viewed as united in the divine love, by the gifts of grace in the virtues of faith, hope, and love: 'Nel suo profondo vidi che s'interna,/ Legato con amore in un volume,/ Cio che per l'universo si squaderna.'[39] As one sees, in the final canto of the *Paradiso*, the principle of that unity, for Dante, as for St Augustine, is the Holy Trinity, 'L' amor che muove il sole e l'altre stella.'[40]

In conclusion, we can hardly complain that James Doull, in the few pages he has devoted to the subject, has not said everything that may be said about the doctrine of Augustine and its influence in medieval culture. Our criticisms, if we have any, are really pleas for fuller explication. Meanwhile, we must be grateful for a magnificent exposition of the logic of the *Confessions*, an important argument about the relation of the *De Trinitate* to the *Confessions* (which is really an argument about the fundamental nature of theology), and some very provocative suggestions about Augustine and Pseudo-Dionysius in the history of medieval philosophy and social institutions. Seldom have so few pages offered so much.

Notes

In these notes, the titles of James Doull's articles are abbreviated as follows: 'Augustinian Trinitarianism' = 'Augustinian Trinitarianism and Existential Theology,' *Dionysius* 3 (1979); 'Christian Origin II' = 'The Christian Origin of Contemporary Institutions Part Two,' *Dionysius* 8 (1984); 'Augustinian Sapientia' = 'What Is Augustinian "Sapientia"?' *Dionysius* 12 (1988).

1 A. von Harnack, 'What Has History to Offer?' trans. from *Erforschtes und Erlebtes*, 1923, in M. Rumscheidt, ed., *Adolf von Harnack: Liberal Theology at Its Height* (London: Collins, 1989), 54.
2 Ibid., 56–7.
3 Cf. A. von Harnack, *Lehrbuch der Dogmengeschichte*, III (Freiburg: J.C.B. Mohr, 1890), 95.
4 Von Harnack, in Rumscheidt, ed., *Adolf von Harnack*, 23–5. As Joanna Scott remarks, Augustine 'is an increasingly invoked source for today's conversation about the moral scope and limits of the state, individual free will, and civil society'; 'Political Thought, Contemporary Influence of Augustine,' in

A. Fitzgerald, ed., *Augustine Through the Ages* (Grand Rapids, Mich.: Eerdmans, 1999), 661.

5 Doull, 'Christian Origin II,' 80.

6 Doull, 'Augustinian Trinitarianism,' 124.

7 'Christian Origin II,' 99; 204 above.

8 Ibid., 80.

9 'Augustinian Trinitarianism,' 123.

10 Ibid., 122.

11 'Christian Origin II,' 80.

12 Ibid., 97; 203 above.

13 Ibid., 100; 205–6 above.

14 'Augustinian Trinitarianism,' 150.

15 'Christian Origin II,' 80.

16 Ibid.

17 Augustine, *Contra Julianum*, IV, 14.72.

18 On the 'circolo ermeneutico,' see G. Reale, *Agostino: Amore assoluto e 'terza navigazione'* (Milan: Rusconi, 1994), 8–9.

19 Augustine, *De Trin.*, XV, 2.2.

20 Cf. R. Crouse, 'St. Augustine's *De Trinitate*: Philosophical Method,' in E. Livingstone, ed., *Studia Patristica* XVI/II (Berlin: Akademie Verlag, 1985), 501–10.

21 Cf. R. Crouse, '*Paucis mutatis verbis*: St Augustine's Platonism,' in R. Dodaro and G. Lawless, eds, *Augustine and His Critics* (London and New York: Routledge, 2000), 37–50.

22 Augustine, *Conf.*, XI, 8.10.

23 Cf. R. Crouse, 'Augustinian Platonism in Early Medieval Theology,' in J. McWilliam, ed., *Augustine: From Rhetor to Theologian* (Waterloo: Wilfrid Laurier University Press, 1992), 109–20. Giovanni Reale observes that while pagan Neoplatonism after Plotinus moves always in the direction of 'systematic complication,' Christian Neoplatonism moves in an opposite way towards 'systematic simplification' (introduction to C. Faraggiana di Sarzana, trans., *Proclo: I Manuali* [Milan: Vita e Pensiero, 1985], ccxx; also Reale, *Per una nuova interpretazione di Platone* [Milan: Vita e Pensiero, 1987], 66, 70). While this could look like a reversion to an older (and therefore simpler) Platonism, its significance is rather that Christian doctrine has overcome those dilemmas about mediation which move pagan Neoplatonism towards infinite complexity.

24 W. Beierwaltes, *Eriugena: Grundzüge seines Denkens* (Frankfurt am Main: Klostermann, 1994), 17.

25 As, for instance, in the first question of the *Summa theologiae.*

26 See, e.g., Bonaventure, *Quaestiones disp. de scientia Christi*, IV (*Opera omnia*, Quaracci, V); Matthew of Aquasparta, *Quaestiones disp. de fide et de cognitione* (*Quaestiones disputatae*, Quaracci, I), Q. V, *de fide*.

27 'Christian Origin II,' 102 n. 124; 209 n. 15 above.

28 See, e.g., S. Menn, *Descartes and Augustine* (Cambridge: Cambridge University Press, 1998). James Doull finds both the Neoplatonic/Procline/Dionysian Augustinianism of the Middle Ages and the Cartesian Augustinianism deficient: 'For a logical exposition of the third level of the "sapientia" one can refer only to Hegel.' 'Augustinian Sapientia,' 64 n. 13.

29 For a criticism of the Augustine-Descartes comparison (and Descartes's own misgivings about it) see M. Sciacca, *Sant'Agostino* (Palermo: L'Epos, 1991), 359–64.

30 C. Dawson, 'St Augustine and His Age,' in M.C. D'Arcy et al., *A Monument to St Augustine* (London: Sheed and Ward, 1930), 77.

31 'Christian Origin II,' 102 and n. 125 (209 n. 16 above); 'Augustinian Sapientia,' 64 n. 1.

32 'Christian Origin II,' 102; 207–8 above.

33 'Augustinian Trinitarianism,' 152.

34 Ibid., 152 n. 48.

35 Ibid., 153, 152.

36 'Christian Origin II,' 101; 207 above.

37 Augustine, *De Civ. Dei*, XIV, 28: 'Fecerunt itaque civitates duas amores duo ...'

38 Augustine, *Conf.*, XIII, 9.

39 Dante, *Paradiso*, XXXIII.

40 Ibid., 145.

chapter five

Neoplatonism and the Origin of the Older Modern Subject[1]

Hegel, beginning his lectures on the history of the older modern philosophy, observed that that philosophy began where the ancient had ended: the new philosophy had its origin in a completion of the old. This completion he found in Neoplatonism: the divine self-consciousness which was for Aristotle the first among substances became in the full development of Neoplatonism the one comprehensive substance which, going into the division of an ideal and a sensible world, was at once the origin of that division and the end to which it returned. The appropriation of being by thought which began with Parmenides was complete. The present paper would clarify the development of Neoplatonism to that completion and the transition at that point to another philosophy.

The primary structure of Neoplatonism is transformed in this transition. Man in this new philosophy is a self-consciousness which knows the division of the finite as its own.[2] Radically opposed to an extended world, its inner freedom externalized, it is also drawn to that apparently alien world and finds a realization of its freedom in discovering its hidden ideality. Hence an insatiable scientific and technical interest, which, while it may distract from the knowledge of God and freedom, is also a way to that knowledge.

The difference of the Neoplatonic from the older modern world is evident where individual freedom and a unified objective end meet in a political community. The highest political realization of a Neoplatonic thought is the unified state of the ending Middle Age. Individual freedom is ordered under a sovereign will. In relation to the sovereignty individuals have an intuition of their primary freedom. The ordered relation of their finite interests to this primary end is sustained by the opposition of an aristocratic or universal class to the class of those in commerce and the trades, however much the interests of the two may interpenetrate. The ruinous consequences when the sovereign fails to maintain his priority or when private persons would usurp the monarchy, where the relation of commoner to aristocrat degenerates into unbounded hatred, can nowhere be studied better than in well known Shakespearean tragedies. The most complete breakdown of the ordered elements is perhaps where Hamlet has the obligation to restore a corrupted monarchy, [and] is destroyed with many in the contradiction of being at once sovereign and subordinate. The free subject of the older modern age, as having the division within his freedom, is himself sovereign and with others constitutes a civil society – a state within the state. The external state of Locke or Rousseau has not for its end to replace the state but to make the unified end of the state also the end of all its members.[3]

So much at this point for the moderns. It remains to follow the course of this present argument more precisely. Its natural division is the following:

A The origin of the free individual and the temporalized Hellenistic world.
B The logic of the conversion of this temporal freedom to the eternal.
C The logical development of Neoplatonism.
D The origin in it of the older modern philosophy.

A. The Hellenic Origin of the Hellenistic Philosophy

Hegel's history of Neoplatonism as the process by which all finitude is known to have its truth in the Aristotelian *noesis noeseos* is difficult from the comprehensiveness of its view. It looks back not only to the Hellenistic schools as the immediate antecedent of Neoplatonism but to the origin of that subjective culture in the older Greek world. The free individual or person, emerging from the substantial life of the *polis* and its gods, found first a temporal realization of its freedom in relation to a temporalized and materialized *logos* and then from an apparent and contradictory freedom sought and discovered its ground in an eternal *logos*.[4] In this return the Neoplatonists read Plato and Aristotle as though containing already the subjective freedom of the following age. The problems of the previous age and its philosophies fell outside their interest. This longer perspective has the advantage that it permits not only a comprehensive view of Neoplatonism and its intrinsic movement but also its limit, if there is that in Plato and Aristotle which Neoplatonism does not contain but became the interest of later philosophy.

The subjective spirit of the Sophists and of the Socratic schools for Plato and Aristotle could either be contained within the qualified freedom of the political community or directed to its true development in a 'theoretic life.' The 'virtuous' relation of the individual to the state was a practical freedom which harmonized the passions to the common good. It belonged to the 'theoretic life' to discover a radical unity of life and thought. The free individual of the Hellenistic schools had supposedly brought all division and particularity to rest in an untroubled self-relation (*ataraxia*).

The reader of *Eumenides* knows that the stability of the *polis* rested on a harmony between the gods of the state and those of the family or natural community. The individual stood in a divided relation to the underworld and to the Olympians. The unconscious potentiality of the one was his end as mortal. In relation to the Olympians he participated in the immortal life of the gods, in whom a poetical vision, life, and self-conscious freedom were united. An ordered human life was made possible by a reason which could hold in check the latent conflict of these opposed ends. The virtuous balance is easily destroyed by war, 'which mostly assimilates the disposition of men to their immediate circumstances.'[5] The resolution of this division at its extreme point also became the interest of tragedy. Oedipus is shown as learning the blindness of political reason in relation to natural particularity. He is then shown also as liberated from the vengeful passions of the natural will, and in relation to his sons and daughter from the opposed ends of family and state. The unity of these ends which is brought into view in these and other Sophoclean tragedies is not that of the Aristophanic comedy, where the individual is raised to a self-conscious freedom in relation to the opposed ends of family and state and their gods. The tragic unification is rather that of the Aristotelian god for whom life is the actuality of self-conscious freedom, not in the medium of poetical language but for that inmost unity of the soul which is the actuality of the potential *nous*.

Aristophanes in *Symposium* defines the primary movement and end in humans and describes it mythically as the liberation from a divided relation to the gods. The comedies present variously through divided and ridiculous characters the divided relation of individuals to their institutions and their gods, and then dissolves these divisions. The spectator is awakened to a knowledge of this content as his own. There is in that awakening the beginning of a new relation of individuals to their institutions. The poet himself in *Plutus* writes not for citizens of the *polis* but for a society of free individuals. At this point of transition the individual through the comic art has a free relation to that same world, human and divine, as the Neoplatonist will regain for himself when the new society into which the *polis* has fallen has come to an understanding of itself. In this return Proclus has still not quite attained that freedom from a plurality of finite gods which is there in *Birds* and others of the later comedies of Aristophanes. Only perhaps in the last flowering of Neoplatonism in the Renaissance does a like completeness recur in aesthetic form.

The logic of this transition from the old substantial world to the world of free individuals is more transparent in the history of Greek philosophy. The movement there is to discover an *arche* in which thinking and being are one, the contrarieties of the many being united in that relation. In this development emerge the categories through which the finite is more adequately grasped, until in Aristotle's 'substance' and 'causes' the world of things is concretely related to thought. But the most comprehensive of divisions remained, that of the *nous* itself in the structure of the *polis* and its gods. In that division, if one speak teleologically of the history with Aristotle, lay the original provocation to philosophical thought, and the inquiry only came to rest with its resolution in the *noesis noeseos* which has life and nature as its own. This *arche* is for Aristotle the object of a *theoria* in which the divided and laborious life of men finds freedom in relation to a divine thinking comprehensive of this division.[6] There is not yet here the free individual of the Hellenistic schools nor the Neoplatonic *nous* in which this individual comes to a true concept of itself. Nor is there the relation of the *nous* to a primary One, the unknowable end and interest of all knowledge.

The new standpoint of post-Aristotelian philosophy is the result of all the previous development. The world as brought within categorial form belongs to the comprehensive category of self-conscious thought; the ideas and their sensible derivatives are within the *nous*. But this unified thought is also divided: the immediate unity of the *nous* in the One is also a divided relation to all that is other than the One. The primary interest of this post-Aristotelian thought is therefore to overcome this division, that the *nous* should so unify its knowledge of the many that in the end its difference from the One will be known as without truth. Philosophical thought would in this way have found its way back to the original Aristotelian concept of the *nous* for which division and plurality was not through a transition to another standpoint but intrinsic to the One.

The Aristotelian philosophy in its original and proper sense responded to the primary desire and need of the older Hellenic world. The undeveloped concept in it of a movement not to the One but from it had however a continuing interest in the ancient world – not philosophical, but as the receptivity and expectation of the Christian revelation. That revelation is unintelligible from a Neoplatonic standpoint as contradicting the primacy of the One over all plurality. But if that presupposition is undone in the completed development of Neoplatonism there may be thought room for a philosophical thought to which that division is intrinsic.[7]

B. The Hellenistic Schools and Origin of Neoplatonism

The world of the Hellenistic schools, if one consider it from the side of Neoplatonism, is a temporal image of the intelligible world. That image emerges at the point of coincidence between the undivided and divided in the intelligible. The image is an immediate existence of the ideal. The noetic self-consciousness of the ideal world is dispersed in that immediacy into a multitude of souls having knowledge of sensible individuals and abstract universals. The individuals who have taken the division of life and thought of the *polis* and its religion into their self-relation find themselves in the immediacy of this result in that sensible world. This temporalized freedom is the antecedent and condition of the conversion from it to the noetic world of Neoplatonism. The individuals of this Hellenistic world bring with them from their earlier formation the assumption that they are free, that the sensible multiplicity and their own contingent relations are not alien but stand in a true relation to their self-consciousness. The Stoic would show this assumption to be true for the individual as universal or thinking, the Epicurean for him in his sensuous immediacy. The Sceptic regards this fixed assertion of opposed dogmas as reason to question whether there is any truth for self-consciousness. He goes on to show that if one assume a unity of these opposed dogmas, reason itself destroys this supposed truth and reduces it to a knowledge of appearances, which can suffice for daily life but is without truth. All three have in common a self-conscious freedom which rests untroubled in itself. The Sceptic has disclosed a world which contradicts this assumed freedom.[8]

Scepticism is thus a disintegration of philosophy and of that world of which it is the comprehensive thought. The 'deconstruction' which nibbles at opposed contemporary dogmas is in comparison frivolous, in that behind a radical subjective freedom and its temporalized world an older Christian order remains. For this ancient scepticism there is nothing but the contradiction of an assumed subjective freedom and an unfree world. The logic of this disintegration is of the greatest importance to a knowledge of Neoplatonism. Through it one knows Neoplatonism not as an extravagant aberration but as a necessary turning of thought. This turning also contains implicitly the subsequent course of Neoplatonism – not simply to go over to an intelligible world but also to know the contradiction of the sensible as resolved in that relation.

The *ataraxia* of the Stoic appeared to be absolutely stabilized against the world: 'Justum et tenacem propositi virum, si fractus illabatur orbis, impavidum ferient ruinae.'[9] The unstable content of sense and imagination was appropriated to the self-identity of thought in the *kataleptike phantasia*, the Stoic criterion of truth. The Stoics thought also that they could advance from that abstract universality, which is indeed the beginning of science, to a demonstrated unity of sensible particularity with it. They would thus have established an unshakeable relation of thinking self-consciousness to its objects. The defect in this relation was that it contained the syllogistic mediation only as negated in the relation of individual to universal. The mediation belonged to a subjective reflection and not to the structure of its objects.[10]

Although the Stoics appeared to have gone beyond Aristotle in detaching the categories from sensible substance and making logic fully the possession of self-conscious thought, in the immediacy of this result they had only an abbreviated and formal relation of thinking to the forms of reasoning. So also at the same time as the *logoi* of nature were taken to be comprehensive of finite categories, the Stoics had hold of sensible objects only through abstract categories of Presocratic thought – somethings, their qualities and relations – through which an objective unity of 'somethings' with their determinations is not discovered.

The Epicurean sought to bind together infallibly the inner security of his self-conscious freedom with the passing good of pleasure. The mediation between the two fell to a discriminating judgment which should relate momentary pleasures to the whole content of a cultivated life. But, as with the Stoic, this mediation was lost in the untroubled self-relation of the individual. In that abstract freedom he is indifferent to the world: 'Nil igitur mors est ad nos neque pertinet hilum.'[11] Similarly the categories in which he thought his sensible world were shifting qualities and atoms having only the most formal differences and properly, as pure objects of thought, only their difference from the void.

The opposition of the Stoic to the Epicurean philosophy cancels itself out no doubt, in that beginning with opposed assumptions each maintains itself so far as it can appropriate the assumption of the other. For themselves the opposition remains, but the Sceptic rightly calls them 'dogmatists' and takes their one-sided assumptions into one view. This comprehensive view leads to the inevitable conclusion that the free individual who is certain the world is not alien to him finds himself in an alien world which has for him no essential and moving interest.[12] The student of Neoplatonism at least is unlikely to confuse this with the so-called scepticism of Hume or Schultze. That scepticism would be called by the ancient Sceptic an empirical dogmatism.

Ancient scepticism is beyond the opposition of rational and empirical positions but can get hold of itself only negatively by demolishing both. The 'tropes' or 'turnings' by which it effects this complete 'deconstruction' are finally reduced to five.[13] These 'tropes' effect an 'epoche' or suspension of judgment in all inquiries. Regarding the 'tropes' themselves in this suspense, the Sceptic both speaks of them empirically as an indefinite plurality and knows the five as complete.[14] In truth they are complete unless for a thinking which knows endless division as a moment in itself and in its objects. That knowledge Plato sought in his concept of an 'otherness' which was not infinite only but a moment in the definite structure of genera and species and their relation to individuals.[15] Aristotle regarded Zeno's problems of the infinite, which still perplex logicians, as belonging to an abstract and undeveloped thought.[16] In his concept of substance they were resolved. That knowledge was however for a thinking which could contemplate universally the formation of increasingly concrete unities of being and thinking. The Sceptic and the Dogmatists, whose positions he would unite, have possession of this development in their self-conscious freedom. But this is a divided self-consciousness, at once universal and as individuals in changing relation to ever changing things. For the Sceptic this division has the form on the one side of a freedom from finite relations resting in itself, on the other of an endless empirical involvement with his world. He is impotent to bring these relations into that unity which is presupposed in the sense of his freedom.

The Sceptical criticism not only destroys the opposed 'dogmas' of the Stoics and the Epicureans but virtually also its own standpoint. There is a progression in the five later tropes in which the endless division from falling in a subjective reflection on the relation of universals to sensible individuals passes into the objective relation of the terms. The fifth 'trope' on the circularity of the relation has all but brought the object into the form of a *logos* comprehending division. Such was the original relation, for the Stoics, of their self-conscious freedom to the universal *logos* and its genera as *spermatikoi logoi*. In that relation the divided moments of self-consciousness, as universal and immediate, are united. This unity itself as immediate is the instant (*to exaiphnes*) in which the divided moments of 'becoming' are one. In this unified relation to the sensible world the free individual is released from the bonds of his temporal cave and reverts to his original concept as a thinking which in its self-relation knows as its own the division of life and the ideal world. Such is the origin of Neoplatonism.[17]

C. Neoplatonism

For one who looks back to the origin of the self-conscious freedom which foundered in Scepticism, the configuration of the world this self-consciousness finds when it has collected itself out of its division and temporal dispersion is evident. Its freedom rests in the unity of the ideal and the sensible world; life and the attendant division of immediate and universal self-consciousness is a manifestation of that unchanging unity. For the self-consciousness itself which has collected itself out of the division and contradiction of Scepticism, its world is not at first so clearly articulated. The *ataraxia* or rest which the free individual had against the division and fluctuation of his world is now the One, his end as unified. The individual finitude of the Sceptic has sunk for a unified thought into that unity. All the sensible has been absorbed into the externalized identity of matter.

In this relation the division the Sceptic could not make his own has been transcended. Self-consciousness is constituted in relation to the One by a division from it and the negation of this division. The division occurs and is negated; the resultant self-consciousness has hold of the moments of its formation as a transition, not at first as a stable knowledge of their relation. For the self-consciousness thus constituted all finitude falls within its self-relation. It comes to a knowledge of this finitude as its own by dividing what is immediately identical with itself and then by appropriating what has been completely divided. For to know its objects as its own is to impart to them its own logical structure of division and return to the undivided. The knowledge of its objects and of itself in this universal thought has thus the form of a procession and return. But this grasp of its objects and of its own freedom is not at first complete. Just as in its constitution and resulting self-relation it did not have hold of its moments, so their relation is not fully articulated in the knowledge of its objects.

Again, when this unified thought itself and its world pass over into temporal manifestation, the sensible world is not fully articulated. The divided self-consciousness of the Dogmatic schools recurs and their unification through Scepticism is lost from sight.

The movement and history of Neoplatonism is from this first incomplete knowledge of itself to an adequate knowledge of its underlying concept, that is, of the sensible world as manifestation of a unified Idea. The development of this systematic thought can only be intrinsic and of the system as a whole, that is, of its elements and primary logical structure. The principal Neoplatonists differ no doubt in their interests. Iamblichus, for example, has a religious interest, which, by the measure of a Plotinian or Porphyrian Neoplatonism might appear unphilosophical. But in this interest lies the need to discover better the relation of the individual to the ideal world than is found in those philosophers. In him, as in Proclus and Damascius, there is a continuing articulation of the system. In that lies their importance and their interest to a philosophical mind.[18]

It is alien to the systematic form of this philosophy that the source of its movement and development should be sought in extraneous and contingent causes. The historical development here is also not that of Greek philosophy before Aristotle, where one philosophy followed another it might seem randomly. The inner logical connection which revealed itself to Aristotle was concealed from his predecessors. There was there an inarticulate movement to systematic form. The development here is within the system.[19]

The knowledge the noetic self-consciousness has of itself and of its world as its own is abstract so far as the moment of division or mediation is transitional only and lost in the return. Its identity with itself is the prevalent moment in its knowledge. The development is towards an adequation of the moments, where each has in it the others: and Being, Life, and Thought are complementary forms of the same totality, differing only as centred successively on each. The One remains transcendent over a more and more unified noetic world until the separation becomes problematical.

The philosophers in the course of this development are attracted by cosmogonic systems which appear to integrate the One and the noetic world. Porphyry would admit such an integration, but at the price of importing finite relations into the infinite One. Others accordingly incorporate these cosmogonies, which serve a religious interest, only at a second level. The intrinsic development of Neoplatonism itself finally passes into a Trinitarian form, as with Maximus Confessor and that great Irishman John Scotus Eriugena.

A further development is still necessary. The subject which contemplates the 'divisio naturae' stands outside the movement itself and can well take from its result a merely formal concept of the divine actuality. That he in his particularity should be comprehended in the movement it was necessary first that a human order should be established, and then this order taken into the infinite Neoplatonic form. This human order was defined by Aquinas through a finite Aristotelian logic. This logic was expanded particularly by Duns Scotus and dissolved in the nominalism of Ockham. That development permitted a return to the standpoint of Eriugena, with the difference that the ascent to the universal and the return to worldly interests were harmonized in one divine Idea. That completion of Neoplatonism was then the turning point to another philosophy.

1. Plotinus

Of all forms of Neoplatonism there is in the Plotinian the greatest distance between the underlying concept and the form of its disclosure in the intelligible and sensible worlds. In all that comes after the One there is no concretion of the undivided and the divided, but only a difference which passes into an abstract self-relation. The *nous,* as it originates in turning to the One out of division, is an undistinguished unity of being and thinking.[20] The primary forms through which a determinate thought is constituted are the *megista gene* of Plato's *Sophist*: being, motion and rest, same and different. In these forms Plato found a response to the Parmenides of his dialogue, who appeared to have shown that there was no true finitude. But of the 'otherness' which thought had through these irreducible distinctions within itself Aristotle had long before observed that it was an 'otherness' of true and false – of the relation of thought to being but not a complete determination of either.[21]

In the first treatise of the sixth *Ennead* Plotinus carries through a detailed criticism of the Aristotelian and the Stoic categories. The criticism is that of an infinite thinking which has in itself its own finitude and that of its objects. It is thus beyond the Aristotelian *gene tou ontos* which only in relation to 'first substance' have that unity of their moments in a manner. The Stoic categories, as modes of an infinite *logos*, are closer to Plotinus. But in relation to both, Plotinus' criticism is extraneous and superficial.[22] It is not that Plotinus might on further reflection have entered the doctrines examined and criticized them on their own ground. The impediment lay in his concept of the *nous* as immediately unifying endless division in its self-relation. Its actual thinking contains first this indeterminate difference and its need is to limit this indeterminacy. Through the Platonic *gene* the *nous* brings its difference into the stability of its self-relation. In this relation it falls into another duality between the result and the way to it: it stands in an abstract relation to its difference.[23]

The Aristotelian categories originated in a profound criticism of the Platonic doctrine that all things were a composition of the One and the indeterminate Dyad. In the Aristotelian categories the Dyad has passed into the moment of 'privation' in a concrete object. For Plotinus only the One is beyond composition out of elements. Aristotle was in error, so the criticism repeats with all the categories, in supposing his categories to have a unity unthinkable from the standpoint of the critic.[24] The Stoic categories appear to Plotinus as a nest of contradictions, which no doubt they are, in that through them the positivity of the 'some thing' and all difference are objectively united.[25] It reveals a complete shift in the Neoplatonism of Porphyry that he can receive into his thought both the Aristotelian and the Stoic logic.

After examining the Aristotelian categories, which, as he regards them, have neither unity severally nor do they together constitute one genus, and the Stoics who cannot without contradiction distinguish four categories within a generic unity, Plotinus asks for his part how there can be a limited multiplicity in thought. The *nous* is different from the One as distinguishing being and unity. For Plotinus the second hypothesis of Parmenides teaches the primary stations in a corresponding formation of being and the negative unity of thinking. The thinking which all but coincides with being is an image of the absolute One. The perfect coincidence of being and activity is the One itself. There appears in their relation as distinguished an indefinite plurality. This plurality is encircled in that as from the One both terms are the whole. The activity of thinking is on the side of the object a timeless motion. The stability of being is the self-identity or rest of thinking. A reflection on the difference of these three terms adds sameness and difference to their number. Plotinus is satisfied that there can be no further primary distinctions or categories. The successive contraries treated in the second hypothesis give rise to derivative distinctions – quality, quantity, and the other so-called categories.[26] The primary genera are distinct only as the movement of thought to itself is distinguished from its original and restored identity. The beginning does not have the division in it nor does the division remain in the end, nor again does the difference have that from which it is different. The noetic world as founded on these distinctions cannot have the triadic form Porphyry sought to give it.

The structure of Plotinus' noetic world is of a universal thought in which differences are implicit; then a multiplication of beings and intelligences in the genera or ideas of a natural order and intelligences particularized in relation to them; then this activity returned to rest in the original identity. The unified and the pluralized thought are exclusive of each other.[27] The same abstract relation of unified and divided moments recurs in the psychic 'hypostasis.' Intelligences in going over to soul both retain their universality and fall into the multiplicity of nature, even to embodiment and to the pure dividedness which is matter. Nature is ambiguously good and evil, according as souls have descended into it or in their intellectual part remain undescended.[28] Souls may order and unify their relations to an external world through the Platonic virtues. But this order assumes and cannot comprehend the primary division of the undescended and the descended soul. In the sensible world the soul does not have that unity which, if abstractly, the Stoic and Epicurean knew.

The ecstatic unity of the individual and the One, in which Neoplatonism has its beginning, is not mediated and confirmed in the explication of the system. The desired freedom appears to be lost unless through a deeper integration of the divided and the undivided.

2. *Porphyry*

If Plotinism be taken as the measure of Neoplatonism, Aemilius and Porphyry will be seen as falling back to Numenius and a middle Platonism which did not yet know fully the primacy of the One and the ecstatic relation of the individual to it beyond all division.[29] But the division which occurred first at the noetic level became at the psychic level an unbridged duality in the individual. A return to the One must be to the One as the source of this division. This step, which occurs immediately to a reflection on the whole Plotinian system, was taken by both his principal disciples.

With Aemilius and Porphyry there begins the series of Neoplatonic commentaries on *Parmenides* which reveal a progressive integration of the system. In Plotinism the One was too abstractly related to permit more than a rudimentary exegesis, which found the three 'hypostases' in the first three hypotheses. Porphyry's exposition differs principally from that of Aemilius in that it denies a difference of principle between rational and irrational souls, and before that has apparently unified more strongly the intelligible and intellective moments of the *nous*. In this he has carried through more fully the same revision of Plotinism. Porphyry's whole exposition is the surest confirmation of that interpretation of his whole philosophy as Stoicism completely Platonized which Pierre Hadot put together from many sources. There is an abstract unity of soul with itself from which negativity has been excluded. Sensible beings appear first as ordered then as unordered, so also matter. The contemplation of the material world relates all finitude first to the identity of the substrate then considers it as a pure detached otherness.[30]

The formation of the noetic world through division of an absolutely unified thought has here a like structure to the mythical generation in Numenius and the *Chaldaean Oracles* of a triadic intelligence. The moments of an undistinguished 'paternal' identity are first distinguished and opposed, then the difference is taken into a thinking turned to its origin. This trinity in which the movement and spiritual connection falls between the 'father' and the 'son' Hadot finds in the writings of Marius Victorinus, as also a conceptual exposition of the same doctrine which can only be thought Porphyrian.

As constituted by this relation to the One which contains the division in it, the self-conscious intelligence likewise unites its 'noetic' and 'noeric' aspects not through an immediate unification of positive and negative moments ('sameness' and 'difference') but as these have been categorially articulated. There is room for the Aristotelian logic through which, as in Stoicism, thought maintains its self-identity. The primary distinctions for this noetic self-consciousness are, however, the categories of the Stoic physics through which thought found relation to the infinite *logos*: the 'something,' the 'not-something,' the positive as 'quality,' the negativity of 'state' and 'relative state.' These distinctions can just as well define the relation of thought to the transcendent One as it brings its content into the contradictory relation of being and not-being. Thinking and thought are united in the exclusion of the contradictory in the constitution of 'beings' and 'non-beings' and the transcendent unity of this opposition in a principle beyond both. This principle is pure act as uniting immediately being and the negative self-relation of thinking. In the self-identical activity of this relation the difference of the noetic level from the One vanishes.

The limit of the standpoint becomes evident when this intellectualized Stoicism has passed over into soul and the sensible world. It is the limit of the Stoic 'dogmatism' which unites individual and universal abstractly on the side of the universal. It is an advance no doubt over Plotinus that souls in their multiplicity and embodiment are inwardly united. But what the opposed Epicurean 'dogma' would save has no place in this relation. Still less is there any understanding of that concreteness which the Sceptic sought and could not find.[31] Because the opposition of universal soul to particular individual souls has been sharpened, as against Plotinus Porphyry is interested more than his teacher in the 'theurgic' arts. They are useful, however, only to souls in their particularity. The soul as thinking needs no extraneous means to its salvation. Porphyry's Neoplatonism leads to a divided relation of humans to the One and is thus an inadequate explication of its concept.

Plotinus had spoken of the One and what came after it according to a Presocratic logic which unites contraries only in the moment. According to the Stoic logic of Porphyry the divided was one with the undivided at the point where its positive and negative moments had the form of contradiction. The unity was abstract and exclusive of the negative, and this abstractness appears in a divided relation of the soul to the One.[32] The inescapable demand for the Neoplatonist was not to revert to Plotinism but to find a comprehensive relation of the One to the divided. Towards this the first step was to set the One beyond all finite relations to what was other than itself.

3. Later Neoplatonism

Although it is true that one would look in vain in Neoplatonism for the logic of a movement from the undivided to the divided and multiple,[33] Iamblichus and after him Proclus and Damascius brought the argument finally to the form where only the limits of human discourse obstructed a knowledge of their equality in a trinitarian relation. In all these philosophers the soul that finds rest in the One is itself unified, its particularity contained without abstract reduction in the relation of individual to universal. The One which is the interest of this unified soul has a like relation to division and to the completed division which is the individual. This concrete relation on the one side and on the other is clarified by degrees in the thought of these three philosophers.

(i) Iamblichus

Iamblichus distinguished before the noetic realm a One without division and a One uniting 'limit' and 'unlimited.' The plurality belonging to this second One is itself unified, that is, it is not subject to the opposition of its constituent moments. It is the plurality of gods through whom the individual in his particular relations to the world is unified and awakened to a sense of the primary One. Thus Proclus reports of Iamblichus' exegesis of *Parmenides* that the first hypothesis was found to be about the One and the gods.[34] There is in this relation a unification of the second with the first One, as also of the individual with the universal soul. But in the one case as in the other the unification is on the side of the universal moment. The henads of Proclus effect, or are intended to effect, a more concrete relation of the many gods to the One, and Damascius' criticism of Proclus moves farther in the same direction.

The difficulties of Iamblichus' formulation come to light more distinctly in the further course of his comment on *Parmenides.* The self-conscious intelligence, while it knows the triad of being, life, and thought as its own, has this knowledge variously in its moments: the noetic intelligence contains the three monads in their undivided totality; in its division and negative return it knows the particular ideas and not their comprehension in the monads.[35] A consequence of this incompleteness of the noetic realm is that the transition to soul and the sensible world is divided: before soul the many gods in the guise in which they appear in the lower world as 'angels,' 'demons,' and 'heroes' constitute an intermediate hypothesis. From the same defect stems also the interpretation of the last two hypotheses as about the celestial and sublunary worlds. Proclus objected rightly that these as not for thought total objects are not properly 'hypotheses.'[36]

The soul for Iamblichus is at an extreme remove from the Plotinian soul untouched by the sufferings of its mortal part. The individual soul, though an inner freedom belongs to it, can attain to that freedom not of itself but only as the gods are moved through the theurgic arts.[37]

(ii) Proclus

The principal division for Proclus of all that is after the One is of gods or henads and beings composite of the undivided and the divided. There is the One, and after the One the whole noetic realm. The relation of the two is that the same total content is in the One without division and contrariety, in the noetic as divided and opposed.[38] The division in the noetic between the 'ontic' and the 'henadic' is that with the one the moment of self-relation or being is first, then procession, then reversion to being; while the 'henadic,' though divided according to the division of being, remains primarily in an undivided relation to the One. The three monads – being, life, and thought – through which the ideal procession and return takes place are the same totality, each having the others in it, and distinguished only by the moments of 'rest,' 'procession,' and 'reversion.' That these moments are divided and timelessly successive results from the original constitution of the noetic: before the concretion of 'being' as the first 'monad' are its abstract elements, 'measure' and the 'unmeasured,' which are unified through their relation to the One. For the thought which considers this unification the first product is 'being'; 'life' and 'thought' then follow as the division and reunification through which the noetic self-consciousness actually knows all things as its own. The realization of self-consciousness in the three 'monadic' totalities, should it be complete, would cancel the assumed priority of the abstract moments and know the derivation from the One as not a composition but through a primary unity of the abstract elements and their product.

Hegel rightly observed that the noetic self-consciousness as realized through the relation of the three monads, each having in its manner the other moments in it, was virtually one idea. Proclus himself, though he speaks similarly of the unity of the monads, is not yet at the point where it can be fully evident.[39] Where the unity of the monads comes most nearly into view is in the reversion of the 'noeric' to the 'noetic' intelligence. That completion of self-conscious thought is also the point of transition to the psychic 'hypostasis' – in the language of *Timaeus*, to the demiurgic construction of the soul. The unification of self-consciousness is spoken of through successive contraries – 'in itself–in another,' 'rest–motion,' 'same–different'; and through syllogistic relations of the undivided and the divided mediated by these categories. It is enough for the present argument to observe that this reflection leads neither to a complete unification of the 'noetic' nor to a concept of soul in which the relation of individual to universal is fully articulated. The latter result demands particular attention if one would see the criticism of Proclan Neoplatonism by Damascius and his revision of its principles as a necessary development.[40]

Proclus, as Iamblichus before him, has need to find a unified relation of the human soul to the One and the whole 'noetic' realm. It reflects the priority of 'being' over 'life' and the activity of thinking that the soul has an eternal being and is embodied in the sensible world through its activity.[41] Although Proclus has moved far from Plotinus and early Neoplatonism towards a concrete concept of man, there is still a distance to go if the sensible individual is to be known as the immediate existence of the whole man. The original concept and desire of Neoplatonism is not yet fully realized.

(iii) Damascius

If with Proclus it is not far from sight that the three monads of the noetic realm make up one idea, Damascius brings fully to light that this unity is the truth of the matter. That the monads which together constitute the infinite procession and conversion of what remains with itself appear as a successive plurality is for a thought which has not hold fully of its own finitude. The primary division for Proclus of all things after the One into composite beings and henads belongs already to a finite standpoint.[42]

The logical method of all the Neoplatonists is an infinite self-conscious thought which can make the finite and divided its own. But in this appropriation the present argument has shown in what ways it might remain held by finite abstractions. Proclus in considering the constitution of self-conscious thought gave an independent 'henadic' status to 'limit' and 'unlimited' – the abstract moments of the division which rested undivided in the One. This initial concession to the finite pervaded his whole system even to his concept of the human soul. Damascius throughout his *Principles* uses a method of 'problems' and 'solutions' which shows a complete clarity about the relativity of finite moments. Problems are formed by fixed finite assumptions. The solution is to situate them as relative in an infinite whole. The application of this method to Proclus' system breaks down its rigid structures and allows its moving spirit to appear far more clearly.[43]

The *Principles* begins with a problem about the relation of the One, considered as principle, to a plurality of which it is assumed to be principle. In this problem lies the difficulty which has beset all his Neoplatonic predecessors of relating the One to the divided: each term has to be at once independent of the other and related to it. There is no solution to these contradictions unless in perceiving that the separation of principle from principled is the product of a finite thought, and that the One is not simply beyond division but has division as its own moment.[44] Damascius' method is perplexing to human thought in that it places the truth, which is its primary interest, beyond its grasp. So with all forms of Neoplatonism, but here, as afterwards with Cusanus, the limit of human discourse is directly exposed.[45]

It would be long here to follow through Damascius' revision of the noetic world already strongly unified by Proclus. The primary opposition of 'ontic' and 'henadic' is all but dissolved in a concept of what is not one as first of all unified – not 'limit' as opposed to 'unlimited,' but transcending this division in relation to the undivided. The intelligible is thus not the product of prior 'henadic' elements but itself equally 'henadic' or divine. It comes into view with this knowledge of a unified division that the ideal world is in truth not a second level below the One but rather, as taught by the *Oracles* and other revelations, the One itself as triune. An intelligible world more within the grasp of a human thought subject to exclusive contraries can be thought no more than that: a world of human discourse.[46]

This deeper unification of the ideal world permitted Damascius to see a concrete unity of the human soul in which the embodied individual in a sensible world is the whole soul, as also the soul as universal is not abstract but the whole soul. That the soul descends from its universality not in its activity only, as for Proclus, but substantially as well supposes an equality and concretion of its moments at one level and the other. This knowledge of the soul and the knowledge of the intelligible as triune and concrete are reciprocal.[47] Proclus was confident that he had learned from Syrianus, his teacher, the true and adequate exegesis of *Parmenides*. The four 'hypotheses' after the first give the complete procession of all things from the One even to the externalized and absolutely divided unity of matter. If the One is, all things both eternal and temporal are. The remaining four 'hypotheses' show that, if the One is not, all things in consequence are not. This exegesis Damascius finds defective, in that it omits from all reality what the world is for souls in a sensible world. Sensible reality it regards as a Stoic would from the side of its identity, not in its otherness and negativity. Damascius, knowing the concrete unity of the soul, regards the sensible world as for such a unified soul. In this, though inwardly, he resumes the standpoint of the Sceptic.[48]

Thus the not-being of the One, as treated in the sixth 'hypothesis,' is an indifference underlying affirmative and negative, such as is the universal side of the Sceptical consciousness. The flux of images which have neither substrate nor definite relation to a knowing subject, presented in the eighth 'hypothesis,' is again sensible immediacy as for the Sceptic. The seventh and ninth 'hypotheses' Damascius concedes to Syrianus and Proclus are about the nullity of all things, if the One is not. These hypotheses he declares to be 'impossible,' that is, contradictory. But he hesitates to reject them as meaningless since all the 'hypotheses' as unified totalities contain like contradictions. It is as though, happy to have found meaning in two of the negative hypotheses, he turns from the anomaly that they should have a different status than the others.[49]

These 'meaningless' hypotheses also have in fact meaning for him. Through them a Sceptical relation of the soul to itself and its sensible objects is converted into that unified soul he knows already, for which also the flux of images is individualized. At that point the development of Neoplatonism appears to be complete; the argument has returned to the divided self-consciousness of Scepticism and made clear what that division of the individual from its universality is.[50]

C. The Origin of the Older Modern Philosophy

1. Neoplatonism from Eriugena to Cusanus

With Damascius the development of Neoplatonism appears to be complete: the ideal and sensible worlds at the point of their complete explication and concreteness disclose through their nullity, as other than the One, that the One is the sole comprehensive truth. There remains with him however an ambiguity and hesitancy in the face of this result: the hypotheses which set forth the procession and return of all things are only for a finite thought, but that thought also finds it absurd to recognize the contradiction and nullity of its hypotheses – to recognize its own finitude and permit the world of its finite discourse to be drawn into the infinite actuality of the One. This further step is taken by Eriugena, guided to it by Dionysius and Maximus Confessor. There is one finite totality or nature, which thought can divide into a creative beginning, a creative *logos* containing a plurality of ideas or created ends, the complete explication of this *logos* as soul and the sensible world, this world as through man united with its exemplar, the exemplary and the sensible thus unified as resting eternally in their creative origin.

A difficulty remains however in the system of Eriugena not far different from that of Damascius. The quadripartite division takes the place of the 'hypotheses.' The movement of the argument no longer depends on a Platonic text but is purely logical, the undivided good as it is for a thought which knows its moments as successive. For this extraneous thought the 'uncreated creative' is divided from 'that which neither creates nor is created' – the principle as returned to itself. And between the two is room for the ideal world and its sensible image. What is the status of this thought and of the structure the ideal and sensible have for it?

The ideal totality 'creates and is created.' As one *logos* it 'creates'; as a plurality of ideas or 'primordial causes' it is 'created.' The structure is very much that of Damascius, the 'unified' in which contraries coincide, and within it the ideas as composed of 'limit and unlimited.' This totality is posterior to the One, from which for the contemplative subject it comes forth and into which it recedes. The particular ideas are at once the objects of an immutable knowledge, and prior to this knowledge is endless 'dyadic' division. The sensible totality has the same ambiguity, that the soul knows a multitude of changing but recurrent images of the ideal content, and when predicated of its material substrate those images dissolve into vanishing appearances.

Souls as returning to the ideal from their dispersion as the sensible totality again return first to their 'primordial cause' or their original state as created, and then through Christ or the *logos* into the unity of the ideal world. The subject which follows the outgoing and return of 'nature' through this twofold movement does away both with its objective divisions and with the gradations in its knowledge of them.[51]

There occurs then the question how beyond the divisions and constructions of a subjective reflection the infinite good is present to what is other than itself, how it is the end to which the rational creature in its finitude is principally drawn. The sense of this question, and how a further philosophical development beyond this point is possible, is readily intelligible if Eriugena's thought be situated in its historical context. The *Periphyseon* was written at a time when politically a unity of ends embodied in the 'emperor' had been established and drew individuals to it for a time, until it succumbed to the counter attraction of divisive passions and interests. The weakness of this restored Roman Empire was that the political good did not inform and give direction to those interests as different and opposed to its realization. For this formation it was not enough that the good should have come into view as that in which for thought all that came after it was enveloped. The good had to have root in the finite: it was necessary that the 'dyad' and the power of contraries be arrested in finite substances. The movement to the good might then have a sensible beginning and be through an ordered human life. Aristotle provided the means for this embodiment of the good.

Cusanus, six centuries after Eriugena, can appear to propose very much the same system. Dionysius and Proclus are also his masters. But between the two systems there is a profound difference: the good for Cusanus is realized in individuals as they have passed through the oppositions of an ordered human world to an infinite unity. His Neoplatonism has behind it a succession of Aristotelian positions in which the mediation of individuals with the good is variously understood. This history makes possible a transformation of Eriugena's system in which the externality of thought to the principle is overcome and the principle known not only by the negation of the finite but positively as the beginning of what comes after it.

The relation of the great Scholastic systems to the resurgent Neoplatonism of Cusanus can be indicated briefly in its general logical structure. It is sufficient in this interest to speak of Thomism, Scotism, and the nominalism of Ockham. Presupposing the one good, these systems proceed to a knowledge of it by another route than that of Neoplatonism – from a sensible beginning variously taken. Aquinas assumes a world of Aristotelian finite substances, and by negating the infinite regress that appears in the mutual relations through which their actuality is sustained, arrives in his five ways at the concept of an infinitely actual being. The subject which carries through this proof knows itself as a substance – as an intellectual form relating to itself all other forms through the necessity of the understanding. Within this unity there is a dispersion of powers, such that sense perception knows the individual directly, the understanding only mediately. The logical movement of the proofs draws together into one the self-relation of substances and their externality, and this unification is reflected into the subject.

Practically, an inner unity of the will with particular natural relations through the virtues is converted into a Stoic individual, whose particularity is inward and has the form of universal rights. Scotism expresses the result of this unification. The individual is not an externalization of the substantial form having its principle in 'materia signata' but belongs to the perfection of the substance. The difference of individual from universal is contained in their relation, as 'formalities' within their community. The thinking individual is likewise more strongly integrated: discursive and intuitive moments of knowledge are more nearly one activity, as are thought and sense perception. The way to a knowledge of God is through individuals in which universals are present, not purely but in a particular content. Universals in their purity are only in the intellect. The question is whether there is a first in the orders of causality, finality, and eminence. The reasoning here is to an infinite being in which the finitude and consequent dependence of substances so conceived has passed into an absolute unity of self-relation and division. This idea is not possible only but actual, since its perfection would be diminished if, as with all else, its universality and its division were not absolutely unified.[52]

Scotism passes easily into the nominalism of Ockham, as the individual substances presupposed in the movement from the world to God are seen to rest on a simpler relation of individual and universal for the thinking subject. The difference of the sensible individual from the universal is the difference in the subject between a sensuous and a thinking intuition. In the one the multiple sensuous content is immediately united; through the other the subject is able to bring the content into logical form of judgment and syllogism.

The nominalist has made for himself a science of contingency in which the movement from the world to God is no more than a possibility without logical cogency. There is no proof that an endless regression is impossible. Practically he lives in a world of free individuals, a democracy where hierarchic order has lost its hold. There is the intuition of a common good, but with it an empirical diversity of ends.

The movement to God at this point is through an inner unification of division and discourse with intuitive unity, not simply their cooperation in relation to a given content, as in nominalism. The necessity which moved in the demonstrations of Aquinas and Scotus has to be discovered as the contrariety underlying contingent relations and their coincidence in the unity of thought. The objects of a thought which has thus taken its external presuppositions into itself are, as Neoplatonists had long known, constituted from logical elements and not alien to self-consciousness.

Cusanus thought to have in the coincidence of opposites a truer knowledge of God and the world than could be obtained by reasoning from finite presuppositions. Only in God and in the intellect as turned to itself out of finite operations was the 'coincidentia oppositorum' actual. All that otherwise was taken for truth was only an endless approximation. The right relation of the mind to this approximate truth was a 'docta ignorantia,' a scepticism fully cognizant of itself. This scepticism is neither the attitude of Damascius nor that of Eriugena to the finite, allowing less of stability to it than either. For Cusanus himself it could not long stand without further foundation. The system set forth in the *Docta Ignorantia* and the *De Conjecturis* is very different from that of Eriugena. The beginning is with God as unity, equality of division, and the nexus of the two – the universal coincidence of opposites, as man, collected into a self-relation which sustains its explication into divided relations, is this coincidence individualized. This concept is not of the God who creates only, but of that which 'creates and is created' – or of the 'unified' of Damascius. But the 'creative' and 'created' moments of that idea are more strongly dissociated. The stabilized finitude of the ideal and the sensible worlds is more explicitly subject to the power of contraries. The mutual limitation and concretion of contraries into 'primordial causes' falls outside the consideration of God and is treated rather in the second book of the *Docta Ignorantia*, which is about the world, as 'correlaria praeambularia ad inferendum unum infinitum universum' (II, 1–6). That the world is the idea under the form of endless division is common doctrine since Proclus. With Cusanus the scepticism latent in that account becomes explicit, in that his attention is on the dyadic form as prior to every content. And inference to God from the world would be mediated by the disclosure through 'learned ignorance' that it has no truth.

The return of the world to God, as treated in the third book of the *Docta Ignorantia*, has likewise another structure than for Eriugena in that the point of interest is the relation of individuals as 'microcosms' uniting uniquely the two worlds to Christ or the universal *logos*. Where in Eriugena's narration of the return individuals are restored first to their original state as united with their primordial cause and then raised to the creative *logos*, here these stages are for the subject the experience of the finitude of his unique independence. The method of 'learned ignorance' breaks through that barrier also, and the individual knows himself as within a unified end (III, 1–3).

Cusanus could not rest with this first system. It was the standpoint of a restless subjective spirit which sought unity beyond division but found it only at the term of a reflection which dissolved the division into an infinite self-relation. The way to this resolution was lost in the result. The 'docta ignorantia' uncovered a unity beyond its reflection but could not overcome itself. This method, coming out of nominalism, found again a reasoned relation of the world to God. In however attenuated a form it assumed a world and a subject which knew it. Here the reasoning which discovered God as the principle destroyed its own assumption – finite relations of thought to corresponding things. The creative principle, at once beginning and end, in which all divisions subsisted became the interest of Cusanus. The 'coincidence of opposites' no longer appeared a sufficient concept of God, nor was he content with a knowledge of God by the 'via negativa.' That way assumed a finitude which was to be negated, an assumption which the 'docta ignorantia' dissolved. Nothing remained to conceal the true principle underlying the divisions.

The system which emerges from this revision is only different from that of Eriugena in that it is for the individual who has experienced the limit of relations to the good through an ordered 'otherness,' ideal and sensible. The simple intuition of the One, which was ever for Neoplatonists the only unqualified truth, has no longer below it another thought which moves to it through oppositions. The 'docta ignorantia' reduced all discourse to scepticism. The conclusion was then drawn that division and difference reside in and belong to the actuality of the creative good. Cusanus works through this revision in successive attempts to speak of it adequately. He proposes to think of God as the 'non aliud,' to be known not simply as beyond the 'otherness' which to the 'docta ignorantia' discloses the untruth of the finite, but as that in which the finite rests. He is then dissatisfied with this name as not indicating clearly that God is not only the indifferent foundation of difference but the primary division and actuality. That infinite potentiality which also is he thinks might better be named 'possest.' But that name has the inconvenience that it suggests a difference and not the absolute unity of these moments. The most appropriate name he therefore finds to be 'posse,' so far as this indicates the infinite actuality of infinite potentiality.[53] Through the succession of these names Cusanus divests his thought ever more distinctly of the externality belonging to the method of 'docta ignorantia.' The transcendence of otherness is transferred thus from a sceptical reflection to the One itself; thereby also the negative theology of the earlier systems passes into an affirmative presence of God in and through division and finitude.[54]

2. Modern Philosophy

The new philosophy began where the old ended, namely where the One beyond all else passed into the self-consciousness which knew the finite as its own. With this transition doubt took the place of the scepticism which had its understanding in Neoplatonism. Doubt has in it a point of certainty and the interest is to know the rest as in a necessary relation to the first certainty thinking has of its own being.

The first systematic analysis of what is in this self-consciousness certain of its being is the *Meditations* of Descartes. The indubitable certainty of self-consciousness is discovered by doubting all that can be doubted

(*Med.* I). The movement to this certainty is a separation of thought from all the content of sense perception, imagination, even of mathematics, which of supposed sciences appeared the most trustworthy. The world from which thinking abstracted itself was opposed to it as wholly other, extension infinitely divisible to the indivisibility of self-consciousness (*Med.* II). But the seeming independence of the subject in this relation was disturbed by a finitude not conformed to its certainty. This instability rested on the idea of an infinite being in whom all perfections were absolutely united – the Neoplatonic One as having in its self-relation all the intelligible and sensible. By a proof of the existence of this idea from the dependence, not of a sensible world, but of the self-certain subject, the relation of the two is discovered to be that of creator to creature (*Med.* III). In that relation the rational creature can discriminate true and false as certainly as it knows itself, through the pure logical form which unites self-consciousness with what is other than itself (*Med.* IV). That this inner truth should become a science also of material objects requires that the extended world which is wholly other than thought be known as depending on the existence of the divine idea. The thinking subject has thus confronting it the divine idea externalized, not a multitude of contingencies without necessary connection, ever dubitable to thought, but in which there is systematic unity and mutual exclusion of identical and different (*Med.* V).[55] Sense perception and imagination as related to that object are not principally doubtful and deceptive but that through which the mind moves to the clear and distinct ideas of the understanding.[56] Finally on this foundation self-conscious thought can discover a necessary connection with that one body which it takes to be peculiarly its own (*Med.* VI).[57]

The new philosophy has thus for its principal interest the same infinite One or Good as the old, only as not beyond the ideal and sensible totalities but in them as their creator. The way to a knowledge of this principle is not by turning from the illusory knowledge and nullity of the sensible world to an intelligible world which thought makes for itself in the light of a primal unity. The idea is sought through a sensible world itself belonging to self-consciousness and the agreement of what is there discovered with the understanding.

The essential problems of this philosophy are also other than those of the old. The logic by which a free self-consciousness would know the natural and the human world contradicts its freedom. The subject finds an abstract freedom in the substance of Spinoza beyond the necessity of its infinite thinking and extended attributes. The monadic individuals of

Leibniz do not define a self-conscious freedom. Free self-consciousness turns therefore to itself and would know God, the world, and its own freedom, should this be possible, through itself and its ideas.[58] This subjective reflection may be likened to ancient scepticism, but is rather an idealism which would know those relations to what is other, in which the subject is unfree, as contained in its freedom, in the concrete freedom present in the transition from the old to the new philosophy. The infinite ideas of the earlier stage of this philosophy – God, nature, and self-conscious freedom – recur in the subjective reflection, first as regulative ideas or as presupposed in the moral will,[59] then as the true substance in which the subject is not first but the moment of return to the good itself through the externality of nature.[60]

The new philosophy in its subjective phase was destructive of the state, that is, of an objective unity of ends.[61] As in relation to the unified good of the state, as realizing variously that unified end, the subject is the bearer of rights established through the revolutions of the eighteenth century. These rights are other than those which attach to the free individual or person of the older world through its various relations to the good. The new philosophy, so far as centred in the subject, was destructive of the concrete freedom of the Christian revelation. In its full explication, where objective and subjective poles meet, this philosophy gives the stability of thought to the Christian 'Vorstellung' of creation, fall, the inner division of the free subject. It provides thus a theological method extending the 'intellectus fidei' of Augustine.[62] This is another method than those which rest on Neoplatonism and the primacy of the negative over positive theology.

What is meant by saying that the new philosophy began where the old ended has perhaps been clarified by a long and difficult argument. One usually takes a shorter route from contemporary subjectivity to Neoplatonism. But what there is more in this subjectivity than in ancient scepticism can easily colour one's perception of Neoplatonism and obscure the development from it of another philosophy.

Notes

1 This is a shortened version of 'Neoplatonism and the Origin of the Cartesian Subject,' originally published in *Animus* 4 (1999) and subsequently edited for this volume by Professor Doull. A briefer exposition still was published as 'Neoplatonism and the Origin of the Older Modern Philosophy.' The *Animus* version remains the most detailed account.

2 The Neoplatonic noetic thought knows the finite as belonging to self-consciousness, but to a self-consciousness itself composite of the divided and the undivided, and having its freedom beyond this relation. For the Cartesian subject a true knowledge of the finite is consequent on its relation to the divine freedom.

3 An end which of course was clear neither to Locke nor Rousseau, who remained with a subjective liberation. The relation of such an individual freedom to a unified political end is only partially disclosed in the 'enlightened' institutions of the United States.

4 This circuitous route corrects a tendency to find too direct a kinship between contemporary subjective freedom and Neoplatonism. The freedom which finds its substantial end in Neoplatonism is that of the 'person' or rational individual of Hellenistic-Roman culture, who is free from his world but does not expect, as in all contemporary doctrines of rights, that it serve and satisfy him in his particularity. The intelligible basis of this freedom is to be sought not only in Neoplatonism but also in the older modern philosophy. Both philosophies are necessary to a correction of contemporary dogmas.

5 Thucydides III (ed. H. Stuart Jones), 82.

6 *Met.* A, 983a29ff.

7 The Aristotelian god, knowing only itself, has also life in it. It knows life therefore as its own *logos* or is self-revelatory. The One of the Neoplatonists is assumed to be productive of all things, but not through its own *logos*, unless as this appears dividedly, e.g., as the 'praedestinationes' of Eriugena. This implication of the Aristotelian divine idea has its further philosophical development in Augustine and then in the older modern philosophy, where one does not have fully the Aristotelian relation but a knowledge at least that the divided and the undivided are complementary.

8 The following succinct statement of the essential structure of the three principal Hellenistic philosophies attempts to extract the intrinsic *logos* of each from the texts of the *Stoicorum Veterum Fragmenta*, Usener's *Epicurea*, and Sextus Empiricus. That is the harder to do in that analogies of that culture to the subjective culture of the present time invite us to read the texts in the light of imported *logoi*. The best defence against anachronistic interpretations is ever Hegel's *Vorlesungen über die Geschichte der Philosophie*, 'Dogmatismus und Skepticismus' (ed. Michelet, 1840), 377–517.

9 Horace, *Carm.*, III, iii, 1ff.

10 *Geschichte der Philosophie* (ed. Michelet), XIII, 399ff.

11 Lucretius, III, 830.

12 On the sceptical life, see St Augustine, *Confessions*, VI, vi ff.

13 Sextus Empiricus, *Pyrr. Hyp.* I, 164–77.

14 Ibid., 135 and 169ff.

15 *Sophist*, 254b ff.

16 *Physics*, VI, 9.

17 'Die nächste Stufe, welche das Sebstbewusstsein erreicht, is, dass es ein Bewusstsein über das erhält, was es so geworden, oder ihm sein wesen zum Gegenstande wird.' Hegel, *Gesch. der Phil.* (Michelet), XIII, 516.

18 Dodds (*E*[*lements of*] *T*[*heology*], xix) can write of Plotinus that 'he stands not at the point of origin but at the culminating crest of the wave ... [W]ithin two generations the dialectical tension of opposites which is the nerve of the Plotinian system was threatening to sink into a meaningless affirmation of incompatibles.' And at xxv: 'Proclus ... is not a creative thinker even in the degree of Iamblichus, but a systematizer who carried to its utmost limits the ideal of one comprehensive philosophy that should embrace all the garnered wisdom of the ancient world.' As if there were less a system in Plotinus than in Proclus! The question, as was clear to the Neoplatonists after Plotinus, was of the logic of the same system.

19 Aristotle, *Met.* I, 984b17ff.; 993a11ff.

20 *Enneads* VI, 2, 6, 18–20. That the *megista gene* of *Sophist*, and they alone, are the primary distinctions of thought, see *En.* VI, 2, 6–9.

21 Aristotle, *Met.* 1089a15–31.

22 Plotinus is often praised as nearer to experience than later Neoplatonism. But the relevant experience here is that of the Hellenistic age. In that regard if Porphyry is Stoicism thought, Plotinism might be spoken of as a thinking of Epicureanism.

23 The logical *gene* are to the unity of thought as parts to the whole: *En.* VI, 2, 3, 20ff. Proclus *E.T.*, 73 on the finitude of this relation.

24 *En.* VI, 1. The examination of Aristotle's concept of sensible substance in Chap. 2 and 3 illustrates the method applied in the rest to the other categories.

25 Plotinus comes to his categories through a certain interpretation of the second hypothesis of Parmenides. The Stoics look for the primary distinctions in an externalized thought in which the absolute negativity of the first hypothesis and the relative of the second are conflated. Of this it can be said at least that the relation of the two hypotheses is not in a subjective reflection only, as for Plotinus, but more objective.

26 *En.* VI, 2, 6–9; on the relation of the 'Platonic categories' to Aristotle's *gene*, see chap. 13–19.

27 Ibid., chap. 20–2.

28 *En.* VI, 4, 13–16, among many places.

29 Porphyry and Numenius: summary of their relation in des Places, *Numenius*,

Fragments, 26–8; Wallis, *Neoplatonism*, 114–17, lists points on which the fragments of the commentary on Parmenides 'mark a return from Plotinus towards Middle Platonism.'

30 Proclus, *In Platonis Parmenidem* (ed. Cousin), 1052, 31 – 1053, 9 on Aemelius; 1053, 38 – 1054, 10 on Porphyry. Analysis in Proclus, *Théologie Platonicienne* (ed. Saffrey and Westerink), I, lxxx–lxxxii [henceforth *TP*]; and on the attribution of the text to Aemelius and Porphyry, ibid., lxxx n. 2 and lxxxi n. 1.

31 The different structure of the soul in Porphyry and Plotinus is well stated in Hadot I, 336ff. The soul as reflecting the intelligible Triad is triadic. The moment of difference in this triadic structure is transitional to the identity of the moments, not an equal moment, as for Proclus.

32 Both in the Triad and in Soul the 'divided' is implicit in the moment of identity and actually in the return, but in both moments abstractly, as in Stoicism.

33 Cf. Hegel, *Gesch. Phil.* (ed. Michelet), XV, 64. In the development from Plotinus to Damascius the structure of the moments of rest, procession, and return becomes ever more concrete, as each contains more explicitly and completely the others. This development is to the concreteness of subjectivity but this expressed through the categories of unity and multiplicity, between which the transition is for a reflection extraneous to both and is not known as the development of the object itself.

34 Proclus, *In Parm.*, 1054, 37 – 1055, 25. *TP*, I, lxxxii–lxxxiii.

35 Dillon, ed., *Iamblichi Fragmenta, In Philebum*, Fr. 4, and commentary thereto.

36 Proclus' criticism of Iamblichus' exposition of *Parmenides*, 1055, 17–25; *TP*, I, lxxxiii.

37 Texts on Iamblichus's concept of the individual soul in its difference from earlier Platonism [are] collected in Dillon, 41–7.

38 In summary form, *E.T.*, props. 1–6; *P.T.*, II, chap.1, III, chap. 1–9.

39 Hegel's brief exposition concentrates on *Platonic Theology* III, chap. 6–14, where Proclus elicits his doctrine of henads from *Philebus.*

40 These remarks condense a long and involved exposition of the 'third intellective triad' in Damascius' commentary on *Parmenides* (ed. Ruelle, II, 169–245). An analysis of the criticism of Proclus contained in this argument is in *TP*, V, ix–xcviii.

41 For Proclus on the relation of the substance of the soul to its activity, see *Elements of Theology*, prop. 191. For Damascius' criticism in his exposition of the third hypothesis of *Parmenides*, see Ruelle, II, 246–73, esp. 252–7, 262–4. See the lucid exposition of the difference of Proclus and Damascius on the structure of the soul in Joseph Combès, *Études Néoplatoniciennes* (Grenoble, 1989), 260–7.

42 *E.T.*, prop. 6: '... le limitant et l'illimité ont l'inconvénient d'apparaître contredistingués comme des termes de même rang, ce que reporte là-haut nos proper oppositions'; Combès, 255.

43 Damascius' method is equivalent to Cusanus' method of 'learned ignorance,' a comprehensive scepticism which knows itself.

44 A conclusion from which nothing separates Damascius, but which he cannot draw, for with it would fall the whole Hellenic world and its gods.

45 *Principles*, 8.

46 For Damascius' criticism of Proclus on the relation of the One to the Intelligible and to finite knowledge, see Ruelle. I, 111–13 (Combès. III, 113–22).

47 For Proclus, see *E.T.*, props. 106 and 191. For Damascius' concept of the soul, Ruelle, II, 251, 19ff.; 252, 7–11, 27–8; 262, 7–26. See also Combès, 189–198, 'L'un humain selon Damascius.'

48 For an exposition of the negative hypotheses, see Ruelle, II, 432–60, and the excellent study of Damascius on the negative hypotheses in Combès, 131–188.

49 Ruelle II, 433.

50 For Damascius, as for all Neoplatonists, the One is the first moving interest of humans, the good through which they are unified; of all else outside this unified relation there is only a human or hypothetical knowledge.

51 As summarily stated at *De Divisione Naturae* V, 1019–21 (ed. Migne).

52 Scotus' proof is explicated fully in Gilson, *Jean Duns Scot*, chap. 2; on the twist Scotus gives to Anselm's argument, see 168ff.

53 Cf. *De Apice Theoriae*, in *Opera* (Paris, 1515), ccxix.

54 'Quando ... mens in posse suo videt posse ipsum ob suam excellentiam capi non posse, tunc visum supra suam capacitatem videt ...' Ibid., ccxx. The comprehensive Proclan monads are appearances of this ground, and [so the opuscule continues] the thinking whose object it is knows itself as having its division and difference intrinsic to it, as with Augustine's trinity of rational powers, which is not intelligible in a Neoplatonic logic. The principle of a new philosophical development has come into view.

55 *Med.* V. The truth the mind has through the pure logical form of demonstration is immutably actual in the necessary existence of God: 'Atque ita plane video omnis scientiae certitudinem et veritatem ab una veri Dei cognitione pendere, adeo ut, priusquam illum nossem, nihil de ulla alia re perfecte scire potuerim' *AT*, VII, 71.

56 *Med.* VI, *AT*, 79. Nature as a mechanical system in which all things are both connected and mutually exclusive is knowable to the understanding which by its logic distinguishes true from false.

57 Ibid., 81.

58 Hume has before him the same infinite ideas as the Cartesian and subsequent philosophies and finds God, nature, and freedom inaccessible to the subject empirically.

59 Kant, Fichte.

60 Schelling, with loss in the 'Identitätsphilosophie' of the difference between the old and the new philosophy; the difference is held together and restored in Hegel's *Phänomenologie des Geistes.*

61 So far as an objective order is not also assumed (Locke) or in some manner derived (Rousseau, Kant).

62 Augustine, converted to Christianity out of the radical conflict of the will, as turned to God or to itself, through a 'Cartesian' self-certainty uncovered conditions of his conversion in a meditation on Scripture. The new philosophy, through its derivation from the old, gives to the 'intellectus fidei' an independence from the text and a greater capacity to distinguish the spirit from the letter.

COMMENTARY

Neoplatonism and Contemporary Constructions and Deconstructions of Modern Subjectivity

WAYNE JOHN HANKEY

Introduction: James Doull, Étienne Gilson, and George Grant

Not many in Canada can be compared to James Doull as the creator of a philosophical school based in an interpretation of the whole history of Western philosophy. When one adds that his school has continued to reproduce itself for a half a century through several generations of students, that it remains central to the life of vibrant institutions, and that this power of regeneration stems from its union of a linguistically and philologically disciplined reading of texts with a total system of philosophy, Professor Doull's accomplishment is virtually incomparable in our country. Only Étienne Gilson's creation of the Pontifical Institute of Mediaeval Studies in Toronto and George Grant's unparalleled drawing of an extraordinarily diverse and large group of Canadians into philosophical reflection on their culture and its future come to mind.

Doull and Gilson have in common that they unite textual erudition with a philosophical project and that institutions and generations of scholar disciples carried on their work. But in North America the institutions with which Gilson was associated have failed or their scholarly work has ceased to serve his philosophical and theological enterprise. Moreover, the texts and Gilson's interpretative scheme ultimately fall away from one another because of Gilson's opposition to Neoplatonism.[1] While the criticism of Neoplatonism unites them, our two philosophical historians separate sharply over its place and character. Gilson opposed Neoplatonism as part of his campaign against modern idealism. In contrast, for Professor Doull, the Hegelian historian, Neoplatonism, though a necessary development, must give way so that the proper freedom of philosophy can be restored in the modern world.

Situating Platonism in relation to modernity was at least as important to the thought of George Grant as it was to that of James Doull or Étienne Gilson.[2] Plato's philosophy represented for Grant the union of knowledge and love which founded a contemplative relation to the cosmos against which he set the contemporary wilful nihilism of the West. Placed against Heidegger's reading of Plato (which he rejected) and Heidegger's account of Western modernity (which he accepted), Grant's Platonism was in a general way Neoplatonic. The Good is beyond knowledge and approached by love through ethical practice and religion. A quotation Grant attributes to Augustine is chiselled into the headstone of his grave, 'Out of the shadows and imaginings into the truth.' Nonetheless, Augustine's identification of God with *esse* made him at best an ambiguous figure for Grant. He found in Eastern Orthodoxy the continuation of the Platonic Christianity the Latin churches had betrayed by the Augustinian *filioque* and their embrace of Aristotle's rationalism.

In fact, though Grant regarded himself as a Christian Platonist he never wrote about Platonism itself. He was not a historian of philosophy but used the history to paint his pictures of our present. Friends and rivals, Grant and Doull divided over the relation between Plato and Hegel, about whom Grant acknowledged that he had learned much from Doull. Grant's work is elegiac because modernity's destructive triumph over Platonism seemed to him irresistible. In this he was close to the anti-modernism of Gilson, even if he set Plato, not existentialist and anti-Platonic Thomism, against Hegel and the modernity Doull embraces.

All three seek freedom from contemporary historicism. For Grant, Plato represents such freedom, but this is a freedom lost. For Gilson, it is attained at one moment. Alone among philosophies the existentialist metaphysic Gilson found in St Thomas was free from the vicissitudes of history. Guaranteed by Exodus 3.14, nothing philosophy or empirical science could discover could touch this metaphysic. With Doull the freedom is in the philosophies which comprehend both what precedes and comes after them: Aristotle and Hegel (and Augustine rendered philosophical by Descartes). The question before us is whether this comprehension, which is at the cost of understanding Neoplatonism through Aristotle and Augustine and understanding Augustine through Aristotle, Descartes, and Hegel, is adequate and complete.

James Doull's Account of Neoplatonism

My comparisons of these three major figures in Canadian philosophy bring us to the elements of Doull's treatment of Neoplatonism. First, as in all Doull's writing, there is an exemplary deep and wide reading of the primary philosophical texts pondered for decades in the languages in which they were written and matched by an extensive knowledge of the best present-day scholarship. Interpretation primarily demands that philosophy be shown to be historical and that this history be the one given it by Hegel. The Hegelian philosophy, which correctly understands the history preceding it, includes as partial moments of itself the thought which succeeds. As a result, the comprehension of the past, shown to have included the totality of the logical moments, contains and determines the future and the relation of future philosophy to the past. What follows Hegel is only worthy of being called philosophy so far as it is written from within his system. Further, Doull excludes a proper return to the pre-modern except through his Hegelian route.[3]

Second, within the history which leads to Hegel's comprehension of it, Neoplatonism is a transitional moment of subjective freedom between Plato and Aristotle, on the one hand, who 'discovered in thought a coincidence of the objective good and individual freedom' [4] and the restoration of that freedom in Christian form by means of what Descartes did with Augustine, on the other. In modernity 'the idea is sought through a sensible world itself belonging to self-consciousness and the agreement of what is there discovered with the understanding.' Consequently, Neoplatonism is properly terminated with the advent of modern philosophy.[5]

Third, Doull's treatment of Neoplatonism is determined by its beginning and its end. Nothing more divides Doull's history from that of the twentieth-century scholars whose work he uses, and from the philosophers and theologians who have retrieved Neoplatonism in our time outside or against the Hegelian perspective, than how these are understood. For Doull the principle of Neoplatonic philosophy is the One as undivided self-consciousness. Its term is Augustine identified with Descartes. In opposition both to contemporary interpreters and to the Neoplatonists themselves, for Doull the Neoplatonic One is the heir not of Plato's Good nor of his One Non-being but of Aristotle's God as self-conscious *Nous*. The history explicates 'the point of unity before division, where the individual had contact with the ground of his freedom.'[6] Doull writes: 'The One as self-consciousness beyond the division of νοητον and νοησις and as absolute good beyond finite relations was Aristotelian and not Platonic.'[7] To this we might contrast, for example, Emmanuel Lévinas commenting on the *Enneads*: 'The unity of the One excludes, in effect, all multiplicity, whether it be that which takes shape already in the distinction between thinker and thought or even in the identity of the identical conceived under the guise of self-consciousness where, in the history of philosophy, one will go someday to find it.'[8]

Augustine's place in the history is equally both exceptional and altogether essential. Already found in Augustine is what the whole development of Neoplatonism seeks.[9] In consequence, Augustine is outside the history of Neoplatonism and is explicitly equated with Descartes.[10] Moreover, Augustine's *notitia sui* is seen as retrieving Aristotle and they are combined.[11] For Doull 'the implication of the Aristotelian divine idea has its further philosophical development in Augustine and then in the older modern philosophy.'[12] In this sense, Aristotle is both the *alpha* and the *omega* of the history and remains above it.

Fourth, Christian modernity is the permanent result of the history of philosophy and religion and neither ought to be nor is in fact escapable. However, modern freedom also needs correction, which it has from Neoplatonism. Neoplatonism and modern philosophy are to be compared as 'the primacy of the negative over positive theology.'[13] These are, in effect, also two Augustinianisms. Doull writes: '[T]he most radical difference occurs between those who saw the completion of Augustinianism in an integration with the Neoplatonism of Proclus and Dionysius and those who brought it together with Cartesianism in the seventeenth century.'[14] In general, the postmodern Augustine is the Neoplatonic one. Doull's assessment of this retrieval is altogether ambiguous. Everything problematic in his representation of Neoplatonism as Aristotelian, in his representation of modernity as terminating Neoplatonism, and what is polemical and exclusive in his relation to contemporary philosophy and theology is found in this characteristically Delphic assessment.

If, in fact, Doull retains the two Augustinianisms as mutually necessary and corrective of one another, we arrive at a result which may be favourably compared to that of the most sophisticated postmodern philosophies.[15] It is true that these involve Neoplatonic turnings to negative theology, to the ethical, and to religion against the Cartesian Augustine, but, as postmodern this turn depends upon and assumes modernity. In response to these, Doull could with equal justice turn back toward the modern in a recognition of the continuing mutual necessity of both Augustinianisms.

If, however, Doull's movement is to the Cartesian Augustine as exclusive successor to Proclus and Dionysius, his result is one-sidedly modern and the position from which he judges is ahistorical. Then Hegel, and Hegel exclusively, holds the Neoplatonic and the modern together and the postmodern retrievals of Neoplatonism are not a movement beyond Hegel. They are a retreat from philosophy to naturalistic immediacy.[16] Philosophy after Hegel 'has known only an historical, temporal spirit.'[17] The 'logical exposition' of Augustinian 'sapientia' disappears and it 'appears ... more as a mixture of religion and borrowed philosophical concepts than as a strict and unified science.'[18] Confronted with this judgment, the historian responds that Doull does not understand what philosophy is for Augustine. For those working to understand Patristic and medieval Augustinianisms in their own terms, philosophy is precisely such a mixture and Doull's description is, in fact, an anachronistic prescription.[19]

Neoplatonism and Augustine on the Way to Modernity or a Way Beyond It

My response cannot engage the full extent of Doull's account. I wish, however, to suggest that Doull is closer to the postmoderns who retrieve Neoplatonism in various ways than he admits. There are two ways of looking at his very negative relation to post-Hegelian philosophy and postmodern philosophy particularly. One alternative is that Doull needs them as a counter to his own one-sided positions, a one-sidedness of which he is unconscious. The other alternative, and the one to which I tend, is that Doull's positions are intentionally polemical when directed against post-Hegelian philosophy. If this should be the case, he would recognize that his own work also comes after Hegel's and is postmodern. He would accept an affinity with his own contemporaries which would make his own position more comprehensive than he represents it as being.

Looking at the juncture between the contemporary scholarship Doull uses and his own interpretation of the phenomena involves considering, at least indirectly, all the elements of Doull's representation of Neoplatonism I have sketched. This is because the French Neoplatonic scholarship on which Doull relies is, in general, associated with anti-modern or postmodern philosophical and theological projects. This scholarship depends on a strong distinction between the One-Good and *Nous.* It also traces a strong difference between a kataphatic and ontological tradition emerging as a possibility out of the Porphyrian interpretation of Plotinus and an apophatic and henological tradition which follows from the Iamblichan reaction against this. In contrast to Doull it does not write one continuous history because it is *set against* erecting

Augustine as the theologian through whom ancient Christianity is summed up and in which Neoplatonism has its result. So far as it turns to Augustine, it is critical of him, if he be seen as the root of modern Cartesian rationalism and its progeny. Alternatively it interprets Augustine to find what stands against this kind of reason.

The French scholars, philosophers, and theologians who are crucially important for present-day Neoplatonic study are usually working against the Hegelian philosophy as well as against the interpretations of Neoplatonism derived from it. Jacques Derrida sums up the French situation: '[W]e are at the dawn of a new Platonism, which is the day after the death of Hegelianism.'[20] Their interpretations of Augustine and of the Neoplatonists, as well as their retrieval of the Greek Fathers, especially the Pseudo-Dionysius, and of the pagan Neoplatonists, are intended as the corrective of modernity.[21] Significantly, Doull's Hegelian opposition to postmodern Neoplatonism also occurs within contemporary French philosophy in the position of Claude Bruaire, who repudiated apophatic theology.[22] In consequence, Doull's account of the relation of Neoplatonism to the 'older modern philosophy' engages the great questions in contemporary philosophy and scholarship. Like those he opposes, Doull writes within a great hermeneutical circle which includes the whole of western philosophy. In responding to him we enter the same circle.

Over the last several years I have published a series of articles which are moving toward a position midway between Doull's Hegelian account of Neoplatonism and that of the French postmoderns and their English followers. With my teacher I see a self-deceiving anti-modern polemic in the postmodern refusal to acknowledge that Augustine belongs to the origins of Latin kataphatic theology, of its elevation of being and thought into the Divine, and of the Western turn to the subject by way of self-certainty established relative to a positively knowable God.[23] From the same attitude derives a refusal to recognize the crucial role of scepticism in constructing pagan and Christian Neoplatonism, to acknowledge Neoplatonism's decisive turn to the subject and, in that turn, the basis and necessity for philosophy as total system.[24] Another false relation to our past, coming out of an acceptance of Heidegger's criticism of Western onto-theology, blinds postmodern theologians and philosophers to the determination of pagan and Christian Neoplatonists to preserve the integrity of philosophical reason and the completeness of *theoria*. Our contemporaries strongly embrace the transcendence of the Good, but the division between the noetic and the sensible and the substantiality of the noetic are rejected. Ancient Neoplatonism is radically transformed when used to squeeze out the intellectual by an immediate joining of the phenomenal and the unthinkable and when employed to sublate *theoria* into a moment within a total *praxis* and *poiêsis.*[25]

However, I am moving outside Professor Doull's interpretation of our history when I judge as polemically one-sided the refusal to accept as authentic the medieval and modern Augustinianisms which discovered the consummation of intellect to be in love beyond rational comprehension. If we would see the logical necessity in the actual historical development, we must recognize that Western thinkers found in the Pseudo-Dionysius either what Augustine lacked or that by which what was unseen in kataphatic, ontological, intellectualist, and anthropomorphic developments of Augustine was disclosed.[26]

The great *summae* of the Latin West and the modern systems which succeeded them owed as much to the Pseudo-Dionysius as to Augustine, as much to Plato as to Aristotle, and as much to Proclus and the dialectic between the One non-Being and the One-Being become a dialectic of subjectivity as to the several sciences of the diverse forms of being.[27] They are total systems as well as complete collections of sciences. Aristotle needs to be supplemented by Plato as much for what he failed to take from his master as for that in which he exceeds him. *Mutatis mutandis,* the same is true for Augustine and the Greek fathers, for Iamblichus and Porphyry, Aquinas and Bonaventure, and so on. The Pseudo-Dionysian tradition is not only important to defining Eastern Orthodoxy in its difference from the more Augustinian West. The Areopagite was even more influential in the West itself. What in Iamblichus and Proclus Doull recognizes as beyond Porphyry[28] is also beyond Augustine, and the need for it explains the persistence of Dionysius within the West.[29] If modernity should in fact be Augustinian in such a way as to require the suppression of this persistent tradition, then the postmodern is not only demanded but will necessarily involve a retrieval of Neoplatonism.

In what follows I look at Neoplatonism in its relation to Aristotle and Augustinianism as these are seen in postmodern accounts which are alternatives to Doull's Hegelian history of the construction of modern subjectivity.[30] The postmoderns are deconstructing modern subjectivity by another account of its construction than Doull's and this requires another account of Neoplatonism. Looking at the two accounts together it emerges that to save Augustine from disappearance in the necessary collapse of an abstract and one-sided modernity erected by subsuming him into what Descartes took from him, he needs once again to be reconciled with the Neoplatonism of Proclus and Dionysius. Were such a reconciliation to take place, then another history of the relation of Neoplatonism and the older modern philosophy would be required, one which recognizes and demands the persistence of what Doull in his polemical moments represents as superseded. To save modernity and Augustine we must recognize more in it and in him than a philosophy and a figure set against Neoplatonism.

Opposition to the modern which also assumes it has characterized philosophy since Hegel. As Doull indicates, for him Descartes is the essential new beginning for philosophy so that reason might regain and expand the freedom which belongs to its ancient Greek origins. Nonetheless, our contemporary postmoderns are following in the path Hegel traced when they retrieve the pre-modern to set the limits of modernity. For Hegel ancient substantiality must ground and correct a Cartesian subjectivity which is as much self-deceived as made self-certain by its immediate givenness for experience, and the Kantian transcendental subject which is as much empty and hidden as it is necessary condition. Beyond Hegel, Marx, on one side, would smash the destructive delusions of bourgeois independent individuality. The historical dialectic which had progressed to a final crisis also found something positive in earlier, more organic, forms. Nietzsche, on the other side, though he would not subordinate the hero to the group, was as concerned as any of our contemporaries to expose the fraud of bad grammar manufacturing a substantial *ego*. When Heidegger uncovered the progressive hiddenness of being by looking to what was before Socrates he followed a path Nietzsche had traced. Wittgenstein would turn us inside out so that there is no beginning from inner depths or substantial self-certainties. For him the depths of the self are excavated from the outside inwards. Equally, Heidegger deposed the Augustinian immortal and historical, rational and sensible individual from its throne where it is established as mirror of the divine. Thrown into time and experiencing history as fatal, it longs for an unveiling of what was also before and underlies. Beside this philosophical movement, and its ally where possible, the anti-modern crusade of the Catholic church is waged.

Neoplatonism in the Battle between Catholic Anti-modernism and Hegelian Modernity

The Christian battle against modernity is waged across the spectrum of the churches. Whatever their differences, the war is generally against the autonomy which modern philosophy claims and which it confers on individuals and secular institutions. During the nineteenth-century post-revolutionary terror, while the Roman church was retrieving Aquinas, the Protestants were reaching back to the Church Fathers. In our time, no one embraces the postmodern more enthusiastically than the theologians. However, uniquely among Western Christians, from the beginning of its reaction against modernity, the Catholic church attacked both rational autonomy and the modern turn to the subject simultaneously.

The nineteenth-century revival of Thomism and medieval scholasticism are explicitly directed against Descartes and what follows on and from him. Being and objective realism are set against the subjective and Idealism. Aquinas is cut away from the history of philosophy and theology to which his works belong. He is represented as an Aristotelian after that came to mean the opposite of Platonist. His thought is supposed to remain within substantial being and is set in opposition to a Neoplatonism for whom the work of theology is to manifest the total system in which the simple Good above being and understanding reveals itself. Unfortunately for the ultimate success of such a characterization, this makes incomprehensible or hidden the logic and origin of theology as systematic *summa*.

With the move among scholars of medieval philosophy beyond an exclusively Aristotelian Thomas, we find that which also separates those who call themselves postmodern, and are our immediate contemporaries, from Marx, Nietzsche, Heidegger, and Wittgenstein.[31] At our end of the twentieth century, Neoplatonism is explicitly embraced to assist the overcoming of modernity. Catholic philosophers and theologians who had been and remained fellow warriors in the war against modernity but who found Thomism, as revived by Pope Leo XIII, to be a bomb that blew up in the face of those who had manufactured it, led the way. A survey of Neoplatonic scholarship employed for philosophy and theology in the twentieth century reveals immediately the dominant role played by Catholics. They move to situate and limit objectifying and calculating reason within the mystical. A crucial figure is the French Dominican André Festugière, a student of the leading French historian of philosophy in the first half of the twentieth century, Émile Bréhier. A notable scholar of Plotinus, Bréhier combined a positivistic disbelief in the metaphysical entities of which Plotinus spoke with a Hegelian interpretation of his thought. Neoplatonism was a transitional moment within a strictly humanistic, secular, and progressive picture of the history of philosophy as the evolution of modern freedom. In contrast, as Derrida indicated, Neoplatonism now belongs to a turn away from Hegel and the modern.[32] The Catholic priests who for ecclesiastical purposes revived and reinterpreted Neoplatonism served philosophical movements deconstructing the modern self in a wider context.

As Doull shows us, the Hegelian system gives absolute priority to self-conscious *Nous*. In such a view, the One of Plotinus and his successors must be another form of the thinking which is both for itself and for us. If thought at the end of its journey were to meet in the One something beyond it, Plotinus would have passed from Western rational freedom to mysticism and thus from philosophy to religion. According to E.R. Dodds and others, the successors of Plotinus in the Iamblichan tradition took this turn. This is not Doull's view. If, as for him, the One be self-consciousness, no move into it could take us beyond what intellect can recuperate as itself.

As in all great shifts, philosophy in our century involves a transvaluation of values. That which freedom aware of itself requires for Hegel is just what closes and entraps it for postmoderns. The conformity of subject and object belongs within the fatal history of the self-closure of subjectivity. The Cartesian logic by which being is established and given its character in the thinking for which it is an object is a trap. This trap is opened only so far as what constitutes thinking, and is the given for thinking, lies always also beyond it. The transcendence of the One-Good in respect to noetic self-consciousness gives it the power to liberate.

It is of the greatest importance, then, that the characteristic reinterpretation of Neoplatonism in our time, against which Doull revives a Hegelian account, has been to rediscover the difference between *Nous* and the One. Contemporary scholarship has reshaped the history of Neoplatonism so as to make the move to the ontological and noetic only one possible tradition in it. Pierre Hadot and others have explored the origins and influence of that direction within Platonism. However, the greatest labour of scholarship, philosophy, and theology in the twentieth century was to recover an appreciation of the Neoplatonic tradition in which the transcendence of the One is the first requirement. Entry into this other tradition is by way of the radically critical negation of thinking and by religious practice elevating us toward what cannot be known. Recuperating this tradition in an effort to liberate the self implies more than a rejection of Hegel. Since for Neoplatonism the human self and the substantial spiritual realities conform, the return of the transcendence of the One and Good involves a deconstruction of the modern self.

Festugière against Bréhier: The Recovery of Platonic Mysticism

For Festugière, in his turn against Bréhier's humanistic positivism and Hegelian Platonism, Plato was, as he had been for Plotinus and his followers, not ultimately a philosopher for whom reality was grasped in the stability of the ideas which united thought and being. Instead, Plato was a theologian and mystic for whom the ultimate was the Good and the One beyond being and knowing. For Festugière Neoplatonism was the true heir of the mystic Plato.

Festugière was only one of many priest-scholars who carried Catholic thought over from what one of them called *une philosophie aristotélico-thomiste*[33] to a Platonic unification of *spiritualité* and reflection by such means as a new critical edition of the Greek text of the *Enneads*, making accessible the works of the later Neoplatonists, locating Augustine within the history of Platonism, retrieving the works of the Greek Fathers (considered to be more securely within the tradition of mystical Platonism than Augustine was), and placing Aquinas and his medieval contemporaries as much within the Platonic as within the Aristotelian tradition. The general aim of these scholar-priests was to exorcise the autonomous rationality of philosophy. Such philosophy established a scientific objectification of reality and divided the knowledge and manipulation of the objectified universe from the religious quest. Philosophy as autonomous reasoning had become the basis of an independent and ultimately atheistical secularity.

One of these scholars, the French Passionist priest Jean Trouillard, must be singled out in this response because he linked the Augustinian and the Hegelian accounts of subjectivity and being and connected these to the problems that all perceived with modern Western rational subjectivity. More importantly, he set against this an alternative which he found primarily in Proclus.

The Neoplatonic Alternatives

Trouillard's Neoplatonic philosophy and theology is anti-metaphysical and essentially postmodern. Proposing that Catholic thought should turn from its Augustinian and Thomist science of God as Being, *ipsum esse subsistens*, to God represented as the One and Good, *to hen*, Trouillard's Procline *hénologie* also stands sharply against Hegelian interpretations of Neoplatonic texts. His negative theology and radically critical philosophy is developed as an alternative to what he regards as the Hegelian conclusion of the way in which Augustine developed what he took from Plotinus. With Trouillard we arrive at a truly surprising point in the twentieth-century turn away from modern subjectivity. The alternatives placed before us are two forms of Neoplatonism.[34] This surprising point is also the place where Professor Doull divides from his French guides. For him both traditions belong to one philosophical movement leading to Augustine.

One of these is the Latin tradition, deriving from Plotinus via Porphyry, which comes to Augustine through Marius Victorinus. This Augustinian Platonism results in a cosmos where ontology is final. Being belongs to *Nous* and is for self-reflective rationality. For this onto-theology at the foundation of modern philosophy and subjectivity in Descartes, alterity is self-othering. For postmoderns this ontological and noetic Augustinianism is the centre of the subjectivity, which must be deconstructed, decentred, or escaped.

One contemporary alternative to this centre is a different account of Augustine, a post- and anti-modern account. With some important caveats, we may agree with Doull in regarding it as a Neoplatonic Augustine who was reconciled with and completed by Proclus and Dionysius in medieval, Renaissance, and contemporary thought. For this alternative Descartes is not the heir but the betrayer of an Augustine for whom reason serves an analogical ascent toward God with whom we are united in the love of love. Reason's inseparability from existence in our thinking is not the self-certain foundation for the grasp and manipulation of the objectified other. The unity of being, knowing, and loving which makes the human mind an image of God is not realized but debased by its modern uses. The trinitarian mind is an image intended to point us to union with its archetype, a union not realized in knowledge, but eternally drawing the self beyond itself in love and *praxis.*

So Augustine may be seen as at the origin of what in Western modernity makes it self-confident and dominating or, alternatively, as a pre-modern spirituality whereby we might find a way within our own tradition which will carry us outside ourselves. Because he may be both, Augustine is at the centre of the questions about our self-construction and de-construction. In consequence, wrestling with Augustine is characteristic of postmodern philosophers and theologians from Hannah Arendt, Wittgenstein, and Derrida to Jean-Luc Marion and John Milbank. However, rather than wrestling with Augustine Trouillard set out a third way.

The third alternative takes up from Iamblichus's rejection of Porphyry's interpretation of Plotinus. Professor Doull agrees[35] with our French Neoplatonic scholars that the tradition from Iamblichus guards the difference between the One and *Nous* and, simultaneously, requires and allows the descent of the human into the sensible realm. However, from the perspective of the scholars, of the Neoplatonists themselves, and of postmodern theologians and philosophers like Trouillard or Lévinas, having started with the One as Aristotelian self-consciousness simplified, Doull could never understand what Iamblichus and his heirs are about. For them all Doull distorts by intellectualizing.

Because of its account of the One and the human self, this Iamblichan tradition demands what Doull inadequately characterized as 'a religious interest,' that is, a spirituality which looks outward and upward by means of liturgy, sacrament, and material symbol.[36] In order for the descended individual soul to ascend toward the ineffable One, theurgic union with the gods is required. As well as sacred objects and rituals, theurgy needs priests who have contact with the gods. Theurgic philosophy is hierarchical, and the great teachers of later Neoplatonism are also priests – and their Christian equivalents are bishops. In this spiritual tradition the self is oriented to the Other, which is always both beyond it and within it, and mounts a hierarchical ladder toward mystical union with the divine One-Good supereminently exceeding Being.

Owing to his exclusively modern (or late medieval) prescriptive conception of philosophy, Doull is unable to recognize that here, as also with Plato, philosophy is philosophy by recognizing its need for religion. Religion in this period is not an 'interest' for philosophy but a necessity. Both Neoplatonic and Patristic theology (including Augustine's) in this period are philosophy in a way Doull excludes. Robert Crouse makes this point in his contribution to this volume. I would modify Crouse's language (though not the substance of his position) by noting that Augustine is to be distinguished from Iamblichus, Proclus, et al. only in so far as the Greeks work out more fully what the mutual relation of philosophy and religion (Crouse's Augustinian 'hermeneutic circle') entails, and by some features of the religions upon which philosophy depends. In fact, in the course of late antiquity Neoplatonic Hellenism and Christianity tend more and more to converge as religions.[37] Augustine has his 'completion' in Proclus and Dionysius precisely because, better than his, their theologies, anthropologies, understandings of religious practice and systems make explicit what is involved in the recognition by philosophy of its need for religion.[38] As compared with them is Augustine deficient because, like Doull, he remains too Plotinian, too intellectualist.

Pierre Hadot's Porphyry

How Augustine's doctrine of the Trinity is understood is at the centre of the questions about the character of these alternatives, and the consequences of taking them. To enter this question, we must concede, as Professor Doull does,[39] the results of Pierre Hadot. He demonstrated that behind the trinitarian doctrine of Marius Victorinus lay Porphyry's telescoping of the hierarchically ordered Plotinian hypostases (the One, *Nous*, and Soul). Augustine followed and extended the crucial steps taken by Porphyry[40] and Victorinus when he understood the persons of the divine Trinity as co-equal and interpenetrating substantial activities of being, knowing, and loving. Augustine is explicit that what he took from Plotinus via Porphyry determined what he made of the human and the divine. But Augustine unifies the selves which in Plotinus are divided and he makes equal the divine hypostases which Plotinus subordinated to the One.

For Plotinus each of us is many. With Plotinus we do not need to deconstruct the unity of the rational self; we are before its problematic unification. This 'before' is part of the attraction of Plotinus to deconstructing postmoderns. There are at least three selves in Plotinus: (1) a thinking individual self eternally established in the divine *Nous*, (2) its psychic image in time, chained to and concerned with the body, and (3) the individuality both founded in and seeking to transcend itself in union with the One. The first self remains always above and exists by a continual contemplation of which the historical self is only rarely conscious. The second, the temporal image of this noetic idea, exists by conversion toward what is established in the realm of true being. The third is the ground of what appears in the other forms of perception but its apprehension is better described as erotic union with the superabundant source than as cognition. Because the self as it exists in the One is certainly not self-reflective, these selves cannot be unified.

With Plotinus as with Augustine, the true self is immortal mind but, beyond Plotinus, the unified Augustinian human self is simultaneously above and below, intellectual and historical, both wisdom (turned toward its archetype in God) and science (turned toward the physical world). Remembering is not only that by which the soul retrieves its knowledge of the principles above, but is also that by which mind gathers its historical experience into its eternally established self. The human individual is immortal and intellectual as well as historical, self-conscious and soul. Its being is as self-related self-conscious subject. The human historical individual is a trinitarian image and placed face to face with God because mind is a circular activity of remembering or being, self-knowing, and self-loving.

Augustine did not achieve this result immediately by a radical transformation of the Plotinian hypostatic hierarchy and the plural Plotinian selves. In between, Porphyry intervenes. As a result, reconstructing what Augustine really did and what its consequences are is preceded by questions about the meaning of what scholarship has identified with Porphyry. These questions become more and more momentous. There is an increasing tendency to find the origins of Greek Christian as well as Augustinian trinitarian theology in what is identified as Porphyry's work. Behind the difference between Augustine and the Pseudo-Dionysius may lie a common filiation from Porphyry. Christian Trinitarian theology – what many would regard as what most distinguishes Christian theologians from pagan Neoplatonists – may in fact have its most fundamental logic in a move within Neoplatonism. The credibility of Doull's account depends in large part on how he locates Augustine's teaching on the Trinity with respect to Porphyry. In fact, as I have indicated, Doull is deeply ambiguous here because Augustine is for him both within the history of Neoplatonism (and so is completed when integrated with Proclus and Dionysius) and outside it as its term (and so is equated with Descartes).

As a result of the intermediation of Porphyry between Plotinus and Augustine, the following questions occur. Is Christian trinitarian theology the development of a logical possibility within Neoplatonism? Is a totalizing ontology one of the alternatives within Neoplatonism? Is this the alternative taken and disseminated by Augustine? Is Augustine taking up possibilities within the Neoplatonic turning of philosophy from substance to subjectivity? Put another way, is Doull's Cartesian Augustine, as well as his Proclean-Dionysian Augustine, contained as a possibility within Neoplatonism. Is Neoplatonism, or better, are the plural Neoplatonism*s* as much at the origins of the modern self as they also contain alternatives to it? To begin answering some of these questions we must return to Hadot's work.

The interpretation of the *Parmenides* of Plato is at the centre of Neoplatonism. In common Neoplatonists made the first hypotheses within the dialogue's dialectic of unity, being, and plurality the primary hypostases, that is, subsistences, of the spiritual world. However, the differences between the great teachers in this school resulted from how they related these primary realities. In general, starting with Plotinus, the

Neoplatonists sharply differentiated the One non-being (as hypostasis, the One, the absolutely simple) from the One-being (as hypostasis, *Nous*, mind). The commentary Hadot maintained to be by Porphyry moved them toward each other by finding a form of being which could belong to the highest, namely, what he designates by the infinitive *to einai* (in Latin, *esse*, which, at the other end of the history which Hadot also traced, Aquinas will call the highest and proper name of God). This 'to be' without subject or predicate is distinguished from particular and participated being. The 'to be' belongs to the One non-being but allows a connection between it and the One-being. At stake here is what Plotinus himself declares to be the greatest of mysteries: how the One is productive, how thinking which is dual because it has being as its object comes forth from the absolutely simple. How does *Nous*, the first emanation of the One, come forth from what has no object of its apprehension, not even itself?

Porphyry's solution may be regarded as illuminating Plotinus or betraying him. Porphyry may be regarded as making a form of Neoplatonism into a step in the systematic totalizing of ontology or as founding a tradition of the negative theology of being which stands against that.[41] Certainly, his *einai* exists in the dynamic between negative and positive, and the intellection for which it exists is not a conceptual grasp of a particular form. The character of Augustine's treatment of being and subjectivity rouses the same questions.

Porphyrian Questions about Augustine and the Answer of Trouillard

Augustine's interpretation of Exodus 3.14, 'I am that I am,' as meaning that God is *ipsum esse*, is decisive for Latin theology and philosophy. It is equally decisive that this *esse* is in the circumcession of the triad of being, knowing, and loving, which is the essence of both God and the human. But the import and fate of these bindings is the pressing question. Has Augustine bound being to knowing so that it is no more than its object and is thus the subject of manipulating will? Or, alternatively, are both being and knowledge pulled away from any such reduction by being carried over to love? (This is the postmodern alternative.) Or is our history the complementarity, confluence, and conflict of these opposed alternatives? (My own view.)

Whichever may be the case about Augustine *lui-même*, Trouillard was conscious of the reductive possibilities within the Augustinian tradition.

With his priestly colleagues Trouillard turned toward the post-Porphyrian Neoplatonism formed in the criticism of Porphyry. His giving of being to the First was strongly opposed, as indeed was his intellectualism. For Trouillard and the later Neoplatonists, the reduction to ontology must be countered by a henology, a strongly negative theology, and a restoration of what in religion raises us beyond what we can understand.

Trouillard found Augustine's trinitarian speculations dangerous. The Augustinian centre in Western thought did not adequately protect difference, otherness, transcendence. For Trouillard, in seeking to found self-reflexive subjectivity in the divine, the Augustinian tradition projects the finite unto the infinite. As he wrote, Augustine's trinitarian speculations

> reduplicate under the pretext of founding them in the Absolute, the distinctions inherent in created spirit. One of the weaknesses of the Augustinian tradition is to work within one side of the Plotinian exegesis of the *Parmenides.* It does not understand the need for a criticism and a religious life which will converge toward the liberation of the Transcendent from all that would draw it within the Intelligible. Without this we risk a perpetual *quiproquo* which finally arrives at the Hegelian dialectic where one cannot tell the difference between the human and the Divine.[42]

Against Augustinian reduplication of human subjectivity in the divine, Trouillard would have us reflect on the power of negation, the indeterminate, and absence. In a move which reminds us of a postmodern deconstruction, Trouillard writes that the Platonic tradition brings before us 'the infinity of absence which all presence implies, more exactly the positivity and efficacy of this absence. A mental intention defines itself as much by that which it excludes as by that which it posits.' He goes on:

> If then the normative dominates presence and absence both, if it commands both possession and privation, the name *Être* is badly chosen to designate it. The normative is 'une hyperontologie.' It is *être* in the measure where it is realized in what derives from it and it also imposes on them 'la distance.' It is unity in the sense that it rules diversity but it is equally the source of the multiplicity and variety of what exists.[43]

This equalizing of the positive and negative is a deconstruction of the ontological and positive account of reality and the self.

I am not able here to explore the postmodern attempts which in diverse ways follow Trouillard in his endeavour to deconstruct or escape the modern Western self. Nor can we complete the exploration of how this effort engages Augustine or Neoplatonism. For example, I cannot and will not describe the variety of Derrida's many engagements with Augustine and negative theology nor what Lévinas takes from Plotinus nor how Jean-Luc Marion's turn to Dionysius belongs to his following of Lévinas rather than Heidegger. I want only to show that this engagement is real, to show that it belongs to the actuality of contemporary philosophy, to indicate why Augustine does not fall outside Neoplatonism, and thus why Neoplatonism cannot be regarded as a surpassed moment. In doing this we must now turn to describe how some postmoderns use the retrieval of what they regard as marginalized features of Augustine's thought or of post-Porphyrian Neoplatonism to open the self-certain and thus closed self.

Why Trouillard and John Milbank Love Eriugena

We can approach something common to these deconstructions and their complementary reconstructions by recalling that for Trouillard the most attractive Christian system is that of Eriugena and by considering why. This enthusiasm for Eriugena is common to Trouillard and the explicitly postmodern English theologian John Milbank, though the reasonings by which they reach it are somewhat different.

For Trouillard, part of what attracts is Eriugena's balancing of Augustine's affirmative theology and exaltation of being with the negative theology of Dionysius. Thus, for Eriugena, non-being, which is beyond perception, is higher than being, which is defined as what we can grasp. That of which we are ignorant is higher, what we grasp in a concept is finite. Humans and God share the privilege of ignorance of what we are because we share infinity. We share God's non-being and we know both of God and of ourselves that we exist but not what we are. This denial of self-knowledge and of *theoria* as foundation makes for common ground with Milbank.

Milbank differs from Trouillard about how to characterize historical positions. His characterization of Augustinianism is the opposite of Trouillard's and he determinedly avoids his exaltation of the negative, fearing the nihilism of modern subjectivity. He has Trouillard's result without his henology because, for Milbank, 'the Platonic Good [is] reinterpreted by Christianity as identical with Being.'[44] Milbank's Augustine is a theologian who subverts philosophical reason. This subversion is necessary because philosophy is at root 'a secularizing immanentism, an attempt to regard a *cosmos* independently of a performed reception of the poetic word.'[45] Performance and *poiêsis* are the requisites for opening the self and overcoming modernity. Plato the theologian pointing *logos* beyond the cosmos is to be recuperated. Certainly the Cartesian use of Augustine's psychology is a perversion, because, for Milbank's Augustine, neither being nor self are grasped in knowledge.

The *esse* of Augustine's God is not particular graspable being. In accord with his formula for understanding Christian theology's identification of God and Being, Augustine's ontology is already the *hyperontologie* Trouillard demands and which was given for him and for Eriugena in the *superessentia* of the Dionysian God. Milbank finds no need to turn to this Proclean and Dionysian tradition as an alternative to Augustine. Instead Milbank's Augustine is reinterpreted so as to draw him toward an apophatic Neoplatonism realized in charity, liturgy, *praxis*, and *poiêsis*.[46] Here we meet what unites Trouillard and Milbank in their embrace of Eriugena.

Eriugena's God creates himself by coming into being, and only as created is known. Thus, knowledge follows on a self-othering *poiêsis* and is subordinate to it. What is true for God is also true for the human. The human fall is a refusal of immediate self-knowledge. We cannot know ourselves in an Augustinian unity of being, knowledge, and love. In contrast to this Augustinian circle, for Eriugena, the primary logic of spirit is substance, power, and activity, a triad he derives from Dionysius and which requires mind to manifest its being in activity beyond itself. God creates and manifests himself through the human and, equally, the human is only known through finding itself in all creation. The human is in the all and is known in the all because all is created *in homine*. Self-knowledge is attained only as a result of a complete externalization through the procession from intellect through reason to sense. Ultimately, self-knowledge is only in the total cosmic *exitus* and *reditus*, a self-othering which is the divine self-creation and the creation of the world in and through the human. Such a human subjectivity has the openness which our critics of its classical modern form demand.

Our postmodern present is getting over theoretical objectivity because to get over the deceits of objectifying reason is to get over modernity. Milbank writes: 'The end of modernity ... means the end of a single system of truth based on universal reason, which tells us what reality is like ... [T]he point is not to 'represent' ... externality, but just to join in its occurrence, not to know, but to intervene, originate.'[47] Thus, *praxis*, *poiêsis*, and *eros* assume *theoria* within themselves. Milbank maintains that 'practice cannot claim to "know" the finality of what it treats as final ... We know what we want to know, and although all desiring is an "informed" desiring, desire shapes truth beyond the imminent implications of any logical order, so rendering the Christian *logos* a continuous product as well as a process of "art" ... Now desire, not Greek "knowledge" mediates to us reality.'[48] Milbank has no need to supplement Augustine with the Dionysian negative theology because he finds what Trouillard discovers in Proclus and Dionysius within Augustine himself.

The Good as Ourselves and the Good Beyond: Henry and Marion

Returning to France, I conclude with two postmoderns, Jean-Luc Marion and Michel Henry, who also turn to what in Neoplatonism is beyond theoretical grasp in order to get the modern subject out of itself, to make it ecstatic. What is opposed in their approaches are the two sides of the presence of the One-Good.

In general we can say that Marion seeks in Augustine and Dionysius what would correct modernity so far as that is Cartesian. Against the Cartesian union of thought and being, he places an Augustinian conversion of the will and a Dionysian eminence of the Good to which we have access not by theory but by praise. Marion's attempt to 'shoot for God according to his most theological name – charity'[49] and thus to move 'hors-texte,' transcending the historical conditions of philosophy, is also Augustinian. Augustine's voluntarism attracts him and, like Trouillard, he detaches himself from the Augustinian ontology, even if he does not follow Trouillard into an explicitly Neoplatonic henology. Trouillard and Marion meet because in charity a Neoplatonic move to the One-Good beyond being and to the will beyond the *noetic* can be united. The context of Marion's postmodern turn to Neoplatonism is defined as much by Lévinas as by Heidegger.

In his first book, *L'idole et la distance*, the religious side of Neoplatonism provides a way around Heidegger's naming of the idols of Western ontology. The Dionysian negative theology is radicalized to stand against Neoplatonic theory. Marion writes: 'The most appropriate name is no more found in the One of Plotinus than in the most gross sensible idol.'[50] The same negation forbids as well the objectifications of ontological metaphysics and objectifying subjectivity: '[T]he distance radically prevents holding God as an object, or as the supreme being, and escapes the ultimate manifestation of the language of the object – the closure of discourse and the disappearance of the referent.'[51]

Instead of seeing himself as a Neoplatonist, Marion associates himself with Dionysius understood to be executing a radical Christian subversion of Platonic philosophy. As with Milbank, the separation of theology from philosophy is crucial to Marion's project, but is, nonetheless, philosophically determined by his acceptance of Heidegger's analysis of the fate of Western ontology – although he and his French contemporaries are distancing themselves further and further from Heidegger's account of the history. However, Marion's own intentions do not, in fact, prevent his position from occurring within the logic of the appropriation of Neoplatonism as a solution to problems philosophy now perceives in modern subjectivity. To move to an emphasis on will and charity in Augustine is not, in fact, to move against Neoplatonism but with it. For Plotinus, we are related to the One through 'Intellect in love,'[52] and later Neoplatonism's exaltation of the One involves simultaneously and necessarily a deepening of the vision of the cosmos as moved erotically. In recent writings, Marion gives both Augustine and Aquinas a Neoplatonic interpretation in order to accommodate their ontological metaphysics to a post-Heideggerian world.

In *L'idole et la distance* and in *Dieu sans l'être*, Aquinas was placed among those who conceive God in terms of being because he made *esse* the first of God's names. But more recently Marion has Neoplatonized the teaching of Thomas as a *théo-onto-logie.* Thus, God is before being, which he gives even to himself, a position in fact found in *Ennead* VI, 8, where freedom and love are ascribed to the One. Marion shifts his Aquinas toward Denys and Proclus in much the same way as Milbank moves Augustine toward them. We have a negative theology of being.

Marion is not the first or only French phenomenologist to take a theological turn and to associate it with a Christian Neoplatonist. Another, Michel Henry, turned to Eckhart, in a move which is complementary to Marion's. Marion aims to prevent the reduction of the source of knowledge to the conditions of the subject and to do so adds to phenomenology a theory of donation. Our knowing presupposes a giving of what is for us. In having an object of knowledge we are thus pointed beyond ourselves and the object; idol becomes icon. Henry wants to protect the affectivity of the subject against objectification, and his analysis, in contrast, is of the subject's internal structure. But there is another difference.

Marion tries to keep philosophy and theology strictly apart. On the basis of his theory of donation, there is to be no move from within phenomenology to a transcendent Giver because phenomenology would thus overreach itself and become metaphysics: '[W]e do not imply that we reclaim a transcendent Donor ... we do not imply that this phenomenology restores metaphysics.'[53] Henry understands Marion's refusals in terms of a proper post-Heideggerian determination not to 'subordinate God to being the preliminary to being,'[54] but sees in his own following of Eckhart a way around this problem.

With Henry the auto-affectivity of the self is represented as true Christianity. In this auto-affection the absolute reveals itself in us. In its immanent activity there is the revelation of the transcendent because the experience of the individual subject is not subjective in the derisory sense. The self is in immediate union with the absolute and exists only in and by that union. Henry turns to Eckhart for support for such a view. Because the God of Eckhart is beyond all representation, He is also at the heart of the self. God determines 'the essence of the immanence and constitutes it.'[55] I quote Henry on Eckhart in a passage which will recall Eriugena. Henry differs from Eriugena because the emphasis is not on the creation of the cosmos but on the self. His aim, like that of other postmoderns, is to open the self to the absolute, but the modern turn to the subject has been conceded in order to be subverted.

> The Life auto-affects itself as myself. If with Eckhart one calls the life 'God,' then one will say with him: 'God engenders himself as myself.' But this Self, engendered in the Life, and holding the singularity of its Self by its thisness, and holding its thisness only in the eternal auto-affection of life, carries here in itself the life, because to the extent that each person is carried by life, he or she only comes to each instant of life by it.[56]

The life is communicated to each from the Son, so there is nothing which does not contain in itself this eternal essence of the life. Henry concludes this passage with another quotation from Eckhart: 'God engenders me as himself.'

With both Marion and Henry we are again in a Christian Neoplatonism which depends on the radical difference of the One and *Nous.* This difference allows God to be both the external source of knowledge beyond reduction to objective conception and also the internal constitution of the subject so that the self is not dependent on its self-objectification. The human subject is affected from within by union with the absolute which constitutes its being. The One is altogether beyond grasp and representation, but it is also the immediacy of my life; therefore, experience is the life of Divinity. With Marion and Henry taken together, in virtue of the indetermination of the One, we are at both sides of the object and the subject simultaneously.

Postmodern Christian Neoplatonism cancels the Platonic division of the sensible and intellectual and believes itself to achieve either the freedom of theology from philosophy or the identity of the two. Henry, Marion, and Milbank call their positions Christian as distinguished from Neoplatonic because Neoplatonism depends upon the division which they have cancelled in virtue of the immediate union between the phenomenal and the Good. In his *The Truth Is Me: Toward a Philosophy of Christianity*, Henry maintains that '[i]n Christianity nothing opposes itself to reality, there is nothing but life.'[57] He turned to Eckhart rather than to Hegel in order to find the unity of self and God because he judged that in Hegel the sensible and the intellectual remain divided.

This brings us to the fundamental question for a consideration of Doull's Hegelian account of Neoplatonism and that belonging to contemporary Neoplatonism. For Doull, the *telos* of Neoplatonism is 'the integrated individual [who] knows his freedom as resting on a unified relation of the two worlds to the One.'[58] In the modern Christian drawing together of the One and the self as the relation of creature to creator, Doull claims that the difference of sensible and ideal is sublated. This is also the result for the postmodern Christian Neoplatonists. Does Doull's Hegelian *telos* of Neoplatonism include that of those he would exclude from philosophy, or does his merely stand against theirs as an alternative?

Conclusion

The aim of my account of the role of Neoplatonism in some postmodern attempts to deconstruct the modern subject has been to take Neoplatonism out of the place Professor Doull assigns it between ancient and modern philosophy. From the perspective of a Hegelian completion of philosophy, Doull placed Neoplatonism between Aristotle and Augustine. Aristotle is its *arche*, Augustine its *telos*, and Hegel the unity of its negative and positive moments. As a result, any return to Neoplatonism is the forsaking of philosophy. I wish to return all three to history not only so that we can be more open to the actual character of the history of philosophy, but above all so that philosophy can be discovered to be actual in the present.

Laws which govern that present have appeared. When would-be postmoderns use a return to the pre-modern against the modern, the connections which link them reassert themselves. The antagonism to modernity which drives the postmodern enterprise results in a distortion of the pre-modern. This distortion manifests the unbreakable bond between all three. The postmoderns remain moderns opposed to an aspect of what they are. Modernity is a proper development of what precedes it, and a representation of the pre-modern set in opposition to modernity must be one-sided. The same logic demands, however, that if modernity be constructed by selecting one element of what precedes it, removing from this aspect the ambiguities of its original context as well as the multiplicity of meanings it acquired in its history, the deconstruction of modernity is both inevitable and good. Excluding Augustine from the history of Neoplatonism and tying him to modernity, and modernity to him, can only result in requiring us to get over them both. A different relation of the contemporary and the modern and of Augustine to both is necessary. The postmodern is a proper corrective, a recovery of something lost or forgotten in the modern, but neither are or can be independent or true and complete simply as alternatives. When we see the two sides together, we understand best how what we are is constructed.

It will have become apparent in what we have surveyed that we are constantly dealing with different sides of the same thing. The alternatives set against each other in the course of history are both present in the origins. In Plotinus, the human soul finds its prior and ground both in *Nous* and in the One. When Augustine unifies the Plotinian selves, both orientations remain present in his *mens*. Porphyry's triad does reveal how the One is and becomes Being, and yet his successors are right to reassert the difference. The self of Augustine's historical journey in the first nine books of the *Confessions* is finally realized by being included in the cosmic liturgy of books 12 and 13, but Augustine is still asserting his *cogito sum* against the Sceptics when *mens* is joining its own activity to the triadic life of God in the last books of the *De Trinitate.* Eriugena and Milbank are right to find Dionysius in Augustine, but Descartes is an Augustinian when he bases his human *cogito* in a positive knowledge of the infinity of God's being and follows Proclus when his Augustinian first philosophy is the foundation of a total system.

If that Cartesian Augustine becomes exclusive and imagines itself to be complete or self-sufficient, we need to be reminded that the persistence of Dionysius in the West is well grounded in the balance of negative and positive in the Neoplatonic origins. Neoplatonism is system because the dialectic of subjectivity is more than science; but it is also philosophical science. If one side asserts itself, the other must appear also.

The postmodern Neoplatonic deconstruction of modern subjectivity consists in breaking its rational hold on being as its object and thus freeing it from self-objectification. The self becomes ecstatic toward and in the other in virtue of a union with the Good. What is eliminated from ancient Neoplatonism in the cancelling of the difference between the sensible and the intelligible is the ascent through theory. For the ancients, the One is only approached by us through *Nous* and theurgy. The union with the holy in the material is for the sake of rising to the immaterial and requires a contemplative theurge. The ancients would be surprised by the postmodern endeavour to unite the transcendent One-Good and the immediate experience of life, by the endeavour to use the Good to remain within an endless temporal *praxis* and *poiêsis*. If our postmoderns have removed the intellectual centre of ancient Neoplatonism, we must ask where it reasserts itself in their own positions. Has modern science in fact disappeared? Or does it remain the presupposition of postmodern ecstasy? Is this the hate which loves what it hates and hates what it loves because it lacks freedom?

The postmodern deconstruction of modern rational subjectivity reveals the logic by which it is constructed such that the deconstruction is a reconstruction. What Marion and Henry take from Neoplatonism makes this clear. First, the inner and the outer are shown to be united in the One and to be united for us in virtue of its generosity as the Good. Second, the union is shown both to be beyond knowledge and for knowledge, constituting it. Postmoderns exhibit the substantiality and acuteness of their understanding by appropriating the unsurpassed systematic representation of the All by the Neoplatonists. But when the contemporary retrieval tries to run away with one aspect of what the ancients united, then the truth of what moderns understood reasserts itself and vice versa. If modern philosophy be Christian, Augustinian, kataphatic, Protestant, comprehending rationality, then to remain philosophy it must needs become Hellenic, Jewish, Dionysian, apophatic, Catholic, and theurgic.

The logic of the history of philosophy is tragic. Perhaps it is more, but it is not less, than tragedy. Professor Doull found in Neoplatonism that by which it might also be comic. In our time to become comic philosophy must write herself into the play, otherwise she will understand neither her past nor her present and will have no future.

Notes

1 On Gilson see W.J. Hankey, 'From Metaphysics to History, from Exodus to Neoplatonism, from Scholasticism to Pluralism: The Fate of Gilsonian Thomism in English-speaking North America,' *Dionysius* 16 (1998): 157–88.

2 See R.L. Bayer, 'George Grant: A Platonist for Our Time,' PhD dissertation, University of Notre Dame, Indiana (April 1999), and W.J. Hankey's review of William Christian, *George Grant: A Biography* in *The Review of Politics* 56 (1995): 173–6.

3 See chapter 5 above, 244 and nn. 59–62.

4 James Doull, 'Neoplatonism and the Origin of the Older Modern Philosophy,' in J.J. Cleary, ed., *The Perennial Tradition of Neoplatonism* (Leuven: Leuven University Press, 1997), 487, 495.

5 See above, 242, 219.

6 'Neoplatonism and the Origin of the Older Modern Philosophy,' 487.

7 Ibid., see n. 4, and pp. 486 and 499.

8 Emmanuel Lévinas, 'De l'un à l'autre: Transcendance et temps,' in Lévinas, *Entre nous: Essais sur le penser-à-l'autre* (Paris: Grassett, 1991), 141.

9 Doull, 'Neoplatonism and the Older Modern Philosophy,' 505 and n. 58.

10 Ibid., n. 9 and 62 and more explicitly Doull, 'Neoplatonism and the Cartesian Subject,' n. 1 and 2.

11 J.A. Doull, 'What Is Augustinian "Sapientia"?' *Dionysius* 12 (1988): 61.

12 Doull, 'Neoplatonism and the Older Modern Philosophy,' n. 9.

13 Ibid., 515 and Doull, 'Neoplatonism and the Cartesian Subject,' 10; above 244.

14 Doull, 'What Is Augustinian "Sapientia"?' 62.

15 I have in mind, for example, Jacques Derrida as represented in K. Keirans, 'Beyond Deconstruction' *Animus* 2 (1997).

16 Doull, 'Neoplatonism and the Cartesian Subject,' 7 and n. 5.

17 'What Is Augustinian "Sapientia"?' 62 n. 13.

18 Ibid.

19 See Robert Crouse, 'The Augustinian Philosophy and Christian Institutions,' in this volume.

20 Jacques Derrida, *La Dissemination* (Paris: Édition du Seuil, 1972), 122–3.

21 See W.J. Hankey, 'French Neoplatonism in the 20th Century,' *Animus* 4 (1999).

22 See D. Leduc-Fagette, 'Claude Bruaire, 1932–1986,' *Revue philosophique de la France et de l'Étranger* 177:1 (Jan.–Mar., 1987): 13; C. Bruaire, *L'Être et l'esprit*, Épiméthée (Paris: PUF, 1983), 6–7, 96ff.; and X. Tilliette, 'La théologie philosophique de Claude Bruaire,' *Gregorianum* 74:4 (1993): 689.

23 See W.J. Hankey, 'Self-knowledge and God as Other in Augustine: Problems

for a Postmodern Retrieval,' *Bochumer Philosophisches Jahrbuch für Antike und Mittalter* 4 (1999): 83–127.

24 See W.J. Hankey, 'The Postmodern Retrieval of Neoplatonism in Jean-Luc Marion and John Milbank and the Origins of Western Subjectivity in Augustine and Eriugena,' *Hermathena* 165 (Winter, 1998): 9–70; and 'Between and Beyond Augustine and Descartes: More than a Source of the Self,' *Augustinian Studies* 32 (2001): 65–88.

25 See W.J. Hankey, 'Denys and Aquinas: Antimodern Cold and Postmodern Hot,' in *Christian Origins: Theology, Rhetoric and Community*, ed. L. Ayres and G. Jones, Studies in Christian Origins (London and New York: Routledge, 1998), 139–84; and '*Theoria versus Poesis*: Neoplatonism and Trinitarian Difference in Aquinas, John Milbank, Jean-Luc Marion and John Zizioulas,' *Modern Theology* 15:4 (October 1999): 387–415; and 'Why Philosophy Abides for Aquinas,' *Heythrop Journal* 42:3 (2001): 329–48.

26 See W.J. Hankey, '"Dionysius dixit, Lex divinitatis est ultima per media reducere": Aquinas, Hierocracy and the "augustinisme politique,"' *Medioevo* 18 (1992): 119–50; and '"Magis ... Pro Nostra Sentencia": John Wyclif, His Medieval Predecessors and Reformed Successors, and a Pseudo-Augustinian Eucharistic Decretal,' *Augustiniana* 45 (1995): 213–45.

27 See W.J. Hankey, 'Dionysian Hierarchy in St. Thomas Aquinas: Tradition and Transformation,' in *Denys l'Aréopagite et sa postérité en Orient et en Occident*, ed. Y. de Andia, Série Antiquité 151 (Paris: Institut d'Études Augustiniennes, 1997), 405–38; and 'Aquinas, Pseudo-Denys, Proclus and Isaiah VI.6,' *Archives d'histoire doctrinale et littéraire du Moyen Âge* 64 (1997): 59–93.

28 See 232–5 above.

29 See W.J. Hankey, 'Augustinian Immediacy and Dionysian Mediation in John Colet, Edmund Spenser, Richard Hooker and the Cardinal de Bérulle,' in *Augustinus in der Neuzeit, Colloque de la Herzog August Bibliothek de Wolfenbüttel, 14–17 octobre, 1996*, ed. D. de Courcelles (Turnhout: Éditions Brepols, 1998), 125–60; and '*Secundum rei vim vel secundum cognoscentium facultatem*: Knower and Known in the *Consolation of Philosophy* of Boethius and the *Proslogion* of Anselm,' in *Medieval Philosophy and the Classical Tradition in Islam, Judaism and Christianity*, ed. John Inglis (Richmond, Eng.: Curzon Press, 2001), 126–50.

30 In order to avoid repeating arguments and references given *in extenso* elsewhere, in what follows I shall take my publications listed above as providing the evidence for what I write below.

31 Although Heidegger has been a very important inspiration to many in the postmodern turn to Neoplatonism, this was not because he either understood it well or himself advocated such a turn. See J.-M. Narbonne,

Hénologie, ontologie et Ereignis (Plotin-Proclus-Heidegger), L'âne d'or (Paris: Les Belles Lettres, 2001).

32 See Eli Diamond, 'Hegel on Being and Nothing: Some Contemporary Neoplatonic and Sceptical Responses,' *Dionysius* 18 (2000): 183–216. The only important study of the Hegelian interpretation of Neoplatonism is W. Beierwaltes, *Platonism und Idealism* (Frankfurt am Main: Vittorio Klostermann, 1972).

33 S. Breton, *De Rome à Paris. Itinéraire philosophique* (Paris: Desclée de Brouwer, 1992), 55.

34 P. Aubenque, 'Plotin et le dépassement de l'ontologie grecque classique,' in *Le Néoplatonisme (Royaumont 9–13 juin 1969)*, ed. P. Hadot, Colloques internationaux du Centre National de la Recherche scientifique (Paris: CNRS, 1971), 101–8 puts the alternatives most clearly.

35 See 232 above: '[T]he first step [beyond Porphyry and Plotinus] was to set the One beyond all finite relations to what was other than itself'; and see 'Neoplatonism and the Origin of the Older Modern Philosophy,' 504–5.

36 Ibid., 496.

37 See P. Hadot, 'La fin du paganisme,' in *Études de philosophie ancienne*, L'âne d'or (Paris: Les Belles Lettres: 1998), 339–74.

38 Doull, 'What Is Augustinian "Sapientia"?' 62.

39 Doull, 'Neoplatonism and the Origin of the Older Modern Philosophy,' 500–2. Doull speaks of the 'telescoping' as 'a deeper integration of the divided and the undivided' (500).

40 Doull observed that Porphyry's integration of the self remains incomplete: '[T]he unity was abstract and exclusive of the negative, and the abstractness appears in a divided relation of the soul to the One.' Ibid., 502 and see n. 34.

41 J.-F. Courtine, 'Métaphysique et ontothéologie,' in *La métaphysique: Son histoire, sa critique, ses jeux*, ed. J.-M. Narbonne and L. Langlois, Zêtêsis (Paris: Vrin, 1999), 157 provides a recent statement of this position.

42 J. Trouillard, 'Pluralité spirituelle et unité normative selon Blondel,' *Archives de philosophie* Jan.–Mar. 1961: 24.

43 Ibid., 27, 28.

44 J. Milbank, *Theology and Social Theory: Beyond Secular Reason* (Oxford: Blackwell, 1990), 295–6.

45 J. Milbank, 'Only Theology Overcomes Metaphysics,' in Milbank, *The Word Made Strange: Theology, Language, Culture* (Oxford: Blackwell, 1997), 49.

46 J. Milbank, 'Intensities,' *Modern Theology* 15:4 (October 1999): 497 n. 142.

47 J. Milbank, '"Postmodern Critical Augustinianism": A Short *Summa* in Forty-Two Responses to Unasked Questions,' *Modern Theology* 7:3 (1991): 225–6.

48 Ibid., 231–5.

49 J.-L. Marion, *God without Being: Hors-texte*, trans. T.A. Carlson (Chicago: University of Chicago Press, 1991), xxi.
50 J.-L. Marion, *L'idole et la distance, Cinq études* (Paris: Grasset et Fasquelle, 1977), 185.
51 Ibid., 178–9.
52 *Ennead* VI, 7, 35.
53 J.-L. Marion, *Étant donné: Essai d'une phénoménologie de la donation*, Épiméthée (Paris: Presses Universitaires de France, 1997), 11.
54 M. Henry, 'Parole et religion: La Parole de Dieu,' in *Phénoménologie et théologie*, ed. J.-F. Courtine (Paris: Critérion, 1992), 144.
55 M. Henry, *L'Essence de la manifestation*, 2 vols., Épiméthée (Paris: Presses Universitaires de France, 1963), 2: 553.
56 Henry, 'Parole et religion,' 137.
57 M. Henry, *C'est moi la vérité: Pour une philosophie du christianisme* (Paris: Seuil, 1996), 297.
58 Doull, 'Neoplatonism and the Older Modern Philosophy,' 488 and see 487, 514–15.

PART THREE

Hegel, Modernity, and Post-modernity

chapter six

Hegel's *Phenomenology* and Post-modern Thought[1]

Introduction

The *Phenomenology of Spirit* is an introduction to the *Science of Logic* and the other parts of the system one calls the Hegelian philosophy. It is introductory in that it brings to light the subjective principle of the older modern philosophy, wherein what is other than self-consciousness is related to it, through a reflective logic, as forms of consciousness. This reflective relation constitutes the 'appearance' of spirit: a creative thinking which, through the rational creature, knows its creation as itself. When all forms of this relation – subjective, objective or historical, the conjunction of the two in religion – are considered in their development and succession, this 'apparent' spirit is found to rest on spirit explicated in its own logical or philosophical form *as* spirit, not simply as for a subject. But the *Phenomenology* does not lead to the philosophical form of spirit as though it were not yet itself philosophy. Rather, it is 'introductory' as comprehensive of, and pointing beyond, what is called 'modern' in distinction from 'ancient' philosophy. In ancient philosophy, though the concept of spirit occurs in its final systematic form as Neoplatonism, there is only the beginning of spirit at the point where all things are returned to their original unity.

Philosophy has its origin temporally in art and religion, so far as these are the forms of a people's knowledge of a concrete ethical freedom. In its three forms, philosophy unites art and religion, showing both to be necessary. Within philosophy itself, the difference between the immediate unity of image and thought in art, and their reflected relation in the *Vorstellung* of religious thought, assumes the form of a self-differentiation of logical stages by which thinking comes to know its object as itself. The first or ancient philosophy which took its beginning in art presupposed a universal principle and came to know what that was through a thinking through of nature. The second, modern or phenomenological philosophy, presupposed nature, this presupposition mediated with the universal through the thinking subject. In the third the mediation is in God or the universal itself.[2] This last philosophy gives adequate form to what is believed in the Christian religion and is the true *intellectus fidei*; a thinking neither extraneous to its content nor mediated only through the subject, as in the Augustinianism become modern philosophy.

The *Phenomenology of Spirit* is a comprehension of modern philosophy in its development of the subject as certain of itself to the truth of that certainty, and the concomitant development of a 'free society.' Following the method given in the introduction of the work, a reader thus oriented can discover the unity and deliberate movement of the work according to Hegel's intention, though it is a standpoint hard to attain for those nurtured in the presuppositions of a later age. That philosophy is a form of 'absolute spirit,' what 'spirit' as absolute or finite is, what philosophy has to do with art and religion – all this is long forgotten.

Though words may differ, to say that philosophy is a form of 'absolute spirit' is in no way an eccentric opinion but that of all philosophers before Hegel, though they might stumble like men drunk[3] and only after a certain development come to know explicitly what they were about. What distinguishes philosophy since the post-Hegelian revolution is the conviction that the new humanized philosophy and culture generally have not lost but taken wholly up into themselves, as their own, everything that had before been ascribed to religion and metaphysics, to the alleged detriment of human freedom. 'Post-Christian' is not said merely of ways of thought antagonistic to Christianity – animism, enlightenment, or whatever – but to the general belief that humanity, as having absorbed Christianity, is able on its own to realize a freedom to which religion had come to be only an impediment and a delusion. The formation of this attitude is not to be explained as an 'overthrow' of philosophy as formerly understood. Those who first spoke of these changes and their successors rather found themselves already on the other side of a wall, and of former philosophy saw only what made sense from that position.

Hegel had not long departed this life when one learned from those who had heard him or were closely associated with his thought that religion was myth or that its proper theme was humanity; that philosophy was the guide to a wholly secular liberation, a liberation not least from religion and metaphysics themselves. If not many at first gave in explicitly to this radical humanization of philosophy, what was called philosophy in the nineteenth century culture after the thirties was nonetheless hardly less remote from the Hegelian concept of philosophy as a form of absolute spirit. Philosophers wavered between more naturalistic and more idealistic versions, losing hold of the dialectic that might have combined these opposed directions and failing to uncover a unity of the two without obscuring the difference.

The logic of this post-Hegelian transition to a humanized philosophy, the history of this philosophy as it sought to unify its divisions, and of the incipient return from it to older philosophies as of other than historical interest, has yet to be fully given. It may be thought that we are for now at a certain lull in the storm where post-Hegelian schools have lost their attraction and the passions which animated their discovery have subsided; where philosophy in any of the three forms Hegel knew only begins to return from a long oblivion.

Phenomenology and Philosophical History

The Phenomenology of Spirit, as an introduction to the *Science of Logic* and the other parts of the Hegelian system, does not lead everyone to the system, whatever presuppositions one may hold as to how, if at all, 'spirit' can be known philosophically.[4] What 'spirit' means is taken to be known through the Christian religion: the triune God in himself, the creation of irrational nature and of the rational creature, implicitly spiritual, the division or 'fall' of the rational creature, the revelation of what God is in the incarnation, death, and resurrection of the Son, the conversion thereby of the division into a moment of concrete spiritual form unifying God and the human individual. That this belief – expressed in a thinking which used natural relations for what was beyond them – could be known as true also for thought, had long been the interest of philosophical Christians; a necessary interest since, for other than philosophical thought, the *Vorstellung*[5] was incredible.

Philosophy is for Hegel a form of 'absolute spirit' and the highest. It is only to be treated after art and religion, being in a manner a unity of the two. That is a hard saying and differs from what since his time one has commonly taken philosophy to be – the most general of the sciences, perhaps, having something more to say of the embodied self-consciousness which is man than psychology and the life sciences or something further than the social sciences about human communal relations; or which perhaps, as logic, can speak of the common form of all inquiries. The unity of mind and body, which man is, is not grasped as 'free spirit,' nor history as the common realization of that freedom. Absolute spirit, as that in which historical reality and subjective freedom are united, which the individual comes to as the knowledge of his freedom, 'has its reality in spirit,' and not in the recurrent evils and precarious goods of historical existence – 'absolute spirit' in that sense appears to a later time as a vain notion, an escape, perhaps an opiate.

But all peoples have their arts in which they realize beauty – the ugly as well, if the world is for them ugly – and some religion in which they have relations to divine beings potent to realize or frustrate human ends. But if all peoples have arts and religions, few peoples have discovered philosophy in Hegel's sense. Philosophy as separate from art and religion, unmixed with myth and image, came into being first among the ancient Greeks. The ground was prepared for that philosophy by the political freedom of the *polis* – not an abstract subjective freedom, but an ethical freedom in which individuals knew themselves free in realizing the concrete objective ends of family and state. To this freedom poets and other artists gave a universal foundation – a religion in the medium of art, nature and freedom harmonized, the harmony not broken by the emergence of the rational individual or person from the domestic and the political community.

It is the emergence of subjective freedom from the collision of natural and political institutions, the formation of an actual relation of individual and universal within which falls also their difference, that permits the appearance of philosophy. In the aesthetic mode both tragic and comic poetry verge on this unified thought, but one on the side of the universal, the other on that of the individual. Philosophy is from the first a free universal thinking which would know all else through forms of itself – concepts or γηνη τον οντος – and these forms as leading to the highest which is 'the thinking of thinking itself.' Not that philosophy knew from the first what it was, as though it could directly appropriate the result of the self-knowledge attained in the aesthetic medium. Though in the order of experience philosophy was dependent on that aesthetic knowledge, once discovered it had its independent growth, at first antagonistic to the anthropomorphizing images of the artists, then recognizing a common end more adequately known in the medium of thought.

After Aristotle, with whom this universal thought discovered what it was, interest turned to the relation of free individuals or persons to that objective end. This relation was sought first in the humanized world of

Hellenistic-Roman culture which drew to it the peoples who did not know the individual freed – or repelled the Jewish people who in their religion knew the root of that freedom [only] in its pure universality. The free individuals of that culture, finding their independence to dissolve into sceptical instability, turned inward to discover that absolute principle in the several forms of Neoplatonism in which ancient philosophy reached its limit.

The limit of that philosophy was that in Neoplatonism the movement to the absolute principle was from the side of the free individual and not also from the principle, though that it should be this as well was contained in the Aristotelian idea of a self-creative thought. The Neoplatonic philosophy knew as the assumed end of its search the intuition of a unity before all division and difference. That philosophy might move from the negativity of this result and come to know that what was other than the principle also pertains to it, and to the free individual, required a new beginning. That beginning, if it would become the end and interest of all, could not exist first as philosophy. Nor could one revert to the aesthetic religion which was the birthplace of the ancient philosophy, since here the need was of the free individual, which had broken with the world to find a world in which its freedom had reality. The condition of such a further philosophy was the Christian religion in which God, knowing division as his own – God as trinitarian – revealed what he was in the incarnation, death, and resurrection of his Son; wherein individuals were not only implicitly free through submission to their creator, as in Judaism, but, as divided and in relation to the creation given over to their passions and finite interests and turned against the creator, were yet drawn by the Son from that division to the concrete freedom revealed in him. In this religion the Aristotelian principle, purged of the presupposed finitude through which philosophical thought had access to it by the negativity of the free individual and its self-knowledge in Neoplatonism, was known as realized in the spiritual relation of God and man in the medium of a thought expressed in language, available to those drawn in faith to the revelation as absolute truth without need of the hard intellectual formation requisite for philosophy.

This *intellectus fidei* had for its medium before the modern age ancient philosophy, especially in the final systematic form called Neoplatonism. Whether thought through more Aristotelian or more Platonic versions of this philosophy, the concrete spirit of the religious belief neither appeared nor was known in a thinking equally concrete. The Neoplatonic philosophy led only to 'the One' before the division of thinking and thought – implicitly 'spirit,' as the source of all things, but not to be spoken of unless in images. For a new philosophy to emerge from this religion it was necessary that the human world, receptive of it and informed by it, should attain the form of a concrete ethical order, where the interest of individuals was to realize objective institutional ends, unitive of nature and subjective freedom. This occurred historically in the reformation of the medieval church by which subjective freedom came to be known as a necessary moment in the reception of religious truth. The reflection of this reform on human institutions was to overthrow the medieval order in all its principal aspects: instead of a celibate ideal to give priority to family life; to set work for one's living above poverty as an abstract freedom from the temptations of economic life; to put in place of obedience a free acceptance of political power.

But in these transformed relations to the world, which rested on the relation of the individual in the religious community to his reconciliation as accomplished in Christ, there was not yet the free self-consciousness which would be the moving force in the modern age, alike in philosophy and in human life generally. The ancient philosophy, in the aesthetic *Sittlichkeit* in which it originated, did not have in it the free rational individual or person. In this second beginning there was only implicitly the free subject, certain of its being and, in that certainty, of its capacity to know the divided or finite and to relate it to the human good. The course of philosophy in the modern age would develop the relation of that subject to the absolute substance, the God of religious faith, and to the radically externalized nature (implicitly the same as that self-conscious certainty), and to develop these relations in the concrete form they had in the religious *Vorstellung*. The principal interest of this philosophy Kant knew to be 'God, freedom, and immortality' – that the subject was free also in its immediate embodied existence. Even so, for the sceptical among the modern philosophers – and scepticism is part of philosophy – what philosophy could not know were these objects-in-general. The general history of that age was disturbed by revolutions which had the same direction as philosophy – to develop subjective freedom. The popular will, which initially saw itself as constitutive of the state and as appropriating it, in the end found its true freedom in returning to the ethical order with which modernity began, only now as having subjective freedom in it.

The aim of *Phenomenology* is to introduce the philosophy of the concrete spirit, of which it can be said it differs from the religious *Vorstellung*, not in content, but only in giving that content a conceptual form appropriate to a reader who is already in the philosophy of the modern age. This modern philosophy begins where the ancient philosophy ended – with the subject certain of itself, as beyond division and the possibility of being deceived as to itself, a subject which finds as its principal idea an absolute substance as cause of its own existence. For this new beginning in philosophy the way to God or the absolute substance is not as for the ancient through nature and its reflection into an ideal world. Having grasped nature as unified, this new thinking radically distinguishes it from itself, and knows it as radically externalized. In this structure, the movement of thought now is, in the light of the divine substance, to find itself by going into the world, which, though separated from the independence of thinking, is implicitly one with it. The objects of primary interest in this reconstitution of the former order are: the freedom of the subject; the laws or necessary connections through which the endless otherness of extended matter is intelligible; the relation of the free subject to itself as a living individual in nature; and God as comprehensive of nature and freedom.

The way to knowledge and the amelioration of human life in this context was by experience.[6] The interest of philosophy was to discover the method of experience, how one might not end in doubting all things but, as a free subject, distinguish true from false. Philosophy not only discovered a method – having which and adapting it to particular subject matters the sciences and technical arts might go their way oblivious to their foundations – but knew itself, in relation to its universal interests, as a knowledge by experience. What was sought before by turning from the world to a divine truth was to be discovered now by turning to nature, not as a distant image of an intelligible world, but as the work of a divine creator, creative alike of the spatio-temporal conditions of nature as of its several orders constituted according to categories of necessity and causality.

Whether taken as constitutive of things or subjectively as 'categories' of the understanding, the free subject knew truly through these forms. But in the subsequent development of this philosophy of the freedom of the subject and the necessity of the understanding, the experience of 'spirit,' which is the subject of the *Phenomenology*, was of the problems the free subject encountered in its knowledge of itself, of nature, and of God in the relation of self-consciousness to what was other than but also belonged to it. As against the older *intellectus fidei* there was here the actual experience – or what is equivalent – the appearance of spirit. The intuition of unity before division had given way to a mediated knowledge comprehensive of division. But in this relation the moment of division and difference is unequal to that of their unity, the mediation being only through the free subject. The movement of the subject is to overcome this inequality and expose the 'spirit' underlying its appearance.

This mediation is first in the subject, its development to a concrete unity of individual and universal, in which the opposition in all its forms of self-consciousness and consciousness is comprehended. The unified individual has then to know the realization in objective or historical form of its freedom. Then the unity of these two developments is known through religion as the free relation of human and divine implicit in this unity which is, through a succession of religions, attained in Christianity. The philosophy as such of phenomenological spirit is finally a reflection on the unfreedom remaining in the religious *Vorstellung*, which draws on the subjective and objective experience, the destruction and restoration of the religious relation in these forms, and through the concept of religion thus attained knows that unfreedom to belong to the form and not to the true content of the Christian religion. In this translation of the *Vorstellung* to the form of thought the subjective mediation gives way to a mediation inherent in the divine idea, which is the standpoint of the Hegelian system.

The third philosophy, to which Hegel first gave expression, has like the second the Christian religion as that in which it exists in the general consciousness. But the relation of the religious to the philosophical form of 'absolute spirit' is not the same. The second, in disciplining an abstract subjective spirit – otherwise destructive of the Christian religion – to the concrete content of the *Vorstellung*, gave to it a philosophical form. The third philosophy founds its relation to nature, and to finite spirit in both its subjective and objective aspects, directly on the Christian trinitarian idea; this as the explicit object of a thinking which, through the first and second philosophies, knows itself and its objects as concrete – as the division and return to itself of an original unity. The movement of this thought, as in the *Vorstellung*, is to a relation of equal 'persons' within which are contained all subjective and objective concepts. On this foundation rests a *Sittlichkeit* in which 'life,' or the immediate existence of spirit, and the relations of individuals in their particularity, are comprehended in a self-governing community wherein the unity of freedom and nature in family, society, and state is equally the unfolding of an objective end and, from the side of individuals, the realizing of that end as their concrete good.

What tribes and peoples take for their gods – as beings capable of sustaining their communities and interests and imparting to individuals some sense of an independence from, or at least a coincidence with, the recurrent course of nature – to such beings mythopoeic fancy has given countless forms, personalized more or less superficially. But that the religion of a people and the expression of itself aesthetically should also take the form of philosophy supposes that its institutions are animated by a subjective freedom – that individuals know the realization of their common ends as a realization also of that freedom. One can say with Aristotle that the tendency to philosophy is present in all men; however, that this tendency develop into philosophy as such – a thinking that knows its determinations as its own and not a thought mixed with myth and image – this thinking must exist virtually in the relation of free individuals to their institutions. From the laborious freedom of political life philosophy could emerge as the science of the free man who knew the principle of that freedom.

Genesis of Post-modern Culture

Phenomenology of Spirit is comprehensive of the subjective standpoint of modern philosophy. Its treatment of that philosophy is different from that of the *Lectures on the History of Philosophy* as not looking back to that history from the new concept of philosophy which emerged from its argument, but, so to speak, from within it, following the development of the subjective principle itself. The infinite substance, existent from its intrinsic necessity, which the Cartesian subject found in itself as its primary idea, was for the Hegelian subject – which not only found a principle of concrete freedom in itself but knew the objective development of that freedom – no longer simply substance but also subject. The relation of human freedom to that infinite subjectivity was not that of Augustinian predestination, as in the Protestant Christianity with which the period began, but of a freedom realized also on the human side.

The new or third philosophy which this argument discovered had no longer the form of a subjective freedom reconciled with the world only in principle, by methodical exploration and ordering of the world finding itself in it but also divided from it. It was no longer the appearance or experience of spirit but spirit itself: nature as a moment of divine freedom; human freedom as a divided subjective and objective relation to that freedom; that division overcome where human and divine meet in the forms of absolute spirit.

The difference of this new philosophical standpoint from that of phenomenal spirit appears in all aspects of human life. In the primary human institutions there is no longer a contest between objective end and individual freedom. The relation of man and woman is no longer a medieval separation of ideal unity and abstract legality; nor is it a unity that is inward and implicit only, not extending to differences; nor again a relation realized in particular interests without inner unity. In the new relation inclination and reason meet, and its realization is through the conforming of nature to the *Sittlichkeit* of the family in children. Moreover, the sphere of private interests is no longer a contest of 'estates' with one another and with a state in course of attaining an effective unity. The revolutions are past in which one sought to centre political sovereignty in 'society.' If 'society' used to be taken to be within the state, as states became more and more democratized, the rights of individuals and of national communities were assumed to be prior to all institutional relations. Thus in both family and in the interrelation of society and state there was at first a deepened spiritual unity, then a falling away from this unity to a priority of individuals in their diverse interests and natural particularity. But neither tendency can be grasped without the other and neither through the antecedent modern philosophy. The rights assumed to belong to individuals and national communities reflect an institutional order in which individuals, as capable of concrete freedom, are the primary end and interest.

In religion the new philosophy worked a like revolution. One is not to suppose that someone of perverse, aberrant genius invented the Hegelian philosophy in the face of common sense and national experience. Rather, as is the office of the philosopher, Hegel discerned and defined logically a universal shift in the self-understanding of peoples, touching all the principal objects of their interest. In religion the shift pertained to the relation of peoples to the primary doctrines of the Christian religion. The belief of the church had been given stable universal form in antiquity, accommodated to the Greco-Roman culture within which it had its historical existence. With peoples who had been converted to the Christian religion, not from that developed culture but from an undeveloped barbarous condition,[7] the need was to form in them that ordered, rational relation to their religion which otherwise must be a mixture of piety and destructive savagery in their relation to the world. Religious belief was both beyond this developing order and mediated by it, expressed through fasts, pilgrimages, and other austerities, reverence to saints in whom faith was actual, and communicated both symbolically and through the discipline of works by a sacred clergy. In this era the philosophical understanding of the concrete spirituality of Trinity, Incarnation, Resurrection and the relation of the faithful to this belief was through the analogies of a finite reason as applied to a unity before all division and discourse. There was no place for the subjective principle of the modern age which radically combined intuition and discourse.

The modern age was founded on a spiritual relation to the spiritual content of the Christian religion; a relation in which substantial unity, division, and subjective return to the origin are not dissipated, as in Neoplatonism, into a primal unity. But, though the relation is now 'spiritual,' it is only as the 'appearance' of spirit: subjectivity, while taken philosophically as the beginning, is extraneously mediated, relating itself to the substantial unity of spirit itself only through a dialectical reflection on the finite, in the course of which reflection it unifies its own divided moments and discloses the objective foundation of this reflection itself.

This 'phenomenal' spirituality brought with it a radical shift in the understanding and practice of the Christian religion and its relation to a secular order.[8] In its religious form it took for its object the *Vorstellung* itself of the principal doctrines, not its translation into the concepts of the Neoplatonic synthesis of Aristotelian and Platonic thought. The intent lay now, not in a virtuous reform of the will against the background of eternal damnation and purgatorial correction, but in the relation of individuals directly to their absolute restoration. Against the purely inward reconciliation in this relation, the subjective moment subordinated in it would on its own make that reconciliation explicit and real by returning to the world and in that relation maintaining a rational self-conscious unity. The phenomenal spirit of the modern age was to become occupied with the relation of religion, as so taken, and enlightened reason; the new beginning which Hegel discerned and delineated at a certain point in its development comprehended the terms of that division.

With that change the phenomenal spirit gave way to concrete spirit: the mere apprehension of the *Vorstellung* passed into agreement with its content. The result is still with us, but as externalized: the subject of the religious relation appears as the existing individual, or as a humanity capable of realizing beyond limit the finite freedom of all its members. When one speaks of a post-Christian or post-modern world what is meant is just this externalized spirit. The consequences for religion, as they have unfolded, are wonderful to consider. Where for Hegel, who had thought through the whole career of the phenomenal spirit, the result was a knowledge of the constant belief of Christians in the unique truth of their religion (as adequate to what is assumed in all religion, other religions as containing a partial truth, a *praeparatio evangelii*), for the externalized standpoint, first, all religions are equal; second, the most primitive is preferable as abstracting least from human existence; third, the Christian religion is of all the most intolerable as most radically founded in thought. The result is a Christianity factualized, resting on a fundamentalism either of image and symbol or of scriptural text.

The confirmation of the Christian religion was for Hegel 'in spirit and in truth'; the historical contingencies of its first appearance, its later tradition, and subsequent division of Christendom into complementary forms having had their truth in that spiritual relation. What separates Hegel from the forms which the new philosophical beginning he articulated assumed after his time, is that there has occurred a conflation of the historical development of Christian peoples in which the original meaning of the modern age has itself been lost from sight. In that conflation, Descartes and his successors appear to have conceived a dualism of mind and body, thought and nature. That their intent was rather to discover a unity such as was not before known is largely forgotten, as alien to a mentality which assumes that unity immediately. The history of this post-Christian, post-modern world has since run its course to the point of a scepticism which no longer knows whether philosophical thought is possible at all; whether there could be a free self-consciousness; where mind is assimilated to body and their relation a mystery. In the practical realm, universal rights are ascribed to individuals as prior to all institutional relations; but what the universality of right and its articulation as a plurality could mean from this standpoint of the externalized spirit, is not intelligible. The meaning of rights and their application becomes in this context a matter of arbitrary and shifting judgment. Institutions as predicated on indeterminate rights lose their cohesion and capacity to unify divided opinions, the exercise of power tending therefore to be arbitrary and tyrannical.

The source of this dissolution and loss of coherent thought is perhaps most easily evident when one considers the origin and meaning of universal rights. The thoughtful historian knows that the 'universality' of the individual – the rational individual or person capable of universal determination in relation to such others – is a concept unknown before the Hellenistic-Roman age. The historian knows also that the more concrete 'rights of man and the citizen' in their various formulations are the product of the rational spirit of Enlightenment. The further extension of rights in modern democracies, including the rights of communities, draws its universality from the concrete spirit expressed in the Hegelian philosophy. Taken in abstraction from that history and the philosophies animating it, rights have the contradictory quality of equalizing all differences while at the same time requiring they be saved; or they appear as a levelling equality and also the immediate reaction to this from the standpoint of a being in nature.

Considered from the side of the Hegelian philosophy, 'post-modernity' is the concrete unity of nature and thought as it appears in the *Sittlichkeit* of family, society, and state set forth in the *Philosophy of Right*. The philosophical science which would grasp the logical structure of post-modernity assumes the system, but in its practical aspect at that first stage of its development – that unification of spirit in ethical institutions as completed in what Hegel calls the 'immediate state.' That immediate state is distinguished in the argument of the *Philosophy of Right* from the state as externalized ('civil society') as a state in which the natural particularity of a people has been united concretely with their common rational universality, existing thus as a particular individual in relation to other such individual states.[9]

That this state does not rest in its ideality (as Plato wished that the *polis* of his Laws remain as isolated as possible from the corrupting relation to other states) is to be understood through the logic of spirit which variously determines the development also of states which have not, as it has, attained a concrete ethical unity. Spiritual unity is not something immediate, but a self-subsistence through division and externality and the negation of it. The externality of the 'immediate' state consists in its natural particularity, and its movement is to unite this its givenness with its inner ideality. But the state as thus unified does not then have a spiritual form. The subjectivity attained in this unification – which is the active or executive power in its constitution – only becomes actual as the unity of the whole people when they forget this ideality and are given over to the multiple internal interests of partial communities – e.g., economic, and other corporations.

In the political system of the nineteenth century, whose dominant form is the nation state, the inner universality of the state is lost from sight in the welter of relations of one to another as particular wills. The instability and contradiction brought to light in these relations is the point of transition to absolute spirit as that on which they depend. This transition is found in some form or other in all human communities, however rudimentary the structure of their domestic, economic, and political institutions. The structures through which individuals have common binding ends – are 'communities' – both liberate and confine or even enslave. So far as members of a community are awakened to a sense of their individual freedom, and of its confinement, they are impelled to 'liberate' themselves from their institutions, whether to remake them and find room for their awakened freedom or only to relapse into the same unfreedom.

In post-modernity, as springing from the completed inner development of the European state, the division into particular and ideal elements[10] also is complete, and appears able to stand on its own independent of the state itself and its religious foundations. If, however, one follow attentively the logical development of post-modernity one witnesses a dissolution of this confidence in its independence of earlier forms. Thus at first only a radical minority went fully over to this division and its utopian confidence in an ultimate human liberation, whether in a Marxist or Nietzchean form or some variation of these. People generally held to the sovereignty of their states, adhering to the abstract or moral aspect of that division or else to its natural extreme, or to some conflation of the two. Power in the states passed to a middle class and formally to a more and more inclusive democracy. The European states found an objective realization of their sovereignty in empires, subjecting peoples of less liberated cultures and providing for the enrichment of the middle class.

The contradiction of this nineteenth-century system – of sovereignties assumed absolute and at the same time particular, and pursuing particular ends of competing economic interests – was brutally exposed in the First World War. Hegel in his time saw in such a collision 'the manifest dialectic of the finitude of these spiritual communities'[11] and the coming into being of a world community whose moving end would be to realize universally that concrete freedom which the particular states attained inwardly in the completion of their historical development. The attempt, following its ruin, to grasp what that inner structure of the nineteenth-century European system was, to grasp what this inner basis of sovereignty might be if purged of its particular embodiments, only resulted in a confused and impotent attempt to form a common world government.

For the logic of the relation of particular sovereignties which had come to the *telos* of a long Christian formation to the recognition of a universal or providential reason working in history to become fully manifest, the states still had to suffer a long and difficult history. The first stage was a separation of their divided externality from a deceptive political sovereignty and of the terms of the division from each. The radical positions of the so-called right and left Hegelians (anti-Hegelians they would better be called) took on a new life in the opposition of an existential nationalism to a universal Marxist will. Contrary fascist and Marxist parties – the two positions are abstractions from the concrete unity of individuals and their institutions – divided European states in more and less virulent forms, seizing power when they could, until the opposition took a general form and collided in the Second World War.

In this conflict of the opposed elements of post-modernism neither appeared in its purity. To attain the dominance it sought, each had to appropriate the spiritual resources of the state, though in a forced amalgamation, not in that which could come into view through their stronger separation. The voluntary union of by now nearly all the European states in the framework of a common state has required a further development in the relation of the elements. The existential aspect, notably in the writings of Martin Heidegger, disowned the violent Nietzschean subjectivity which animated Nazism and became more passive in nature, more receptive of an older spirituality temporalized, defining its opponent more generally as a universal economic-technical will. 'Technocracy,' on the other hand, is pluralistic, a segment of the 'global economy' without its own political centre, as in Leninized Marxism.

The competition of these forms had thus been blunted in Europe by their inclusion within the bureaucratic framework of a common state. Linguistic, cultural communities coexist with the equalizing force of the global economy. In this structure both aspects are democratized: the universal rights of individuals are given primacy over constitutional arrangements, as over legislative and judicial powers. In this relation, while one knows in general what the underlying rights of individuals are, how they are to apply to them in their endless particularity is ever provisional and uncertain. In the same way, as the philosophical confidence of Feuerbach, Marx, Nietzsche, Heidegger in his phenomenological stage, and the other recent schools generally has been broken, so now it is uncertain whether there can be philosophy at all, as in the practical sphere government, in the relation of public opinion to legislation and its judicial interpretation, has become a contingent reflection of these elements one on the other.

In this context a recognition of the unity of the divided elements may take the form of an admiration of the primitive, for in all human communities there is something of objective, institutional form – of family, economic relations, governance – in relation to which individuals are in some manner unified. Within primitive institutions the least of subjective freedom. But into such forms an existential subjectivity can read its own freedom and make of primitives guardians of nature against technological destruction. Individuals in flight from a Christian religion, considered oppressive of anarchic freedom, can more easily recognize the religious interest common to humanity in religions that have not much of reason in them. Thus, according to an opinion now current, Canada is an association of aboriginal peoples and English and French linguistic-cultural communities – of those at the first beginnings of a rational freedom and those who would be liberated from reason.

But one knows that humans, as rational, are unable for long to live within finite ends. That is true even if, as in Enlightenment and post-modernism, there is present also a universal end – happiness, the realized good of individuals, or however named. The scepticism of indefinite difference does not suffice. There is need to go beyond ever-receding limits. The less and more adequate forms in which an infinite end is discovered by post-moderns deserves the closest attention. The process leads in the end to a recovery as actual of the whole historical mediation which led to a knowledge of a concrete spirituality, a mediation lost in the externalization or temporalization of that standpoint in its initial realization.

For as by successive stages the post-modern, post-Christian world has lost intrinsic stability and begins to look beyond itself, a new relation opens to former philosophies. It was not as if the giants of that world had actually overthrown religion and philosophy. The relation is analogous to that of the subjective culture of the Hellenistic-Roman age where individuals, against the ethical order of the *polis* and the hard objectivity of the *res publica Romana*, thought to have freedom and the enjoyment of their right as persons in a human world – only to experience the disintegration of that world in a scepticism which could not find a universal inclusive of particularity. In that age one turned inward from the chaos of temporal life to an intelligible world and a unity before division, of which nature and the sensible world could then be known as a well-ordered image.

That contemplative reconciliation already appeared superficial to Augustine as not concretely unitive of the two worlds, nor subjectively of the human individual. In the post-modern, post-Christian world the awakening to a need to know what its own standpoint is, is satisfied only in the recognition of a concrete spirituality, a 'third philosophy,' which it supposes itself already to possess. But as awakening in the contemporary division between a desired existential concreteness and the equalizing freedom of the technical-economic society, philosophical thinking more readily gives weight to one or the other pole of this division. Thus some find their way from the later Heidegger to medieval Christianity, mediated to the world through some form of Christianized Neoplatonism. For them our loss of religion and philosophy has its source in the subjectivity of the modern age, the mistaken turn philosophy took with Descartes, reaching its extreme in Hegel. For others a benevolent development of the global economy grounded in Protestantism and morality is the way to the spiritual as well as economic liberation of humanity. Both have in them a certain unification of the divided terms of post-modernity, but extraneously from the standpoint of the older and of the modern philosophy.

The first of these two forms finds relation to the existential aspect of post-modernity, holds to nature, and would limit the exploitation of it by the subjective thought of the modern age. The other has confidence that democracy and a technical-economic culture globalized, if guided by a morality rooted in Protestant faith, can advance the well-being of humanity indefinitely. Neither form has place for the Hegelian argument that the ancient philosophy, reaching its limit, gave way to the modern, and this in turn to the third philosophy of whose historical existence post-modernity is a certain form.

More generally, to attempt in the 'post-modern' world to separate what is 'pre-modern' from what is 'modern' – Protestantism, Enlightenment – would be to use in vain a Procrustean sword. The philosopher, whose office is to understand the world in which he is, cannot stay with the common division of post-modernity into an existential side and a technological having its roots in modernity. People do not in reality live in one or the other but in both. To rediscover the historical mediation forgotten in post-modernity is not to retreat or divide but to attend to the whole mediation, ancient, medieval, and modern. If one would know what the universal human rights presupposed in post-modernity mean, and in what institutional order they could be given definite and stable interpretation, one must look impartially at both aspects of post-modernity, including also the recovery of the spirit of modernity and on what basis its excesses, unbound in post-modernity, can be converted to the good of free individuality as their proper end.

Conclusion

The dissolution of the post-modern society as a contradictory relation of existential particularity and equality of differences is for Hegel the disclosure of the ethical order of the state in its third form – as world history. The concrete freedom in which European nations reached the term of their historical development, as giving to their institutions and their freedom in them the form adequate to that of their Christian belief, is no longer borne primarily by peoples of a particular national temperament, language, and culture, but, as universal, draws all peoples to it. The historical scene has radically changed from the age of the nation states and their empires. There is now a common technical-economic culture equalizing individuals and 'liberating' them to an anarchic freedom, eroding the authority of traditional cultures and religions.

In this awakening to a universal world order, a post-modern freedom in a global economy can appear as the primary reality and controlling force. But there is present also in this society the need to reflect on itself and discover anew what it is; to grasp its own historical development and antecedents in earlier cultures and religions. The reason moving in that history – the conflict of substantial unity and subjective freedom, the unification of the two, and the transition of this unity into ethical institutions – has, however, an objectivity unattainable from the standpoint of the post-modern society as such. For those of a Christian tradition in its post-Christian form, this transition might appear as to an immediate unity of divided economic and communal moments – a return to the primitive as healing the division. But the authority of the primitive, as having in it the least either of intrinsic stability or of subjective freedom, tends to give way to the attraction of cultures that are strongly stabilized but repressive of individuality.

Where the condition of peace among nations has been for some time the fear of mutual destruction, a fear that does not depart but has become more unregulated with the end of the 'cold war,' the need is more urgent than in Hegel's time to discover on what this finite actuality of competing states rests, what the historical spirit taken universally is and what its relation to absolute spirit. Hegel's response to these questions must remind the reader of the *Civitas dei* of Augustine, where the principal opposition is found to be between the human subjectivity awakening in relation to the absolute creative God of Judaism and the subjective freedom mediated by the Greek and come fully into its own in the Roman world. The Christian religion, which had its historical preparation in these peoples, Augustine could only treat as guided by Scripture and a Pauline expression of its essential content. This representation or *Vorstellung* imposed on him the requirement of an absolute separation of the 'two cities' and prevented the recognition of truth in the religions and institutions of other than the Jewish people, unless in the Roman Empire and the philosophical grasp of its culture in Neoplatonism.

The Hegelian philosophy, containing the content of the Christian religion in conceptual form, could remove that radical division, enter into relation to other peoples and cultures from the most primitive to the original Paradise, finding in the Greeks and Romans the logic of the *preparatio evangelii.* Hegel can then find in history the immediate relation of individuals to an absolute end, and the conversion of a falling away from that end into a free subjective relation to it. Christian history mediates between Augustine's *civitas dei* – as possessing the absolute truth in separation – and historical existence. There takes shape a world more and more conformed in its institutions, and in the spirit moving in them, to the unchanging belief of all peoples. And philosophy, in responding to the reason of the world that has broken from the *Vorstellung,* gives to its religious content the form of thought. At first in this work one drew on the ancient philosophy. Then, finding that this could not contain the concreteness of the *Vorstellung,* the need of which the structure of medieval institutions made felt, a new philosophy emerged founded on the religious belief itself and able to relate that belief to a secularity apparently radically opposed to it. And from that modern world in turn has emerged a more deeply Christianized secularity and a new philosophy.

Notes

1 This is James Doull's final essay and was posthumously published first in the philosophy journal *Animus* 5 (2000), from written drafts collated and edited by F.L. Jackson. For fuller editorial details the reader is advised to see the article published there. All notes below are by F.L. Jackson.

2 Following Hegel's account of the historical appearances of philosophy, *Enc.*, 574-7.

3 The simile is Aristotle's. Having brought Presocratic metaphysics to completion in the idea of *nous,* Anaxagoras is spoken of as 'a sober man among drunkards.'

4 JD follows Hegel's characterization of his *Phenomenology of Spirit* as 'introductory' to the system in the specific sense that it recapitulates the history of philosophical culture from the standpoint of its consummation in the full-blown consciousness of freedom. Phenomenological reflection is the 'proof' of the standpoint which forms the basis of the system.

5 Here and in what follows, reference to 'the' *Vorstellung* is JD's (as Hegel's) shorthand for the specific theological content of Christian faith, the image of God as Trinity.

6 JD follows Hegel in understanding modern thought from Descartes to Kant as a reflection on God, world, and self from the standpoint of the self-certain subject – in Hegel's terms the finitely existent or 'phenomenal' spirit. The simple term for the relation of a conscious subject to everything that appears as given is 'experience.' Modern philosophy is thus essentially 'philosophy of experience,' and Hegel accordingly titles his summary of it 'Science of the experience of consciousness': 'Phenomenology' (*Phenomenology of Spirit*, Intro.).

7 The Christianized Germanic peoples, the European nations.

8 Protestantism.

9 On the 'externalized state' see *Philosophy of Right*, 183. By the 'immediate' state is intended rather the modern nation state, particularly the older European monarchies whose claim to political identity rested on a contradictory fusion of the Christian principle of *universal* freedom and some immediate, naturalistic feature of boundary, blood, language, or lineage definitive of a *particular Volk*. This inner inconsistency made violent conflict between the several European *Volksgeister* inevitable, as also the emergence of a post-nationalist, *world*-historical political spirit. JD sees the comprehension of this historical dialectic as the chief inspiration of Hegel's *Philosophy of Right*.

10 The same elements whose unification on the side of a finite, historical humanity is the basis of the 'immediate state' discussed on p. 293 above.

11 In the celebrated passage referenced (*PhR*, 340), Hegel describes the dialectical logic according to which, out of the historical conflict of the European nation states, a post-national or world-historical spirit is to emerge, motivated directly by the demand for a *universal* human freedom. JD follows up Hegel's insight, viewing the cataclysmic wars of the twentieth century as the self-inflicted death throes of European nationalism. The question then becomes what to make, politically and philosophically, of the aftermath; the emergent post-nationalist, post-Christian, post-modern world. JD is

concerned to show that while 'post-modern thought' reflects the awareness of a vast spiritual sea-change, it expresses this most unclearly as a liberation already (or never) accomplished, a position negatively sustained through outright abandonment of the whole spiritual legacy, which it reduces sceptically or linguistically to inconsequential rubble.

COMMENTARY
The Hegelian Idea

F.L. JACKSON

To appreciate the force of James Doull's 'Hegel's *Phenomenology* and Postmodern Thought' it is necessary to emphasize the uniqueness of its account of Hegel's *Phenomenology*, especially with regard to its relation to the philosophical system as a whole, an account which departs significantly from most established traditions of Hegel interpretation. There are those on the left who give phenomenology precedence over the system and those on the right who view the earlier work as but an imperfect prelude to the system. A common approach is to describe the argument of *Phenomenology* as a sort of existential experiment in which the naive reader would be self-educated into the 'absolute standpoint,' then to argue the project is bound to fail since there is no such standpoint. The systematic philosophy is in this way deprived of its starting point and exposed as a metaphysical fantasy wisely to be ignored.

For more sympathetic commentators the *Phenomenology* has been seen as suggestive, once shorn of its pretensions, of a general philosophical method, a 'science of consciousness' perhaps, in the manner of Husserl. Or it has been read as a grand philosophical critique of historical culture, full of interesting themes – scepticism-stoicism, master-slave, freedom-terror, morality-wickedness, state-society, and so on – that might prove productive once adapted to other contexts and purposes. The best-intentioned commentaries on the relation of *Phenomenology* to the system have, however, been wanting in a key respect: in failing faithfully to consult Hegel himself on the matter or, having done so, in having missed the significance of what he plainly says. In the end, how phenomenology and speculative philosophy were in Hegel's mind equal in importance, how the one is indeed the necessary introduction to the other, remains for the most part a mystery.

The great virtue of James Doull's approach is that he makes no attempt whatever to disclose or interpret hidden meanings in Hegel or to carry out a critique of his work from some ultra-Hegelian point of view.

Such approaches he considered plainly un-Hegelian, bound to miss or distort Hegel's meaning. Bringing to bear a breadth and depth of philosophical and historical learning legendary among those who knew him, Doull remained devoutly resolute in letting Hegel's arguments speak for themselves. It is this devotion over a lifetime to understanding the Hegelian philosophy on its own terms and no other that earned Doull the reputation among any who knew him as certainly the most subtle, thorough, and reliable Hegelian of his generation, if not of his century. It is for this reason necessary not to read Doull on Hegel as an interpretative gloss on certain of the latter's views, taken as already known. Rather they represent a fastidious elucidation of these views themselves, just as they are, precisely as Hegel wrote, spoke, and propounded them, together with Doull's own considered reflections on their implications for more recent thought.

In the present essay reference is repeatedly made to a rarely mentioned account Hegel gives of the relation of the philosophy of the past to his own, a matter he considered so important to the understanding of what philosophy itself is that it forms the concluding argument of the 'handbook' of the system, the *Encyclopedia of the Philosophical Sciences.* There (at *Enc.* 574–7) philosophy, as a form of the 'absolute spirit,' is said to have had three successive historical manifestations, in the course of which human thinking is educated to the fullest consciousness of what its own essential idea is. These appearances are identified, somewhat cryptically, on the model of infinite 'syllogisms' wherein the principal moments of speculative thinking take the role in turn of premise, mediating term, and conclusion. Thus, in the metaphysical thought of the ancients, that there is a reason in things – *logos* or *archē* – is assumed as intuitive; thinking is reflection on a given world ordered as *physis*, nature, whose ground is ultimately disclosed in the principle of the thinking mind or spirit itself, the Aristotelian *nous.* Christianity takes up the standpoint of this spiritual inwardness or self-conscious subjectivity; nature is assumed an otherness which it seeks to reconcile to itself. The theme of the subsequent modern form of philosophy is, accordingly, about the 'experience of consciousness': the thinking subject reconciling otherness to itself according to an idea of their infinite unity, an idea appearing in it as innate: 'It is the syllogism of spiritual reflection in the idea; philosophy appears as a subjective knowing whose end is freedom and which is itself the way to realize it' (*Enc.* 576). The third syllogism is a thinking from the standpoint of this infinite idea itself; the modern principle of free subjectivity and the ancient principle of rational substance – 'spirit' and 'nature' – are as premises of which it reveals itself to be the common ground.

Doull's summation has entirely to do with these historical appearances of philosophy as Hegel describes them, and especially with the emergence with Hegel of a 'third' philosophy coincident with the emergence of a post-modern age and culture. It is the philosophical history of European-Christian-modern ('Western') culture, consummated in the modern awakening to the explicit consciousness of freedom, that forms the theme and content of the *Phenomenology of Spirit.* But as every consummation is at once culmination and recommencement, Hegel apprehends in his own time both the end and completion of Christo-European modernity and its philosophy – the owl of Minerva has already flown[1] – but in this also the transition to a third, world-historical era and mentality, the philosophical principle and logic of which he would sketch in a new 'outline of the philosophical sciences.' Doull's essay has in view at every point this argument of the *Phenomenology* concerning the culmination of modern philosophical history, specifically in the 'absolute knowledge' of the idea of freedom, which at once becomes the presumed principle of commencement in a new, post-historical world and philosophy.

As one writing from the 'other side of a wall,' that is, from a time well beyond Hegel and on this side of the cultural divide of which he writes, Doull is interested also in tracing the subsequent history of this transition: the course of decline of the older European culture and the initial forms in which a 'third,' post-modern mentality sought to assert and articulate itself. For as Hegel frequently observes, cultures do not simply fade away or displace one another; they self-destruct, passing into decay precisely in virtue of a new inconsistency of principle emergent within them. Renewal and decay initially form a single confused movement; the new culture asserts itself in an absolutism wherein the older traditional forms of life and thought are repudiated and yet clung to. This ambiguity passes into a more definite conflict between revolutionary and reactionary ideologies, each claiming to represent the new world order, but whose mutually destructive opposition finally gives way to total scepticism. The initially negative forms of 'ultra-modernity,' having completed their destruction of all former traditions, now reveal the emptiness and violence of their own merely abstract, dogmatic grasp of the principle of freedom on which they purport to rest. What is actually destroyed in this new scepticism, however, is just the post-modern standpoint itself so far as it knows its own principle only in this dogmatic, negative form. Out of this emptiness arises the necessity of a recovery of the philosophical tradition,[2] and it is for this reason that, for Doull, what Hegel has to say on the question of the historical 'appearances' of philosophy is of the greatest interest and significance

One has an earlier model of such a world-altering transition in the fate of classical culture, whose corruption, decline, and fall was one with the emergence of a whole new order and mentality, founded on the principle of spiritual inwardness. This new Christian-European principle reaches its fullest articulation in modern philosophy and the modern state, where self-conscious individuals come to know freedom as the very essence of their being. But it is in this same cognition of freedom as merely moral or individual that Hegel saw modernity to have reached its apex and crisis in a conflicted freedom that is at once infinite and finite: a freedom that *would* be universal and substantial but in fact is dependent on the subjectivity of particular individuals, in whom it becomes indistinguishable from impulse and caprice. The great question for Hegel is thus knowledge of the *idea* of freedom itself as the measure of man rather than man as the measure of freedom.

It is indeed this idea of an unconditional freedom beyond subjective or moral autonomy, the standpoint of modern individualism, which Doull sees as latent in post-modern culture, though it has had the greatest difficulty getting hold of and articulating it. The idea of an infinitely actual freedom it can affirm only retrogressively by appeal to older forms, most generally in the elevation of subjective freedom itself to the rank of a political and existential absolute. It is from this presumption of absolute individualism that the mutual destruction of the European nation states and the coincident intellectual deconstruction of traditional Western art, theology, and philosophy has been carried out. The result is a stand-off between the politics of global humanism on the one side and, on the other, those of cultural particularism. The end both would achieve is the final overcoming of modernity, the one in its final globalized perfection, the other in its total terroristic destruction. What this conflict itself actually advances, however, is the further slide of modernity into decadence; for subjectivity, rendered absolute as unlimited individualism and justified by appeal to linguistic, historical, or fanatical anti-rationalism, does not yield unconditional freedom but universal arbitrariness and violence.

The positive concept of an infinite freedom which for Hegel is the 'idea' of philosophy thus lies buried under the ruins of a degenerate post-modernity, repressive of any and all traditions, especially those like philosophy which would appeal to reason. From this post-philosophical standpoint, notoriously, it is the Hegelian philosophy *especially* that is declared absurd, abhorrent, and unintelligible. It is Doull's aim, not only to bring back into focus the great cultural and intellectual shift which Hegel knew and wrote about, but also to show how developments since that time are consistent with the perspective explicated in Hegel's *Phenomenology*, *Philosophy of Right*, and other works. And as it is this perspective which Doull at all points assumes and adopts in his commentary, it would seem useful, in what follows, first to summarize the basics of the Hegelian philosophy of the 'idea.'

Freedom

In spite of the vast literature of bewilderment as to what the Hegelian philosophy is about, Hegel himself was surprisingly forthcoming: it is simply the idea of *freedom*, he says: freedom as supreme logical principle, as *telos* of nature, as pure form of individual self-certainty, as basis of all legal, moral, and institutional life, as the universal theme in all art, religion, and philosophy. This is not to 'interpret' Hegel in any way: that freedom is the ruling idea of philosophy, that philosophy is nothing other than the will to bring this idea to light, to comprehend and articulate it, this proposition Hegel returns to on every other page. The centrality of the principle of freedom is made most evident, of course, in connection with the philosophy of the spirit – that is, freedom manifest as human freedom. The following excerpt offers a directly available example of the importance he attaches to it:

> No idea is so generally recognized as indefinite, ambiguous, and prone to the greatest misconceptions – to which it ever falls victim – as the idea of *freedom*; and yet none so readily accepted currently. Because it is as free that the human spirit is *actual*, so misconceptions concerning freedom are of enormous consequence in practice. Indeed, once individuals and peoples have got the abstract concept of realized freedom fixed in their heads it has an invincible power, simply because freedom is of the very essence of the human spirit, indeed, its very actuality. Whole continents, Africa and the Orient, have not [up to Hegel's time] possessed this idea ... The Greeks and Romans, Plato and Aristotle, even the Stoics, never had it – they believed it

> is only by birth (as Athenian, Spartan, etc.) or by strength of character or culture or through philosophy ('the sage is free even while a slave and in chains') that one might be called free.

Hegel continues:

> This idea entered the world through Christianity, according to which the individual *as such* is judged of *infinite* worth as the object and aim of the divine love; who, standing in absolute relation to God as Spirit, is determined as having this spirit dwelling also in himself – which is to say: the human being is *as such* destined to the highest freedom. As in religion man is aware of a relation to absolute spirit as his very essence, so, when he steps into the sphere of *worldly* existence, he has this same divine spirit present with him as the substance of the state, the family, etc. It is this same spirit that engenders these [institutional] relations and constitutes their measure, while in turn it is through their influence the individual becomes endowed with an ethical disposition, so that even in the sphere of particular existence and everyday feeling and willing, the individual is *actually* free. (*Enc.* 482)[3]

These remarks conclude Hegel's psychology of the 'subjective spirit' (*Enc.* pt. 3.I), which argues that freedom is indeed 'human nature,' that is, the determinative factor in every mode and dynamic of psychological life. This is prefatory to the further argument that freedom is also the animating principle of all social and political institutions, the principle of 'objective' spirit. But for Hegel freedom is again more than this; it is also the hidden *telos* of nature as well as the essential theme of all artistic, religious, and philosophical searching and expression. What can justify such sweeping claims for the principle of freedom and how is Hegel's emphatic account of it more than dogmatic or arbitrary?

Thinking

Philosophy as a form of thinking can have no ring of truth, Hegel observes, where its principles are merely picked out of the air, assumed a priori, or acquiesced to on wholly positive, non-intellectual grounds. Nor do ideas simply reflect the circumstances of their time; on the contrary, it is only on being first initiated in thought that ideas acquire their historical force. Hegel's philosophy owes everything to the proposition that freedom is not some notion merely conjured in thinking or which thinking draws from an extraneous source; this because *thinking is itself nothing but freedom,* freedom in its most immediate form as self-consciousness, inwardly self-determinate activity.

> [T]hinking is *my* activity, the expression of my spirit, of myself as a thinking subject in my own simple self-initiated universality as self-existent 'I' – in short, it is my *freedom* ... In thinking freedom is directly implied, since it *is* nothing else but universal self-relativity or indeterminate being-unto-self *qua* subject, which at the same time, with respect to its *content,* is wholly concerned with determinations of *fact.* (*Enc.* 23)

Everything in philosophy turns, Hegel insists, on firmly holding to this Cartesian point: it is as thinking-being, and only so, that one is free. It can accordingly make no sense to speak of 'thinking' in the abstract and 'freedom' as some content that may or may not come within its ken. Freedom cannot be an arbitrary content for thought for the compelling reason that to think at all is to bring this very principle into play. It follows, moreover, that descriptions of thinking as neural process, language, or whatever are absurd on their face simply because, were such judgments literally true, they would render the experiential testimony, tests of validity, or other appeal to a standard of cogency necessary to make and defend them quite unthinkable. Hyper-metaphysical accounts of what thinking is fare no better – thought is not so subtle an art as to privilege the deep thinker; as Spinoza says simply, 'Man thinks.'

Contemporary sophistication now generally rejects the *res cogitans* as a psycho-linguistic fiction. It is indeed a prime concern of post-modern philosophy to show that there simply is no such thing, in spite of the ubiquity of the presumption in ordinary science and everyday life. But even were 'reasonable' to mean no more than 'persuasive,' without the presumption of thinking persons capable of persuading and being persuaded, it can hardly be imagined what 'convincing discourse' concerning any matter – including the present one about whether there is thinking or not – could possibly mean; unless the claim is that words and arguments are really only as sticks and clubs and discourse mutual hypnosis. In the end it is the post-modern repudiation of thinking autonomy that is implausible, strained, and metaphysical.

In any case, Hegel's account of thinking hardly lends itself to the caricature of the 'absolute subject,' the breeder of abstractions and an abstraction itself. As his psychology seeks to demonstrate, 'thinking' is what it is for the ordinary experience of it rather than what might be made of it by a Heidegger or Derrida: a 'gathering apprehension' or the mere abstraction of 'writing.' It is ordinarily witnessed as the act of freely bringing some content or other 'to mind,' becoming subjectively absorbed with it, withdrawing reflectively into oneself so as first to render it objective, then comprehending it through the powers of imagination, linguistic signification, and conceptualization. These intellectual acts are not separate steps on some abstract epistemological ladder; they are organically inseparable moments in the everyday subjective life of human beings who, finding themselves 'there' in a given world, permeate and transform it through their own self-conscious activity, thereby rendering it a world of their own, conformed to their freedom.

For Hegel, in its fullest definition thinking is neither apprehension, reflection, nor abstraction alone but the total dynamic of self-generative, self-determinative, and self-authenticating subjective activity. The possibility of philosophy – indeed, that there can be insight, judgment, persuasion, argument, comprehension at all, that anything can be meaningfully uttered or understood – hinges entirely on this presumption of the free act of thought. In Hegel's view, philosophy *is* nothing else but the self-conscious exercise of this freedom through which the individual's inward and outward life acquires an altered character, no longer appearing as a world extraneously given and passively reacted to but as a subjectively inhabited, *self*-given world in which freedom has reality, scope, and effect – a distinctively *human* world. The question then becomes: what is the form of the object of thinking?

The Concept

> As other sciences take their commencement from something subjectively presupposed ... space, number, or whatever, it might seem philosophy too must begin by making 'thinking' the object of thinking. But the free act of thinking is precisely this: to place itself at the standpoint where it exists for itself, thus *generates and provides for itself an object distinctly its own.* (*Enc.* 17)

It is as a thinking of thinking that philosophy has long been defined. But that thinking is freedom cannot be taken to mean one can literally 'think what one likes.' On the contrary, to take up the free standpoint of thought is precisely to suspend one's *particular* point of view – 'what one likes' – to allow thinking itself to determine what its true object must be. That thinking is inevitably the thinking of some particular individual does not preclude this necessity that, once entered into, thinking can and must begin only with itself. For this, active being in and for self is precisely what 'thinking' is.

As purely self-determinate activity, then, thinking cannot in principle have an object extraneous to it in any absolute sense; for what it *is* is the free merging of itself with a content and its mediation and positing of that as its own. *Thinking* prehension is not a 'gathering' in the weak Heideggerean sense, but a coincident *self*-prehension, which together is a *com-prehension*: thinking finding in its other itself, and in itself its other. Hegel everywhere lays great emphasis on this character of thinking as comprehension, the specifically positive resolution of a content to self-determinate form. And this free, self-determinate form of the object of thought is precisely what Hegel calls the *concept* in a unique and telling sense.[4]

The concept, *Der Begriff*, is for Hegel the object proper to thinking, not contingently but essentially. A term much misunderstood and mutilated in the literature, the Hegelian concept bears little resemblance to the English notion of a class or generalization wherein particulars are abstractly summarized in terms of some common feature and assigned an arbitrary signifier, or to the Kantian synthesis of representations according to categories a priori. Hegel certainly recognizes this abstractive-categorizing mode of thinking (he calls it 'understanding' – *Verstand*), but as only one moment in the larger dynamic of 'comprehension' (*Begreifung*), whose object, as concept, is grasped *un*conditionally, that is, as what specifically is in and for itself.

'Object' and 'objectivity' have in the Hegelian argument both a weak and a strong sense. 'Ob-ject' can generally indicate something 'standing over against,' a *Gegenstand*: objectivity in the conditional sense in which most modern philosophers from Descartes to Kant belaboured it. The ambiguity of the object in this weaker sense is that its distinctness relative to a subject is also a dependency on it. In the stronger sense (for which Hegel reserves the term '*Object*'), the object rather means that which stands independently on its own, is 'self-objective,' revealed for thinking as it is in itself – in the older metaphor, as 'innate.' Here the distinction-from and the being-for thinking are not extrinsically related factors, but are determined as moments within the logical structure of the object itself. 'Concept' is Hegel's term for the unconditional objectivity any content has and must have to be 'comprehended' in thought – a meaning much closer to the everyday sense of the word. The concept is the object proper to thinking in the precise sense that what is grasped conceptually, 'comprehended,' is not merely 'given' but *self*-given, known in its *intrinsic* necessity; and only so as compatible with thinking itself as free, self-determinate activity.

This is why, Hegel insists, thinking beings can never rest with a world looming inexorably and contingently 'there,' contrary in principle to their freedom. Nor can they be content with worlds conjectured or conjured in imagination. Thinking is only at home – *bei sich* – in a world in which it can find its own freedom confirmed, in which its self-determinate character is reflected. The com-prehension of otherness in self and self in otherness is thus precisely what thinking is; again, an absolute Other cannot exist for it. Accordingly, only when grasped *conceptually*, as determined in itself, is anything actually 'intelligible' for me, that is, does my world and my freedom become transparent to one another, a unity-in-difference of subjective and objective, universal and particular, articulated equally on the objective side as on the side of thinking itself. Which is to say in sum: only a conceptually comprehended world can be real for freedom.

Freedom, in other words, is the formal principle of the conceptual object of thought. Hegel can thus write: '[T]he concept is what is *free* ... [what] *is determinate in and for itself*' (*Enc.* 160). To grasp anything conceptually is to grasp it in its 'actuality' in the Aristotelian sense or, as for Spinoza, *sub specie aeternitatis.* It belongs to the unconditioned objectivity of the concept that in it the moments of freedom itself are exhibited: first, simply as reduction of some content to universality, then as a determinate content distinguished from its determining ground, then as this distinction resolved to a *self*-determinate whole. Further, as self-determination is the ruling principle on the subjective side, that is, in thinking itself, the relation between thinking and its unconditional object is one of infinite reciprocity: each has the other's principle in it, each discloses itself in the other. Conceptual comprehension is thus as much thinking as self-sublimating subjectivity, as its concept is self-evidencing objectivity. On this account, the relation of thinking to actuality cannot be described as if a relation of one thing to another, nor, as in the grand modern tradition, as a 'correspondence' of thinking to a content that must remain empirically alien to it. Nor is it the relation of thinking to something posited by itself, the reduction of reality to a figment of representation, of which Hegel, like Plato, frequently stands accused in post-modern literature.[5] Hegel emphasizes the very opposite: to apprehend the world empirically or phenomenologically is only to formalize how it appears; only in its conceptual comprehension is it comprehended as it actually is. This is the basis of one of Hegel's more striking claims, namely, that it is only by bringing clearly to light the conceptual nature of its own thinking that philosophy rises to self-consciousness as to what its true standpoint is, from which standpoint alone can it comprehend the actual world in its living concreteness. 'The concept of philosophy ... must come to be grasped by philosophy itself. This is indeed its unique aim, action, and goal: to attain to the concept of its concept, thereby to secure its completion and satisfaction' (*Enc.* 17).

The 'concept of the concept' in this sense of the concept fully developed philosophically, is what Hegel calls 'the idea.' It is thus more than rhetorical to describe the whole aim and burden of Hegelian philosophy, philosophy's third and final historical 'appearance,' as precisely to identify and articulate this idea in the full range of its meaning and ramifications.

The Idea

As earlier noted, Hegel speaks of the history of philosophy as the disclosure in three historical forms of this philosophical idea. He also represents these forms *logically* in an infinite trinity whose terms are the perennial absolutes of philosophical thinking, namely: 'nature,' the given order of things; 'spirit' as self-conscious thinking life; and 'idea' as their common underlying, unconditional principle. Ancient philosophy sprang spontaneously out of the impulse of human beings to discover a reason in their immediate life-world, culminating in the Platonic trinity of One, *Nous*, and Cosmos, grasped in an ontological thinking for which these terms are only intuitively unified. The Christian trinity established the form of the modern philosophy: to a rational, indwelling spirit an infinite principle of freedom is revealed, a freedom which, through the theoretical and practical sublimation of nature and its own historical action, it would seek to bring to life.

For Hegel the limit of these first and second historical philosophies lies in the fact that, in them, thinking commences with the assumption of a principle other than its own – Substance, Subjectivity – which then dominates the form and course of its reasoning. Thinking does not have hold of its own principle, it is not 'for itself,' is not the *self*-thinking Aristotle described as the divine life. Philosophy is properly consummated, therefore, only where it no longer addresses a principle other than its own but attains to a properly *conceptual* form in a *post*-historical philosophy where the idea of freedom itself is made the explicit point of departure for thinking which now knows what it is and what it does. Such a philosophy will develop this principle as the true basis of nature and spirit alike, as the hidden *telos* of the given world as also the realized end of human life and action.

And this explication of the various forms of the philosophical idea is what the Hegelian system is, as set forth in the *Encyclopedia of the Philosophical Sciences in Outline.* It is the standpoint Doull assumes at all points in his essay. Developed in thinking itself, it is the 'self-thinking' or 'logical' idea. As a principle of *infinite* self-determination, however, it has the implication already in it of infinite self-differentiation, self-externality, and as such is the reason of the external world – the idea of nature. And as it also implies infinite reflection inward out of difference into a relation to self it is equally freedom as the principle of human selfhood and life – the idea of spirit.

(i) The Logical Idea

For the most part Hegel's science of the logical idea has been written off by formal logicians as a bag of dialectical tricks, what logic properly should never be.[6] Even among the sympathetic the impulse is to 'interpret' it, to make something of it other than what is there, perhaps visit a few initial categories ('being-nothing-change') with a view to discovering whether or not 'dialectic' actually works. The tendency in short is to fail to appreciate Hegel's science of logic as he himself describes it: as the speculative genealogy of the basic unit of philosophical thinking, the 'concept,' the reflection wherein thinking renders itself cognizant as to what its proper object is. This survey of the range of recognizable pre-conceptual logical categories is, however, no mere aggregation where each stands on its own to be only abstractly related to others, as in classical metaphysics and in formal logic. Rather, it is the elicitation of all the pre-conceptual forms of the concept carried out from the standpoint of the latter's fully developed form: the 'concept of the concept,' the logical idea.

Hegel describes the logical system as a 'circle of circles' in the sense that its main divisions, and divisions of divisions, mark the evolution of thinking itself into its properly conceptual form. It is divided accordingly into a succession of proto-logical reflections. As 'ontology' thinking is immediate, intuitive, and pre-reflexive, its object what exists in itself as such, being *qua* being, and logic the distinguishing of its accidental determinations as categories. As 'metaphysics' the particularity of being is assumed as given and thinking is the reflection which elicits its essential categories by reference to a noumenal ground. As 'formal logic' thinking is directed to its own conceptual act, but only to observe in it a set of static, 'formal' relations: 'rules' of judgment, forms of inference, and so on. The final argument of Hegel's logic consists in a speculative critique of these abstract and static categories of formal logic, aimed at showing that, and how, they are rooted in the self-determinate dynamic of conceptual thinking itself.

The intent of the science of logic overall is thus to present traditional ontology, metaphysics, and formal logic as *pre*-conceptual forms of conceptual thinking, their categories pre-conceptual forms of the concept. Being, quality, one, quantum, identity, difference, substance, causality, universality, predication, inference, etc. – these are concepts *in principle* but clearly not explicitly so; they appear rather to describe noumenal entities, relations, or operations given intuitively, transcendentally, or formally such that thinking is not fully aware of its own action in them. Accordingly for Hegel, the onto-meta-logical categories brought to light in ancient and modern philosophy are and are not philosophically valid. But while the science of logic may be viewed on its one side as a wholesale *de*construction of all traditional categories, found unstable as measured against the self-determinacy of the concept, it is equally the positive *re*construction of these same categories, revealing each to prefigure the logic of the concept itself. It is in terms of this intention that Hegel's logic is the logic of freedom, its sole presupposition the principle of self-determinacy, the concept. The logic is thus thinking's complete systematic demonstration of what its own principle is. It is systematic since the principle of its procedure is its own. It is complete, not in the absurd sense of incapable of refinement and comprehensive of every particular (Hegel rejects such a trivial notion of what 'absolute knowledge' is), but complete in that it concludes with the concept with which it begins, but developed as the consummation of the whole lineage of its own incomplete forms. This 'realized' concept Hegel calls the logical idea, the principle of freedom intellectually self-articulated.

For Hegel the further task of philosophy is to establish the rule of the idea in all regions of unconscious and self-conscious life. Again, analytically considered, as the principle of the infinitely self-determinate, the idea has three connotations, each of which emphasizes a different dynamic. First, simply *as* principle, the idea is the simple thought of the infinite unity of identity, determinateness, and self-relation, the logical idea. But as a principle of infinite *determination* it is a principle of substantial necessity, externality, 'reality': the idea as principle of nature.

Finally, as determination is at once self-determination, externality is not absolute but a self-externality which implies the corresponding movement of infinite return to self, and in this aspect the idea is the principle of the human mind and spirit.

These modes implicit in the idea itself form the basis of the larger Hegelian system of the philosophical sciences. Freedom is throughout the principle: as the inner necessity of nature, as free, self-conscious activity, and as the infinite idea comprehended in philosophy. Though the triune principle is found in one form or another in virtually every culture, Hegel wholly intends the correspondence here of the Hegelian idea with the Christian doctrine of the Trinity. Where in the latter the Persons are represented as at once one and distinct, co-equal and yet all-inclusive, the same holds for the principle that founds the philosophical sciences. Logic is their 'theology,' the logical idea the template for the systematic ordering of the philosophies of nature and spirit. In the Hegelian idea, as in the Christian Trinity, the divine, the natural, and the human worlds flow freely into and imply one another.

(ii) Idea as Nature

If *logos* forms the first person of the Hegelian trinity of the idea, the second is *physis,* the order of nature. Commentators have had the greatest difficulty making sense of the conclusion of Hegel's logic, where 'the idea, appearing as its other-being, resolves to let its own moment of particularity, determinateness and externality issue freely forth as *nature*' (*Enc.* 244). This transition is familiar enough in the religious image of divine creation – nature as the explicit act of God. In Christian theology it appears more definitely as God's self-emptying and incarnation as the Son. The difficulty in appreciating Hegel's logical formulation of the same idea lies partly in an obscure grasp of what exactly 'nature' is, partly in the overwhelming dominance of that particular view of nature formed in modern philosophy, elaborated in contemporary natural science, and whose outlook and method is considered absolutely authoritative.

On the first point, the idea has more in it than the principle of freedom as ordinarily understood, that is, as free agency, absence of restriction, free choice, or whatever: views which properly belong to the human context, where freedom has the conditional form of a human quality or practical ideal. The idea, however, is freedom thought *un*conditionally, that is, as infinite, fully actual *self-determination.* As Hegel puts it in a theological metaphor, the idea is 'God as he is before the creation of nature and the human world.' It belongs to the concept of infinite, unconditional self-determination, however, that the *whole* dynamic be fully manifest in each of its moments, and so the logical idea, the idea in and for thought, is equally the idea of infinite other-determination, of external necessitation, which is the principle according to which nature is 'nature.' It is in this *logical* sense that the idea may be said to 'issue freely forth as nature,' for what nature here means is not, as in the common modern notion, a world that mysteriously exists 'outside us.' Rather it is nature grasped as external *in principle*, thus as an infinite order which has 'other-determinateness,' externality, as its essential inner dynamic. And this nature is a 'real' external world, not relatively but in itself, since 'othering' and 'externality' do not describe how nature appears relative to human consciousness, but are the characteristic mode of being or activity of anything *qua* natural.

Such a view of nature, while familiar enough in the common experience of it, is wholly foreign to what has become authoritative in the modern science of nature. There nature stands wholly in relation to human cognition and practice, its otherness not an essential externality but an otherness-for-man. Nature has come accordingly to be defined as the realm of the non-human, non-anthropomorphically described as a realm of literally 'mind-less' elements – particles, forces, mechanisms, whatever – a view extended also to physiology and human psychology, yielding the absurd modern contradiction of scientifically minded human beings scientifically convincing themselves of their own mindlessness, thus of their incapacity for science. Practically expressed through nature-domineering industry and technocracy, this humanized science of nature inevitably breeds its opposite: the aesthetic-existential insistence on the oneness of nature and man, each ambiguously intrinsic to the other's meaning. Where nature is defined as a spiritless universe incorporating the human, or alternatively as nothing but a moment in human self-experience, the paradox is generated of a nature that both is and is not independent of the human perspective, which is and is not liberated from it. The on-going ever hotter war between scientific technocracy and various expressions of neo-romanticist naturalism expresses this contradiction at the heart of the modern view of nature.

In Hegel's account, nature is the idea of a self-external and self-externalizing order: endless iteration of the same, endless proliferation of differences, endless regeneration of forms, structures, and processes, which endlessness expresses the essential finitude of nature. Nature is nonetheless ordered, though not in the sense of a hierarchical generation of lower from higher forms, nor a complexification in which higher evolve from lower: emanation and evolution are for Hegel explanations imposed on nature after the fact.[7] The order of nature is quite simply nature itself as a living system, the dynamic interdependency and interrelation of whose constituent elements, structures, processes, and realms have their principle, their *telos*, in the idea. It is the mark of nature that while events and processes are ever unique and endlessly particularizing they express and obey nonetheless the inner law of the whole. This ambiguous collusion of contingency and necessity is, however, essential: that what is necessary be contingent, and what is contingent necessary, expresses precisely the dynamic of other-determination which is the form self-determination assumes in and as nature. Accordingly, nature is a whole in which everything falls outside everything else *in infinitivum*, where universal natural laws are always manifest in something particular and contingent, and where whatever comes about or is produced is something other than its cause.

The Christian doctrine of *creatio ex nihilo* suggests that the origin of nature is not itself a natural event. Hegel argues the same on rational grounds: nature cannot be thought as grounded in itself; it is not itself a natural event or entity; nor can it have a beginning in time since there is no before and after time itself. Nor for similar reasons can one sub-realm of nature be thought reducible to another or to have its genesis in it: the chemical in the electrical, the biological in the chemical, conscious life in the biological. It is only for a finite, analogical thinking that natural forms appear as springing out of one another, matter from energy, life out of chemical soup, human beings from frogs. The relations between the cosmic, mechanistic, physical, chemical, and biological spheres of nature are of quite another order for Hegel; they belong to a universal ecology the logic of which must form the primary interest of a speculative natural philosophy. In this ecology, there is certainly interdependency and symbiosis within and between the suborders of nature; but the deeper dynamic of this interdependency lies in a progression of the form of organization manifest at each level and it is through this progression that nature is known as a totality. In cosmic or mechanistic suborders sheer abstract externality prevails; the principle of self-determination whose moment this other-determinateness is remains wholly covert, a 'blind' inner necessity as in the laws of motion. In higher orders this 'inner' necessity itself comes more explicitly to the fore in electromagnetic interaction, thermodynamics, chemical affinities, and so forth. And in biological nature the externality of part to part is dominated by a yet more definite principle of order in the form of organic life, where in the organism externality has a more concrete shape as *self*-externality, as evidenced in self-preservation, self-reproduction, self-animation, etc. Nature is thus known as a system of systems, external to one another but such that the purely abstract form of natural otherness and other-determination is progressively sublimated such that the principle of self-determination underlying it comes to be more and more distinctly prefigured – where blind force becomes inner necessity, inner necessity interaction, and interaction the self-activity of living things.

As endless process of self-manifestation, self-differentiation, and self-sublimation, it follows, nature cannot rightly be thought of as a completed whole with a definite origin and end. The postulation of primal energies or a 'big bang,' theories of evolution, and the like are inspired by the wish to render nature complete, self-original, and self-subsistent. But this is just what nature is not, as it everywhere demonstrates. It is non-original, endless, open-ended not simply in fact, but *in principle*; in short, nature is as such a finite order. If there is consummation, it is not in the completion of nature *as nature*, but in that specific natural form in which the limit of nature's principle is itself revealed and in which, accordingly, nature itself is sublimated. This consummate natural form is that animal 'which has its own species for object,' that is, the conscious and self-conscious human animal in whom is accomplished, not the perfection of nature as nature but the passing over of its externality into a fully explicit self-externality, a being-for-self: and this is consciousness, thought. In the self-objectivity of the human being there is the end of nature itself and the genesis of a trans-natural order of 'immortal' being, that is, of a freedom no longer hidden as necessity, but as a present and living freedom. In this human self-conscious life the idea recurs once more, but as the return into self out of nature, the idea as 'spirit.'

(iii) Idea as Spirit

The Hegelian idea of spirit has been the subject of endless mystification as to what it means and what is to be made of it. Yet in one form or another its essential theme and problematic, the psychology and sociology of human freedom, was to become the principal preoccupation of later times and, in Marxism and existentialism, of the philosophy and politics of the twentieth century. Hegel certainly thought the question as to what spirit is definitive, not only for religion and philosophy, but for the very fate of humanity:[8] 'To discover the definition [of spirit] and grasp its meaning and burden was, one can say, the ultimate goal of all education and philosophy, the point toward which all religion and science has ever tended, and the impulse according to which alone the history of the world can be comprehended' (*Enc.* 384).

As earlier indicated, what Hegel meant by 'spirit' he makes plain enough. It is again freedom, self-determination, but neither as abstract principle nor as the covert necessity driving nature, neither *logos* nor *telos*, but freedom as actual, self-conscious life. This living freedom, abstractly considered, is self-mediating activity, or more logically put, the activity of 'being-for-self-in-otherness.' This self-activity implies reflexivity: on the one hand it suggests 'return-out-of-otherness-into-self,' on the other hand 'positing-of-self-in-otherness' – in Kantian terms, theoretical and practical reason. The distinction provides the basis for Hegel's triune division of the philosophy of the spiritual idea. Considered as a free turning inward into self out of otherness, spiritual self-activity is *mental life*; as a self freely willing a world as its own, it is *ethical life*; as the completer life which has freedom itself as its very intuition, aim, and object, which comprehends it, that is, aesthetically, contemplatively, and intellectually, it is the 'absolute' spirit.

To English ears, the word 'spirit' has an unearthly, superstitious ring, its use mostly confined to rhetorical, poetic, or theological contexts. How Hegel would define the term is again plainly enough stated – 'the substance of spirit is *freedom*, non-dependence on another, relation of self to itself, ... the concept of that which exists for itself, has itself alone for object' (*Enc.* 382 and *Zusatz*) – and Hegel is also always clear that spirit denotes something altogether concrete and familiar, akin to what in ordinary parlance is simply called 'Life,' the organic metaphor being used to express the uniquely human world of experience and thought, desire and action, circumstance and fate; the world as actually shared with other self-conscious beings. Religion pictures the spirit as a divine life, inwardly animating individuals and prevailing over the whole course of human affairs, bringing it to completion. Hegel's purpose was to bring this religious image of the spiritual life within the reach of concrete philosophical thought, to 'comprehend' it in more than metaphors: 'The word and *image* of spirit is found early on: the chief theme of Christian teaching is to come to know God as Spirit. To grasp in its own element of conceptual thought the essential reality given here as an image is the task of philosophy, a task not genuinely resolved so long as the concept of freedom is not its very object and soul' (*Enc.* 384).

It might be argued that the employment of an old term like 'spirit' in a modern, post-Enlightenment theory of human psychology and practice is atavistic, but that would be to miss the whole crux of Hegel's argument, which is that no theories which purport to account for human beings and their actions can be genuine if they fail to make freedom itself, *specifically and at every point*, the essential concept. The use of the term 'spirit' signals and carries with it just this import: that the only philosophically valid psychology is a psychology of freedom, the only valid political theory one that makes freedom the principle of society and the state, the only true religion or philosophy that which knows freedom as its proper form and content. Spirit is thus freedom fully articulated in, for, and as human life. As such it is again idea, but as the system of all the inward, outward, and infinite expressions of self-conscious life.

In its inward form as mental life, spirit is not to be thought a *given* existence of any kind: not a soul-thing, an ego, a *Dasein*. It arises as the infinite reflexive self-conscious activity wherein all givenness whatever is rendered 'ideal' in the distinctly Hegelian sense of that term.[9] The mental life of the individual (and *Geist* has this meaning in everyday parlance) – the full range of psycho-somatic dispositions, sensory-motor reactions, emotions, and habits, conscious and unconscious selfhood, powers of imagination, representation, language, and thought – is genuinely understood only as the system of the modes of subjective self-activity, drawing everything given into itself and imposing upon it the form of its own inner freedom.[10]

But free subjectivity, the Aristotelian soul as 'potentially all things,' is but one aspect of spirit as infinitely self-reflexive activity. The other aspect is self-resolution-in-otherness, figuratively a self which, inwardly certain of its freedom, wills an objective world conformable to itself. This practical spirit, spirit as the will to liberty (and *Geist* has also the common meaning of *esprit*), is the basis of Hegel's account of the *ethical* universe, the idea as the system of the forms of free institutional life. Here again freedom is the operative and constitutive principle of the whole range of legal, moral, domestic, economic, social, and political human assumptions and arrangements. It is of all Hegel's doctrines the one that has had the greatest influence on later speculation, especially in the realm of political philosophy, due principally to the widespread influence of Marx's infamous caricature of it.[11]

Thus, considered immediately as it appears in and for human beings as self-conscious individuals, spirit is a dual process of liberation: free reflection-inward (*Erinnerung*) out of otherness – freedom as subjectivity – and self-active individuals determining how and what their world ought to be – freedom as ethical activity (*Sittlichkeit*). Hegel refers to both the psychological and the practical free spirit, considered in themselves, as finite or incomplete forms: 'finite' relative to the fuller spiritual self-consciousness which explicitly knows and wills freedom itself as its own principle – the in-finite, im-mortal, or absolute spirit (*Enc.* 386 and *Zusatz*). Freedom as subjectivity is finite in the sense that the world it internalizes is not one it gives itself but one it finds given for it. It is thus a freedom sustained only in the destruction of everything given and objective; in the end, an anarchic, chronically unrequited spirit. Freedom as practical freedom is finite in the opposite way: any human-initiated arrangement is contingent upon the will to sustain it, and so arrangements based on no more than the free choice of particular individuals cannot found an order of freedom that is substantial or stable. Thus, existential inwardness remains fatally entangled in an otherness it would at the same time suspend, while practical activism remains unrequited due to the finite character of its motivation and end. The one has the *form* of freedom only, the other is ever *on the way* to it. Standing in unreconciled division, they as much limit freedom as realize it; an issue to become of momentous significance, as will be argued, for the post-Hegelian era, where these forms of finite freedom are raised to the absolute.

The 'absolute spirit' which Hegel distinguishes from its finite form is not this human freedom raised to infinity as an existential or ideological absolute. Rather in mind is something more like what Aristotle calls the divine life, spirit as the explicit knowing and willing of freedom as its own constituent and ruling idea. If as *Dasein* freedom is without a world of its own (or *only* its own), or if as *praxis* it is fatally and forever unconsummated, for the spirit which exists for itself *as spirit*, freedom is unconditional, recognized and willed as universal reality, not the contingent property of 'I, this individual' nor again the abstract end of an endless project called 'Man.'

Appealing to a common religious image, Hegel describes the absolute spirit as self-conscious openness to the divine love 'in which all are made free.' To this infinite spirit the finite, human forms of spirituality certainly belong, but only as moments in it – indeed only as such do they have their true form and inspiration. The individual sense of self, of an inward independence subliminal of natural existence, has its deeper significance in the recognition of nature *itself* as, in Schelling's phrase, the realm of the pre-self, the prefiguration of self-conscious freedom, the latter's immanent or unconscious life.[12] On the other hand, the practical or moral vision of an order of human freedom which ever ought to be brought about but never quite is has its deeper justification in the recognition of freedom as an eternally *realized* end, a recognition occurring only where 'spirit exists for spirit,' that is, in and for aesthetic, religious, and philosophical experience. It is in this latter, unconditional spirituality that personal and practical freedom have their proper model, instruction, and redemption.

Art, religion, and philosophy are for Hegel forms of the 'absolute' spirit in the sense that their object of interest is not the 'phenomenal' spirit, not the realm of the human in its psychological or political meaning, but the *idea* that informs this worldly spirit and establishes its end. Their perennial and essential interest, however far they may actually stray from or corrupt it, is in grasping this idea of freedom as the ruling principle alike of all human life and history. In these absolute-oriented forms of life a creative, pious, and speculative human spirit gives itself over entirely to bringing forth from itself this, its essential and universal meaning, rendering it visible, alive, and intelligible.

Philosophy for its part is that 'speculative' mode of spiritual activity which seeks to grasp the idea in a form expressly adequate to it, that is, under the free form of thought. Philosophy in principle is, in Aristotle's formula, the 'thinking of thinking,' or in Hegel's, 'the self-thinking idea.' Its whole justification thus lies in its claim that, as itself a wholly free, that is, a 'speculative' thinking, it possesses in itself the standard and ground of its own veracity.[13] The inspiration of philosophy stems, not from any impulse to flee the world into abstractions; the world for philosophy is no other than the concrete, familiar world of ordinary experience. But it is this world brought, whole and intact, under the explicit form of freedom, that is, of *thought*. It is the essential unity and reciprocity of the ideal and the worldly, the infinite and finite, the spiritual and natural, which in the arts is given a sensible shape, which forms an object of worship in religion, and which philosophy would comprehend in the pure thought of freedom as 'absolute idea.'

After Hegel

James Doull's brief survey of the fate of political culture since Hegel is predicated on a strict reading of Hegel's own account of the consummation of Christian modernity and the advent of a new age and philosophy. The express intent of the *Phenomenology of Spirit*, he notes, is what Hegel says it is: to recapitulate the intellectual history of the Western world from the point of view of a principle which modern philosophy has yielded up, and in which this second world-historical form of philosophy brings itself to conclusion and opens the way to another standpoint of thought. Taking over from the Christian religion its key doctrine of God as spirit and making this its assumption and aim, modern philosophy had been the development of the Christian principle of spiritual freedom to its fullest conceptual clarity. Doull frequently cites the formula in which Hegel expresses the insight in which the philosophy of modernity is consummated: 'spirit has come to know itself *as spirit*,' that is to say, no longer a religious mystery or a political yearning but a philosophically comprehended idea, freedom has entered into general human consciousness as the acknowledged foundation of all human life, culture, and history.

But at this point emerges the ambiguity of the emergent post-modern era to which Doull refers. The great principle of human freedom which Western culture and thought laboured over centuries to bring to clarity is, at the very point of its consummation, abruptly and decisively resolved to the status of an absolute fact, a foregone conclusion and dogmatic presupposition, the immediate truth of which is negatively justified and sustained through the wholesale suspension, critique, overthrow, and deconstruction of everything that would pretend to mediate it, including particularly the very historical and intellectual mediation out of which in fact it arose. Hegel and all his ancestors are especially singled out and reassessed as prime enemies of human freedom in having allegedly restricted it to being something finite and unrealized, a mere idea, an otherworldly 'spiritual' freedom, thus in essence a sham. The appeal is now to an utterly this-worldly freedom wherein individuals are assumed to be immediately and unconditionally free, free absolutely even in their natural or social contingency, and having the absolute right to bring everything in heaven and earth into relation with this their subjectivity.

Where freedom is affirmed as being what belongs *directly* to naturally existing self-active individuals, its rational basis is or course denied. But from the standpoint of the powerful dogma of absolute human freedom which sustains the spectacular technocratic-ideological transformations of the post-modern era, as well as the various forms of the opposition to it, the twilight of gods and moralities is not at all considered catastrophic; indeed, it is the necessary precondition of entry into the new age and mentality to be founded on more than mere gods, principles, or principalities. Accordingly, post-modern theology and philosophy (as Feuerbach and Marx, Kierkegaard and Nietzsche) invert traditional Christian doctrine itself to render it compatible with an assumed apotheosis of the human. The hierarchy spiritual-human-natural is to be altogether repudiated, or else turned on its head. The post-modern revolution demands an end to all mediations, whether divine, rational, linguistic, or historical, that would imply a limit to a radically post-Christian, post-rational, post-historical freedom. To undermine and demolish all such mediations has become the chief thrust and task of post-modern 'critique' in its ever-changing forms. Its point is especially to show how philosophical rationality in all its forms has been inspired specifically by the will to repress the absolute freedom of individuals, and so, even in Hegel's own time, the Christian-Hegelian doctrine of spirit had already being declared wanting in the crucial respect that its freedom was no more than the mere thought of it, that it was enough one believe in it; in short, an inhuman freedom 'not of this world.' Commensurate with this wholesale deconstruction of traditional art, theology, and philosophy and their relegation to the trash heap of mere language or to a history superseded is the collapse, of which Doull writes, of the older European culture of the nation state, through two world wars and the subsequent, still unresolved conflict between the politics of global humanism and neo-fascistic particularism. In this stand-off, what is generally affirmed as the final overcoming or perfection of modernity is at once the latter's descent into decadence, where subjective freedom, rendered absolute as unlimited individualism, becomes at once a principle of arbitrariness and of terror.

Yet remarkably, in its attempt to articulate a new standpoint beyond the modern, post-modern thought cannot do otherwise than continue to make use of the language and concepts deriving from the very traditions it seeks to undermine. Derrida has allowed it is necessary to continue the study of the history of philosophy just so one know what it is that must be repudiated. In such duplicities the post-modern critique reveals that it ever corrupts its own position: in seeking more and more extreme ways of accomplishing its task of putting an end to philosophy – ideologically, existentially, analytically, linguistically, deconstructively, etc. – it can find nothing to appeal to which is not again, in some way, philosophy, not itself a 'position.' This ambiguity is not without precedent. Christian theology knew itself to occupy a new ground comprehensive of the standpoint of Roman and Greek thought; yet having at first only the latter's language and schemata available to it, it continually corrupted its own standpoint and it took centuries for its image of spiritual life to become established in a certainty, language and polity of its own. The circumstance with post-modernity is similar. So far as it possesses its principle only in a dogmatic form it can assert it only as a negative, revolutionary, and hyper-sceptical deconstruction of the whole of the past. In this form, however, as Doull implies, it cannot know what its real basis and inspiration is. It only knows, and indeed only is, modernity itself in its decadence.

This is quite the same issue Hegel himself had in view in his own day in speaking of a 'third' philosophical era arising out of the modern, an era whose idea he would seek to disclose in broad logical terms. He too insisted that in freedom lay the necessity that it be more than a merely metaphysical or moral principle; that it be actual in human life and history. But while describing 'spirit' as the 'highest definition of God or the absolute,' Hegel did not take this to be its *sole* definition: freedom is also 'idea,' and again 'nature.' This is why 'absolute spirit' could not be for Hegel what it later came to be thought, namely, a radicalized existential subjectivity or an ideal revolutionary order. It is for him art, religion, philosophy – those forms of human activity wherein freedom is acknowledged as an *eternal* life,[14] the soul no less of the natural as of the human world. To inherit this eternal life requires of individuals that they surrender to a freedom they know and affirm as more than themselves. Only so does it become incarnate in them. Or put otherwise, only in express acknowledgment of the infinity of the idea is the human spirit truly free.

By contrast, post-modernity has as yet only got hold of the principle of freedom in an abstractly negative – and so far abstractly affirmative – manner. It is human freedom raised to its extreme pitch, first, in dogmas of universal praxis and existential ontology, more lately, in strained scepticisms that would reduce freedom to no more than 'undecideability' or the limitlessness of human progress, caprice, or power. Freedom is the particular, subjective individual rendered absolute, self-given, and self-active, free by nature and by right, whose personal-practical world is all there is, into which everything actual and possible is drawn, there being nothing whatever behind or beyond it. Where individuality has become the measure of freedom the divine and the natural become mere extensions: religion celebrates the individual as God-in-the-world; 'spirituality' is the human feeling of divinity; art, religion and philosophy express the right to arbitrary and ideocentric creativity, belief, and speculation.

Already in Hegel's time, post-Christian Christianity had shifted the emphasis from God to the people of God, faith to religiosity, the principal object being to believe something, preferably something believer-friendly and therapeutic but above all theology-free, since from the new perspective religious truth is the enemy of religious freedom. As for nature, the older view of a created cosmic, organic system real and necessary in itself is supplanted by nature solely relative to human interests: whether theoretically as evolutionary pre-history, practically as a resource for endless exploitation, or aesthetically as the free individual's own preconscious life. What is utterly lost in the radical post-modern humanization of nature and divinity is of course the idea of freedom itself, freedom as *infinite* self-determination, as an *intelligible* principle intuitively present as nature and experienced as the motive and end of human life. It is the idea which Hegel specifically formulates in the closing section of the *Encyclopedia* as forming the distinctive theme of a third world-historical philosophy to comprehend and supersede the ancient and modern, whose outline he would only barely sketch in the system. Its starting point is neither the ancient assumption of reason in nature nor the modern one of spiritual self-activity, but rather the idea of freedom as a self-intelligible and self-instituting truth for thought, in which idea alone the earlier forms of philosophy have their unity, fulfilment, and ground.

The manner in which this new insight first presents itself, however, is as the ambiguous rejection-retention of the older modern philosophy whose principal fruit it has gleaned, namely, the certainty of human freedom. This certainty it would radicalize in a humanistic absolutism which inevitably degenerates by stages into little more than the particular feeling of being at once finite and unlimited in one's individuality, a feeling expressed perhaps as existential melancholy or in an anarchical activism never propitiated since accepting no natural or institutional limits. It is a degeneration whose political progress/regress Doull brings out clearly in his essay. As he there points out, what is chiefly remarkable in the post-modern era is how the same principle of freedom which forms its positive basis is the source also of the unique forms of decadence to which it is prone – illimitable technocracy, libertarian extremism, terroristic politics, radical scepticism, collapse of all moral and institutional structures, and so forth. Human freedom, once rendered absolute, becomes a powerful engine of frivolous excess and fanaticism, of violence and malevolence – forms of decay all the more intractable since specifically justified in the name of freedom.

Hegel everywhere points to the gross ambiguity of a *literal* freedom-in-time, entirely contingent on individual subjectivity and finite human arrangements subject to the vicissitudes of chance and political power. From it he clearly distinguished the 'full blown' idea of human freedom which Christianity introduced into world history 'according to which the individual *as such* is of *infinite* worth as the object and aim of the divine love, and who, standing in absolute relation to God as Spirit, is determined as having this spirit dwelling in him – which is to say: the human being *as such* is destined to the highest freedom' (*Enc.* 482). Hegel saw modern philosophy from Descartes – the 'second syllogism' – as the clear and distinct development in thought of this Christian principle. It is the same principle which, its religious and speculative underpinning later abandoned, was embraced after his time as a cultural and political absolute, thereby at once recognized and conserved, but also corrupted. Much as the Romans inherited the speculative accomplishment of the Greeks, transforming it into pragmatic and intellectual dogmas of their own, the modern principle of human freedom has become, since Hegel, a universally acknowledged precept, the unquestioned first premise of private and public life. As such it has been the source at once of an incorrigible energy and revolutionary optimism distinguishing the last centuries of the millennium, but also has sown the seed of a new kind of corruption: the perversion of freedom into egomania and a justification for public anarchy or global terrorism.

Hegel himself stood on the cusp of this passage of modernity into post-modernity somewhat as Aristotle stood in the twilight of the ancient Greek world. He already knew there was no escaping the momentous eventuality of the idea of a realized freedom; no retreat from the new culture it was to breed with its illimitable capacity for unprecedented human progress and, at once, unprecedented devastation; no route back into older standpoints of Asian or Greek philosophy, of Christianity or Islam, of the greats of modern philosophy. The culture of radicalized freedom has by now virtually run its course; the only route beyond it is through it, a comprehension of the idea of freedom on deeper, more universal terms, inclusive of its own philosophical and historical legacy. Hegel's system is the first attempt to delineate such a rational, post-modern philosophy, such as would make the idea of freedom its centre and starting point. As Doull makes clear, the burden of the *Phenomenology* is the comprehension on the part of philosophy of the history of its own proper idea, a coming to know what it has been, and through this to complete its own history. It is with coming to grips with this vast cultural transition first consciously enunciated in the Hegelian philosophy that contemporary thinking and culture continues to be primarily occupied

Notes

1 The metaphor from *The Philosophy of Right* is far from enigmatic, as often alleged, as Hegel is everywhere clear on the imminent collapse of European Christian modernity through its own subjective principle.
2 See my 'Post-Modernism and the Recovery of the Philosophical Tradition,' *Animus* 5.1 (1996) (www.mun.ca/animus).
3 Translations are for the most part the author's, using Meiner's 1959 edition of the *Werke.*
4 The link between 'concept,' 'grasp,' 'prehend,' 'comprehend,' etc. is less vivid in English than in German where *Begriff* (concept) yields *begreifen* (comprehend), *begrifflich* (conceptual), *Begreifung* (comprehension), etc. Standard English translations have further obscured this whole matter by translating *Begriff* as 'Notion,' a wholly atavistic and now meaningless term.
5 As to how Hegel differentiated the standpoint of earlier modern from his own, see *Enc.* 19–83. Also, e.g, 'the Kantian philosophy may be most accurately described ... as containing the propositions only of a phenomenology, not a philosophy of spirit' (*Enc.* 413). As for the accusation of a reduction of reality to representation, see my 'The Postmodern Attack on Plato,' *Animus* 5.3 (1996) (www.mun.ca/animus).
6 A small example: Derrida construes Hegel's logic as ignoring 'difference,' the technique of *Aufheben* being the arbitrary sublimation and identification of differences. This completely ignores Hegel's own account of identity/difference at *Enc.* 113–20 where, in its extreme form as 'opposition,' difference is *self*-difference, thus *self-cancelling* difference, the result of which is not identity again but the concept of identity-in-difference, 'ground.' As to dialectic, see Hegel's very specific views on its limited role in speculative method at *Enc.* 79–82.
7 *Enc.* 249 and *Zusatz.*
8 Unquestionably the most influential of all the forms of the Hegelian idea, the full outline of the philosophy of spirit is found at *Enc.* 377–577, with portions of the argument further elaborated in *The Philosophy of Right* and in his various posthumously published lectures.
9 As Hegel uses the terms somewhat obliquely, the sense of 'ideal,' ideality,' etc. is another major source of confused Hegel-interpretation. 'Ideal' does

not signify an abstraction, paradigm of perfection, purely mental entities. etc. Rather it is a *logical* term describing the status anything acquires once taken up into a context comprehensive of it, wherein it then serves as a subordinate, component function, or 'moment.' Listening to a recorded sonata, electronic and physiological events are certainly in play, but they exist only 'ideally' in the experience: one hears the *sonata*, not an eardrum or a whirling disc. So too (*pace* Derrida) writing is only 'ideal' in relation to what is communicated, sensory events in perception, organs in an organism, ministries in a government etc.

10 See my 'Hegel's Psychology of Freedom' in *Animus* 5 (2000) (www.mun.ca/animus).

11 Marx's theory of the state and history rests on what he calls his sole assumption, viz., that 'individuals exist.' In this is contained the intrinsically ambiguous view of man as a need-driven animal who is yet consciously capable of action, and of freedom as no more than the disinhibition of such need-satisfaction. Marx's account of the Hegelian philosophy of spirit is accordingly spurious in forcing upon it a view of these matters which Hegel explicitly rejects.

12 Spirit as having nature for 'presupposition' and as yet also the 'truth' of nature are propositions absolutely key to the whole Hegelian standpoint, as clearly set forth in 'The Concept of Spirit,' *Enc.* 381.

13 Which is not say that philosophy, as art and religion, is not given over a good deal of the time to the promotion of utter nonsense. Its self-verifying character makes this inevitable, however, which is why philosophical thought can *only* be authenticated through itself and from no other standpoint. The most sublime and civilized principles and intuitions fall victim to the prevailing prejudices and superstitions of the time, as has been the fate of the principle of freedom throughout the twentieth century.

14 Aristotle, *Meta.*, xi.7, which Hegel quotes in concluding the *Encyclopedia*.

chapter seven

The Doull Fackenheim Debate – Would Hegel Today Be a Hegelian?[1]

1. Fackenheim

While taking its departure from James Doull's review of my *The Religious Dimension in Hegel's Thought* (*Dialogue*, December 1968: 483–92), the present note is not intended to be an author's reply to a reviewer – always in bad taste, and in this case quite unwarranted when the review in question shows all the fair-mindedness and care any author could ask for. My note is much rather part of a dialogue, agreed on in advance by both participants, in which Hegel, not a book on Hegel, is the subject. I have stated my belief that Hegel would not today be a Hegelian, and I gather that Professor Doull disagrees. Since, however, we share the conviction that without recourse to Hegel no profound contemporary philosophizing is possible, both our articles, their disagreements notwithstanding, may be considered as contributions to the celebration of the bicentenary of Hegel's birth.

I begin with an objection Doull takes to a question I ask of the *Phenomenology*. Hegel's work purports to hand 'the individual ... the ladder to the standpoint of philosophical science' by 'showing him that standpoint as it is in him,' while at the same time rejecting any suggestion that 'unscientific consciousness' – which has 'the right to demand' that ladder – be 'instructed in science.' Philosophical science alone is the judge of its internal self-development; all external judgments, far from having an independent foundation, are themselves taken up and transfigured into philosophical science. I myself make these points and indeed stress that the Hegelian system is at once as hospitable to empirical reality as any empiricism and as comprehensive it its scope as any rationalism, thus being immune to attacks from the right and the left alike. Doull thus seems rightly to object when I *ask one* external question of the *Phenomenology* – 'Can there be a form of non-philosophical human life which makes the rise to the scientific standpoint on the one hand possible and on the other still necessary, and if so, what justifies Hegel's claim that in the nineteenth century that form of life has become actual?'

I do not ask (as 'the Understanding' might) external questions abstractly and indiscriminately. I ask *one concrete* question. This particular question, moreover, does not seem un-Hegelian if 'the individual,' while denied instruction in philosophical science, is yet granted the 'right to demand' the ladder to that science. Or at least *some* individual or individuals must be able to ask that question if Hegelian 'science' is ever to come into *any* man's possession. How does Hegel himself – or, for that matter, James Doull – reach philosophical science and its standpoint since neither man was born a Hegelian philosopher?

Doull is too profound a student of Hegel to need my instruction either in the inevitability of this question or in the proper Hegelian answer. 'We' *already are,* on the one hand, 'free,' post-French-revolutionary Europeans, and, on the other, modern-Protestant Christians; and in addition we have also internalized the whole history of Western philosophy we need but integrate the totality of our spiritual existence in the sphere of speculative thought to be transported into Hegelian science. In short, while actually at one end of the Hegelian ladder, we are already, potentially, at the other as well. And the external question we might wish to ask of the *Phenomenology* dissolves in the asking.

At this point, however, I am forced to lodge a protest. Hegel and Doull are Christians for whom Patristic and Protestant Christianity are part of their being before they ascend the ladder to Hegel's philosophical science. I am a Jew. I can study Patristic and Protestant Christianity. I can imaginatively identify with them. I cannot, and indeed must refuse to, make them part of my being. Unlike Hegel and Doull, I am not, therefore – at least so far as the religious aspect of my existence is concerned – at both sides of the Hegelian ladder but at one side only. And my grasping of Hegel's ladder requires of me a leap of faith quite un-Hegelian in nature – a faith in Hegel's premise that philosophical science will 'do justice' to all religions (and hence to my own) such as, according to Hegel, no religion, the Christian included, can do to any other.

The necessity for this leap of faith might in itself suffice to justify my external question addressed to the *Phenomenology*. I am forced, however, to go further. For while I am tempted to grasp Hegel's philosophical ladder on faith (his philosophical promise being as a rule extraordinarily trustworthy), he fails to deliver on his promise to do justice to Judaism. This is not the place for a critical discussion of the relevant parts of Hegel's *Philosophy of Religion.* Suffice it to say that Hegel's account of Judaism can find no room for Jewish Messianism but must rather treat Judaism in terms of Christian Messianism; and the result is that the Hegelian 'justice' renders Judaism superseded and Jewish existence anachronistic. It is no accident that the Jewish Hegelian Eduard Gans in 1819 founded a *Verein* for the express purpose of rejuvenating Judaism in the light of Hegelian principles – and became a convert of Protestant Christianity six years later.

The above protest may seem guilty of parochialism. I therefore add that what applies to Judaism applies, *mutatis mutandis,* to other non-Christian religions as well. Most assuredly Hegel's philosophy seeks to do 'justice' to all religions which (he holds) they cannot do to each other; but surely nothing in Hegel's writing justifies Doull's statement that 'the translation of religion into philosophy, in Hegel's intention, is not of *one* religion but of *all* religions *considered as mutually complementary*' (489; italics added). For Hegel, Christianity – and Christianity alone – is 'the absolute religion'; and in making his own statement Doull himself is a post-Hegelian. So, I suggest, would Hegel himself be were he alive today, for he would surely identify himself with those post-Constantinian tendencies in contemporary Christianity which are most radical in their acceptance of religious pluralism. But what, we might ask, would happen to the unity of the Hegelian system, if its religious-existential basis is not one absolute religion but rather a radical and unsurmountable religious plurality?

This takes me from my first to the second external question I ask of the Hegelian philosophy. Of the *Phenomenology* I have asked: how do I get *into* Hegel's philosophy? Of the system as a whole I ask: could any *occurrence whatever* in the 'actual world' force me out of it? Is the system hospitable to *all conceivable* empirical realities and immune to *all possible* threats? Or merely to such as Hegel in his own time can reasonably be expected to have perceived and anticipated? In partial answer to this question Doull (taking a slightly left-wing but, I think, justified turn) maintains that nineteenth-century European colonialism is not part of the 'free' essence of Hegel's Europe but rather contrary to it, representing 'possibilities for evil in modern subjectivity' (p490) which neither destroy nor fragment that essence. I am inclined to agree with him on this example, for I see little justice in the Marxist or quasi-Marxist view that Hegel's essence of modern 'free' Europe is destroyed or invalidated in its root by the colonialism (or, for that matter, the oppressive capitalism) which in the nineteenth-century was part of it. Indeed, such a view seems incongruous when, as Doull hints, the new post-colonized nations are themselves inspired, to a large degree, by that essence.

I have my doubt, however, about Doull's choice of example. Nineteenth-century European colonialism may be understood as an arbitrary – 'subjective' – by-product which at most tainted the European essence. Twentieth-century Nazism was a total collapse with which post-Nazi Germany – and Europe – has yet to come to terms. No accidental taint of an essence, it had a demonic essence of its own, which would surely have destroyed the Europe Hegel believed in but for an accidental event – Hitler's loss of the war. Hegel did not anticipate any such essence; indeed, its possibility remains unaccounted for in his philosophy. For while he accounts for evil he fails to account for *demonic* evil; it is Schelling, not Hegel, who writes: 'Just as there is an ardor for good, there is also an enthusiasm for evil' (*Werke* I, 7, 372). For Hegel, evil is 'separation from the universal, which latter is the rational, laws, the determinations of spirit' (*Werke* [Glockner], 16: 264). In Nazi Germany it was evil which had become the universal, the 'rational,' the 'laws,' the 'determinations of spirit,' and when the second world war ended Hegel's 'true modern state' was all-but-replaced by quite another state – the Nazi murder camp (see Alexander Donat, *The Holocaust Kingdom* [New York: Holt, Rinehart & Winston, 1963]). The enthusiasm Schelling speaks of was displayed when millions of Germans (and many other Europeans) embraced Hitler's ideology. It showed a terrifying power when the murder camps began to run themselves – an 'objective spirit' which might well have conquered Europe. And it was supremely manifest in the 'absolute' anti-spirit displayed by Eichmann, who diverted trains desperately needed for military purposes in order to dispatch men, women, and children to their death at Auschwitz.

Were Hegel alive today, how would he respond to the eruption of demonic evil in the heart of twentieth-century Europe? Not , I think, by joining in the present virtually unanimous philosophical conspiracy of silence on the subject of the Nazi holocaust: his philosophical integrity and his sense of history were too profound. Nor do I like to think that he would respond as he in fact occasionally did respond to the technological dehumanization already manifest in his time – by seeking refuge in a 'separate philosophical sanctuary' of thought from the turmoil of the 'actual world.' I like to think of a Hegel torn between the 'peace' of a philosophical system and fidelity to the 'actual world' as choosing the latter. And since the Hegelian 'World Spirit' is no abstract universal but rather embodied in epoch-making particulars, I can picture a Hegel of whom the 'World Spirit' during the second world war rested on the victims of Auschwitz, objects of groundless hate, abandoned by the world, witnesses in their suffering of an 'untruth' then permeating the world which has not yet vanished. And I seem to perceive the outlines of a post-Hegelian philosophy arising from this testimony. This would, negatively, abandon all claims to systematic finality and god-like self-confidence. And it would, positively, affirm a human freedom which, while radically ambiguous, has indestructibly *human* possibilities and a divine Grace which, while in unprecedented obscurity, has not vanished forever from human history. And it would understand itself as a thought-activity which, though radically fragmented by the grim revelation of demonic evil in the twentieth century, nevertheless stoutly seeks such comprehensiveness and transcending wisdom as remain within its grasp.

(Written during the final agony of Biafra and completed on January 27th, 1970, the twenty-fifth anniversary of the liberation of Auschwitz.)

2. Doull

Hegel, now alive, would be a Hegelian still. Subsequent history would seem to have made obvious and accessible to many a way of thinking hardly any but himself could see demanded already at the time of the French Revolution. Already then the radical will to dominate the world through science and technology had overthrown traditional authority. What this freedom was, its possibilities for good and ill, how the demonic Faustian evil that was inseparable from it might be turned to good – it was from these reflections that the Hegelian philosophy sprang.

What distinguishes the Hegelian answer from all other answers before or since is that, neither turning from revolutionary freedom nor overlooking its evil and ruinous possibilities, he shows on what its hope of human liberation is founded: the idea of a unity of theory and practice in which the contradiction between arbitrary subjective freedom and the universality of science and technology is overcome.[2] Neither the Pelagian optimism of liberal democracy nor the Kabbalistic vision of original human solidarity that inspired Marxism suffices him. In liberal democracy it is supposed that particular interests have a primary right to independence, from which they yield to the general interest only so much as may be required in given conditions. Thus the evil implicit in the assertion of the particular is usually hidden from view. The conflict is resolved in an endlessly adaptable pragmatic subjectivity. Marxists would eradicate the conflict of interest but at the price of that subjective freedom which permits the individual to make the unity of interests his own. Hegel would save the truth of both positions.[3]

To answer Emil Fackenheim's grave and deeply considered objections to the Hegelian philosophy I have first moved the argument from religion to secular freedom. I do this because the 'ladder' to the Hegelian philosophy – the *Phenomenology of Spirit* – does not move directly to philosophy through the Christian or any religion but through religion as this recurs on the basis of secular atheism. For this reason the 'leap' from experience to pure thought which the *Phenomenology* asks is not more closed to a Jew than to a Christian. One may rather say that it is equally closed to both.[4]

And the second objection – that in the face of the holocaust Hegel must abandon the rational confidence of the system – this too has another appearance if it be so that the system has its origin in the consciousness of radical evil. From the standpoint of the Hegelian system it would be said that the degradation of European culture in Nazism was through the association of an abstract morality (Kantian and the like) on the one side and a naturalism on the other – an association which permitted the hypocrisy of endless attachment, for example, to the particularity of race.

This extreme conflict of modern secular freedom, where the highest scientific accomplishments and the purest moral conscience can show themselves as, rather, barbarous unreason and the tyrannical will to dominate – this depravity occurs short of the system. Where this corruption reaches the point of blind nihilistic will, out of this collapse of arbitrary freedom begins the possibility of pure thought and philosophy. Europeans fell in the unacknowledged, unrepented evil of the holocaust (so Hegel would say) because they had become incapable of their culture in its deeper and forgotten possibilities.[5]

The Hegelian philosophy is peculiarly the philosophy of Lutheran Protestantism and the Prussian state.[6] This is not untrue. Yet by neither was it accepted, unless for as long as needed to reject it and turn from it with abhorrence. If a Jew cannot follow Hegel unless at the price of this religion, Christians have always found the same difficulty. For a moment Hegel seemed to find a congruence of Protestant faith and revolutionary freedom in the heroic Germany of Goethe and Beethoven. The system outlived Hegel in antithetic post-Hegelian philosophies, chiefly Marxism and the various forms of Existentialism. In however little they might agree besides, the post-Hegelians in common find the ascent beyond experience to pure thought intolerable.[7]

The ladder to the philosophical science seems unscalable to Christian and atheist alike. It is indeed unscalable to whoever adheres to any form of experience as ultimately authoritative. The *Phenomenology* is the way of total scepticism in which all the seeming certainties of science and practical life, all of religious beliefs, are dissolved.[8] To whom is some form of experience not authoritative?

The destruction of differences in the ascent to philosophy Fackenheim would accept from Hegel if then the system restored and confirmed experience, as it promises to do. The demand that the Hegelian philosophy be capable of giving a true account of the Jewish religion is a demand that Hegel himself would certainly acknowledge.[9] That the system fails to provide what it promises is felt no less strongly by Christians, as Kierkegaard, or by atheistic Hegelians, as Marx, on being asked to reconcile himself to the Prussian monarchy.

But the system does not so much promise to restore, whether it be a particular form of religion or a practical attitude, on its own terms. Rather the Hegelian logic professes to measure by its own standard – the Idea. Thus the *Philosophy of Religion*,[10] which examines religious phenomena in the light of the Idea, does not propose to give an account of any religion such as would satisfy a believer in it *qua* believer. Instead it intends to sort out in each from the total phenomenon where it conforms, or fails to conform, with the Idea. The truth of each religion, so defined, is for Hegel what remains of each as a moment also in the absolute religion. It was in the sense that, reviewing Fackenheim's *Religious Dimension*, I spoke of 'the translation of religion into philosophy' as 'not of *one* religion but of all religions *considered as mutually complementary*.' Certainly Christianity is for Hegel the absolute religion, but philosophy shows the absolute religion as unable to exist adequately to its concept unless the other religions are also present, preserved as well as transcended.[11] So far as for Christians the experience of other religions is foreign they might *believe* Christianity to be the final religion, but they would *know* it as one among other religions.

The dissolution of religious, as of linguistic and cultural differences Hegel thought neither possible nor desirable unless in the general movement of history towards human freedom. Some religions, as the Greek and the Roman, had ceased to have independent existence as religions. They survived in the education of Europeans, as containing the experience through which the Christian religion had been mediated. The various forms of Catholic and Protestant Christianity Hegel saw as grounded in the special character of the European peoples, no less persistent therefore than the nation states themselves. Nor does he appear to have thought that Calvinistic Christianity with its affinity to the pragmatic Anglo-Saxon temper would soon come together with his Lutheran form.

Even less could Hegel according to his principles expect that Judaism would become assimilated to some form of Christianity. So long as for Christians a division persists between the logic of secular and of religious experience, and faith thus remains inward, personal, unreal, Hegel would see the continuing existence of Judaism as a separate religion as a necessary element in European culture. Modern secular culture indeed assimilates Jew and Christian to each other. It does so not onesidedly, however, to Hegel's mind but because it tends to, and implicitly is, the unity of both attitudes. The unity of secular with religious experience in which the *Phenomenology* concludes its argument is on the side of religions, the dissolution of the antagonism between Judaism and Christianity.[12]

At that point it is true Hegel sees no more place for Jewish Messianism but only for Christian. But it would be a Christian Messianism in which the abstract inwardness of Christian subjectivity had regained its starting point in the Jewish experience of divine transcendence. But the unity of secular life, which was the condition on which the two true religions would tend to coalesce, seems remoter to us than to Hegel. The conflicts of civil society, which he saw united in the state, in our time appear as the division between liberal democracy and communism. Religious division therefore also seems more fixed than when Jew and Christian seemed to be losing their difference in a common secular life stronger than the attraction of either religion.

The 'ladder' to the philosophical science seems not to be there for any in our time. And yet is it not here, and for everyone, in the secular despair which feels rather horror or indifference at the triumphs of technology, which looks with indifference or disgust at liberal and socialist democracies alike? Nor is this contemporary experience peculiarly Christian or Jewish or atheistic but has elements of them all, as of other cultures and religions as well. The Hegelian philosophy is accessible because it is the philosophy of the scientific-technical age, the demand and necessity that this come to an adequate consciousness of itself. The elements are there, as in Hegel's time, in the dividedness of secular freedom and in the religions through which it is sought to understand the divisions. What bring these elements together, says Hegel, is the common need of men that they think. The system is the self-conscious thought of the modern age.[13]

Twentieth-century Nazism was a 'total collapse' of European culture, in which was disclosed a 'demonic essence' such as Hegel had not anticipated and could not account for in his philosophy (see 333 above). What has happened in twentieth-century Europe I would describe as Fackenheim describes it. In the Hegelian philosophy I find the clearest consciousness of demonic evil in modern culture and the only way possible to contain it.

'Just as there is an ardor for good' in men, 'there is also an enthusiasm for evil.' In the same work Schelling defines evil as the capacity of men to use the spiritual or rational in their nature in the service of limited and irrational ends. Evil does not lie in following particular interests or passions as such, but if reason and will – the universal in man – should subserve these ends against the universal good itself.[14]

Hegel speaks in just his way: 'Evil is the self-certainty of conscience which gives itself the content of a subjective or particular interest against the good.'[15] Evil has its source in knowledge, in the rationality of man, whereby the consciousness can occur of a universal end in opposition to the multitude of natural and particular ends.[16] This opposition of the natural will to the universal, itself raised to universality, is not only demonic but the devil himself.[17]

The demonic of Schelling, and as Fackenheim understands it, is indeed other than Hegel's devil overcome. The nothingness of the devil's work is for Hegel also human experience in the nihilism of abstract conscience. Therefore the Hegelian would not speak of a 'demonic essence' in man.[18] For the 'demonic,' says Goethe, there are countless names; all religions and philosophies have sought to solve the riddle of it; it may set itself against the moral order as such, or the two may rather be interwoven as the warp with the woof.[19] Hegel reduces the latter or finite form to the former and would resolve the contradiction in the human will. But in this he intends not to dissolve the mixed realm of good and evil, as one might say of Marx, but to take from it any claim to ultimate independence – not only theologically, but also within the secular order.

Hegel does not overlook the 'demonic' in a Kabbalistic sense, such as is found in Schelling's *Wesen der menschlichen Freiheit* (to which Fackenheim refers). Nor do I think it can be said to fall outside the system. The teaching on evil of the Old Testament Hegel regards as true and invaluable but incomplete. No less necessary and true – and also incomplete – is that Stoic subjectivity which in the decay of ancient public life sought happiness in imperturbable self-certainty. These are the elements of his one doctrine wherein is resolved the contradiction; of a contentless monadic self and a self that is endlessly caught in the divineness of finite interests.[20]

The place in this resolution of the Hellenized Judaism of the Kabbal Hegel distinctly recognizes.[21] The later Hasidic Judaism, which arose alike in response to Spinoza and to Messianism of a Christian kind within Judaism,[22] Hegel does not appear to have known. Nonetheless he sees such a form as not only possible in the modern world but as necessary and as antithetic to a moralistic Christianity.[23]

Hegel's teaching on good and evil is that of Augustinian theology as developed against the Pelagians. Revived and given its extreme theological expression by Luther, Hegel then gave it logical form and made it the foundation of this doctrine of right.[24] The meaning of this doctrine in secular and practical form is that it would correct and overcome the separation of reason and experience, of conscience and passion. Conscience and reason, outside this unity, it regards as themselves altogether suspect.[25]

Protestant faith, so Hegel thought, was the preparation for the modern scientific culture and its aggressive, unlimited will precisely in that the consciousness of evil attained there its extreme point at which legalism and abstract subjectivity dissolved into concrete ethical life or *Sittlichkeit.* This was the principle by which medieval flight from the world was overcome. The flight was overcome because in this principle the extremist conflict of interest even to a Faustian pact with the devil was in principle transcended.

The modern state derived its sovereign power from the consciousness of this reconciliation. In immediate and natural form the state was the realization of Protestant faith. It rested on the confidence of men that they could both pursue their several interests and find in the end that their work was the interest of all.[26]

No state of course attained this ideal unity of interest, whether before or after the revolutionary movements of the eighteenth century. Yet the vitality and strength of the state lay in nothing else than confidence that the common interest was in general attained within the given possibilities.

Hegel was conscious alike of the truth and the limits of this conviction. That in the end the European states would destroy one another by war, as happened in the Great War of 1914–18, Hegel saw to be implied in the unresolved contradiction between their idea and its reality.[27]

Hegel was conscious that in the longer history of the European idea the dominant role was likely to be played by North Americans and Slavs, by whom the conflicts of the coming industrial society would have to be resolved more universally – not within the natural limits of a state, but directly on the basis of the Enlightenment and universal right. The Hegelian state absorbed revolutionary freedom, but not so that the argument would not be reopened in another and more difficult form.[28]

The nation states of the period between the two great wars were hardly any longer states in Hegel's sense. Traditional and accepted sovereign power had vanished or was an empty form. The conflicts of economic society were anyway no longer within the power of single states to resolve. The states were dissolving into their elements and the only new forms of unity to be seen were either a world capitalism or world revolution. The Nazi state, and like appearances, was a response to these conditions. It sought to unite interest again through the natural solidarity of the 'Volk.' In the Nazi state abstract democratic freedom and 'race' coalesced and in this unity set themselves against liberal democracy and communism alike. There was no primary reduction of national sentiment to universal humanity such as was present alike in the traditional state and in Hegel's ideal.[29]

Science and technology – the works of reason – and reason itself were made the servant of offended, resentful national passions. The degradation of Europe, but of a Europe, Hegel would say, that was incapable of its idea. Europe, he would have said, had fallen back to forms of thought long superseded. But then this was because the problems of the revolutionary wars were again with us and demanded a more thorough solution than Europe had lived with in the nineteenth century.

Would Hegel, in the face of this ruin of Europe, retreat to 'a post-Hegelian philosophy' which 'would, negatively, abandon all claims to systematic finality and god-like self-confidence' (see 334 above)? I have indicated why I cannot think so. Between Emil Fackenheim and myself the question appears to be whether modern subjectivity – Hellenic and Christian first, then the moving spirit of the scientific-technical culture – has to be, and can be, abandoned. It seems certain to me that without this spirit the holocaust could not have happened. And endless capacity to confound good with ill must have been present in the German people and other Europeans. But neither the knowledge of a primary unity of interests nor the confidence whereby individuals or nations need not pursue their advantage beyond measure – the evil is not in the system and a self-confidence which can act but exactly in the absence of them.

A philosophy which, with Emil Fackenheim, affirmed 'a human freedom which, while radically ambiguous, has indestructibly human possibilities and a divine Grace which ... has not vanished forever from human history' Hegel, now living, would have no difficulty in making his own. But he would continue to require, as formerly against Schelling, that the ambiguity of freedom be also resolved in man himself. Or can science and technology learn modesty and bring Faustian ambition within limit? In antiquity Prometheus could be subdued and taught to live under the power of Zeus. But now he has captured the citadel of Zeus and founded technology on the sovereign right of the individual. The principle of the modern age is the unity of theoretical and practical. A more dangerous principle there could not be. But Hegel would, as before, see no other course than to awaken in men a clear knowledge of this principle. Danger he would see to lie exactly in a seeming modesty which left it open to human passions and false certainties to seduce reason and science from their natural end of serving humanity.[30]

Notes

1 Originally published as 'Would Hegel Today Be a Hegelian?' *Dialogue* (1970), 222–35 (with Emil Fackenheim).

2 E.g., *Enzyklopädie* (1830), sect. 481.

3 E.g., *Phil. des Rechts*, sect. 260.

4 *Phänomenologie des Geistes*, ed. Hoffmeister, 382–3.

5 On the last, e.g., *Phil. des Rechts* (Hoffmeister), Vorrede, 8f. On the paragraph generally, ibid., sect. 140.

6 Fackenheim, *The Religious Dimension in Hegel's Thought*, 223f.

7 On the dissolution historically of the Hegelian philosophy, see Löwith, *Von Hegel zu Nietzsche*, generally.

8 *Phänomenologie* (Hoffmeister), Einleitung, 67f.

9 E.g., *Phil. der Religion* (Lasson), I: 71f.

10 *Phil. der Religion* (1840), 76–7.

11 Ibid., pt. 3, 208–9.

12 Where the former takes the form of Spinozism and is no longer separate from Christian subjectivity, but the immediate and substantial form of it. Cf. *Phänomenologie*, 'Das absolute Wissen; von dieser selbstlosen substantialität zurück, und behauptet die Individualität gegen sie' (Hoffmeister, 559–60).

13 *Enzyklopädie* (1830), sect. 9–12. Cf. Bacon's *Insturatio magna*, praefatio, 132 (Spedding). For the concept of human freedom implied therein, see Hegel's inaugural lecture in Berlin (*Berliner Schriften*, ed. Hoffmeister, 3–21).

14 'Die allgemeine Möglichkeit des Bösen besteht darin, dass des Mensch seine Selbstheit, anstatt sie zur Basis, zum Organ zu machen, vielmehr zum Herrschenden und zum allwillen zu erheben, dagegen das Geistige in sich zum Mittel zu machen streben kann.' *Werke*, 7: 389.

15 Cf. *Enz.* (1830) sect. 511.

16 *Phil. der Religion* (1840), pt. 3, 254f.

17 Ibid., 261.

18 *Enz.*, sect. 511.

19 Cf. Goethe, *Dichtung und Wahrheit*, bk. 20.

20 *Phil. der Religion* (1840), pt. 3, 270f.

21 *Geschichte der Philosophie* (1844), pt. 3, 23–5.

22 Buber, *The Origin and Meaning of Hasidism*, English trans. (New York, 1960), chap. 3.

23 It is instructive, for example, to consider in relation to Buber, loc. cit., *Phänomenologie* (Hoffmeister), 559–61.

24 Ibid., 343 on the true reconciliation of secularity with religion.

25 *Phil. des Rechts*, sect. 139, 140.

26 Ibid., sect. 331.

27 Ibid., sect. 340.

28 *Phil. der Geschichte* (1848), 107.

29 Hegel's attitude to such a state may easily be gathered from his criticism of Rousseau, related in part to a book of a certain von Haller. See especially *Phil. des Rechts*, sect. 258, note. As to how he regarded the anti-Semitism of his time, see note to sect. 270. On the relation of the Nazi state to law and the universal see H. Picker, *Hitler's Tischgespräche* (Munich, 1968), 36ff. As an example of Hitler's political Darwinism the following: 'Wenn ich an ein göttliches Gebot glauben will, so kann nur das sein: die Art zu erhalten!'

30 Cf. *Enz.*, sect. 482.

COMMENTARY

Two Interpretations of Freedom and Evil – Hegel's Theory of Modernity Revisited

KENNETH KIERANS

Over thirty-five years ago, Emil Fackenheim published an important book on the religious significance of Hegel's philosophy. Referring to the *Phenomenology of Spirit* (1807) and the *Encyclopaedia of the Philosophical Sciences* (1817, 1827, and 1830) as well as to the posthumously published lectures on religion and the history of philosophy, he argued that no one before or since has mounted so powerful a defence of modernity. He maintained that Hegel succeeded admirably in showing how modern 'secular' freedom is implicitly 'Christian' in content, and how it can recognize and overcome much – if not all – of the 'evil' that is bound up with it.[1]

Fackenheim basically agreed with what many others – notably Marx and Kierkegaard – had said about Hegel, that is, that his philosophy was the ultimate and final 'bourgeois-Christian' synthesis.[2] But he was much more radical in his insistence that the synthesis could not be sustained. Thus Hegel was so committed to Protestantism that he could not grasp the truth of Jewish and other non-Christian religions. And he was so deeply attached to nineteenth-century European freedom that he could not even imagine the evil that in the twentieth century would expose the fragility and contingency of that freedom, namely, Nazism.[3]

The past few decades have done much to clarify these issues. Everyone now speaks of a post-modern consciousness that would recognize non-Western religions as well as the abstract and one-sided character of liberal and socialist ideals. Radical critiques of modernity, of the various forms of Christianity, and of the ancient sources of Western culture are commonplace. These critiques frequently present Hegel as the point of departure, and sometimes even the point of arrival, for thoughtful reflection on these issues.[4] While the summaries and comparisons offered are often too vague to be genuinely helpful, they have helped to bring out striking conflicts both in Hegel's position and in the modern world.

What makes James Doull's work so interesting and valuable is that he developed these conflicts not only in their negative, but also in their positive, significance. For more than fifty years – in his teaching, his writings, and his scholarly contacts – he worked towards a true understanding of Hegel and of the continuities between modernity and Christianity. Furthermore, in an effort to accommodate conflicting and opposing forms of thought, ancient and modern, he pursued this understanding in the broadest philosophical and historical context. This is no doubt why he was able to engage in such a fruitful exchange with Fackenheim.

Doull was quick to recognize the virtues of Fackenheim's book, wrote a glowing review of it, and subsequently agreed to a public debate on Hegel.[5] The method he followed is at once fascinating and instructive. For he did not reject Fackenheim's interpretation out of hand, but rather built upon it in order to advance a deeper – and more perfect – knowledge of Hegel and of the modern world. This kind of argument – Hegel himself called it 'immanent' or 'determinate' critique – is a lost art, and stands as a model for us today.[6]

In the debate, Doull acknowledged Fackenheim's 'deeply considered' rejection of Hegel, but then connected the reasons for that rejection with Hegel's own philosophy.[7] Fackenheim had remarked that Hegel could account for a relatively mundane kind of evil – 'colonialism' and 'oppressive capitalism,' for instance – but not for the kind of evil that possessed Hitler. In Nazism, a '*demonic* evil' appeared that transcended the categories of modern freedom and reason (333 above). Doull replied that Nazism had indeed degraded Europe, that Hitler's 'will to dominate' was 'tyrannical,' but that this 'depravity' in no way escaped the inner logic of Hegel's philosophy. On the contrary, the evil that could give rise to the holocaust has a central place in his philosophy and therefore 'occurs short of the system' (335).

Doull's reply is to the point, and invites us to look again at Hegel, to see more clearly the relation between European freedom and evil, and to consider how that freedom can find expression in a philosophical system. If one attends to Hegel's thoughts on evil, on which his whole theory of modernity turns, one finds that he presents it as an imperfect form of freedom. In the *Phenomenology*, evil is part and parcel of the freedom which leads humans to distinguish themselves from instinctive and natural life, as well as from religious feeling and every possible form of social existence. Evil essentially involves reasoning and consciousness, and leads – particularly in modern times – to the most extreme contradiction between the freedom of consciousness and the world as it actually is. But for Hegel the contradiction between the two sides disappears at the point where consciousness becomes 'explicitly' aware of its own 'negative' attitude and returns to the identity of being with thought: only in its 'pure' form is the activity of thought perfectly free and unopposed.[8]

It is significant that Hegel does not immediately connect the purely philosophical idea of freedom with the freedom of social and political life. While he always weaves political life and philosophy together in complex and mutually supportive ways, he never confuses the two. In fact, the *Phenomenology* directly condemns the modern view that we can attain 'absolute freedom' through a revolutionary transformation of society and government. This kind of freedom – Hegel saw it at work in the Jacobins – is so intense and fanatical that it makes all forms of institutional order appear external and oppressive. The result can only be a formal and contentless self-will, a freedom that contradicts and annihilates itself.[9]

The *Encyclopaedia* gives us a more positive view of modern social life, in the form of a post-revolutionary political world, yet even that work emphasizes the difference between the historical form of the state and the true idea of freedom. Hegel states clearly that political power reveals a 'onesidedness' that can 'infect' its implicit truth and result in the 'demoralization' of the state. Hence the difference between the true state and the actually existing state persists, even though they are 'one' in the 'mind'.[10] This is for Hegel a point of huge importance. It is the very onesidedness of historical life, the division and fragmentation of temporal and external existence, transposed into a concentrated discussion of religion, that finally moves him to a philosophical knowledge of freedom.[11]

Nevertheless, the connections of Hegel's philosophy with religion and modern freedom, and their connections with one another, are for Fackenheim more than just doubtful. In his book, he noted that religion as Hegel understood it embraced everything of value, including memory, intellect, love, and trust in divinity. The problem was not that Hegel leaves religion behind, but that he reduces it to his own moral self-activity and pride in knowing the truth.[12] In other words, Hegel's philosophy fails precisely because its affirmation of religion is so intimately bound up with the typically modern freedom to think and know all. Such freedom for Fackenheim involves the most appalling vanity, and, from that point of view, can be regarded as one with wickedness and sin – the ultimate glorification of self. He returns to this theme in his debate with Doull when he urges us to abandon 'all claims to systematic finality and god-like confidence' (334).

Fackenheim believes with all the passion of his deeply held Jewish faith that the comprehensive nature of Hegel's thinking betrays an incoherent conception of divinity and humanity. His critique highlights the conflict of Hegel's philosophy. At one extreme, God is nothing but the thought of modern freedom – humanity as active and practical, the basis and ground of explanation of all things. At the other extreme, God is all in all – the sole ground of explanation of finite existence – and humanity is nothing but the medium through which he manifests his perfection. For Fackenheim, the two extremes meet, not in the completed 'system' of Hegelian 'science,' but rather in the mystical transcendence of it, that is, in 'a radical and unsurmountable religious plurality' (332).

Fackenheim comes to the spiritual centre of his position when he speaks of 'post-Hegelian' philosophy.[13] On the one hand, God is completely beyond the finite world as it appears in nature and in history, and on the other hand, the finite world is the scene of a terrible separation or fall from God. But the abstract opposition of modern self-will and the world reveals a gulf between the finite and the infinite which humanity can bridge first by clearly distinguishing the divine nature and the human and then by opening itself to genuine forms of faith and love. This is the process by which a humbled humanity finally comes to recognize its own 'radically ambiguous' freedom as well as the possibility of 'divine Grace' (334). For Fackenheim, the modern denial of the finite is utter folly, but in an ironic twist this negative attitude is the condition of our turning to God, beyond the mind, and apprehending that infinite being as it reveals itself to us in the heart and the imagination.

It is particularly in reference to Schelling – Hegel's great antagonist – that Fackenheim develops this notion of spirituality.[14] Human beings are divided within themselves: the self-will which separates them from God and their innermost life or love. History is the process by which the difference between the two sides, the opposition between self-will and universal will, is superseded by harmony and reconciliation. But for Fackenheim this result – summed up in Hegel's concept of modern political life – only makes it clear that there is more to human evil than the 'separation' of self-will from universal will. He thinks Schelling was right to insist that human beings have an 'enthusiasm for evil' that appears not despite but because of their intelligence and capacity for political life. As Fackenheim puts it, 'demonic' evil is self-will in the form of universal will, and its appearance in Hitler's Europe compels us to seek wisdom and goodness in ways that go beyond modern subjectivity (333).

We have here an implicit endorsement of Schelling's conception of God as substance and substance only. Schelling was by faith a Christian; but his way of seeing things, according to which all the finite seems feeble and transient, is consistent with Fackenheim's emphatically Jewish conception of history. For Schelling, God is that irresistible universal power which reveals the nullity of the finite world and produces from itself nothing that has positive subsistence of its own. Accordingly, he speaks of the 'overcoming' of human reason, of human 'will' (*Willens*), which occurs 'through the extreme, though at the same time voluntary, submission to divinity' (*Gottheit*).[15] Elsewhere Fackenheim sums up Schelling's position as follows: 'If God is radically outside human reason, feeling, and will, then He can become accessible only if He reveals Himself ... If there is a God, He is the God of Abraham, Isaac, and Jacob.'[16]

Hegel took this Schellingian – and Jewish – view of the unity of substance as the basis for his own understanding of world history, but, like Fichte before him, held that it had to be harmonized with the principle of the West, the principle of individuality and freedom. Schelling put substance at the summit of his philosophy, and defined it to be the unity of thought and being, of subjectivity and objectivity, without showing how the opposition arises in the first place, or how he can trace it back to the unity of substance. 'What is lacking in Schelling's philosophy,' Hegel says, 'is thus the fact that the point of indifference of subjectivity and objectivity [viz., the unity of substance] ... is absolutely pre-supposed, without any attempt at showing that this is the truth.'[17] Doull thinks Fackenheim is vulnerable to the same criticism.

Fackenheim would say, rightly, that he can affirm the unity of substance, the reality of God, without denying human individuality and freedom. He follows Schelling in his notion that the endless confusion of good and evil in historical life stimulates and arouses us to a higher, more spiritual conception of freedom. In yet another place, he argues that moral freedom for Schelling is a consequence of the timeless act by which an individual's life in time and history is determined. To choose between good and evil is to act in response to the demands of the moment, but outside of time and above the conflicts of history. In a strange and paradoxical way, history must be vulgar and impure, a mixture of good and evil, of universal will and self-will, for otherwise human individuality and freedom would have no material through which to realize themselves. Fackenheim, in fact, thinks that Schelling did not go far enough in acknowledging 'irrationality' and the role of 'accident' in the historical world.[18]

Doull does not deny the contingency of historical life, the confusion in it of reason and unreason, of good and evil. Yet he is certain – as Hegel was – that the linear movement out from self-will to universal will, and from universal will to self-will, bends back on itself, as it were, and turns round into a circle. The endless movement back and forth of universal will and self-will, of good and evil, of inward and outward, is overcome, 'not only theologically, but also within the secular order' (338). With Fackenheim, these conflicting sides, or motions, can only be potentially the same; the endless alternation of opposed principles is a necessary characteristic of the finite world of nature and history. With Doull, the unity of principles is not potential only, but also actual; the necessity of nature and history has been unveiled and made known. Modern freedom is in principle unlimited, or infinite, but it can make itself at home in the finite world even and especially at the point where the conflict of opposed principles becomes 'extreme' (339).

Evil for Hegel is not just the alternation and confusion but also the opposition of universal will and self-will. It is the appearance of self-will naked and undisguised, first in the abstract moral demand that individuals be left to themselves to decide what is good, and then in the contempt that these same individuals show for existing moral practices and customs. Evil is at once a contentless moral right and a subjective passion which is contrary to the actual world. But then it is also, as Hegel says, a mere 'semblance' of will that 'collapses of its own force'; it cannot be sustained.[19] Indeed, the appearance of evil is for him the point of transition to a rational social and political existence. Doull concurs, adding that this unity with the good is accomplished in 'human will' (338).

Hegel did not imagine that the modern state could abolish contrary passions or eliminate the confusion of universal will and self-will. In his view, the unity of the state, of universal will and self-will, exists in nature, in history, and thus retains the appearance of something imperfect and 'external.'[20] This is not to say that the unity of the state was an ideal confined only to Hegel's head, or that its unity was so frail that its existence or non-existence depended on the will of this or that individual. On the contrary, as Doull remarks, the ideal unity of Hegel's state really was present and active in the 'confidence' of Europeans that 'the common interest was in general attained within the given possibilities' (339). But the reality of nineteenth-century European states obviously conflicted with their past as well as with Hegel's ideal.

Doull observes that both traditional sovereign power and Hegel's ideal version of it 'vanished' to the extent that the European states failed to subordinate their various kinds of 'national sentiment' to the higher claims of 'universal humanity' (340). With this failure come the well-known evils of twentieth-century European history: war, economic oppression, nationalism, racism, anti-Semitism. The problem is always that the ideal unity of the state appears, on the one hand, as a quite abstract form of moral reflection and, on the other, as an outright contingent, national existence. In this respect, both in its different nationalities and in its moral self-reflection, Europe represents not just opposition, but unmediated opposition, the endless alternation of opposed determinations.

Doull agrees with Fackenheim that this divided European culture made the holocaust happen. As it appears in science and reason, this culture is called liberal or socialist: as given in nature and history, it is a mass of 'resentful national passions' (340). As a rational possession, this culture has a subjective form, a form that has more to do with the future than with real present life. Similarly, as a tradition and inheritance, this culture seems to be a thing of the past and to lie outside of the contemporary world. Doull and Fackenheim come together at this point. Yet it is also here – in the gap between past and future, tradition and reflection – that they part company.

Fackenheim sees the freedom that comes out of European culture as something endlessly negative and urges us to return to forms of consciousness which precede modern life. Doull's critique is not simply negative in this sense – rather, he presents the freedom of modern scientific culture as a necessary result of a long history that began with the ancient Greeks and continued through the Roman Empire into medieval Europe. This connected view of history allows him to criticize the abstract conscience of modern Europeans in a determinate way, and thus to see the nihilism of modern scientific culture as a defective – not excessive – form of Western rationality and freedom. It gives him the means to attack the subjective form of modern freedom in a thoughtful way, in an effective way, by identifying it with a forgotten but still 'moving spirit,' as well as with a possible 'system' of rights and duties by virtue of which individuals and nations can again have the 'self-confidence' to limit themselves (340–1). Fackenheim's splendid vision of God in history is only a potential liberation from the onesidedness and egotism of modern subjectivity. By contrast, Doull insists that the nihilism of modern reason and science gives us no choice but to develop and perfect European freedom into an intelligible world, a fully present reality. For us too, now that we are beginning to put the twentieth century into some kind of perspective, Fackenheim's fixation on the gulf between the divine and the human, the infinite and the finite, may be too limiting. There may be, as Hegel thought, a deeper paradox at work in Western history, that is, that the idea of God appears more clearly and adequately in modern times than in pre-modern times. If so, Doull is surely right to think that we can appreciate this paradox only by closing the gap between traditional and modern thought. Hence he takes the secular form of freedom to be the most objective form of religious content; hence, in harmony with Hegel's conception of the subject, he holds that the opposition of modern self-will and the world must be resolved at once in God and 'in man himself' (341).

The marvellous result is that modern freedom appears in a positive light. True, a freedom that is in principle unlimited may hold the world in contempt and make religion a means to its own self-consciousness and self-assertion; but it has its origins in a thinking that is implicitly substantial and comprehensive and thus guided, as Doull points out, by the need both to affirm the world and to reconcile 'all religions' (336). As manifest in religion – Oriental and Western – this thinking is tied to given content, to a direct vision of the world, and to an inner feeling for its meaning. As developed in philosophy – ancient and modern – it expresses the substance of religion, the objective world distinct from the feeling for it, and the content of self-consciousness distinct from the form of its activity. Thinking, in this Hegelian sense of the term, means that one not only enters into opposition with the life of the world, but also deepens the opposition to the point where one breaks free of the oscillation between one side and the other, one religion and another, and attains true self-knowledge, true self-activity.[21]

It is not just in passing that Doull links the 'need' to think to secular and religious divisions that are deeper in our time than in Hegel's. When the European states divide into hostile nations and classes, when liberals and socialists concentrate only on the individual, one may well say that the spirit of Europe is lost. Europeans over the last two hundred years, Doull says, have reacted with 'horror' or 'indifference' to what Europe has become. They have experienced 'secular despair' and turn in increasing numbers to religious beliefs and philosophical schools that offer escape from the present social reality (337). In this respect, Doull is no less despairing of European political life than Fackenheim. For both of them, the collapse of the older institutional order in Europe has revealed a mass of conflicting atheistic and religious beliefs, of contradictory modern and pre-modern attitudes.

But for Doull the true spirit of Europe – to be realized in North America, if not in Europe itself – still lies in the identity between the Christian religion and private, social, and political life.[22] Does this mean that he expected Christian believers, either separately or in combination with non-Christian believers, to restore secular life to some kind of order? We should be surprised if he did. As someone who lived with Hegel's writings for many years, he knew of his strong and repeated denunciations of conservatives who would turn to religion in order to curb or limit modern freedom.[23] For Hegel, religion can prevail in modern society only on the basis of an independent and secular freedom. Likewise, Doull boldly declared that modern freedom need not and cannot be 'abandoned' (340–1).

Hegel's claims on behalf of the secular form of reason were uncompromising; he pursued this reason even to the point where it seemed to destroy Christian belief.[24] For him, religion must appear external and restrictive except insofar as it passes through the experience of an all-conquering and all-consuming secular atheism. But then it follows that religion and secular atheism are both forms in which the idea of freedom exists. It is this idea of freedom that moved Hegel to speak both of evil and of the reconciliation of the religious and secular conscience. And it is this idea that inspired Doull and Fackenheim to engage in their remarkable debate, the excellence of which is to reveal just how profound and provocative Hegel's theory of modernity really was.

Notes

1 Emil L. Fackenheim, *The Religious Dimension in Hegel's Thought* (Bloomington: Indiana University Press, 1967), 10–12.

2 See Karl Löwith, *From Hegel to Nietzsche*, trans. David E. Green (New York: Columbia University Press, 1964), 28–9, 327–8; and the comments in Martin Heidegger, *Nietzsche* (San Francisco: Harper and Row, 1987), vol. 3: 225–6.

3 Fackenheim, *Religious Dimension*, 235–6.

4 See esp. Jacques Derrida, 'L'âge de Hegel,' in *Qui a peur de la philosophie*, ed. GREPH (Paris: Oublier-Flammarion, 1977), 73–107.

5 J.A. Doull, review of *The Religious Dimension in Hegel's Thought* by Emil L. Fackenheim, *Dialogue* 7 (1968–9): 483–91 and see chapter 7 above. See too Doull's 'Comment on Fackenheim's "Hegel and Judaism,"' in J.J. O'Malley et al., eds., *The Legacy of Hegel* (The Hague: Martinus Nijhoff, 1973), 186–95.
6 G.W.F. Hegel, *Phenomenology of Spirit*, trans. A.V. Miller (New York: Oxford University Press, 1977), 36. German: *Phänomenologie des Geistes*, in *Werke*, ed. Eva Moldenhauer and Karl Markus Michel (Frankfurt am Main: Suhrkamp, 1970), vol. 3: 57. Henceforth called *PhG*. I shall give page numbers from both the translation and the original, with that of the translation first.
7 See 335 above. Henceforth page references to this debate will appear in the text of my commentary, within parentheses.
8 *PhG*, 408–9/493–4.
9 *PhG*, 361–3/439–41.
10 G.W.F. Hegel, *The Encyclopaedia of the Philosophical Sciences*, trans. William Wallace (Oxford: Oxford University Press, 1971), pt. 3, *Philosophy of Spirit*, sect. 552, 290. German: *Enzyklopädie der philosophischen Wissenschaften*, III, *Die Philosophie des Gesites*, in *Werke*, vol. 10: 363–4. Henceforth called *Enc*. After indicating the section number, I shall give page numbers from both the translation and the original, with that of the translation first.
11 *Enc*., sect. 571, 301/377.
12 Fackenheim, *Religious Dimension*, 70–1, 193–214.
13 See also Emil L. Fackenheim, *Encounters between Judaism and Modern Philosophy* (New York: Basic Books, 1973), 159ff.
14 Emil L. Fackenheim, *Metaphysics and Historicity* (Milwaukee: Marquette University Press, 1961), 20n., 36–7n., 90–1n.
15 F.W.J. Schelling, *Schriften zur Religionsphilosophie*. 1841–54, in *Werke*, ed. Manfred Schröter (Munich: C.H. Beck, 1959), vol. 6: 560; my translation.
16 Emil L. Fackenheim, 'Schelling's Philosophy of Religion,' *University of Toronto Quarterly* 22 (1952): 11–12.
17 G.W.F. Hegel, *Lectures on the History of Philosophy*, trans. E.S. Haldane and Frances H. Simon (London: Routledge and Keegan Paul, 1955), vol. 3: 525. German: *Vorlesungen über die Geschichte der Philosophie*, III, in *Werke*, vol. 20: 435.
18 See Emil L. Fackenheim, 'Schelling's Conception of Positive Philosophy,' *Review of Metaphysics* 7 (1954): 581. Fackenheim brings out the moral implication of the irrationality of history in the conclusion to an article on Kant: 'Nothing in heaven or earth is more important than the moment in which a man – any man – makes himself good or bad. And whenever a man makes such a decision, the universe, so to speak, holds its breath.' See his 'Kant and Radical Evil,' *University of Toronto Quarterly* 23 (1954): 353.

19 *Enc.*, sect. 512, 253/317.

20 *Enc.*, sect. 513, 253/318.

21 G.W.F. Hegel, *Introduction to the Lectures on the History of Philosophy*, trans. T.M. Knox and A.V. Miller (Oxford: Oxford University Press, 1985), 31–3. German: *Vorlesungen über die Geschichte der Philosophie*, I, in *Werke*, vol. 18: 88–9.

22 In one of his last articles, Doull has claimed for North American states a concrete unity of Protestant Christianity and modern freedom that is now impossible for European states. Catholic Christianity was for him a subordinate – perhaps vanishing – part of this unity. See Doull, 'The Philosophical Basis of Constitutional Discussion in Canada,' chapter 9 below.

23 Hegel was critical of Catholic Christianity and Platonic philosophy for failing to resolve the conflict between religion and secular freedom. For him, Protestant Christianity makes a resolution of the conflict both necessary and possible, precisely because it heightens the antagonism between the two sides. See, e.g., *Enc.*, sect. 552, 284–91/356–65.

24 *PhG*, 348–9/422–4.

PART FOUR

The Post-modern State

chapter eight

Heidegger and the State[1]

In the context of Heidegger's thought it is not easy to say what the state is. The state has always been in some sense a complete society as having power to regulate the lives and private interests of a people, however far these powers might be neglected or abused. For Heidegger the relation of individuals at the present time to the system of their private interests, which he calls 'Technik,' is not only other than but threatens to overwhelm what might be called their political community or state. This latter has its existence for him not in a common political will but in the medium of poetical language. The true form of his national community is for him that of a *polis* in its particular geographical situation, where mortals live poetically under finite gods, themselves within the world.[2] The government of this community he thought for a little to find in the Nietzschean will of the 'Fuhrer.' When he gave up that hope it is hard to say how his was an actual state. States and other institutions, if they are actual and not in the language and fancy of poets, exist primarily in a practical thought which unites the universal and sensible immediacy.

When interviewed late in his life by the German publication *Der Spiegel* Heidegger showed himself true to the structure his political thought assumed, once he had through his study of Nietzsche purged himself of National Socialism. He continued to hope that his nation might be saved if, having given up its aggressive will, it could live in its language and natural situation and through Holderlin and other poets find the inner unity and truth of that world. Only such natural communities were capable of a creative spiritual life in relation to their history and traditions.[3]

How such a community could save itself from 'global technology' Heidegger confessed that he did not know.[4] It would not be saved by the designs and contrivances of mortals: 'Nur ein Gott kann uns noch retten.'[5] The god who could save was of course not the Christian God, but a finite god of those who know their mortality. He could have no confidence in democracy. What was the democracy founded on the radical rights and freedoms of individuals but the political face of 'Technik'? What matter, he would surely say if pressed farther, whether it was the totalitarian democracy of Marxists or a pluralistic American democracy?

Heidegger's thought has been immensely influential because it articulates more completely than other contemporary philosophies the world in which Europeans find themselves after the ruin of imperial states which, held by the universal spirit of the Christian religion, had for several centuries dominated all peoples and cultures. Drawing back into themselves and resting from their historical labours they saw the cause of their evils in an excess of thought. The intellectual world of Christian belief – an omnipotent God, creator of nature and finite spirits, who had their end in him – and a secular order inspired by this belief were in truth but predicates of humans in their natural particularity. This lost world, on condition it should not be actual, remained of endless interest to scholars and others. Its images and ideas as imprinted on language and entering the arts of peoples liberated from its authority might still be the source of a cultivated life. This tenuous relation to what was once the highest truth might itself be lost if one were drawn into the world of 'Technik,' where there were no more gods and nature was but a resource for human exploitation.

The thought of Europeans in this return to their natural particularity either sought to retain a concreteness in the medium of language or fell into the endless finitude of contemporary logic where individuals can find no unity and self-relation. The only way it seems in which the two forms of thought can be fitted together is if somehow 'Technik' can be limited and made the servant of the cultivated who live in harmony with nature.[6]

But the two in fact exist side by side: the European nations both remain particular linguistic communities and in a common economy give free play to the forces of 'Technik.' In this division the national communities are no longer states. A state or complete society would be that in which all the interests of the common economy would be centred and capable in some measure of political regulation. This limitation of 'Technik' is not that which the national communities might hope to have in themselves.

The function of the common state might however be taken as principally to limit 'Technik' in the interest of the national communities and their cultivated life. Heidegger does not comment on such an accommodation, which had not advanced as far in his day as since.[7]

Graeme Nicholson, in the concluding remarks of his *Illustrations of Being*, an excellent work which both sets out with great clarity the structure of Heidegger's thought and is sensitive to its limits, looks in both directions: the relation of national cultures to 'Technik' might be stabilized by a common state or, as in Marx's thought, state and economy might find their centre in the free individual who would draw on abundant goods for the enjoyment of a cultured life. The logic of this European world pulls in both directions. There is the danger in a common state that national communities be drawn out of their particularity to the universality they have fled. How is the other direction, which Nicholson finds more interesting, more than utopian?

It can perhaps help to make the structure of this contemporary Europe more distinct if one considers the form of religion appropriate to it. To the common state corresponds a common church, what one might call a Euro-catholic Church. Its practical function would be to oppose the excessive freedom of a technological humanism destructive of family virtue and social justice, and to encourage a passive acceptance of life and nature. The clerical government of such a church should be above what it would regulate, having an affinity thus with the celibate clergy of the medieval church. For access to the scriptures and ancient doctrines of an older church, the Church of a post-Christian humanity would depend on the hermeneutic arts to disclose what the language, but not the thought, of former times meant to the existential individual. The weakness of this church lies obviously in the distance between its actual work and an ancient doctrine and belief no longer actual.

In older Christian times, to give over the world of thought and rational belief to individuals in the particularity of nature and language was to give oneself to the devil.

> Verachte nur Vernunft und Wissenschaft
> des Menchen allerhochste Kraft,
> Lass nur in Blend – und Zauberwerken
> Dich von dem Lugengeist bestarken,
> So hab ich dich schon unbedengt.
>
> Goethe, *Faust*[8]

This reversal and the dogma of the present time that reason and the authority of reason are the source of evil confuse reason with the abuse of reason for finite ends. The evils of the Nazi time were from the universality of a Nietzschean will and from the obedience of the German people to authority. The evil in this is not reason but the absolute assertion of a national will. In giving up its aggressive will has a nation exorcized the devil or lulled him to sleep? By the measure of the Greek state which serves Heidegger for a model, the correction of the evil will in this relation is inward and potential. Is the individual of 'technology' another than the one who flees from it? Or is there in 'technology' a harder but more complete purgation of the natural particularity which as active has been the cause of atrocious evils?

The further course of the argument will be first to situate Heidegger's thought in the revolutions of the nineteenth and twentieth centuries which, as some Sampson, have brought down in ruins the temple of Christian belief and philosophy. It will then ask what bearing this revolution has on North America, where there are not national states.

The revolutionary spirit of the nineteenth century, whether in its more moderate liberal or its radical forms, had in it the assumption that we were done with thinking about the world and had now to change it. Heidegger finds in Nietzsche the completion and inner collapse of this revolutionary will. This completion had for him historical reality in the Nazi movement. His own philosophical thought, beginning at this point, looks back at the world the revolution had demolished and defines itself in that relation. The nineteenth-century revolutions and their completion in the twentieth attain thus a circular form – an incomplete circle in that the older order is regarded from the standpoint of its ruin. Towards the older world Heidegger has an ambiguous relation: partly it was beyond the strength of the later generation to uphold it; partly the liberation is final and philosophy has found its true form beyond the errors of the past.

An analogy from a simpler age may help towards bringing into one view the revolutionary movement of the past two centuries and Heidegger's relation to it. Plato in the *Statesman* tells a myth about the course of human history according to which it is ever a repetition of two phases: in the one phase a people grows from childhood to maturity, in the other it reverts again to childhood. The growth from childhood has in it a separation of needs and interests from an immediate unity. This division is the source of conflict and oppression, but the growth to maturity is the process of ordering this division to one end. There is thus formed a political community in which at the point of its full development all have part. Constitutionally, as the dialogue later explains, this growth is a development from monarchy through aristocracy to an ordered democracy.

The other phase has its beginning in the completion of the first: the individual, freed by this development, finds the structures by which he was freed an impediment to his freedom. There sets in that process of deconstruction which Plato sets forth at length in the *Republic*. In the need to make his own the freedom he enjoyed in the political community the individual does not rest until he has broken down every form of constitutional order and has remaining only a self-conscious freedom without other content than that of an arbitrary tyrannical self-will, from which state he lapses into childhood.

The political thought of Plato and Aristotle is centred on the question how this process of construction and destruction might best be stabilized. By what education can the knowledge be awakened in individuals that their freedom has its concrete realization in a well-ordered *polis*? What is the best possible order of the *polis*? If there is to be a *polis* at all the radical freedom disclosed by the circle has to be limited. But the Owl of Minerva flies late: the awakened freedom could find satisfaction only in a polity which had room for subjective freedom.

The Greek world of Nietzsche and Heidegger is inhabited by those whose historical finitude is contained in a certain temporal infinity. They live in the medium of language and the arts; philosophically they are before Socrates, with whom began the articulation of a *logos* underlying language and myth. From the finitude of political freedom the Greeks in their own time moved in another direction – to the discovery of an eternal actuality and a knowledge of nature and human finitude through their first causes, that is, through the form of their dependence on eternal actuality. The positive phase which the revolutions of the last two centuries have deconstructed had its completion when the reason moving in the finite content of family, society, and state was no longer another reason than that known in religion – in the relation of human and divine freedom. As in Plato's myth the individual would have this result as his own, theology turned overnight into anthropology, the eternal into a predicate of temporal existence. Philosophy was no longer, as since Plato and Aristotle, the conversion of what was first for some human interest or standpoint into what was first in an objective and universal thought but some 'Weltanschauung.' There are many philosophies and an unheard of philosophical production. But by an older measure the contemporary question might be asked of this whole revolution whether there was any longer philosophy.

Once this negative phase had begun its course it was as though the antecedent phase on which it depended had never been. F.L. Jackson shows with great clarity in a series of articles how polemics against the old order invariably have for their target not that forgotten order but another aspect of the revolution. The revolutionary will which would change the world is not the abstract sophistic which Plato exposes. Neither is it the rational freedom of eighteenth-century Enlightenment (of which more below) which would unite thought and nature as radically opposed. It is the freedom of a particular individual who supposedly is beyond the abstraction of the understanding by which the enlightened individual set mind against body, thought against nature – as Heidegger will say, beyond metaphysics. This individual has a sense of his concreteness but does not know it explicitly. Hence in reality he is ever divided, as he gives prominence to his unique embodiment or to his humanity.

The movement of this revolutionary deconstruction turns on the relation of these divided moments of the individual who in the world would make the realm of belief and thought and rational human institution into what they are for him. Heidegger discerns clearly the lines of this history, which for him is a history of the moments of time. If time be taken to be in truth the 'now,' the difference between past and future is lost in a timeless identity. An eternal realm opens for the individual. Nor has he freed himself from an intelligible world if he has still to wrestle with a division between the stable objectivity of things – their pastness – and their immediate sensory presence. Only in so far as past, present, and future are for him one process in the division of the moments is he free as this particular individual. Being is not God and an intelligible world but time and becoming.

Heidegger would force the whole history of philosophy into this mould, as a history of the moments of time. Already with Plato had begun a forgetting of being as infinite process and a preoccupation with the being of beings, and this forgetting had reached its extreme in the full development of that Christian world immediately antecedent to the nineteenth-century revolution. The history of philosophy, considered on its own and not within this revolutionary interest, was rather always about infinite being and the finite structure of beings. Neither Plato and Aristotle nor later philosophy had forgotten being but would know less abstractly than Parmenides how being and beings were one totality.

Heidegger also was not content to make an end of the metaphysics which was about the being of beings. In the full development of his thought a metaphysics of language takes the place of a conceptual metaphysics.

As an account of the progress of the nineteenth-century revolution Heidegger's history of the moments of time is of great interest. The demolition of the old Christian order was not accomplished in a day but in the course of a century and by successive stages. It appeared indeed to novelists of the early century that with the release of a boundless human will the old order was gone. To Balzac or Thackerey the new world was a 'vanity fair,' the expression of irrational passions without centre and unity of ends. But as long as the work of the revolution appears as vain servitude to an aggressive will, as for Schopenhauer, an interest remains and is even strengthened in the objective authority and direction of the old order. In this situation, for example, the opposition of earlier times to an infallible centre of authority in the Roman church has no ground left to stand on. Churches resting on scriptural authority, having no longer any rational relation to that authority, can only adhere to it literally. Individuals in these relations are abstractly outside the revolution, while also in but not committed to it.

Until the fiasco of 1848 liberals expected the restored monarchic states to pass easily into their hands. An abstract subjective freedom instead capitulated to the political will of the state. The relation of the revolutionary individual to the state assumed a more concrete form after the mid-century. The vain interests of the liberated individual were stabilized in a state which, while it might retain or, as in France, attempt to restore, a monarchic form, had in effect gone over to the middle class. In this relation was formed what in Britain and its colonial satellites is called Victorian morality. Elsewhere an equivalent structure had other names. The revolutionary will had found a political centre, but its relation to it was divided. Against an inner morality stands a natural immediacy and the interests arising from it. An evolutionary naturalism looks to find a relation of the two from the side of nature; a revived idealism would find a concretion from the side of thought. From neither side is a concrete unity to be discovered. There is at best for this idealism a synthesis of ideal and real moments for a subjective reflection. The virtue of the ruling middle class is a synthesis of nature and reason; as against their inferiors there is more of reason in the mix, and thus also a more evident conflict of the elements.

The political life of the states animated by this divided spirit displays a glaring contrast of ideal and brutally realistic moments. There is room in imperial states for an unbounded expansion of economic interests, at home a growth on all sides of the arts and sciences, but always within the limits of the divided will. As with the 'timocratic' and 'oligarchic' polities of Plato's *Republic* there emerged here a dissatisfaction with this abstract ordering of a will which would be free in its natural particularity. In response there appeared in the later years of the century a prophet and liberator in the person of Nietzsche, who revived the radical freedom of Feuerbach and Stirner for a time which was ready to receive it. To attain the desired concrete freedom the revolutionary individual had at once to go over more deeply to life and nature and in this relation to know all division and change as within an infinite circle. The world might be said to have become the property of the free individual.

The whole culture of the last decades of the nineteenth century and the beginning of the next was in the throes of this discovery, receptive of nature and desirous of knowing nature as symbolic of an ideal truth. This twofold movement settled variously into one whole, in which the revolutionary individual had his fulfilment. In philosophy this development had the form of a reaction against the idealism of the time to a realism more idealistic than it, which would gather all finitude into one whole and make it available as never before to human purposes. For this unification all logical differences were to be mathematicized or equalized and treated on this basis, in which logic might be said to return to Zeno. Or the phenomenology of Husserl might look for a unity of thought and the world through concreter ideal structures and find guidance for its collecting and dividing in the logic of language.

This logical revolution was incomplete so far as its ideal and real elements had not settled into the individual in his natural particularity as their subject. The residual idealism of the early Russell or of Husserl was lost in the completion of the revolution. The overthrow of bourgeois culture in this and other manifestations was also incomplete in that it was the work and possession of cultivated circles only. Through the collision of the imperial states in the Great War of 1914-18 its result passed into the general culture.

The war required of the citizens of the imperial states a unification of the divided interests of their bourgeois culture. In relation to the state it effected therefore a like revolution to that which individuals had been carrying through among themselves. The war as forming a community in which the division of morality and the natural will was negated freed individuals inwardly from the authority of a state so ordered. It imprinted on them a concrete freedom which remained with them as members of a community living in their particular interests.

The post-war Germany in which Heidegger began his philosophical work had completed the nineteenth-century revolution; the individual in his particularity had taken possession of the former Christian world: only such part of that world as could be predicated of this individual was any longer true. This revolutionized world was however divided in itself: it was a plurality of national communities tempered by their particular environment and expressing their community in the medium of a natural language, and it was 'global technology' or an economic society which reached to the ends of the earth for resources to supply the unlimited interests and desires of the same individuals as lived also within the confines of their national communities. This division is not accidental but belongs essentially to this achieved revolutionary freedom. It had been the interest of the former Christian world in the whole course of its history to overcome this division. In an older theological language the 'global technology' was the region of the Fall, which fell between an original and a restored justice. The corrective work of an intellectual culture within the operation of divine grace had for its end to draw this realm of violence and self-will within the relation of the original to the restored justice. The nineteenth-century revolution supposes this history completed and its fruits to be the possession of individuals in their natural particularity and their national communities. But such communities and their members when they have freed themselves from the residual authority of the old order, whether they take themselves as in a passive paradisiac relation to the world or as animated by a Nietzschean will, find that they do not contain within themselves the system of their particular needs and desires. Only a community whose particularity rests on a universal or divine order can find its original freedom continuing in the competitive realm of particular passions and interests.

This inevitable division of revolutionary freedom in the first years of Heidegger's academic life took the form of a struggle for domination between the two parts. That is the structure of the contest between 'fascism' in its various forms and Marxist socialism, which pervaded Europe between the wars and exhausted itself in the Second World War. National communities trusted their fortunes to the genius of leaders who could supposedly discern the relation between their inner sense of themselves and the changing circumstances of the moment. So also Marxists found that the government of free individuals had to be exercized by the supposed genius of one such individual.

The classical exposition of this freedom as that of the members of a national community is Heidegger's *Sein und Zeit*. 'Dasein' has in his 'Seinsverstandnis' or sense of being an unbroken self-relation in his various ways of being in the world. As he acts and the momentary actuality of his designs passes into memory, what he has done remains with him and is the ground of new decisions which have again the same cyclic course. It is unnecessary for the present purpose, which is to situate Heidegger in the context of the nineteenth- and twentieth-century revolutions and the world they would overturn, to follow the successive structures of 'Dasein' as they are developed in *Sein und Zeit*. Instead certain difficulties of the whole standpoint have to be examined. 'Dasein' who accumulates his particular experience of the world and would keep it his own or 'authentic' is the object in *Sein und Zeit* of a transcendental phenomenology to which it belongs to know universal objects such as a 'world.' What the world in which 'Dasein' lives and moves and has his being, is for himself, has difficulties analogous to those of the Humean empiricism, if it would speak of a 'world,' even though here the experience of 'Dasein' has a formal unity through the moments of time. When the argument of *Sein und Zeit* considers the structure of a common discourse among the many 'Daseins' or 'existers,' as Nicholson conveniently names them, this difficulty becomes explicit. The language in which 'existers' communicate must, it seems, derive its objectivity from an underlying universal, if it would fashion the contingent experience of individuals into a common stock of words and meanings. But if, as philosophers had thought since Plato, logic was the ground of language and logical judgments the model of linguistic statements, the supposed primacy of 'Dasein' in his particularity was endangered.

In Plato's *Republic* what confines prisoners in the Cave is a supposed primacy of the moment and then of language and opinion. Liberation is through the knowledge of a rational spirit as primary. But for revolutionary freedom this is neither an acceptable way nor a way easily avoided. A concrete logic is concealed in the capacity of 'Dasein' to make its own the flux of its own experience. But the humanized world of 'existers' in their particularity and finitude requires that that logic be held within a particular embodiment.

Heidegger found his way to the mature formulation of his philosophy, where being would be housed in language and 'Dasein' live not in the singularity of authentic experience but in the truth of language – in a poetical discourse which could hold language from collapse into the abstractions of the understanding – not directly but through a confrontation with Nietzsche or, in the realities of his time, with National Socialism. The uncertain relation of 'Dasein' in his particularity to a universal thought derived not only from the phenomenological method of that work but also from the structure of its object. 'Dasein' as fully explicated and free in its historicity is the Nietzschean individual. In a protracted occupation with the thought of Nietzsche Heidegger pronounced him the last metaphysician – the end of philosophy save in the new form he would give it. In Nietzsche the aggressive will of the modern age had reached its extreme point in that with him the common error of philosophers – to go inward to a cause or principle of all things – had the form of a will which negated all distinctions and willed only itself. A dissolution of the world which the modern age from Descartes to Hegel had accomplished in thought Nietzsche had also realized.

It should be clear from what has been said already that this history is in truth about the course of the nineteenth-century revolution. The 'Hegel' of this history is in its reality that unity into which the divided will of an incomplete revolution was constrained by the first war, out of which sprang the completed revolutionary will of Nietzsche's thought. This freedom has still in it a relation of time and immediacy to the universality of thought. Individual and community do not save their particularity in that relation.

Heidegger made a new beginning of his thought with being itself, not with the 'Dasein' in whom it was concealed and hidden. The free individual could not make his world but lived in a world given him by being itself. There is no thought here of the creation of a world in which finite spirits live and recognize in it and through a human order its creator. The interest of *Zeit und Sein* and of those works which, depending on its logic, define the fourfold structure of heaven and earth, mortals and immortality, and the nature of that poetical inspiration which constructs this world and enables one to dwell in it – their interest is to situate human freedom in a realm of language and imagination which in older philosophies falls between immediate intuition and thought.

There is a difficulty in Heidegger's development of a world from the side of being that he must use images of 'giving' and 'reaching' to describe how a finite content is made present. Being is active, but the source of its activity is hidden. The human attitude which can receive its disclosures is that of waiting and listening, and letting the world disclosed *be*, without the destructive intrusion of the aggressive will which with Nietzsche fell in upon itself.

Being makes itself present as an 'Ereignis' or appropriation of all finitude, in which concealment and unconcealment – negative and affirmative – are united and divided. The content of this *logos* in language can have a great but not unending stability. Individuals do not make, but receive, their language. Through its mutable stability peoples have a culture and a history. They live poetically in a given world then eventually reduce it to prose and have need of a new beginning.

In the successive forms of this poetical history there is a common structure. The inner *logos* of language has an external expression in a nature where the relation of heaven and earth has an Empedoclean structure of a mixing and separation of the elements. Humans live in a like relation to their mortality to more stable and universal entities, which might be called gods, but which also are subject to a fatal 'Gotterdammerung.'

In our time the relation of a poetical living to its prosaic levelling is of national communities to the 'global technology' in which there are no longer mortals and gods but the release of an atheistic Marxist will. Heidegger asks whether some balance of the two might not be possible. But against him rise Derrida and the deconstructionists, who delight to show that in poetry and language there is no unambiguous truth – neither in that nor another medium any truth at all. As Hector to Aeneas in the flames of Troy, Heidegger might truly say that if the freedom of the revolutionary individual in his particularity could have been saved, he would have saved it. The national communities of Europe may long continue to feed on their cultural memories while they also put themselves under a common state. In that relation they can hope to live well without the oppression of their culture and national differences.

Hegel, who lived before the revolutions of the nineteenth and twentieth centuries and knew that philosophy is not prophetic but speaks of what is actual, could all the same from the old order take a more comprehensive view of the approaching revolution than was available to those within it. The states and their members in the freedom they had attained would go over to their national particularity and make for themselves a world which would know only a historical and finite spirit. It was in the logic of that historicized culture that the states would experience the limit of their national particularity, that their active spirit would fail and their continuing history be somewhat as that of the Greek states in a larger historical world.[9] If they found security in the middle realm of language and imagination, the actual course of this history would expose the contradiction that lay in the attempt of humans to make the eternal realm of religion and philosophy their own. Heidegger's world where being dwells in language has in it not only the instability of its historical forms but also an uncertain actuality. Is his fourfold structure actual or of an imagination living in itself? To enter into the logic of Hegel's argument it is necessary to go farther than Heidegger in dismantling the revolution of the nineteenth and twentieth centuries.

It would appear that Heidegger's philosophy could be of little interest to North Americans. The fear that national linguistic communities be engulfed by global technology has no direct pertinence here.[10] Neither Canada nor the United States is a nation in the European sense. Europeans in migrating to North America left behind them their homelands and that natural embodiment of a universal belief and culture which to Europeans remain as the medium in which they still find relation to that older belief and culture. If Europe was to be rebuilt in the forests of America it could only be on a more inward and universal foundation. It is thus understandable that in the United States one people, more strongly unified perhaps than any, could be fashioned out of immigrants from every nation and culture. That in this new Europe national differences should be melted down and not have a certain room on a common basis (as they do, for instance, in Canada) is not necessary to the reconstruction. Nor is it necessary that the language of the new Europe should be uniquely English. Global technology and the destruction of nature are problems as well to the new as to the old Europe, but it is unthinkable here that their solution should be sought in the restored relation of particular nations to their homelands.

Heidegger in fact has been of considerable interest to North Americans. In asking why and within what limits this interest has occurred, it is convenient to attend principally to the United States, which more than two centuries ago separated itself from the old Europe and took on itself the task of building a new and universal Europe, which should be a model for mankind. Some remarks can then be added on Canada, which to this day continues in a certain cultural dependence and has no clear sense of its sovereignty on a North American basis.

It is perhaps useful to observe in passing how little the new Europe as built in the United States can be understood through Heidegger's philosophy. For him 'Americanism,' as he calls it, and the Marxism of the defunct Soviet Union were more or less equivalent forms of 'global technology.' It could not enter his view that the state and its relation to society and individual freedom are conceived altogether differently in the two systems. According to the Marxism which Lenin and his successors imposed on the peoples of the Russian Empire, civil society – the realm of private freedom and competition – was to be done away with. The state also, as the instrument of the dominant economic class, was to be abolished. Both state and society were to be made predicates of individuals in their natural particularity, to whom would belong the fruits of labour without competition or political oppression. But where there is not a society and a state, within which a reconciliation of interests and the experience of community and a common end can occur, all authority and government must be partisan – of some part over the rest. Government by a part however is bound to be felt as oppressive and alien to the rest. And the particular will of a leader or a central committee is the agent of unbounded tyranny and oppression. The system inevitably erodes all sense of community and collapses of itself when it can no longer be maintained by terror.

The revolutions of the eighteenth century had another structure than those of the following centuries. Their interest was not to destroy the state but to find room within it for a society of free individuals. The arbitrary will of kings would be limited by the reason of society, and the unreason or evil will of society would be contained by the relation of society to a sovereign will. The state might be spoken of as constituted by a contract among the members of society. This account explained why the sovereign must find agreement with the will of society. But the unified will in which society could be thought to make the contract being itself through relation to the state, the true account was rather that a state already existing was modified by taking the rational will of society into it.

Thus the eighteenth-century revolutions like subsequent revolutions, if their movement would be well understood, have to be taken with that which they work against. They also are the negative phase of a cyclic movement. In this case what lay behind and incited the revolutionary spirit was a state to which the interests of classes had been effectively subordinated, which still was for them the centre on which in their interests they depended. The destructive passions of individuals had also found an inner centre in a sense of community in the multitude of their occupations: there had been formed what is called the 'work ethic.' And the family had come to have an intrinsic end in which nature and reason coincided. So the state, civil society, and family were all there before the revolution set in, but without a self-conscious principle.

The defect of this ethical order for the revolutionary will was that the concrete unity present in institutions was not the work of individuals in their self-conscious freedom. Their relation to it, as to the Christian religion, was rather the free acceptance of a given order and truth. What the revolutionary will put in place of this antecedent order was a society of their own making, in which the division and unification of interests existed for rational individuals in pursuit of their natural interests and their general well being. Political life was the process of bringing this freedom of society into an acceptable relation to the sovereignty of the state.

The political and social freedom which the revolution made for itself was not equivalent to the order it opposed. Hume, who was among the first to reflect on the new order, found the relation of individuals in their immediate experience to the common benevolence and interest in the useful inscrutable to reason,[11] as was also the relation of their freedom to the state and to religion. The intrinsic movement of the revolutionary was however to know itself and that which it supplanted. This revolution had a history in that the freedom assumed to be present in society was also unfreedom.[12] Enlightenment has a history in which the free individual from an immediate and felt unity of the natural and the rational will comes to know their difference and opposition and then their unity as thus opposed. In the course of this development society both finds it must draw more on the sovereignty of the state and would take this dependence into itself.

The society of free individuals as having in it a unity of natural and rational interests appears to be beyond the old order, whose religion and institutions served to awaken a sense of this unity and to maintain its priority over all division. The concrete freedom enjoyed in society was at first contingent and in the enjoyment of goods. The inner division of the will and the origin of evil – which the religion and culture of the old order knew is concealed in the society of free individuals – could only emerge as that society found need to have a deeper hold on the unity of natural interests and rational freedom. But first the division has itself to be deepened and the rational individual take itself to be a product of nature.[13] The revolution in its course has thus two faces: it is turned against the old order and at the extreme of its separation replaces it by a religion of nature and radical equality;[14] its movement is also towards the lost concreteness in which the conflict of good and evil is overcome not primarily in social programmes but inwardly, a general recognition that liberalism is bad because it demoralizes people.

These general reflections on eighteenth-century revolutions have diverted attention from the question asked: why is Heidegger of interest to North Americans? The answer, in relation at least to the United States is this: the free individual of the American revolution appears at a certain stage of its development to have an affinity with Heidegger's *Dasein.*[15] The following observations on the revolution in America will show the limits of that affinity.

The community in which Americans primarily know their individual freedom is the state. Although supposedly constituted by a prior freedom of rational individuals, the unity of the state once constituted is regarded as the condition of popular government by and in the interest of the people. No people has a stronger sense of its political unity than the American. This primary relation of individuals permits radical changes in the understanding of individual freedom to occur within the constitution. The eighteenth-century constitution is thus for Americans not a historic relic but actual, as the ground on which also the evils of the present time can be corrected. Hence the continuing confidence of Americans and a capacity to act politically no longer found in Europe.

Their relation to the state is for Americans the point of connection between the old order and the new. It is possible therefore for Americans to be in some manner Christian at the same time as they live in an enlightened freedom opposed to the Christian religion. Their history is only to be understood when regarded in this total context.

The rational freedom through which Americans are related to the state has in it the division of the individual as immediate and as universal and his self-relation in this division. The individual is free in relation to his natural needs and desires; and the multitude of such individuals in the division of work, the subordination and mutual dependence of the economic system, are a community. This concurrence of interests is at first an attitude of benevolence and a common relation to things as useful. An individual may or may not in fact through his work realize at once his private satisfaction and community with his neighbour. Such is the natural right of Americans to life, liberty, and the pursuit of happiness.

The contingency of this freedom was not strongly felt in the first decades of the Republic, where resources were abundant and individuals had room to escape the oppression of society and begin anew the pursuit of happiness – the worldly realization of their rational freedom. Society in these conditions required a minimum of correction by the state.

The economic relations of an industrial society exposed the contingency of an individual freedom so conceived. To explicate what lay in the concept of the individual free in the satisfaction of his natural needs and interests Americans imbibed for a time the idealism of Kant and his successors, and a clearer concept of the rational subject permitted also another concept of his relation to nature, namely as the pragmatic individual. In this concept the free individual is divided from himself. His relations to himself and to others are from his own activity. But the order which individuals and the society of free individuals make for themselves in the satisfaction of their needs and desires has only the relation to rational freedom that it is not bound by the order it has laid down in particular circumstances.

The free individual in this form has made his freedom objective to himself. But the subject who observes this freedom is rather the social scientist or the agent of the state. The state is related to individuals in this externalized freedom through programmes and all the apparatus of a liberalism which would improve and correct the evils of society extraneously. Or the individual turns himself over to the direction of another to fashion his psychic states acceptably to himself and the current social order.

What the pragmatic synthesis of rational freedom and man as emerging from nature passes into here, as already with Rousseau, is the individual for whom all acceptable social relations derived from his freedom. Heidegger's *Dasein* is a pragmatist of sorts, but differs from the pragmatist of enlightened thought in that he knows the divided moments of his activity as the process of his freedom. The pragmatist proper has not brought into one relation his universality or sense of being and his activity. He is less than *Dasein* in that he does not have that concrete unity. But he is also more in that he would come to the unity of the natural and rational in man in the medium of thought. *Dasein* knows this concreteness as fact: the radical division of the moments is known not in thought but in the medium of language.

What the pragmatic synthesis of rational freedom and man as emerging from nature passes into here, as already with Rousseau, is the individual for whom all acceptable social relations derive from his freedom. This rational subject is at once also the living individual. But this rational freedom is abstract, an equality outside which fall living individuals and the multiple interests of society. Equality has thus in part the form of a right of choice in relation to nature, while from this freedom life and nature are repelled and declare against it a right to life. Adherence to life does not have in it the reason and freedom of family life. The equality again of the general will, while it is the beginning of a rational political freedom, has not in it the ordered relation of particular goods to a unity of ends in the state, a relation to which enlightened freedom from its intrinsic logic tends.

If life and equality do not oppose and repel each other but consolidate, one has the rebellious individual who is outside society, who being provoked burns down cities, forms gangs which prey on society and on themselves, sustains his high on drugs. As moving more widely in society this destructive will appears as a love of violence and pornography and the erosion of all institutions. The characteristic evils of American society have in short their origin in this abstract equality which had not taken difference and finitude into its self-relation. Out of this social ruin the elements of a more adequate concept of individual freedom and its relation to the state can perhaps be discerned. The objective institutions of the old order acquire a renewed interest when the liberation from them has been completed. On the side of enlightened freedom a general disbelief in pragmatic liberalism has occurred. Partly this has the form of a nostalgic relapse into an unregulated society and to older tradition as in that relation. Partly an acceptable liberalism has to address the relation of the liberated, alienated individual to the state and an ordered freedom. The problems of society have to become the affairs of individuals as well as of programmes. From being destructive of the old order an enlightened freedom which in its universality begins to have hold of its division has interest rather in finding a stable and concrete end in society and the state.

There is widely in the United States the insight that the proper functioning of the constitution is impeded by the power of special interests. Special interests impede, for example, the interest of the American government in providing health care equitably to its citizens. Enlightened freedom in its several forms is a relation of special interests to a common social freedom and to the state. The whole system of special interests in its contemporary form is what Heidegger calls 'Technik' or 'technology.' Enlightened freedom in its full development would take this system into the political good, so that it serve the whole interest of individuals, at the same time as individuals were converted to a knowledge of the political good as prior to their private interest.

Any such complete explication of the logic of enlightenment in the realities of American life is of course remote and conjectural. There is not at any rate to such an explication the obstacle of nationality and cultural particularity. Enlightened freedom in all its forms, as containing a unity of nature and reason, has a Trinitarian Christian structure. A development of this freedom is to a concretion and adequation of the Trinitarian moments. Enlightenment is thus, as Hegel said of it, a realization of Christianity: an abstract and positive relation at first to its content, then a developed opposition of the rational and natural will, in the end an 'aufhebung' of the Fall for self-conscious freedom. Through the enlightened freedom of the United States, so far as there is in it some sense of its whole structure and tendency, there is access to the religion of Paul and Augustine for thought and as actual.

Canada has been receptive both of nineteenth-century European culture and of its dissolution in the twentieth century. To both we have been in a relation of colonial dependence. An illustration: some years ago George Grant in a well-known book lamented the demise of Canada; a Canadian nation, betrayed by its politicians, had fallen prey to the great technological empire to the south. But in truth neither was Canada a nation nor, as the argument has shown already, is the United States rightly defined as a centre of 'global technology.' What then were we to lament? George Grant grew up in the ruins of Victorian culture in Ontario and Heidegger was for him a principal interpreter of the culture which took its place. *Amicus Plato, sed magis amica veritas.* The effect on Canadians of this twofold relation to the Old World has been to make possible the question, what are we as a North American people, whose freedom and its political articulation has a different basis than for Europeans? After the constitutional experiments of recent years English-speaking Canadians are at least at the point where they do not know what they are as a people. Quebec has perhaps gone farther, in that it prepares for a sovereignty, not of a linguistic and cultural community only, but of a people who should be able to hold their own in North America. Had Canadians of English speech a sense of themselves as sovereign, the two peoples might have no great difficulty in agreeing on a common sovereignty of equals, in which there was ample room for their differences.

But to clear the way for the independence of both peoples and a constitutional order which would be wholly their own there is needed not only an attrition, now largely completed, of the older colonial dependence but a recognition also of the new as inappropriate. So long as the political centre for English Canadians was the Empire, the Confederation was for them an extension of Great Britain in which French Canada could not have an equal part. Quebec had meantime its centre in Rome, a relation if it afforded a cultural security impeded the formation of an independent political spirit. While the two peoples were in this different dependence a common sovereignty at home must be incomplete. In particular Quebec could not entrust the amendment of the constitution to an English majority.

When Pierre Trudeau completed formally the sovereignty of Canada he revised the Constitution at the same time in the image of the European democracies of the day, giving primacy to a charter of rights and freedoms. What sovereignty as defined in the older constitutional act meant in this relation was left in obscurity. Trudeau in this imitated one aspect of the European states but not that in which they are national communities. He would destroy Quebec nationalism. But the same European model could serve his nationalist opponents just as well. From that point political discourse in Canada has largely been guided by a European model, this taken in various ways.

At Meech Lake an accord was reached in which the offence done to Quebec by Trudeau was undone and the beginning at least found of a common and accepted sovereignty. But a foolish politician from New Brunswick obtained acceptance of a parallel accord which cancelled the first, treating Canada as a congeries of individuals, cultures, and tribes, not a sovereign political community. The acceptance of that McKenna accord by the Mulroney government was the origin of the Bloc Québécois, now the official opposition in Ottawa.

The subsequent Charlottetown Accord, in which the Canadian people did not find an acceptable expression of their sovereignty, carried this new colonialism to the extreme. Canada was made up first of the aboriginal peoples who as in nature were its guardians against the aggressive European will. The second ingredient was the many cultures of immigrant peoples. At the same time the equality of individuals and the free operation of 'global technology' were assured.

In Europe these ingredients have a certain coherence through the customs and political traditions of the national communities. Where neither French nor English in Canada, and much less the many cultures and aboriginal peoples, are national states, the effect of this manner of thought is to dissolve the political community. Heidegger is of course only a part of this thought, which contains as well what he opposed. For Canadians the experience of contemporary European culture in its whole extent, from which they cannot take shelter in some national *Heimat*, can only work as a purgation and a disclosure of the universal basis on which, like the Americans, they have to build a political community and give appropriate expression to the sense of themselves as beyond the passions which divide, for example, the English and the Irish, or the south Slavic nations.

Notes

1 'Heidegger and The State,' essay presented to the Contemporary Studies Programme, University of King's College, 1992. First published in this volume.
2 The eloquent description of the life of the Athenian state in *Einfuhrung in die Metaphysik*, 117, though it needs revision to be taken into his later philosophy, remains close to his ideal; see also *The Thing, Building, Dwelling, Thinking*.
3 French version (Mercure de France, 1977), 47, which alone I had at hand during this writing.
4 Ibid., 59.
5 Ibid., 49.
6 *Erlauterungen zu Holderlin's Dichtung*, 178–9.
7 Heidegger would hardly have followed with approbation the movement of the European states to a common state, which had barely begun in his time.
8 *Faust, Ein Fragment* (Insel, 1958), 72.
9 *Die Philosophie des Rechts.*
10 Quebec, determined to preserve its language and culture, nonetheless strongly supports North American free trade.
11 In Hume's moral philosophy, the relation of individuals to the structure of society is not through reason but through 'feeling.'
12 Where Adam Smith sees capitalism as benevolent, Ricardo sees in it a grinding necessity.
13 As in the materialism of the French Enlightenment.
14 The French Revolution.
15 As Heidegger's *Dasein* is a particular individual who has a relation to his world through an inner idealism so, as the argument will show, the pragmatic American individual is an embodied natural idealist.

COMMENTARY
Heidegger and the Dialectic of Modernity

GRAEME NICHOLSON

1. Introduction: The Rupture of Natural and Ideal Self in the Twentieth Century

In 'Heidegger and the State' James Doull has outlined with his customary depth and power the relationship in which Heidegger stands to the history of recent times, the history of the 'nineteenth- and twentieth-century revolution,' a history that he treats as a dialectic of the post-Enlightenment era.[1] The nineteenth century was for Doull the period of reductionism: the politics, religion, commerce, and science that made our tradition were reduced to the free and autonomous individual, to become his possession, reclaimed, as Feuerbach argued, from the alienation that had originally precipitated metaphysics. Yet as this was actually lived through during the whole nineteenth century, there were divisions, many of them, that repeatedly appeared. This radically free individual was inwardly divided in principle, and so was the world occupied by this individual. The individual Victorian combined a stern personal morality with an unprecedented rapacity in business affairs. The world was a congeries of distinct national states and languages, on the one hand, and an emerging world economic order, on the other. Doull expresses this world often in terms of a self divided between a natural self and an ideal self, and in the pages to come I shall follow him in this way of seeing the matter.[2] Unmediated, these two selves ultimately passed into explicit and open opposition to each other, which I take to be Doull's analysis of the transition from the nineteenth century to the twentieth.

Both the economy and the literary-philosophical culture of the period around 1900 demanded that the natural self be utterly liberated: buccaneer capitalism, the glorification of war, and the Nietzschean will. With the general conflagration of 1914–18, the opposition between the natural self and the ideal self, now openly divided from each other, 'passed into the general culture,' as Doull says. From this arose on one side the activist idealism of international Communism, which would enshrine the victory of universal man over nature, and on the other side Fascism, which celebrated the natural will and one's particular national heritage, denying the unity of mankind in the name of racial theories. This struggle was the master division of the twentieth century, Fascism versus Communism, the outward collective war between the natural self and the ideal self whose opposition had been concealed in the preceding century. It is true that today Fascism and Communism are both lost causes, and yet the division that they expressed has not gone away and has not been reconciled. Indeed, the central political struggle in our day is that between a reformist statism and a libertarian capitalism, and I shall be making the claim that these two forces are, in principle, the same as the ones Doull has identified.

A deeper comprehension of this dialectic would require one to situate it in relation to what preceded the nineteenth century, and there are many references in this and other articles by Doull to the long history that led up to the Enlightenment, giving deeper intelligibility to his account of our own modernity. But although I will try to bear that history in mind, I shall not bring it into this paper. Instead, I will pick out one thread from his account of the nineteenth–twentieth century revolution for a closer look: the changing fortunes of the state.

Certainly the nineteenth-century reduction to the free individual precipitated a revolution in the state (and here it is Europe, not the United States, that I have in mind). Liberals expected a constitution of individual freedom in 1848, but, as Doull points out, they did not get it. What they got instead was the divided self and the divided world, in which increasingly a 'brutal realism' prevailed in the 'imperial states' which made 'room for an unbounded expansion of economic interests,' that is, the victory in the state of the natural over the ideal self.[3] Before the nineteenth-century revolution, the state was, in theory and to some extent in practice, the home of reason, justice, and law, an agent of Enlightenment. But when the liberals of the nineteenth century attacked *that* state, they left a vacuum behind which was quickly occupied by the representatives of 'civil society,' so that Marx could describe the state after 1848 as the mere executive committee of the ruling class: 'The executive of the modern State is but a committee for managing the common affairs of the whole bourgeoisie.'[4] In that era, it was only in personal morality and in voluntary charity that the ideal self could find its scope. Of course, this was no small thing, for the later nineteenth century was marked by innumerable causes of voluntary idealism that left a wonderful heritage for our own times: the abolition of slavery, the emancipation of women, universal manhood suffrage, trade unionism, schools for the children of workers and peasants, evangelical and medical missions, Germany's Inner Mission, hygienic nursing, settlement houses, etc., etc. All this was conceptualized by the participants as free and voluntary action, which meant outside the state. It was in the twentieth century that reformers and socialists, small in number at first, yet steadily growing, began to make the case that these social causes, being in the public interest, ought to be promoted and supported by the state, and to the extent that social democracy gained a foothold, that became the reality, a new socialization of the state, correcting its brutal nineteenth-century realism.

But with the rupture of the natural self from the ideal self, with the unprecedented violence of the First World War, there emerged new ideologies that made it the business of the state either to conduct revolutionary warfare worldwide in the name of the new Communist man or to guard the nation or *Volk* and breed it for the future. The rational, enlightened works of humane reform could wait. Reality was threatening and strong measures were needed. The Fascist state is the same in principle as the Communist state, even if one is national and the other international, as I think Doull has also conceded with his remarks, later in his paper, about Lenin and his successors.[5] Both combine revolutionary urgency with the rule of one partial group over society ('proletarian' dictatorship or the *Führerprinzip*).

In our own time, with the defeat of both movements, we have not reverted to a social democracy, but rather, all throughout the West, to a mixed order which enshrines an unending oscillation between social reformers inclined to statism and advocates of untrammelled capitalism inclined to libertarianism: that is, essentially a return to what Doull has described as the divided self of the nineteenth century, with the state tilting now this way and now that.[6]

2. The Early Heidegger

In the midst of this history stands Heidegger, whose thought began to take shape at the very juncture where the nineteenth-century self was broken and the violence of our own times began. The first point that Doull makes a propos of Heidegger is that it is difficult to see what Heidegger makes of the state, and surely the entire progress of Doull's paper gives the deeper rationale for this observation.[7] If philosophy is its time comprehended in thought, we could never expect from Heidegger an eighteenth-century-type, Enlightenment account of the state; nor should we expect from his discerning, radical mind a return to the nineteenth-century idea, for instance, in celebrating Bismarckian *Realpolitik* (in fact, Heidegger's parents had suffered under Bismarck's anti-Catholic *Kulturkampf*). What then of the state, the universal community, the regime of law and justice in Heidegger's early period?

His earliest thought was Catholic, which is to say, universalist in scope, not remotely nationalist or German, and hence it expressed an integrated self and world just as fully as James Doull could ever wish. But it was not original philosophy, not yet the Heidegger of the twentieth century. As he stepped beyond his *heimatliche* tradition, it was above all to enter into neo-Kantianism and the phenomenology of Husserl. Consideration of Heidegger's beginnings should not omit the influence upon him of Kant, Husserl, and phenomenology, and I'll come to that presently. But what of the social world, the condition of state and society in which Heidegger began to work?

To put it briefly, this public world was in the midst of catastrophe. As he began his work of thought, the two sides of the splintered Victorian unity were in the very midst of their violent mutual destruction. Never, perhaps, in the history of the world had the objective domain of state, law, diplomacy, and the military exhibited such folly and failure. After Germany's loss of the war, the old Wilhelmian-Bismarckian order collapsed without warning, leaving nothing in its place, and after successive catastrophes (the failed Bavarian soviet, the failed Spartacists, the failed peace accord of Versailles, the collapsed economy and currency, perpetual failures in the Weimar parliament) German students and the intelligentsia, I believe, expected nothing from politicians, diplomats, or soldiers. The objective world was for them a vacuum. Heidegger and his generation were in search for what was unconditionally true, authentic, absolute, what had unconditional being, what withstood every doubt, a principle for life, a religion, God. No social order, no state, they thought, could meet that test. And if we think of their situation in the light of Doull's dialectic, we have to recognize that it expressed a separate but genuine moment of the dialectic: the very moment of dissolution and nothingness, where no order has begun to establish itself. I have sometimes imagined the thought of Plato, too, as beginning with the very collapse of Athens, or of Greece, a moment quite distinct from the later efforts of Sparta or Thebes or Macedonia to rebuild a society and state.

Obviously these young people were not to shape the political future, though that future was already present in incubated form. Outside the circles of the existentialists with their Kierkegaard and their Dostoyevsky were the right-wing militants, with an utterly different agenda, principally one of revenge, and the left-wing militants, with some degree of hope and a very high degree of determination – two groups whose ultimate clash would result in Nazi victory and shape the future, two groups who, as Doull has shown, represent the unmediated sides of the foregoing dialectic.

As Doull presents Heidegger's thought, he was from the beginning inclined to the same side as Nietzsche and other advocates of the particularistic and natural self, the self, in Doull's view, that became defined as Dasein in *Sein und Zeit,* the self that knows its own freedom in the form of individual authenticity (see especially sections 50, 53, and 60–2 of *Being and Time*).[8] And yet I think that judgment needs to be modified. Heidegger's thought was profoundly shaped by Husserl's, and Husserl's thought belongs clearly to the opposite stream in the Doullian dialectic, that of ideality, idealism, and the ideal self. It is no small task to see how Heidegger assimilated Husserl, yet surely he did. And just as Husserl expressed allegiance repeatedly to Descartes, so did Heidegger to Kant. His Kantianism is found in the very idea of an analytic of Dasein as an a priori for all experience; likewise in his doctrine of the temporality of this Dasein, which gives the pattern for all other temporalities. The Heideggerian idea of conscience is a replica of Kant's practical reason, and the latter's doctrine of our finitude is invoked by Heidegger himself as grounds for maintaining against the German Idealists the unknowable thing in itself. Heidegger saw himself as working *on Kantian grounds* to overcome the Kantian prohibition of an ontology. This is the burden of the 1929 text *Kant and the Problem of Metaphysics,* though it is also evident in *Being and Time* (sect. 64, for instance), and in the *Basic Problems of Phenomenology* from 1927. To understand Heidegger, we need to recognize that idealist heritage, even as he rejected the abstract transcendental method of Husserl and the accompanying transcendental Ego. From the standpoint of Doull's dialectic, it can appear that the phenomenology of *Sein und Zeit* is an incoherent position: the effort of the natural and particular self to absorb the ideal self and to express it in all its universality, rationality, and truth. Can Heidegger be defended at this point?

Doull is right to criticize *Sein und Zeit* as particularist or naturalist in its uncertainty about logic, or *logos,* or universal reason – Heidegger seems to have only factual historical languages at his disposal, no truly universalist account of thought, even though such an account would seem to be required by the project of a phenomenology of Dasein, its world, and being itself.[9] There is little reason to think that, if a phenomenology is utterly committed to and immersed in the particularity of a given historical language, it could ever fulfil the scientific task it sets for itself. Here is one of Heidegger's early dilemmas, and it showed itself clearly in his ongoing dialogue with Husserl. Husserl was suspicious of Heidegger's 'fundamental ontology' focused on Dasein. For Husserl, this constituted a relapse into naturalism and psychologism. The interaction between Husserl and Heidegger can be found in many documents of the time: one of the most illuminating is found in volume 9 of Husserl's collected works.[10] According to Husserl, First Philosophy ought to free itself, not only from hasty ontological commitments, but also from any psychological or existential account of the philosophizing Ego. Thus we see, in the volume edited by Biemel, that when Husserl was working with Heidegger in 1927 in a joint effort to produce an article on phenomenology for the *Encyclopaedia Britannica,* Husserl's drafts of the article repeatedly sought to establish a pure and ideal consciousness, distinct from the historical and psychological ego, as the fundamental principle of phenomenology. The drafts by Heidegger, by contrast, which Husserl ultimately rejected, sought always to attribute this 'consciousness' to a historical and embodied Dasein.[11] For Husserl, Heidegger's account of the historicity of Dasein brought a contamination of the philosophical domain – here history was constituting us, whereas Husserl's transcendental method insisted that, at all costs, it must be ourselves who constitute history. It is also well known that, in a conversation with Karl Löwith in Rome in 1936, Heidegger said that the doctrine of historicity in *Sein und Zeit* was the link that tied it to his National Socialist activity in the 1930s.[12]

Yet it would not be right to interpret *Being and Time* mainly as a vindication of a 'historical' self or a 'natural' self – rather this self, which is assuredly finite in its historical and natural life, is being thought here above all as the discloser of being. In place of any account of an ideal self, we have Heidegger's question as to the *being* of Dasein, and the question as to the meaning of being as such. If we look in Heidegger for clues as to his ultimate topic, we shall be led, not to any self or spirit at all, but rather to being, the being of beings, and the meaning of being.

Heidegger's question of being was introduced into a context of modern philosophy (and a modern state), but the question as he understood it was not a particularly modern question. Years of immersion in Aristotelian studies had defined for Heidegger his question of being, and it is no accident that *Sein und Zeit* opens by quoting a key passage from Plato's *Sophist* probing a question about being. In later times that question had 'subsided as a theme for actual investigation' (*Being and Time,* 1), and yet Heidegger offers evidence that Augustine, Aquinas, Descartes, Kant, Hegel, and recent authors had become entangled in difficulties by leaving indeterminate 'what you actually mean by the expression "being"' (*Sophist,* 244a – quoted on the opening page of *Being and Time*). His work is raised above the level of mere 'technical' or 'analytical' philosophy because of the hypothesis that gives him his start – that we all possess a pre-ontological understanding of being, which is no mere command over certain concepts and words, but is our opening to being and being's self-manifestation to us, a togetherness of *Sein* and *Dasein.* It is this coupling of *Dasein* and *Sein* that stands in the place where Doull had hoped to find a natural self together with an ideal self. What makes Heidegger different from Husserl is not merely his rejection of the transcendental Ego, but his indication that being is close to us, and yet enigmatic and in need of questioning. I am convinced that this ontological position of *Dasein* differentiates Heidegger from Nietzsche and all naturalisms, even if, in 1927, its political meaning remained still obscure.

3. The Middle Heidegger

Let us look next at Heidegger at a somewhat later stage, that of his National Socialist commitment. Under the influence of National Socialism, Heidegger takes account of a wider community than the individual authentic Dasein, but it is still a particularistic one, a *Volk* which knows itself above all through its particular language.[13] There is some accord between the phenomenology of *Sein und Zeit* and the political writings of the 1930s: it seems they both overstress the one self at the expense of the other. In addition, Heidegger is now polemical against the church, and proclaims with Nietzsche the death of God.[14]

But in this period, Heidegger does undertake to engage with the state: in 1933–4, he offered a seminar, together with a Freiburg professor of law, on Hegel's *Philosophy of Right* (though hitherto no protocols have appeared from that occasion.) The rectoral address of 1933 contains the outline of a philosophy of the state. It is un-Hegelian, and closer to Herder and the Romantics in that the *Volk* is its substratum: one and the same entity exists, first of all as a *Volk,* then as a state (*Staat*), and then as a nation (*Nation*). The *Volk* is defined essentially by language (it is not a race, *Rasse*) and by the communities of labour and family, building and dwelling.[15] The state is that institution whereby the *Volk* comes to know itself, in a knowledge accomplished by way of deliberation and especially decision: the state is where the *Volk* is capable of self-assertion, which is the condition for self-government and self-knowledge.[16] The nation is the same entity regarded in the long vista of history: it is the guardian of trophies, memorials, and defeats, the subject of pride and shame, it is the record of soldiers, conquerors, and heroes. The being of the nation is expressed in fate and destiny, the ultimate categories of history.[17] The actual purpose of the rectoral address, I think, was to inject the resolute questioning of academia into the midst of the state, sharpening the self-knowledge of the *Volk*. The power of *Geist*, intellect, which alone can guide the strengths of a people, is expressed in the decisions of the state. Of course, Heidegger's initiative failed, and one could express this by saying that the Nazis had even less of a philosophy of the state than Heidegger did. All they wanted was a racial *Volk*, with symbols of the nation employed by a *Führer*. So in the vista of Doull's dialectic, should we say that Heidegger's 1933 conception of the state was the expression in thought of the current actuality of the state as the National Socialist state? Was philosophy, in this case, its age comprehended in thought? I must say – if it is not an affront to true dialectic – that in this case the thought was better than the age.

Of course the age was worse than anyone at the time could have known: the true horrors of National Socialism could still hardly be suspected. The inner heart of Nazism was, I suppose, a thirst for revenge, the determination to punish those who were thought to have caused Germany's collapse. It was led by men of the same generation as Heidegger's, for whom the *only* self was a natural self, in its blood and its egoism. Even the brownshirts, however, had not surmised the immeasurable depth of hatred and malice in their Führer's heart. What they all wrought goes beyond any harm and damage that a 'natural self' might be thought capable of. For my part, I think of these deeds, the Holocaust, in a Christian perspective: it was the devil and all his angels busy with their work. We admire those who resisted National Socialism even in its early stages, but we do so without imputing to them the power to gaze into the future. We admire and respect the judgment that Nazism was wrong when the evidence was barely there how very wrong it was. Heidegger is not among that group. But neither was he among the crowd of bullies who constituted the active part of the Nazi party. He *sought* to introduce into the Nazi discourse some principle of intelligence, knowledge, and, perhaps, even justice, in the doctrine of the state in his rectoral address. The power of collective decision is clearly assigned here to the state. We know that Heidegger failed, and, moreover, that he regretted his complicity. The account he gave later of these events[18] should not be read as statements of a defiant self-vindication, but as a chastened report to posterity. He has been judged too harshly by those who have commented on his work, though it is evident that Doull is not one who condemns Heidegger this way in retrospect, like such authors as Victor Farias, Tom Rockmore, and Richard Wolin.[19]

It appears strange on the Doullian view that, after his own political catastrophe, Heidegger did not undertake to study seriously the philosophy of the state, whether in Plato and Aristotle, in Renaissance and modern authors, or in Fichte and Hegel. Nor did his lived experience of history lead Heidegger to an engagement with dialectical philosophy. He moved first of all to the poetry of Hölderlin, and subsequently to a lengthy study of Nietzsche and his metaphysics. One might be tempted to see a merely bohemian, existentialist distaste for real politics and economics in the middle Heidegger, yet I think that would not do him justice: he did give profound thought to questions of state and politics.

In the rectoral address, he broadened his view of human existence away from the singular individual at least to the *national* community (admittedly, not to the international scene). But this national community, for all Heidegger's rhetoric of struggle and force, is not seen as having the power simply to impose its will on its surroundings. The self-assertion of each nation is met in the end by the power of fate and destiny, the arbiter of history, by comparison to which the nation's power must yield. That is the meaning of his quotation from Aeschylus's *Prometheus*, which he renders 'Knowing is less mighty by far than necessity.'[20] As I read the text, fate and destiny (i.e., history in its ultimate constitution) stand over against each singular national community in the same relation as being does to the individual Dasein in *Being and Time*. And as the decade of the thirties ran its own fateful way, Heidegger continued to resist the national worship of the *Volk*. He continued to see the folkish ideology of the Nazis as the ultimate false version of subjectivism. This is all well documented by the text on which he worked privately in the late thirties, now published as *Contributions to Philosophy*.[21] He speaks throughout the work in a mood of melancholy, lamenting nationalist triumphalism, the link of politics and racism, the reduction of art and thought to folkish 'culture,' and the glorification of conflict. The book concludes with the vista of the possible opening of humankind to the promptings of being, now seen in the guise of the *Ereignis* (that virtually untranslatable term that Heidegger's translators now render as 'en-owning'). These are all enigmatic thoughts, and the work as a whole has that character, but nothing is clearer than Heidegger's horror at the spectacle of technologically enhanced displays of mass subjectivity. Indeed, I think the dialectic of modernity showed its most malignant face in the terrible 1930s. Like many other intellectuals, Heidegger was trapped on one side of a vast and gruesome process – not imprisoned in a Nazi camp, to be sure, like many powerless persons, but trapped nevertheless in a world process of which he could not gain a complete view.

4. The Late Heidegger

Doull understands the late Heidegger to be insisting that the true and universal interests of humanity in our age cannot be found in a system of administration, bureaucracy, cost–benefit analysis, micro-management, production quotas, and competition incentives.[22] This indeed, and much else, is what Heidegger called *Technik*. Rather, our true interest is to live a life according to the multiform disclosures of language, a poetic life lived with other mortals under the sky where the gods have their dwelling.[23]

Doull is not well disposed to these poetic longings expressed by the late Heidegger. The issue is brought to a head by way of the concept of the state. Doull insists that our existence is properly in a real, actual state and other real, actual institutions that 'exist primarily in a practical thought,' and that our existence is not to be found primarily 'in the language and fancy of poets.'[24] Moreover, according to Doull, this later thought of Heidegger is the characteristic expression of a Europe that has begun to transfer state authority to the European Union, while still maintaining the languages and cultures of its ancient *patriae*. For post-modern Europeans, moreover, Christianity is interesting just as long as nobody believes it, and the nation is important as long as it has no power. Doull even visualizes a post-Christian European church where hermeneutics would mediate to its members a non-binding religion of merely finite gods.[25] And Heidegger is the philosopher of this culture! Doull's is a strong reproach.

What then should one say? Is it possible to defend the later work of Heidegger from this reproach? One possibility of a reply might be this: it can seem that, today, the machinery of government and even law has become utterly intertwined with the bureaucracy, the management, the system – what Heidegger called *Technik*. Doull's view, I think, is that that is not possible. He would say, I think, that the 'real, actual state' of post-modernity is something more than the system of management and incentives that is Heidegger's *Technik.* Perhaps Doull sees even in the post-modern state the image of a nobler state, the Platonic-Aristotelian state, perhaps, or the Hegelian state. Perhaps the state in its idea is still operative today in Canada and other countries of the West. If that is the case, then, Doull can argue that we ought to have expected something better, something of that idea, from a philosopher like Heidegger. There are points where Doull seems to invoke a Platonic-Aristotelian idea of the state, seemingly presented as the *true* idea of the state. He speaks at the start of the 'complete society,' and claims that actual, that is, true states 'exist primarily in a practical thought which unites the universal and sensible immediacy.'[26] At points as well, he invokes the Hegelian terminology of an ethical life comprehending family, civil society, and state in an intelligible order. So he may believe that this ideal is actual in our times, and was in earlier times. Nevertheless, the following challenge might be put to Doull: perhaps the current reality of the state really does not incarnate in any credible degree the true idea of the state as the great tradition of philosophy conceived it. We would need a fuller investigation to determine this question. But my appeal to Doull would be that, surely, one could *not* go so far as to claim that *if* post-modernity gives us nothing better than a government of administration, micro-management, etc. (i.e., the Heideggerian *Technik*), then our true and universal interests would *still* lie more with *that* state than with a poetic life lived under a god-filled sky. If Heidegger *were* right in seeing the state as part of *Technik, das Ge-Stell,* it would not be here that our true interests are found. I am in agreement with Doull, if I understand him correctly, that the Platonic-Aristotelian, view, and the Hegelian view, are better than what came after them. But what if reality were in discord with Platonic, Aristotelian and Hegelian philosophy?

Heidegger's relative silence, in his first and third periods, on the question of the state is indeed regrettable. But we might seek to probe behind this relative silence, and learn if there are reasons for it, by following the dialectic of modernity that Doull has sketched for us. Doull has been speaking of a divided self in the nineteenth century, then of an open clash between the natural self and the ideal self in the twentieth century. If we are to conduct a further discussion about the state I do not think that Doull would object to substituting a different concept for that of the self; so let us follow Hegel and consider the state as an expression of *will.* We would then consider that the *will* was divided in the nineteenth century, inwardly and not openly, between a natural will and an ideal will. The outward clash of the twentieth century was that between a natural will exemplified by the Nazi state and an ideal will exemplified by the Communist state. We must not suppose that these were the only antagonists, and in particular we must recognize that the ideal will was certainly expressed by many governments and states that were socialist, social-democratic, or liberal. They legislated for freedom, for justice, and for welfare.

But there is a further dialectical possibility that I would like to look into, which I shall call the degeneration of the ideal will. In a general way, this idea is familiar to everyone. It has guided countless programs for reform and revolution that were aimed against previous governments and institutions, with a rallying cry against corruption. But very often, corruption meant that the ideal will had been overcome by a natural will: corruption in office driven by greed, party spirit, and so on. The further possibility that I mean here, however, is a degeneration in the ideal will, arising not from the temptations of the natural will but from an excess of idealism, a possible degeneracy of the ideal will *as such*, degeneration *as* the ideal will. There is a familiar transition, in which the will, as an *ideal* will, begins with the intent to provide some benefit or accomplish some good. It then undertakes to streamline, instrumentalize, and universalize this benefit, and, if that takes some bureaucracy or even a bit of coercion to accomplish the end, then so be it. This is the point where legislation is introduced, and therewith we provide the personnel and 'infrastructure' to accomplish the end. Yet there are both public consequences and moral consequences.

(a) The project of *legislating for freedom* can yield a thicket of guarantees for privacy and for private property, regulations for the conduct of elections and public meetings, citizenship rules, defined rights for patients, prisoners, students, and so on. This is a *legalism* that has a *moral equivalent* in our everyday life, where we show an obsession with personal autonomy (today often called 'getting control' or 'my power') and a generalized indifference, egoism, what we now call possessive individualism.

(b) The project of *legislating for justice* can yield a thicket of regulations for human rights, rights of specific groups, judicial and procedural regulations, and so on. This *procedural* methodology has its everyday *moral equivalent* too: sticking up for 'my' rights and 'our' rights; suing your doctor and your lawyer; denouncing your old teachers and priests on television; and so on.

(c) The project of *legislating for welfare* can yield a virtually infinite bureaucracy of social work, intervention, payments, redevelopment, redistribution, affirmative action, and employment equity. As the *moral equivalent* I see a utilitarianism, for which the point is to deliver the goods and never mind too much about how we live and interact as persons. Better a rude and patronizing official than none at all.

And I am suggesting not only that these forms of degeneracy are evident all around us today, but that they represent a degenerative process in the state, in the ideal will. They signify the degeneration of the state into *Technik*. After the transition in which we 'instrumentalize' the benefits, there is no remedy for the self-righteousness that infects that person or office who is providing a benefit. When we put procedures like these in place, we become immune to that dialogue or encounter with another human being – now the 'client'! – where our own human motives might have been put into question by that human being. The degeneration is just the point in the dialectic where the ideal will, expressed in a state, can make the transition to a universal regime of *Technik*. Admittedly, *Technik* also consists of science and production, but the transition I describe is the degeneration of the *state* into *Technik*.

Presumably it is Doull's position that degenerations like this are to be expected from time to time in an imperfect world, but that the true visage of justice, the idea of the state, is still intact, not degenerated but imperfectly administered. What is actual is rational. This would be one territory where the issue between Doull and Heidegger could be pursued. What Heidegger proposed in his early work was, of course, not a dialectic, but a phenomenology, of Dasein: its theme was Dasein's being as a whole, especially in view of its alternative possibilities for inauthenticity and authenticity. It was not devoted to the political life in particular. But in this early period, Heidegger insisted that the regime of 'the public' and *das Man* does actually constitute our daily life – and this degenerate will I have been speaking of would be the *Verfallen*, the 'falling prey' of Dasein. Nor was the authentic will a hidden condition, already existing, for this 'falling prey' – only a possibility lying in the future.

Heidegger's later work certainly continued the questioning about being, although there was a change of terminology, an effort, on the whole, to speak in a simpler language. But it is still his view, I think, that the foreground and the present age are actually constituted by forces of inauthenticity, which, in their accumulated power as *Technik*, have reached deep into social life, political life, and even into the individual psyche. Our North American society offers ample evidence of the reach of medical technology, even into human reproduction; of electronic technology, so that today everyone tries to look like television characters; of cybernetic technology, to the extent that you can hardly borrow a library book if you can't use e-mail.

Doull wonders whether this question of being ever received an answer, and refers to late texts, *Zeit und Sein*, for instance, which appear to him unsatisfactory in this respect.[27] They do seem to be texts which, whenever they succeed in making statements, generate ever further questions. That is perhaps characteristic of Heidegger's later thought, that it does not terminate in authoritative formulations. Some will praise that kind of thought, others will dismiss it. For my own part, it is not precisely the indecision and lack of closure that I welcome in Heidegger. He does not seem capable of authoritative formulations about being. If he were able to do that, it would be most welcome to me. But short of that, I find in his writing a closeness to the subject matter of thought and a power to let us see 'the things themselves' (see especially *Being and Time*, sect. 7). His texts exhibit the characteristics that express his own interpretation of truth: disclosure, unconcealedness – the positive fruit of a philosophy that lives within the coupling of *Dasein* with *Sein*.

In conclusion, I might suggest that, while Heidegger's thought is not the culmination of the dialectic of modernity – probably there will be none – it does belong within that dialectic, showing one possibility that remains open to us to disclose the being and truth of all things.

Notes

1 See 'Heidegger and the State' (above), 360.

2 Ibid., 363–4.

3 Ibid., 364.

4 K. Marx and F. Engels, *Manifesto of the Communist Party* [1848], reprinted in *The Marx-Engels Reader*, 2nd ed., ed. R.C. Tucker (New York: Norton, 1978), 475.

5 See above, 370.

6 Ibid., 363–4.

7 Ibid., 357.

8 Ibid., 366.

9 Ibid., 366–7.

10 Edmund Husserl, *Phänomenologische Psychologie* (*Husserliana Band IX*), ed. W. Biemel (The Hague: Nihjhoff, 1968).

11 Ibid., 237–301. The details of the interaction of the two phenomenologists, and Ludwig Landgrebe, are laid out in the 'Text-Critical Appendix,' 590–615. I have offered an overview of this failed effort at cooperation in *Seeing and Reading* (Atlantic Highlands, NJ: Humanities Press, 1984; now reprinted in Amherst, NY: Humanity Books, 1989), 117–22.

12 One documentation for this is available in Thomas Sheehan, 'Reading a Life,' in *The Cambridge Companion to Heidegger*, ed. C. Guignon (Cambridge: Cambridge University Press, 1993), 85–6.

13 See my article 'The Politics of Heidegger's Rectoral Address,' *Man and World* 20 (1987): 171–87, where I maintain that, in his 1933 rectoral address in Freiburg University, Heidegger conceived a *Volk* as constituted by its language rather than by any biological characteristics.

14 *Die Selbstbehauptung der deutschen Universität* [1933], now published under the editorship of H. Heidegger (Frankfurt: Klostermann, 1983), 13; English trans. K. Harries, *Review of Metaphysics* 38 (1985): 474.

15 *Selbstbehauptung*, 13–16; Eng. trans., 474–6.

16 See my 'Heidegger's Rectoral Address,' 175–6.

17 *Selbstbehauptung*, 15–16; trans., 477.

18 'The Rectorate: Facts and Thoughts,' trans. K. Harries, *Review of Metaphysics* 38 (1985): 481–502; see also the *Spiegel* interview, now available in *The Heidegger Controversy*, ed. R. Wolin (Cambridge, Mass.: MIT Press, 1993).

19 See *The Heidegger Controversy*.

20 *Selbstbehauptung*, 11; trans. 472.

21 *Beiträge zur Philosophie* (Frankfurt: Klostermann, 1989).

22 See above, 357, 367.

23 See essays such as 'The Thing' and 'Building Dwelling Thinking' in M. Heidegger, *Poetry Language Thought*, trans. A. Hofstadter (New York: Harper, 1970).

24 Ibid., 357.

25 Ibid., 359.

26 Ibid., 357.

27 Ibid., 367–9.

chapter nine

The Philosophical Basis of Constitutional Discussion in Canada[1]

The present constitutional crisis in Canada resembles that of the United States in the interval between gaining its independence and the discovery and ratification of the constitution which was to give stability to its revolution. The 'patriation' of the Canadian constitution did away with the last remnant of colonial dependence on Great Britain. We have not yet on our own discovered an acceptable formulation of our most difficult constitutional problem – how communities of a British and a French culture can constitute one political community without subordination or assimilation. The thirteen former colonies would have sunk into impotence had they not found a constitution expressive of a common political loyalty stronger than all divisive interests, a common loyalty which could accommodate loyalties to particular sovereign communities. Canada likewise will not long survive as one state unless we can define constitutionally the common loyalty and attachment of both historic peoples and cultures – a loyalty which can coincide with an undiminished loyalty to particular sovereignties.

The differences are of course very great between our crisis and that of Americans after the War of Independence. We do not have to replace with a new sovereignty a former sovereignty which we have rejected. For us, after 'patriation,' the question is whether Canada is capable of an internal political unity, on its own and without reference to a third party. We have a federation which works better and more to the satisfaction of its citizens than most states. Quebec and other Canadians have had a common political formation in which as we passed from colonial dependence to complete independence we made our own the developing democratic freedom of the most advanced states.

Thus the patriation of the Canadian constitution might seem little more than a formality. Or the 1982 amendment with the charter and an amending formula might be thought sufficient to give Canadians a sense that the constitution was their own. The 'bilingualism' of an elite would allow a common Canadian spirit to break through the isolation of the two linguistic communities. The experience of the following fifteen years has shown that Trudeau's reforms are no more than the beginning of a true patriation, that is, the discovering of an internal unity and common loyalty adequate even to sovereign differences. The 1995 referendum makes evident the limits of Trudeauism.

To discover the basis of a unified Canadian sovereignty is more difficult in two respects than the formidable task of the American founders. The member states of the American union had all a common culture and political tradition. We have to find a constitution and political loyalty freely acceptable to peoples of two of the great European cultures, at home ever more or less antagonistic to each other. Secondly, Americans had in the British constitution of the time a model which with certain modifications served to define their freedom. The European Union is often seen by Canadians as a model in one way or another for a new federation. How the model might apply to Canadians who, European in culture, are also North Americans has not been explained.

Those who designed the institutions of the American republic were often well acquainted with the French culture of the time. Americans in their subsequent development have drawn also on other European cultures and can with reason regard themselves as heirs to the whole European tradition, however much they continue to be regarded by some Europeans as barbarians. But their borrowings have been of a primarily British and empirical orientation. They have not had to accommodate on its own the more intellectual spirit of French culture. In the European Union the British and French with other peoples have submitted partially to common institutions. But in this relation they also maintain the illusion that they are as before independent nation states. Such a relation of the two peoples as exists imperfectly in Canada, and threatens to dissolve, is without precedent.

The European Union is an unlikely model for Canadians looking to find an internal unity or an actual sovereignty, in which there can be substantial agreement about amendments to our primary political institutions. Both separatists and federalists in Canada tend to a rather superficial view of the union. To the one party it appears to confirm a conviction that a small Francophone community in Quebec could on its own do quite well in a world of continental and global economic associations. The other party learns from the union that closed national communities are an impediment to success in the new economic order and must give way to a culture of equal individuals having common rights and freedoms – among which is the right to be part of a linguistic community. Both parties derive from that model an aversion to the authoritarian structure of the nation state in the time of its independence. The model draws Canadians into the disintegration of the European nation states and the uncertain emergence of a common state. In no way does it illustrate how Canada in North America might understand and define institutionally its difference from the United States which has not, as the European states, lost a confidence that it can order its own affairs and maintain a dominant role in world politics. Separatists assume in an independent Quebec a unified political will, not to be derived from the European model.

The true implication of patriation is that we have to give up looking to Europe as a model and guide to the independence whether of Canada or Quebec. It is still a species of colonialism when now the European Union takes the place of the British Empire or a Catholic France. Like the former American colonies we have to modify and make our own the political formation we have received in the course of a long colonial dependence.

It is possible in the manner of nationalist historians to regard the history of Quebec as essentially the development of New France to its destined completion as an independent French nation state in North America. The Conquest and the two centuries and a half of English domination can appear as an episode which the Quebec people lived through, intact in its inner core and able since the Quiet Revolution to prove its inner strength in economic, political, and cultural achievements. If the English power assured to the Quebec nation its survival, that power was ever also a threat against which it must find security in itself. The time has evidently come in this view when the English relation is no longer necessary to Quebec, virtually irrelevant unless for common economic advantages.

A parallel narration of Canadian history from the side of the other 'nation' has often been told. From colony Canada has developed to the point where it is an independent replica of post-imperial Britain. Part of the story is also of the weakness of this Anglo-Canadian nationalism; confronted by the forces of a continental or global economy it laments impotently its passing. There is not the confidence of separatists in Quebec that a balance can be found between national particularity and economic union with the United States.

It is hard to bring down to earth the idea of Canada as 'two nations,' to envisage them as actually existing. They are abstractions which have no existence unless in European conditions. Were the history of the 'two nations' such as nationalists recount, they would already have separated painlessly enough, seeing mutual benefit and little loss in their separation. But it is inexplicable on that view that a majority of Quebecers remain attached to Canada. Of this the recent referendum is the most obvious proof. A deceptive question and a campaign of historical distortions were not enough. It was enough that the federalists presented only an abstract choice between Canada and independence. And Canada in that choice was defined in the manner of Trudeau as the economic individualistic antithesis to nationalism; a choice so defined makes nationalists of many who know its dangers.

That Canada after patriation should be more than a contest between antithetical aspects of the European Union has a certain recognition in the argument often made by Lucien Bouchard, an argument which reflects his own experience and perhaps a continuing difficulty with fiercer and more abstract nationalists. The first choice of Quebecers, the argument runs, would be to remain in a Canada where there was an equality and mutual recognition of the two peoples. Successive attempts to obtain such recognition have been rejected by English Canadians, who appear to have no understanding of what is sought. Independence is the only remaining option.

The weakness of this argument is obvious enough. Strictly speaking there has been but one serious attempt to accommodate Quebec in the patriated constitution – that of the Meech Lake Accord. That Accord might be said to be post-colonial in that it sought a reconciliation in a deepened understanding of the relation of sovereign provinces to one another and to the federal sovereignty. It was the beginning at least of such an understanding. That the Accord looked in the right direction for a reconciliation of the two peoples is amply proven by the vehement reaction of Quebecers at its rejection and by the consistent finding of repeated opinion polls that a strong majority would support a solution along these lines. The defeat of the Meech Lake Accord only proves that no other course than separation remains if one can assume that English Canadians are incorrigibly wedded to the Trudeauite liberalism that destroyed the Accord from within and then externally by the agency of

Clyde Wells. It was destroyed from within when Brian Mulroney, more skilled as a mediator than in his grasp of what was mediated, allowed to be associated with the Accord a concoction of demands of another inspiration proposed by Frank McKenna. The Accord in itself was no doubt ambiguous, read differently by many in Quebec and English Canada. Trudeauites, seeing disguised nationalism in it, opposed it consistently from their standpoint. What the other Canada is capable of towards Quebec is not evident in its defeat.

Joe Clark's subsequent attempt at a reconciliation was a mishmash of discordant elements in which neither community could recognize itself. The basic structure of the Charlottetown Accord, if it can be said to have a structure, conceived Canada as a plurality of cultures within a common economy. The two historic peoples receded into the background; what was said of their relation made no sense in that context. The proposed Accord is not, however, without value in that it spelled out rather fully for Canadians the implications of the European model. For the latter's representation of the elements of such a union – of many communities united in one economy – is fictitious when applied to Canada. So far as anything is proven by the defeat of this proposal, it is that such a juxtaposition of nationalism and economic individualism appeared alien to most Canadians.

What is true in the assertion that all attempts at reconciliation have failed is at most this, that a reconciliation on the basis of the European model is not possible, that we have to move beyond the residual colonialism which to this point has largely controlled the constitutional argument since patriation. Lévesque and Trudeau deserve to be honoured by all Canadians, not exactly for what they directly intended, but for bringing the argument to this provisional conclusion. René Lévesque, though as a nationalist he advanced arguments pertinent to a European context, was, as well as a citizen of a free Quebec, a North American. As such he could take *le beau risque*, he could collaborate with the premiers of other provinces in their opposition to a unilateral patriation. He could also be seduced from that alliance because of the instability of his relation to it.

Mr Bouchard, taking a like risk, found himself deeply distressed at its apparent failure; so with others whom Mulroney persuaded to give federalism a chance. The conclusion that separation is the only course remaining rests on personal feeling and a misreading of certain events. It has no general cogency. The well-founded conclusion from recent Canadian history is rather, as indicated, that the reconciliation of the two peoples, implied and demanded in patriation, is to be found neither in nationalism nor in economic individualism, as conceived in the European model. There is not only a separate history of Quebec and another of a British 'nation'; there is also a common Canadian history more basic than either of these abstractions. Quebec is not externally related to the Canadian federation, from which it might extract itself at will on the assumption that it is the replica of a European nation state. The vitality and survival of a French people in North America require that through its culture it be engaged in the history and the problems of the continent, and not be at home save in economic relations only within the confines of a linguistic community. So long as the two peoples were in a colonial relation to Europe, they might be federated but their common relations to the federation could not but be distorted and more or less concealed. Superimposed on it was a divergent relation to a European centre. In recent years the British Empire in the one case, Catholic France in the other, have given way to a common relation to the European Union, as that in which the British and French peoples would find a stability they no longer have in themselves. This mode of dependency too must break down before the two peoples can find a common centre which is their own in their North American setting.

This post-colonial colonialism, so to speak, continues to inform the relation of Ottawa to the separatist government in Quebec. The antithetical positions in which this ultimate dependence is expressed are perhaps in both cases in course of revision. The federal government after the 1995 referendum can no long adhere to a pure Trudeauism. The referendum has also made evident that the pure separatism of Parizeau cannot prevail. In neither case is more than the semblance of revision possible without going beyond the European model from which they are derived. We are at a point of uncommon difficulty, where, as the Americans two centuries ago, we have to define our independence constitutionally, in our case in conformity with the sense the two peoples have of their own freedom.

There is need to be clear why neither an independent nation state in Quebec – or in other parts of Canada – nor the antithetical form of a basically economic union is a real possibility for Canadians. Against these opposed positions and their application to Canada there are two fatal objections: the first is that there are no longer in Europe nation states such as the separatist supposes; the second that in North America there are not, and never have been, nation states. The Trudeauite position succumbs to the same argument.

1. The European Union

The Quiet Revolution in Quebec was contemporaneous with a shift in Canada generally as to the ends of government and the rights and reasonable expectations of individuals in relation to the state. Largely through the agency of the federal government the network of social programs was established which are an important element in the attachment of Canadians to their common government. Canada became a social democratic state in line with the more enlightened European states and distinct in new ways from the United States. For English Canadians also there was a Quiet Revolution, which remains even if some give in too much to an American conservatism or to the pressures of a global economy.

In Quebec the revolution began at a different point than in the other Canada, out of the aversion of a church-oriented society to the seductions of a modern industrial economy. The result was generally the same in both cases, if one allows for cultural differences in the attitude of individuals to government.

The revolution from older and more limited concepts of individual rights to the idea that the general well-being of individuals is the direct concern of governments is not in itself nationalistic. The revolutions of the seventeenth and eighteenth centuries had obtained the right of individuals to pursue their reasonable interests freely and rights to legal and political equality. The European states as reconstituted after the ruin of the French Revolution had implicit in them a deeper revolution in which the state in collaboration with the democratic will of its members undertakes also to correct the abuses of a free economy and to secure to individuals essential human goods to a tolerable level.

The states so humanized in the course of the last and the present centuries were particular peoples. Universal rights were realized and understood variously according to the characteristic temper and mentality of the European peoples. States so constituted are appropriately called nation states, a designation which suits less well earlier forms of the European state.

Quebec nationalists equate the Quebec which has resulted from the Quiet Revolution with such a nation state; Quebec as part of the Canadian federation appears as an incomplete or improper state. It has not a full sovereignty of its own. But the Europe to which they look for a model is also part of an economic and political union. In those relations the nation is no longer a sovereign state simply but has imparted something of its sovereignty to these larger associations. There thus would recur apparently for Quebec something of the same contraction of sovereignty as it suffers in the Canadian federation.

There is a difficulty in the concept of a nation state. It is at the same time a particular national community having its own language, customs, animation, exclusive of other such communities, and is founded on universal human rights which are not abstract but pervade the whole range of its interests. The difficulty of this relation, long felt by those who live in the French or British state, may escape the eye of an external observer who sees only the ordered freedom of a particular people, a model to which his own people tend as the fulfilment of their history. A young Lucien Bouchard, as many another, admired the heroic figures of Churchill and de Gaulle who in a critical time drew their peoples from deep divisions to receive for a little the spirit of their institutions.

During the nineteenth century and until the First World War the political division of the universal and the natural and particular elements of the European state was in general held in check. In the French state, to say of it what may be said *mutatis mutandis* of the British or German state, there were radical divisions, but submerged in the attachment of the people to their sovereign state, which asserted the universality of French culture in an empire comprising many peoples and regimes. The collision of the European imperial states in the First World War made evident the human cost of greatness. Individuals fell back on themselves; the union of nationality and universal rights was shattered. In its place emerged a divided and antagonistic relation to nation and to universal humanity. The political life of all the nation states was dominated by an opposition of nationalistic and socialist parties.[2] In the one part individuals sought an intuitive relation of their national particularity to the state through a supposedly inspired leader. In the other the inspired leader would guide them to the satisfaction of their desires in a perfected economy which took the place of the state. In both forms the universality of an older European world was pulled down to earth and centred in the individual, as worker or as member of a national community.

The Second World War made evident what was in these opposed forms and the tenuous relation they provided of individuals to the rational freedom of culture and tradition. The reaction of individuals from the ruin these forms had brought upon them was a still deeper flight from the authority of political and other institutions. In the medium of language was sought a community anterior to the tyranny of thought and the universal. Language might be taken in a fragmented and empirical form (Wittgenstein) or as inspired and unified poetical utterance (Heidegger). But the pre-rational community sought in language was before long subject to its own 'deconstruction.' The community of individuals in the medium of language was found illusory. In truth, endless division or difference stood in the way of community.

A pleiad of writers in France have drawn out these ultimate consequences of founding the universality of a people and culture on its exclusive particularity. Thus, 'deconstruction' makes evident, if not to themselves, to an observer why the European states had need of a political union, if individuals were to have a basis of community beyond endless diversity in relation to themselves and others.[3]

The constitutions of European states as revised after the Second World War are normally prefaced by such a charter of individual rights as was added to the Canadian Constitution in the 1982 amendment. The experience of the European states as sketched makes evident that these rights, if they be regarded as predicated of the members of a particular linguistic and cultural community as such, are contingent only – not 'inalienable,' as in the older American or French declarations. Rights were predicated formerly of individuals in virtue of their common rationality. According to the latest European thought such individuals do not exist. Rather, one should say, they only exist so far as a common state and community is given priority over particular national communities.

Europeans, for all anyone can know, may continue indefinitely in an ambiguity where now the Union, now the member states appear prior. So the Union through its institutions appears empowered to act as a state. But its actions only take effect so far as the particular states can bargain their way to agreement. A Thatcher or Chirac can gratify national sentiment by acting as though their countries were still nation states – sovereign in a strict and older sense. One knows how to take such shows of independence.

The Union allows to Europeans a sense of the freedom they do not have in their national communities. It provides at least an abstract relation to a common culture. The Union is necessary to contemporary Europeans, but not much loved by them. In all member states there is a nationalist element that would be free of Union. What part of Quebec separatists, situated in a like Union, would be of that party? Is there a right of separation from the Union? Countries joined often by the vote of a small majority. They are only bound to the Union by treaty. A like small majority would seem adequate ground for terminating the treaty.

But it is an abuse of language to call the power to revert to an independence no longer possible a right. To encourage such a reversion can only be the work of a faction, not of a unified people.

The argument given is more easily grasped when one has considered the difference of North American from European states: as not founded on nationality they need not succumb to the logic which has made the nation state obsolete as the primary form of political community. The conclusion stands: the European nation state no longer exists. It continues only as subordinated to a common European state.

2. The North American States

There are no nation states in North America.[4] By the time of the discovery and occupation of the Americas the political institutions which had taken shape in Europe on the ruins of the Roman Empire and beyond its boundaries had in some cases attained the unity and stability of a state. The several European peoples who took part in this great work of discovery and occupation might be called nation states, though they were still far from that fusion of sovereignty and nationality which they would come to after the French Revolution. They had reached or were approaching a point where feudal divisions were brought firmly under the unified sovereignty of monarchs. In their common relation to a monarch, individuals were not nobles or commoners first but Englishmen, Frenchmen, or of whatever nation – even though the dynastic and other interests of the monarch might diverge from and be destructive of the interests of his subjects. There was not yet room within that sovereignty for a civic and economic freedom and the right to participate on equal terms in the various goods of society.

The political institutions which these nation states built in the New World were not simply replicas of those they lived in at home. Immigrants might indeed take themselves to be exiles condemned to live in savage and unformed lands.[5] But if they would have for themselves in America the ordered life they knew at home, they and their descendants had to build this order on a new ground. They had to subdue the wilderness, so that it would serve their needs and desires, and at length beyond these works of necessity to fashion a cultivated life not borrowed but their own. They brought with them the religions, institutions, culture of a particular European people. This model was receptive of further developments in the original but what they built in the light of this model was another and freer relation to it than was possible for those who had remained in Europe.

Those who had migrated to America could not revert to the state of a Germanic tribe which knew its culture in the medium of language and custom, not also in the common medium of thought. They had behind them the long formation by which they had brought together the inner world of belief and thought and their relation to nature.[6] The humanistic and afterwards the rational-scientific culture of the modern age addressed itself to individuals as human and only secondarily as of a particular nation and language. That culture, as modified by the particular bent and character of the several European peoples who had part in the occupation was the model for the new beginning in the Americas.

First in this construction is not to build a particular nation but to establish in America the Spanish or French or British version of this common culture. There was room for many Spains, Britains, Frances in the New World. New Spain, New France, New England (with the other English colonies) are not names of particular nations but, potentially at least, of continental empires. The home countries fought one another over the domination and division of the New World. As the political powers passed from European nations to their colonists this general relation to a common culture remained. Colonial empires tended to pass into federations – not as alliances of nations, but as a twofold relation of individuals to the federation and to a particular state. In that division of sovereignty and of individual loyalty, the more general relation to the union gave stability also to the parts.

This transition of empire to a type of federation previously unknown is no doubt most evident in the case of the United States. Colonies which had gained but were in imminent danger of losing this independence found stability in a union which expressed more distinctly their common culture and institutions. They remain sovereign states, giving in common a part of their sovereignty to the Union. Individuals are subject to two coincident sovereignties. Inseparable from the Union is a sense that to it belongs all North America, at least between certain latitudes. However unjust it might appear to aboriginal peoples, to Mexicans or Canadians, the Union expanded as by a certain destiny into a continental empire. Virginia, New York, or any State can be likened to a European nation state. But to Americans their relation to the Union was also essential.

The United States was founded explicitly not on race or language but on universal humanity. A common language, the descent of a large proportion of its population from British immigrants, the continuing British quality of its culture, do not make the United States a nation state. Universal rights, so far as they do not derive from the universal culture of the Roman Empire, became known through the revolutions of the seventeenth and eighteenth centuries in certain European nation states. It became evident in the present century how insecure is the relation of universal right to race, language, and cultural particularity in the nation state, where at least these differences are taken to be primary. The European union tends to purge the nation states of this ambiguity. The United States was built on this modern freedom; there are racial divisions and hatreds, but the impulse also to overcome them. Hence the capacity of the United States to absorb and convert to Americans in a generation or two immigrants from all nations.

It is less evident perhaps that the independent states of Latin America may not be equated more or less to European nation states. They are fragments, however, of former empires which imposed a common Spanish or Portuguese culture on native peoples, into which they have gradually been drawn while retaining something of their origins. The mixed populations of Mexico or Brazil are not nation states like Spain or Portugal but participate in a common European culture of a particular type. However much the mixture of European and aboriginal peoples varies among Latin American states, the pattern remains that they are fragments of an imperial culture or cultures and, without political unity, define themselves readily as distinct from the radically individualized culture of the United States. In their internal structure the principal Latin American states are federations, borrowing in their institutions from the American model. Even where there are unitary states these also by the general argument given should not be accounted nation states.

Is Quebec an exception to the rule that there are no nations states in the Americas? As New France it had become a continental empire. If after the Conquest the Quebec people retreated into themselves for survival and were largely excluded from the western expansion of Canada, they thought themselves at times to have a spiritual role in Canada and North America as against a British culture devoted to economic interests. What is called separatism at the present time is rather a demand for recognition as an essential and equal part with the British element in Canada.

The modern scientific and technical culture, detached from the conditions of its origin, has of course spread to all peoples and becomes a world culture. The free subjective spirit moving in this culture from its beginnings and the democratic institutions and concern for individual rights which developed from it have been received with more difficulty. The reception of this culture by most peoples has been on the basis of a native culture which continues with the new, the one side variously modifying the other. With the Japanese and some other peoples of the Far East the solidity and social cohesion of the old culture have aided greatly in their rise to near supremacy in the 'global economy.' In other cases, notably with Islamic peoples, a deep antagonism between the old and the borrowed culture simmers and is easily awakened to violent reactions. In general it is not yet evident how far the free subjective spirit of the western culture will invade the old and how far it will stagnate under the weight of rigid customs and immovable institutional structures.

In the United States and Canada this culture has room to unfold, neither enclosed within national communities nor modified by the alien spirit of other cultures. With modifications the same may be said of Latin America. There the Spanish invaders encountered splendid empires in Mexico and Peru. But the bonds attaching individuals to these empires were weak and gave way almost on contact with the free resolute will of a few conquistadors. European culture in its Iberian form gradually took root in a passive enslaved multitude. In Canada and the United States the aboriginal people were largely thrust aside and those formed to a more general and freer relation to European culture were European immigrants and their descendants. With the end of the independent states in Europe people so formed have come into their own.

The European culture which has had its own unique growth in the New World has several variants according to the particular culture of the occupying powers. These variants differ primarily in the way in which they have integrated into an older state the subjective freedom of the modern age:

- A Latin American states after two centuries of independence have not found a stable relation of free individuals to the state.
- B In the United States the society of free individuals is taken to be primary, but is stabilized in relation to a state limited by the division of legislative and executive powers. The state sustains but does not dominate the society of free individuals. An unresolved tension occurs between individual freedom and a recognized obligation of the state to correct and complement the competitive economic society.
- C In Canada the society of free individuals exists within the state. There is not the aversion of Americans to the state when it is felt to impinge on individual freedom. Canadians expect the state to provide for their general well-being through social programs etc. Unique to the Canadian federation is that it is composed at the same time of provinces,

sovereign and equal to one another, and of two great European cultures in which the relation of individual freedom to the state is understood in different but complementary ways.

The interest of the present argument is to clarify the Canadian form of political freedom by drawing out its difference from the American – a comparison far more pertinent than the analogy of the European Union.

A. Latin American Polities

Of the Latin American form it is enough to ask why it has not settled into the stability of the American and Canadian structures. Spanish and Portuguese conquerors brought to the New World their version of a Renaissance Catholicism which had in it the ideal of a humane government of aboriginal peoples converted to their religion. The reality of the conquest was rather the enslavement of the aborigines to a landed aristocracy. Two centuries of liberal ideas and institutions have not eradicated an assumption that political power belongs primarily to an aristocratic military class.

Liberal ideas are the leaven of recurrent revolutions. Revolutions fail in that the enlightened concepts of individual freedom and equality and of democratic government do not inwardly transform an older feudal structure. There is not a strong society of free individuals, as in the United States, in which feudal distinctions pass into a general equality and differences of wealth and power are thought to be within that primary equality.

Political power may pass from those of pure European descent to wider sections of the mixed population. An underlying resistance of Iberian culture to the individual freedom of the American and French revolutions remains. In Britain and France the emergence of the free rational individual, and the society of such individuals out of an older communal solidarity, was a native growth. These countries were the seat of the revolutions which transformed the substantial absolute state into the democratic state. In Spain and Portugal this revolutionary spirit was an alien force. In their colonies it was easily received by those who would be independent of a home country or, after independence, would overthrow oppressive regimes, only in its victory to revert to another form of the old order. That in turn awakens discontent and new revolution.

The most successful of Latin American governments has been that of the PRI in Mexico – the government of institutionalized revolution, where popular government, or the appearance of it, rests on an antecedent agreement among the powerful elements of society and is not permitted to fall into extreme divisions. Presidents name their successors. A continuing revolutionary ferment falls within an underlying Catholic culture, accepting of authority, into which the aboriginal and mixed populations have been drawn. Resurgent democratic forces and NAFTA may destroy this arrangement. For good? Or only after a time to renew the former cycle?[7]

B. The United States

In the United States democratic government does not need a unified authority outside the process proper – a *deus ex machina* – to save it from its own divisiveness. The revolution does not need to be 'institutionalized,' as in Mexico, but has an intrinsic stability. The political institutions settled upon in 1787 have been found adequate in their essentials to the profound changes of two centuries in the mentality and interests of the American people.

Americans are deeply attached to their political institutions, which they always regard as a model for all peoples. At the same time they dislike government as ever tending to encroach on the freedom of individuals to pursue the good as they like. There is demanded at the same time a maximum of private freedom and, as required, a unified and effective political will. A strongly competitive divisive spirit is contained within a unified political community. How this relation of seemingly discordant elements is possible is a difficult matter.[8]

Derived principally from the institutions of a particular European people, of mixed Germanic and Celtic stock, American institutions are dissociated from that national particularity and able to attract to the idea of individual freedom moving in them people from many nations. American political history is not a national history but the working out on a larger playing field of those ideas of individual freedom and a democratic state which occupied Europeans in their national communities in the seventeenth and eighteenth centuries. Not that Americans, as Europeans, have not moved on to a later age. But Americans have not left behind them as something done with and of cultural interest only the problems of their origins and older formation: individual freedom as then understood and its changing relations to the state. The problem is not dissolved, as for Europeans, into an antithetical relation of linguistic communities to an individual freedom without intrinsic limit and direction.

The constitution of the American Union modified the British constitution of the time in that it divided the powers of government more radically, limited the executive power temporally, and derived it by election by the people. These and related modifications were agreed upon by representatives of the now independent colonies and ratified by their legislatures, representative in turn of their peoples. The constitution thus adopted might in a common language of the time be regarded as a 'social contract.' In a strict consideration this, as other forms of a 'social contract,' does not found a state, which exists already, but defines the terms of assent of free individuals to its authority and builds this assent into its structure.[9] The union of the thirteen independent colonies replaced their former common relation to Great Britain, removing from it the 'tyranny' of royal power which had been imposed provocatively without due assent of the governed.

The states of the Union, which had already existed for as long as a century and a half, modified their institutions similarly. The formation of the federal constitution is of peculiar interest as revealing distinctly what is in these modifications, in particular, the limits of a contract theory of the state. The 'social contract,' however variously understood, assumes a voluntary association of individuals in a system of cooperation. It overlooks that the individuals who thus choose to cooperate are already in a political community which the 'contract' qualifies but has not invented: before as after the 'contract' the state had power to make and enforce laws, for the good or detriment of the people, to override the particular ends individuals or subordinate communities might set for themselves. The state is not a voluntary association, but, if a state of a free people, protects the rights and freedoms of its members, and inclines them to prefer when necessary the good of the whole political community to their private ends and interests.[10]

The American people both during the War of Independence and in their first attempt at a union in the Articles of Confederation experienced fully the limits of a cooperative federalism. The Union was not on its own a state capable of carrying out what was expected of it – to consolidate the independence won in a difficult war, internally and in relation to foreign powers. Individuals and communities closer to them had reason, as ever, to prefer those nearer to a more remote interest on which their freedom principally depended. The War however and the imminent dissolution of the federation awakened a sufficient sense of their common good in the American people to devise and accept a federal state in which sovereignty and coercive power and the assent of free individuals – an effective state and private freedom – found a firm and stable balance.

The American Union is not derivative from particular communities in the manner of the European Union, but is directly the common state of all Americans.[11] In this relation the founders of the Union agreed in fact to a political relation beyond the scope of a contract, in which a priority of the contracting parties, in this case the States, is assumed. For individuals this relation was equal to that which bound them to a particular state. States and the Union had a shared sovereignty. The Union as the common state of all Americans and that which defined their relations with other states, had a priority over the particular states. As the States were not prior to the Union, once founded, so were they not subordinate but shared a coincident sovereignty distinguished by the powers appropriated to each.

The Union has also another primacy. In its first invention it was the product of a profound reflection: Americans in that relation came to know what their freedom was, not as a fact only, but in its general form. The tension between the free movement of private interest and the common good is most evident in that relation. At that level conflicts can be brought back to the principles of the Constitution and the American idea of freedom. It falls likewise to the federal state to resolve the conflicting interests of States according to commonly accepted principles.[12]

European states in the time of their full sovereignty when their interests and ambitions collided beyond negotiation resorted to war as the final arbitration. In the American Union, with one great exception, divisions among sovereign bodies have been resolved peacefully. There is present effectively, as not in that Europe, a common political state and a common political will, to which such differences give way short of war. It only extended its own experience at home when twice in the present century the United States persuaded the great powers to initiate a world government in the interests of peace.

The American federation is a relation of sovereign States to a sovereign Union, but that as ordinarily viewed from the standpoint of free individuals. The Union is the ultimate support of 'government of the people, by the people and for the people.' Political power derives from the people who made and can amend their institutions. But the constitution on which the self-government of free individuals depends, so far as it expresses and gives objective form to their freedom, is in a proper consideration only amendable in its essentials if the amendment is thought to be more adequate to that freedom. The individuals who constitute for themselves a state are 'created equal' and have rights in virtue of that equality, among others, to 'life, liberty and the pursuit of happiness.' Government exists to support and make room for these 'inalienable rights' and has thus a corresponding stability in its primary structure not subject to arbitrary amendment.

The equal individuals having a common end in their individual and mutual well-being or 'happiness' are assumed to be already a 'society' before they have instituted a political order. The free individuals of that society may, with Hobbes, be regarded as in a state of war as soon as they compete for the necessities of human life. So regarded, they are actually free only through the state. They may also be regarded as having through their rationality power over the conditions of their needs and well-being and thus be accounted free prior to the state. So variously Locke, Rousseau, Kant, and others. The history of the American republic illustrates amply that neither the idealistic view of the free individual nor that which sees him enslaved in a struggle to survive and advance himself in competition with others is true by itself, that both are abstractions from a comprehensive view. Abundant resources and an open frontier invited individuals to seek their good with the least reliance on the state. Urban life and an industrial economy at length contracted or nullified that individual freedom, unless the state intervened to provide a tolerable equality of opportunity and support for those whom fluctuations of the economy made destitute. The dependence of 'society' on the state thus became less formal, and the assumption that 'society' was antecedent to the state more dubious.

The political history of the United States, considered in its essentials, is of the development and clarification of the relation of individual freedom, and the society of free individuals, to an underlying political community. This development remains incomplete. The tension between a liberal state which took on itself to assist individuals directly according to their need and the conservatism which would leave the maximum possible to the competitive society is now at a certain extreme. There is to be an end to 'big government,' at the same time as more is expected and required of government to regulate environmental and other basic conditions of human well-being.

The development is not to a European socialism which at the extreme in Marxism obliterates the distinction of state from society. Nor is it the chaotic capitalism following on the breakdown of Marxist regulation which is not a 'civil society,' that is, a society of free and rational individuals. Nor again is its terminus a 'global economy' beyond the scope of regulation by nation states. The developing relation of society to state in the United States holds firmly to this difference: as the well-being of individuals becomes more fully the interest of the state, the demand remains that these individuals pursue and find their 'happiness' by their own talents and exertions, and that they have a fair opportunity to do so. The competition of 'civil society' is for individuals the way to their good, the political community the end, but an end partially concealed. The way to the community sought is not broken by an endless regress as in the European Union and the necessity thus imposed of choosing between cultural community and individual freedom.[13]

What is the 'free individual' of the American republic and of the eighteenth-century 'enlightenment' which is its origin? Hume in his analysis of the free individual discovers a moral sentiment whose object is the 'useful' and the 'good,' his own and that of others. The individual who has in himself this unified relation to what serves his needs and desires and to himself as their end, and a like interest in realizing the need and the good of others, is the 'free individual,' and the community of individuals so moved is 'civil society.' Community and individual freedom belong together. The many arts by which individuals satisfy their needs and desires are, as beyond the capacity of each for efficient production, divided among them. They thus create an economic society in which they compete for its goods. But underlying the competition is the original moral structure, according to which ideally in seeking one's own good one seeks also the good of all.[14]

The general structure of this society can perhaps be made evident most directly if one considers its origin in the socio-political structure immediately antecedent to it. Montesquieu defines the moving principle in individuals in relation to the consolidated monarchies of the early modern age as 'honour.' By 'honour' he meant a relation in which particular needs, desires and interests of individuals were centred in service to the monarch and in virtue of that interest given up as required. 'Honour' is the relation of individuals to the unified state in which feudal privileges have been subordinated to the political community. 'Honour' Montesquieu distinguishes from 'virtue' as the prime motive which can hold together a democratic state. Through 'virtue' the individual takes to himself that unity of needs, desires, interests, which in a monarchy he received from above by his complete loyalty.[15]

The 'liberty' of the 'virtuous' man is to be able to do what he ought to do, what agrees with that rational spirit he has in common with others.[16] It is the principle of 'civil society,' and the polity of a monarchic state, to become democratic, has to be so modified as not to impede the society of free individuals. The 'political virtue' of the free individual was this same rational freedom as operating in the legislative power of the state. By itself in that relation political virtue would be subject to corruption through the intrusion of special interests. For those who represent society in the legislative branch, as those who chose them, are not only moral or rational but serve as well many interests, their own as well as others. The executive on its own easily passed from the will of the people, as embodied in laws to which they had assented, to an arbitrary and tyrannical personal will. The correction of this twofold tendency of the state to corruption and tyranny was that it be controlled through popular representation by that part of society which had imbibed the spirit of the modern age and were certain they could regulate their affairs in their own and the general interest. But they had to be bound to that intention by an executive power, itself obliged to act lawfully. The moral virtue of this class, transferred to the state as political virtue, made possible a common rational freedom. On the ground of their common rationality individuals had rights to their freedom as against arbitrary intrusion from the side of the state.[17]

In England this beginning of modern democratic government was confined to a propertied class and coexisted with an aristocracy of birth and class gradations inconsistent with the universal equality and freedom contained in its principle. The monarchic unity which the state had attained in subordinating feudal freedoms to itself continued in the new division of powers. Government was not so far in the possession of a society of free and equal individuals as to be 'of the people, by the people and for the people.' In the United States the idea that government was instituted by free individuals for their good had much less to oppose it. The religious freedom of a largely Protestant people had passed into the inner rational freedom of 'enlightened' individuals in their worldly relations. And in America it was incomparably more open to free and equal individuals to seek their good independently. The community or society of such individuals appeared primary, a unified sovereign state the source of tyranny. The divided power of the state might be unified against an external enemy in the President as Commander-in-Chief, but the Presidential office was itself limited temporally and derived from the people.

The American federation appeared to early observers to be a weak state which could hardly survive deep divisions among its constituent parts, should these become actual. The society of free individuals was minimally dependent on the federal state.[18] Its members had established loyalties to their particular states. In what did a stronger loyalty to the federation consist, which could sustain whatever centrifugal forces might work against it? In this, that the federal state expressed most purely that 'virtue' which was the moving principle of democracies, the sense of freedom as against particular and divisive interests in the individual and the society of free individuals. The following stages may be discerned in the development of the recognition of this fact.

(1) The society of free individuals is unable short of war to maintain their common relation to the federal sovereignty when centrifugal interests take the form of a division between a slave and a free economy, of a different social order and understanding of the principles of the Revolution. Through the Civil War is awakened in Americans the sense that they are one people, that the free society has its ultimate support in the Union, which as able to sustain the deepest divisions is henceforth regarded as indivisible. For individuals in this relation natural interests are subsumed under virtue or the inalienable rights of the Revolution.

(2) On the basis of this final unification, the society of free individuals can in the second stage react to the negation of its freedom in the inequality and dependence of an industrial economy. The political relation of society is so far strengthened that the state gives support to the independence of individuals against the power of wealth and would restrict the influence of private interests in the election of representatives of the people. The individuals of society are to be moral and their state is the proponent of morality at home and abroad. In compensation to this strengthened universality of the individual, pragmatists would found the relations of individuals in society on their experience as natural and embodied. Neither morality nor pragmatism sufficed to save the real freedom of individuals against fluctuations of the economy. To stabilize the freedom of its members a new relation of society to the state was demanded.

(3) The state which would secure the freedom of individuals both as rational agents and in their natural needs threatened the independence and assumed priority of society. At the same time society could not do without a state to save it from its divided freedom. It might be proposed from the side of the state to eliminate or reduce to a minimum poverty and other natural ills. The bureaucratic apparatus which would accomplish these works was oppressive to the free society. Individuals in rela-

tion to 'big government' might forget the rational virtue of the free society and, while they became consumers of its bounty, rebel against its authority and that of the state, against the inequalities of an ordered freedom.

The 'conservative' society, which would diminish the state to find stability against the 'liberated' individual for whom everything is as he chooses, falls back on an objective good and makes contact thus with the state it rejects. The 'liberated' individual ambiguously destroys the distinctions of society which extended its equality to those excluded from it. Unknowingly he also in this way does away with what distinguishes society from state, and at the same time with his own arbitrary freedom.

(1) In the first decades after the adoption of the Constitution there were a number of secessionist movements in the United States. The rights of States as sovereign entities in relation to the federal sovereignty were indeterminate. Not that the Constitution was in fact unclear on this relation. The Union was not an association of States which their citizens had fully consented to join, from which they might also freely secede if that was the will of their people. The Union was the common state of all Americans individually, over whom it exercised sovereign authority directly in the powers given it by the Constitution. This common sovereignty it plainly did not fall within the particular sovereignty of a State to nullify. Madison commented on one such attempt: 'For this preposterous and anarchical pretension there is not a shadow of countenance in the Constitution.'

The Constitution was clear that States had no right of secession but only over time did the adopted constitution become established in the thought and habits of Americans. The original States of the Union had been in existence as long as a century and a half, and to them their citizens were accustomed to look for the protection of their interests and as the basis of their political freedom. That in the powers assigned to it the Union was a state, and that its legislation was directly binding on all individuals, was only to be known actually and fixed in the political habits of Americans through the conflicting interests of States and regions and their containment and resolution by the federal state. The constitution of a free people, if well designed, is a structure which permits a resolution of even the most difficult divisions acceptably. The habit of accepting its authority and of recognizing in it the objective expression of their freedom one should expect to be difficult; a federal constitution, such as the American and the Canadian, is only well established when the loyalties of individuals to the whole and to a sovereign part coincide and are articulated according to the division of powers.

At that point it can also become evident that the relation of individuals to the federation has a precedence over that to the partial sovereignty. For in that relation conflicts among sovereign parts have the ground of their resolution, and the relation of the principles of the constitution to individual freedom is there most evident.[19] The nation states of Europe in the time of their independence when they could settle on no agreement to their differences sought a resolution by war. A federation which is not an association merely of sovereign parts, such as the European Union, but a common sovereignty having particular sovereignties within it, has the great virtue that every difference among the parts can be resolved peacefully. The Civil War, as the great exception to the strength of the Union to sustain differences, belongs to and completed the formation of the American federation accordingly. In foreign relations, while economically aggressive, the United States has been mostly free of the tendency of the former European nations to universalize in empires their particular sense of themselves. Instead it has promoted a structure of world government to make wars unnecessary.

It was at first not evident to Americans whether they should understand the Constitution as giving to individuals the right to pursue their good independently with the least intrusion possible of the state into their freedom or as unifying and protecting the general interests of society. The formation of ordered government under the President might seem to followers of Jefferson hardly less than a return to the tyranny of a king. To followers of Alexander Hamilton, Jefferson appeared an anarchic Jacobin. That the free individual having in large measure power over the conditions of his well-being and the state as supporting a society of such individuals, who in the means to their good were dependent and competitive, as well as free, were abstractions became clear as Republicans in the realities of office were found to differ little from Federalists. The sense of the division of powers in the Constitution was at the same time to check the arbitrary power of a sovereign and to ground the rational freedom of the individual. The independent individual and the monarch, thus constrained by the legislative power, were complementary not exclusive.

This unstable relation of individual freedom to the federal state on the occasion of the Sedition Act of 1798, which in restricting seditious speech was taken to exceed the power of Congress, gave rise at least to the beginning of a states' rights theory of the Constitution. A claim was made in the 'Virginia and Kentucky Resolves' that States might interpose their authority between individuals and the federal state to declare void and demand the repeal of federal acts they judged to be unconstitutional. These documents, one the work of Madison, the other of Jefferson, did not assign a right of nullification to the people of a single state. But if the peoples of a number of states concerted in their demand, might this not be taken as equivalent to the will of the people as the ultimate source of political authority? But there was in this doctrine an assumption that the Union was a contract among states which they might revoke.

Stronger formulations of doctrine were to follow, not as defending individual freedom against the federal state but in defence of some regional interest. The war of 1812–14 was of particular interest to the states bordering on Upper Canada. To New England it was of no interest and the ruin of its commerce. A proposal to draft a new constitution protecting New England interests, to submit it to the original thirteen states, to go their own way if it were not accepted, did not prevail at the New England Convention of 1814. The disaffection on that occasion subsided with the termination of the war.[20]

The original Republican and Federalist parties – the parties of Jefferson and Hamilton – passed into Democrats and Whigs, both committed to maintain the Union. But the division of interests became more intractable as North and South diverged farther from each other with a rapid growth of manufacturing in the one, while the other drew its wealth in great part from the export of cotton grown by slave labour. The interests of the new states of the Northwest diverged from both. The North required tariffs for the protection of its industries; tariffs against British goods threatened the export market for Southern cotton. Other underlying differences gradually emerged than those between free and slave states. The South, to retain its political power in Congress, would extend slavery to the new states of the West; the North, if it could not abolish slavery, would keep it within existing limits.

If the South could not maintain its interest politically within the Constitution, the only line of defence remaining appeared to be the states' rights doctrine: the Union is a compact among the sovereign States and within the Union they retain fully their former sovereignty. The federal government is only the agent of the States, which are therefore competent to annul on their territory any legislation they judge to exceed its powers.[21] Against a tariff act, South Carolina in 1832 sought to give effect to this doctrine: a convention called by the government declared in the name of the sovereign people that the tariff act was not authorized by the Constitution of the United States, was null and void on its territory and not binding on its agents.

The counter position was thus formulated by President Jackson, though a southerner and friend of states' rights: 'whether it be formed by compact between the States, or in any other manner, it is a government in which all the people are represented, which operates directly on the people individually, not upon the States. Each State having parted with so many powers as to constitute jointly with the other States, a single nation, cannot possess any right to secede, because such secession does not break a league but destroys the unity of a nation.' Both sides made preparations for war, but a compromise on the tariff act averted the crisis for the moment.

Underlying the divergent economic interests of North and South was a different concept of liberty. The free individual of the Declaration of Independence – the enlightened individual – had potentially in his self-relation the means to his own and others' well-being. His freedom was compatible with the Union which in its relation to the divided powers of state was ideally capable of resolving all conflicting interests of the society of free individuals without the imposition of an extraneous tyrannical will. The type of the free individual had been for Jefferson the independent farmer who in great part had in his power the means to his well-being. This 'enlightened' freedom belonged essentially to all men as expressive of their common rationality. Jefferson and others of his clan might incidentally have owned slaves. In the subsequent development of the Republic, in which the whole relation of society with its conflicting regional interests came into view, it was made evident that the particular freedom of a slave-owning class was incompatible with the Union.

In defence of slavery the argument of the ancients was advanced that a free and cultivated society was not possible without the labour of an enslaved class. The dependent employees of Northern factories were virtual slaves. In this defence the 'enlightenment' concept of freedom was forgotten, that the free relation of individuals to themselves and others did not abstract from but was realized in the useful labour which had formerly been thought servile. An aristocratic freedom resting on slavery retreated from the principles of the Revolution and could only live with a modified Union.

While the South by this doctrine was only conditionally attached to the Union, a fanatical spirit in the North began to demand the emancipation of the slaves as the fulfilment of the Revolution. To this demand was opposed the attachment of Southerners to their sovereign States. The war between these immovable forces made evident what lay in the doctrine that there was not right of secession from the Union as directly the state of all Americans. In that relation the society of free individuals had the objective constitutional structure in which democratic government – government of the people by their own agency and for the common well-being and the reality of their freedom – was possible. Through the primary concurrence of individual freedom with the operation of the federal state the Union was indivisible. Individuals might again find themselves unfree in the free society, but from that time with the sense of themselves as one nation – not as an association only of sovereign communities.

Through a development which had its completion in the Civil War the United States, from being a union of sovereign parts, became a nation.[22] 'Nation' is used of course in an extended sense, in which it refers not to a linguistic or racial community but to a unified democratic community to which individuals of whatever origin may belong as adhering to the rational principles on which it was founded. Particular sovereign states continue within the common state but without a temporal or other primacy on which a right of secession might be based, if one assumed that the union rested on a contract of some kind among them.

Separatists in Quebec argue on the same assumptions with only the difference that the contracting parties – the 'two nations' – are said to be nation states – linguistic and racial communities naturally separate and thus incapable of constituting together a 'proper' state, nation, or people. These assumptions apply no more to the Canadian than they did a century and a half ago to the American federation. But in neither case is the formal constitutional argument sufficient to preserve the federation unless the common sovereignty is known and felt by individuals to be congruent with and the foundation of their attachment to a particular sovereignty. How Americans came to recognize the federal state as the object and support of their democratic freedom is exemplary for Canadians, who in this regard are still at the first stage of constitutional development.

The relation of the American state to the society of free individuals who are said to found it is somewhat clarified in the first stage of its development. By the separation of powers and by the Bill of Rights individuals are at the same time to have stable government and protection against the tyranny – the arbitrary will – of a king. The Republic once founded was threatened much less by a tyranny of the executive power than by the conflicting interests of society, which at the extreme government found impossible to resolve and contain. The Union could not be saved without civil war and in the direction of that war a virtual unification of the powers of the state and the President as Commander-in-Chief. To that unification corresponds on the side of free individuals a sovereign popular will supposedly free from the special interests of the same individuals in the competition of society. The popular will and the unified will of the political community coincide. In that coincidence a priority one to the other of the will of the people and the unified political expression of it vanishes. But the relation of the one side to the other is not fully clarified so long as the particular divided interests of society fall outside that point of coincidence. It is a striking aspect of American political life that in a long series of presidents, many pedestrian enough in character indeed, a few heroic figures continue to hold the affection and respect of the people. In these heroes who stand at the beginning of the Republic and the principal points of transition in its history the American people appear to find a political embodiment of the popular will, thus a precedence of state to the divided will and interests of society. Eminent among these heroes is Abraham Lincoln, with whom the Republic passes from problems about its unity and survival to divisions within an established and unquestioned unity.

(2) In the decades following the Civil War the rapid growth of an industrial society tended to make obsolete the concept of the independent individual as the bearer of American freedom. The means to his happiness or the reality of his freedom was a system of economic relations controlled by the rich and powerful. One might go West and begin anew a more independent life, until the same confining structures followed – and eventually there was no more open West. The inequalities, the poverty and uncertainty of life for many might seem to demand some form of European socialism where the state would attempt to equalize the effects of an unregulated capitalism. Americans, although the Union had become a nation or people, would maintain on that basis a freedom of the individual in society. A socialist assimilation of society to the state was intolerable. How could the sense of individuals that this 'happiness' or success in society depended principally on themselves, was the realization of their freedom, be sustained in the dependent situation of workers in a capitalist economy? Defenders of slavery in the South had argued that the condition of factory workers in the North was hardly different, and might be worse, than that of slaves. The response of reforming presidents in what is called the 'Progressive Age' was partly to restrict the tendency of corporations to combine and eliminate competition, saving thus something of an equality of opportunity. For the 'en-

lightened' freedom of the Revolution demands that the individual, potentially free in his rational self-relation, have in society conditions which permit a tolerable realization of that inner freedom.

Some part again of a solution was to restore to individuals the sense that the state was not, as appeared, the instrument of powerful interests but served the popular will, that is, all individuals as equal. To that end the election of federal senators was taken from State legislators, subject to corruption by powerful interests, and given directly to the people. The introduction of 'primaries' again was expected to weaken the control of parties and the special interests they commonly served over the choice of candidates for election to Congress.

These and like reforms reflect an altered relation of society to the state. The virtue of the independent individual pursuing his good had become a common morality, and the relation of individuals to the state was on the basis of this morality. The state in this way imparted at least an inward and formal freedom to individuals in the capitalist society. Americans thus abstractly unified knew themselves as among the great powers of the day. They took part with the European nation states in the work of dividing the world among them. But they also distinguished themselves as moved, not to dominate, but to promote among others their unique freedom. When the European powers from the competition for empire turned on themselves in the First World War, the United States in this moral temper determined the victory. President Wilson would establish a moral world order. But for this flight neither Europeans nor his countrymen were prepared. The Europeans knew only their national interests; the real interests of Americans prevailed over their moral elevation.

The division in this moral politics was nowhere more conspicuous than in the relation of the United States to Latin America which it began to dominate at this time. Partly Americans intended to bring to Cuba and other Latin states democracy and the application of modern reason to their affairs. But of the goods flowing from this 'enlightened' reason Hispanic culture is not easily receptive. They brought also an economic domination which developed and used the resources of Latin countries in American interests. And for the protection of these interests they preferred compliant and dependent dictators to democratic forces better attuned to American political ideals.

To American culture of the time belongs also a correction of this universalized individual freedom. The true subject of American freedom was rather to be thought the 'pragmatic' individual: the living individual who shaped his world not in the light of universal ideas and ends but empirically in structures found to serve his needs and desires. A realization and concretion of the individual as moral or universal, the 'pragmatic' individual could not on his own find his way back to that universality. The inalienable rights of the Revolution and the principles of the constitution were not to be discovered from that standpoint but only shifting, evolving social structures.

For James or Dewey, who were formed and lived in the universality of a scientific culture, the consequences of Pragmatism for that culture might not be evident. One can look for the discovery of freer social forms in the light of growing experience. But going over themselves to the standpoint of their discovery they could not but agree with Richard Rorty that the 'pragmatic' individual is cut off by an ever-recurrent negativity from an ascent to the universal. The 'enlightened' freedom of the American political tradition would have to be thought illusory.

In this second state the Republic appears to founder, as for different causes it came near to ruin in the first. What is lacking here is a relation of the 'pragmatic' individual to the universal principles of the Revolution. The resolution in this case also is through a clarified relation of the free society, taken in its dividedness, to the state.

The conversion of Americans at that time to another concept of the state and its relation to the society of free individuals had first a negative side. The moral optimism which had carried them through the First World War showed itself in the war and its aftermath to be inadequate to the reality of life. From the universality of institutions individuals turned to relations seemingly truer to life. If the 'liberation' from an abstract morality was then only at its beginning, a rebellious and dissatisfied sentiment pervaded the general culture.

This cultural shift was played against the background of the old order – of a capitalism confirmed by morality. The break between this order and real life was imposed by the Great Depression. If the relation of the state to society be that which came into being in this second stage, President Hoover rightly concluded that nothing could be done politically about the unemployment and misery of a large part of the American people who were displaced from the free economy. State intervention would be immoral. If the state were to respond to the need of the impoverished, there would lie in this response an assumption that its concern extended to the conditions of life, which, not attended to, made meaningless the rational pursuit of their 'happiness' by individuals. Corresponding to this obligation on the side of the state would be a new dimension in the rights or rational expectations of individuals – a new concept of their freedom.

The American state in thus overreaching the free society and setting conditions to its operation, in sustaining the whole interest of individuals, may be said to have bridged in principle the division between the pragmatic individual and the free rational individual of the Revolution. The intention was not, as in Marxism, to annul the difference or assimilate society and state to each other, but, what is more difficult, to save the free society through a new relation to the state.

(3) Franklin Roosevelt initiated a change in the understanding by Americans of the ends of government and of their freedom such as has given him a place among the heroes of the Republic – even if this third revolution remains incomplete and of uncertain issue. There are still those after fifty years who propose to undo the New Deal, but only if somehow its benefits can continue on their own without 'big government.' That the whole material interests of its citizens was the proper concern of government had in a gradual process since the mid-nineteenth century become accepted doctrine in the more advanced European states. This revolution had other impediments and took another course in the United States than in Europe. Conceivably in the end it may be better established there than in Europe, where its causes have long been obscured in a dichotomy between nationalism and the economic society.

In the United States the argument has not been as in Europe within nation states which had appropriated or supposed they had appropriated the revolutions of the seventeenth and eighteenth centuries, and thus had the affairs of civil society within their scope. The argument has been instead between the society of free individuals, which would maintain its priority, and the tendency of a state whose object was the concrete and unified interest of its citizens to assume a primacy over society. It is not that Roosevelt or Americans since his time have ceased to take their stand on the side of society and to regard the revolution from that point of view. But the logic of the revolution has itself tended to undermine the ground on which they stand. Thus what seemed stable in society has become unstable: the institutional relations of individuals have fallen into an extreme turmoil, and many ask whether the Republic can long survive.

In the present argument the essential difference between society and the state which encroaches on it is that in society, although the individual in his rational freedom and in his divided relations to a natural world is taken to be one individual, this unity is only partially explicit. A multitude of individuals as rational make up a society, but they are also competitive and divided. The state is called a complete community in the sense that it has room for the divisions of society with a unity of ends. The New Deal brought into the free society a unity of ends, in that it proposed to complement its independent operation when this does not extend to the whole range of human needs, to regulate *ab extra* in various ways its natural fluctuations, to conform the justice of the courts to the needs and economic rights of individuals, and so on. So far as these interventions were like a *deus ex machina* and did not take into them the order of society they must be disturbing to that order and the sense individuals had of their freedom through that order.

The social reforms initiated by the New Deal can appear to be only an addendum to the society of free individuals when it fails of itself to meet the needs of its members. The right of individuals to what belongs to their general well-being and development may appear to have its realization ordinarily through participation in the free society. But the seeds were sown for a revolution in the relation of society to state and of individuals to both. A society, John Rawls observes, having in mind the American society, is neither an association nor a community having a unified end. An association one joins from an interest in its purposes, and may leave if it no longer interests. The state, according to a long tradition, is thought to be a 'complete society' uniting in relation to itself the diverse ends of its members. A society is a community continuous over generations, into which individuals are born and in it pass their lives, in which individuals pursue a plurality of goods but not one unified political good.[23]

But in the New Deal is implicit such a unified relation of the state to individuals having in themselves relation to a comprehensive good. The pragmatic individual, in whom abstract morality and that from which it abstracts are united, is potentially a political animal, regarded from the side of life and nature. There is in him a sense or intuition of a unified end underlying the process of his development. The experience of the limits of the pluralistic competitive society in the Great Depression awakened this political dimension and made individuals so constituted receptive of the New Deal, just as this has as the subjects of its reform individuals having in themselves an intrinsic principle of development of whatever is in them.

This incipient relation of the individual to a state, in which he overreaches his relation to society, has in part a negative aspect. Institutions shaped on the assumptions of the competitive society can be felt unfree. The family, as nurturing the independent individual of society and as reflecting this relation in its discipline, gave way to a family unified by a more immediate affection. This weaker bond was then less able to contain the divisive ambitions of society. A radical subjective freedom, indifferent to natural distinctions, promoted as alternate families a number of socially destructive relations.

The division of parties in society tended to extremes. To 'conservatives' in the time of Joseph McCarthy 'liberals' might seem virtual Marxists – destroyers of the free society. In the 'political correctness' of the present time it is hardly safe to be a conservative. Only by moderating extreme positions within themselves do parties win support enough from the people to govern. Those who hold, or would hold, office are subject to a negative criticism by journalists who expose every deviation from a political virtue they would destroy.

Society itself has become more intensely competitive, as institutional loyalties have dissolved and success or survival depends on abstract criteria. With a weakening of social bonds individuals become more easily an end to themselves for criminal and other antisocial works. The noble work of those who liberated blacks from a submissive and subordinate place in American society or the attempt of liberals to create a 'great society' in which there would be no more poverty or urban slums – these and similar works ended otherwise than intended. The freedom of those liberated had not in it generally an intrinsic order and direction. The ghettos became more violent and drug-ridden, cities dangerous to live in.

The freedom which a liberal state has brought to individuals is widely the banality of the consumer society with its endless satisfactions and nothing for the rational spirit. In the 'consumer society' and the technological apparatus which caters to its needs and passions, the rich grow richer and the poorer find it hard or impossible to hold their ground. Where are the equality and rational independence to which all at last are to have been liberated, the end in which that equality and their natural goods might fall together?

The economic society which the state was to regulate for the good of individuals is to be deregulated and have a life of its own as a 'global economy' ever expanding in an inexhaustible market. But it is not the former society which has as its mover the free rational individual. Its god is change and those flourish who produce and keep up with the change. Neither in the individual nor in society is there a centre which can dominate change and bring order into it.

Such most briefly is the negative side of this third stage in the Revolution, which is not accidental to it but the consequence of its pragmatism. The pragmatic individual, who has implicit in him relation to a comprehensive good, is at first the interest of a beneficent liberal state in its external and material relation and not in its inward rational direction. The individual is in this way freed from the moral or rational society, but to a freedom which knows neither that order nor a new integration of it with the state.

Americans might – Richard Rorty tells them they must[24] – remain with this result and abandon the ideas of the Revolution: that all men have inalienable rights – rights pertaining to them not accidentally but in consequence of their rationality; that as rational they are not simply involved in or enslaved by the great economic system by which together they undertake to satisfy their needs and multiple desires, but in and through it they have the right to seek their happiness, that is, the sense that this system is for them, that they are free in it. The 'enlightened' freedom of Americans has always had in it this unification of ends, whereby free individuals are not simply a multitude but have with others a common end and are a society. The logic of this unification has become more evident from one stage to another of the 'enlightened' freedom. The primary sense of the development indeed has been that this freedom has become clearer and more stable, as belonging to a rational self-consciousness.

When the free individual gave body to his morality as the pragmatic individual, he had hold virtually of the connection and transition between his involvement in the many ends serving his needs and transient or more stable desires and his universality. The many ends were for him as an endless but seemingly progressive process. Rorty, imbued with contemporary European thought, attends to the ever-unsurmounted negativity in this process and pronounces a comprehension of that recurrent division, and thus a referring of the many ends to one end or the good, to be impossible. In that he is the victim of an alien logic and has forgotten that 'Enlightenment' even in its less developed forms knows this unified relation to self-conscious freedom of what is other than itself, and which appears to be only a disparate multitude.

The positive side of this third stage in the American revolution is that society is drawn farther into this unity of ends or the state, to the point where the assumed priority of society loses all stability. For the free individuals of society this movement can appear anything but positive – a recurrence of the old tyranny of the state against which Americans gained their independence. But the movement here is from the side of society, and the state which threatens to emerge from it is a more unified democratic state, which does not detract from but gives stability to the society of free individuals. In the various forms of 'enlightened' society the animation is from individuals who seek their good through particular ends. The competition of individuals in the advancement of their particular ends is within a society or community which it divides. Individuals in the 'enlightened' society know themselves as free so far as this division does not alienate but is known as their own. But the community, and thus the recognition by individuals of their freedom, is incomplete so long as the division and the competition are taken as primary and not comprehended in the community. That this is true Americans before 'Enlightenment' knew in the medium of their reformed Christianity, and the moving spirit of 'Enlightenment' from the first was to give universality and historical existence to the freedom of the 'elect.'[25]

The present perplexities of the Republic have awakened a great deal of reflection among Americans. Within the perspective of a society engrossed with the goods which an ever more sophisticated technical economy provides for the satisfaction and anticipation of every need and desire the 'enlightened' tradition of a rational and practical freedom is lost from sight. But that tradition also remains alive among Americans, for whom the Constitution and their democratic freedom have an almost sacred quality. The need, practically and for political thought, is to bring together that rational tradition and the irrational culture of the present time. How is contemporary individual freedom, in which rights are detached from their universal and rational basis, to be thought continuous with that tradition?

In regard to these and like questions the writings of John Rawls are of particular interest. Rawls would revive in a contemporary context an old doctrine that the state rests on a 'social contract,' and has in view the whole 'enlightened' tradition and the origin of 'Enlightenment' in pre-revolutionary America. His interest is to save the society of free individuals by finding in it for the developed individual freedom of the present time a justice or confirmation of their freedom. This justice as political would define the relation of individuals to the state, and would maintain the difference and priority of society in relation to the state.

Especially in his *Political Liberalism*, Rawls, although the 'enlightened' concepts of his thought are universal, writes of their embodiment in the political history of the United States. Since the United States was founded on 'enlightened' principles and not on national particularity, the course of its political development, considered in essentials, exemplifies the development and clarification of these principles. Thus it is not an extraneous imposition when Rawls situates himself in the Kantian philosophy, the last and most developed expression of 'enlightened' thought. Pragmatism had its source in that philosophy, and in this development is brought back to its source.

Rawls' use of the Kantian philosophy is novel and pertinent to his time. Various answers were given to the question What is the good or unity of ends? These answers, whether utilitarian, intuitional, or pragmatic, related the good too directly to the finite ends of society, confusing thus the difference of society from state. Rawls has in mind, and would have his readers assume, a well-ordered society. The general conditions of such a society are that 'everyone accepts, and knows that everyone accepts, the very same principles of justice'; that 'its basic structure – its main political and social institutions and how they fit together as one system of cooperation – is publicly known, or with good reason believed, to satisfy these principles'; that 'its citizens have a normally effective sense of justice, and so they generally comply with society's basic institutions, which they regard as just.'[26] What principles of justice sustain in Americans such a confidence in their basic institutions and their normal functioning? In what context are these principles voluntarily accepted and preferred to other principles?

This 'well-ordered society' Rawls knows is a highly idealized concept of the society in which he lives, where many have lost confidence in their institutions, their just operation and that their fellow citizens normally act justly. But the Republic since its founding has rested on such an idea, free individuals realizing tolerably their own and the general good under institutions adapted to that end. When the working of their institutions was felt not to be just, the resilient spirit of Americans, as the present argument has shown, was able so to revise them as to restore a general confidence in them. Rawls' question is how such a restoration is possible in present circumstances.

Rawls supposes that his readers have from their tradition concepts of justice and the good – of ends and a just ordering of them. He supposes also that they recognize the common good of the free society. These primary social goods are: (a) basic rights and liberties, (b) freedom of movement and free choice of occupation, (c) powers and prerogatives of office and positions of responsibility in the political and economic institutions of the basic structure, (d) income and wealth, (e) the social bases of self-respect.[27] Not that for Rawls these are the only or the highest human goods. His interest is that in the light of comprehensive ideas of the good, individuals discern a just order in the pursuit of these goods, to know themselves as free in finite and limiting ends.

This is pure 'Enlightenment' doctrine: from the contemplation of ultimate ends one is to turn to the world, to what falls within the human understanding and is useful for the improvement of human life.[28] But this confinement of humans for their good is only free if held in relation to the infinite good from which they have turned. The Kantian philosophy of the understanding rests on a higher standpoint of practical reason, and this on a comprehensive religious standpoint. These levels are not to be conflated. Rawls' inquiry has for its object to articulate the relation of the comprehensive good to the goods of society by discovering a concept of justice such as persons situated in that higher standpoint would prefer to other concepts which tended to obliterate the difference.

Rawls invites the reader by 'a device of representation' to place himself behind a 'veil of ignorance' where he knows nothing of society explicitly. He retreats, that is, to the universal good, which is without the division and determinations belonging to the society of free individuals. The object he has before him through this construction is the same concept of the good as that in which the contentious religious sects of an earlier America consented to tolerate their differences and work together for worldly ends.[29] Or it is the principle of 'Enlightenment,' in whose light people in the eighteenth century were moved to bring reason and justice into human affairs.

The situation of the reader who has placed himself under the 'veil of ignorance' is analogous to that of the representatives to whom initially Americans entrusted the work of designing their political institutions. The demand then was to find institutions which supported and did not oppress the freedom individuals knew in society. With the likeness there are great differences between the one situation and the other. The good which the 'enlightened' were to bring into the world through determinate political and social structures was not a representation which a self-conscious thought knew as its own, but the abstraction of a highest being – inaccessible, though presupposed, to a Humean scepticism, variously knowable to other philosophies of the time. More like Hume than like Kant, the founders lived in the world of that older modern philosophy. And the tolerance of religious diversity which 'Enlightenment' brought was of religion so far as reasonable by the measure of that abstraction.[30]

For Rawls' Kantian standpoint this comprehensive idea has more explicitly the form of the good, not beyond but inclusive of finite ends. Theoretically 'regulative' for that philosophy, it is for practical reason the assumed but unattainable end of its striving. Rawls' 'device of representation' can serve as a measure in choosing the appropriate concept of justice for society because it is not, as in the earlier 'enlightened' thought of the Founders, a being concealed behind finite ends, but that in which they are centred. The preferable concept of justice is that which, allowing the dispersion and multiplicity of goods in society, also draws it into a unity progressively more apparent.

In the light of this measure Rawls finds two principles of justice. One is the equality of individuals as rational and their rights or particular forms of this rational equality. The other is the 'difference principle,' that through which in pursuing the common particular goods of society individuals have relation to the concealed unity of ends, and thus to that perception of their freedom which belongs to a 'well-ordered society.' The 'difference principle' is succinctly stated as follows. Social and economic inequalities are to satisfy two conditions: first they are to be attached to positions and offices open to all under conditions of fair equality of opportunity; and second, they are to be to the greatest benefit of the least advantaged members of society.[31]

Equality of opportunity maximized approximates as far as possible a realized or concrete equality. Differences in natural capacity and interest cannot be wholly eliminated and ignored, as by lot in ancient Athens or as in Andrew Jackson's belief that government offices were such that everyone was capable of them. The other clause reduces farther this disparity: economic competition reaches beyond its divisive tendency and is made the servant of all according to their need. The ambitious pursuit of wealth and power is voluntarily converted into the common end of giving to all the benefits of economic and technical progress and thus the sense of a real and improving freedom.

To the participation of individuals in this 'just society' there is the condition that they be members of society, that is, moral and rational agents who freely chose a particular work among those offered in society; that in pursuing their individual good in that way, with and against others, they come to recognize that society is not competitive only, but beyond competition a system of cooperation. Many in the indulgent, debauched, and, it may be, rebellious society of the present time define their freedom by negating that condition. The 'justice' of Rawls' well-ordered society does not respond to this deeper dissatisfaction, but defines only a 'should be' or a moral and voluntary restraint on the aggressive pursuit by individuals and economic associations of their particular good.

The moral restraint of this social and political justice is grounded and stabilized in the good to which individuals represent themselves as subordinated. In this representation the many ends through which individuals in society would attain their good and a realization of their freedom are not opposed to their common end or community but drawn into it. In society itself the communal relation which is the basis of justice has priority over the good which there exists in the multiple ends through which individuals freely pursue their good. So long as the good in which this division is unified is a representation only, it is of no effect towards bringing into society more than an indefinite approach to a realized community – a community, that is, whose primary end is not the particular goods of the competitive society but the inclusive good of individuals as living and rational beings.

The 'represented' good further is only supportive of a voluntary and moral justice if it is not a construction only, to which the free individuals of society who construct it are prior, but is the *prius* for them. This transposition is the central interest of contemporary American culture. It appears most distinctly in a deepened opposition of 'right' and 'left' in society. The 'right' no longer simply defends economic freedom against the state of the New Deal or virtue against permissiveness, but has need to find a relation underlying reflection and choice, which it finds in family and the 'right to life.' This attitude may assume many forms: care for the environment, idealization of primitive society, hostility to reason and 'technology.' Taken in its American context, it is rather a recognition of life as created and of the relation of the rational creature to an absolute good. A 'religious right' so understood has no quarrel with the free economy or with 'technology' so far as this respects life. The primary opposition to a 'right' so founded is an unlimited 'freedom of choice.'

The 'left' in this opposition is a subjectivity which is not the moral and rational subject of the free society nor simply the subject 'liberated' from that morality, but has for its interest to surmount that division. This freedom animates what is called 'political correctness.' It pervades the popular arts. There is in it the contradiction that one would destroy reason and morality and in so doing exceed the morality of those one exposes and destroys. This negation and restoration is practised not only on others but by the individual on himself, especially in the destructive aesthetic frenzy of the arts, which in its negativity turns also to morality and the universal. This freedom has of course nihilistic Nietzschean forms, but, taken in its opposition to the good in which the 'right' would find stability, its object likewise may be seen to be a unity before, but capable of, division – the attempt of the individual to make the good his own.

'Enlightenment' in its development and various forms would realize freedom through the knowledge of nature and its application to the improvement of human life. The society of free individuals who pursue this work know their freedom through the common relation of their particular good to the common good. So far as this relation to the universal is inward and concealed from them in their relations to a world confronting them, as for instance in Hume's account of the structure of 'enlightened' reason, their freedom is abstract and divided: there is a community and a multitude of individuals pursuing competitively diverse ends. As the present study has brought out in relation to the United States, whose institutions were founded on this concept of a society of free individuals, a development of this society has the meaning of drawing together and articulating the relation of its inner end or common good, the many useful arts and their competitive application, and the individuals who have their freedom in relating the two. The term of this development is that the system of particular ends should be known as realizing the common end, and the freedom of individuals in their particular ends as within their common end. There is a point in this movement where the freedom of individuals in society conflicts with the common end and the attempt to realize it directly. The state since the New Deal takes for its object the whole good of individuals. In society that work is the prerogative of free individuals, who would have also their particular good. Essential to free individuals is that the good be effected by them, not simply that it be done.

Rawls' concept of justice has the great interest that it shows the limit of this accommodation to each other of the state and the free society. Beyond this point either the free moral subject recedes into a relation to the good prior to its divided moral relation to society or the 'liberal' who was the agent and advocate of a direct political realization of the good finds that he can maintain his freedom only as an absolute freedom of choice, as beyond the division of moral and immoral. In the one case the division of society as primary is given up, in the other as meaningless it is virtually given up.

That the positivity of 'Enlightenment' when it has the form of a relation of a would-be concrete moral will to the good passes into a radical opposition of good and evil, or the individual will absolutized, has its classical exposition in Kant's treatise on religion[32] considered from the side of 'enlightened' reason. The aversion of 'Enlightenment' to the Christian doctrine of a radical propensity to evil in man rested on an abstract concept of the good which the intrinsic development of the position has corrected. The idea of a concrete good to be freely realized, which is implicit in 'Enlightenment,' is derived from that part of the Christian community which admitted a free subjective movement in the reception of grace. What in early New England and the other colonies was known in the various Protestant communities the 'enlightened' proposed as a universal human work to be realized historically by a society of free individuals turned to their finite interests. The condition of such a work, known in the Augustinian-Calvinist theology of American sects, namely a unification of the divided good and evil propensities of the human soul, was forgotten in the structure of the society of free individuals. Protestant Christianity remained in general the belief of enlightened America, moralized more or less and recalled to its concrete doctrine by degrees through experience of the limits of enlightened freedom at its several stages. The term of this development would be to grasp what 'Enlightenment' is and to retract the assumptions of the society of free individuals and its apparent priority to the state.

In Europe the revolutions of the eighteenth century had their result in the formation of the democratic state which has place for society and individual freedom within it. On this basis the universal social programs, which in the United States are felt to impinge on individuals, are more easily accepted. In relation to the state, individuals can feel themselves not less but more free than in society. As predicated of particular national communities this distinction survives in cultured habits and tends to be negated in relation to the common economic community.

At such time as out of the present disposition of forces in the United States the state might emerge more clearly as the basis and support of the society of free individuals, both sustaining the goods and interests of society and bringing them under more universal human ends, that state, as resting on universal principles, would have a far greater stability than the one-time independent nation states of Europe. If the present tendency to give over to the states a greater part of what the central government has taken to itself since the New Deal were to continue, the federation would have more life. For the sense of individuals that in the central state and the Constitution they have the ultimate security of their liberties is best maintained by strong differences among the particular sovereignties and between them and the federal state, with the more developed concept now of individual freedom.

The separation of powers in the Constitution suited better the relation of private interests to the incipient state of the early republic. In place of a fear of tyranny there is now a sense that the state is beholden to special interests and cannot respond to the recognized needs of the people. Montesquieu, having before him the unified state of the early modern age, would correct through the division of powers both the arbitrary will of the sovereign and the capricious will of the people. A primary unity of the powers remained and the idea of the judiciary as a third power, which occurred to him, he quickly corrected, seeing its function in the interpretation of laws and their application to particular cases as part of the executive power. Rousseau, discerning the unity of the rational and the sensuous will and that the state is occupied with the relation of the two, denied that the powers were primarily separate. Still less from the Kantian standpoint of Rawls should one allow such a separation of the popular will as determined by the representatives in Congress from the Presidential power. And the Supreme Court, which on its own declares the content of individual rights, thus taking on itself to legislate for the people, shows the worst consequences of the tripartite division. Domestically and in foreign relations there are two competing powers, of which each would be the state, and law and policy in consequence proceed rather from compromise than a unified view of the common interest. In a recognition of the priority of state to society the relation of powers would be seen differently.

These and like institutional changes are implied if Americans are to respond to the deepest division of society at the present time. When and in what ways they might find an acceptable response in continuity with their political traditions is for the future to disclose. One who attends to American freedom and the spirit moving in their institutions can hardly doubt that, whenever it might be, they will resolve appropriately also this most difficult of divisions. It is sufficient for the present inquiry to have shown that the whole movement of American political history is towards the reversal of an assumed priority of society to state. What lies in the opposite assumption of Canadian history, that the state underlies the free society, has been given precision by this inquiry.

The United States is the first post-national state, the first state based not on national particularity but on rational principles, whose history is essentially the development of those principles. Americans were from the first conscious that they attempted something new, and of consequence for the human race: there began with their independence a 'novus ordo saeclorum.'

C. Canada

What is Canada? Not a 'proper' state, some would reply, taking for their model the now obsolete European nation state. Not like the United States, most would agree whether of the Anglophone or Francophone community. This difference, which shows itself in many forms, is rooted in a different perception of the relation of the state to the private freedom of society. Canadians in all parts of the country accept and are strongly attached to universal social programs, which are less felt to be an affront to private freedom.

Provinces in Canada because of this difference have a stronger sense of their sovereignty than is usual in the United States. They can on this account more easily take themselves to be independent, and thus like nation states. In Quebec, which lives in another language than the English-speaking provinces and in another form of the common European culture, a developed provincial sovereignty easily passes into a movement to separate from a redundant federation. The only adequate response is that Canada is a federation of sovereignties which on the basis of a common European culture can contain different national forms of that culture. Not just any difference, but that of the two peoples who in the seventeenth and eighteenth centuries discovered and brought into being the rational democratic freedom of the modern age. The peculiar spirit of this federation is that neither culture should dominate or suppress the other, but, as complementary, the tension between the two should enliven the whole and make evident to both their common freedom.

That Canada is either a federation so defined or a historical blunder at the point of dissolution can be judged objectively by an argument structured as follows: (1) The common history of the British and French peoples in Canada during a long colonial dependence is essentially of the formation of a federation so conceived. (2) Canadian history since the 'patriation' of the Constitution is essentially a continuing attempt to make our own what we had become in the course of that dependent development. This second stage has two movements in it: in this our Canadian revolution, as in all successful revolutions, there is need first to be 'liberated' from the authority of received institutions, then to review and appropriate from the standpoint of that freedom what was before found oppressive.

Since, unlike Americans, we suspended our revolution until the complete development of democratic institutions in one federation, in its positive development we have less need to amend than to understand the principles of our freedom.

(1) The English and the French occupation and colonization of North America both began in the first years of the seventeenth century. The political institutions and government of the two peoples at that time were both divergent and founded on common principles. In a parallel but also different development, both had subjected the feudal estates to a monarchy which as beyond this division is called 'absolute.' This reduction was carried out more radically by the French kings, who soon ceased to summon the estates. In England, after an apparent accommodation of king and parliament to each other rival claims to sovereignty were fought out in the Civil War and at length adjusted to each other. In France only the Revolution made room for popular freedom within the unified state.

There is a different development of common political principles. The subjective freedom of the modern age required a radical revision of the medieval state, where finally the would-be independence of the estates was stabilized under an absolute monarchy. In this revision the English maintained better a continuity of the old with the new, glossing over in their empirical temper the deep divisions latent in the process. The French held logically to the implications of absolute monarchy, restraining the subjective freedom which moved strongly in them, until this, assuming a radical form, destroyed the monarchic state.

In the philosophy, the science, the arts of the time, there was a reciprocity where what might be discovered on one side of the Channel was taken up and carried farther on the other. The movement began in many matters with the British; what they had done the French genius would then raise to a more rational form. In political matters to carry divisions to extremes can be destructive, as French history illustrates. To live with a constitution which is not grasped in its principles, given conceptual and written form, is however unworthy of a cultivated people. In such federations as the American and Canadian an unclarity about the principles of the constitution is dangerous.

For a century and a half France and Great Britain contested which would dominate North America beyond Mexico. The British conquest of

New France was followed shortly by the independence of their American colonies. In Canada conqueror and conquered came under one monarch. The subsequent political history of Canada is the common development of that, at first formal, relation.

That peoples should pass from one monarch to another was a frequent occurrence at the time. Alsace and afterward Corsica were, for example, taken into the French state. Such transitions became more difficult when government in the nineteenth century had passed from kings to peoples and their elected representatives. When the basis of government in European states passed from rational principles to race, language, and cultural particularity, these transitions must appear impossible. If one would follow the political development of Canada, the initial relation of the two peoples should not be taken anachronistically.

Religion, language, and the civil law distinguished the conquered people from their conquerors. In a political relation these differences were tolerable to an 'enlightened' age. That the subjects of a Christian king had to belong uniformly to one part of the Church, as Louis XIV had been persuaded to think in the previous century, had ceased to appear a necessary basis of political cohesion. Still less to those who had some part in the common European culture of the time need language and the conventions of another law seem radical impediments to a common polity.

The conquered also from their own culture could not be without inclination to the freer form of government the Conquest had brought within their reach. New France had appeared a model of conformity to the absolute monarchy and to a monarchic church. But the realities of life in North America awakened also incipiently an independence and equality of individuals which tended to make of feudal forms of land tenure merely formal distinctions. The religious beginnings of subjective freedom in Jansenism and Calvinism might be suppressed but not the response to life in the New World. Peculiar to the French among European peoples is an adherence at the same time to a unified authority in king or pope, which will have no individual freedom unless as subordinated to it, and to the Cartesian freedom of the modern age which is its own centre of authority. A common government and common loyalties between this people and a British people in whom the same division occurred in a more moderate and subdued form might be a difficulty, but, given favourable conditions, in no way impossible.

To know how the common polity of these peoples which now exists, if imperfectly, came to be, one must attend not only to the events of their common and special histories but to the spirit moving in them. The moving principle of the French monarchy, which ruled in New France until the Conquest, was the quality Montesquieu calls 'honour.' 'Honour' he distinguishes from 'virtue,' the animating principle and source of loyalty in democratic constitutions. The latter quality he observes particularly in the English state of his time. The 'virtuous' man is the free moral individual of the American revolution, but considered as in relation to the English monarchic state. The difference of these subjective principles and of the constitutions they sustain is the best beginning if one would grasp the initial relation of the two peoples. In 'honour' there is not yet the subjective freedom of the modern age but a striving towards it, in that the individual discovers his highest secular good in loyal service, it may be at the cost of his possessions and his life, to the monarch. In this he has brought into one relation his various interests and passions. The object of that unified relation is called in political discourse 'the good.' For the particular goods which he is thus ready to sacrifice he can ordinarily expect benefits to be conferred on him emanating from the monarch. The 'virtuous' man has in his self-relation, and not from above, his relation to the many particular goods he needs or desires.

'Honour,' so understood, is the virtue first of an aristocratic class, then derivatively of a bourgeoisie who would be something in the world. The one class tends to an excess of independence and finds submission hard. The monarchic government operates through a relation of this to the more compliant middle class. The peasantry fall outside this direct relation to the monarch. Thus in New France the will of the monarch is executed by the divided authority of the military Governor and the Intendant. But the relation of the country people to this system is different almost from the first in New France. There is not a half-servile peasantry, but the 'habitant' with a strengthened sense of his independence and equality. One reads with admiration of the heroic characters who made New France – Champlain, Frontenac, and many another; of the wars with the Indians and the English enemy; of the great explorations which extended the French empire to the western plains and the Gulf of Mexico; of the heroic missions of the Jesuits, in a like service of 'honour' to the Papal monarch. The formation of a Quebec people has in it also the beginning of a 'virtue' which could survive the termination of this ordered relation of individuals to their political centre in the absolute monarch.

The disappearance of the old order can appear in a nationalist perspective as an immense shock from which to this day French Quebecers have hardly recovered. It is also said that they were already a 'people' or a 'nation,' in which case they would have in themselves a political order to replace that from which they were severed. It would be better said that the Conquest stabilized their relation to the culture earlier imposed from above, that French culture from that point took root in North America and was capable of an intrinsic development. The conquered were not in a later nationalist sense a 'nation' or 'people,' but the bearers of French culture of the 'old regime,' towards which they must find a freer relation.

The British community which came into being in Canada after the Conquest and would soon consist in great part of royalist refugees from the American Revolution, had in common with the French community a devotion to the monarchic state as the source of its freedom. It differed from the French community in that it had in it also the 'enlightened' subjective freedom to which Church and State were alike inimical in New France. The conquered people, in the sense of themselves as now on their own, were readily receptive of that freedom.

Towards the conquered people the British government followed an ambiguous and shifting policy. Were that possible, it would assimilate the French to the British community. But the Quebec Act of 1774, in recognizing the right of the French community to its religion and law, envisaged a coexistence of the two communities. And the Constitutional Act of 1791 granted equally to both the beginnings at least of representative institutions. Lord Durham hoped that the union of the two Canadas in 1840 would lead to the assimilation of the French to the English community. But with the 'responsible government' which he also recommended, coexistence was found to be irreversible.

Two communities existed side by side under a common government, to one its proper government, alien to the other. But the relation of the French community to the conqueror was far from defensive only. Holding simply to the authoritarian structures of the old regime, it would have generated from itself that revolutionary reaction which thirty years after the Conquest was to destroy the French monarchy. In Canada the nearest equivalent to the American and French revolutions, in which the society of free individuals took possession of the state, was the rebellion of 1837 in both Canadas against governments which excluded the popular will from their councils. Had those rebellions prevailed, both communities would have been absorbed quickly into the United States.

However well in the old and the new France monarchy and Church might suppress the emergence of a subjective spirit in religion, when this subjectivity took on secular forms and became the spirit of a free society they were impotent against it. The limited and ineffective participation of both communities in government since 1791 provoked them to rebellion. The 'responsible' government then granted to the Canadas and to the Atlantic colonies was capable of uniting with the monarchy the individual freedom of society.

How monarchy and individual freedom could be mutually supportive Burke, in reaction to the French Revolution, best explained to English readers. So far as the freedom of society in relation to the state is not abstract and equalizing only, but through the resolved opposition of parliamentary houses contains acceptably the whole public interest, it is not at odds with a monarchic will which intends the same general interest. The right of rebellion from the side of society lies with its representatives, as those who know most definitely the essential interests of the state, if, as on the occasion of the expulsion of James II, the monarch has undertaken to destroy the liberties of the people and reverts to an absolute monarch. However badly this doctrine is articulated in British or Canadian institutions at the present time, it expresses accurately what lies in the transition from the revolutions of the seventeenth and eighteenth centuries to the democratic states of the following century, where society is taken one way or another to be contained in the state.

It could easily appear to Lord Durham, a liberal of the time when the British state was passing to a democratic form, that the two Canadas could live under a common government responsible to the popular will, and that in that relation the particular cultural and religious attachments of the French community would lose their hold. The deeper sense of particular freedom in both communities nullified so direct a union. The attempted union rather gave form to their difference as democratic communities.

The difficulties of a union whose components would not unite one knows were among the causes of the Canadian federation. Why would not a wider union inclusive of the Atlantic colonies have the same and further difficulties? Some might think that finally in that federation the French community would be assimilated to the British. But having their own government in the federation the French community might just as well consolidate its difference. Apart from reasons of security and the pressures of the British government on the colonies to unite, why an interest in the federation? As North Americans neither the British nor the French in Canada can make of themselves nation states only but, as the Americans, through a federation would know the common principles of their particular states. From a like impulse the British and French in Europe gave universality to their culture through their nineteenth-century empires. What they attempted then to do severally by the domination of others they now began to do together through their relation to a still abstract community.

The French and British communities in Canada, though their first union failed, had advanced a long way since the Conquest towards a common polity. The opposition of the English people to an absolute monarch and to the absolute authority of the Roman church had been a large part of their history in the seventeenth and eighteenth centuries. Since the Conquest the former subjects of the French kings had taken from the conqueror the principles of an ordered popular government on a British model and not that of the successive constitutions of an attempted restoration in France. Both the Protestant and the Roman parts of the Christian church, as the religion of 'enlightened' peoples, had lost much of the ground of their implacable hostility towards each other. What then were the obstacles to a federation in which both communities with others could find a common expression of their freedom? The answer is given by the history of Canada since Confederation.

The debates among the political leaders of the several colonies, in which they devised and agreed to the constitution of a federation very much as the British parliament would enact, show little understanding of the principal questions, how provincial and federal sovereignty would be related to each other, and how the difference of provinces, especially of Quebec, would be saved in their federal relation. As themselves colonies and not sovereign states they could not but assume the British constitution as it was, and then ask with what distribution of powers it could be applied to a federation. As the federation would have a sovereignty subordinate to that of Great Britain, so the provincial would be subordinate to the federal sovereignty. Canada would be a dependent unitary state, containing dependent sovereignties in it. But the idea was also expressed that Canada would form a new 'political nationality' – a society in which British and French Canadians alike could appreciate and understand their position relative to each other.[33] Only as this idea has come to be partially realized is Canada a proper federation.

In concept the provinces have the structure of a complete state according to the Burkean model, where popular sovereignty and the unified sovereignty of the monarch coalesce, where the powers of government are at once divided and unified in the collaboration of king and parliament. Provinces, so conceived, are equally sovereign with the federal state in the matters assigned them. The priority of the federal state is only that it acts for all the people domestically and *ad extra*, and that in its operation it should be capable of resolving acceptably the most difficult division of interests among provinces. The history of the federation in its first century is essentially a movement towards the realization of this concept.

The British constitution of the time was in important aspects a bad model for the Canadian federation. Burke's idea of a state which in its sovereignty would hold together the potentially destructive forces of a free society was lost in the nineteenth-century state, where the monarchic or unitive power came to be largely ceremonial, the 'upper house' more or less redundant, and parliament virtually the 'Commons,' and where actual sovereignty was concentrated in the Prime Minister. This model suited badly a federation of particular sovereignties which in its central government had need to represent not only Canadians individually but also the substantial interest of provinces. A Senate in the patronage of the Prime Minister could not fulfil that function. Again, the collapsed parliamentary structure adopted must give weight too directly to the populous central provinces, whose difference when they were united had made evident the need of a larger federation. A Canada of 'two nations' was unworkable. This duality of the Canadas, if it would not be disruptive but beneficent, had to be situated within the primary equality of a number of provinces.

The French people, as they sought to reconstitute the state after the Revolution, could not be satisfied with the British solution. The presidency, as representing people in their fundamental equality and solidarity, could not be confined within the parliamentary structure which represented them in their various interests. If unstable, it expresses better than the British structure the rational equality of individuals, and thus the French mentality and tradition. But the centralizing tendency of this structure, as reductive of differences, is also inadequate to a federation of sovereign provinces.

That Canada was founded by 'two nations' is not without truth, if it is taken to mean that within a colonial context the political leaders of the united Canada recognized that their common and particular sovereignties had to be separated and ordered to each other on that basis, and that with others they found and proposed to the imperial power a constitution tolerably adapted to that end. How the common sovereignty would secure the opposed ends of the 'two nations' was to say the least unclear. The one 'nation' saw itself as part of, and perhaps nearly equivalent to, a British North America extending from sea to sea. The other supported the union as permitting a more independent growth of the French and Catholic culture centred in Lower Canada.

There was thus in both 'nations' the beginning of a common but differently qualified loyalty to the federation. For both that qualified loyalty was subordinate to a higher loyalty – to the Empire for the one, to the Roman church for the other. The Maritime provinces in joining the federation exchanged their former colonial independence for a chronic dependence. Their attachment to the federation was and remains at once disinterested and servile. They never doubt their equality with the central provinces, and in this are complete Canadians, but in an economy not favourable to their interests they have learned to expect external assistance. Contrariwise, the western provinces, which knew little or nothing of a prior independence, having become economically self-sufficient, have need that their sovereign equality be recognized by the central provinces. Newfoundland, which alone of the provinces joined the federation from an independent status, can less than any doubt its equality with the rest.

It is evident that while Canada was in a colonial relation to Great Britain, even if it were latterly only for constitutional amendment, provinces could have no right of secession from the federation, this resting on an act of the British Parliament. It is mythical to think of the federation as a compact between 'two nations.' The question of secession arises however in an interesting form at the point where the provinces have attained fully that sovereignty which belonged to them in concept from the beginning. As sovereign, why can a province not choose to exercise that sovereignty independently, if it so chooses? That is in truth the constitutional basis of Quebec separatism, and to answer the claim requires great clarity about the nature of the Canadian federation.

The process is well known by which the Judicial Committee of the Privy Council in a series of cases gradually corrected the initial assumption of the federal government that the Parliament of Canada through its power of disallowance and its general power to provide for 'peace, order, and good government' could overrule provincial legislation. 'What the Judicial Committee did was to give official legal sanction to a theory of federalism congenial to those who, at the time of Confederation and afterwards, could not accept federalism.'[34] Rather than a theory one should say that it is of the essence of North American federalism that states or provinces be sovereign in their assigned powers. On the view of John A. MacDonald that 'the true principle of a Confederation lay in giving the General Government all the principles and powers of sovereignty,'[35] Canada could not long have survived. The effect of that principle must be to impose the will of the one 'nation,' centred in Ontario, not only on the Quebec 'nation' but on the diverse interests of the other sovereign provinces.

The interest of the present study, however, is not so much the step-by-step attrition of insufficient views of the Constitution through court decisions, as in its principles and the spirit moving in them. So long as the centralized federalism of the beginning prevails, the sovereign provinces are not secure in the exercise of their powers. But if the federal invasions of their particular powers were stayed, a more difficult problem would remain. The difference of provinces, conspicuously of Quebec but also of the others, is not confined to their particular constitutional powers but extends to their whole culture and its linguistic medium as well as to their religion. The sovereignty of a province which would care for and secure its difference in this comprehensive sense cannot be formal or ceremonial only, as that invested in a Lieutenant Governor, but that which imparts to the divisive interests of society the unity of a political community – of a particular political community.

The movement here has an opposite direction to that of the United States, where the individuals of a free society are drawn by degrees more fully into a political community. In the Canadian federation the political community is assumed, and a relation of individuals to it, at first abstract, has to take into it the divided freedom of society. The correction of a federal power which as general can dominate the particular provincial sovereignties is thus through a development and clarification of the ends of government. The relation of individuals to the state which Canada became in adopting 'a Constitution similar in Principle to that of the United Kingdom'[36] is implicitly that in which the development of the American state, as given above, terminates. That is, it is implicitly what it actually became after the Second World War – a state having the general well-being of its members for its end. Initially both federal and provincial sovereignties in Canada were far from this ideal. The federal state concerned itself with the general conditions (tariffs, railways, etc.) of a free economic development and touched little the ordinary lives of individuals.

The development of post-revolutionary states in Europe had a very different structure from that of the same states when they were in course of being revolutionized during the seventeenth-and eighteenth centuries. The society of free individuals, which both endangered the absolute state and transformed it into an ordered democratic state, was in that new relation both inwardly integrated into the state and drew the state into its interests. Hence the separation in the British state between a royal sovereignty and the sovereignty in the House of Commons of the leader of the majority party – a separation which gradually took place in the nineteenth century there and analogously in other European states. To a radical thought which abstracted from the inner unity it could appear that the old difference of state and society had vanished. But the history of the time reveals much more a need and desire to hold together the relation of free individuals to the inner substantial unity and their life in the state which collaborated with private interests in creating an earlier version of the 'global economy.' A unity of the two aspects was sought in the competing world empires which the nation states made for themselves. The empires held the loyalty of their citizens by drawing together their dispersed interests and ambitions with their inner communal relation, which, far from ceremonial only, confirmed the assumption that society was contained in the state or political community. The ordering of the economy to the good of individuals is an imparting to it of this concrete relation.

These considerations are essential to an understanding of the long protracted colonial dependence of Canadians. So long as Canadians of British stock or formed by that culture knew an integration of the elements of the nineteenth-century state in relation to the Empire and not at home, their political loyalty was centred in that relation and not in their own federation.

The way to independence is thus the appropriation of that unity of the elements of the state which was the source of attraction to the Empire and a hardly questioning loyalty to it. That appropriation is at the same time a development of the Canadian state towards a concrete unity of ends – a capacity to use the goods of society for the common good and the needs of individuals. With this is formed a stronger attachment of individuals to the federal state, and through a parallel formation to their provinces. As there is greater clarity about the ends of government and both the general and the particular sovereignties deepen, the abstract relation of the beginning, where power descends from the federal to the provincial level, passes more into an equal and shared sovereignty.

In this more developed relation it is thought appropriate for example to transfer revenues from the federal to provincial governments, to permit them to fulfil their recognized obligations to the people with a tolerable equality. Through tariffs and various natural conditions the economic development of the country was concentrated in the central provinces. The tension between a unitary economy and the right of sovereign provinces to provide for the particular needs and interests of their people had far greater recognition in Canada than in the American federation, as follows from their different principles. Canadians are receptive of such measures provided that the federal state supplies the provinces with the means to a reasonable equality. Through the strength of that relation they are able to moderate the tendency of the sovereign provinces to maximize their wealth. One may observe that were Canada still Quebec and Ontario only and their common sovereignty not strongly separated from their particular sovereignties this equalization would not occur.

The most difficult division in Canada is between the primarily French culture of Quebec and the primarily British culture of the other provinces. But towards the resolution of that division in a common sovereignty the differences among the English-speaking provinces are of the greatest importance. Through their resolution to federate provincial states have come to be related not as hierarchic but as primarily equal sovereignties, the provinces as particular sovereignties and sovereign over their particularity. Quebecers require something more if they are to recognize federal sovereignty as fully their own. The federal state has to reflect also a different sense of the elements of the same concrete sovereignty, that is, not only economic but cultural equality. But the Canadian federation, like the American, is a realization in North America of a common European culture and can contain on the same principle the difference of French and English cultures.

The liberation of Canadians of British culture from dependence on the Empire was effected historically by their participation in the two great European wars of this century. They were in this way required to find in themselves that unified relation to the state which hitherto they had through the Empire. After the First World War their dependent relation came to be recognized as a relation of equals.[37] Domestically that integration of the state was the ground of the deepened relation of federal to provincial sovereignty spoken of above, and of the better understanding of the ends of government. But that unification was British still and in relation to the Empire. It pertained differently to French Canada.

The Second World War was the external cause of a more complete independence and of a relation not primarily to Great Britain but to Europe. For Europeans that war was the point of transition from nation states to the European Community which began to take shape shortly afterwards. The nature of that war has already been considered, but not the somewhat complex relation of Canadians to it. The opposed fascist and socialist positions, which fought out their differences in the war, were not national only but occurred variously in all the European nation states. In Canada they were borrowed and hardly felt except in certain circles. Some favoured and even fought for the government side in the Spanish Civil War; some in Quebec felt an affinity with the Vichy regime in France. These forces were pertinent however to a post-national independence in Canada. The Commonwealth in which Canada was equal to the British nation state was not a national community but gave to its members only a formal unity. The relation of nation states in the European Union which would emerge from the war is very different: the constituent parts are there taken into the union to the extent that the union is a state. The Canadian federation is only a community having states within it when its unity is at least that of the European Union. It is only altogether on its own and independent when it no longer looks to the European Union, but turning to itself finds a relation of sovereign parts to the federal state which is no longer ambiguous.

In the war Canada had part in a process by which the independent nation states were subsumed at least in principle under a common state. The opposed fascistic and socialist forms which are drawn into that union are already in a manner post-national. The Nietzschean nationalism of the one has in it a temporalized universality, and in the universal economic process of Marxism national communities have only an accidental being. In these forms the inner universality to which in the previous war the nation states sacrificed their particularity is externalized and temporalized. What is then sought is to regain the universality lost in this externality, and that is to bring to light the common state which underlies the particular national states and their mutual relations.

For Canadians the reflection into their own state of this dispersion and collection of the particularity of the European nation states provided the basis on which we could 'patriate' the Constitution, confident that we could resolve without reference to an external authority even the most difficult of differences – those between Quebec and the British culture of the other provinces. We appeared to have found a common sovereignty in which the two peoples were equal and their difference stabilized.

The route by which Quebec moved from a French and Catholic to a European colonialism, finally to a recognition of North American independence, can appear very different, but is essentially the same as for Canadians of British culture. The differences, as always, are those of the two cultures – of that which draws back from radical divisions and that which lets them appear. Having attempted briefly in 1837 a revolution of the American or French type, Quebec came under the authority of the restored Roman church, which set itself against the more radical secularity of the nineteenth century. The Church could not undo this new revolution or the structure of the nineteenth-century state already described, but held to one element of that state against the rest – to its substantial unity. On this account in Quebec it gave its blessing to a rural and family-oriented life, and was averse to the industrial society forming in the cities and controlled by Anglo-Canadian or American enterprise. Clerical power was not contested as in France by a liberal society no less French than itself – the other aspect of the nineteenth-century state.

The Church carried to an extreme the division there in another form in New France between absolute authority and subjective freedom – a division always at some point intolerable to the free spirit of the French people.[38] In the nineteenth-century form the division is unstable in that the subjective freedom of the modern age is implicit in the substantial aspect of the restored state. The Second World War provided the turning point to a unification of the divided state. France succumbed to the opposed existential and Marxist forces of the time. The Church, thinking it had affinity with the former, aggravated the division and made way for a mediated return to the substantial basis of the state through the heroic work of de Gaulle. The reflection on this restoration on Quebec facilitated the 'quiet revolution' and the end of an abstract clerical power.

Through the historical development of Canada to independence all that divided the French and British communities following the Conquest has passed into the difference of two forms of a common European culture within a post-national state. Initially different in religion and the form of their freedom, when both attained self-government under the same parliamentary institutions, their relation to each other was no longer external and imposed only. The conditions of a common polity and a common political loyalty began to be present. The first attempted union of the two peoples failed, not having room for their difference. In the federation of these with other North American colonies, the difference of Quebec from the other provinces, and of these from one another and Quebec, had the form of particular sovereignties within a common sovereignty. That relation was implied in the Constitution and gradually realized. The two peoples were still divided in their political loyalties by their different response to the revolutions of the previous century. Catholic Quebec and a British Canada centred on the Empire were deeply divided until this division was taken into the common structure of the nineteenth-century state, and through the unification of its elements to a post-national state.[39]

(2) In the difficult transition – in Canada to independence, in Europe to the beginning of a post-national state – there are two essential considerations: (i) the point of transition is the nineteenth-century state restored to the unity of its elements; (ii) the common state as initially discerned in this relation is not an abstraction, nor the particular state in a recurrent division between nationalism and a society of equal individuals. The common post-national state came into view through the hard conditions of war. That this external mediation be replaced by a stable relation to the post-national state as primary in time of peace requires of individuals that they appropriate what was more done to them by the course of history than is their own work.

(i) Canadians for a little after the Second World War appeared to have a sense of what they were as a people. As uncommonly free from the hatreds which set nation states against one another, Canada seemed to have a particular role in the new world order. Domestically we were capable of the enlightened social programs of a state which knew the true ends of government. In Quebec the authors of the 'quiet revolution' not only released the economic talents of their people but appeared to know what the state is. Then this initial clarity faded. Canadians seemed to lose all sense of what they had become. Institutions through which their freedom was able to develop were felt oppressive. Authority in all forms was felt alien by an anarchic freedom. Then also on the basis of this 'liberation' the desire awakened to have in some form or other the lost direction and universality, but as yet hardly that in which their freedom was formed and which underlies their free rejection of it.

In Quebec the 'quiet revolution' was soon fragmented. Some adopted Lévesque's interpretation that the state of Quebec was primarily a linguistic and cultural community which could only be itself as separate from Canada. Some, following Trudeau, took the state of Quebec to be the common centralizing relation of a multitude of equal individuals. Support for both interpretations was sought in analogies with the European Union – colonialism after its time. Trudeau's position permitted a federalism only superficially related to the Constitution and to the common Canadian loyalty formed by our history.

While these opposed interpretations of the revolution animated political life in Quebec for a time, the same – or a more radical – collapse of institutions occurred in the Canada of British culture. To an anarchic individualism neither nationalism nor democratic centralism has much attraction; still less, it might seem, the rational freedom of a common post-national state to which our history has led us.

A like collapse has befallen the state of Quebec and all parts of the federation. At the same time the true federalism to which historically we have come remains strongly attractive and is sought in Quebec and the rest of Canada. The Canada in which Quebec and the provinces of a British culture are equal and their differences secured eludes contemporary political discourse. An attempt to discover it at Meech Lake foundered: there was no sufficient consideration of principles and of the relation of what was proposed to nationalism and to the democratic centralism of Trudeau. By themselves in their opposition these positions beget recurrent referenda – or until, a multitude of accidental forces conspiring some day in that direction, the nationalists prevail. We are at an impasse, and do not know how to move beyond it.

(ii) The current impasse, where everyone is weary of the recurrent contests between nationalists and democratic centralists but discovers no new positions in their place, where the interest of the general culture is to dissipate institutional structures and live the Heraclitean freedom of incessant change – these phenomena need not be thought negative only. In every successful revolution[40] – and for Canadians their independence is a revolution against a long colonial dependence – it is necessary first to loosen the hold of former things, to give oneself a distance from them. This destructive retreat in this as in other cases will then be found to be a *reculer pour mieux sauter.* The question occurs at that point: what then are Canadians moved to put in the place of the old? The answer is evident in many ways.

In Quebec there was an expectation that a renewed federalism would follow 'patriation.' This expectation explains the vehement reaction there to the defeat of the Meech Lake Accord, in which there was seen to be at least the beginning of such a renewal. It explains the continuing attachment of Quebecers to federalism, and the refusal to accept separation simply. The exasperating immobility of Canadians of British culture in the face of an impending ruin to their country has in part a like explanation: somehow Canada will remain together; the constitutional problem is not as bad as it appears to be, that is, an undefined solution is assumed.

The positive impulse is to make our own what we have become through our history, to know our constitution as the basis of our freedom. As with Americans when they had to give form and stability to their independence, our history was a series of episodes received from colonial powers, assented to but never taken wholly upon ourselves. To make it our own we have to dwell again with its stages, know their limits and the causes of our dissatisfaction with them. The objective measure in this renewed experience is the last stage, in which our dependence ended and consequently we had need to know our institutions and the freedom formed in them.

The difference of North American from European nation states has already been examined. At the beginning of a Canadian reflection on our independence this difference is not wholly apparent. We see the incipient structure of our independence not as it properly is for us as Canadians but by reference to the analogous transition of the European nation states into the post-national state of the Union. This reference is necessary and useful, but also misleading. In the model, nation states, understood as linguistic and cultural communities, are there, and with them the common economy in which individuals are equal. The political union can appear as added to these communities, a 'superstate,' not a proper state. In the Canadian, as in the American federation, the particular states and the economic relations of individuals fall within the union. The nationalist and the democratic centralist in Canada, relying on the model, give priority, the one to the nation, the other to the economic community; or as combining them, treat their unity as derivative. The contortions by which in post-modern European thought the difference of these communities in relation to each other and to the political union is both maintained and undermined have already been noticed. These difficulties point to but never reach the North American comprehension of particular states in the post-national state. The model for us is thus properly a device serving to bring this unified relation into view.

When this difference is grasped the appropriation of our independence and developed freedom can be seen to have a definite logical form. We must ask first what we have when the dispersed elements of the European Union – the national communities and the multitude of equal economic individuals – are taken into the common state, which in this relation would no longer be a 'superstate' but the central state of a federation of the North American type. Then of this realized union we must ask what form of freedom is in it – whether that which we have come to in our history or another and less complete freedom.

Perhaps with little clarity as to method, this construction was offered to the Canadian people in the Charlottetown Accord. Canadians in all parts of the country with an uncommon unanimity rejected the Accord. The people, being sometimes clearer than their leaders about their ultimate political interests, one can reasonably suppose, did not find in it an adequate and acceptable definition of their freedom.

Absent from the arguments of separatists and federalists, which look from the one side to the European Union, from the other to the Charlottetown Accord, is anything more than a trivial consideration of our difference from the United States. That we are different, Canadians, whether of British or of French culture, have commonly assumed. Assumed also has been that in some way our freedom and our political institutions are to be preferred to the American form. This difference, if one would determine methodically and not by some prejudice or arbitrary opinion what it is, must be considered as the difference of one type of North American polity from another.

Historically Canadians retreated from the revolutions of the eighteenth century and were barely touched by them in the 1837 rebellions. But the nineteenth-century state, which in one form we received in responsible government and in the 1867 Constitution, is a response to those revolutions and contains them in it. Only with NAFTA and the growing integration of the Canadian with the American economy are the conditions present in which we can experience fully that enlightened freedom and measure it by our sense of ourselves and our freedom. If as with the definition of our freedom in the Charlottetown Accord we find dissatisfaction also with the American model we could then attend to the measure by which we made those judgments, namely the freedom contained in our type of post-national federation.

The interest of a reflection on the history of the Canadian federation would then be to make our own that correction and unification of the elements of the nineteenth-century state which was imposed on us externally by the wars of the European nation states and their consequent transition to a post-national state.

This threefold reflection through which our independence would not be immediate and abstract but of what we had become in the course of our history needs to be set forth more precisely:

(a) The first attempt to grasp our new found Canadian independence and the polity appropriate to it broke down into an opposition of nationalist and democratic centralist positions, and the pursuit of these positions has weakened for a new generation either into indifference or into an aesthetic rather than a political relation to them. The logic of this division, and the changing relations to this division and to an underlying unity is a matter of great interest: it has been the object in Europe of a 'post-modern' culture. This culture is beyond the contest of fascists and Marxists in the inter-war and war years, in that a unity of the opposed positions is recognized and they are on that account pacified. The elements of the political structure are a plurality of linguistic and cultural communities, a common economic society in which cultural differences are predicated of equal individuals, and the common state.

In any political community there is an initial solidarity, the separation from it of a multitude of competing and cooperating interests, and a unified relation of these interests. In the European Community the several linguistic and cultural communities take themselves to be sovereign states, that is, to have their relations to the common economic society and the common state centred in them. They enter these larger communities by treaties and with the consent of their peoples, and to secede from them is likewise within their power and their affair only. But this conviction is belied by the fact that they do not singly have power to regulate the economic relations of their citizens and the fact that the common state is essential both to their internal unity and to prevent a recurrence of wars among them. It is thus equally true to say that the economic society and the common state are prior to the linguistic and cultural communities, and that sovereignty is situated rather in economic society and eminently in the common state. In this consideration the supposed power of the nation states, which these linguistic communities take themselves to be, to join or secede as they like from the larger community appears more illusory than real.

But if the order of priority is reversed and the common state taken to be first, there is the difficulty that the members of the linguistic and cultural communities do not find the multitude of habits, traditions, familiar ways in which they live and are a particular community preserved in that relation, but rather an abstract bureaucracy for which they feel no affection. The common economy, while offering a field for the expression of particular interests and talents, and satisfying needs and desires more abundantly, also levels and subjects individuals to blind economic forces in which they feel themselves unfree. There occurs thus a dialectic which instates and destabilizes one element and then another in a recurrent circle.

These linguistic and cultural communities are not states in an older and common sense, in that there is not in them a unity of ends. Or, better, a unified end exists in them in the medium of language and imagination and in cultural habits, not in thought and thought realized in action. Thus the post-modern culture of these communities is averse to thought and assigns a primacy to language as the seat of a cultural content formerly taken to be founded on the universality of thought.

The members of these confined communities as equal in their common economic community touch on the universal, and are uncomfortable with language and the fixity of cultural habits. It belongs also to 'post-modern' culture to expose the instability of language and the life enclosed within it. It is easily shown that there is an 'otherness' or negativity which ever eludes linguistic expression, so that what is said and accepted in the discourse of cultural communities is no more true than untrue.

The society of equal individuals, if its members thus free themselves from the tedious confines of a particular cultural community, is itself exposed to a like criticism. It is at home in an abstract equality, and thus in turn oblivious of 'otherness' or difference. Here too an apparent stability is exposed to doubt and instability, incorrigible from its standpoint.

Thus the relation of individuals to the common state recurs as that on which both the linguistic and the economic community rest. But how from the recurrent 'otherness' and thus unfreedom of these communities can one enter the common political community in which this negativity is circumvented, if indeed there is in that community what formerly one expected of a state – a unity of ends? If there is to be experience of that common state, it must be encountered first as other, as externalized and temporalized. One is attracted to the image of aboriginal peoples living not far from a 'state of nature' where there are no longer a multitude of tribes but they have begun to think of themselves as a people. Those whom we formerly thought barbarous and unfree are thus made our guides to freedom: from the rational order we imposed on them, thinking ourselves free in it, we must be saved by their example. But then the beginning of experience is not its end and when we have made that temporalized state our own, that preference for the primitive and immediate is reversed: we know the common state for what it is – as that on which the other communities depend. The movement of these divided communities to the unity of a state is analogous to the unification of the nation state before Enlightenment and the formation of civil society within it.

Thus we have in the transition of the European nation states to a post-national state, in a first reflection on their consequent dependence, a relation like that of their original formation into sovereign states. Here this relation is not of a particular state but of a common state. The particular states, considered in that dependence, are not primarily linguistic and cultural communities, nor the multitude of equal individuals in their particular interest, but themselves sovereign in the same sense as the common state, particularized sovereignties.

In the European Community this dialectic of 'post-modern' culture is not carried through to its conclusion. The cultural and linguistic habits, the former independence of the nation states as embodied have too strong a hold. The common economy and common state which are perforce accepted are also resisted. But the dialectic which allows a sceptical freedom from the national and economic communities is a no less necessary element of this culture. In a North American situation there is not the same resistance to the argument which here only discovers a form of the 'post-national' state in which in fact we live.

On the stages of this dialectical drama as played in Canada not much need be added. An attempt was made in the Charlottetown Accord to draw together the elements of the argument. Canada, it was said there, is composed of linguistic and cultural communities and a common economy. There is an enveloping political community best perceived through the spirituality of the native peoples.[41] To serve this role the content of this spirituality had to be extended from the particularity of tribes and a particular way of life. The many tribes are seen as a people and constituting thereby an immediately existing state, which serves as a model or symbol of the unified political community which the Canadian state would be. The further step of referring this externalized polity to the actual Canadian state is not taken. If this first reflection were completed, one would know the Canadian state as unified, not the further development of individual freedom within it.

When we bring before us the whole articulation of the argument, some consequences of great interest become evident. The first is that the assumed democratic right of national communities to secede from the Canadian federation rests on an incomplete reflection on the European model which is assumed to confirm it. Secondly, the acceptance by the democratic centralist that such a right exists, though requiring perhaps a stronger proof than 'fifty percent plus one,' rests on equally unstable assumptions. Thirdly, since the linguistic and cultural communities in the light of the whole argument have only such sovereignty as the common state imparts to them, they have on their own no right of secession.

It is also evident that the freedom individuals have in relation to the common state, so far as this is defined by the present argument, is not adequate to that which they acquired in the course of our history. It is rather the concept of freedom with which our history began. Likewise federal and provincial sovereignties, as defined by the whole argument of the European model, are not what we know from our history. There is lacking to it both the subjective freedom of Enlightenment and the incorporation of that freedom into the post-revolutionary state. How in our independence do we make our own this further development of our freedom and our political institutions? Not certainly from the European model.

(b) The further development of an independent Canada towards an appropriation of its history and political freedom is in relation to the United States. We have both to be open to the 'enlightened' freedom which opposes the state unless as the servant of free rational individuals and to hold to our historic differences from the United States – to a state which has that freedom in it but can draw particular interests into the whole interest of its citizens. Western Canadians and their governments tend to fluctuate between a conservatism of the American right and a socialistic liberalism. This conservatism has a political instrument in the Reform Party, which would replace a traditional conservatism more attached to the state. Ontario, which in the time of the Empire was sure of its difference from the United States, has seen the disintegration of a British conservatism and its replacement, at least for the moment, by an American conservatism like that of the Reform Party. Ontarians feared the North American Free Trade Agreement (NAFTA). But the conjoint opposition of socialism and an older conservatism, which might define a distinct Canadian position, hardly appears. Quebecers, having in them an 'enlightened' freedom akin to the American, are commonly at home more easily in the United States than in Ontario. So far as Quebecers retain something of the sense of a state they had in the first bloom of the 'quiet revolution,' and thus of the difference of Canada from the United States, they could with reason accept NAFTA more confidently than Ontarians. The nationalist and centralist fragments of that revolution, which look to the European model, have no ground for that security. The people of the Maritimes have in common with Quebecers that they feel an affinity with New Englanders especially more easily than with Ontarians, and with that an inarticulate sense of a Canadian difference. Newfoundlanders, basically in a pre-enlightened society until recent years, received Americans enthusiastically during the Second World War,[42] and that attraction continues along with an indifference to Ontarian culture.

In what way these diverse relations will develop and out of them a clear perception take shape of a common difference of Canada from the United States, that for the present is unclear. The reaction to the pressures of a common economy should however tend to make the difference more distinct. At the same time, as the argument has shown, there is great need in the United States that the relation of society to state approach more nearly the Canadian model.

(c) As the centre of constitutional interest in Canada shifts from the abstractions of linguistic and cultural communities and democratic centralism, and from the first form of a post-national state on which they depend, to the deeper problem of the difference of our post-national federation from the American, the answer to current questions about a right of secession will be evident. The question will be asked in relation to the Constitution and not in terms of 'democratic rights' in abstraction from a context giving meaning to 'rights' and to 'democracy,' or of loose analogies with other peoples of a very different history and political experience. The beginning of an appropriate answer is to recognize what a post-national federation, ours or the American, is, and what it means to say that it is indivisible. The present study of American institutions has shown not only that it does not belong to a particular sovereignty within the federation to dissolve for its own citizens or those of other particular sovereignties the integrity of their common state; it was also shown that the freedom of a particular sovereignty and the knowledge of its freedom are dependent on the federation. From which it followed that only if there is a democratic right to destroy and debase one's freedom is there a right of secession from such a federation. What was said of the American case applies by the same logic to the Canadian.

But there is more to the appropriation of what we became through our history than to distinguish generally our concept of freedom and the relation of society to the state from the American. There is also the divided colonial relation of French and British in Canada from Confederation until the point of independence, when we thought ourselves capable of regulating this difference internally. It has been shown in the historical part of this inquiry on what this capacity rests, namely, that our federation, like the American, is based not on the culture of a particular nation state but on a common European culture. Within that common culture the two national cultures can have free play, and by their reciprocal relation bring to light their common basis.

A comparison with the United States can illustrate the essential operation of such a federation. Occasionally the debates of the American Congress carry the argument back to the principles of the Constitution on which ultimately political decisions depend. Such debates are a continuing education to the American people, who are both loyal as no other to their constitution, whose principles are written and known, and who ordinarily regard government as a matter of deals, capitulation to special interests, etc. In the first spectacle their loyalty is confirmed, and respect for the state and those in political office can outweigh an everyday cynicism. The debates of the Parliament of Canada are uniformly confined to particularities, to partisan retorts, and the like. The relation of decisions to their constitutional basis does not appear. The loyalty of Canadians and a stronger than American tendency to respect government are not informed and strengthened by the actual operation of government. How many Canadians know or have any definite sense of their constitution?

The relation of peoples of French and British culture in Canada is in good part controlled by prejudices, ignorance, old hostilities, etc. of which politicians sometimes take advantage for their own ends, which as recorded in public opinion polls they sometimes regard as defining the limits of the politically possible. The primary condition of a more principled consideration of this and other deeply divisive matters is that the Constitution be known and its operation become conspicuous as need be. Public opinion can in this way be brought into contact with the stable and reasonable loyalties of the people, and the limits of the possible greatly extended: 'Les bornes du possible dans les choses morales sont moins étroites que nous ne pensons.'[43]

The constitutional correction which could assure the minority of French culture in Canada of their equality and of a protection of their particularity not subject to the fluctuating opinions and prejudices of the majority and their elected representatives is first that state sovereignty be removed from the now meaningless symbolism for most of an all but defunct British monarchy and attached to the office of a president as protector of the Constitution. Canadians might then know what their Constitution is and relate thus political loyalty to a visible and present head of state. Secondly, the effective sovereignty of the state should not rest in the Prime Minister all but exclusively, but as well in the twofold representation of the people individually and as sovereign provinces.

Canadian sovereignty, which is properly neither French nor British but inclusive of both, can let this difference have its place in the structure of the senatorial representation of the sovereign provinces. Fundamental questions about the relation of the two cultures could then be brought back to constitutional principles and the common and equal loyalty of the peoples of both cultures.

The security of Quebec and as well of the other provinces in their particularity is to be obtained partly and primarily in an articulated relation to the federal sovereignty. The further and also essential protection is in the recognition of provincial sovereignty, within the powers assigned, as an unqualified sovereignty. For to particular sovereignties within the federation belong not only powers which might in altered circumstances be divided differently, but primarily their difference itself. In the case of Quebec that difference is the French language and culture. Others might care to protect lesser qualitative differences.

Canadians after Meech Lake and Charlottetown know the difficulty of amending constitutional principles. Neither an unstable consensus among Premiers and the Prime Minister nor the consultation of experts and special interests is an appropriate method. Because the Constitution defines the primary conditions of political agreement in Canada it cannot fall to any particular interest or collection of interests to amend its principles. Those who would with some clarity amend it must abstract from these particularities, discern the simple operation of the principles, and ask by what changes in continuity with their history the Constitution would better reflect the fundamental loyalties and sense of their freedom of the people. Once in this manner we have brought our independence into agreement with our history, we should be as reluctant to amend constitutional principles as the Americans. May Quebecers and others long be spared the partisan constitutional aggressions of recent years!

One might reasonably think that our independence was complete if we could regard the operation of a federation in which different partial sovereignties could subsist, even the difference of national cultures, where difficult conflicts among the parts could occur and be resolved without oppressing the differences. In the particular sovereignties as in nation states, individuals do not know their rights and freedoms immediately, but as distinctions which emerge and show their primacy in the resolution and clarification of differences. And the clarity a particular sovereign community has about its ends and the order pertinent to their realization it maintains not within itself simply, but through its sometimes difficult relation with other sovereign communities of the federation and their resolution through the common principles of the constitution. Our independence is complete if the differences, for example of Ontario and the West – centralization and the sovereignty of provinces – are seen as in the course of their resolution realizing the federation and making possible a knowledge of our freedom. The different spirit of French and British culture and the consequent collisions and misunderstandings of the two not only sharpen in each the sense of its difference but permit a recognition of the common European freedom which our federation and the American would variously realize.[44]

Conclusion

The present argument has shown that questions about the democratic right of a linguistic and cultural community in Canada to secede from the federation belong to a preliminary stage in the definition of our independence. It has shown that the counter-position which takes Canada to be a centralized community of equal individuals belongs to the same stage. The two positions have in common that they recognize a democratic right of secession.

This democratic 'right' has two distinct meanings, as one may learn from the European model from which these positions derive. One is the right of linguistic and cultural communities to self-determination. Pure examples of that right are the demands of Basques, Irish nationalists, and many other ethnic and linguistic communities within European nation states that they be given independence. An equivalent in Canada is the claim of native tribes to self-government. Whatever else may be said of this 'right,' it is not democratic but communal, and exercised by leaders who think themselves authorized to realize it by whatever means.

The other meaning is the right of nation states to decide by simple majority whether or not to apply to join the European Community. Considered in its content, this is the right of members of a nation state, who no longer have the political will to maintain an internal unity or sovereignty, to choose whether by joining to acquiesce in their historical situation or at an unmanageable economic cost to remain on their own.

Nationalists in Quebec use the word ambiguously in both senses. Partly the leaders of an ethnic community have the right to obtain the independence of their people by a *coup*. Partly the whole Quebec community is said to have a right to choose democratically whether or not to be part of a Canadian or North American economic and political association. The content of this right is not so clear as in Europe, since Quebec is not in transition from the status of a nation state to that of a universal or post-national state. Nor is Canada or the United States in such a transition. Nor does the ethnic right to self-determination apply well to old stock Quebecers who are neither a politically undeveloped tribe nor a linguistic and cultural community absorbed into a nation state in the process of its formation; and now that the unity has slackened, demanding to be free from it.

Quebec independence and Canadian unity have thus to the present been discussed largely in borrowed and unreal concepts, in which no solution is to be found. The unreality of current arguments would become evident were Quebec to become independent. First, the ethnic and economic meanings of the 'right' to independence would collide: who belongs to the state of Quebec? Secondly, an economic and political association with the United States and/or Canada would not be with former nation states but with post-national states in which the political freedoms of the older modern age had not collapsed into cultural habits giving way to the levelling pressures of the common economy and state. In these relations an independent Quebec, if it would not be absorbed, would have to define its political freedom through the constitutions of those federations. In this process it would discover that the constitution in which uniquely its language and culture would be secure and could flourish was that which already belonged to it though its common history with those of British culture in Canada. What concealed this reality from Quebecers would be seen to be the unreal abstraction of a first reflection on a common Canadian independence.

The same abstractions have their hold on Canadians of British culture. But having slight contact with political realities in Canada and the United States these abstractions are certain to fade and lose their attraction. A sign that we are moving from this first formulation of Canadian independence is the decision of the Government of Canada to ask the Supreme Court to define the so-called democratic right of secession in terms of the Constitution. While the opposed abstractions of nationalists and federalists held the field the constitution from which governments received their powers appeared to have no bearing on these constitutional differences!

One does not know whether the Supreme Court will answer the questions submitted to it directly according to the principles of the Constitution or will interpose concepts limiting their application to contemporary conditions. At the least the Court cannot but declare that there is no unilateral democratic right of secession; that a legal secession is only possible with the agreement of the federal and the other provincial sovereignties. It might not add that agreement could not be about economic and financial matters only but also and principally about federal and provincial sovereignty. At that level it must become evident that no agreement was possible, and that the Canadian federation, like the American, was indivisible, and for the same reasons. True separatists such as Mr Parizeau knew well that discussions towards agreement must be futile. To semi-separatists that may not be so clear.

By what arguments could the federal and the provincial governments, if they were true to their primary constitutional obligations, be persuaded to give up the territorial integrity of Canada, the common country of all Canadians? What could persuade them to a course ruinous to all Canadians? To Quebec even more, if possible, than to others, since they would lose the only security possible for their distinct language and culture? So long as federalism could be equated with the democratic centralism of Pierre Trudeau the illusion might stand that these primary political questions need not enter the argument, that the real interests of Canadians were economic and not rather the freedom they had through their history and federal institutions.

Until Canadians have gone farther in the understanding of their common history and institutions it must be uncertain whether in some referendum a majority of Quebec might choose to secede. Public opinion as evoked in referendum campaigns is unstable and fluctuates in response to changing circumstances. Mr Bouchard or another may seize an opportune moment and persuade a majority to vote 'Yes.' A *de facto* Quebec may be there and the Government of Canada required to take account of the fact. If that government had become clearer than in the past about the Constitution, about the desire of most Quebecers to be equal and distinct under it, and in the only true and possible sense sovereign at home, its appropriate response is evident enough and of no great difficulty. Its response would be to carry on as usual in Quebec according to its constitutional obligations, and to leave it to the illegal government in Quebec to realize its independence. Since no *coup* can do without an army, the Government of Canada would be less negligent than before and make certain that the Canadian military knew whom they were obliged to serve. The federal government would only respond to force clearly initiated by the secessionist government, and then only to the minimum degree. So far as its services to the Quebec people, and their federal obligations, were disturbed, that would be unmistakably the work of the secessionists.

The Government of Canada would await the internal collapse of the *coup* from the opposition of a near majority of federalists; from the division of true separatists from semi-separatists who were led to think that independence was an easy matter; through the repressive methods the leaders of the *coup* must use to control disaffections and criticisms; through a general repugnance to the methods necessary to dislodge the federal presence; through economic confusion and hardship. The *coup* would not survive many months if at the same time the Government of Canada had the will at last to implement, it might be at first on its own, those reforms which would assure the Quebec people that they had their full recognition and their sovereignty in the Canadian federation. Since by the same reforms Canadians in the other provinces would come to a clarity about their freedom and its appropriate institutional structure, and thus have common cause with Quebecers, it would not be a great matter in those circumstances[45] for political leaders, if they were tolerably adequate to their offices, to awaken in their people a sense of their fundamental interest as Canadians and as citizens of a particular province.

Notes

1 Originally published as 'The Philosophical Basis of Constitutional Discussion in Canada,' *Animus* 2 (1997).

2 The opposition was characteristically more muted in Britain; at its extreme in Germany; qualified variously by national differences in France, Italy, Spain, etc.; the one side suppressed in the Soviet Union.

3 Foucault, Deleuze, Derrida, etc. These writers, situated in a national culture, would one way or another be free in that particularity by sheltering it under an endless otherness.

4 The same may be said of South America, but for simplicity the present argument has primarily in view North America (Canada, United States, Mexico).

5 They might, as in New England, also think themselves delivered from religious oppression and free to build a world better conformed to their beliefs.

6 The class structures which in an older world kept their hold tended to dissolve in the New World.

7 The Mexican polity is treated here in a few words simply to complete the structure of the argument. For a more extended treatment see F.L. Jackson, 'Mexican Freedom: The Ideal of the Indigenous State,' *Animus* 2 (1997), to which the writer is much indebted.

8 The constant problem of the older modern political philosophy which would find place for private freedom within the state. Without, as with Marx, Mill, etc. making the state a function of private freedom.

9 For this relation to be evident the construction of society from an antecedent state of nature must be seen to belong to a subjective reflection without historical objectivity. So far as his standpoint permitted, Hume already had a sense that this was so in calling the contract a 'fiction' (*Treatise*, bk III, part II, sect. 1: Of Justice). But it is a rational construction (Rousseau, Kant, recently Rawls).

10 That the state is not a voluntary association of individuals Aristotle showed against the subjective philosophy of his time: man is by nature a 'political animal,' who has only as much of individual freedom as the state can contain. Contemporary Aristoteleans (A. MacIntyre, etc.) revive that teaching in some form. The enlightened modern, however, can only tolerate a state in which there is room for a society of free individuals. The priority to society of such a state is both proved and resisted in the course of American history.

11 *The Federalist*, XLV (Madison).

12 *The Federalist*, IX, X (Hamilton).

13 The difference of society from the state does not collapse as for Marxists into either anarchic freedom or the rigid domination of a party. From the side of the existential individual even so acute a philosopher as Heidegger did not distinguish American liberalism from Soviet Marxism.

14 Hume, *Treatise*, book III, part III, sect.1.

15 Montesquieu, *De l'esprit des lois*, III, iii; III, vii.

16 Ibid., XI, iii: '... la liberté [sc. politique] ne peut consister qu'à pouvoir faire ce que l'on doit faire, et à n'être point contraint de faire ce que l'on ne doit pas vouloir.' This universal relation of individuals to the constitution is the basis of their confidence in the laws and the expectation that they will generally be obeyed. Cf. XII, ii.

17 Americans, regarding the state more from the rational self-relation of the individual (Jefferson) or of individuals in their economic relations (Hamilton) than from their common rationality, conceived the division of powers, which made political liberty possible, more loosely than Montesquieu. They attended less to the primary unity of the legislative and executive powers, on which Montesquieu is not far from Rousseau's doctrine of a primary

indivisibility (*Du contrat social*, II, II), and did not concur in his consequent reflection: 'Des trois puissances don nours avons parlé, celle de juger est en quelque façon nulle' (*De l'esprit*, XI, vi): the judicial power is that part of the executive which interprets the laws in relation of particular cases.

18 Notes 10 and 11 *supra.*

19 On the New England Convention, see S.E. Morrison, *The Oxford History of the American People* (Oxford, 1965), 396–7.

20 New England Convention; see Morrison, 396–7.

21 Calhoun's Exposition of 1828, see Morrison, 432.

22 'Before 1861 the two words "United States" were generally used as a plural noun ... After 1865 the United States became a singular noun.' J.M. McPherson, *Abraham Lincoln and the Second American Revolution* (Oxford, 1991), viii.

23 John Rawls, *Political Liberalism* (New York, 1993), 40–3.

24 Richard Rorty, 'Pragmatism, Relativism, and Irrationalism,' in *Consequences of Pragmatism* (Minneapolis, 1982), 160–75, esp. 165f.

25 See below.

26 *Political Liberalism*, 35.

27 Ibid., 181.

28 Kant, *Kritik der Reinen Vernunft*, Vorrede.

29 *Political Liberalism*, 24.

30 Ibid., 195ff.

31 Ibid., 6.

32 *Religion innerhalb der Grenzen der blossen Vernunft.*

33 George-Étienne Cartier, quoted by Peter H. Russell, *Constitutional Odyssey*, 2nd ed. (Toronto, 1993), 85.

34 ibid., 43.

35 Quoted in Russell, 43.

36 'The Constitution Act, 1867,' preface, in *The Constitution Acts 1867 to 1982* (Department of Justice, Canada, 1989).

37 James Ross Hurley, *Amending Canada's Constitution* (Canada, 1996), 24.

38 On the French spirit, see *De l'esprit des lois*, XIX, chap. 5.

39 The Quebec people might turn inward from an un-Catholic secularity. The Church might attempt to give a Christian direction to that secularity through neo-Thomism and other forms antecedent to the subjective freedom of the modern age. But the division could only be bridged by the subjective freedom latent in that post-revolutionary Catholicism, which must appear.

40 Not like the Russian revolution, which has failed to transform the character of the old Russian society.

41 There is the memorable image of the prayerful chanting and drumming of the native chief at the hearings on the Charlottetown Accord conducted by Joe Clark.

42 F.L. Jackson, *Newfoundland in Canada: A People in Search of a Polity* (St John's, 1984) 7–29, esp. 17ff.

43 *Du contrat social*, III, chap. 12.

44 In France the older culture of the people enters contemporary life as refracted by the assumptions of the post-modern culture; similarly in Britain. The spirit of each can move more freely in Canada.

45 And not only in those circumstances ...

COMMENTARY ONE

The Critique of Naturalistic Individualism: James Doull's Political Thought, 1960–1983

HENRY ROPER

George Grant, perhaps Canada's best-known political philosopher, frequently acknowledged James Doull's influence upon his intellectual development.[1] But Doull's own writings show that his contribution to Canadian political philosophy has not been confined to inspiring the creative work of others. It is my intention here to provide an outline of his political ideas during the 1960s and 1970s, when Doull not only wrote about the radical changes taking place in Canada but also became directly involved in politics.

Doull was a founding member of the Nova Scotia New Democratic Party, serving for several years in the early 1960s on the executive of the Halifax Federal Constituency. In 1962 he acted as chairman of the Draft Program Committee of the Nova Scotia NDP.[2] Doull did not provide an account of his reasons for becoming a political activist. Nevertheless, it is possible to discover from his writings his ideas on the alternatives open to Canada during this period.

Doull's basic preoccupations about the country would seem to have been rooted in his belief in the need to impose some sort of limit upon the pursuit of self-interest in capitalist society, particularly as expressed in American democracy. American affluence had been achieved through the elevation of the individual at the expense of the community. In a paper written in 1962 for the NDP, entitled 'Liberalism and Social Democracy in Canada,' Doull argues that the Canadian Liberal party was becoming, like the American Democrats, a coalition of interest groups. If the newly born NDP were to differentiate itself from the Liberals, and help to prevent Canada's absorption into the United States, it had to stand for more than Pearsonian Liberalism in a slightly pinker form. Doull asserts that simply to turn to traditional socialism as an antidote to this danger would not be successful, for the sense of alienation fundamental to European socialism had been dissolved in North America by prosperity. 'What is required is plainly a socialism for the affluent society. It would be more exact to say a socialism for the American or unalienated society.'[3]

But why did Doull think that any form of socialism was necessary in the early 1960s if alienation had been overcome in North America? In his view socialism was needed to overcome an alienation more far-reaching than that generated by economic deprivation. Liberal America, despite its economic success, had given rise to another form of alienation through its elevation of wealth, attained by the pursuit of individual self-interest, to the position of supreme good. The extreme individualism embodied in America destroyed freedom, as did its opposite, the bureaucratic centralism of the Soviet Union. Both societies exalted equality, one through encouraging acquisitiveness, the other by denying it through state control and ownership. Doull concludes that the NDP must become a socialist party which worked to find a way between these two extremes, both of which made impossible a proper relation among individuals and between individuals and the state. This new way would be a socialism in which the state would act to limit competitiveness, but would, through planning, ensure that individuals and groups were compensated appropriately for their labours.

> Resentment would be outweighed by the more important fact that there was order in society – that social differences made sense and did not represent as now merely greater success in the competitions. The supreme art of government is to enable the governed in their disparate interests and abilities to find satisfaction in what they contribute and receive ... and to respect the different and greater contributions of other groups. Democratic socialism has to achieve in some measure this organic society or it will achieve none of its more limited purposes.[4]

To Doull, socialism would overcome the alienation created by liberal individualism by teaching each group in society its proper role and expectations. Canada, he suggests, although North American, is fortunate in being able to accept the greater role played by the state in European countries through its closer ties with British and French traditions.

'Liberalism and Social Democracy in Canada' reveals the preoccupations that are developed in Doull's other writings on political philosophy. He begins with the assumption that individual freedom cannot truly exist without its being perfected in the state, which makes possible the right relationship between individuals, families, and other social entities. In his article 'The Theology of the Great Society' (1967), he provides a critique of the limits of individualism and its inadequacy as an avenue to human freedom. The article took the form of an analysis of Harvey Cox's book *The Secular City*, which had been published in 1965. Doull describes this work as embodying completely the presuppositions and hopes of liberal America. Cox had no doubt that the principles of equality expressed in the American Revolution, combined with the abundance made possible through technology, would bring about the universal liberation of the individual. According to Doull, this belief, and the pragmatism on which it is based, is simply a faith with no philosophical foundation. It is based on a particular idea of freedom, but cannot explain why this conception of freedom should be considered as absolute, man being, to Cox, 'creator of the meaning he lives by.'[5]

The liberal faith, resting on such shaky foundations, also has ambiguous ends. Where, Doull asks, does this movement towards human liberation lead, or is it simply an endless process of becoming? He concludes that Cox's position raised dilemmas that must lead back to the very philosophy and theology that it was supposed to have transcended:

> In the 'secular city' we see neither the perfection of human freedom nor, as some fear, the end of western culture. Pragmatic man has shown how to cope with limited problems using limited methods. In doing so he has forgotten other forms of reason. He has extended immeasurably the means to human freedom, and has forgotten freedom itself. It is not possible to live humanly in 'Technopolis.' But neither is it necessary to abandon it. Instead technology can be overcome and contained within human freedom.[6]

Doull asserts that it is just as false to flee from 'the technology of human freedom' as it is to embrace it completely. It must be understood as one aspect of Christian freedom, of which it is simply an outgrowth, being 'the theology of the active men for whom it is sufficient to strive for limited goods – for whom thought, truth, beauty, enjoyment, everything ultimate is pursued only in subjective and unreal form.'[7]

Doull does not explain in 'The Theology of the Great Society' how, from the political perspective, man can move beyond technopolis. It is sufficient for his purpose to show what it is to live within it, that the freedom attained by pragmatic man is partial, and the liberal road to freedom illusory. He further develops his critique of liberal individualism in 'Naturalistic Individualism: Quebec Independence and an Independent Canada,' published in 1983. He opens this essay with the assertion that the situation of both English and French Canada is much the same. Both have lost contact with their common tradition, which was the subordination of individual economic interest to institutional life, whether expressed in the family, the church, or the state. French Canadian preoccupations with language and identity are symptomatic, not of a resistance to modernity, but of an acceptance of it, in the form of a belated nineteenth-century nationalism:

> Both nationalism and economic individualism of the present time are to be understood as steps in the decline of Europe and of the American extensions of that culture – a decline that has some parallels with the decline of the free states of ancient antiquity. There individuals in the course of time freed themselves from an objective system of rights and duties and came to regard themselves in their private interests as elements of the state and other institutions.[8]

Doull hastens to emphasize that he is not drawing a simplistic parallel between the decline of the ancient world and modern developments, but making a point about the consequences of individuals' becoming liberated from public obligations. Indeed, he goes on to posit that the history of institutions since the decline of Rome has been based on a factor that had no existence in ancient times, Augustinian Christianity. This has been the basis of secular freedom in the West, for in time it led to the emergence of secular institutions based on thought rather than nature. To Doull, the fundamental truth about Christian institutions is that in them nature, in all its aspects, particularly as an object of the human will, is shaped and contained by reason. Marx, in his argument, is both the prophet and instrument of the destruction of free institutions in the West, for Marx asserts that freedom lies in the overcoming of man's alienation from nature; freedom can be found not in the rational but in the exploration of the natural. This is what Doull means by 'technological naturalism.' Marx's views lead to the exaltation of natural individual desire; community in the traditional Christian sense cannot and must not exist, for all institutions, to the degree that they are expressions of reason and not nature, are modes of repression. In Doull's words, 'the state is to be absorbed into civil society and made the servant of the natural will. Family and church are forms of suppression. The economy is to be taken in hand and made to serve free individuals.'[9]

Doull proceeds to argue that the implications of Marx are present most explicitly in the technological societies of the West rather than in the bureaucratic states of the eastern bloc. In Western societies the end of Marxism – the liberation of the individual to live according to natural will – has been much more fully realized. Increasingly, the only limit placed upon natural rights in Western societies is that imposed by the natural rights of others. The decline of reason as a measure of anything must lead inevitably to the destruction of traditional distinctions between human and non-human; natural rights are thus extended beyond the human realm as, for example, in the animal-rights movement.[10]

To Doull, evil in the twentieth century has been understood in a new and sinister way. As liberated persons cannot face the reality that the horrors of this century, for example those perpetrated in the name of communism or fascism, are the result of human natural will, these are perversely attributed to an incomplete liberation from reason. In other words, evil is defined as the very opposite of its traditional Christian meaning.[11]

The contemporary situation, in his argument, is revealed in the proliferation of religious cults, the 'knowledge industry,' and the other endless avenues to self-fulfilment available in a society of naturalistic individualists. They believe their liberation is the culmination of human intellectual and spiritual history and so they are free to appropriate whatever part of their heritage that can fulfil their own particular natural desires. This is 'technological naturalism' because it is based on the presupposition that technological change and individual liberation are not only compatible but inseparable.[12]

Doull distinguishes this 'technological naturalism,' originating with Marx and triumphant in the United States, from the naturalism of Nietzsche and Heidegger, who recognized that 'technology and natural freedom are incapable of being combined – that their unity is a nihilistic will in which nature is not fulfilled ... but destroyed.'[13] Their view of natural freedom stripped away the illusion that liberation can be achieved through the medium of technological reason as the partner of the natural will, as they grasped that this particular form of the union of reason and nature is impossible. Indeed, their position led them to the view that if freedom is to be found in nature, it must be in a flight from technology altogether.[14] The naturalism present in Nietzsche and Heidegger (and by implication existentialism generally) simply furthers the disintegration of society, as individuals flee from their institutional obligations to the pursuit of private and particular ends.[15]

Doull's treatment of naturalism is reminiscent of his approach to the liberalism of Harvey Cox. Both positions are based upon the idea of subjective human freedom; in neither case, however, is that presupposition grounded in reason. The naturalistic examination of nature, turning it into an absolute and reducing reason to nothing, must reduce nature, which loses all conceptual content, to nothingness too.[16] It will be recalled that Doull sees liberalism as foundering upon the contradiction between the elevation of individual freedom as an absolute and the lack of any justification for this faith in pragmatic philosophy.[17] For both liberals and existentialists, the impossibility of sustaining what is fundamental to their positions will lead them back, in Doull's view, to a consideration of first principles, to a rediscovery of philosophy, so that they can rediscover the true content of reason, its proper relationship to nature, and, as a consequence, the truth of human freedom.

Doull devotes the last part of 'Naturalistic Individualism' to a consideration of Canada and Quebec. Having portrayed the United States as dominated by 'technological naturalism,' he sees the question as whether Canada will resist this fate, for the relationship between French- and English-speaking Canadians is subordinate to this fundamental decision facing both:

> It is generally thought that Canadians, whether English-speaking or French-speaking, have not much will to Americanize. If this means, as it may, that however inarticulately, they are too strongly drawn to an older Christian and European culture to revel in the free natural individuality of contemporary Americans, then it is possible to define the peculiar quality of being Canadian. The problem is set for them that either they can be nothing, either receptive and imitative, or they can define their rejection of technological naturalism by means of the old tradition. To that tradition and the rational freedom it contains their relation is commonly nostalgic: it is not their actual culture. It is not impossible that it should be their culture, and there is quite certainly no other way of repelling the servitude of free natural individuality or technology. But whether the desire of rational freedom will ever be strong [in] so apathetic a people, none can say.[18]

This lengthy quotation provides a clear insight into Doull's thinking about the possibilities and dangers facing Canada in the era of 'naturalistic individualism.' It also shows that his ideas remained consistent throughout the 1960s and 1970s. In 1962 he attempted to show that socialism in the North American context must serve as a means by which the individualism of America can be contained if it is not to be destructive. Canada, which had not fully accepted American ideals, could, through its closer contact with Europe, avoid the extremes of excessive state planning and individual self-assertiveness, thus becoming a society incorporating the strength of both traditions. He foresaw the danger that the NDP would turn into a version of the Canadian Liberal party, capable only of acting as a broker among interest groups; the development of the Canadian political process since the 1960s has surely borne out his fears. The ideal of an organic society, which had a central place in the ideology of both Canadian conservatism and socialism, has disappeared, to be replaced by the politics of individual and group rights. Doull's analysis of this development in 'Naturalistic Individualism: Quebec and an Independent Canada,' by placing it within the context of contemporary Marxism and existentialism, raises the level of argument about the Canadian polity from the parochial to the world-historical.

It is worth noting again the connection between Doull and George Grant. Both seem in the late 1950s to have been possessed by a cautious optimism about the possibilities open to Canada, and perhaps even North America. As we have seen, this is present in Doull's essay on 'Liberalism and Social Democracy in Canada.' It can also be found in Grant's first book, *Philosophy in the Mass Age*, published in 1959 and written when he was still under the sway of Hegel. As Grant put it in the preface to the second edition, which appeared in 1966:

> It cannot be insisted too often how hard it is for anyone who believes in the western doctrine of providence to avoid reaching the conclusion that Hegel has understood the implications of that doctrine better than any other thinker. I therefore attempted to write down in non-professional language the substance of the vision that the age of reason was beginning to dawn and first in North America.[19]

Grant then explains that his thinking had been led away from this optimistic vision by his moving from Nova Scotia to Ontario, where he experienced fully the effects of technological change upon the Great Lakes region of Canada. But even in *Philosophy in the Mass Age* Grant warns that freedom is increasingly denied as much in capitalist as in Marxist societies. Both East and West are dominated by the idea of humans as the makers of history, an idea that pushes aside any spiritual tradition which can contain the will: 'The question thoughtful people must ask themselves is whether the progressive spirit is going to hold within itself any conception of spiritual law and freedom; or whether our history-making spirit will degenerate into a rudderless desire for domination on the part of our elites and aimless pleasure-seeking among the masses.'[20]

Like Grant in the writings that followed *Philosophy in the Mass Age*, Doull moved away from the optimism of 'Liberalism and Social Democracy in Canada' to a more pessimistic view in the late 1970s and early 1980s. His attitude towards the United States, for example, hardened to the degree that he saw America primarily in relation to the triumph of the natural will; as he put it in 'Naturalistic Individualism,' in a colloquialism unusual in so austere a stylist, America has 'gone natural.'[21] There is little optimism in this essay, only a suggestion of what Canadians must do if they are not to follow Americans into the swamp of unfreedom to which they will be led by the pursuit of nature rather than reason.

Doull, who had given up his involvement with the NDP in the late 1960s, returned to non-partisan political activity in 1980 as a result of the Canadian government's decision to repatriate the Canadian constitution. He considered Prime Minister Trudeau's willingness to ignore the provinces as revealing a determination to 'reduce to a secondary level the historical and traditional aspect of Canadian sovereignty and put in its place a technocratic centralism representing primarily individual rights.'[22] Furthermore, Trudeau wished to substitute an abstract populism based on the idea of individual rights, as embodied in the Charter of Rights and Freedoms, for traditional liberties sustained by parliamentary sovereignty at both the federal and provincial levels. In 'An Open Letter to Members of the House of Commons and Especially the Senate of Canada,' Doull argues that the exaltation of human rights and the notion of government as a face-to-face relationship between citizen and central authority, notions basic to Trudeau's constitutional reforms, could lead only to bureaucratic rule. 'The fanatical advocates of this system are everywhere zealous for democracy and human rights in theory. Both are trampled on in practice, for the reason that there is no power able to contain the technocratic leadership itself.'[23] He returns to this point in 'Naturalistic Individualism,' where he suggests that the more society becomes fragmented by naturalistic individualism, either in its Marxist or existentialist guise, the greater the probability that individual desires can only be reconciled by the authority exercised by bureaucratic elites.[24]

If James Doull's writings by the early 1980s reveal a deepening pessimism, his conviction remained secure that rational freedom can only be attained by rediscovering the philosophical truths by which it came into the world. All his writings about Canada, implicitly or explicitly, call his fellow citizens to an understanding of that tradition of thought, in the hope that Canadians would turn from the slavery of naturalistic individualism to a knowledge that would enable them to realize a better destiny.[25]

Notes

1 Larry Schmidt, ed., *George Grant in Process: Essays and Conversations* (Toronto: Anansi, 1978), 64. 'Doull, who was my own age and really educated in a way I was not, led me into Kant and Plato ... Of course Doull's great teacher has been Hegel, and I am not a Hegelian. That has led Doull and me apart. But that doesn't make one forget one's debt. He was the person who made me really look at western philosophy.' See also David Cayley, ed., *George Grant in Conversation* (Toronto: Anansi, 1995), 56; and William Christian, *George Grant: A Biography* (Toronto: University of Toronto Press, 1993), 139–40.

2 See the New Democratic Party Collection, vol. 1353 #2, MG 2, Public Archives of Nova Scotia [PANS], and the James H. Aitchison Collection, vols. 1326 #2, 1326 #3, and 1328 #3, MG 2, PANS. I am grateful to Mr Dennis Theman, former provincial secretary, Nova Scotia NDP, for permission to examine certain items in the NDP Collection, PANS.

3 J.H. Aitchison Collection, vol. 1328 #3, MG 2, PANS, 'Liberalism and Social Democracy in Canada,' 4. This unpublished paper was written in Doull's capacity as chairman of the Draft Program Committee, Nova Scotia NDP, and is dated November 1962. Hereafter cited as 'Liberalism and Social Democracy.'

4 'Liberalism and Social Democracy,' 5. Cf. George Grant, 'An Ethic of Community,' in Michael Oliver, ed., *Social Purpose for Canada* (Toronto: University of Toronto Press, 1961), 17–19.

5 Doull, 'The Theology of the Great Society,' *Canadian Journal of Theology* 13 (1967): 5–18.

6 Ibid., 14.

7 Ibid., 18.

8 Doull, 'Naturalistic Individualism: Quebec and an Independent Canada,' in Eugene Coombs, ed., *Modernity and Responsibility: Essays for George Grant* (Toronto: University of Toronto Press, 1983), 33. Hereafter cited as 'Naturalistic Individualism.'

9 'Naturalistic Individualism,' 34. Cf. James Doull, 'The Christian Origin of Contemporary Institutions Part Two,' *Dionysius* 8 (1984) and 'Hegel and Contemporary Liberalism: A Defense of the *Rechtsphilosophie* against Marx

and His Contemporary Followers,' in J.J. O'Malley, ed., *The Legacy of Hegel* (The Hague: Nijhoff, 1973), 224–48.

10 'Naturalistic Individualism,' 34–5.

11 Ibid., 36.

12 Ibid., 37.

13 Ibid., 40.

14 Ibid., 40–1.

15 Ibid., 41–2. Cf. Doull, 'Augustinian Trinitarianism and Existential Theology,' *Dionysius* 3 (1979): 111–24.

16 'Naturalistic Individualism,' 45–7.

17 'The Theology of the Great Society,' 7–8 and passim.

18 'Naturalistic Individualism,' 50.

19 George P. Grant, *Philosophy in the Mass Age*, 2nd ed. (Toronto: Copp Clark, 1966), vii; reprinted in vol. 2 of the *Collected Works of George Grant* (Toronto: University of Toronto Press, 2002).

20 Ibid. (2nd ed.), 76.

21 'Naturalistic Individualism,' 48.

22 Letter from J.A. Doull to His Excellency Edward Schreyer, Governor-General of Canada, 15 December 1980.

23 Doull, 'An Open Letter to Members of the House of Commons and Especially the Senate of Canada,' 1 December 1980, 1

24 'Naturalistic Individualism,' 34–5.

25 I wish to thank Rev. A.H. Bassett and Dr W.J. Hankey for providing me with material useful in the preparation of this paper. Special thanks are due to Mrs Phoebe Roper for her assistance in matters of style and content. Responsibility for any shortcomings, needless to say, remains my own.

COMMENTARY TWO
North American Freedom: James Doull's Recent Political Thought

DAVID G. PEDDLE and NEIL G. ROBERTSON

1. Introduction: North American Freedom and the Post-Nation State

For James Doull the true measure of political institutions is human freedom, the principle of which is most fully actualized in the development of the modern state. Doull finds that the logic of this freedom is given its most articulate expression in the philosophical writing of Hegel. Following Hegel, Doull argues that individual freedom achieves its fullest expression only through participation in social and political institutions, that individual freedom is thoroughly mediated by institutional life. What this means is that the individual is not the sole locus of freedom, and thus freedom cannot be situated simply in the individual will. Rather, individuals discover their freedom in institutions – above all the state – which actualize freedom and whose constitutions give determination and specification to freedom, making it real in a world of family, economic, and social life. For Hegel, to emphasize either the freedom of the 'ancients' or that of the 'moderns' is to provide a necessarily one-sided account. To treat freedom as primarily the enjoyment of individual rights and self-interest is to give it only a partial, 'modern' expression. Likewise partial is the 'ancient' view which treats freedom as above all attained in self-government through participation in the political sphere. For Hegel, the ancient and modern accounts of freedom – self-government and individual rights – belong together in the fully developed modern state.[1]

The Hegelian account of the state has formed the constant background to Doull's considerations of post-Hegelian political developments. Doull's consistent view has been that European political life and cultural life more generally has suffered a profound 'revolution' or corruption. His argument is that this history has not been without shape or logic, but rather from the Hegelian standpoint can be understood through the presuppositions that animate it. For Doull, the movement in

European culture has been necessarily bipartite: on the one side is a technological humanism embodied in socialism and liberalism, while on the other side is an existential naturalism given political voice in fascism and the protection of linguistic and other communities. According to Doull, while both aspects of this revolution were given expression in nineteenth-century European culture, it was only with the destruction of the older European nation state in the trenches of the First World War that these 'elements' of that older state came into their own. He contends that even today's European Union is crucially formed by an ambiguous relation of these elements or abstractions from the modern state.

From the 1960s to the present, Doull's hope has been that while European culture and political life has suffered this profound 'revolution' or corruption, the Canadian state might embody modern freedom more adequately than was possible even in the nation state of the nineteenth century. While there has been a notable consistency in his political thought and his sense of what is possible in Canada, at the same time there has been in his recent thought a crucial development by which he has been able better to articulate his intuition that there is present in Canada, in its history and institutions, a Canadian freedom which is not reducible to the one-sided expressions of freedom that have beset contemporary Europe. In short, Doull's recent political thought finds in Canada a freedom comprehensible through a renewed Hegelianism.

What has made possible this later, more developed account of Canadian political institutions and history has been Doull's rethinking of North American political forms and history. Particularly decisive here has been his changed understanding of the United States. Through the 1960s and early 1980s, from the standpoint of the 'Canadianism' of the time, Doull equated the United States with one side of the bipartite collapse of European culture. Within this account of post-Hegelian Europe, twentieth-century American consumer culture might readily appear the most complete realization of technological humanism.[2] From this standpoint, why Canada is not itself fully given over to the 'revolutionary' standpoint of Europe must be understood as simply an intuition. While Doull might contrast the violent naturalism and revolutionary upheaval of American civic life with the stability of the Canadian state, finding the source of this stability in a more conservative relation to the traditions of Europe, especially those of Christianity and constitutional monarchy, the explanation for this in his early writings remained largely undeveloped. He maintained, for example, that Canadians' resistance to

Americanization indicates that 'they are too strongly drawn to an older Christian and European culture to revel in the free natural individuality of contemporary Americans.' Doull takes as the consequence of this suggestion that to obtain political maturity Canadians must 'define their rejection of technological naturalism by means of the old tradition.'[3] But why this resistance to the 'technological naturalism' of the United States arises from an attachment to the older tradition, and not rather out of a relation to the other side of the contemporary, existential naturalism, remained largely unexplained.

In the late 1980s and early 1990s, through a deepened reflection on Canadian constitutional disputes, such accounts both of the United States and Canada disappear from Doull's analyses of the political situation in North America. He does retain his account of the history of nineteenth- and twentieth-century European political culture as a twofold corruption which is implicitly still dependent upon the more comprehensive reality of the state realized at the end of the early modern period and articulated by Hegel. However, Doull has recognized that this account is not applicable to North America. North America has, of course, participated in and been crucially informed by the developments in Europe; however, these developments were always in some sense at arm's length, and when taken into the North American context took on a different significance. North America did not suffer the world wars as cataclysmic events, destructive of institutions. Neither the United States nor Canada had empires of any note to lose in the course of the century, nor was their politics beset by the rise of fascism or Marxism. In contrast to the European states after the Second World War, which looked beyond their borders to a union that might serve to stabilize rights and welfare, both the United States and Canada, in their distinct ways, retained their institutions and found in them, however imperfectly, vehicles for the resolution of the divisions and conflicts that beset North American societies.

What especially underlies Doull's new account of North America is the claim that its political forms and cultural life did not fall into European division and immediacy, but retained, however incompletely, the distinction of society and state, so that the state was able to recognize and relate the differences and divisions of society and so give unity and direction to social and political life. In short, Doull still finds in North America the structure of the Hegelian or European state prior to its contemporary collapse. Nevertheless, according to his later account of North America, Doull's earlier 'European' reading of North America is not so much simply wrong as it is inadequate. There is a certain corruption to contemporary political life in North America that can be likened to, and in part has been influenced by, that of Europe, but for Doull their difference is more fundamental. For Doull, North Americans have been brought to a point where while they have lost sight of the full character of their institutions, these institutions nonetheless still animate them and hold their loyalties. We shall come to a more precise sense of this contemporary North American confusion when we look at first its American and then its Canadian forms.

For Doull, what allows the North American state to remain in the face of the collapse of the European state is not simply the geographical fact of being continentally removed from Europe's century of horror and the profound reworking of political and culture life this has necessitated. More fundamental is the very derived nature of North American political life; it is not the original, but a reworking of the European original in a new context. The refounding of forms of European culture in the New World meant that the colonials would have a freer relation to the culture they would refashion in the wilderness. Because of the non-autochthonous nature of North American states, they cannot be spoken of as nation states in the European sense, but more as particular forms of the common humanist and later enlightened culture of Europe.[4]

Doull's argument is that North American states escaped the confusion endemic to European nation states, namely a confusion of the universality of their cultures with the particularity of their given nationality, class divisions, and so on. In the transition to North America, the universal character of European culture emerged as primary. As Doull puts it, 'First in this construction is not to build a particular nation, but to establish in America the Spanish or French or British version of this common culture.'[5] That these colonies are not nations is given institutional expression in their development toward continental federations. Built into all New World colonies, therefore, is a capacity to interrelate and integrate not only a diversity of peoples and various particular sovereignties (states or provinces), but indeed different 'nations.' Precisely because both French and British North America were different versions of a common European culture, they were capable of a union that could respect their differences in a manner unthinkable in Europe.[6]

This North American freedom establishes the political and cultural forms of Europe in a freer and more universal context. While Doull argues that this is easiest to see in the United States, he nevertheless maintains that this development is applicable to the New World as a whole. The institutional expression of this more articulated relation of the universality of European freedom to its particular manifestations is the federation. Here there can be a twofold sovereignty: one general, applying to all citizens directly, and as a medium for relating particular sovereignties to one another; the other, a second level of particular sovereignties in and through which citizens can maintain particular forms of freedom and culture. These federations, first the American and then more generally throughout the New World, were unknown in Europe, and expressed the distinctive character of North American freedom.

Doull divides this North American freedom into three forms: Latin American, American, and Canadian. Each of these forms is distinguishable by the way it relates the individual freedom of civil society to the state as a unity of ends. Doull only briefly discusses the Latin American form, finding there an unstable relation of individual freedom to the state.[7] More central to his consideration of North American freedom is his analysis of the United States and Canada, where he discovers stable, but importantly distinguishable, ways in which society is related to the state. Doull contends that the United States begins by supposing the primacy of the society of free individuals, supposing at the same time that this society can nonetheless be given stability in a state organized through a separation of powers. The history of the United States is, according to Doull, 'towards the reversal of this assumed priority of society to state.'[8] For Canada, the initial assumption is rather 'that the state underlies the free society.'[9] The history of Canada has, then, an opposite tendency to the American; rather than a movement by which the society of free individuals comes to see its dependance on the actuality of the state, the history of Canada is the unfolding of society into its differences and divisions upon the presupposed basis of the state. In terms of federal relations, the American federation had need to reverse the assumed priority of states to the Union; in Canada, the federation had need to give a more complete recognition of the sovereignty of provinces within the federal sovereignty. However, Doull's central contention is that while importantly distinguishable, both Canada and the United States are species of the common genus of North American freedom. In both, there is still a distinction of society and state which makes room for particular differences, even to the point of national differences, but does so in such a manner as to see these differences not as exclusive but as complementary ways of realizing a common European culture in North America. Doull argues that North American institutions are able to mediate and relate what in the European Union has taken the form of immediacies of the linguistic community, human rights, and an expansive economy. In Doull's recent thinking, North American states are still states in the Hegelian sense, those of Europe are no longer.

For Doull, the beginning point for a truly Canadian consideration of Canada's constitutional arrangements is to become clear about its character as a North American polity. Doull recommends that Canadians need to free themselves from the categories of contemporary European political life – the logic of the EU – as the basis of analysis. He suggests that the last twenty years of constitutional discussion in Canada, the opposition of Trudeauite democratic centralism and nationalist Québécois separatism, is animated by terms borrowed from Europe in its contemporary corruption. The impasse of contemporary constitutional debates, the sense of their futility, may awaken Canadians to see that the terms of the debate thus far have in fact been inadequate to Canada's history and institutions. Trudeauite centralism has proved itself incapable of uniting the country. Quebec separatists seem unable to move their compatriots to a clear determination for independence. In calling for a more home-grown analysis of the nature of the Canadian polity, Doull is not suggesting that Canadians simply turn from European categories to those of contemporary America. Rather he contends that a better understanding of the United States is the first step in clarifying for ourselves the character of North American freedom and the possibilities for a kind of polity beyond the European model of the nation state. But this is only a first step, for, as we have noted, Doull sees Canada as importantly distinguished from the United States. However, even before this step, Doull would see the need to come to a more adequate understanding of the American polity than that directly available to us from contemporary American thought. Implicit in his argument is the claim that abstractions have also beset American political thinkers. They, too, have an inadequate account of their own political order. In order to become clear about Doull's analysis of the American form of North American freedom, it is first necessary to see how he presents a more comprehensive account of the American political order than that found on either side of the liberal-communitarian debate that has dominated American political thought in the past twenty years.

2. Doull on the United States: The Constitution and the Common Good

In its recent history, North American political thought has been shaped by the position of the liberal philosopher John Rawls and the response of his communitarian critics, notably Alasdair MacIntyre, Charles Taylor, and Michael Sandel.[10] Rawls's *Theory of Justice* (1970) was considered by communitarians to be articulating a conception of the state as a society of abstract choosers, moralized consumers who are radically individuated in their conception of the good, and in this sense deeply secularized pursuers of empty self-interest. Against this conception of the deracinated chooser, communitarians could rightly point to individuals as deeply embedded in community, discovering ends and goals only through a hermeneutic of larger traditions and practices. As a result of productive debate, each of these sides has developed through the 1980s and 1990s more concrete and nuanced conceptions of their respective positions. Both sides have seen the need to connect more directly their philosophical considerations to the actual history and institutions of the United States. Rawls, led by a recognition of the historical and cultural specificity of his view, has become a 'political liberal,' while communitarians have shifted from more psychological and phenomenological concerns to an emphasis on political institutions and citizenship; they have become republicans.[11] The debate now takes place on more explicitly political grounds – Rawls moving away from the abstractions of a *Theory of Justice*, and communitarians moving away from the coercive moral exclusivity which marred their earlier positions.[12] Sandel's *Democracy's Discontent* indicates possibilities for a more robust expression of communitarian concerns under a republican rubric; his emphasis on the metaphysics of the embedded self is replaced with an emphasis on citizenship and virtue.

Equally, in terms of American historiography, the opposition of Hartz's (and later Strauss's) conception of America as foundationally liberal to the claim of Pocock and others to a civic republican foundation has given way to a more sophisticated *rapprochement* of the two sides. Those who lean towards a liberal conception of the American founding now recognize the need to weave republican elements into their account; civic republicans have been forced to find room for the role of Lockean elements in their renditions of the establishment of the United States. From Doull's point of view, the only further step is to see the liberal and republican accounts of the founding, like the liberal and communitarian considerations in contemporary political theory, as abstractions of an actuality that encompasses both. For Doull, the considerations of contemporary American political theorists and historians are inadequate to the freedom that defines American institutions and history. Doull's Hegelian account of the United States permits a unification of the universalist interest of liberal justice with the historical institutional focus of the communitarians-cum-republicans. The logical premise of this account is that a common good animates, preserves, and relates the differences in the public political life of the United States.[13]

For Doull, the logic of how the common good is effective in the particular goods of American society and political life is itself articulated in the history of the United States. In this sense, Doull sees the historical development of American political life not as a story of the contingencies by which ideals were either realized or thwarted, but rather as crucially determined by an American freedom which is as much real as ideal. Doull sees the peculiar character of American political life, in contrast to other North American polities, as resting in its account of the relation of civil society to the state. The United States was founded on an enlightened revolutionary sense that civil society, the society of free individuals, is independent of and prior to the state. Doull's claim is that the dynamic of American history is toward the dissolution of this assumption. In this history the American people are not reversing their revolution, but rather seeking to make it more institutionally effective.

Doull's analysis of the history of the United States as moving toward a sense of the priority of the state to civil society falls into three central divisions. First, he treats of the period from federation to the Civil War as a working-out in Americans of the recognition that the union expresses their character as one people and upholds the freedom and civility of their society. Because the union comprehends and preserves on a rational basis the distinctiveness of and differences between states, associations, and individuals, it is thought indivisible. Second, he considers the Progressive Age and its attempt to temper the excesses of an industrialized economy on the basis of pragmatism and respect for a moral universality inclusive of both employer and labourer. For Doull, this standpoint was inadequate to accomplish the institutional development required to correct capitalism. Finally, he considers the New Deal, which achieves a certain concreteness in its concern for the rational and natural aspects of the individual, and develops on this ground a deepened sense of the priority of the state to civil society. However, the relation of the state to civil society discovered in the New Deal is conceived in too immediate a manner, and the individual who looks to government for the direct satisfaction of his needs finds, on the one hand, an unfreedom in the divisions and ethic of civil society and, on the other, more a benevolent bureaucracy than a deepened form of self-government. Against this immediate unification of individual and state, libertarian conservatives, such as Robert Nozick, turn to a similarly immediate union with civil society of the individual, who finds in government the destruction of its freedom. Against both, the communitarian calls for a return to republican self-government and the preservation of local, intermediary bodies. For Doull, none of these positions achieve an adequate account of American freedom because they do not see the state as comprehensive of civil society; in its own way each position remains in the standpoint of civil society. Rawls articulates a position relative to a well-ordered society, Nozick relative to an anarchic society, and Sandel relative to a pre-existing community. Doull's Hegelian consideration of American freedom argues that in the relation of governmental institutions to society, these various elements are related and subordinated to an effective common good. So long as contemporary theorists interpret the state from the standpoint of civil society, the concrete relation of state to civil society achieved in the New Deal remains only implicit. However, Doull's view is that the actual history of contemporary America is toward drawing out more fully this concreteness. What Doull has achieved in a developed philosophical conception of the common good which animates the political life of the United States is the recognition of a principle which underlies the divisions of civil society and is prior to it. In the founding of the Constitution, the Civil War, and the New Deal Doull finds historical moments which demonstrate the necessity of a constitutional citizenship beyond the unstable associations of civil society, of an individual freedom beyond the abstract choice characteristic of the unfettered consumer. What is distinctive in Doull's standpoint is a recognition and articulation of an objective historical development of the conception of freedom in its relation to the economic, moral, and constitutional life of the United States.

However, to measure the validity of Doull's account, it is not enough to show that the Hegelian account of freedom is superior to or comprehensive of other accounts. That is too general. Doull's argument rests upon his capacity to articulate more effectively than others the distinctive character of American freedom. What distinguishes the United States is that it is the first enlightened, secular state founded in the New World, a state which is grounded in an explicit way in a distinctive sense of freedom and whose history is peculiarly tied to this sense of freedom. To better gauge Doull's considerations of the United States we will examine four concerns that go some way toward adumbrating the peculiar nature of American freedom: (1) the federal character of the United States; (2) the enlightened relation of church and state in the U.S.; (3) the relation of American history to its conception of freedom; and (4) the limits of American freedom.

(i) The Federal Character of the United States

A central weakness in both liberal and communitarian accounts of political life is that neither can provide a principled explication of the United States as a federation. Rawls's account of liberalism provides a theory of society that is inherently centralist. It is unclear what constitutes the borders, both internal and external, of the just society. In particular, the role of the more limited sovereignties of states remains underdeveloped in Rawls's account. This centralizing aspect of Rawls's liberalism emerges in his support of a strong Supreme Court with powers to override state and local laws. By contrast with this emphasis on the judiciary, communitarians see themselves as supporting self-government, both federal and local. Communitarians oppose the centralizing monological tendencies of liberalism with a defence of the integrity and self-government of communities. However, the relation of these communities to the institutional structure of federalism remains undeveloped. Sandel, for example, cannot give institutional expression to the multi-layered self, constituted through a plurality of communities. The priority and distinctive character of federal institutions is swallowed up in an ambiguous sense of a vague plurality of communal attachments.

Doull acknowledges the liberal concern for a universal justice and the communitarian sense of the United States as a self-governing community and community of communities. His argument is that what is lacking is an account of the role of the federal institutions that make effective both sides of the liberal-communitarian debate. Doull argues that American freedom must be grasped constitutionally as achieved through a distinction of federal and state institutions which within their respective powers both secure individuals in their liberty and draw them together into a common will.

In coming to a sense of Doull's conception of American freedom as institutionally mediated it is instructive to look at his account of the character of the movement from the Articles of Confederation to the constitution of 1787.[14] A sense of the United States as a federation – neither a unitary state nor a simple cooperative of states – can be captured by looking in more detail at the transition to the constitution of 1787.

Alexander Hamilton, among others, made explicit the limits of the Articles of Confederation. The central defect of the Articles was that, according to them, the federal government was not directly related to individuals but merely to state governments. As a result, Congress could raise neither men nor money by direct conscription or taxation of individuals, but relied on the states' fulfilment of various congressional requisitions. With 'neither troops, nor treasury, nor government,' the security of the confederation and of the freedom of individuals was in question.[15] Individuals thus had a more stable allegiance to their particular states, which they knew as the basis of the security of life and property and whose authority they knew in the sanction of law and taxation, than they had to the federal government. Therefore, so long as the primary division was between state government and Congress, the people's loyalty remained with the state. Hence Hamilton's description of the confederation: 'Each state yielding to the persuasive voice of immediate interest has successively withdrawn its support till the frail and tottering edifice seems ready to fall upon our heads and crush us beneath its ruins.'[16] However, just as the confederation could not bring institutional stability to the revolutionary will, so too a division emerged between state legislatures and the will of the people. State legislatures engaged in paper money schemes and enacted laws which confiscated property and suspended established ways of debt collection. Private property, the determinate expression of individual freedom, thus became insecure and the legislative expression of the people's will, so far as it was in opposition to the subjective freedom which is its basis, appeared as capricious and arbitrary as that of a monarch.[17] As Madison stated: 'The legislative department is everywhere extending its activity and drawing all power into its impetuous vortex.'[18] Here the Revolution had turned back on itself, destroying the institutions which gave stability to its will and making its freedom vulnerable to outside interests, those of other states or foreign powers.[19] In critical reflection upon the defects of the Articles of Confederation and upon the tyranny of state legislatures there was, thus, the deeply felt need of institutional reform. As abstracted from its contemporary political structures, the revolutionary freedom of Americans returned to the unified will forged in opposition to British dominion. This will, however, was now mediated not merely by the negation of external dominion but likewise by the negation of its own incomplete political forms, specifically the Articles and the priority of particular states which it sustained. Madison among others made clear that only republican government could give institutional enactment to this mediated freedom while remaining true to the character of the American people, the fundamental principles of the Revolution, and self-government.[20]

As Doull argues, what emerges here is not properly articulated in accordance with contract doctrine. First, the War of Independence and the confederation which followed were not original associations out of a state of nature. Rather they mark transformations of a public culture already established.[21] Secondly, the constitution, which overcomes the limitations of the initial confederation explicitly denies the immediate priority of individuals and their particular or naturalistic allegiances to various states. Finally, the logic of the time demanded that political institutions express the universality of the rational individual – not simply the competitive relations of individuals and local cultures, but their implicit unity as well.[22] What emerged from this demand is a federal government based on the freedom and equality of all citizens.[23]

(ii) The Constitution as the Relation of Religion and State

Distinctive of the American constitution, especially for its time, was not only its federal structure but also its conception of the relation of religion to the state. The enlightened spirit that made possible the distinctively New World relation of states to a federal government also moved the founders to establish in the Constitution a novel relation of government to religion. The exact character of this relation is today very much a matter of debate. It can be framed as a question of how higher goods are to be related to the political good. The liberal-communitarian debate brings out the elements of the question, but in such a form as to make the actual Constitution of the United States appear inherently contradictory. Is the American constitution inherently secular and secularizing, or is it rather a forum that safeguards and encourages not only religion, but also the connecting of religion to political ends?

For sophisticated liberals such as Rawls, higher or comprehensive accounts of the good, while part of the background of 'political liberalism,' must remain firmly in the background and do not properly belong to the public reason by which a well-ordered society determines its political and social relations. The executive, the legislature, and above all the judiciary are to eschew distinctively religious, or indeed any, comprehensive accounts as rationale for law or policy. The state is to be resolutely agnostic about the comprehensive character of reality or human life. For liberals, the use of higher ends, most especially religious ends, in public policy and law is inherently tyrannical and oppressive – the imposition of one account to the detriment of others.

For communitarians, such an evacuation of the public sphere by higher goods is either impossible or the surreptitious domination by one comprehensive account over others. Where the liberal account, grounded in the autonomous chooser, parades as neutral, a highly contestable comprehensive account is allowed to dominate without debate. For communitarians, public debate must allow room for the articulation of higher ends. Without such articulation the relation of individuals to the public sphere is attenuated, and the democratic process is itself in danger of corrosion. Communitarians see a strong relation between the growing inarticulacy of the role of higher ends in public deliberation and a deepening discontent and malaise in American public life.

Doull's argument suggests that both the liberal and communitarian accounts have merits, but merits that must be seen as complementary and not exclusive. For Doull, the American constitution is a work of enlightened secularity – but a secularity which cannot be divorced from a relation to religious ends. He comments on Rawls's account of liberalism: 'This is pure "Enlightenment" doctrine: from the contemplation of ultimate ends one is to turn to the world, to what falls within the human understanding and is useful for the improvement of human life. But this confinement of humans for their good is only free if held in relation to the infinite good from which they have turned.'[24]

For Doull, the logic of the American constitution, and enlightened secularity more generally, rests on a determinate account of higher ends: a reformed Christianity. He notes: 'The idea of a concrete good to be freely realized, which is implicit in "Enlightenment," is derived from that part of the Christian community which admitted a free subjective movement in the reception of grace.'[25] According to Doull, the American constitution is neither directly Christian nor post- or non-Christian. Enlightened secularity both presupposes the concrete relation of good and evil that belongs to Augustinian-Calvinist theology and is forgetful of it in its turn to enlightened self-consciousness: 'Protestant Christianity remained in general the belief of enlightened America, moralized more or less and recalled to its concrete doctrine by degrees through the experience of the limits of enlightened freedom at its several stages.'[26] In Doull's view, what makes possible a stable enlightened secularity is a knowledge of the concretely unified reformed Christian standpoint.

Doull agrees with Rawls that higher ends are not to be made directly effective in political deliberation; the state is not to serve religious ends. On the other hand, he also agrees with communitarians that the political sphere cannot simply be divorced from higher ends. Rawls's agnosticism and purely pragmatic relation to comprehensive doctrines is not sustainable; lost from sight is the indirect but foundational relation of Protestant Christianity to the enlightened secularity Rawls would defend. Rawls's external and pragmatic account of the relation of higher ends and public reason is as problematic as communitarian confusion between the two.[27] What is not recognized by either account is the role of American institutions not only to embody an enlightened secular conception of the common good, but also to (a) educate towards that good and (b) embody a recognition of the limits of that good.

To come to a more definite sense of Doull's conception of how higher ends and political life are related in the American constitution there is need to turn to the work of the framers.[28] What is remarkable here is that each of the competing interpretations of the relation of church and state expresses from its own standpoint not only the distinction between religious and secular realms but also the existence of a unifying principle. By turning to the framers it is possible to recover the logic by which religion and secularity could be distinguished and separated, but on the basis of a common rationality.

Starting from a Lockean position which radically separates church and state, Jefferson moves to a position of universal Unitarianism, where the separation of church and state dissolves, and each realm is conceived as grounded in the rational powers of the ethical individual. Where Jefferson would separate church and state to defend against irrational enthusiasm, he also expected a Unitarian conquest of irrational religion. He states: 'I rejoice that in this country of free inquiry and belief, which has surrendered its creed and conscience to neither kings nor priests, the genuine doctrine of one only God is reviving, and I trust that there is not a young man now living in the United States who will not die a Unitarian.'[29] One might say that Jefferson expected an establishment of Unitarianism through the assent of the free will of individuals, not through state support.

By contrast with Jefferson, who pursued the question from the standpoint of the rationally free citizen who had not given up his right of conscience, the eighteenth-century evangelical standpoint stressed that the source of one's religious views lies not in the individual's rational morality but in the commands of a sovereign God. From the evangelical side, the separation of church and state was not intended to protect the state from enthusiasm, but rather to protect religion from secular corruption.[30] However, from the standpoint of faith, evangelicals also conceived a unity between the two realms, recognizing God as sovereign in both.

James Madison, in his *Memorial and Remonstrance*, brought these standpoints together, recognizing the need both to prevent religious warfare and oppression and to permit individuals to follow absolute duties. On a Madisonian view, then, there is an important reciprocity between religious and political life. On the one hand, the state can provide substantial protection for the free practice of religious duty, while on the other hand, religious ethics can promote virtue among citizens. Madison, in fact, contends that the duty to God is 'precedent both in order of time and in degree of obligation to the claims of civil society.'[31] However, while Madison accepted the priority of divine commands in times of conflict between religion and state, his position is intelligible only if one recognizes that he assumes a general agreement between the claims of religion and those of the state – government would be impossible if there were a radical separation between constitutional and divine law.

What underlies the standpoint of the Constitution and its relation to religion is the recognition of an objective good which comprehends the universal and particular expressions of the individual's will. The Constitution reconciles the rational and natural interests of the individual at the level of secularity, as does reformed Christianity at the level of religion: in their difference the two sides reveal a common principle. Still, politics and religion in their finite interests, as particular governments or sects, may indeed conflict. In a situation of conflict, both religion and state are rendered abstract or one-sided, and either may be on the side of justice or injustice. In such instances, a standpoint compatible with the spirit of the U.S. Constitution will not simply subordinate religious interests to those of government, assuming government to be comprehensive. Rather, under the 'free exercise clause' of the First Amendment, it will permit exemptions which enable believers to enact their religious duties.[32] These exemptions recognize both the limit to the political good pursued in the institutions of the state and a continuing relation to higher ends. But the character of the constitutional exemptions is of such an order as not to allow individuals to dissolve their adherence to the American polity. These exemptions uphold the awareness that, in times of conflict, either side may be untrue to their concrete identity. Indeed, it is through the protections of freedom of religion that the Constitution frees individuals to relate and reconcile worldly and spiritual ends. The deeply religious character of American life persists not in spite of, but because of, the constitutional protections of religious worship.

What then distinguishes Doull's account from both the liberal and the communitarian standpoints is that he grounds enlightened secularity not only historically, but also logically, in the standpoint of Augustinian-Calvinism that the first settlers brought with them from Europe. In relation to a secular world of finite interests, the Freedom known to the Puritan settlers became actual in the institutions of the American constitution, together with a recognition that this accomplished worldly freedom was finite relative to a more comprehensive end.

(iii) The History of the Constitution as Realizing American Freedom

Doull's account of American freedom is grounded in a consideration of the framing of the constitution of 1787. However, his claim is that the freedom embodied in that document was not simply and directly realized; rather the whole history of the United States must be seen as animated by the working out, the making actual and concrete, of the freedom first articulated in the Constitution. Doull reads the history of the United States in a Hegelian manner: American freedom is not primarily a moral principle, vulnerable to the contingencies and accidents of history, but rather is historically effective in the institutions and culture of American public life. For Doull, the deepest testimony to the sovereignty of the United States is that its history is at the deepest level constitutional. That history can certainly be told so as to emphasize liberal or republican moments. More comprehensively, however, the history is not about moral or cultural perspectives on the public sphere; rather, it is most concretely gathered together as a history of the constitution through which American freedom is by stages more fully articulated.

As already stated, for Doull this history is divided into three stages: (1) from the founding to the Civil War; (2) from the Civil War to the Depression; and (3) from the New Deal to the contemporary period. At each stage in this history, Doull sees both a deeper realization of American freedom and a heightened sense of the limits of that freedom. Through their history, Americans grow increasingly attached to their institutions, and come to know them as realizing an ever more concrete sense of freedom. With that contentment, however, there arises a more developed sense and demand for the fullest concretion of freedom – the concretion known inwardly in reformed religious belief.

The first stage in this history (the period that ends in the Civil War), Doull argues, has as its central problematic the movement to realize the indissolubility of the union and thereby the priority of the state to civil society.[33] The Civil War established the freedom of the Constitution as effective in the union, both federally and at the state level. In this conflict, the federal government, as the protector of the universality of human freedom as against the institution of slavery, demonstrates its right over the secessionist interests. However, once achieved, this unification of popular will and common good – the result of a generation's Herculean struggle – becomes not a conclusion but a starting point for succeeding generations, a given heritage in which the sacrifices which give birth to union are lost in a certain immediacy. As Doull notes, the sense of a coincidence of popular will and the unified will of the people is achieved in the Civil War, but their relation is 'not fully clarified so long as the particular divided interests of society fall outside the point of coincidence.'[34] The next two periods of American history will be efforts to draw the divided interests of society into a relation to the sense of Americans as being one people. Doull describes inadequate efforts in the first phase, from Reconstruction to the Depression, to relate the divided realm of society to the unified will of the state through the figures of the moral and then the pragmatic individual. The moral individual strives for an inner freedom from an industrializing society which seems more and more to fully undermine his actual freedom. The pragmatic individual assumes that the accomplishments of a long history are immediately present in the common sense of the individual. What is required from this pragmatic standpoint is the free expression of individual desire and ingenuity and a policing of the excesses of civil society. However, from this standpoint it proves impossible to correct the inequalities of economic and social life.

The further development of a universal constitutional freedom achieves concretion in the New Deal precisely through the recognition of the limits of the assumptions of pragmatism. The capitalist order which gives expression to pragmatic individualism is unable adequately to express the universality of the human spirit, unable to secure its freedom and equality, unable to be corrected on merely moral grounds. The continuing presence of racism in the laissez-faire civil society of the late nineteenth and early twentieth centuries is a particularly striking symptom of the inadequately realized relation of state to society that belongs to this post–Civil War period. The equality of blacks, although recognized constitutionally, is not made effective in the social and political life of the union. Though the growth of capitalism has substantial roots in the elimination of slavery, it was not itself inimical to racism, as exemplified by the popularity and influence of Herbert Spencer's intellectual legitimation of laissez-faire, voluntarist capitalism.[35] This prototypical Darwinism legitimized not only the accumulation of wealth by those at the top of the economic order and its resulting privilege but also the placement of blacks at the bottom of the social order. With this 'scientific' doctrine of white supremacy, the ideology of the South had, in a sense, become the ideology of the nation.

This shared racist ideology was, ironically, an important aspect of the reintegration of the South into the union. Reintegration was furthered by the non-interventionist stance of the federal government. Ralph Henry Gabriel makes the interesting point that the federal government's retreat from intervention was crucial to the re-emergence of southern loyalty to the union. In 1877 the army was withdrawn. Further, the decision in the civil-rights cases of 1883 limited the power of Congress to interfere in state matters, and in consequence gave the states power over race relations, subject only to the limitation that slavery not be reestablished. Gabriel states: 'In 1883, only eighteen years after the surrender of Lee, the Court accepted Calhoun's principle that the disposition of the race problem should be denied to the central government and be left to the local community.'[36] This sense of sovereignty over the issue of race restored the relationship of the South to the Constitution and contributed greatly to national unity. While reunification helped reestablish the patriotic unity among states, it infringed upon the universality of the rights of the citizen, but in such a manner as perfectly to embody the general character of American freedom which Doull describes as belonging to this period: slavery had been abolished and the supremacy of the union realized in the Civil War. However, before making actual in southern states and American society more generally the full implications of this new status for blacks, the federal government withdrew from interference in race matters.

Doull's general observation that the achievement of national union in the Civil War left outside that realized union the divided relations of society applies not only to the forms of economic slavery experienced in the laissez-faire industrializing economy, but also to the relations between black and white. It was left to the era of the New Deal to raise explicitly the demand that American freedom more concretely penetrate into the divided realm of society.

The New Deal originated, of course, in response to the massive unemployment and financial chaos brought on by the collapse of industry and the economic system during the Great Depression. Left to itself, the free play of individual interest produced an inherently unstable economy, with dramatic effects on the political and socio-economic lives of all citizens. One could no longer have faith in the combination of laissez-faire and survival of the fittest to provide a workable social order. Both rich and poor were devastated by the economic collapse. The Depression marked a practical demonstration that laissez-faire capitalism was not a natural order, success in which was a measure of the virtue of citizens; even those who were successful and were judged to be the fittest suffered during the Depression. By contrast with the Spencerian laissez-faire hierarchy of race, the New Deal implicitly recognized a universality of suffering; all humans, black and white, were thought to have the same needs. Sandel characterizes the civil-rights movement as a moment of self-government and civic engagement, the active participation of blacks in their own political fate. By contrast, Sandel characterizes the New Deal as the origin of the procedural republic that he would oppose. Doull's argument suggests that the New Deal and the civil-rights movement belong to a shared but new conception of American freedom.[37]

(iv) The Limits of American Freedom

Doull finds implicit in the New Deal and in the subsequent development of American society and institutions a demand for freedom that exposes the limits of freedom as articulated by the Constitution. As he indicates, there is a certain externality to the U.S. Constitution expressed in the mechanisms which prevent tyrannies of one sort and another. The separation of powers which allows the concretion of American freedom at the same time prevents its positive fruition, resulting in institutional gridlock and a certain impotence in the development of important social programs, in areas such as health insurance or campaign finance reform. Certainly at vital moments American leaders and their citizenry are able to rise above these divisions and make effective the unified sovereignty of the state, but such occasional moments as much expose the limits of the Constitution as they exemplify the power of American political culture to rise above those limits.

It is just here that the Hegelian character of Doull's account emerges most explicitly. Doull suggests that American freedom will only achieve stable realization in a relation of state to society such as is embodied in the Hegelian account of the state.[38] What he has argued through his consideration of the United States is that such a resolution might occur on the basis of the logic inherent in American history. Doull's 'predictions,' just as much as his analysis of the development of the United States, rest upon his sense of the form and limits that belong to the particular character of American freedom. To know more fully the nature of what Doull understands by North American freedom in general, we must turn to his analysis of Canada.[39]

3. Doull on Canada: Comprehending the Constitution

For Doull, a proper understanding of the United States is the necessary beginning to an understanding of Canada at two levels: (1) the United States, in contrast to contemporary Europe, retains an actual sovereignty in that the state is a unity of ends that is seen to be both the basis of the freedom of individuals in society and also able to recollect individuals out of the divisions and differences of society into an effective political will – in this sense, the early modern European state, though modified by the history of the U.S., is still effective; (2) the United States is a post-national federation where sovereignty is divided into particular and general forms, giving institutional reality to a North American freedom beyond anything accomplished by the Europeans, even in the nation states of the nineteenth century. Together these considerations make clear the inadequacy of considering Canada in terms derived from contemporary European political thought and culture.

For over a decade, in various papers and submissions to government commissions, Doull has argued that Canada remains colonial so long as it carries out its constitutional debate in terms borrowed from the European Union. He does see that there is something compelling in this turn to a European model. Canada is importantly distinct from the United States, whose political categories cannot adequately comprehend the realities of Canada – which include not only its two distinct nationalities, but also Canadians' sense of the role of government in realizing the well-being of its citizens. Canada thus shares with Europe the question of distinct nationalities as well as the desire for a social democratic state that would subordinate economic life to welfare. Indeed, the European Union seems in many ways analogous to the Canadian situation: a common government ensures through human rights the welfare of the citizens of Europe, while allowing the distinctive linguistic and national groups freedom to retain their particular cultures.

Nevertheless, Doull sees the limit of this model and its application to Canada in terms of both its own concept and its foreignness to the realities of Canadian history and institutions. The inherent weakness of the EU, in Doull's analysis, is that it is defined by the relation of two opposed abstractions (universal citizenship and linguistic particularity), and not by their unity effected in and through an actual sovereignty. Doull sees post-modern culture as the most complete reflection on this state of affairs in Europe: each of the opposed elements that define the EU is shown in post-modernity to be capable only of dissolving institutional expression of individual freedom. Beyond the insight of the sceptical negativity of post-modernism, however, there appears to be no movement to recognize an actual sovereignty capable of uniting and giving stability to the opposed aspects of contemporary Europe. Doull argues that the inherent direction of the European Union is towards a post-national federation, but that to reach that condition would require Europeans move beyond the ambiguity of post-modernity and subordinate universal citizenship, linguistic community, and sceptical negativity to an effective sovereignty.

Doull's argument about the United States suggests that in spite of negative aspects of its contemporary situation, the U.S. is an effective sovereignty. So also is Canada, were it to recognize and more fully animate its institutional structures and gain a better sense of their history. But it is precisely here that an apparent ambiguity in his account emerges. In the conclusion to 'The Philosophical Basis of Constitutional Discussion in Canada,' Doull argues that, on the basis of both the European Union rightly understood and the United States as displayed by its history, there exists no right of any kind for the separation of Quebec from the Canadian federation.[40] The country is 'indivisible.'[41] However, Doull speaks of Canadians as 'looking to find an internal unity or an actual sovereignty,'[42] and thus his account might at this point appear ambiguous: the country is indivisible and yet in danger of division. Also apparently problematic are Doull's statements about constitutional amendment. He states: '[W]e have less need to amend than to understand the principles of our freedom.'[43] However, there is also, according to Doull, a need for constitutional amendment to 'assure the minority of French culture in Canada of their equality and of a protection of their particularity.'[44] These do not represent confusions on Doull's part, but rather express his conception of the central ambiguity in Canada's present constitutional situation. Doull finds in the present situation in Canada a division of subjective reason from the reality present to it in the institutions and history of the country, a division generated by abstractions taking the place of a real knowing of what is before Canadians.[45] What is required for Canada to 'define constitutionally' the basis of the federation is not so much to rework or re-establish the constitution on new grounds, but to comprehend it, and in this comprehension to make our constitutional documents more adequately reflect and embody the reality of Canadian freedom. In order to have a viable country, the American people had to engage in the work of defining their independence with their break from Britain: they had to appropriate for themselves the forms of freedom they had received both from Britain and from their engagement with the New World. Doull argues that Canada, in spite of a long transition from colony to self-rule, has only begun to appropriate its own forms of freedom, to truly patriate its constitution. What Doull captures in his portrayal of this frustrating division between the reality of Canadian freedom and our incapacity to be reconciled to it is the combined sense in Canadians, on the one side, of being more victims than agents in their history – so that constitutional discussions become bouts of mutual grievance, even to the extent of efforts to separate – and, on the other side, an extraordinary and seemingly inexplicable loyalty and attachment to the federation – without which the intensity of grievance would itself be inexplicable. No Canadian seems satisfied with the confederation and yet no change to it is generally acceptable, nor in the end does there seem to be an adequately determined will to leave it.

Doull is not so naive as to suppose that everyone is, in fact, happy with confederation and just doesn't know it. Rather, he maintains that the elements of the constitution are not adequately integrated or understood in their mutual relation. Aspects of our constitution have become corrupted or are inadequate to the freedom that underlies the constitution as a whole. So, for instance, Doull complains that the way Parliament operates in Canada, where there is virtual rule by the Prime Minister's Office, tends towards turning the federal government into an instrument of central Canada, thus generating (among other problems) western grievance. In addition, the Charter, as presently understood by the courts, tends to separate rights and individual freedom from the work of democratic self-government. Further, federal centralizing tendencies tend to encroach upon provincial sovereignty, and thus fail to accord to the provinces their proper status within the federation. In reaction to these perversions of the constitution, Quebec must claim for itself complete independence, and see the only benefit of the confederation as purely financial.

Doull's analysis is that these imperfect realizations of the constitutional order actually present in Canada result from the hold of certain abstractions upon Canadians. He sees these abstractions as stemming from the influence of contemporary European categories upon Canada's own efforts at self-understanding. Canadians tend to see the federal government as a promoter of individual social democratic rights: the courts are seen to secure and define these rights, the government to administer them. Parliament in such a view is reduced largely to a debating chamber for the evening news. For English Canadians who fail to see themselves as possessing a distinct culture, the provinces can appear primarily as administrative units, occasional defenders of ways of life threatened by centralist national policy and economy. The Quebec separatists essentially agree with this account, having contempt for the lack of culture in English-speaking Canada. Further, taking up the side of linguistic communities in the European Union, the Quebec separatist would argue their right to a distinct way of life, seeing in the centralist universalism of Canadian liberalism a desire to assimilate and undermine their rights to a distinct society.

According to Doull, what is lacking in the accounts of Canada that are premised on the categories of the European Union is the standpoint of subjective freedom in its relation to the state, namely, the conception of sovereignty that lies at the heart of the early modern state and, according to Doull, is still to be found in North American political forms.[46] Where the state is seen as capable of uniting the ends of society, and so limiting, ordering, and reconciling various interests (including economic, linguistic, institutional, and communitarian interests), the abstractions of 'liberal rights' and 'linguistic community' can be related to one another, and seen as aspects of a more substantial reality, that of the state. In this, the immediacy and directness of liberal rights and community rights can and must be overcome, and must be related to the more complete good of the state in all its distinctions and aspects. It is only from this standpoint that the state may be seen not simply as external authority, but as the ground of freedom. In North America, and particularly in the Canadian state, which recognizes more fully the rights of communities as well as of individuals, the apparently intractable oppositions that derive from a European perspective on Canada become resolvable, not by levelling but by preserving differences and relating them to one another so as to bring to light a common freedom.[47]

Central to Doull's argument is that a Hegelian solution to Canada's constitutional dilemma is not an imposition, but is rather that to which the history of Canada has led. Canadians need only recognize what has been accomplished in their history. The explanation for Canadians' apparent ignorance of their own reality is, for Doull, the result of a long colonial submission and tendency to experience their history passively, together with a contemporary rebellion from that history: 'In every successful revolution – and for Canadians their independence is a revolution against a long colonial dependence – it is necessary first to loosen the hold of former things, to give oneself a distance from them. This destructive retreat in this as in other cases will then be found to be a *reculer pour mieux sauter.*[48]

Only in 1982 did Canadians begin actively to appropriate what had been accomplished in their historical development. Yet why is it that Canadians, in coming to define their polity after its long historical development, turn to the categories of the European Union? Doull has called this a 'post-colonial colonialism.' On his account, in the revolution towards a Canadian independence we have not in fact sufficiently freed ourselves from our dependence upon others and in particular Europe. On a separatist account, Canada is in fact not a sovereign state and does not have actually present within itself the capacity to gather its elements into a united will. By this latter reading the turn to European models is reflective of the artificial and external nature of Canadian unity. On the face of it, this appears a more plausible explanation: Canadians tend to see their liberty secured not through the relation of society to state accomplished in Parliament and its relation to the executive, but through the courts and the welfare bureaucracy or, by contrast, through the absence of these institutions and participation in the global economy. In these terms, the unity with Canada appropriate to Quebec is at best sovereignty association. As Doull himself points out, however, if Canada is nothing other than can be grasped by the categories of the EU, it is not a proper state and must dissolve. Is Doull then engaged in wishful thinking when he tells us that Canada is more than an artifice of colonial policy? How are we to decide between these two possibilities? Is there a way to determine which is the reality: the actuality of the Canadian state and Canadian freedom, or the recognition that Canada is nothing but an artifice relating, but not uniting, liberal rights and linguistic community? Peter Russell's pertinent question can be rephrased: 'Are Canadians a sovereign people?'

Doull suggests at the end of his piece that the fullest development in this self-understanding is reached when Canadians ask these questions about the character of their country in relation to the constitution. It was after the publication of 'The Philosophical Basis of the Constitutional Discussion in Canada' that the Supreme Court delivered its judgment about the right of Quebec to separate. The judgment seems to capture just the ambiguity that Doull recognizes as belonging to the present confusion in Canada about what constitutes the country. Thus the court, rather than directly answer the question, pointed to the need to negotiate in the occurrence of a 'yes' vote on a referendum. Rather than prejudging whether the country is in fact a sovereign people, the court outlined the means necessary to determine this matter. A constitution can be the legal document that outlines the basic political structures of a country; it can also be the practices, customs, and institutions by which a people order their lives. Doull suggests that it belongs to a modern state that a people not only live within a constitutional order, but that they understand it. In this understanding of a constitutional order there is the need not only to have a sense of the ordinary practices of government, nor simply to know the positive requirements of constitutional law, but equally to place these into a concrete history, above all a history comprehended as a history of freedom. When Doull states that the principles of the constitution are not in need of amendment, he means 'principles' in this sense, principles of freedom that have come to realization through the historical life of Canadians. Thus, the call to negotiate to which the Supreme Court points need not be simply a business or treaty negotiation. Rather, it may be an opportunity for the sovereign elements of the country – the federal government and the provinces – to discover the principles of freedom which in the first place animate their grievances, and which, better understood, can be seen to animate a constitutional order capable of comprehending all the sovereignties of the country, without requiring one aspect to dominate over the others.

Doull tells us that Quebec does not have any right to secede from the federation unless 'there is a democratic right to destroy and debase one's freedom.'[49] One might add that the rest of the country has no right to continue to display indifference to Quebec's legitimate demand to have its distinctness and sovereignty better articulated in the constitution. In his *Lectures on the Philosophy of History*, Hegel argues that freedom is self-consciousness. Doull's argument is that while Canadians may in some manner have a sense of their freedom, in their loyalty and their refusal to give up the confederation they are inadequately self-conscious, and so by that measure remain slaves to abstractions. That this is the truth of the Canadian situation and not rather that Canada is itself an abstraction cannot find its proof simply in the display by Canadians of a stubborn loyalty to the confederation mixed with a dissatisfaction with all contemporary understandings of the country. Nor again is it a proof of Doull's position that he can place the present dilemma within a reading of the larger history of Canada as a 'history more basic' than that of the two 'nations' which comprise it. While in those terms his account may be found to be both compelling and powerful, perhaps more persuasive than other accounts, neither level of analysis is sufficient to state that Doull has got it right. Doull's analysis of Canada is based upon a broader consideration of the nature of freedom as this came to be realized first in Europe and then in new terms in North America. In this sense his consideration of contemporary Canada rests on a much wider understanding of the whole history of Western culture and the ultimately philosophical grounds such an understanding must have if it is rise to the standpoint of objectivity. It is the relation of this total history to the distinctive history and constitutional principles and institutions of Canada that forms the proof of Doull's contention that Canada is in fact a sovereign state inadequately conscious of its own freedom and not a colonial artefact. In turn, according to Doull, it is only insofar as Canadians can recognize the rational reality of their sovereignty that the country will be capable of an effective constitutional reconciliation of the forces that appear to threaten its dissolution.

Notes

1 Cf. Hegel, *The Philosophy of Right*, trans. T.M. Knox (Oxford: Clarendon Press, 1967), para. 260.

2 Equally, Quebec's independence movement could appear to be 'fascistic,' indistinguishable from similar movements in Switzerland, Wales, or Spain. See chapter 9 (above), 406.

3 Doull, 'Naturalistic Individualism: Quebec Independence and an Independent Canada,' in Eugene Coombs, ed., *Modernity and Responsibility: Essays for George Grant* (Toronto: University of Toronto Press, 1983), 50.

4 See above, 398, 402.

5 Ibid., 403.

6 Ibid., 415.

7 Here Doull draws on F.L. Jackson's 'Mexican Freedom: The Ideal of the Indigenous State,' *Animus* 2 (1997).

8 See above, 433.

9 Ibid.

10 For the communitarian view cf. especially Alasdair MacIntyre, *Whose Justice? Which Rationality?* (London: Duckworth, 1988), Michael Sandel, *Liberalism and the Limits of Justice* (Cambridge: Cambridge University Press, 1982), and Charles Taylor, *Sources of the Self: The Making of the Modern Identity* (Cambridge, Mass.: Harvard University Press, 1989). For the republican development of this position cf. Michael Sandel, *Democracy's Discontent* (Cambridge: Harvard University Press, 1996).

11 John Rawls, *Political Liberalism* (New York: Columbia University Press, 1993).

12 A key development of the Rawlsian view is the recognition of cultural belonging as necessary to individual freedom. Cf. esp. Will Kymlicka's *Liberalism, Community and Culture* (Oxford: Clarendon Press, 1989) and *Multicultural Citizenship* (Oxford: Clarendon Press, 1995).

13 To speak of a common good as effective in American history is to point to the principle that unites communitarians and liberals. For Rawls this common good is that point of unity discovered in the original position that relates and reconciles individuals to one another and is informative of a well-ordered society; for republicans and communitarians the common good is what binds individuals to a sense of community and interrelatedness beyond and, in a sense, prior to their individuality. Doull's account of an actual and historically effective common good points to a standpoint that unifies liberal and communitarian.

14 See 408 above.

15 Alexander Hamilton, John Jay, James Madison, *The Federalist Papers*, ed. Clinton Rossiter (Chicago: Mentor Books, 1961), sect. 15. Hereafter references will name the author responsible for the specific section, with section number.

16 Hamilton, *Federalist*, 15. For example, various states ignored the nation's treaties with foreign countries, waged war on the Indians, built their own navies, and refused to fulfil national requisitions. Cf. Edmund S. Morgan, *The Birth of the Republic, 1763–89* (Chicago: University of Chicago Press, 1977), 124.

17 Cf. Gordon Wood, *The Creation of the American Republic 1776–1787* (Chapel Hill: University of North Carolina Press, 1969), 403–9. Morgan states: 'Rhode Island where a wildly depreciating paper currency had been made

legal tender, was the notorious example. Hordes of happy debtors were paying off their obligations in worthless paper, leaving their creditors bankrupt.' *Birth of the Republic*, 124.

18 Hamilton, *Federalist*, 15.

19 Hamilton, *Federalist*, 6.

20 Madison, *Federalist*, 39.

21 See 408–9 above.

22 Doull finds the clearest philosophical expression of this principle in the thought of David Hume. Ibid., 411.

23 Cf. Ibid., 410.

24 Ibid., 428.

25 Ibid., 432.

26 Ibid.

27 Cf. Rawls, *Political Liberalism*, 159, 160, 160 n.25, 163.

28 Cf. the excellent historical analysis of this First Amendment question in Michael W. McConnell's 'The Origins and Historical Understanding of Free Exercise of Religion,' *Harvard Law Review*, 103, no. 7 (1990).

29 Letter from Thomas Jefferson to Dr Benjamin Waterhouse (26 June 1803) in McConnell, 'Origins,' 1450.

30 Cf. McConnell, 'Origins,' 1437–43.

31 Madison, *Memorial and Remonstrance*, quoted in McConnell, 'Origins,' 1453.

32 These exemptions must be subject to the proviso that the duties they protect must not violate human rights and dignity. Such violations contradict the spirit which animates the Constitution.

33 See 409–10, 413 above.

34 Ibid., 419.

35 Richard Hofstadter, *The American Political Tradition and the Men Who Made It* (New York: Vintage Books, 1948), 168.

36 Ralph Henry Gabriel, *The Course of American Democratic Thought*, 2nd ed. (New York: Ronald, 1956), 142.

37 Cf. 431 above. For an excellent account of the relationship between the New Deal and the civil-rights movement see Harvard Sitkoff, *A New Deal for Blacks: The Emergence of Civil Rights as a National Issue, Volume I: The Depression Decade* (New York: Oxford University Press, 1978).

38 See 432 above.

39 Doull remarks: '[T]here is great need in the United States that the relation of society to state approach more nearly the Canadian model.' 456 above.

40 Ibid., 454.

41 Ibid., 456.

42 Ibid., 394.

43 Ibid., 435.
44 Ibid., 457.
45 Cf. *Philosophy of Right*, para. 12, where Hegel notes a like division in his own day.
46 Doull would include among such accounts the recent work of Will Kymlicka and Charles Taylor. Kymlicka too directly subordinates community to the service of liberal individualism; in political terms, according to Kymlicka's logic, the implication is that the 'distinct society clause' must be subordinated to the Charter of Rights. Taylor, by contrast, sees individual freedom as simply an aspect of modern communities, and insufficiently recognizes that Quebec's freedom rests upon its place within confederation. For Taylor, then, there can be no inherent limit to the powers that rightly belong to Quebec; the federal government and the other provinces appear external to the substance of Quebec. Both sides have as their object the concrete unity of Canadian life, but they conceptualize it in contrasting one-sided forms.
47 Doull captures this articulated sense of freedom at 457–9 above.
48 Ibid., 449.
49 Ibid., 456.

Bibliography of Essays by James Doull

Published

1959 'Review of J. Maritain, *The Degrees of Knowledge*, translated by G. Phelan.' *Dalhousie Review* 39, no. 4: 546–7.

– 'Review of G.S. Kirk and J.E. Raven, *The Presocratic Philosophers: A Critical History with a Selection of Texts.*' *Dalhousie Review* 39, no. 4: 550–1.

1961 'Review of F. Clairmonte, *Economic Liberalism and Underdevelopment.*' *Dalhousie Review* 41, no. 3: 404–7.

1967 'Review of *Hegel's Phenomenology: Dialogues on the Life of Mind* by J. Loewen-burg.' *Dialogue* 5: 96–101.

– 'The Theology of the Great Society.' *Canadian Journal of Theology* 13: 5–18.

1969 'Review of Emil Fackenheim, *The Religious Dimension in Hegel's Thought.*' *Dialogue* 7: 483–91.

1970 'Would Hegel Today Be a Hegelian.' *Dialogue* 8: 222–35 (with Emil Fackenheim).

– 'Comment on Quentin Lauer's "Hegel on the Identity of Content in Religion and Philosophy."' In D.E. Christensen, ed., *Hegel and the Philosophy of Religion,* 279–83. The Hague: Nijhoff

1972 'Review of *Hegel's Philosophy of Nature,*' translations of the *Philosophy of Nature* by A.V. Miller and M.J. Petry. *Dialogue* 11: 379–99.

1973 'Hegel and Contemporary Liberalism, Anarchism, Socialism: A Defense of the *Rechtsphilosophie* against Marx and His Contemporary Followers.' In J.J. O'Malley et al., *The Legacy of Hegel,* 224–48. The Hague: Nijhoff, 1973.

– 'Comment on Fackenheim's Hegel and Judaism.' In J.J. O'Malley et al., eds, *The Legacy of Hegel,* 186–95.

1975 'Review of *Hegel's Philosophy of Right, with Marx's Commentary: A Handbook for Students,* by Howard P. Kaintz.' *Owl of Minerva* 7, no. 1: 5–7.

1977 'A Commentary on Plato's *Theatetus.*' *Dionysius* 1: 5–47.

1979 'Augustinian Trinitarianism and Existential Theology.' *Dionysius* 3: 111–59.

– 'Dante on Averroism.' *Actas del V congresso internacional de filosofia medieval* (Madrid, 1979), I: 669–76.

1982 'The Christian Origin of Contemporary Institutions Part One.' *Dionysius* 6: 111–65.

1983 'The Logic of Theology since Hegel.' *Dionysius* 7: 129–36.

– 'Naturalistic Individualism: Quebec Independence and an Independent Canada.' In Eugene Coombs, ed., *Modernity and Responsibility: Essays for George Grant* (Toronto: University of Toronto Press), 29–50.

1984 'The Christian Origin of Contemporary Institutions Part Two: The History of Christian Institutions.' *Dionysius* 8: 53–103.

– 'The Concept of Enlightenment.' In Frushsorge, Mannger, and Strock, eds, *Digressionen: Wege zur Aufklarung* (Festgabe für Peter Michelsen), 25–31. Heidelberg: Karlwinter Universitat Verlag.

1985 'Findlay and Plato.' In R.S. Cohen, R.M. Martin, and M. Westphal, eds, *Studies in the Philosophy of J.N. Findlay.* Albany: State University of New York Press.

– 'Hegel's Critique of Hellenic Virtue.' *Dionysius* 9: 3–17.

1986 'Faith and Enlightenment.' *Dionysius* 10: 129–35.

1988 'What Is Augustinian "Sapientia"?' *Dionysius* 12: 61–7

1992 'The Relation of the Charter of Rights to the Canadian Constitution.' *Machray Review* 2: 13–25.

1997 'Neoplatonism and the Origin of the Older Modern Philosophy.' In *The Perennial Tradition of Neo-Platonism.* Leuven, Belgium: Leuven University Press.

– 'The Philosophical Basis of Constitutional Discussion in Canada.' *Animus* 2.

1999 'The Argument to the Hypotheses in Plato's *Parmenides.*' *Animus* 4.

– 'Neoplatonism and the Origin of the Older Modern Philosophy' (extended version). *Animus* 4.

2000 'Hegel and the English Reform Bill.' *Animus* 5.

– 'Hegel's *Phenomenology* and Post-modern Thought.' *Animus* 5.

2001 'The Problem of Participation in Plato's *Parmenides.*' *Dionysius* 19.

2002 'Secularity and Religion.' *Animus* 7.

2003 'Heidegger and the State.' Essay presented to the Contemporary Studies Programme, University of King's College, 1992. First published in this volume, 357–77.

– 'The Hypotheses of Plato's *Parmenides.*' First published in this volume, 83–139.
– 'Liberation and History.' Lecture to the Foundation Year Programme, University of King's College, 1999. First published in this volume, 3–17.

Unpublished

1962 'Liberalism and Social Democracy in Canada.' Paper prepared for the Draft Programme Committee of the Nova Scotia New Democratic Party.
1974 'What Is the Proper Business of Philosophy Today?' Debate with David Braybrooke.
1978 'Is a Union the Only or the Best Way?' Essay presented to the Dalhousie Faculty.
1980 'An Open Letter to Members of the House of Commons and Especially the Senate of Canada.'
– 'Canadian Constitutional Reform and the Monarchy: Reflections on the New Canadian Federation Proposed by the Constitutional Committee of the Quebec Liberal Party.'
1981 'Provincial Sovereignty and the Canadian Constitution.'
– 'What Can the Provinces Concede to the Federal Government in the Coming Constitutional Conference?'
1989 'The Concept of Enlightenment II.' Presented to the Atlantic Eighteenth-century Society Conference, University of King's College, Halifax.
1990 'The Opposition to the Meech Lake Accord and Premier McKenna's "Companion" Resolution.' Submission to the Special Committee on the Proposed Companion Resolution to the Meech Lake Accord. St John's (February).
1991 'The Canadian Constitutional Crisis.' Presented to the Memorial University Philosophy Society.
– 'The Amending Formula and the Constitution of Canada,' presented to the Joint Committe on the Amending Formula. St John's (April).
1992 'The Relation of the "Canada Clause" ...' Brief to the Special Joint
– Parlimentary Committee on a Renewed Canada. St John's (January).
1995 'Using the European Union as a Model for Quebec Independence.'

Contributors

Robert Crouse is Professor Emeritus at Dalhousie University and at the University of King's College, Halifax. He has written widely on medieval thought and has been Visiting Professor of Patrology at the Institutum Patristicum Augustinianum, Pontifical Lateran University, Rome. Crouse is a member of the editorial board of *Dionysius.*

Paul Epstein wrote his PhD thesis under the supervision of James Doull. He is a student of ancient Greek poetry, and its relation to Greek religion and philosophy. Epstein is Associate Professor of Classics at Oklahoma State University and a member of the editorial board of *Animus: A Philosophical Journal for Our Time.*

Wayne Hankey is Carnegie Professor of Classics at Dalhousie University and the University of King's College, Halifax. His doctorate is from Oxford University, whose press has just republished his *God in Himself, Aquinas' Doctrine of God as Expounded in the Summa Theologiae* in the series Oxford Scholarly Classics. His recent work is on medieval Neoplatonism, the formation of Western subjectivity, and contemporary French Neoplatonism. He is secretary and editor of *Dionysius* and has just finished terms as Visiting Fellow at Clare Hall, Cambridge University, and as a Visiting Scholar at Harvard University and Boston College.

Dennis House has taught ancient philosophy in the Dalhousie Classics Department since 1975. He is a Carnegie Professor of Classics at the University of King's College and Dalhousie University, Halifax, and is a member of the editorial boards of *Dionysius* and *Animus.* Currently House is writing a commentary on Plato's thought.

F.L. Jackson is a professor of philosophy retired from Memorial University. He is author of *Surviving Confederation* and has written widely on the philosophical history of the nineteenth and twentieth centuries. Jackson is a member of the editorial board of *Animus.*

Angus Johnston is an associate professor of humanities and social sciences at the University of King's College, Halifax. He is a former vice-president of the college and director of the Foundation Year Programme. He completed his doctoral dissertation on Aristotle's *Physics* under the supervision of James Doull. He is a member of the editorial board of *Animus.*

Kenneth Kierans is an assistant professor of humanities and social sciences at the University of King's College, Halifax. His research and teaching focus on the history of philosophy and political philosophy in the early modern and contemporary periods.

Graeme Nicholson is a professor of philosophy, retired from Trinity College, University of Toronto, and a member of the Centre for the Study of Religion. He is co-editor of *Fackenheim: German Philosophy and Jewish Thought* and *Hans-Georg Gadamer on Education, Poetry and History: Applied Hermeneutics,* and the author of *Illustrations of Being: Drawing upon Heidegger and Upon Metaphysics* and *Plato's Phaedrus: The Philosophy of Love.*

David Peddle is an assistant professor of philosophy and teaches in the Humanities Programme at Sir Wilfred Grenfell College, Memorial University. His interests and writings centre on contemporary political thought and Hegel. He is a member of the editorial board of *Animus* and managing editor of the James Alexander Doull Archive.

Neil Robertson is an associate professor at the University of King's College, Halifax, where he is director of its Early Modern Studies Programme, a member of its Contemporary Studies Programme, and a coordinator of its Foundation Year Programme. Robertson's interests and writings centre on the French Enlightenment, Leo Strauss, and Reformation thought.

Henry Roper was, until his retirement in 1998, professor of humanities at the University of King's College, Halifax, where he also served as vice-president, registrar, and director of the King's Foundation Year Programme. He is co-editor, with Arthur Davis, of *The Collected Works of George Grant, Volume 3, 1960–1970,* to be published by the University of Toronto Press.

Colin Starnes, Professor of Classics at Dalhousie University, has been President of the University of King's College, Halifax, since 1993. He is author of *Augustine's Conversion: A Guide to the Argument of Confessions I–IX* and *New Republic: A Commentary on Book I of More's Utopia Showing Its Relation to Plato's Republic.*

Index

www.ingramcontent.com/pod-product-compliance
Lightning Source LLC
LaVergne TN
LVHW040754070826
844660LV00025B/1146

* 9 7 8 1 4 8 7 5 9 2 7 7 6 *